# *Saints* of
# NORTH AMERICA

# *Saints* of
# NORTH AMERICA

**Vincent J. O'Malley, C.M.**

Our Sunday Visitor Publishing Division
Our Sunday Visitor, Inc.
Huntington, Indiana 46750

Copyright © 2004 by Our Sunday Visitor Publishing Division, Our Sunday Visitor, Inc. Published 2004

09 08 07 06 05 04   1 2 3 4 5

ISBN: 1-931709-52-1 (Inventory No. T29)
LCCN: 2004111701

Cover design by Monica Haneline
Interior design by Sherri L. Hoffman

PRINTED IN THE UNITED STATES OF AMERICA

*To my deceased parents,*
*Vincent Joseph O'Malley*
*and*
*Mary Rose O'Connell O'Malley,*
*in gratitude for their having imparted God's gifts of*
*family and faith,*
*the desire for love and truth,*
*and*
*the value of respect for all peoples.*

# CONTENTS

# ACKNOWLEDGMENTS

Mrs. Robin Nardi, my secretary, assisted me throughout the process of preparing this book. She generously volunteered countless hours and limitless skills for organization and computerization. Her writing to, and maintaining records of, on-going communications with almost one hundred fifty dioceses, religious communities, and guilds for information, photos, and photo-use permissions required extensive organization and dedication. Along with Robin Nardi, my sister Frances O'Malley assisted me in the final stages of gathering materials and reviewing them for sending to the publisher. These two women took complete responsibility for obtaining the photos and the necessary photo-use permission forms.

As the annual preacher at St. Lazare Retreat House in Spring Lake, Michigan, I enjoyed the time and opportunity to write this book. I thank my provincial, Father Thomas F. McKenna, C.M., for this preaching assignment, and I thank the retreat house director, Father Michael Shea, C.M., for the freedom and support in doing this project. The retreat-house secretary Florence Morris was a life-saver whenever I needed assistance in the daily activities of living and working. The local pastor of St. Mary's Church in Spring Lake, Michigan, Father Anthony Vainavicz, invited me to use his extensive private library, which I did frequently.

Persons abroad assisted me greatly. In México, Msgr. Gerardo Sánchez Sánchez, an author of many books on the saints of México, and Father Miguel Mendoza provided immeasurable assistance. My Vincentian confreres provided me with hospitality in México City, as did the Daughters of Charity in Guadalajara. In Montréal, Sister Patricia Simpson, C.N.D., and Sister Simone Poissant, C.N.D., provided information about the Canadian saints and candidates for canonization. Sister Simone proofread the text for the French-language accents. Mr. Fernando

Fuentes, a Mexican native living in Holland, Michigan, reviewed the text for the Spanish-language accents. In Central America, two Vincentian confreres helped to identify local candidates for sainthood and to provide information about them. I thank Father Gregory Gay, C.M., provincial of the Central American Province, who lives in Guatemala City, Guatemala, and Father John Prager, C.M., of the U.S. Eastern Province, who lives in Puerto Armuelles, Panama. Father Gregory Gay and George Herbert Foulkes, postulator for four Mexican candidates, kindly discussed with me the complexity of the historical background of the Church in Central America and México.

My former colleagues at Niagara University, Father Joseph G. Hubbert, C.M., chairman of the Religious Studies Department, and Doctor John B. Stranges, university professor and Canadian citizen, thoughtfully recommended bibliographies to help me understand the history of the Catholic Church in the United States and Canada.

The biographies for the one hundred forty-four entries required the assistance and critical reading of countless postulators, vice-postulators, historians, archivists, shrine directors, museum curators, guild presidents, librarians, devotees, promoters, and secretaries. In each biography, where applicable, I try to recognize the person(s) primarily responsible for providing information and reviewing the draft of the biography. Many more people could have been thanked for each entry, especially secretaries.

Besides enjoying daily prayer, ministry, and community life, how else does one keep proper perspective in the midst of this comprehensive project? I thank my sister and brother-in-law, Margaret and John McGinley of Poughkeepsie, New York, for introducing me to the game of golf. And I thank my regular golfing buddies in Western Michigan for sharing one of life's happiest pastimes.

# INTRODUCTION

The purpose of *Saints of North America* is to enlighten and inspire readers by the lives of the saints and official candidates for sainthood, as well as to encourage readers to seek the intercession of these deceased holy souls. This purpose coincides with the threefold role of the saints: to enlighten, to inspire, and to intercede.

The *scope* of this book embraces North America, and the saints and candidates for canonization who lived there for a significant time. North America, for the purposes of this book, is understood to include the countries of Canada, the United States of America, México, Central America, and the Caribbean. Biographies are provided for those whom the Roman Catholic Church counts among its canonized saints and those officially in the process toward canonization; this is the *primary criterion* for inclusion in this book. There are four classifications:

1) *Servant of God*, which is the title bestowed by the local ordinary, after an introductory process has determined that the person possessed a "reputation for sanctity" and a documented history of "heroic virtues or martyrdom."

2) The honorific title *Venerable* is bestowed by the Vatican's Congregation for the Causes of the Saints, when this Congregation decrees, after its thorough study of documentation detailing a candidate's history and reputation of holiness, that the candidate truly practiced heroic virtues.

3) *Blessed* is the title which the pope declares after verification of a miracle which is attributed to the power of God through the intercession of the candidate. A local cult of the beatified person is permitted and promoted.

4) The title *Saint* is bestowed by the pope after a second miracle is verified. Then the universal cult of the saint is permitted and promoted.

Some few persons included in this book are not included in the Vatican's *Index ac Status Causarum*, which the Congregation for the Causes of the Saints compiles. The causes for those few persons, however, have undergone the initial step of the process, whereby the local ordinary has permitted that prayers be prayed seeking that person's intercession, and that inquiry be made about miracles allegedly attributable to that person's intercession. In accordance with the decrees promulgated by Pope Urban VIII in 1625 and 1631, this author fully respects the authority of the Vatican in naming saints, and does not anticipate decisions regarding the naming of saints. The entries for the few persons who have not been designated servants of God, to the best of my knowledge, are Pierre Chaumonot, Demetrius Gallitzin, Charles Nerinckx, Georges Vanier, and Pauline Vanier. The author would have included other potential candidates, but either no action has been taken at the local level or other action has been suggested at the Vatican level. For example, regarding the four Churchwomen of El Salvador, who were brutally raped and murdered in 1980, no authority has as yet introduced this cause. On September 23, 1941, Denis Cardinal Dougherty of Philadelphia, in a meeting with Pope Pius XII, intended to introduce the cause of the "one hundred sixteen priest and brother missionary martyrs of the U.S.A." who died during the sixteenth to nineteenth centuries. The Sacred Congregation of Rites, however, replied that the causes of these proposed martyrs should be treated individually rather than collectively. Similarly, other outstanding servants of the Church in North America, whose causes have not been introduced officially, are not included in this text.

A *second criterion* for inclusion in this book is that the person spent a significant amount of time in North America. Blessed Damien de Veuster (d. 1889), a priest from Belgium, ministered for a quarter-century in Hawaii, which in 1959 became the fiftieth state of the U.S.A. Jérôme Le Royer de la Dauversière never set foot on North American soil, but Canadians regard him uniquely as one of the six founders of the Church in Canada. He allegedly received inspiration from the Blessed

Mother to develop Ville-Marie (now Montréal) as a center for evangelization. With great determination, he assisted others in fulfilling his Marian mission. As such, he is included in this book. A half-dozen seventeenth century Spanish Franciscans, each of whom labored for some years in México before being assigned to the Asian missions where they were martyred in Japan, are included.

On the other hand, the German native Blessed Frances Schervier, who founded the Franciscan Sisters of the Poor, and twice made official visitations in the United States, is not included; she remained in the U.S.A. less than a year, with each visit lasting five months. The Spanish Franciscans Blessed Louis Baba and Blessed Louis Sotelo lived in México en route from Spain to their missions in the Philippines and Japan, but for only ten months; therefore, they are not included. The Ukrainian Catholic bishop, Blessed Vasyl Velychkovsky, C.Ss.R., died a martyr in Winnipeg, Canada, where he spent the last year of his life trying to recuperate from chemical, physical, and mental tortures suffered for decades at the hands of the Soviet Union's KGB; he is not included. Those whose presence here was a year or less are not included.

Some people in this text may be considered as *representing more than one country*. Isaac Jogues, S.J., ministered more than eight years in Canada before being captured and imprisoned for one year at Auriesville, New York, where he was martyred. Kateri Tekakwitha was born in Auriesville, New York, and was raised five miles away at Fonda; at the age of twenty, she fled to Caughnawaga, near Montréal, where she spent the last four years of her life. Catherine de Hueck Doherty lived and worked in the United States for almost ten years before returning to Canada and settling down at Combermere, Ontario, for almost four decades. Father Marie-Clement Staub, A.A., spent five years at Worcester, Massachusetts, before spending twenty years at Sillery and Montréal, Québec. In addition, many Spanish missionaries to México during the sixteenth to eighteenth centuries labored in territories which at that time belonged to Spain but became part of the United States in the nineteenth century. Antonio Margil (d. 1726), Eusebino Kino (d. 1711), and Junípero Serra (d. 1784) labored respectively in Arizona, Texas, and California, all of which became part of the U.S.A. between 1848 and 1853. In this book, current boundaries are used to identify people with places.

There are one hundred forty-four entries in this book: forty-five entries for Canada; forty-five for the United States; forty-five for México; five for Central America; and four for the Caribbean. Since more than half-dozen of those entries include multiple martyrs — namely, the Martyrs of Georgia, the Martyrs of Virginia, the Martyrs of Oaxaca, the Martyrs of Tlaxcala, Anacleto González Flores and Companions, Cristobal Magallanes and Companions, and Pedro Baptist Blazquez and Companions - the total number of persons considered in this text increases by fifty. Some martyrs, like the Mexican catechist María de la Luz Camacho and the boy soldier José Sanchez del Rio were killed singly in separate incidents, and are therefore treated individually. The author intended to be comprehensive for all countries and regions except México. All of México's nearly thirty saints, blesseds, and venerables were included, but only one-third of their nearly sixty servants of God. México ranks third in the world, after Italy and Spain, for the highest number of current candidates for sainthood.

A challenge arose in deciding what name to use for vowed religious who ceased using their baptismal and family name in public life after they took a new name in religious life. The author decided each case on an ad hoc basis. Blessed Damien of Molokai and Father Solanus Casey are known best by their names in religion; who would know them respectively as Joseph or Bernard? The same holds true for Sister Theodore Guerin and Mother Angela Teresa McCrory; who would know them as Anne Thérèse or Brigid? On the other hand, Mother Maria Fitzbach and Sister Dina Belanger are known more often by their secular names, than their religious names: Mother Mary of the Sacred Heart, or Sister Cecile of Rome.

In the stories of these saints and candidates for sainthood, the author focused on presenting, in limited space, two things: first, the personality and spirituality of the individuals, and second, the place(s) and fame with which the person is associated. Especially, the author tried to include as often as possible the words of the individuals themselves, in this book as in his previous books. In each biography, in the highlighted space for "Place," the author highlighted only a few places; there was no desire to be exhaustive. In the highlighted space for "Fame," the author identified, first, some outstanding trait of personality or spirituality, and secondly, some outstanding achievement.

Entries are arranged according to the calendar year. Rome assigns feast days for saints and blesseds, but not for candidates whose status is venerable or servant of God. Therefore, the Church-assigned feast day is used for saints and blesseds, but venerables and servants of God are placed under the date of the individual's death or a date used by the promoters of the particular candidate when they remember privately the candidate whom they are promoting. In providing calendar dates for venerables or servants of God, the author, again, does not anticipate the Church in assigning calendar dates for liturgical celebration. When two or three people share the same date of celebration, they are all listed on that one date. The "Index of Saints and Feast Days" on page 541 provides a way of looking up individuals by name.

The saints herein represent a great geographical expanse. Of the fifty states of the U.S.A., these saints or candidates labored in over half of them — mostly in the Mid-Atlantic, Midwest, South, and Southwest. Of México's thirty-one states, all but a few of the least populated states are represented. Among Canada's ten provinces and two territories, over half are represented, with the highest number being from Québec and Ontario. Of the seven countries in Central America, four are represented: Costa Rica, El Salvador, Guatemala, and Nicaragua. In the Caribbean, three of the four Greater Antilles are included, namely, Cuba, Santo Domingo (now Haiti and the Dominican Republic), and Puerto Rico. A listing of "Countries, Provinces, and States in Which Saints Lived and Ministered" is provided on page 535. This breakdown by geographic location will enable readers to look up saints and candidates who represent a given area.

The overwhelming number of these saints and candidates for sainthood represent the clerical and lay religious vocations. They were missionaries, martyrs, founders and foundresses, and a few mystics. There are more than three dozen laity included in this study. They include married couples, married individuals, and single persons with vocations including governmental leaders, nurses, catechists, and mystics. Six teen-agers are included among this book's saints and candidates.

Sources sometimes provide contradictory information. Therefore, in an attempt to ensure accuracy in historical detail and in the descriptions of the individuals' personality and spirituality, the author sent drafts of the biographies to people with expert knowledge of the particular saints or candidates for critical review. The utmost gratitude is extended to the many people who provided biographical information and who reviewed the drafts.

# JANUARY

⌘

### 4. ✠ Saint Elizabeth Ann Seton

*Places: Emmitsburg, Maryland, and New York, New York*
*Fame: Wife, mother, convert, educator, and care-giver of orphans*
*and widows. Foundress of the Sisters of Charity.*

The desire to do God's will inspired Elizabeth Ann Bayley Seton (1774-1821) throughout her life.[1] In her youth, she read the Scriptures daily. As a young wife and mother, she appreciated that "I must answer for my children in judgment."[2] As a widow, she converted from the Episcopal Church to Roman Catholicism in order to pursue the "right faith."[3] In founding the Sisters of Charity, the first community native to the United States for religious women, she instructed her sisters, "The first end [of the congregation] I

ELIZABETH ANN
SETON

propose in our daily work is to do the will of God; secondly, to do it in the manner He wills; and thirdly, to do it because it is His will."[4]

Elizabeth Bayley, the middle child of three daughters, was born into a prestigious colonial family. When Elizabeth was almost three, her mother died, and thirteen months later, her father remarried. The new couple gave birth to seven more children. Because the stepmother favored her natural children over her stepdaughters, siblings Mary and Elizabeth spent almost half of their childhood, from 1782 to 1786 and from 1788 to 1791, with their paternal uncle and his wife at New Rochelle, New York.

In January of 1794, nineteen-year-old Elizabeth married twenty-five year-old William Magee Seton. Contemporaries described her as beautiful, vivacious, conversant in French, and an accomplished horsewoman. She enjoyed great popularity at parties and balls. The newlyweds, who probably were introduced about 1791, seemed headed for a storybook future. William worked for his father, who had co-founded a prosperous import-export business as well as the Bank of New York. Elizabeth remained at home, where she cared for their five children.

Elizabeth called her beloved sister-in-law, Rebecca Seton, her "soul's sister."[5] The two assisted the poor of the city, and in 1797 helped to found the Society for the Relief of Poor Widows with Young Children; Elizabeth and her sister-in-law became known as "the Protestant Sisters of Charity."[6] The young Seton family began experiencing financial difficulties when piracy on the high seas and an undeclared war between Britain and France put a stranglehold on transatlantic shipping. William's father died in 1798; then William declared bankruptcy in 1800. William's health also failed; he had contracted tuberculosis. Elizabeth describes this period as their "worldly shipwreck."[7]

On October 1, 1803, the couple and their eldest daughter, Anna Maria, sailed for Livorno, Italy. They left their four other children with Elizabeth's soul-sister Rebecca. The Setons planned to rent an apartment at Pisa, where William would experience clean country air. After arriving at Livorno on November 19, the family trio was quarantined until December 19 in the dungeon-like *lazaretto*. The Italian authorities hesitated to issue a clean bill of health for passengers who had just come from New York City, where a yellow fever epidemic was raging.

After William died just eight days after his release from quarantine, Elizabeth visited his grave and "wept plentifully over it with unrestrained affection."[8] Mother and daughter Seton were prohibited from returning immediately to the United States because of inclement sailing weather, followed first by the daughter's and then by the mother's sickness.

During her stay in Italy, Elizabeth began considering converting to Roman Catholicism. The Filicchi family, business friends of William's, invited Elizabeth and her daughter into their home. The hosts and guest oftentimes discussed religion. Elizabeth wished to discover the one true religion. Antonio urged her to "pray and inquire."[9] While visiting Italy's countless Catholic Churches, Elizabeth was moved by the artwork, music, and piety that she observed. In the Pitti Palace at Florence, she was affected for hours by the life-size *Descent From the Cross*; Elizabeth identified profoundly with the maternal experiences of the Blessed Mother. She read St. Francis de Sales' *Introduction to the Devout Life* and prayed St. Bernard's *Memorare*. Having been struck by the Church's unbroken apostolic tradition and belief in the Real Presence, she reveals, "I read the promises given to St. Peter and the sixth chapter [of] John every day."[10] Years later she wrote, "I determined when I came home, both in duty to my own children and my own soul, to learn all I was capable of understanding on the subject. If ever a soul did make a fair inquiry, our God knows that mine did."[11]

Nine months after her return to the United States in June of 1804, Elizabeth formally converted to Roman Catholicism. She had made a concerted effort to discern whether Protestantism or Roman Catholicism possessed the "right faith,"[12] and entered into discussions with her minister, later bishop, John Henry Hobart. Her family and friends, shocked to hear of her considering conversion, threatened to ostracize her, and to cut her off financially, even though she was a widow with five children under eight years of age. In mid-January 1805, having decided to become Catholic, she wrote, "I will go peaceably and firmly to the Catholic Church, for if faith is so important to our salvation, I will seek it where true faith began, seek it among those who received it from God Himself."[13]

How would she support her children and herself? She tried and failed at two enterprises in New York City: teaching in one school, and managing a boarding house for boys attending another school. In June of 1808, Elizabeth arrived at Baltimore, and in September, she opened a girls' school on Paca Street, next to St. Mary's College and Seminary. The next year, a donor purchased land at Emmitsburg, Maryland, and Elizabeth moved her school for girls there. The first day-pupils were admitted on February 22, 1810, and the first boarders in May of that same year. Both poor and well-to-do boarding students attended St. Joseph's Academy and Free School, whose enrollment soared to sixty students by 1817. Mother Seton is regarded as the pioneer of American Catholic Schools.

Elizabeth wished to live a religious life. On March 25, 1809, in front of Bishop John Carroll and her daughter Kate, Elizabeth professed private vows. On December 7, 1809, one young woman joined Elizabeth Seton at Baltimore. By the end of December, 1809, another five young women joined Elizabeth's community; more women followed.

In January of 1812, Archbishop Carroll approved the modified rule of the Paris-based Daughters of Charity for the Emmitsburg-based Sisters of Charity.[14] Elizabeth was elected superior, and received from

Carroll the title of "Mother." On March 12, 1812, at the age of sixteen, Elizabeth's daughter Anna made her profession of vows as a Sister of Charity on her deathbed. On July 19, 1813, Elizabeth and eighteen women took vows as Sisters of Charity at Emmitsburg.

The sisters' community grew rapidly. Prior to Mother Seton's death in 1821, the community had grown to approximately sixty sisters. The sisters served at St. Joseph's Academy and Free School in Emmitsburg, performed domestic and infirmary services at Mt. St. Mary's College and Seminary at Emmitsburg, and administered an orphanage and attached school in Philadelphia and another orphanage in New York City. A quarter century after the death of Mother Seton, the community founded by her underwent major reorganization, resulting in six separate communities.

Elizabeth's spirituality consisted of desiring to do God's will as it was revealed in the Scriptures and through the advice of her directors, all of which she contemplated before the Real Presence. She prays, "O my God! Forgive what I have been, correct what I am, and direct what I shall be. From break of day I seek thee, till the dead of night. All is solitary where you are not, and where you art is full of joy."[15] Possessing a great trust in God, she writes, "There is a Providence which neither slumbers nor sleeps."[16] Consistently, she acceded to God's will, praying, "If it succeeds I bless God, if it does not succeed, . . . I bless God, because it will be right that it should not succeed."[17]

What became of Mother Seton's five children? The eldest, Nina, died at sixteen after making a deathbed profession as a Sister of Charity. William and Richard attended Georgetown College in Washington, D.C., Saint Mary's College in Baltimore, and Mount Saint Mary's College in Emmitsburg. After serving an apprenticeship with the Filicchis, William enlisted in the United States Navy in 1817, and served for almost seventeen years before retiring as a lieutenant. Richard pursued an apprenticeship with the Filicchis and served as a civil servant in the United States Navy. He died at the age of twenty-five, off the coast of Liberia, from a fever he contracted while nursing a passenger back to good health. Catherine, who was the only one of Elizabeth's children present at her mother's deathbed, joined the Sisters of Mercy in New York and devoted the next fifty years of her life to prison ministry. The youngest child, Rebecca, died at fourteen in

Emmitsburg from complications of a hip injury she had suffered when she was eight.

*For further information, contact*
Archives, Daughters of Charity
333 S. Seton Avenue
Emmitsburg, MD 21727 U.S.A.

## 5. ✠ Saint John Neumann

*Places: Buffalo, New York; Baltimore, Maryland;
and Philadelphia, Pennsylvania*
*Fame: Extraordinary educator of youth, Archbishop of Philadelphia,
first male saint from the U.S.A.*

As a twenty-year-old seminarian at the University of Budweis, Bohemia (now the Czech Republic), John Nepomucene Neumann (1811-1860) first read and became inspired by letters from European missionary bishops who described their challenging and satisfying ministries among the Native Americans in the United States.[18] John dreamed of dedicating his life similarly to preaching the Gospel in the New World. On October 1, 1834, he wrote in his spiritual journal:

JOHN NEUMANN

> It's underway then, this final year of my seminary studies. How shall I thank You, my God, for all the help You have given me to reach my goal? This will be my thanksgiving: I shall make You known and loved, while for myself I ask of You and the whole court of heaven the light I need to follow the way of Your law. Holy Spirit, give me the courage I lack. You, my God and my Creator, well know how frail I am. Without your help I can achieve nothing at all. Make me a worthy priest, worthy of You, the all-holy God.[19]

At the completion of his studies, this brilliant and industrious student was disappointed that none of the American bishops to whom he had written to offer his services had responded. With forty dollars in his pocket, and no guarantee of a bishop in the United States willing to ordain him, he left home on February 8, 1836, and arrived at New York City on June 2. Two days later, John met the bishop of the diocese of New York, John DuBois, who informed the seminarian that three weeks earlier this bishop had sent a transatlantic letter in which he had agreed to accept John. The bishop quickly made plans to ordain John. Within the same week, DuBois ordained John sub-deacon and deacon, and on June 25, a priest of the diocese of New York

Two days after ordination, John departed New York City for his first assignment, namely, a nine-hundred-square-mile crescent of the western frontier of New York State, which stretched north to Niagara Falls, south to Erie, east to Batavia, and west to Buffalo. He was assigned to take special interest in the German-speaking Catholics since only three priests in the entire diocese spoke German. He studied German in order to converse with these immigrants. "Because he wanted to be a missionary, helping to foster the faith of the immigrants, he learned Spanish, French, Italian, and English. With Czech, his mother's language, he was able to understand Polish and some other Slavic languages."[20] He also learned some Gaelic in order to serve the Irish.

From his diocesan headquarters at Williamsville, New York, Father John Neumann worked zealously among the immigrants. In Western New York, this studious priest, whose mother had nicknamed him "the Bookworm," built churches and schools. He believed that Catholic education was a key factor in teaching and promoting the faith. When he stopped for a few days at Rochester, Neumann met the Redemptorist priest Joseph Prost. Four years later, Prost advised the lonely diocesan priest to consider joining the Redemptorist community.

After pondering his vocation for months, Neumann decided in 1840 to transfer from the diocese of New York to the religious community of the Redemptorists. He desired the emotional and spiritual support of community life. John, who was the Redemptorists' first novice in America since their arrival in the U.S.A. in 1832, did not enjoy the traditional tranquility of a typical novitiate. He began his novitiate in October of 1840, but during these eighteen months, he was asked to continue as a parish priest, and was moved eight times, including stays at Pittsburgh, Baltimore, New York City, Rochester, Buffalo, and Norwalk, Ohio. Back at Baltimore, he enjoyed a respite of six weeks from labor in order to pray intensely before making religious profession on January 6, 1842.

John discovered that life as a Redemptorist was quite similar to life as a diocesan priest. Because the new country had so few priests and the population kept booming with new waves of immigrants, he and other priests traveled great distances in search of and service to Catholics scattered over burgeoning towns and villages. At Baltimore, John traveled by horseback throughout Maryland, north to York, Pennsylvania, and south to Richmond, Virginia. In January of 1845, he was assigned to Pittsburgh, where he founded fifteen parishes, started many societies, and welcomed many converts. In one year, of the eighty-five converts, one-third were black. In the midst of his missionary activity in Baltimore and Pittsburgh, he assisted with administrative and financial advice for both the School Sisters of Notre Dame de Namur, and the Oblate Sisters of Providence. Beginning at thirty-six, he was named successively religious superior of the forty Redemptorists living in the U.S.A., a member of the provincial council, and assistant provincial. In 1848, after a dozen years in the U.S.A., he applied for and received American citizenship.

In March of 1852, Neumann was ordained the fourth bishop of the Diocese of Philadelphia, which at that time included the eastern and central portions of Pennsylvania, the lower half of New Jersey, and the whole state of Delaware.

Neumann's accomplishments at Philadelphia astounded observers. During his eight-year reign as bishop, he built eighty churches and thirty-five schools, and increased the number of clergy from one hundred to over one hundred fifty.[21] He founded the Sisters of the Third Order of St. Francis at Glen Riddle, Pennsylvania, to help to provide teachers for the schools he had helped to establish. This unassuming bishop is credited with being the founder of the Catholic School System in the United States of America. He authored a catechism for school children and adults; then he translated it into German. He also wrote a Bible history book for adults.

Bishop Neumann introduced into the United States the practice of the diocesan-wide Forty Hours Devotion. Right after the Synod of Bishops in Baltimore in 1852, he convened his priests the following year to share with them the bishops' decisions regarding church doctrine, liturgy, and pastoral matters. Although concerned about the diocese's debt, he built anyway, fearing that the faith of the immigrants would be lost if the Church did not serve them in their towns and villages. Two issues that caused him special consternation were the Know-Nothing Party's violence and vandalism against Catholics and their buildings, and the intransigence of the lay trustee advocates.

This itinerant bishop traveled throughout his diocese. He enjoyed preaching, teaching, baptizing, confirming, hearing confessions, visiting the sick, and settling disputes. He lived simply, much to the chagrin of the blueblood leaders in society, who thought the bishop should cultivate the wealthy and powerful people. But the bishop preferred to visit the country people rather than dine with the powerful.

The story is told about Bishop Neumann and his nephew visiting a small town where the local pastor borrowed a horse and wagon to pick up his guests. Unfortunately, the wagon was filled with manure.

> Uncomplainingly, the bishop climbed on the plank and motioned to [his nephew] Father Berger to join him. The two of them sat with their backs to the driver and their legs dangling from the back of the wagon. The horse-drawn conveyance bounced and jounced along rough roads. It began to rain, and the Bishop and Father John were splattered with mud. A head of steam, generated by the rain, rose like a cloud of acrid incense from inside the wagon. Neumann bore all this with grace and good humor. "John," he said to his nephew, " have you ever seen such an entourage for a bishop?"[22]

After sixteen years as priest and eight years as bishop, this highly energetic man succumbed to sickness and death. At forty-eight, John collapsed, of an apparent heart attack, a few blocks from the bishop's residence at Logan Square. Thousands of people, from every class in society, passed by his bier to pay their final respects. After Masses were celebrated at the cathedral, and at the nearby Redemptorist parish, John Neumann was buried with his confreres. He writes in his directives, "I cannot be with my confreres in life. I want to be with them in death."[23]

*For further information, contact*
The National Shrine of St. John Neumann
1019 North Fifth Street
Philadelphia, PA 19123 U.S.A.

## 6. ✠ Blessed Brother André Bessette

*Place: Montréal, Québec*
*Fame: Miracle-worker. Founder and fund-raiser for
the Oratory of St. Joseph.*

The "miracle worker of Montréal," Brother André Bessette (1845-1937) possessed a great humility.[24] He frequently said of himself, "I am ignorant. If there were anyone more ignorant, the good God would have chosen him in my place."[25] When people began calling him "The Miracle Worker," he retorted, "How can anyone believe that I, Brother André, poor and ignorant as I am, might heal them, or perform miracles? Well, I don't. The Good Lord is the only author of all

ANDRÉ BESSETTE

these miracles."[26] At other times, Brother attributed the healing power to the intercession of his heavenly patron, by saying, "It is St. Joseph who cures."[27]

From four years after his religious profession at thirty-five, until his death at ninety-one, miraculous powers emanated through Brother André. Thousands of canes and crutches left with Brother testify to their former owners' sudden healing.

The cures associated with Brother André covered a wide gamut of afflictions and people. The common thread was the recipient's belief in the power of Brother André's intercession. When a virtually blind priest was assigned to assist Brother, the priest explained that his infirmity would limit his contribution. Brother replied that he would ask for St. Joseph's help. The priest was cured within one day of his arrival. When a stonemason begged Brother to cure the laborer's crippled legs, Brother prayed for the man, told him to throw away his crutches and to report to work the next day to help Brother construct his chapel. The wife of the doctor at Notre Dame College developed a hemorrhage which neither the doctor nor his learned colleagues could cure. The woman asked her husband to bring Brother to their house. The skeptical doctor acceded to his wife's wishes. Brother arrived, prayed for the woman, and rubbed St. Joseph's oil on her. Instantaneously, the hemorrhaging ceased. A railroad supervisor suffered mangled legs when a marble slab fell on him. For two years, doctors could make no improvement. When the man approached Brother, he simply rubbed St. Joseph's oil over the wound, prayed, and told the man to throw away his crutches. The man stood up and walked. He headed directly to the offices of the newspaper *La Patrie,* which announced the cure in the next day's headlines. Cures abounded. "In 1916 alone, four hundred thirty-five cases of cures were reported, which amounted to more than one cure per day, not including those not reported."[28]

Not all miracle-seekers received their desired cures. To some seekers, Brother simply said, "I'll pray for you."[29] In other cases, he advised the devotees to pray a novena to St. Joseph, or to rub on the affected area either a St. Joseph's medal or St. Joseph's oil.[30] To many seekers, he suggested that they pray, "St. Joseph, pray for me as you yourself would have prayed, had you been here on earth, in my shoes, with my troubles."[31] If André perceived no faith in a miracle-seeker, he rejected the request. He urged those approaching him to do penance and to receive the sacraments of reconciliation and Holy Communion. The primary goal of Brother's ministry was not to cure people's bodies, but to lead people to God, who might cure them. When some petitioners came seeking only physical results, Brother would comment, "It's odd . . . I'm often asked for cures, but very rarely for the virtue of humility, or the spirit of faith."[32]

André received both praise and criticism on account of his healing ministry. Many members of his religious community called him "Old Smearer," and "Old Greaser," and teasingly asked him "How many people did you grease today?"[33] The school doctor and other medical personnel regarded him as a quack. Students at the school nicknamed André "Brother Greaser."[34] The majority of contemporaries, however, honored this holy man, and praised God for what He achieved through Brother.

Brother André had been born in the village of Saint-Grégoire, thirty miles southeast of Montréal. The eighth of twelve children, he was baptized Alfred. Reflecting on his childhood, Brother recalled years later that "probably due to the fact that I was the most sickly, my mother showed more affection to me than to the other children, and also took greater care of me. She kissed me more often than I deserved... And also, how I loved her!"[35] His father, a carpenter, died in 1855. The mother tried to raise the ten living children, but the task became impossible, and she put up for adoption all of her children except sickly Alfred. The other children were absorbed into the homes of family members and neighbors. Two and a half years after his father's death, Alfred's forty-year-old mother, succumbed to tuberculosis. Alfred's Aunt Rosalie then cared for him until the mayor of the village adopted him.

What work might this sickly young man find? "He tried his hand at a dozen different trades, wandering from town to town. With no education or trade, he could do only menial tasks and obtain unsteady jobs. Bakers, cobblers, tinsmiths, and blacksmiths hired him, but always only as an apprentice."[36] He wandered for eight years, searching for but not finding steady work. In 1865, Alfred moved to the United States to find work in the textile mills of New England. In 1867, he returned home and settled down at Saint-Césaire, where the parish priest perceived Alfred's singular prayerfulness, and after three years' observation, encouraged Alfred to consider the religious life.

In 1870, Alfred's pastor wrote to the Holy Cross Fathers at Notre Dame College in the Côte-des-Neiges neighborhood of Montréal. He recommended Alfred's candidacy for the seminary, and added, "I am sending you a saint."[37] A month after being received at the college, Alfred entered the novitiate. One year later, the religious superiors voted not to admit André to religious life on account of his poor health. His novice master, however, pleaded, "Even if this young man becomes unable to work, he will still be very much able to pray."[38] In 1872, André took temporary vows, and was named porter of Notre Dame College. He held that post until he was appointed Guardian of the Oratory in 1909.

Talk about Brother's power to heal arose as early as 1874. One of Brother's earliest alleged cures occurred at Notre Dame College, where a student lay in the infirmary. Brother visited him, and when the boy explained that he was sick, Brother replied, "No, you're not . . . Why don't you go and play with the others?"[39] The boy ran outside and joined his classmates. The school doctor was furious, and checked for a relapse, but none occurred. In 1884, two men carried a woman crippled with rheumatism into the kitchen where Brother was scrubbing the floor. Without ceasing his work, Brother said, "Let her walk by herself . . . You're no longer sick. You can go home now."[40] Rejoicing, the lady walked out of the room. In that same year, the father of two students at the college lamented to Brother that the man's wife lay seriously crippled at home. Brother assured him that as they were speaking, the wife was feeling better. When the husband arrived home, his previously paralyzed wife stood up, walked over to, and greeted him.

Crowds of miracle-seekers began amassing on the grounds of Notre Dame College, in the hope of encountering Brother André. A chapel needed to be built where the faithful might pray. André's friends constructed an open-air chapel which held ten people. Worshipers came by the hundreds, and the chapel was enlarged in 1904 to hold one hundred people. In 1908, the nave was extended farther, and in 1917, the crypt chapel was built to hold one thousand people. Seven years later, construction was begun on the basilica, which was finished in 1966.

How did Brother André develop such an efficacious devotion to St. Joseph? Brother informed his friends that his devotion had originated with his mother, who had taught him to pray to the father of the Holy Family. As a youth and a teenager, he developed the devotion by much prayer. As a novice and young lay brother, André prayed for hours before the Blessed Sacrament and the statue of St. Joseph.

Two weeks before he died, the aging André commented to a friend that he looked forward to death and eternal life. He explained, "If one can do good on earth, he can do far more in heaven."[41] Brother took sick that very night, suffering terribly with acute gastritis. He prayed, "I thank God for giving me the grace to suffer; I need it so much."[42] He requested of his religious superior, "Pray for my conversion."[43] Two weeks later, on the feast of the Epiphany, Brother died. His remains were waked publicly for six days and nights. One million people filed past his casket to pay their respects. After the Mass in the Cathedral of

Montréal, a service was held in the oratory crypt, where Brother was laid to rest.

*For further information, contact*
Oratory of St. Joseph of Montréal
3800, chemin Queen Mary
Montreal, QC H3V 1H6 Canada

## 10. ✠ Venerable Félix de Jesús Rougier

*Place: México City, D.F.*
*Fame: Open to the Spirit. Founder of the Missionaries of the Holy Spirit.*

Born and raised at Meilhaud in central France, Félix Rougier (1859-1938) grew up as the oldest of three sons.[44] At eighteen, he was inspired to become a missionary after hearing a French bishop describe at a school assembly the spiritual and material poverty of his congregation at Oceania. Félix was one of four hundred students in the audience. He wrote in his diary:

FÉLIX DE JESÚS
ROUGIER

> At the conclusion of his talk, the bishop asked, "Who among you wish to promise me right now to come to help me to save these poor souls? Raise your hands. I [Félix] looked around. No hand was raised. I felt interiorly an irresistible movement, and I determined in a second that I would go with the missionary bishop. And I raised my hand.[45]

Félix entered the seminary and community of the Society of Mary, commonly known as the Marist Fathers, in 1878. Nine years later, he was ordained a priest. For the next eight years, he taught Sacred Scripture at Barcelona, Spain. In 1895, his community assigned him to Colombia, and in 1902, to México, where he served as religious superior and pastor in a church which served French immigrants.

One year later, on February 4, 1903, Félix had a providential encounter with Concepción de la Cabrera, popularly known as Conchita, who was the mother and mystic who inspired the Works of the Cross. The two had never met previously. He writes to his superior general, "she told me it was necessary to shake the spiritual lethargy which had invaded me; that I needed to surrender myself to God seriously, and that I should start a new life."[46] Félix responded wholeheartedly to the invitation. He spent hours before the Blessed Sacrament and practiced great austerities.

Conchita, who had already founded three communities of women religious, told Félix that she perceived it as his God-given vocation to found a men's religious community, to be named the Religious of the Cross. Bishops and priests with whom Félix had consulted about this possibility agreed with the proposal. The superior general, however, refused Félix permission, and transferred him immediately to Spain. Félix, having promised obedience beforehand, obeyed exactly.

For the next ten years, Félix served at Barcelona, Spain. During that time, up to seventeen archbishops and bishops wrote many times to the superior general requesting that Félix be freed to found the new congregation. Even Pope Pius X became involved. He agreed to allow the foundation, but he prohibited Félix from leaving the Marists in order to found the new congregation, and the pope changed the name of the proposed Religious of the Cross to the Missionaries of the Holy Spirit. The Marist Fathers agreed to lend Félix to found this new apostolate. He traveled to México at a time when bishops and priests were fleeing the country because of the anti-Catholic persecution.

In México, Félix founded the Missionaries of the Holy Spirit on Christmas Day, 1914. Because of the persecution, he was forced by the concern for safety to move the novitiate many times. The number of vocations grew, especially from seminarians who had been forced to leave other closed seminaries. The Marist community kept extending his period of being "on loan" to the Missionaries. Finally, in 1925, the new Marist superior general promised no further opposition to whatever the Vatican desired for Félix's role in México. On Easter Sunday, 1926, Félix, at age sixty-seven and after forty-eight years as a Marist, took vows in the community which he had founded a dozen years earlier.

Félix witnessed the tremendous spiritual and institutional growth of the Missionaries. The charism of the Missionaries of the Holy Spirit, which Father Félix Rougier discovered in the Gospel, emphasized Jesus' status as victim and priest who is consumed on the cross. This character is expressed by means of three expressions: Christ crucified, Christ the priest, and Christ the victim. The founder taught that it was impossible to prescind from any one of these three elements, since each one affected the other.

Ahead of his time, he opened a house for priests' ongoing formation and integration of health and holiness. To promote writings on the spiritual life, he edited the magazine *La Cruz*. He worked with Conchita in developing her five communities, and he founded another three women's communities who devote themselves to the service of priests and evangelization among the Mexican Indians: the Daughters of the Holy Spirit (1924), The Guadalupean Missionaries of the Holy Spirit (1930), and the Oblate Sisters of Jesus' Priests (1937). "In addition to the religious congregations mentioned, Father Rougier played a decisive role in the birth and growth of an additional nine Mexican religious families started by his followers, which form part of what is now called "the Family of the Cross." The groups are now present in a majority of Latin American countries and the United States."[47]

Two years before he died, Father Félix, burdened with a series of physical illnesses, wrote, "I went through everything: colds, exhaustion, fevers, rheumatism, and strong headaches that forced me to go to bed."[48] Just two months before he died, he was re-elected superior general, but he could hardly function. On the day of his death, some of his missionaries gathered around his bed, and he replied when invited to give some final words of advice, "That you love the Father in heaven a great deal, as Jesus did. And that you be able to say with him: I always do what pleases my Father."[49]

*For further information, contact*
Missionaries of the Holy Spirit
Félix Rougier House of Studies
P.O. Box 499
St. Benedict, OR 97373 U.S.A.

# 12. ✠ Saint Marguerite Bourgeoys

*Place: Montréal, Québec*
*Fame: Montréal's first teacher. Foundress of the*
*Congregatión-de-Notre-Dame.*

In her hometown of Troyes, France, twenty-year-old Marguerite Bourgeoys (1620-1700), while participating in a procession in honor of Our Lady of the Rosary, glanced up at a statue of Our Lady positioned in the portal of the Abbey-Church of Notre Dame aux Nonnains, and her life became changed forever.[50] Marguerite wrote, "I found it [the statue] very beautiful. At the same time, I found myself so moved and so changed that I no longer recognized myself.

MARGUERITE
BOURGEOYS

When I returned home, this was apparent to everyone... From that moment, I gave up my pretty clothes and withdrew from the world to give myself to the service of God."[51]

To express this momentous grace from God, Marguerite joined the "extern congregation" that the local cloistered nuns of the Congregatión-de-Notre-Dame-de-Troyes had founded to instruct young women who, as uncloistered protégés, would go forth into the city and its environs to catechize young people. After working at this ministry, Marguerite applied for admission to two cloistered communities of nuns. Both communities, we know not why, refused her admission. In 1643, she took a private vow of chastity, and later poverty. Her spiritual life deepened, and Marguerite's spiritual director advised her to consider founding an uncloistered community of women. Marguerite accepted the invitation, and two women joined her. The three lived together under the direction of Sister Louise de Maisonneuve. Soon, one woman died and the other married. Alone, Marguerite continued her dedicated life.

In 1653, Paul de Maisonneuve, the Governor of Ville-Marie (now Montréal), visited France to recruit a lay teacher to journey from village to village and instruct settlers' children and Amerindians in the faith. Maisonneuve's sister, Sister Louise, who had directed the "extern congregation," recommended Marguerite Bourgeoys. The governor asked

Marguerite to consider his invitation, so she conferred with her spiritual director and agreed to labor in New France.

After departing Troyes in February of 1653, Marguerite arrived at the port of Saint-Nazaire, where a Carmelite priest hand-delivered a letter accepting her into that community in France. Feeling pangs of guilt, she prayed before the Blessed Sacrament. Later, she described the experience: "In a moment, all my sorrow disappeared, and there I received great strength and great certainty that I must go to Canada."[52]

The ship set sail in mid-June. At departure, the passenger list included one hundred eight men and about fifteen women. When rough seas and an outbreak of scurvy caused the deaths of eight men, Marguerite took the initiative to care for the sick and dying. At this time, the men on board began calling Marguerite "Sister" and that title remained with her after the passengers came ashore.

Arriving at Québec in late September, the new volunteer was introduced to Jeanne Mance by Marguerite's fellow traveler Governor Maisonneuve, who said, "I have brought with me an excellent young woman, named Marguerite Bourgeoys, a person of good sense and lively intelligence, whose virtue is a treasure which will be a powerful help in Montréal."[53]

During her first five years at Ville-Marie, where there were too few children to teach in this village of two hundred inhabitants, Marguerite occupied herself by helping the townspeople, in every way possible. She gathered the women of the village and taught them how to care for a home, and how to manage a farm. An excellent seamstress, she sewed clothing for those in need. Generously she provided food from her table for the hungry. When the townspeople balked at the difficult and dangerous task of re-constructing a cross on the Iroquois-controlled hilltop overlooking the village, Marguerite suggested building a chapel and cross at the more convenient but equally visible location at the river's edge. She oversaw the early days of the chapel's construction in 1655, exchanging others' commitments to construct the chapel for her services in sewing. When some men quit building because of a work-related dispute, she and other women assisted in the stone-laying work.

Finally, the need for a school arose. In late 1658, the governor granted Marguerite an abandoned stone stable for her schoolhouse. She gathered helpers to clean the building, to construct a fireplace, and to transform the loft into a dormitory. This space above the school provided lodging for her, and for the "the king's wards," i.e., women who traveled to New France for the purpose of finding a husband and settling the land. Even after they married, these women gathered every Sunday and feast day at Marguerite's house for instruction in the faith. Eventually, some of the women who joined her in living above the school, joined her in religious life. In the school, Marguerite provided vocational training to the sons and daughters of the settlers, whether farmers or merchants. Viewing all students with the deepest respect, she writes, "It [teaching] is the work [most] suited to draw down the graces of God if it is done with purity of intention, without distinction between the poor and the rich, between relatives and friends and strangers, between the pretty and the ugly, the gentle and the grumblers."[54]

Returning to Troyes in 1659 to seek members of the "extern Congregation" who might assist her at New France, Marguerite rejoiced in three highly cultured women who signed away their family inheritance and willingly embraced poverty. In 1670, she returned to France for additional volunteers, and six more women came with her.

This group of women, who committed to living a communal life and teaching the faith, represented the beginning of Marguerite's Congregatión-de-Notre-Dame in New France. "Her inspiration in founding such a community was Mary the mother of Jesus, whom she saw as the first and most faithful disciple of the Lord, going about teaching and doing good in the primitive church."[55]

The years 1679-80 proved for Marguerite to be a time of particular trial with the sisters and with the bishop. She and the sisters had disputed about the admission of a candidate, and Marguerite felt that the sisters had lost confidence in her. She suggested that she step down and they elect a new superior. Providentially, the governor's wife was traveling to France, and Marguerite felt it best for the community if she absented herself for a while. Upon her return to Montréal, she was greeted with the news that additional Canadian-born women wished to join the congregation. By 1681, the community had grown to eighteen members, including seven Canadian-born and two Amerindian Iroquois women.

In 1693, Marguerite relinquished the role of leadership of the community, in which capacity she had served for over thirty years. Her successor was the community's first Montréal-born member. Marguerite continued in these later years to work to maintain against opposition the uncloistered character of the community. In 1698, just two years before she died, Marguerite received Vatican approval for the Congregatión-de-Notre-Dame.

On the last day of 1699, the community's young mistress of novices, who had been seriously ill for months, appeared to be dying. The community rushed to pray beside her bed. Marguerite prayed with the community, and then added, "O my God — why do you not take me — I who am useless and can do nothing in this house — why not take me instead of this poor sister who can still do great things for you!"[56] The next day, the young sister's health improved dramatically, and the near-octogenarian Marguerite became seriously sick with fever and pain. On January 12, Marguerite died.

*For further information, contact*
Marguerite Bourgeoys Museum
400 St. Paul Street East
Montréal, QC H2Y 1H4 Canada

## 19. ✠ Frederic Baraga

*Places: Great Lakes region: Michigan, Wisconsin, Minnesota, and Canada*
*Fame: Snowshoe priest; indefatigable missionary to Native Americans.*
*First bishop of Milwaukee, Wisconsin.*

Baptized Irenaeus Frederic Baraga (1797-1868), Frederic never used his first name.[57] By fourteen, this middle child of five siblings lost his brother, sister, mother and father. On the advice of his priest-teacher Clement Hofbauer, now canonized, Frederic entered the seminary, in 1821.

At the time of Frederic's ordination in 1823, Jansenism was rampant in his native Slovenia. In his enthusiastic opposition to Jansenism,

FREDERIC BARAGA

however, Frederic became unpopular with the Jansenist emperor and lukewarm bishop and clergy. He was transferred from his initial assignment of the cathedral parish to a poor, neglected, remote parish. After learning from the missionary-sending Leopoldine Foundation about the urgent need for missionaries in North America, Frederic applied to and was accepted by the bishop of the frontier diocese of Cincinnati. Upon arriving in New York harbor on New Year's Eve 1830, this young priest traveled to meet his bishop, who assigned young Father Baraga to the northern part of the diocese, namely, western Michigan.

Baraga's flock consisted of Ottawa and Chippewa Indians, occasional fur traders, and eventually immigrant miners in a triangular territory measuring 80,000 square miles and extending in the east from Sault St. Marie, Michigan, northwest to Grand Portage, Minnesota, southwest to Fond du Lac, Wisconsin, south-central to Marquette, Wisconsin, and southeast to Harbor Springs and Grand Rapids, Michigan.[58] He established missions in various villages along the way. In 1853, he was named the Bishop of Sault St. Marie, which see was relocated in 1866 to Marquette because of that city's more central and accessible location.

Baraga loved the Native Americans. He possessed utmost respect for the tribal members and their system of elder meetings. Lamenting the white man's manipulation of the Indians by promoting abuse of alcohol and removing Indians from native lands, he complained to governmental authorities. He prayed for his people, for justice to them, and peace among them. After ten years on the mission, he developed the practice of rising at four o'clock each morning to spend three hours in daily prayer. This holy man writes joyfully of the Indians' growth in Christianity:

> The hearty welcome of my dear good children of Arbre Croche [now, Harbor Springs, MI] and their faithful adherence to religion which they manifest in all their dealings, re-paid me in many ways for the difficulties of the journey. They manufacture their sugar close together in twelve adjoining sugar cabins. On entering the sugar district, I was delightfully surprised to find a little chapel which these good Indians had erected for the per-

formance of their devotion. It was unusually touching and in many ways shaming to the Christians of Europe to find in this virgin forest so far removed from any settlement, a devout group of newly converted Indians who for the short time that they pass here have built for themselves a chapel for the performance of their spiritual exercises.[59]

Travel was conducted by foot, horseback, and canoe most of the year; and by snowshoes in the winter. Baraga explains in a letter to his bishop at Cincinnati some of the difficulties encountered in his missionary journeys.

> In winter a person cannot travel otherwise than on foot. As the snow is generally deep and there are no traveled roads, the only way to travel is on snow-shoes. These snow-shoes are from four to five feet long and one foot wide and are tied to one's feet. With them a man can travel even in the deepest snow without sinking in very much. But this style of walking is very tiresome, especially for Europeans, who are not accustomed to it. . . .
>
> Another hardship is the sleeping in the open air in a northern winter, for there are no huts in which to stay overnight. Generally speaking, a man may travel four or five days in this extensive and thinly settled country before coming to another Indian settlement. It is true, a large fire is made, but this soon goes out, for the Indian guide, who accompanies us, sleeps the whole night as if he were in a feather-bed, and then a person suffers much from the cold.[60]

This polyglot spoke and wrote fluently Slovenian, French, German, English plus Chippewa. His first pastoral letter, he wrote in 1853 in the Chippewa tongue. He authored seven prayer-books in Slovenian, twenty books in English on scriptural, doctrinal, and liturgical topics with pastoral applications; a sociological description of the tribes he knew; a dictionary and grammar of the Chippewa language, plus a catechism and hymnbook in Chippewa. His daily diary amounted eventually to three volumes.

The bishop died midwinter in Marquette. While attending the Council of Baltimore in 1866, he had suffered a stroke. The bishop begged the priest who had accompanied him to take him back home to die in his wilderness diocese. He survived another sixteen months. The funeral Mass was filled with worshipers, Catholic and non-Catholic, Native Americans and European immigrants, rich and poor. All believed Bishop Baraga to be a saint.

*For further information, contact*
Bishop Baraga Association
P.O. Box 550, 347 Rock St.
Marquette, MI 49855 U.S.A.

⚭

## 21. ✠ Mother Angeline Teresa McCrory

*Places: New York City, and Germantown, New York*
*Fame: Daughter of Carmel, and Mother of the Aged, Foundress of the Carmelite Sisters for the Aged and Infirm*

As a young child, Brigid McCrory (1893-1984) was moved to care compassionately for the aged, for the love of God.[61] At nineteen, Brigid entered the Little Sisters of the Poor, who cared for the destitute aged. At thirty, inspired by a new way of serving senior citizens, she left the Little Sisters and founded a new community, the Carmelite Sisters for the Aged and Infirm.

MOTHER ANGELINE TERESA McCRORY

Brigid's family had provided her with the context in which her faith and love grew. Growing up in Ulster, Northern Ireland, this second of five children experienced firsthand the socioeconomic conditions of being Catholic in Protestant-dominated Northern Ireland. Although the Penal Laws had been repealed in 1829, prejudice remained ingrained in the population at large and in political structures. Almost three and a half million Catholics felt compelled to emigrate from their homeland between 1851 and 1901.[62] Brigid's family, when she was eight, moved to

Scotland, where her father found employment in a steel mill near Glasgow.

Brigid entered the Little Sisters of the Poor in February 1912. Years later, she explained her motivation. "I guess first of all it was my close association with my eighty-two-year-old grandfather in County Tyrone. . . . As a child, I remember that I always thought of the elderly as lonely, hungry, and cold, and my heart went out in sympathy to them."[63] After eighteen months, Brigid received the name Sister Angeline of Saint Agathe. After professing her vows, she was assigned to Brooklyn, New York, where she arrived in October 1915. For nine years there, she cared for the sick, begging for the daily food for the sisters' and patients. In October 1926, she was named the superior of Our Lady's Home in the Bronx, New York, where now Mother Angeline became responsible for eighteen sisters and two hundred thirty elderly residents.

Mother adapted the community's care for the aged to the spirit, culture, and needs of the United States. She made the living arrangements less like an institution and more like a home. She desired to preserve the independence, privacy, dignity, and standard of living to which the residents had become accustomed after seventy or eighty years of living. Whereas the community's rule stated that the homes were to accept only the indigent poor, Mother interpreted "poor" in a broad sense. Knowing that many elderly had some money, but little companionship, purpose, and joy; she welcomed these "poor" into the Little Sisters' home.

All went well until 1927, when Mother General visited from France. She ordered Mother Angeline to adhere to the community's rules as written. Mother Angeline faced a dilemma. If she adhered strictly to the instructions of her superiors, would she be keeping the vow of hospitality as she perceived it? Almost all of the Little Sisters in the local community agreed with Mother Angeline that the French rules needed adaptation to the situation in the United States.

Two years later, Mother Angeline, after much prayer, discussion, discernment, and two official canonical visitations, decided to transfer from her original community in order to found a new community. Six companions opted to join her in departing the one community and founding another. Mother Angeline felt sadness, but no animosity, in the departure. "Although heartbroken at leaving a community we loved and where we had spent many happy years," she and the other sisters felt called by God to serve God's elderly in a new manner.[64] Mother Angeline writes further, "I have always loved my former Congregation and value the spiritual foundation that was mine and the reverence and respect for the aging that I learned in the Congregation."[65]

On August 11, 1929, Sister Angeline and six other sisters left the Little Sisters. In transition, they received hospitality from the Sparkill Dominican Sisters at St. Martin of Tours Parish, in the Bronx, New York. On September 3, 1929, the sisters moved, through the kindness of Cardinal Hayes, into the old rectory at St. Elizabeth's Parish, in New York City. The sisters regard this date as the community's foundation day. In spring 1931, Mother Angeline inquired of Father Lawrence Flanagan, provincial of the Carmelite Province of New York, if her sisters might affiliate with the Carmelite Order. He responded enthusiastically. On July 16, 1931, with all the necessary approvals having been received, the Church recognized the foundation of the Carmelite Sisters of the Aged and Infirm. The community Constitution received papal approval in 1957.

At the end of September 1931, the Carmelites moved into St. Patrick's Home in the Bronx. The number of vocational candidates, and admissions of elderly into the Home increased rapidly. During the next four decades, seven expansions were made at St. Patrick's Home for the elderly and the sisters. In 1947, the sisters moved their mother-house to Germantown, New York, one hundred miles north of New York City, at Avila-on-the-Hudson.

Permeating the growth of the community and its apostolate was Mother Angeline's vision. She wanted the guests to feel at home. She writes:

> Loving care means planning little parties and surprises to break the monotony; being concerned when an old person is sick and confused. It means bidding an old person the time of the day, and saying a few kind words to them. In short, doing all those little thoughtful things you would want someone to do for your own mother or father. . . . A priest very kindly told us that our vocation was the greatest in the Church. . . . That we, in caring for the aged, were taking care of the lonely, dying Christ. All of us can reflect well on this thought.[66]

The source of Mother Angeline's vision lay with Jesus Christ in prayer. She writes, "We all know that labor done for God is high and holy, but it must not replace habitually the spiritual exercises of the Rule. We must, as Carmelites, lead a contemplative and active life, giving the required time to prayer which is more important than our work."[67] The following prayer, which was found among her personal effects, describes her heart and soul.

> Dearest Lord, may I see Thee today and every day in the person of the aged and sick, and while caring for them, minister unto Thee. Though Thou hidest Thyself behind the unattractive guise of the irritable, the exacting, the unreasonable, may I still recognize Thee and say, Jesus, my Patient, how sweet it is to serve Thee. Lord, give me this seeing faith. Then my work will never be monotonous. I will ever find a new joy in humoring and gratifying the fancies and wishes of all the aged. O beloved sick, how doubly dear you are to me when you personify Christ, and what a privilege is mine to be allowed to nurse you.[68]

After living fourteen and a half years as a Little Sister of the Poor, and another fifty-five years as a Carmelite Sister for the Aged and Infirm, Mother Angeline returned to God on her ninety-first birthday. During her almost half a century as superior general, from 1929 to 1978, the community experienced prodigious growth, in members and foundations: to over three hundred sisters serving at over fifty sites in thirty dioceses, plus one site each in Ireland and Scotland.

*For further information, contact*
St. Teresa's Motherhouse
Avila on the Hudson
600 Woods Road
Germantown, New York 12526 U.S.A.

# FEBRUARY

❧

## 1. ✠ Venerable José Ramon Ibarra y González

*Places: Chilapa, and Puebla, México*
*Fame: Evangelization through education, pastor and scholar*

In the small town of Olinalá, in the state of Guerrero, José Ramon Ibarra y González (1853-1917) was born the only child of his father's second marriage, thus joining his sisters from his father's first marriage. Because of the dangers presented during the guerrilla war, the family moved to Izucar of Matamoros, and later to Puebla.

The young boy conducted himself well in studies and in relationships with his peers. A seminarian classmate remembers that José was like "a teacher" and "a superior" to all the other students.[69] The bishop too appreciated José's brilliance and goodness, and sent the lad to Rome to complete his studies. He attended the Latin American Pontifical College, beginning in May 1877, and was ordained in 1880 in the Basilica of St. John Lateran. The bishop asked José to remain in the Eternal City for two more years to take advanced studies. During the young man's total of five years at Rome, he earned doctorate degrees in sacred theology and canon law from the Gregorian University, a degree in civil law from the Institute of St. Apollinaris, and a doctorate in philosophy from the Roman Academy of St. Thomas Aquinas. Pope Leo XIII awarded him with a medal for outstanding academic achievement.

Upon returning to his home diocese of Puebla, he was assigned to teach in the seminary, and to assist in the chancery. On his own, José, having been sensitized by the loss of both his parents before he had left for Rome, chose to visit the sick and dying. A born organizer and leader, he oversaw the First Diocesan Pilgrimage to the shrine of Our Lady of Guadalupe, and the next year he organized the first-ever diocesan pilgrimage to Rome, on which journey two hundred persons accompanied him. Associated with Concepción Cabrera de Armida and Father Félix Rougier, he promoted devotion to the Sacred Heart, and urged pastors to establish in their parishes the Apostolate of the Cross. For ten months, December 1887 to September 1888, he governed the diocese.

In January 1890, at the Vatican, he was ordained bishop and was appointed to the Diocese of Chilapa. During his dozen years in that see, he founded numerous *colegios*, free schools, a night school for adults, and a vocational school; and encouraged pastors to establish parish schools. He took a special interest in educating the indigenous population, and in promoting vocations to the priesthood among them. This energetic bishop also began for this relatively new diocese, founded in 1863, the construction of its first cathedral, and reorganization of its administrative structures. For the sick and poor, he founded the hospital Sagrado Corazon. To develop a communal vision for the diocese, he convened three synods: in 1893, 1895, and 1901. To foster communication and transportation he initiated the construction of a railroad within the state of Guerrero.

The pope transferred Bishop Ibarra y González to the diocese of Puebla in July 1902 and, a month later, elevated that see to an archdiocese, with Ibarra becoming the first Archbishop of Puebla. As archbishop, he opened many new schools, including a seminary to promote vocations among the indigenous population, and saw the local Palafox Seminario seminary raised to the status of Catholic University. He formed the Asociación de Misioneras Guadajupanos to respond to the social needs of the Native Americans, and worked diligently with Concepción Cabrera and Félix Rougier to obtain in Rome the approbation of the Congregación de los Misioneros del Espíritu Santo to advance the works of the Cross.

Great sadness and suffering afflicted the archbishop in his last few years on earth. The anti-Catholic activity that had been advocated by revolutionary forces became heightened beginning in 1910. By August 1914, the archbishop was forced to flee his diocese. He found refuge in México City. "The news that arrived from Puebla was tragic: priests were being persecuted, dispersed, and assassinated; worship was suspended for a time, the Church faithful were frightened, the seminary was dissolved, some churches were profaned."[70] Physically, he had been suffering for years. At the end of 1916, gangrene set in, which made it impossible for him to celebrate Mass. His greatest spiritual consolation became reception of the Eucharist. On February 1, 1917, he died, an exile from his archdiocese, in the home of the lay leader Concepción Cabrera de Armida.

*For further information, contact*
Arquidiócesis de Puebla
Curia 2 Sur #305
Centro
Apartado Postal #235
72000 Puebla, Puebla, México

∞

## 3. ✠ Mother Mary Lange

*Place: Baltimore, Maryland*
***Fame:*** *Educated children of color when the custom of slavery prohibited it.
Founded the Oblate Sisters of Providence, the Catholic Church's
first religious community of women of African heritage.*

The Oblate Sisters of Providence, founded in 1829, by Mother Mary Lange (c. 1784-82) believe that Providence originated and protected their community despite decades of prejudice, poverty, and instability.[71]

MARY LANGE

The Oblates are children of Divine Providence. They had a beginning without human planning. Although the community was founded in Baltimore, those who founded it were not natives of Baltimore nor of Maryland. That city had become a place of refuge from uprisings, rebellions, and political upheavals. Mother Mary Lange and her early daughters were refugees. This community, always poor, almost coming to an end once, persevering, taking on new life, was supported always by the foundresses' abiding confidence in God. Mother Mary Lange began her work, increased in numbers without resources. When authorities of the Church abandoned her, God, in unexpected ways, raised up champions for her cause. She lived through terrible disappointments and rose above hard opposition. As difficulties mounted, her hope grew.[72]

Historical documents provide little information about Mother Mary Lange's early years. She was born to refugees from the revolution that had swept across Saint Dominique (now called Haiti, on the western half of the politically divided island of Hispaniola, whose eastern half is called the Dominican Republic). Elizabeth Clarisse, as she had been baptized, entered the United States around 1812. She made her way to Baltimore, which city had become a haven for French-speaking refugees from France and Haiti.

Elizabeth learned upon arriving in antebellum Baltimore, that "colored folk" did not possess the same constitutional rights as "white folk." The customs of slavery prohibited educating "colored" children, even those who were freed. Regardless of the custom, Elizabeth, around 1818, began educating Negro girls. A Haitian friend, Marie Balas, joined Elizabeth in the teaching project. Elizabeth transformed her home to a children's school.

Just as many Catholics had fled the revolution in Haiti, so too many Catholics had fled the French Revolution and its subsequent Reign of Terror. From France came the Sulpician Fathers, who, like almost all the religious communities in France at that time, had been disestablished, and were forced to leave the country. The Sulpician Fathers headed for Baltimore, where they founded the United States' first seminary, St. Mary's, in 1791. The Sulpicians, whose primary apostolate was educating seminarians for the priesthood, assisted the Haitians. Both peoples shared a common background: the French language, the Catholic faith, and the tragedy of violent revolution in their homeland. The Sulpicians offered to the Haitian Catholic community the use of the downstairs chapel in the seminary while the seminarians used the upper chapel. From the seminary's *la chapelle basse* grew the first African-American congregation in the United States.

In 1804, Jacques Nicholas Joubert arrived at Baltimore. His parents took the family from France during its continuing revolution, and found refuge in Saint Dominique. Revolutions erupted there too, and he alone of his family escaped. In Baltimore, he entered St. Mary's Seminary, and was ordained a Sulpician priest. He would play a significant role in helping to found the future Oblate Sisters of Providence.

Father Joubert and Elizabeth Lange thought on the same wavelength. Without having met each other, each perceived the injustice which prohibited Negroes from being educated. Providentially, the Sulpicians assigned Joubert to pastor the Haitian refugees.

Joubert approached Archbishop Ambrose Marechal, another Sulpician, and asked him to found a school for colored girls. The archbishop was receptive, but soon died. His successor, James Whitfield, sensed that "the finger of God is in this thing," and ordered in March 1828, that such a school be started immediately. The next month, Joubert approached Elizabeth and suggested that they start a religious community of Negro women who would educate Negro girls. Elizabeth, who already had been teaching girls for the past ten years, agreed immediately.

Four women became the founding members of the Oblate Sisters of Providence. Elizabeth Lange, who took the name Sister Mary in religious life, and her assistant Marie Balas, who called herself Sister Mary Frances, were joined by another refugee Rosanne Boegue, now Sister Mary Rose, and one of the boarding students, Almaide Duchemin, who became Sister Mary Theresa. The women elected Sister Mary as their first superior, and thenceforth called her Mother Mary. These four women moved into a rented home at 5 St. Mary's Court, where many students enrolled immediately. Before the year ended, the owner informed the sisters that he planned to renovate the home; therefore, they had to vacate the premises. The sisters looked for other lodging in the area, but discovered that homes were either too expensive or "unavailable" when the owners realized that the sisters were Negroes. Eventually, the sisters rented a home at 610 George Street, until a house, donated by a dear friend, Dr. Ferdinand Chatard, was readied on Richmond Street.

Because Mother Mary spoke French as her native tongue, and Spanish as her second language, she did not feel as comfortable in speaking or writing English. Father Joubert, therefore, wrote the Constitution and Rules for their community, with the help of the sisters. Archbishop Whitfield approved the Constitution in late June of 1829. A few days later, on July 2, the four women took vows as Oblate Sisters of Providence. In December, the archbishop granted the sisters permission to reserve the blessed Eucharist in their house. Two years later, Pope Gregory XVI approved the constitution, thereby making the Oblate Sisters of Providence the first community of religious women of African descent. The founding of the Oblate Sisters of Providence represents a milestone in the history of the Catholic Church.

In 1832, when a cholera epidemic swept through New York City, Philadelphia, and Baltimore, the trustees of the Baltimore Bureau of the Poor inquired if the sisters might assist in caring for the sick. All eleven sisters volunteered. Only four, however, including Mother Mary, could be freed from teaching for this temporary assignment. The four sisters dedicated their time and energy for a month. One of the sisters, Sister Anthony Duchemin, mother of Sister Mary Theresa, contracted the dreaded disease while nursing the archbishop of Baltimore. He survived, and she died. The secretary of the trustees wrote to the sisters a letter expressing his and others' deep gratitude for the contribution, which the sisters made in the time of public crisis.

For the community's first years, the sisters' homes doubled as schools. The convent's community room served as the students' classroom during the day, and the sisters' sewing and ironing room during the evening. After dinner, the sisters and students took recreation in the common room. By 1845, the school enjoyed an enrollment of twenty students, of whom ten were non-paying orphans. Fourteen sisters had joined the community at this point. With the growth in student body and religious vocations, the new superior felt confident in expanding the number of schools. Between 1857 and 1866, the Oblate Sisters opened four new schools: one in Fells Point, Maryland; one in Philadelphia; one in New Orleans; and another one in Baltimore.

> Ecclesiastical authorities (with some few exceptions) made no provisions for the Oblates' spiritual life. The sisters had no Mass, no regular confessor. They stood in front of St. Alphonsus Church hoping for spiritual comfort from some busy Redemptorist who might speak French. They were cold, hungry, and discouraged, since even the ecclesiastical authorities suggested the dissolution of the community and the sisters' return to the

world. As day succeeded day, it looked as if they and their institute would be abandoned.[73]

The administration of the community passed easily from Mother Mary to other sisters. Mother Mary led the Oblates from the founding in 1829 until 1832, when she requested not to be re-elected. In 1835 and 1838, she relented, and allowed herself to be a candidate. After both elections, she was named superior. Mother served, therefore, a total of nine years as superior. In 1841, Sister Mary Theresa, one of the four original sisters was elected superior. In an attempt to facilitate her raising funds for the poor community, she proposed legislation whereby the sisters would change the community's constitution and name. Having failed in those initiatives, in 1845, she left the community "to be free to serve God as a true and accepted religious."[74] She founded a new community, the Sisters Servants of the Immaculate Heart of Mary, at Monroe, Michigan. One other Oblate sister left with Sister Mary Theresa. The departure of these sisters broke the hearts of the remaining sisters. Mother Mary, who in Sister Mary Theresa had lost a dear friend, co-founder, and fellow sister, had been busy earning with a second sister the only two incomes available to the community, by working as domestics at St. Mary's Seminary in Baltimore.

The Oblates suffered terrible prejudice, poverty, and instability from the very beginning of their institution. Some white people disliked black people in general. Many others opposed black children becoming educated. And some did not like seeing Negro nuns; "The sisters had to endure verbal insults, along with threats of physical abuse from some of Baltimore's white Catholics who objected to colored women wearing the habit of a nun."[75] When the sisters were teaching in Philadelphia, the sisters were forced to step off the sidewalks and into the muddy streets so that white people could pass.

Poverty afflicted the sisters. Whatever monies the community possessed at the outset had come mostly from inheritance, which Mother Mary had received from her father, "a gentleman of some financial means and social standing."[76] The inheritance evaporated quickly, however, and the sisters' meager income came from the small amounts paid by students, and the monies received from their needlework, sewing, mending, and working as laundresses, first at the seminary and later at Loyola College.

Instability burdened the sisters in their properties, apostolates, and lack of hierarchical support. In1828, the sisters' landlord forced them to move, and in 1870, the City of Baltimore required the sisters to move to 501 East Chase Street, but without the city's providing either adequate advance notice or sufficient financial compensation. All the sisters' schools, which had been opened between 1857-1866, were forced to close for financial reasons before 1871. After Archbishops Marechal and Whitfield, the sisters felt that no other archbishop during Mother Mary's lifetime cared whether the community survived or not. One archbishop had commented, "*Cui bono*" (to what benefit) when a plea was made to keep the community functioning.[77] This archbishop suggested that the sisters might disband, and return to the lay state.

Fortunately, the sisters enjoyed a succession of dedicated chaplains. The Sulpician Joubert, who had suggested founding the religious community, served the sisters admirably from 1828 until he died in November 1843. The Redemptorist Fathers took over as chaplains in 1847, assigning Thaddeus Anwander to care for the sisters. While begging on his knees in front of the archbishop not to abandon the sisters, the young priest Anwander spoke on behalf of his vice-provincial John Neumann that Neumann personally would guarantee the care of the sisters. Anwander's begging continued. He went door-to-door in Baltimore seeking donations, and recruiting students for the sisters. In a short time, the school's enrollment jumped to sixty boarders, and one hundred day students. The number of sisters doubled. A boys' school was started. When Neumann discovered that the sisters had received no retreat for three years because they had no money to pay for a priest's travel and services, he sent a priest to them. Neumann himself traveled to Baltimore to serve as the sister's extraordinary confessor four times a year. In 1860, at the suggestion of Archbishop Kenrick, the Jesuit chaplain P. L. Miller dedicated himself to assisting the sisters. When the sisters needed an additional house, but could not afford to purchase one, members of the Society of Jesus arranged that the Jesuits would buy a house for the sisters if the sisters would do the laundry at Loyola College and receive payment for their labor. In 1879, the Josephite Fathers were given responsibility as chaplains, and appointed their confrere Michael Walsh to the position.

In 1879, at still thriving Saint Frances Academy on Chase Street, Mother Mary celebrated her golden jubilee as a religious sister and foundress. The community rejoiced with her, but Mother was feeling the effects of her age, and the tiredness brought on by a lifetime of service to others. Mother Mary remained in her room for hours at a time, not leaving for any length of time, except for Mass on Sundays and holy days. Her joy came from visits in her room, surrounded by her sisters and students. On February 3, 1882, the devoted Father Anwander happened to be visiting for early morning Mass. After Mass, he took Communion to Mother, and found her near death. After receiving Communion, she extended her hands to receive the anointing. In that posture of hands outreached and opened, she breathed her last, and returned to God.

*For further information, contact*
Mother Mary Lange Guild
Our Lady of Mount Providence Convent
701 Gun Road
Baltimore, MD 21227 U.S.A.

❦

## 4. ✠ Venerable Délia Tétreault

*Place: Montréal, Québec*
*Fame: Mystic and missionary. Foundress of Missionary Sisters*
*of the Immaculate Conception.*

Délia Tétreault (1865-1941) felt interiorly so filled with God's love, that she felt exteriorly called to share God's love with others.[78] She may be described as simultaneously a mystic and missionary. This twofold movement, like inhalation and exhalation, results from the one God-given experience of grace. This contemplative envisioned and originated the first missionary institute founded in the Americas for women religious. Délia felt empowered, and perhaps even compelled, by the grace of God, to bring Christ to others.

Délia was born at Sainte-Marie-de-Monnoir (now Marieville), in the diocese of Saint-Hyacinthe, in Québec. Her parents already had six children. In the mysterious ways of God, the frail Délia, who from birth needed constant care, lived; whereas her twin brother, robust at birth, became ill and died after seven months. Two

DÉLIA TÉTREAULT

years later, just before Délia's mother died, she handed her infant daughter to the mother's sister Julie and her husband Jean Alix, Délia's godfather, who adopted and raised the child.

From early childhood, Délia was attracted to and inspired by stories of missionaries, who sacrificed their lives in foreign countries, where they propagated the faith, and provided for people's most basic material needs. In the attic of her adoptive parents' home, young Délia discovered literature from the Propagation of the Faith and the Holy Childhood societies. Frequently, she ran to the attic to read this inspirational literature. She dreamed about the stories she read.

> I was kneeling beside my bed when, all of a sudden, I saw a ripe field of wheat extending as far as the eye can see. At a given moment, all the ears of wheat changed into heads of children. At the same time, I understood that they represented the souls of pagan children. I was struck by this dream, but it never occurred to me to tell anyone about it, not even my mother to whom I usually told everything.[79]

As a teenager, although she felt pulled in opposite directions, i.e., to give her life to God as a missionary nun or to pursue worldly allurements, the attraction to serve in the foreign missions never left her entirely. When missionary priests from Canada's Northwest Territories visited and preached in her parish church, the desire was rekindled and became rooted more deeply in her imagination and desire. At fifteen, she took a private vow of virginity, so sure was she that God was calling her to a religious and missionary vocation. A dilemma presented itself, however, in that the universal Church had no congregations of women missionary religious. Mother Cabrini's community of the Missionaries of the Sacred Heart, the first community of women missionary religious, would not be founded until 1880.

Over the next eighteen years, Délia pursued five options. At eighteen, she applied to the cloistered Carmelites, but they refused her admission based on her frail health. That same year, she lived as a postulant with the Grey Nuns in Saint-Hyacinthe, until an epidemic erupted. Délia's parents rushed to the convent and took her home, where she remained for the next seven years. An itinerant missionary White Father, who was preaching throughout Canada about the Church's ministry in Africa, met and invited her to come to that continent. She responded wholeheartedly, but the day before she was to depart for Africa, she became seriously ill. The twenty-five-year-old young lady was heartbroken: "The day I was to embark for Africa the rain came down in torrents and I believe I shed as many tears as the sky poured drops of water!" Shortly thereafter, Delia encountered, during a retreat at Saint-Hyacinthe, the French Jesuit priest Almire Pichon, who recently had been assigned to Montréal after having served for a short time as spiritual director for Thérèse of Lisieux, and who now desired to found a work for the poor. Délia, perceiving that this might be God's way of preparing her for the missions, volunteered her services at Bethany House at Montréal, where she visited the sick and poor in their homes, especially the recently arrived Italian immigrants, whose language she learned. Ten years later, Pichon asked Délia to leave the organization because she maintained the conviction that Our Lord was calling her to found a missionary order for religious women, while Father Pichon felt sure that her vocation lay with helping his work at Montréal.

Now thirty-five, Délia approached, in autumn 1900, the archbishop of Montréal, Paul Bruchesi, and shared with him her missionary dreams. The inspiration that she had received nearly twenty years earlier in a spiritual experience was two-fold. She was to found in Canada not only a missionary community of women religious, but also to work to establish a similar society of men. The bishop expressed his general support, but was concerned that her work might become a financial burden on the diocese. Délia assured him, promising that she and her companions would provide for their needs by their own labor. Shortly thereafter, her parents lost all their wealth in a bank crash, and she became infected for a time with a lung disease, which required treatment for tuberculosis.

Undaunted, the irrepressible Délia began in 1902, an apostolic school to train missionaries for various religious communities. Her interior call, however, remained to found a missionary institute for women religious. In 1904, Bishop Bruchesi, at Rome for the celebration of the jubilee of the Immaculate Conception, shared Délia's dream with the pope, who responded enthusiastically to the concept and urged the bishop to grant immediate approval to the project. From Rome, Bishop Bruchesi wrote affirmatively to Délia, who was delighted with the news. Thus the apostolic school evolved into the Institute of the Missionary Sisters of the Immaculate Conception, whose name was given by the Pope himself. In 1905, Délia took perpetual vows in the community, and took as her religious name Sister Mary of the Holy Spirit.

The Institute grew rapidly ever since its foundation in 1902. In 1908, Délia involved her Apostolic School students in promoting the Holy Childhood Fund. Three years later, she introduced retreat weekends "to develop, among women and young girls, zeal for the interests of God and the Church." When a wave of Chinese immigrants flooded into Montreal, she took on the ministry of visiting them in their homes, teaching Sunday school instruction classes, and opening a school and hospital to serve this Asian population. In 1920, she founded the missionary magazine *Le Precurseur* and, three years later, began the English edition of the same magazine, which continues to be published to this day. In 1921, when the Canadian bishops agreed to found the Foreign Missions Seminary, Delia advised them. With regard to her own community of missionary nuns, between 1909 and 1934, the foundress opened thirty-nine houses, mostly schools and orphanages: six in Southern China, including a leprosarium; eight in Northern China, including dispensaries and catechumenates; three in the Philippines, including a nursing school; four in Japan; and in Rome a clinic and a school for the poor. In Canada, the foundress had opened sixteen houses in ten dioceses, including hospitals for the Chinese at Montreal and Vancouver.

In 1933, at sixty-eight, Délia suffered a severe stroke. She remained bedridden for the next eight years, until she died. Suffering from aphasia, she knew what she wanted to say but could not give voice to the words, which eluded her. In her private world with little communication, she found consolation in fully conscious contemplation.

Délia's spirituality revealed the heart and soul of a missionary. Her heart found joy in living simply so that others may simply live. She immersed herself in the situations of the poor: visiting their homes, and learning their languages. With the eyes of her soul, she envisioned peoples of every nation being invited to and welcomed into the Church. She was filled with spiritual fire to propagate the truth and love of Jesus. Soulfully, she sought to know and to do God's will, so that she might experience and communicate God's way of grace. Humbly, admitting that she could not always perceive God's will, she abandoned herself to Divine Providence, as she faced life's realities. Délia's model in living the virtues of faith, hope, and love was the Blessed Virgin Mary. The saints whose lives and writings inspired and guided her include especially Saint Thérèse de Lisieux through *The Story Of a Soul*, Saint Louis de Montfort, and Saint Francis de Sales.

"The Foundress left no 'treatise on spirituality' which would be the condensed version of a doctrine, but she drew from the very lives of Jesus and His Mother a 'life spirit' which can be actualized in everyday situations and is a source of inspiration for those who share her vocation."[80]

One author has perceived three aspects of Délia's spirituality: first, to do the will of God as made manifest by Jesus' Holy Spirit; second, to honor the Immaculate Virgin Mary, who reveals in the Annunciation and Visitation the twofold virtue of receiving and sharing the grace of the Holy Spirit; and third, giving thanks to God through joyful living. Each of these aspects will be expanded.

First, Délia instructed her sisters to be "servants of the Holy Spirit," and allow themselves to be transformed by the Spirit.[81] She herself prayed,

> O adorable Trinity, Father, Son and Holy Spirit, God in three persons.... I come to thank you for all that you have done and have permitted. Everything is good; everything is for the best. Thank you. Here are my hands, my feet, my humble being; do all that you wish with me, I wish to do only your holy will. And she counseled her sisters, "Do whatever God wishes, and in the way

He wishes; to live that way, have little regard for the human manner, but keep your eyes on God, which matters the most."[82]

Second, the foundress asked the sisters to regard Mary as the true superior of the community. Mary guides and directs them; she graces the sisters' lives as she graced Jesus' life. Délia prays for her sisters, "May you let Mary Immaculate obtain for you, who imitate her purity, the grace that empowers you to become temples of the Holy Spirit . . . that you become faithful imitators of our Immaculate Mother."[83]

Third, Délia encourages her sisters, "Our expression of thanks ought to be incessant."[84] A consequence of giving thanks is joy, "which is the best gratitude that one can express to God."[85] "Expressing gratitude is an expression of love . . . which needs to be concretized in a particular action."[86] Délia's missionary motivation penetrated her gratitude. She writes, "The apostolate among pagan peoples has been given us, it seems to me, by the Holy Virgin, as an exterior means of manifesting our thankfulness. God has given us everything, even his own Son; what better way to repay Him . . . , than to bring to Him children, who will sing of His goodness from one century to the next."[87]

> The spirit of joy and thankfulness ought to be the true spirit of our Institute. Take for a daily resolution to make an offering of a little joy. Do a kindness, sow some joy! . . . If there are too many people who are poor in the material blessings of good fortune, there are even more who are poor in receiving acts of kindness. I suggest that you always present yourselves like joyous rays of sunshine. How much good are we able to attain by a simple smile.
>
> Say to the good God a thousand times each day: "My good Master, be present to my affairs, and I will be present to Your affairs.[88]

The Missionaries of the Immaculate Conception regard the following letter of September 4, 1916, as an inspirational statement of the community's charism, and "way of life" which the foundress wanted the sisters to live. Délia was writing to Sister Marie-Immaculée, the superior of the local community at St. Bruno,

> Your letter speaking to me of your joy, your good dispositions and those of your companions makes me bless God. You are con-

tent with everything He permits, with everything that He gives you: that is to say that the good Master also is content with you.

Seize every occasion to cultivate virtue, especially the virtues that ought to characterize our Institute: humility, charity, obedience, joy, silence and thanksgiving. As to this last virtue, each moment brings opportunity to practice it.

Oh how I would like to speak with you at length about this important and delightful duty of thanksgiving.

The more Our Lord makes me penetrate into the spirit of our vocation, and further it appears to me that the principal reason for the existence of our Society, is truly thanksgiving in union with Mary our Immaculate Mother and all the blessed souls in heaven. The apostolate to the unchurched has been given to us, it seems to me, by the Holy Virgin as an exterior means to manifest our interior thanksgiving. God has given us everything, even His own Son; what better means to repay Him — as if a feeble creature might be able to do so in this world — than to give to his children, chosen ones who will also sing His goodness for unending ages. That our life might be given for all, by prayer, sacrifice and work, a perpetual song of thanksgiving for ourselves and for those who forget to thank Him, to whom they owe everything. Let us be imbued with this idea; let us live it; let us do it so well, that we leave this heritage to those who replace us.[89]

When Délia died in 1941, the community, which she had founded in 1902, had grown to five hundred fifty-four sisters who were working in six countries.

*For further information, contact*
Cause Délia-Tétreault
100, Place Juge-Desnoyers
Laval, QC H7G 1A4 Canada

# 5. ☩ Saint Felipe de Jesús de las Casas

*Places: México City, México*
*Fame: First native saint of México and all North America.*
*Martyred in Japan.*

Just over a hundred years after Christopher Columbus is credited with having discovered the New World, a native son of México suffered martyrdom in Japan. Thirty years later, his mother attended in Rome the ceremony at which her son was beatified. Two hundred years later, in 1827, Felipe de Jesús de las Casas (1572-97) was declared a saint of the Church, the first from México, and the first from North America.

Felipe's parents originated from Spain. His father came from Toledo, and his mother from Salamanca. They met, and soon married in November of 1570 at Seville, Spain. In August of the following year, they sailed for México, arriving in October after a terribly threatening voyage. Interestingly, at this early date, the sea captain kept in his chapel an image of Our Lady of Guadalupe. The newlyweds settled first at México's southernmost province of Chiapas, but within the year moved to México City to enjoy a significant inheritance of property and wealth. Although some scholars claim that Felipe was born at Chiapas, other sources report that it was more likely that he, who was born on May 1, first saw the light of day at México City.

The future martyr was the oldest of eleven children. At times he accompanied his father in his professional duties as customs agent and international importer to the port at Acapulco, where Felipe saw the ships that sailed the trans-Pacific routes. Upon completing elementary school, he attended a Jesuit school in the capital city for his secondary education. This youth, who always had been in his childhood "wild, self-willed and easily provoked"[90] fell in with the wrong crowd in the Colegio Maximo de San Pedro y San Pablo. His mother used to say oftentimes in exasperation, "Felipe, may God make you a saint."[91] To which the house-servant would reply, "Felipe will become a saint when the fig tree matures."[92] At sixteen, at his parents' suggestion, Felipe entered the Franciscan seminary at Puebla, but remained there only a short time before returning home. Desiring to become a businessman like his father, at seventeen he left México in January 1590 for the Philippines.

After about three and half years in business at Manila, he again entered a seminary administered by the Franciscans. One year later, he completed the novitiate and took vows in May 1594. Two years later, while sailing home to México for the purpose of being ordained there, the ship on which he was a passenger encountered a great storm. The ship, having lost its masts and rudder, was blown to the island of Shikoku, from where it was towed by Japanese to their harbor at Hirado, where the ship was purposely run aground.

The local *daimyo* Masuda greeted the rescued sailors and passengers, about two hundred people altogether. He suggested that the friars might offer some gifts to the governor Masuda and the most powerful *daimyo* Hdeyoshi at Kyoto. The friars happily consented. Meanwhile, Masuda goaded on by his Buddhist priest-advisor, plotted to confiscate the goods on board the ship. To the surprise of Fray Felipe at Kyoto, "the conspirators had accused the Spaniards of planning to invade Japan, and claimed that the missionaries were merely the forerunners of the soldiers."[93] With that, Hideyoshi declared, "I will kill all the missionaries and also the Christians."[94] Guards were sent to surround the houses of the Franciscans and Jesuits at Kyoto and Osaka.

For the sake of background information, in Japan the Catholic Faith had been spreading rapidly. In less than four decades after St. Francis Xavier's arrival in 1549, "it is said that by 1587 there were in Japan over two hundred thousand Christians."[95] The rising Christian population was causing alarm and anger among the emperors. In 1588, all Christian missionaries were ordered to leave the country within six months. Some obeyed, and others sought to assimilate themselves into the native population. In 1596, another emperor reacted with fury to the claim of a Spanish naval captain that "the object of the missionaries was to facilitate the conquest of Japan by the Portuguese or Spaniards."[96]

Returning to the story about Felipe, the Emperor Tagcosama ordered his soldiers to round up both native and foreign Christian clergy and lay leaders. Initially, twenty-four Christian clergy and laity were arrested, and were marched to the jail at Nagasaki. Along the way, two more Christians were arrested so that the group totaled twenty-six persons.

The twenty-six Christians included six Franciscans, three Jesuits, and seventeen Third Order lay Franciscans, among whom were three young altar boys. The first person to step forward and to be killed among these victims was Felipe de Jesús de las Casas. Like almost all of the religious prisoners, he had his left ear cut off. Soldiers force-marched the prisoners through numerous towns to the execution site at Nagasaki. At their destination, "they were allowed to make their confessions to two Jesuits and, after being fastened to crosses by cords and chains about their arms and legs and with an iron collar round their necks, they were raised into the air, the foot of each cross falling into a hole in the ground prepared for it."[97]

*For further information, contact*
Franciscan Friars
Provincial Curia
Caballocalco 11
Coyoacán, México D.F. 04000 México

❧

## 7. ☩ Frank Parater

*Place: Richmond, VA*
*Fame: Precocious in spirituality, and prescient of his death.*
*Seminarian who died at twenty-two.*

The death of twenty-two year-old seminarian Frank Parater (1897-1920) seemed at first like the very sad death of any other young person. Within a few hours after his death, however, when Frank's "Last Will and Testament" was read, the contents revealed an extraordinary aspect about the death.[98]

FRANK PARATER

Frank Parater had been born and raised in Richmond, Virginia. After his father's first wife and the several children to whom she gave birth had died, he married a devout Episcopalian who converted to the Catholic faith. Having grown up in the city's Church Hill neighborhood, Frank served Masses at the monastery of the Visitation Sisters, attended the local Catholic grade school, where the Xaverian Brothers taught, and graduated from Benedictine High School. Desiring to become a priest for the Diocese of Richmond, he entered Belmont Abbey College Seminary near Charlotte, North Carolina. Upon Frank's completion of studies at Belmont, the bishop of Richmond sent his promising candidate to North American College at Rome, where the bishop expected the seminarian to complete his studies in philosophy and theology, and be ordained. Frank arrived at Rome, in mid-November 1919, and officially enrolled and began classes on November 25.

At Rome, in the less than three months that he lived there, Frank made a positive impression on observers. His peers liked him, as exemplified by his having been elected in early January to emcee the seminarians' festive evening on the feast of the Epiphany. His easy smile conveyed an apparent happiness, which proved contagious to others who reciprocated in kind. At prayer and in conversations, he demonstrated a piety typical of many seminarians, although, some of his passing comments revealed glimpses of an unusually profound spirituality. His death was sad particularly because of its suddenness, his youth, and his promise.

When his "Last Will and Testament" was discovered, however, observers suddenly perceived an extraordinary spiritual maturity, and a mystery surrounding his death. Readers should keep in mind that when Frank Parater wrote his will on December 5, 1919, he was enjoying the best of health, with no hint of sickness on the horizon.

On January 22, he suddenly felt ill with "rheumatic pains, first in one arm and then spreading."[99] Five days later, he was admitted to the Blue Nuns Hospital with "increasing pains in his arms, hands, back and chest."[100] Doctors diagnosed his illness as rheumatic fever. One week later, on February 5, with his poor health continuing to worsen, he was placed on the critical list. The next day, the rector of the seminary offered the community Mass for Frank's recovery, if it might be God's will. Early on February 7, Frank, who already had received the sacraments of Penance and Anointing of the Sick, attempted to get out of bed to receive the sacrament of Holy Communion, but being too weak to do so, he knelt on his bed and received. "The last action he made was a slow and labored sign of the cross. Towards the end, his lips moved constantly in prayer; his death was like falling asleep."[101] That morning, Frank died.

Later that same day of Frank's death, the rector of the seminary assigned one of Frank's classmates from the diocese of Richmond, to sort through the dead man's belongings. In this process, the classmate discovered a sealed envelope, marked "My Last Will," with the caveat, "To be opened only in the case of my death."[102] The seminarian immediately carried the envelope to the rector. The entire contents reads as follows:

> I have nothing to leave or give but my life, and this I have consecrated to the Sacred Heart to be used as He wills. I have offered my all for the conversions to God of non-Catholics in Virginia. This is what I live for and, in case of death, what I die for.
>
> Death is not unpleasant to me, but the most beautiful and welcome event of my life. Death is the messenger of God come to tell us that our novitiate is ended and to welcome us to the real life.
>
> Melancholic or morbid sentimentality is not the cause of my writing this, for I love life here, the college, the men, and Rome itself. But I have desired to die and be buried with the saints. I dare not ask God to take me lest I should be ungrateful or be trying to shirk the higher responsibilities of life; but I shall never have less to answer for — perhaps never to be better ready to meet my Maker, my God, my All.
>
> Since I was a child, I have desired to die for the love of God and for my fellow man. Whether or not I shall receive that favor I know not, but if I live, it is for the same purpose; every action of my life here is offered to God for the spread and success of the Catholic Church in Virginia, I have always desired to be only a little child, that I may enter the Kingdom of God. In the general resurrection I wish to always be a boy and to be permitted to accompany Saints John Berchmans, Aloysisus and Stanislaus [all of whom died between eighteen and twenty-three] as their servant and friend. Do we serve God and man less worthily by our

prayers in heaven than by our actions on earth? Surely it is not selfish to desire to be with Him Who has loved us so well.

I shall not leave my dear ones. I will always be near them and be able to help them more than I can here below. I shall be of more service to my diocese in heaven than I could ever be on earth.

If it is God's holy will, I will join him on Good Friday, 1920, and never leave him more — but not my will, Father, but thine be done!

Rome, December 5th, 1919<br>[Signed] Frank Parater

Had Frank known of his impending death? Was it a natural premonition, or a supernatural prescience? In any case, the content of the will was startling. News spread about the mysterious foreknowledge. The will was translated, and was printed in *L'Osservatore Romano*. Pope Benedict XV asked for a copy, as did his successor Pius XI. One of the seminarians commented about the seminarians' change in mood from sadness to joy after they had read Frank's will: "We actually rejoiced because we felt a saint had been in our midst."[103]

*For further information, contact*
Diocese of Richmond
3805 Cutshaw Ave, Suite # 307
Richmond, Virginia 23230

## 9. ✠ Martyrs of Virginia

*Place: Williamsburg and Yorktown, Virginia*
*Fame: Martyred on account of hatred of the Christian life.*
*Proto-martyrs of Virginia.*

In February 1571, eight Jesuits including two priests, three lay brothers, and three novices died for the faith at the hands of Indians in Virginia.[104] One priest and two lay brothers were martyred near Williamsburg on

February 4 and 5. The remaining five Jesuits were slain in a village, perhaps near Yorktown, on February 9.

On an exploration which Captain Angel de Villafañe had led, Spanish sailors discovered a large bay, which they named the Bay of the Mother of God (now Chesapeake Bay). From this region, the explorers returned to Spain with the usual fruits and vegetables, plus an Indian youth whom the sailors named Don Luis de Velasco, in honor of the boy's godfather Don Luis. Young Don Luis was baptized in New Spain, and was educated in Spain.

After numerous failures to convert the Indians of the Florida Mission, which extended along the Atlantic Coast for almost six hundred miles (between present-day Miami, Florida, and Charleston, South Carolina), the Jesuit superior Father Juan Bautista de Segura (1529-1571) decided to close this mission. Segura wrote to the superior general Father Francis Borgia that the missions were bearing no fruit. In consequence, Segura ordered all Jesuits to return from this mission to their headquarters at Havana, Cuba. Before leaving the area, Segura decided to make one last effort at evangelizing the Indians. He decided to travel to Ajacan, the Great Tidewater Peninsula in Southern Virginia, where no mission had yet been undertaken.

In an attempt to make this evangelizing effort different from other failed attempts, Segura decided to prohibit any soldiers from participating in or even being present at the mission. Segura had witnessed how soldiers at Santa Elena (now Charleston, South Carolina) and Guale (now Golden Isles, Gerogia) had mistreated the Indians, which resulted in jeopardizing the success of the missionary effort. Recently, the Franciscans and the Dominicans had prohibited the Spanish military from particiapting in their missions among the Indians. Segura believed it was time for the Jesuits to employ the same *modus operandi*. Instead of taking along soldiers for protection, Segura reasoned that he would take the Indian convert Don Luis, who already knew the language and customs of the Powhatans, and whose blood brothers reigned as chiefs at Ajacan. Don Luis, Segura surmised, would best serve the purpose, plan, and perception of the mission as evangelical in nature, and not political in any way.

Father Segura put together a mission team. He chose two recently arrived Jesuit educators, the priest Luis de Quiros and lay brother Gabriel

Gomez. Another lay brother, Sancho Zeballos, who had appealed directly and successfully to the governor at Cuba, came from Spain to join the mission. Segura chose a third brother, Pedro Linares, and three novices, Gabriel de Solis, Juan Bautista Mendez, and Cristobal Redondo. The eight Jesuits embarked from St. Augustine, and put into port at Santa Elena, where they replenished their supplies. At Santa Elena, a young boy named Alonso Olmos, the son of a colonist, asked to join the mission. The lad had been serving as an altar boy at Santa Elena, and explained that he wished to assist the missionaries in the same way. The boy's father, and the Jesuits approved of the boy's joining them.

On September 10, 1570, the ship carrying the missionaries arrived at the Bay of the Mother of God. From there, the captain sailed sixty miles "up the James River to College Creek, which is just below Jamestown Island (later the site of the first permanent English colony in America). The expedition probably debarked along College Creek near Williamsburg." From that site, the missionaries traveled up a creek until they selected a site, which "was one of the Chiskiac Indian villages [possibly] near the York River, in the vicinity of Queens Creek or Indian Fields Creek. The supplies were unloaded from the ship along College Creek, carried overland to Queens Creek, and then transported to the site by Indian canoes."[105] Segura ordered the ship to return to Cuba without delay, and to return in spring with food, clothing, and seed for planting. The Chiskiac Indians in the region were suffering a famine, and the missionaries wished to do all that they could to help the natives. On September 12, the ship headed out of the bay.

The new arrivals applied themselves to the tasks at hand. After making initial contact with local Indians, Don Luis went off in search of his relatives. The Jesuits got busy with building a cabin, which would provide them with living quarters and a chapel, which became "probably the first Catholic Chapel in Virginia."[106]

In primitive surroundings, the Jesuits set up religious life. They opened a school for Indian boys. There was daily Mss, and daily spiritual instruction. The three novice Brothers were professed into the Society of Jesus — the first religious profession recorded in the United States.[107]

When weeks passed without Don Luis returning, concern arose among the Jesuits for his whereabouts. Local Indians relayed rumors to the Jesuits that Don Luis was safe, and "that Don Luis had returned to native ways and was leading a life of unbridled vice."[108] For months, Segura tried through intermediaries to persuade his convert and hand-selected guide to rejoin the mission. As time passed, winter weather set in, and the food supply lessened. The Jesuits suffered severe cold and hunger that winter.

"In 1571, Father de Segura dispatched Father Quiros to attempt again to persuade Don Luis to return."[109] The Jesuit superior sent two novices with the priest, in order to assist in carrying the much-needed supplies, which Quiros might receive from Don Luis and the other Indians. Quiros located Don Luis, and urged him to return to the faith, and to the Jesuit camp. Don Luis "promised to follow them back to the village. Instead, he took several fellow Indians and overtook the three missionaries near the present site of Williamsburg, and killed them. It was Sunday, February 4, 1571."[110] The Algonquins shot the Christians with bows and arrows. Quiros and Gabriel de Solis, now wounded, were beaten to death by club-wielding braves. Bautista Mendez, although wounded, escaped to the forest. The next day, he was discovered, gravely wounded but still alive. His enemies finished him off.

On February 9, Don Luis and fellow Indians visited the Jesuit cabin. Father Segura welcomed Don Luis with open arms. The Indians "asked for axes with which to cut wood, [and], receiving the axes, they killed all the remaining missionaries with the exception of the boy Alonso."[111] All five missionaries lay dead on the spot. Alonso successfully implored Don Luis to give the dead a decent burial. With the others assisting in burying the five victims, Alonso placed a crucifix in the hands of each of the deceased.

A few months later, a Spanish supply ship sailed up the James River. The sailors noticed that the Indians on shore were wearing the religious cassocks of the Jesuits. Soon, two canoes full of Indian warriors attacked the Spanish ship. Battle ensued. The Spanish captured two Indians, who reported the deaths of the Jesuits and the capture of Alonso. Eighteen months after the martyrdom, i.e, August 1572, the Governor of Cuba, Pedro Menendez de Aviles, arrived on board a ship to investigate the whereabouts of the Jesuits and to rescue Alonso. The rescue succeeded.

Many early witnesses testified to the details of the martyrs' deaths. Alonso reported the facts to his rescuers. Several Indians corroborated Alonso's story. Sailors on board the rescue ship saw the Indians dressed in the Jesuits' cassocks, and wearing the Eucharistic patens as necklace jewelry. Three other contemporary accounts support the story as told by Alonso. Jesuit priest Juan Rogel visited the Chesapeake Bay in 1572, researched the events, and wrote an account. The Jesuit lay brother Juan de la Carrera, who had stocked Segura's ship at Santa Elena in 1570, also visited the Chesapeake area in 1572, and wrote a similar accounting of the facts. Bartolomé Martinez, a colonial official who resided at Santa Elena during the time of the martyrdoms at Ajacán, supported the above evidence in his account. Significantly, in all accounts, Don Luis' motivation for killing the missionaries, and in choosing not to kill Alonso, lay in his hatred of the missionaries, and the Christian moral message. Alonso's life was spared because he was not a missionary.

What little information is known about the background of the martyrs is summarized below.

The superior of the mission, Juan Bautista de Segura, was born at Toledo, Spain. Apparently, he studied with the priesthood in mind, as he learned Latin, Greek, and Hebrew on his way to earning a Master of Arts degree at the University of Alcalá, after which he studied theology and Sacred Scripture at the same institution for four more years. Upon completing his studies, he entered the Society of Jesus at Alcalá in 1556, took vows two days later, and was ordained the following year. During the next ten years, he taught for three years, and then served as rector at three successive Jesuit colleges. Always desirous of going to the missions, he was assigned to the Florida Mission. On September 26, 1567, he was named vice provincial of that mission. Nine months later, June 1568, he arrived at St. Augustine, Florida. Eight extant letters reveal that he "traveled to all the mission posts at Tegesta, Calus and Guale, teaching the natives and the Spanish garrisons, and . . . his letters retain a spirit of bold determination. He insisted on the freedom of movement of the Jesuits, and refused to let them be relegated to the status of garrison chaplains as [Governor] Menendez preferred."[112]

Jesuit priest Luis de Quiros was born in Andulusia, Spain. He taught at Jesuit schools in Trigueros (now Huelva) beginning around 1562, and at Seville beginning in 1567. For two years, he served as superior of a mission among the Moriscos (Jews who converted to Catholicism) near Granada. In June 1570, he arrived at the Florida Mission.

The three lay brothers appear to have been quite young. Gabriel Gomez, who came from Granada in Spain, had entered the Society of Jesus in 1568. He taught at Seville before being assigned to the Florida Mission. Sancho Zaballos taught at Seville before entering the Jesuits, and shortly thereafter was missioned to Florida. Superior General Francis Borgia, on November 14, 1570, sent a stinging criticism to the provincial for sending a confrere so young to a mission so difficult. Pedro Mingot Linares was born at Valencia, Spain, and entered the Jesuits on May 31, 1564. Four years later, he arrived at the Florida Mission, where he taught catechism at Santa Elena for several months before going to Ajacan.

The three novices, Cristobal Redondo, Gabriel de Solis, and Juan Bautista Mendez, had originated their stay with the Jesuits as lay catechists. The earliest evidence of these three, namely, a letter written in December 1570, describes the trio as *mancebos de doctrina*, [catechists], whereas a letter written by the same author in August 1572, calls them *hermanos* [brothers]. These three Jesuit novices represent the first vocations to the priesthood and religious life in the geographical area. "If they were not Jesuits, perhaps they would have been spared as Alonso was."[113]

*For further information, contact*

Office of the Postulator
3805 Cutshaw Ave., Suite 307
Richmond, Virginia 23220 U.S.A.

# 10. ✠ José Sánchez del Río

*Place: Sahuayo, Michoacán, México*
*Fame: Volunteer in the army of the Cristeros. Boy martyr.*

Mature in faith and courage well beyond his thirteen years, the life and letters of José Sánchez del Río (1915-28) might inspire older readers to deepen their faith and courage.[114]

Although young in age, and the youngest in the family of six children, José wanted to join the Cristero movement in armed rebellion in defense of the faith against the anti-Catholic government and its army. Clearly José's two older brothers could not leave their jobs and join the army since they were busily providing for José's entire family in place of the father who had died already. José reasoned that his brothers were needed at home, and that he was free to leave.

José pleaded with his mother to allow him to join the Cristeros. She argued that he was too young to join the Catholic soldiers and fight in their army. Prolonged discussion persuaded neither mother nor son to change their minds. When she pointed that even the head of the Cristero army would agree that José was too young, he countered by suggesting that he would write to General Mendoza, and let him decide the question that so divided the mother and son. In desperation, and confident of her position, she agreed to follow her son's suggestion.

José wrote to the general, who responded as the mother had said all along, that the thirteen-year old boy was too young to fight in the army. José, however, was undaunted. He wrote to the same general a second letter, suggesting that the lad, although not permitted to carry weapons, would be available to assist the general in any way needed. After this second request, and the limited role proffered, the general agreed to let José join the Cristero army, but on one condition, namely, that the boy's mother would approve of his volunteering. Upon receipt of the general's letter, the mother kept her word, and allowed her son to leave home at this tender age to fight in defense of the Catholic faith.

After only a few months in the army, José was taken prisoner. At a battle near Cotija, General Mendoza's horse was shot and killed. When the young assistant saw what had happened to the general, the youth rushed to the general's side, and offered his own horse to the military leader. José is reported to have said, "General, take my horse. You need one. I do not. I will remain here, and I will see what happens later."[115] The ensuing battle went badly for the Catholics, and when they retreated, the youth was left standing alone against the advancing enemy army. José was captured by the federalist troops, and was presented to their commander.

The enemy general admired the courage of this young warrior. The general invited the boy to switch sides, to fight with the government, and assured him that the life with the federal troops would be better for him than life as a captured Cristero. Without hesitation, José rejected the enemy general's offer, viewing such betrayal as a sin. "Never, never. Death first. I do not want to join the enemies of Christ the King."[116] When word reached the general about the boy's intransigence, the general ordered the youth to be jailed for the moment, and later to be shot to death. Soldiers took José to his hometown to be jailed. The place in which they held him was the parish church, which had been converted to a jail, and a horse stable. José, shocked by the sacrilegious reduction of the church from its sacred to secular purpose, became even more confirmed in his resolve to remain faithful to Christ and His Church.

During his last week on earth, José wrote two letters, one to his mother and another to his aunt. The letters demonstrate the boy's outstanding faith and courage. He writes on February 6, 1928:

> My dear mother, today, I was taken as a prisoner of combat. I believe that in a little while I am going to die. But that is not so important, mama. Resign yourself the to the will of God. I will die content, because I will die in duty at the side of Our God. Do not worry about my death, that is why I have sacrificed myself. Before you say to my two brothers that they ought to follow the example which their younger brother has given them, and that you might do the will of God, take courage and, you my mother with my father, bless me. Give my regards to everyone, for this last time, and you receive the heart of your son who so much desires to be with you and see you before he would die.
>
> [Signed,] José Sanchez del Rio.[117]

Four days later, José writes to his aunt,

I have been sentenced to die. At 8:30, the moment will have arrived that I have desired so much. I thank you for all the kindnesses that you and Magdalena have shown to me. I am not able to write to María. Tell Magdalena that that the authorities have granted permission for me to see her one last time, and I think they will not prohibit her coming. Greetings to everyone, and you, please receive as always and to the very end, the heart of your nephew who loves you much and desires to see you. Christ lives. Christ reigns. Christ rules, along with the Holy Virgin of Guadalupe! — José Sanchez del Rio, who died in defense of the faith. Don't forget to come. So long.[118]

When one of the soldiers, just before shooting him, asked José what he would like the soldiers to say to his mother, the youth replied, "That we will see each other in heaven. *¡Viva Cristo Rey!* [Long live Christ the King!]" Those words were the last thing said by José. The soldiers then shot him to death.

*For further information, contact*
Promotores de la Cause de Canonización
Diócesis de Michoacán
Abasolo 45,
Sahuayo, Michoacán, México

## 11. ☩ Venerable Maria Luisa Josefa of the Blessed Sacrament

*Places: Atotonilco el Alto and Guadalajara, Jalisco;*
*and Los Angeles, California*
*Fame: "I belong to God." Foundress of the Carmelite Sisters*
*of the Most Sacred Heart of México and the Carmelite Sisters*
*of the Most Sacred Heart of Los Angeles.*

As a young teenager, Maria Luisa Josefa de la Peña Navarro (1866-1937) expressed interest in becoming a contemplative nun.[119] Pursuit of her vocation, however, was delayed by her parents, two successive bishops, and the Mexican government. Meanwhile, Luisita, as her family and friends affectionately called her, kept trying to discern and to the do God's will. Eventually, at fifty-five, she founded a religious community, the Carmelite Sisters of the Sacred Heart at Guadalajara, and within the decade established a second branch at Los Angeles. Her vocation is a testimony to perseverance in discovering and doing God's will.

Born at Atotonilco el Alto, a small town fifty miles east of Guadalajara, Luisita grew up in comfort as the third of fourteen children on the parents' extensive ranch lands. She enjoyed the benefit of a tutor, and progressed in studies without difficulty. Interpersonal relationships, however, presented a challenge. In the company of others, she remained reticent and even reclusive. Her behavior appeared haughty and aloof. Her father became annoyed when, as he and his daughter would ride in a wagon on the ranch, he would greet his employees, but his daughter would turn away her head, and would refuse to speak to the ranch hands. He scolded her, "My little daughter, will your tongue wear out if you simply greet these people?[120] Her mother took a more direct approach. "She spoke not only an occasional word of reproof, but she sought every available opportunity to humble this proud young girl, yet with a kindness and charity that was most effective.[121]

Fortunately, Luisita underwent a growth spurt in personality, when she and an elderly woman relative of the family struck up a friendship. Both were reflective and spiritual in personality. As the pair would walk throughout the grounds of the sprawling ranch, the elderly woman helped to develop within the young girl an appreciation of God's presence in the beauty of all creation, especially in each person. During these walks, Luisita developed the desire to enter the religious life, and in particular the contemplative life.

Her parents had plans for Luisita. According to the custom of the time and place, the parents would choose a husband for their daughter. The parents selected a prominent physician, who was delighted with he arrangement to marry Luisitia. She, however, was fifteen; and he thirty. Yielding to her parents' wishes, and after months of extensive preparations, Luisita married Doctor Pascual Rojas on February 9, 1882. As the couple was approaching México City on their honeymoon, the husband asked his wife what sites she would like to see. She replied the Convent of the Visitation Sisters. When the married couple arrived, Luisita requested to speak in private with the superior. Luisita sought permission to join the religious order then and there. Luisita returned to her husband, with whom the following exchange took place.

"You may go now, Pascual. I am going to stay here. I have asked for admission, and Reverend Mother has accepted me." Pascual could not believe her words. Yet she had been very clear about what she said. She was going to enter the convent and she said that he could return to Atotonilco. Slowly he walked to Maria Luisa's side without speaking. As he stood beside her, it was the superior who broke the silence. "Dear child," she said kindly, "you must do as your father asks." These words shook Pascual back to his senses. "She is not my daughter, Mother," he explained with vehemence. "This is my wife. We were just married and came to México City for our honeymoon." That presented a totally different situation, and the superior told Maria Luisa that although she had acceded to this marriage because of her parents' wishes, she was then not free to enter the convent. . . .

It was with much reluctance that Maria Luisa listened to the superior's words, for she had set her heart on joining he Sisters of the Visitation. Pascual took her gently by the arm and with real sympathy said, "If you will return with me now, Maria Luisa, I promise I shall let you come back to the convent some day."[122]

The couple lived together for the next fourteen years, until Pascual died. They had desired children, but when God did not grant them offspring, the pair devoted themselves to the care of the sick, and opened the first ever hospital at Atotonilco. Meanwhile, Luisita kept maturing in warmth and relationships, compassion in service and skill in organization. The hospital flourished under Luisa's leadership. On her husband's deathbed, he encouraged his wife to fulfill his promise that he would let her return to the convent.

Luisa applied to the Visitation Convent at Morelia, but the community refused to admit her because of her weak health. She turned to the Carmelites, who accepted her in their branch of Discalced Carmelites of St. Teresa at Guadalajara. Luisa loved this life, whereby she began fulfilling her youthful dreams.

At Atotonilco, however, the hospital was faltering without Luisa's leadership. Proper medical care was not being provided, medical supplies were not available when needed, and the building was falling into disrepair. The townspeople begged Archbishop José de Jesus Ortiz Rodríguez at Guadalajara to urge Luisa to return to them. The archbishop, perceiving the same deterioration of the institution, and knowing no one else could administer the hospital, went to the Carmelite convent, and asked the novice Luisa to consider leaving the convent and returning to the hospital. "After much prayer and listening to the archbishop, she chose to return to the hospital and accede to his wishes as she felt they represented God's manifest will for her."[123]

Luisita returned to the hospital. "Her heart ached for the poor and afflicted who had been so badly neglected. She immediately set about putting things in order. News of her return brought many of her friends to her aid, but this news also brought many of the sick. This made it necessary for all to work long hours. Day by day, improvements were made. Maria Luisa was tireless in her efforts."[124] As soon as the hospital was restored to good operations, Maria Luisita set about opening in town a school for poor girls. Volunteers stepped forward to assist her in this work too.

Women of similar vision and virtue gathered around Maria Luisa. On Christmas Eve 1904, in a simple ceremony, seven of these women dedicated themselves to caring for others. Within three years, the number burgeoned to twenty women. The archbishop grew suspicious of these laywomen who were living like religious. He opined that if they wanted to act like religious, they ought to become religious. He suggested that they might affiliate themselves with the Sisters of Perpetual Adoration at Guadalajara. Maria Luisa requested time to ponder the proposal. In the meantime, the bishop died before Maria Luisa could respond to him. The new archbishop, Francisco Orozco y Jimenez, however, thought like his predecessor, except the new pastor recommended that the women join the Sisters Servants of the Blessed Sacrament.

Maria yielded, and left her hospital and school to join the religious community at Guadalajara with nineteen of her colleagues. She entered the community on May 22, 1913, and almost two years later, she made vows in that order. Only months after she had left

Atotonilco, the same archbishop visited her and lamented that without her leadership the hospital was collapsing and the school had closed. She offered to pray for the situation. He wanted more. Like his predecessor, he said, "You must leave the convent and return once more to your work of caring for the sick and educating the young. That is where you belong — not here."[125] Maria was shocked. It was the archbishop who had sent her away from the social ministry to the convent. Now he was requesting her to return, after she had vowed herself in this community.

Obedient as ever, and perceiving God's will in the archbishop's will, she returned to Atotonilco in May 1917. Of the nineteen women who had joined the Blessed Sacrament Convent with her, only five came out with her, and these were elderly and illiterate. By this time, the hospital had no patients, and the school had no teachers and students. Maria Luisa threw herself into restoring both institutions. Again, young women joined her in the effort. Soon, they numbered twenty. And again, the archbishop accused the laywomen of trying to live like nuns. He urged them to join a convent from which they could continue this ministry, but as nuns. Maria Luisa replied that she wanted to be a nun, but a contemplative one, although she appreciated the spiritual and temporal needs of the people. The bishop and Maria Luisa compromised. Maria Luisa would found a third-order Carmelite community, whose members would remain contemplative, wear the Carmelite habit, and provide some time each day for apostolic service. In 1920, the archbishop wrote to Rome for approval of the community. Approval was received the next year, and Maria Luisa founded at Guadalajara, the Carmelite Sisters of the Sacred Heart.

Four years later, when President Calles promulgated his anti-Catholic ordinances, he dictated that seminaries and convents were to be closed, priests and nuns were to be exiled abroad, church properties were to be confiscated, and priests and nuns who resisted were to be killed. Mother Luisita and her community took refuge in Los Angeles, California. There, Mother established another foundation of her community. After Calles fled from the presidency and sought refuge in he U.S.A., Maria returned to México. There she labored from 1929 until her death in 1937.

Her life evidences development in personality and flexibility in responding to the changing demands of times, archbishops, and governments. Wife, widow, in and out of two religious communities, and foundress of a Carmelite community with two branches, she leaves a legacy of trying to discover and do God's will, as manifested in superiors and in the signs of the times. She advised one of her sisters:

It is very necessary to have recollection and detachment and above all, detachment from your own will. Really and truly, you cannot have any other will but that of the Beloved. You still lack very much, but God our Lord will make you very virtuous and give you what you are lacking. Humble yourself, asking Him to do everything for you and with tranquility continue working for the good of your own soul which is the most urgent thing for you to do. See God, your soul and eternity, and for the rest, do not preoccupy yourself. For greater things, you were born. Pray for me. I wish to be what I should be.[126]

Mother Luisita sums up in one of her retreat meditations the spirit that guided her life.

I belong to God. He created me. Therefore he can dispose of me according to his holy will. The eleven o'clock conference was about desiring to attain perfection. We will never find this perfection in contemplation, nor in consolations, nor in sensible fervor. It will only be found in promptly and joyfully carrying out the will of God, solely because God is asking it of us through our superiors. We should obey without paying any attention to our own inclinations, conquering ourselves without trying to figure out whether we like of dislike whatever is asked of us through obedience. That's what our fervor is all about — doing whatever God wants promptly because He wants it and our rules, regulations and superiors commands' demand it from us, even if we ourselves don't want to do it.[127]

*For further information, contact*
Carmelite Sisters of he most Sacred Heart of Los Angeles
920 East Alhambra Road
Alhambra, California 91801 U.S.A.

## 16.  ✠  Stephen Eckert, O.F.M. Cap.

*Places: Dublin and Kitchener, Ontario; Detroit, Michigan;*
*New York City, New York; and Milwaukee, Wisconsin.*
*Fame: Zeal for souls. Apostle of African-Americans.*

Franciscan Friar Stephen Eckert (1869-1923) gained renown for his sanctity and service to Catholics and non-Catholics, and especially for his dedication to members of the African-American community.[128] His obituary reads:

STEPHEN ECKERT

> Love for his divine master consumed him in his work for the poorest of God's poor, the neglected and despised Negro. God, the eternal Judge, alone can number the sacrifices which Father Stephen made for the Negro Mission in the last ten years. How many painful experiences he underwent! But no obstacle, no difficulty, no sacrifice could deter him. On behalf of the Negro he wrote appeals and articles and letters for the newspapers.... For the Negroes he traveled from city to city, to bring home to their white brethren the duty they have toward the colored race. The extensive propaganda he carried on during the last two years, the prejudices he removed in the minds of bishops, priests and the laity, will surely be one of his brightest pages in the book of life.[129]

Father Stephen's vocation began at home. At St. Columban, near Dublin, Ontario, about fifty miles west of Toronto, his parents John Eckert and Kunigunda Arnold, who individually had emigrated from Bavaria in 1858, met in Ontario, and married at Stratford, Ontario, in August 1858. The couple quickly gave birth to nine children, of whom John was the middle child. The parents raised the children firmly in the faith in the midst of the surrounding predominantly Protestant population. Every week, if weather and road conditions permitted, the family traveled on horseback the six-mile distance for Sunday Mass. The same trek was made for confessions on Saturday once each month. When the Eckert and neighboring families could not travel for Sunday Mass, Sunday services were conducted locally by neighbors, oftentimes in the Eckert farmhouse.

After John received his elementary education at the local public school in Berlin (now Kitchener), he attended for six years and graduated from the apostolic school at St. Jerome's College, also in Berlin. In his final year of study at Berlin, two Capuchin friars preached a mission in the local parish. Having heard the friars preach, John joined the newly established society of Third Order Franciscans at St. Jerome's Seminary. Feeling attracted to the Capuchin charism, and wanting to know more about them, John spent a few days in the summer of 1890 with the Franciscan community at St. Bonaventure Monastery in downtown Detroit. That December, John asked to join the order. "He was attracted to the Capuchin Order because of its otherworldliness, its simplicity, its apostolic work, its spirit of penance and of prayer."[130]

John formally applied to the Capuchin community, and on December 17, 1890, the Capuchin provincial accepted John as a candidate. In spring 1891, John Eckert traveled to St. Bonaventure Friary in Detroit, where the provincialate and the novitiate were located. On May 21, 1891, he received the Capuchin habit, and the religious name Stephen, in honor of the Church's first martyr. One year later, he pronounced temporary vows. Advancing to the major seminary, he spent the next four years at St. Francis Friary in Milwaukee, Wisconsin. Throughout his seminary days, Friar Stephen Eckert demonstrated purposefulness to the task at hand. He applied himself diligently to studies, although he never manifested great scholarship. Sports, especially football, he enjoyed immensely and entered into enthusiastically. Prayer, he practiced faithfully, at meditation and Mass, at devotions and visits to the Blessed Sacrament. Nothing exceptional stands out about him except his desire to become a missionary, and his emphasis on preachers learning to preach well. "He deplored the lack of a more adequate training in elocution, and set aside a special time for the practice of this art. He loved to listen to sermons and discussed them with his fellow students to acquire greater proficiency in preaching."[131] On May 24, 1895, the seminarian took his final vows. On July 2, 1896, Stephen was ordained a priest.

The next seventeen years, from September 1896 until summer 1913, Father Stephen experienced, with one exception, a series of short-lived assignments. He began ministry in New York, at St. Fidelis Friary and St. John the Baptist Parish in New York City (1896), and Sacred Heart Friary and Parish at Yonkers (1897). For a brief time, he worked in the midwest, preaching retreats at Detroit (1905), serving as hospital chaplain at Fond-du-Lac, Wisconsin (1905), and again preaching missions at Detroit (1906). He returned to New York City, where he ministered at Our Lady of Angels Parish (1906), St. John the Baptist Parish (1907), Our Lady of Angels Parish again (1909), and St. Boniface Parish in Harlem (1911). In all these assignments, Father Stephen manifested great zeal for souls. His popular and effective preaching of parish missions and retreats, especially for men, brought many fallen-away Catholics back to the Church. He reached out to the unchurched and inactive Protestants, and brought hundreds into the Catholic Church. He achieved this evangelization through house-to-house visitations and distributing Catholic literature in public places. For young people, he organized spiritual, educational, and social activities, including, First Communion classes, Confraternity of Christian Doctrine classes for public school children, Eucharistic Leagues, and Apostleship of Prayer groups. "His first experience with blacks came when several families moved into the parish [St. John's on West 30th Street in midtown Manhattan]."[132] Because the blacks felt like minorities in a basically Irish parish, Father Stephen investigated purchasing a vacant Protestant church, and using that for his black Catholic population. But he was transferred again, to Harlem, which was "predominantly Slavic and Italian."[133]

While at Yonkers, Father Stephen traveled to Cornwell Heights, near Philadelphia, to visit with and learn from the Sisters of the Blessed Sacrament, which community Mother Katharine Drexel had founded in 1891, to work specifically with "Indian and Colored People." As early as 1905, Father Stephen had begun expressing to his superiors his desire to live among and work with African-Americans. He suggested that an itinerant ministry be started among the blacks of the southern United States. In January 1906, his provincial superior began investigating that possibility, but the superior general at Rome rejected the proposal. In 1907, Father Stephen, in the midst of performing his assigned duties, made time to work with the black population as well. In 1909, he had a chance meeting with Bishop O'Gorman of Sierra Leone, Africa. This meeting occasioned fanning into greater flame the spirit of the priest for ministering among blacks.

In early 1911, the archbishop of Milwaukee entrusted to the Capuchin Friars the newly established St. Benedict the Moor Mission for the Colored. The Capuchins needed Franciscan priests and brothers who felt a special calling to serve the African-American community. Father Stephen was assigned to the mission two years after it had opened. He would spend the last ten years of his life laboring for the Mission for the Colored.

> In July 1913, Father Stephen was appointed pastor, and the Servant of God took up his residence in a small, poorly furnished room. The Blessed Sacrament was kept in the small chapel, and the Servant of God spent long hours there late at night in prayer for his Mission. The Servant of God accomplished an immense amount of good at the Mission in the almost ten years of self-sacrificing activity. It was like working in a foreign mission field, great was the need and few were the workers. Father Stephen actually spent himself most heroically for the spiritual and temporal good of his colored flock.[134]

Simply, Father Stephen continued in this mission what he had done in previous missions, but this time for the African-Americans for whom he felt a great affection and calling. He visited hundreds of families. The school enrollment grew by leaps and bounds. To attract students from a wider geographical base Father Stephen conceived of, constructed, and fund-raised for a boarding school. To ensure a future for all the graduates, the priest-founder instituted both academic and vocational tracks. Ahead of his times, he opened a day nursery for working mothers, and a residence and employment agency for young women. He begged locally and preached nationally to promote and provide for the school. In 1921, when another Capuchin was named pastor, Father Stephen was appointed the mission's fund-raiser. In his fund-raising, he instructed his audiences about the plight of the American blacks, and urged donors to give generously in support of the Church's works for justice.

While ministering to the black population, the zealous priest encountered much criticism. Fellow priests accused him of financial folly for trying to found and fund a boarding school, a nursery school, and a residence for women. Laity criticized him for his affection for the black population. Father Stephen remained, however, undaunted in his vision and mission.

The apparently indefatigable Father Stephen suddenly became seriously ill after preaching and hearing confessions at a Forty Hours service in Britt, Iowa. Returning to Milwaukee, the priest suffered the onset of pneumonia. As he lay in bed, he lamented, "Here I lie idle, while thousands of souls are perishing!"[135] His strength continued to fade, and he died peacefully on February 16, just shy of fifty-four years of age.

At the wake services, many among the steady stream of mourners commented, "He was a saintly man."[136] At the funeral Mass, people of all religions and races, especially blacks, prayed for the repose of the soul of the beloved priest. In testimony to the gratitude for his life, inspiration, and service, more than eighty priests attended the funeral Mass. The official newsletter of his religious community writes at the end of Stephen's life, "all were convinced that Father Stephen was a saint in life and in death."[137]

In 1958, members and friends of St. Benedict the Moor Mission erected in the churchyard a life-size statue of the beloved priest. The inscription reads: "Apostle and Champion of the Colored Race."[138]

*For further information, contact*
Capuchin Archives
1820 Mt. Elliott Avenue
Detroit, MI 48207 U.S.A.

# 18. ✠ Francisco Orozco y Jimenez

*Place: Chiapas, Chiapas; and Guadalajara, Jalisco; México*
*Fame: Suffered exile five times. Zealous bishop, then archbishop.*

Among the prelates of the Mexican Church in the twentieth century, the most esteemed Francisco Orozco y Jimenez (1864-1936), archbishop and defender of the church of Guadalajara, stands out above the others, without a doubt. An outstanding humanist, he developed the course of clerical studies and historical investigations, and bequeathed to others the valuable collection of documents. Like a good shepherd, he resisted the anticlerical efforts of the revolution, sometimes in the forefront, and other times hiding in the mountains, in order not to abandon his flock.[139]

Orozco is called the new St. Athanasius (c. 297-373), that famous archbishop of Alexandria, Egypt, who during the Arian-led persecution of the Church in North Africa, suffered exile five times during his seventeen years as shepherd of the see. Orozco, too, was exiled five times in the course of his twenty-three years as archbishop of Guadalajara (1913-36). Like Athanasius, Orozco returned to his archdiocese shortly before his death, so that he might die among his people, for whom he had spent his life.

This extraordinary man was born at Zamora, Michoacán. After his mother died when he was nine, he left for Rome at twelve to pursue studies for the priesthood. At the prestigious Gregorian University, he achieved the highest grades among his classmates in philosophy. Ordained in 1888, he was assigned to teach at the seminaries in Zamora and México City, to which ministry he assiduously dedicated the next fourteen years. In 1896, he received a doctorate in sacred theology from the Pontifical University of México. By the time he finished studies, he spoke and wrote four Romance languages, namely, Italian, Portuguese, French, and Spanish; plus English, and had learned two Native American dialects, namely, Tzotzil and Cachiquil.

This gifted man, at thirty-eight, was named Bishop of Chiapas, and was ordained for that see at the national shrine of Our Lady of Guadalupe on the feast of the Assumption in 1902. Within the next ten years, he oversaw the reconstruction of the cathedral, built the Church of the Sacred Heart, repaired and restored several chapels, rebuilt the local seminary, founded a *colegio*, opened an orphanage and a hospital, and successfully invited into his diocese several religious orders whose members took over responsibility for various parishes. For the main plaza of the city, he donated a statue of the original Franciscan missionary Bartolomé de las Casas, who had worked in that city and region for the evangelization and protection of the Indians. From his sizeable inherited wealth he made a generous donation to the city of Chiapas, so that the city fathers could purchase electrical lights and provide other public services. Eventually, after a lifetime of having dispersed his monies, he would die a penniless man.

After serving successfully for a dozen years as Bishop of Chiapas, Orozco was appointed by the Vatican as Archbishop of Guadalajara. He began his service there in 1913.

> An interminable series of events in his long episcopacy showed this man to be father, shepherd, and teacher. The tragedy of the times matured his soul, and while he grew, so did the sons and daughters of the diocese grow and become strengthened, so through courage and determination, they became adults who defended their faith and developed stronger ties than ever to the Church.[140]

At the beginning of 1914, the government, literally at the last minute, withdrew its earlier approval for a long-planned church-sponsored procession in support of the national bishops' decision to consecrate México to the Sacred Heart of Jesus. Many thousands of people stood ready to march. A meeting was hurriedly held among government officials, four representative women of the society sponsoring the parade, and the archbishop. The government relinquished and agreed to allow the procession to go forward, but on the condition that the route would be changed, and that only women would be allowed to march. The route was changed: the procession marched from the plaza in front of the cathedral to inside the cathedral, where the crowd remained from 4 p.m. until 9 p.m., praising God. As for the participants in the procession, the men insisted that they go to protect the women, the children wanted to be with their mothers, the laborers wanted to participate in order to protect the youth. The priests and bishop, at the time of marching, fell in behind the thousands of faithful. Spontaneously, the crowd started singing a hymn to the Sacred Heart of Jesus. The participants' religious fervor had increased beyond measure.[141]

Religious persecution increased during the next few months, and Orozco fled to the United States and Rome. Two years later, 1916, he returned, to México, but under an alias and in secrecy. The archbishop continued his ministry among his people, but frequently changed his residence, lest he bring harm to his hosts, and if captured, loss of ministry to his flock. In the summer of 1918, he was captured and was exiled to the United States. Fifteen months later, he again returned to organize important diocesan-wide events, namely, the First Franciscan Provincial Congress, the Diocesan Eucharistic Congress, and the National Workers Congress. In May 1924, the government again expelled him from the diocese, but allowed him to return one year later. In 1926, when President Calles promulgated in February, his harsh anti-Catholic laws, the bishops of the country responded in July, by prohibiting public worship anywhere in the country, until the government would revoke its discriminatory laws. Shortly thereafter, government workers burst into the home of Orozco, and stole his valuable collection of Mexican artifacts and antiquities. In October, the government ordered the arrest of the archbishop. Orozco fled his home and hid. "He suffered extreme poverty, privations and sickness. He did not abandon his flock; he strengthened them with his personal presence and pastoral letters."[142] An excerpt from one of his pastoral letters from this era follows:

> Let us not pass over in silence the local examples [of heroic suffering]: the five Mexican martyrs whom we venerate on our altars: Saint Felipe de Jesus, and the *beati* Laurel, Zuñiga, Flores and Gutiérrez. Does not this honor, though, extend to many others who with their blood and sweat watered this beloved soil such as the martyrs of Cajonos de Oaxaca, those of Etzatlan in Jalsico, and the Jesuits in Tepehuanes, and the Franciscans and Dominicans and Augustinians, whose memory now it is right to revive? There is not one means [of sanctity] for the primordial times [of the Church] and another means for later times. Neither the faith nor the Christian religion, or the Catholic Church, are changing with the times: there is only one faith, one baptism and

one God; one community of believers, one sacrament of Baptism, one Lord, according to what the apostle handed down.

But it seems right to me to note here some names whom the public already knows. In the first place is the good priest David Galvan of Guadalajara, who died some ten years ago, like some priests from Zacatecas, and in these last months, the senior priest Batis from Durango, some youths who were sacrificed at Zacatecas, one man from Guanajuato, and another man from the state of México, to which list we can add a dozen youth from various places who belonged to the respected Catholic Association of Mexican Youth.

Current circumstances, unfortunately, do not provide me with the necessary data, at this moment, to expand more fully on this news. But in order to give weight to this sorrowful moment, today, I raise my voice which I hope resonates throughout the land. I announce the great glory and the incomparable halo with which my beloved Spouse, the Church of Guadalajara, raises its head. Consider the names that will be remembered forever of the seven brave priests and seven laity, without mentioning at the moment the names of those not less glorious persons who have fallen heroically in the field of battle for their religion.

The seven priests include: Padre Jenaro Sánchez, hanged and stabbed; the senior pastor of Nochistlan, Ramon Adame, executed cruelly and criminally in Yahualica, even after [the government] had demanded and received from one or another neighbor the six thousand pesos for his ransom; Padre Sabas Reyes, heroically fulfilling his priestly ministry, yet with a cruelty equal to Nero's, was sacrificed at Tototlan; the pastor of Teocolotlan, Don José Maria Robles, cruelly sacrificed on a mountain; the most respectable and worthy pastor of Totatische, Don Cristobal Magallanes, who accompanied the new and exemplary priest Don Augustín Caloca, both of whom were shot at Colotlan; closing for now this series with the humble and self-sacrificing priest Don José Isabel Flores, who for more than thirty years directed the vicariate of Mazatlán, where he was hanged after having heroically endured scurrilous threats and torments.

The names of Ancacleto Gonzalez Flores, Luis Padilla, Jorge and Ramon Vargas, brothers, and Ezequiel and Salvador Huerta, also brothers, are well known, and so are the details of their heroic deaths.[143]

At the end of the Cristero Rebellion in 1929, Archbishop Orozco came out of hiding. The Church and government had signed a *Modus Vivendi* calling for a cease-fire and for Masses to be celebrated again. But the truce was respected by only one side; the defenders of the faith laid down their arms, while the government broke the treaty to seek out and slaughter those who opposed the government. Bishop Orozco fled the country. He used this time abroad to foster devotion to Our Lady of Guadalupe. He was invited to celebrate Mass with the pope at Rome. Leaving Italy, he preached and lectured widely in London and the U.S.

Returning surreptitiously to México in March 1930, he stayed away from Guadalajara and the state of Jalisco. He communicated with his people through pastoral letters, while the coadjutor bishop and the vicar general administered the diocese. Years later, however, when he felt he was approaching the end of his life, he risked returning to his see. He returned in August 1934, but remained in hiding and away from his residence. While visiting from place to place, and conferring the sacraments, the physically weak septuagenarian would sometimes interrupt the ceremonies and lie down in a pew.

On February 3, 1936, the archbishop suffered a heart attack. He continued working. The very next day, he released a circular letter, promoting a campaign to develop the faith among the Mexican youth. About two weeks later, February 18, he died. Virtually the entire city of Guadalajara came to the cathedral, where they paid their respects before the opened coffin. In the opinion of many, although the archbishop had not died a martyr's death physically through a single act of violence, nevertheless, he had died a martyr's death spiritually. Every day, he had given his life for his people, and the privations and persecutions which he had suffered for them, caused him to lose his life early.

*For further information, contact*
Arzodiócesis de Guadalajara
Liceo 17 Centro – Apartado Postal 1-331
C.P. 4100 Guadalajara, Jalisco México

## 20. ✛ Pierre-Joseph-Marie Chaumonot

*Place: Ancienne-Lorette, QC*
*Fame: Apostle of the Huron, Iroquois, and French.*
*Founder of the Huron parish at Our Lady of Lorette.*

The apostolate of Father Chaumonot is not explained as a life of intense prayer. For him, to catechize, to preach, to console the sick, to meditate, or celebrate Mass were one and the same occupation. His ministry among the Hurons was nothing other than radiating the presence of Christ among those with whom he lived.[144]

As a young priest, Pierre-Joseph-Marie Chaumonot (1611-93) experienced the honor of working with and learning from three saintly Jesuits: the universally revered Jean de Brébeuf, the ever-generous Antoine Daniel, and . . .

PIERRE-JOSEPH-MARIE
CHAUMONOT

Charles Garnier.[145] The former was not only mentor for Pierre in his second assignment as a young priest, but also served as superior for all Jesuits in the North American mission. The latter guided Pierre in his third assignment in the New World, and intervened to save Pierre's life, when a hostile Indian, after beating Pierre with a rock, was on the brink of swinging a hatchet to sever Pierre's head from his neck. For eleven years, from 1639 to 1650, the newly ordained Pierre served courageously and generously in various Jesuit missions emanating from the central mission at Sainte-Marie (now Midland), Ontario.

Pierre possessed a gift for linguistics. He quickly grasped the various languages used among the tribes of the Huron and Iroquois. He composed a grammar and dictionary of the Huron language, from which other Jesuits studied. When the Onandaga tribe of the Iroquois Nation expressed interest in receiving missionaries, the Jesuit superiors selected two men to travel to what is now central New York State; Pierre was sent in part because of his deep respect for the Indians, and on account of his linguistic skills.

The young cleric was gifted also with a strong faith in Jesus, and deep devotion to Our Lady of Loreto. After hearing a homily on the feast day of the great Jesuit St. Francis Borgia, Pierre asked to be admitted to the novitiate of the Society of Jesus. After reading letters written by Jean de Brébeuf in *The Jesuit Relations*, Pierre volunteered to give his life to Christ to evangelize the Native Americans. Three times he made pilgrimages to the shrine of Our Lady of Loreto, located in central Italy. First, at twenty, when after traveling throughout France and northern Italy, he begged the Blessed Mother to cure him of a "body rot" on the top of his head. Later, in his mid-twenties, as a Jesuit scholastic teaching at Fermo, he visited again his beloved Lady of Loreto. Finally, at twenty-seven, after having volunteered to minister to the Native Americans in North America, he made a pilgrimage from Rome to Loreto, to beseech Our Lady's blessings on his voyage and vocation among the Native Americans. In 1673, when he was assigned to a newly developed Indian reservation, he built a chapel there, and named both the village and chapel Notre-Dame-de-Lorette.

Courage characterized this priest. Despite the Iroquois having murdered five Jesuits, Nöel Chabanal, Antoine Daniel, Jean de Brébeuf, Charles Garnier, and Gabriel Lalement, between July 1648 and September 1649, and thousands of Huron, Pierre opted to remain in the North American mission. Another priest, with whom he had traveled to the New World, opted to return to Europe. People had good reason to fear the Iroquois. This tribe treated their enemies, Native American or French, with the greatest brutalities. In his autobiography, which he wrote at the command of his religious superiors, Pierre reveals what he witnessed.

> As they [the Iroquois] massacred one of the women, named Dorothy, with blows from hatchets and knives, at the entrance to the village of Onnontague [in Central New York State], she saw tears falling from the face of a little eight-year-old girl who had visited the Ursuline school. The woman said to the girl, "My daughter, do not cry at either my death or yours. Today, we will ascend to the heavenly assembly. God will have pity on us for all

eternity. The Iroquois will not be able to steal from us this great benefit. In dying, she cried out, "Jesus, have pity on me." And her daughter was killed by means of beatings and stabbings over the course of the next hour. She kept saying the same words her mother had spoken, "Jesus, have pity on me."

Two other children were burnt over a little fire. They cried out in the midst of flames that they would die Christians. They considered themselves happy that God saw them in their torments, and that he knew the disposition of their hearts. Mothers held their infants tight, lest they play in these flames, and lest they not be able to separate their children from the excess of all these barbarous cruelties. So much is it true that the faith and the love of God are stronger than fire and death.[146]

In May 1649, when the mission could no longer be maintained safely, all the Jesuits chose Ile St. Joseph (now Christian Island) as a place of refuge and asked Pierre to lead them and three hundred Hurons to safety. The next year, the same group moved to Ile d'Orleans, outside of Quebec, where they remained safely for the next five years. In 1655, the Jesuit superiors sent Pierre along with another priest and fifty Huron and Frenchmen to the Onandaga Indians in central New York State. The visitors lived in imminent danger for two and a half years. Sensing a trap whereby the Iroquois might kill as many Huron and French as they could at any one time, the Canadian Catholics fled for their lives, in the dark of night. Returning in 1658, Pierre soon received two successive assignments: to Montréal, where he founded the Confraternity of the Holy Family; and to Fort Richelieu. Beginning in 1666, he stayed with the Huron at their campsites, moving as they did, first to Beauport, then Sillery, and ultimately, Notre-Dame-de-Lorette.

The gifts that Pierre brought with him in 1639 he used liberally in the service of the Native Americans, especially his beloved Huron, until his death in 1693. Fourteen months after ordination at Rome, he sailed from Dieppe, and debarked at Québec ten weeks later. Sailing in the same flotilla were two other ships, with a total of nine missionaries: three Jesuits, three Sisters Hospitallers, and three Ursulines, including Sister Marie-de-l'Incarnation. After a week layover, Pierre set out on a nine-hundred-mile journey by canoe, which took him from Québec to

Huronia, at Georgian Bay. At Huronia, he ministered for eleven years. Sent eastward with the Huron survivors of the Iroquois attacks, Pierre spent most of the rest of his priesthood with this tribe. Forty-eight of his fifty-four years on the Canadian missions he had spent among the Huron. His last nineteen years in ministry he passed at the mission which he had founded and named Notre-Dame-de-Lorette. There he built a chapel in honor of and according to the exact design of the shrine of Our Lady of Loreto in Italy. Five years before he died, he celebrated his golden jubilee of ordination; he was "the first priest to celebrate such an anniversary in the New World."[147] At his death, his religious superior observed that Pierre was the oldest and most famous of the Jesuit missionaries of his era. At his death, the Huron gave Pierre the same name by which they had called Jean de Brébeuf, "Echon," signifying a healing tree with medicinal properties. The Huron saw the same kind of person in Pierre as they had in Jean de Brébeuf.

Pierre had taken a most unusual path to priesthood. After being born and raised in Bourgoyne, France, and having been taught to read and write at the age of six by his school-teaching grandfather, and from age twelve having been instructed by his priest-uncle at Chatillon, Pierre ran away from school with a classmate at seventeen. The classmate had suggested that they might study Gregorian Chant at the Oratorian monastery at Beaune, and Pierre was willing to go along. To help finance the journey, Pierre waited until his priest-uncle was busy with a church service, and then stole money from him. The two youths traveled to Beaune, but took their time getting there, and an even more circuitous route afterwards. Because of his act of thievery, Pierre felt he could not return home. After running out of money at Beaune, Pierre adopted the lifestyle of an itinerant homeless person, begging his way through Lyon, Chambery, and over the Alps into Anconia on the Adriatic Coast in central Italy. He was traveling to Rome, to confess his thievery, and other sins.

Tired of running and starving, he felt sick in body; his clothing, hair, and scalp were full of lice. Desperate, he entered the Basilica of Our Lady of Loreto, and begged the Blessed Mother to cure him. Outside the basilica, a young man approached him, and offered to help him: the stranger cut off most of Pierre's hair, and scrubbed his scalp clean. Pierre believed this person was heaven-sent. On the way to Rome, he found employment at Terni, where he also found a Jesuit priest to whom the youth could confess his sins. Confessing in Latin, the youth impressed the priest, who encouraged the youth to consider the seminary. After some months, Pierre went to Rome, but soon returned to Terni, where he took up his former employment and classes at the Jesuit College. "While in Terni, Peter, to better his Italian, read the lives of the saints and as a result of the readings decided that after Rome, he would return to France and become a hermit."[148] Shortly thereafter, while listening to a sermon about the sanctity of Francis Borgia, Pierre was inspired to enter the Society of Jesus, which he did in May 1632. Two years later, he was assigned to teach at Fermo, and in 1637, he was sent to Rome to study philosophy. The next year, having been inspired by the letters of Jean de Brébeuf, he requested to be missioned to Canada. In March 1638, without having studied theology, he was ordained a priest. Fourteen months after ordination, he embarked for North America, where he labored for the next fifty-four years, until his death in 1693.

Although he never suffered martyrdom, as did his Jesuit companions, nevertheless he suffered great privations in the wilderness and in the reservations, where he gave his whole life in praise of God and in service to the Native Americans. No less an authority than Marie-de-l'Incarnation, says, "He has endured as much as and even more than the greatest martyrs of Canada."[149]

*For further information, contact*
Gilles Drolet
1562, rue Jandomien
Ancienne-Lorette, QC G2E 1T8 Canada

# 21. ✠ Blessed Didace Pelletier

*Place: Sainte-Anne-de-Beaupré, QC*
*Fame: Humble builder of churches in early Canada.*
*First Canadian-born lay brother of the Franciscan Recollects.*

Didace Pelletier (1657-99) lived a simple life, as a Franciscan Recollect brother laboring as a carpenter. [150] He achieved, however, the highest of places in the opinions of his contemporaries: "the devotion of the people is such that they have already canonized him in popular belief."[151] The Catholic Church recognizes his holiness and honors him as an official candidate for sainthood.

The parents of Didace emigrated from Dieppe to Beaupré, where their only son, Claude, was born. Because no Catholic parish and church existed at Beaupre in 1657, the child was baptized at home by an itinerant Jesuit missionary. When the first church was built, and the parish of Sainte-Anne-de-Beaupré was established, Claude Pelletier headed the list of persons whose names were inscribed in the new baptismal registry. At eight, Claude received the sacrament of Confirmation from Québec's first bishop, François de Laval. For his education, Claude studied at the vocational school, which Bishop Laval had founded at Saint-Joachim, a dozen miles north of Beaupré. Claude learned the trade of carpenter.

At twenty-one, wanting to dedicate his life to God in the Church as a lay brother, Claude entered the religious order of the Franciscan Recollects at the community's convent at Notre-Dame-des-Anges. Half a year later, he received the religious habit, and his religious name, Didace, in honor of a lay brother saint from Seville, Spain. The next year, after completing his one-year novitiate, he pronounced the religious vows of poverty, chastity, and obedience. For the next fourteen years, Didace remained at the Convent of Notre-Dame-des-Anges, where Father Joseph Denis, Canada's first native-born priest, was already residing. Brother Didace asked Father Denis to serve as his confessor and spiritual director.

Under the direction of his spiritual director, Didace grew steadily in the Christian and religious life. Didace kept the Rule perfectly. He practiced poverty and mortification to a high degree. Work, he performed admirably. Becoming a famed builder of churches, he labored at Percé and l'ile Bonventure from 1684-89, at Plaisance and Terre-Neuve from 1689-92, and at Montréal from 1692-96.

When Father Joseph Denis was named provincial, and moved from Beaupré to Québec; Brother Didace moved too, to Trois-Rivières. There, while preparing wood in the cold weather for use in the warm weather to build a chapel for the convent, he contracted pleurisy during the winter of 1698-99. Confreres rushed the sick brother to the Ursuline Sisters' hospital at Québec. There a physician examined him, and diagnosed the illness as not life-threatening. Brother Didace, however, suspected something worse; he asked for and received the last rites of the Church. He died within twenty-four hours of his arrival at the hospital. Of his forty-one years on earth, Didace had spent twenty years as a lay brother in the community of the Recollects.

Brother Didace enjoyed a reputation for sanctity. An historian of the Ursuline Sisters comments, "One of the most touching memories of our early days in our hospital is the death of a holy Canadian, Brother Didace Pelletier, a Recollect, a native of Sainte-Anne-de-Beaupré, who died in the odor of sanctity in our Hotel-Dieu, on February 21, 1699, and whom God would honor with the gift of miracles."[152] Brother's spiritual director, and long-time superior, Father Joseph Denis comments, "Brother Didace maintained during his whole life not only the first fervor of the novitiate, but even the grace of his baptism."[153] The same witness writes about Brother,

> I pointed out to him (Brother Didace) that he would not live a long time if he gave no relaxation to his body. He begged me, not only as his confessor but even more as one who nearly always had been his superior, to allow him to continue to live as he had been doing. He preferred to die ten years sooner and to have the consolation of having obeyed the Rule, than to live ten years longer and to reproach himself for having spared himself the rigors of the Rule. His religious order had existed long before he ever joined it, and it would continue long after his death, [Brother reasoned]. The work which gave the greatest honor to the state of his soul was to become holy."[154]

Brother was buried at Trois-Rivières. His memory remains alive at the Basilica of Sainte-Anne-de-Beaupré. There, a statue of the humble brother, holding a hammer and chisel, portrays him as the saintly builder of churches throughout the St. Lawrence River region in the first century of the propagation of the faith in Canada.

*For further information, contact*
Les Franciscains
5750, boul. Rosemont
Montréal, QC H1T 2H2 Canada

❧

## 23. ✠ Venerable Samuel Mazzuchelli

*Places: Michigan, Wisconsin, Illinois, Iowa*
*Fame: "Always on call." Missionary to Native Indians and pioneers.*
*Founder of Sinsinawa Dominican Congregation of the Most Holy Rosary.*

Dominican seminarian Samuel Mazzuchelli (1806-64) volunteered to leave the comfort and culture of Milan, Italy, in order to serve in "the poorest diocese in the world."[155] Samuel was the youngest child of a wealthy Milanese banker and widower; Samuel's mother had passed away when the boy was six.[156] The father had tried but failed to dissuade his son, first from entering at seventeen the religious community of the Dominican friars in Italy, and now from volunteering at twenty for the foreign missions in the United States of

SAMUEL MAZZUCHELLI

America. The Diocese of Cincinnati for which the young man was volunteering was coextensive with the entire Old Northwest Territory, which embraced the current states of Indiana, Illinois, Michigan, Ohio and Wisconsin, and which measured almost two hundred fifty thousand square miles. The bishop, Dominican Edward Fenwick, had sent his vicar general, Frederic Rese, to Rome to recruit priests and to raise funds. After Rese met Mazzuchelli at the Dominicans' headquarters,

Santa Sabina in Rome, Mazzuchelli sought and received the permission of the Dominican provincial to go to the United States. Young Mazzuchelli writes, "Let us set out for any place where the work is great and difficult, but where also with the help of the One who sent us, we shall open the way for the Gospel."[157]

Mazzuchelli traveled from Rome to Milan, where he bade farewell to his family, and continued on to Paris. At La Havre, he departed on October 5, 1828. Forty-five days later, he arrived at New York City. He headed south to Baltimore, and west to Cincinnati, where Bishop Fenwick welcomed him on November 5, 1828. The seminarian spent the next year at Somerset, Ohio, completing his theological studies. With four other Dominicans, he lived in a log cabin, and worshiped in the first log church built in Ohio.

The bishop ordained Mazzuchelli a priest on September 5, 1830, two months before his twenty-fourth birthday. Less than a month after ordination, Mazzuchelli set out by himself for his destination eight hundred miles north to Mackinac Island. No priest had ministered in the Upper Peninsula for the past sixty years, when the Jesuits had left the region when the order was suppressed worldwide in 1773. Mazzuchelli refers to the Jesuits as the "unforgotten padres."[158] For an entire year, the newly ordained priest ministered alone. In his second year, Mazzuchelli was joined in the region by Frederic Baraga, who after three years of ordination transferred from a diocese in Slovenia to the diocese of Cincinnati.

From 1830 to 1835, Father Mazzuchelli, whom the Irish settlers and even the French Bishop Mathias Loras called "Matthew Kelly," lived and worked among the Menominee, Winnebago, and Chippewa tribes, Canadian fur traders, and American pioneers. The young priest proved to be an indefatigable missionary, traveling on foot, snowshoes, horseback, or canoe to reach his congregation among the seventy-three thousand square miles of the Wisconsin Territory and the Upper Peninsula of Michigan. He administered the sacraments to his flock in every season, under all weather and travel conditions. He founded many parishes, and built three churches in the region, including (in the winter of 1830-1831), the first church in Wisconsin at Green Bay. He built for Menominee children a school which was moved later to Keshena, Wisconsin. In 1833, he published a compilation of prayers for the

Winnebago Indians; this book represents the first publication in that tribe's dialect. In 1834, he authored a liturgical calendar in the Chippewa language. The young priest led the singing of the psalms in church in alternate verses of Latin and the vernacular.

As more priests gradually came to the Upper Peninsula, Mazzuchelli felt called to evangelize farther south, where he discovered a growing population of Catholic miners. From 1835 until his death in 1864, he ministered in the tri-state Upper Mississippi Valley region where Wisconsin, Illinois, and Iowa meet. He chose as his chief residence Sinsinawa, Wisconsin. Again, selflessly, he ministered sacraments to the people, founded approximately thirty parishes, built approximately fourteen churches, founded St. Thomas Aquinas College and St. Clara Academy. The college became closed at the end of the Civil War. The academy became a college for women, and is now Dominican University at River Forest, Illinois.

The tri-state territory burgeoned in population after lead was discovered and mines were opened in the Upper Mississippi Valley. The region's population soared from eighteen thousand in 1838 to seventy thousand seven years later. When dioceses were founded at Dubuque (1837), Chicago (1843), and Milwaukee (1843), the bishops actively recruited priests to serve the area. In 1839, the first bishop of Dubuque, Matthias Loras, appointed Mazzuchelli vicar general for the diocese.

After suffering a serious illness in 1843, Father Mazzuchelli returned to Milan for a year to recover his health. There he wrote and published his *Memorie*. The *Memorie* is not a work done at the end of Father Mazzuchelli's life; he wrote it at thirty-seven to acquaint the Italian people with his ministry in America. Within months of publication of the *Memorie*, Mazzuchelli returned to the United States, where he labored for another twenty years, and died at fifty-seven on February 23, 1864. He writes eloquently about the missionary vocation:

> It is almost incredible that the comforts of this life, relatives, friends, love of country, and love of riches, can be an obstacle to the apostolic vocation for anyone. Such motives would shame anyone who, dominated by them, would sacrifice the very least of the gifts of Heaven. This action would reveal a smallness of soul of which it is best not to speak, in order to avoid the supposition

that there are any persons in the divine vocation of the priesthood who would debase it it by such weakness. To preach the faith is a work so meritorious, so worthy of the clergy, so like that of the Messiah, that it should revive the noblest sentiments of our hearts and inspire a multitude of apostolic laborers. Yes, Christ tells the contrary: "The harvest is plentiful, but the laborers are few" (Lk 10:2). Let us wake up then, open our eyes in apostolic charity; and if we are called, set out for any place where the work is great and difficult, but where also, with the help of him who sent us, we shall open the way for the Gospel and where, through him, our labors will meet with good success according to the assurance of St. Paul: "I planted, Apollos watered, but God gave the growth" (1 Cor 3:6).[159]

Before he returned to the Upper Mississippi Valley, Vatican officials named Father Mazzuchelli a Missionary Apostolic, which position gave him the authority "to establish the Dominican Order on the banks of the Upper Mississippi."[160] In the next few years, he started a novitiate, and founded in southwestern Wisconsin, Sinsinawa Mound College as an apostolic school for boys. Because his colleagues could not endure the frontier as well as he, the province ceased to exist as a separate entity after six years. To further the mission of the Church in evangelization and education, he founded in 1847, the sisters' community of Sinsinawa Dominicans of the Most Holy Rosary, which community continues to this day. Five years later, in 1852, he transferred the sisters' community from Sinsinawa to Benton, Wisconsin, where he served as pastor for the last fifteen years of his life, from 1849 to 1864.

Because he possessed skills as a designer and builder, he was asked by local governmental leaders to design several civic buildings, including the Market House in Galena, the state capitol in Iowa City, and the courthouses in Galena, Illinois, and Fort Madison, Iowa.

Despite initial apprehension concerning the foreigner, Native Americans, fur traders and pioneers, and Protestants subject to anti-Catholic bigotry, grew to love and admire Father Mazzuchelli. His manner was gentle, his teaching clear, his preaching mellifluous, and his efforts effective. When critics disparaged the Indians and their customs, the priest defended their inherent human dignity and generally virtuous living. He warmly welcomed Indians to study and convert to the Catholic faith. An immigrant himself, he nevertheless approached the offices of the governor, United States Congress, and president of the United States as advocate for the Indians. For the benefit of the Catholic population, the priest traveled great distances at great personal sufferings to serve their pastoral needs. A Presbyterian church leader at Mackinac describes the priest in glowing terms:

> There is a priest in this locale, an Italian, who, they say, came from an opulent family of Rome, and who, despite the characteristics of Italians of his rank, the softness, the refinement and the luxury, is content to take food and room with an Indian and adapt to the conditions of the place in order to propagate the church of Rome. He is a true and faithful servant of his master and manifests a zeal, a patience and a perseverance that the Christians would do well to imitate. In coming to Mackinac he had certainly to sacrifice all that is dear to a man: hearth, family, friends and country, naturally dear to his heart as life itself, and exchange this for a "home" upon this isolated island with only the company of French in a culture of savages.[161]

On a bitterly cold morning of February 23, 1864, after traveling to minister the sacrament of anointing of the sick to two parishioners, Father Mazzuchelli contracted pneumonia. That same evening, he died, remembered fondly by all who knew him.

*For further information, contact*
Mazzuchelli Guild
585 County Road - Z
Sinsinawa, WI 53824 U.S.A.

## 25. ✠ Blessed Sebastian de Aparicio

*Places: Puebla, México City, Veracruz, and Zacatecas, México*
*Fame: Lay pioneer road builder.*
*A delayed vocation as a Franciscan brother.*

Born and raised at Gudena, Spain, Sebastian (1502-1600) worked as a shepherd until he was fifteen. Then he found a series of jobs: a servant for a wealthy widow, a valet for a rich man, a farmhand. He sent the bulk of his wages home to his parents and siblings. He preferred the simple life. He emigrated to México at thirty-one in 1533, four decades after Columbus discovered the New World, and a dozen years after Cortez defeated the Aztecs at the site of current-day México City.

He settled at Puebla do Los Angeles. Discovering that the colonizers lacked sufficient tools to till the soil, and sufficient vehicles to transport their produce to larger markets, he set out to manufacture plows and carts, to tame oxen, and to construct roads. His first roadway project extended from Puebla to the port city of Veracruz, a distance of almost two hundred miles. He then added a branch extending from Veracruz to the capital at México City, another eight-five miles away. Thus Puebla became linked with two major cities. Now that the eastern coast and middle were connected, he added during the decade beginning in 1542 a road from México City to the large silver mines at the far northern city of Zacatecas, despite the obstacles of rugged mountainous terrain and hostile Chichimecos Indians. He achieved these feats in less than twenty years.

At this stage in his life, at fifty, he had acquired much wealth and fame; and decided to settle down to a ranch just north of México City. As in his youth, he still preferred, however, the simple life. He remitted debts to widows, donated dowries to young girls, fed the hungry, provided free transportation to whoever was traveling; in general, he went about doing good. He sought nothing for himself.

As he started his sixtieth year, he agreed to marry. The young bride and he lived, however, as brother and sister. After one year, she died. He married again, and the same thing happened; they lived the celibate life, and she soon died.

As he entered his seventieth year, he became acutely ill. He thought he would die. The event impacted him so much that he decided during his recovery that he would distribute all his wealth, giving most of it to the Capuchin Poor Clares in México City, for whom he asked to be allowed to work there as a servant and Third Order Secular of St. Francis. After a while, he thought he'd like to become a full member of the religious life. In June 1573, he requested admission as a lay brother to the Franciscans. Only after a year's waiting, did the order allow the seventy-two-year-old candidate to enter. After completing the year novitiate at the Church of San Francisco on Madero Avenue near the famous Zocolo, he was missioned to his native Puebla with the assigned task of collecting alms daily for the more than one hundred friars who lived in the local monastery. "For the next twenty-five years, until his death in 1600, Brother Sebastian wandered around as a begging brother throughout the region of Puebla, Cholula, Atlixco, Huejetzingo, Tlaxcala and Huaquechula."[162]

Over three hundred incidents of miracles and exceptional powers were attributed to Sebastian at the time of investigation of his life for beatification.[163] Blessed spirits accompanied him, guided him, provided food, light, song, and safety in his journeys. He possessed a way of communicating with animals that astounded those who found the same beasts unmanageable; he could tame them with ease and gentleness.

*For further information, contact*
Capilla de Beato Sebastian
Iglesia de San Francisco
14 Oriente & Boulevard 5 de Mayo
Barrio del Alto, Puebla, Puebla, México

## 25. ✛ Félix Varela

*Places: Havana, Cuba; St. Augustine, Florida; and
New York, New York, U.S.A.
Fame: Exemplary pastor, prolific author, social reformer.
Servant of the immigrant Church*

Born in Havana, Cuba, Félix Francisco José Maria de la Concepción Varela y Morales (1788-1853) desired from an early age to become a priest. [164] After having lost both his parents by age six, he was raised by his grandparents and other relatives. At fourteen he entered the diocesan Seminary of Saint Charles and Saint Ambrose in Havana. Nine years later, December 21, 1811, he was ordained a priest in the cathedral at Havana.

FÉLIX VARELA

For his first ten years as priest, Father Félix taught in the seminary. Students were inspired not only to study the arts and sciences because of Father Félix's love of the subjects, but also to dedicate themselves to God, God's people, and the fatherland of Cuba, in imitation of their teacher's moral and spiritual life.

During this period of his life, he earned degrees in philosophy, theology, chemistry and civil law, all the while editing several reviews and publishing a number of books, one of them being a three-volume course in philosophy that remained the standard philosophy textbook in Cuban universities and seminaries for many years. By the age of thirty-three, he was widely considered the foremost thinker and writer of Cuba.[165]

In 1821, he was appointed to represent Cuba at the Court of the Constitutional Monarchy in Madrid, Spain. Initially he resisted accepting the position, but eventually he yielded to his bishop, who urged Father Félix to accept this opportunity to serve Spain and Cuba. In this parliament Father Félix advocated for the abolition of slavery and freedom of Cuba's black slaves, racial equality, equal education for boys and girls, constitutional government for all Spanish colonies, and reform of Spain's antiquarian criminal laws. Two years later, when the Absolute Monarchy returned to power, and executed over one thousand reformers, he fled for his life to New York City. The bishop there hesitated to accept this reformer, but upon further investigation, welcomed him into the diocese.

In New York City, Father Félix served in three assignments: in 1825, as curate to the Cathedral parish of St. Patrick on Mulberry Street in lower Manhattan; in 1827, as pastor of the neighboring Christ Church parish; and in 1832, as founding pastor for the parish of the Transfiguration of Our Lord on Mott Street. In this last assignment, he remained for twenty-five years, serving a congregation of immigrant "Irish, Poles, Germans, Austrians, Swiss, French, Spanish and Cubans."[166]

[Father Varela] wrote articles for several English and Spanish monthly and weekly publications, prepared a new edition of his three-volume work on philosophy, composed a catechism for the diocese, opened day-schools for boys and girls, created a diocesan newspaper and established an orphanage that was staffed by the Sisters of Charity. . . . He struggled mightily for public assistance for Catholic school children, succeeded in forming several helpful relationships with Protestant leaders, both clergy and lay, and became a hero throughout the city for his daily care of victims of a cholera epidemic in 1832. . . . He brought parish missions to the diocese. He won a place for Catholic chaplains in public hospitals and charitable institutions. He entered into all manner of controversies about Church doctrine. He preached the need of religious schools for children and youth. He formed valuable alliances with the scientists of the City of New York, such as André Parmentier, the founder of the Brooklyn Botanic Garden. And he served as theologian to both Bishop DuBois and Archbishop Hughes. There was hardly a sector of New York life in which he was not somehow involved.[167]

During these same three decades, he started nurseries and orphanages for poor children, organized the New York Catholic Temperance Association for those suffering the affliction and addiction of alcohol, and in this virulently anti-Catholic period, courageously declared and defended the Catholic faith. In 1832, during the cholera epidemic, Father Félix literally moved into the hospitals in order to make his rounds more easily and more thoroughly. "Varela also founded the first Spanish newspaper in the U.S, publishing articles about human rights, as well as essays on religious tolerance, cooperation between English and

Spanish-speaking communities, and the importance of education."[168] He worked indefatigably for Cuba's right of political independence from Spain. Because of his exemplary service to the Church, Father Félix was appointed Vicar General of the Diocese of New York.

During the last few years of his life, he suffered from much sickness. Worn out by decades of service, he became less active and less public. He died alone and in poverty in St. Augustine, Florida. "His spiritual strength lay in the Eucharist."[169] His physical remains lie within the Great Hall of the University of Havana

Out of respect for the extraordinary contributions made by Father Félix, the United States Post Office, in 1997, issued a commemorative stamp in Father Félix's name and image.

*For further information, contact*
*Félix Varela Foundation*
Immaculate Conception Seminary
7200 Douglaston Parkway
Douglaston, New York 11362 U.S.A.

❧

## 26. ✠ Saint Pedro Baptist Blasquez and Companions

*Places: México City, México*
*Fame: They left home to preach the gospel in foreign lands.*
*Martyred at Nagasaki, Japan*

Five Franciscans, including four priests and one brother, who once had served as missionaries in México, later died as martyrs in Japan. The five had responded to the call of Father Pedro Ortiz, the superior general of the Franciscans, who around 1593 asked for sixty volunteers to serve in mission fields abroad. At that time, Spain was perhaps the most developed country in the world. Its wealth in art, architecture, education, vitality of religious spirit, and physical comforts was unequalled in other parts of the world. To leave Spain to serve in the New World or the Far East would require great sacrifices on behalf of any volunteer. Highly cultured Spaniards would have to enter cultures much less sophisticated than the one they had grown up in. Father Ortiz, nonetheless, received his sixty volunteers.

Along with the Mexican native Father Felipe de Jesus Casas, whose feast is celebrated separately on February 5, the four Spaniards, namely, Pedro Baptist Blasquez and his companions, died on the same day at the same place.

Father Pedro Blasquez (1546-97) had volunteered for the missions long before Father Ortiz made his celebrated call for missionaries. Pedro, back in 1581, had left the challenges of academia where he had been working as a professor of philosophy, to undertake instead the rigorous challenges of mission life abroad. He departed the Old World in April 1581, and arrived at the capital of the New World, i.e., México City, two months later. The subjects of his mission were no longer students but colonists in the capital and Chichimecos Indians on the outskirts of the city. Even though the Chichimecos had a reputation of behaving cruelly to most outsiders, they befriended Father Pedro. After two years' service in México not only as missionary but also as religious superior, Father Pedro was assigned to the Philippines as "visitor," i.e., religious superior of all the friars and community houses in the Philippines. Leaving Acapulco, he arrived at Manila in the same year, 1584. During his nine years in this assignment, he expanded the number of personnel and houses for the missions, and increased the number of native people who converted to the Catholic faith. The growth was so rapid and extensive that he helped to define and design the ministry in the Philippines as a new province which served three hundred thousand Catholics. Not only the church but also the local government appreciated his abilities, resulting in the governor of the Philippines asking Pedro to serve as ambassador to the court of Hideyoshi, the *daimyo* and de facto ruler of Japan.

The Basque-native Martin de Aguirre (1567-97) decided at eighteen, when studying at the University of Alcalá, to dedicate his life to God as a priest. He entered the Franciscan order, and took vows one year later. As a young priest, he labored in Spain for six years, before leaving from Madrid, Spain and traveling to Churubusco, México, where he taught liberal arts in the local friary. This assignment lasted one year, and in 1594 he went to Manila to replace Father Pedro Baptist Blasquez, who had gone to Japan. After teaching for two years at Manila, Father Martin followed Father Pedro to Osaka, Japan.

Francis Blanco (1571-97) was the youngest of these four Spaniards. He left his native region of Galicia in northwestern Spain to study at the University of Salamanca. There he decided to join the Franciscan order. As a deacon, he responded to Father Ortiz's invitation for volunteers to serve abroad. Francis sailed with Father Martin, who was four years older, and during the trip and in México the older Franciscan instructed the younger. Although it is not known definitively, it seems that Martin was ordained a priest during his time in México. Father Martin visited the Philippines briefly, and in 1596 continued his journey to Japan. Again, Father Francis traveled with Father Martin, and again, studies were continued in the new land.

The eldest among the foursome was Brother Francis de San Miguel (1543-97). Brother had been a trusted companion of Father Pedro Blasquez ever since the two had left Spain in 1581. They ministered together at Michoacán and México City, in México; at Manila in the Philippines; and at Osaka, Japan.

The deaths of these missionaries is attributable to the mercurial *daimyo* Hideyoshi and his medical doctor and former Buddhist monk Jaquin. Before this brutal pair rose to power, the previous *daimyo* Nobunaga (1533-82) had welcomed into Japan in 1549 and tolerated with great religious freedom the famous Jesuit missionary Francis Xavier and his companions. But because the central authority was not powerful, there was constant struggle and civil war among the feuding *daimyos*. When the tolerant Nobunaga died in 1582, he controlled thirty of the sixty-six provinces in Japan, and about one hundred thousand persons had converted to Catholicism. Nobunaga's successor, however, named Hideyoshi (1582-98), oscillated between supporting the missionaries sometimes, and persecuting them at other times. In 1587, he promulgated a decree expelling all Jesuits from Japan. Only three or four left, and the others remained on or near Japan's southernmost island of Kyushu. Three years later, this *daimyo* sent a letter to the governor of the Philippines threatening an invasion unless the governor sent an ambassador who would give political recognition to Hideyoshi. The governor sent a Domincan priest Cobo as one of two ambassadors, and after meeting the priest, Hideyoshi requested that ten more like him be sent as missionaries. Father Cobo died in a shipwreck on the way back to the Philippines. In 1593, Hideyoshi repeated his threat to the Philippine governor. Again, the governor sent ambassadors: this time, four Franciscans. In his court, Hideyoshi made initial angry and bombastic response to the ambassadors, then agreed to support the Franciscan religious mission not only politically but also financially. In a couple of years, the Franciscans built four religious houses and four hospitals. By 1596, over twenty-five thousand Japanese had converted to Catholicism. And Father Peter had successfully interceded so that the Jesuits who had been expelled previously were now allowed to stay, ostensibly to minister, but without preaching.

The respite from the mercurial *daimyo* was short-lived. The Spanish galleon San Felipe suffered damage in a storm on its route between Manila and México, and when the ship's captain sought refuge at Hirado on the west coast of Japan, Hideyoshi ordered the ship and its contents to be confiscated. Japan had suffered earthquakes within the year and the coffers of the *daimyo* needed to be replenished. Because seven clerics were on board and the ship contained much military weaponry, the clerics were charged with being spies. Hideyoshi declared summary executions for these and other clerics. Three weeks later, he relented on the advice of his advisors. He insisted, however, that some missionaries would have to die. He drew up the list which consisted of six Franciscans and eighteen Japanese. Two more were added later to make the total twenty-six. On January 3rd, all were paraded through the public squares at Kyoto, Osaka, and Sakai. A week later, they began their forced march to Nagasaki, which lay twenty-six miles from their jail cells at Kyoto. The group of martyrs is known in the universal church as Paul Miki and companions.

*For further information, contact*
Franciscan Friars
Provincial Curia
Caballocalco 11
Coyoacán, México D.F. 04000 México

## 26. ✠ Alexis-Louis Mangin

*Place: Masson, QC*
*Fame: Prayer-filled pastor. Founder of the Congregation*
*of the Servants of Jesus-Mary.*

Born in Belgium at Liegè, Louis Mangin (1856-1920) was his parents' sixth and youngest child, and the only boy.[170] Seven months later, his father inherited an uncle's large estate at Rambervillers, France, and the family's moved there. Blessed with a quick mind, Louis learned to read and write at five, before attending school. Blessed with a prodigious memory, he could remember a lesson after having heard it just once. Possessing an active imagination, he would

ALEXIS-LOUIS MANGIN

entertain his sisters by saying Mass at a homemade altar, and preaching to them from a pulpit which he had constructed. The lad possessed a natural ability for learning handyman crafts, which contributed nicely to the work needing to be done on the family farm. When his father died in 1864, the eight-year-old son promised his mother that he would not worry or sadden her. The lad kept his promise. Part of his desire to live virtuously flowed from his devotion to the Eucharist and the Virgin Mary. In the minor seminary at Chatel, and the college seminary at Nancy, he excelled academically, morally, and spiritually. By nineteen, he earned two bachelor's degrees in both letters and science. At this time, he prefixed his first name with Alexis. In 1875, he entered the Major Seminary of Saint-Die in Alsace. The final year of theological studies he took at the French School of Theology at Rome, where, in April 1881, he was ordained a priest in the Carmelite chapel in Velletri, on the outskirts of Rome.

During the next four years, Father Alexis-Louis Mangin taught at the college in Metz, in Rambervillers, where he created a Circle of Catholic Youth. In 1885, Monsignor Avila Labelle was visiting from Saint-Jerome, Québec, when he persuaded Father Mangin to cross the Atlantic and to minister abroad. The young priest accepted the offer.

His new bishop assigned him to the parish at Chénéville in late 1885, and in late summer 1889 to the church at Masson.

Father Mangin's sister Marie moved with him to the New World. She assisted him in the rectory, having agreed to cook and clean until the time when he would find a suitable housekeeper. In April 1890, after the brother had completed a novena to St. Joseph with the petition of finding a housekeeper, twenty-five-year-old Eleonore Potvin appeared at the rectory door, asking if she might find employment there. Having been hired, she worked diligently. And after having spent many hours before the Blessed Sacrament, she radiated the presence of God as she went about her work.

In 1892, Eleonore joined the Third Order of St. Francis of Assisi, which had been newly established in the parish. She took for her religious name Sister Zita. Sometime before April 1893, she added "Jesus" to her religious name, calling herself Sister Zita of Jesus. Continuing to perform her tasks, and praying at length in the parish church, she asked Father Mangin if he would serve as her spiritual director. He accepted that role.

At the end of April 1893, Sister Zita of Jesus reported to Father Mangin that recently she had experienced extraordinary spiritual phenomena. At the beginning of one week, the Blessed Virgin Mary appeared to her, and asked her to continue praying for priests: "I take care of my divine Son, and you are to take care of priests who are representatives of my Son."[171] At the end of the week, Jesus appeared to her, holding two crowns, one of flowers and another of thorns. He asked which of the two she desired. When she replied, "the crown of thorns," Jesus placed that crown on her head. So, she began her work of praying for priests. Father Mangin listened and rejoiced. He responded to Sister Zita that for some time he himself had been considering a similar work. He interpreted the events that had happened to Sister Zita as a sign that perhaps God wanted her to found the work that he had been envisioning. Sister Zita, who was happy to do whatever God might ask of her, considered the priest's invitation. Half a year later, Father Mangin suggested to Sister Zita that she might make an extended retreat in order to test the depth of her virtue. At the end of the retreat, Sister Zita sought to do whatever God, or his priests-representatives, might ask of her.

Father Mangin provided Sister Zita with a space of her own, where she might enjoy peace and quiet, which was not only conducive to but also necessary for contemplative prayer. The space provided was an unused stable. Sister Zita and friends thoroughly cleaned the space which the animals had vacated. Sister Zita viewed the "little stable" as a monastery wherein she might praise God and pray for priests uninterruptedly.

A religious community was in the making. By spring 1895, three other women had joined Sister Zita in her apostolate of prayer. One woman who had been Sister's prayer-companion for the last three years was Sophie Chauvin, who also had joined the Third Order, and who had taken as her religious name, Sister Delphine. Another woman was Sister Zita's cousin, who called herself Sister Veronica. As the work kept attracting new members, Father Mangin realized that he ought to alert the archbishop about the developments at Masson.

The archbishop, giving his full support to the project in 1896, assigned Father Mangin full-time to the ministry with the burgeoning community. The priest instructed the sisters in theology and spirituality. An excerpt from one of his instructions follows:

> The divine psalmody said in front of the Blessed Sacrament is esteemed, after the Mass, as the most exalted, most holy, and most powerful means of prayer. The words of the Holy Office are the unerring groaning of the Holy Spirit. Let your prayer become a humble supplication from the Church militant joined to the eternal *Sanctus* of the Church triumphant.[172]

The founder worked with the foundress to propose articles for the community's *Constitution and Rules*. After these were reviewed and discussed by all the sisters, he refined them, and prepared them for presentation to the archbishop and pope. Diocesan approval, he gained in 1904. Papal approbation was sought and received ten years later. The charism of the Servants is described in the *Constitution*:

> The solitude of the cloister, embraced in full fidelity, makes possible a presence and openness to Christ, and, in Him, a communion with the entire world. Also, the Servants of Jesus-Mary, although separated from the world, carry in their hearts and their

contemplative prayers, the joys and sorrows, the hopes and anxieties of all people, who are their brothers and sisters.[173]

As the community continued to grow, Father Mangin continued to offer advice regarding the housing of the sisters, and the balancing of the budget. Between 1895 and 1902, the community moved various times, from the stable at Masson to a convent across the street, then to Aylmer, and later to Hull, where the motherhouse remains to this day. When the financial situation of the community became perilous, even to the point of threatening their continued existence, Father Mangin discussed financial options with the mother-servant and bank officials and the archbishop. The archbishop provided a loan from Church monies.

When the Foundress Mother-Servant Zita of Jesus died in May 1903, Father Mangin played a significant role in continuing the community's vision, mission, and living history. He instructed the sisters, "Mary has chosen you and has separated you from the world in order that you may be, like her and by her, the servants of Jesus, the eternal priest."[174] He reminded the sisters, "You are contemplatives. Your life ought to be a life of continual prayer."[175]

The administrators of the community continued to seek his counsel, which he gave happily and humbly, never forgetting or transgressing the inherent limitations of that role; he did not impose himself or his views upon the sisters. He gave his agreement when the Mother-Servant decided in 1918 that the sisters had become so numerous that the time had come to form another monastery. He recommended Rimouski for the location, so the sisters started a second foundation there.

Two years later, an epidemic of Spanish influenza circulated at Hull, and in the mother-house of the sisters. In January, although he seemed to have contracted the disease, he continued to bring Communion to the sick sisters in the house. He struggled to maintain his usual schedule. Never fully recovering; gradually he weakened. On February 26, 1920, Father Alexis-Louis Mangin died.

*For further information, contact*
Les Servantes de Jesus-Marie
210, rue Laurier
Hull, QC J8X 3W1 Canada

# MARCH

❧

## 2. ✠ Blessed Bartolomé Gutiérrez Rodríguez

*Places: México City, D.F.*
*Fame: Years of service were followed by years of imprisonment*
*and torture. Missionary-martyr in Japan.*

Bartolomé Gutiérrez Rodríguez (1580-1632) was born and raised in México City.[176] At sixteen, he joined the Hermits of St. Augustine, and the next year pronounced his religious vows. Continuing on to priesthood, he studied at Yurirapundaro and was ordained at Puebla.

Shortly after ordination, the young priest left his native land to perform missionary ministry in the Philippines and Japan. After laboring in the Philippines for six years, he was missioned to Japan in 1612. Although quite young, he was named prior of the Augustinian house at Osaka. Two years later, he and other missionaries were exiled during the general persecution of Iyeasu, and returned to Manila.

Surreptitiously, Bartolomé returned to Japan in 1617, and for the next dozen years evaded the grasp of government enforcers. Time after time, he narrowly escaped capture. Once, he hid under a blanket of cobwebs, where his pursuers refused to search. Another time, he ran down a street with opponents in hot pursuit, and he ducked into a home whose residents he knew. Grabbing a guitar, he started entertaining the family. A knock came at the door, Bartolomé's pursuers entered, and Bartolomé invited the government officials to join the family's festivities. The men left without investigating further. In another home, he hid in a closet while soldiers searched the house for him. Another time, while Bartolomé was hiding in a home, the woman of the house answered the front door with so much "courtesy and friendliness" that the soldiers concluded that she could not be hiding anyone.[177]

In 1629, a cruel persecution broke out under Nagasaki's newest governor, Takenaka Uneme. Numerous Christians apostasized. One apostate informed authorities about Bartolomé. At the village of Kikizu in Arima, Bartolomé was captured on November 10. He was sent immediately to the prison at Omura. By the end of the month, four more missionaries were sent to the same prison. For two years in prison, the missionaries were allowed to celebrate Mass, to receive Christian visitors, and to meet with persons interested in receiving instructions and converting to the faith. Then the five prisoners were transferred to Nagasaki.

In this capital city of the province, the prison situation proved much more difficult. "All five [missionaries] were confined to cramped quarters of only eight square yards; and next to them were fifty-four Christians in an area that measured twenty-four square yards."[178] Many times, the authorities and their enforcers tried to persuade the inmates to abandon their Christian faith. No one succumbed despite either the offer of greater comfort, or the threat of greater punishment. In early December 1631, the five missionaries were transported to the hot sulphur springs at Unzen, which is a large complex volcano on the Shimabara Peninsula, east of Nagasaki

> Repeatedly they were immersed in the sulphurous water until the skin all over their bodies was burned by the acid. A doctor was on hand to apply remedies so they could be tortured anew. This barbarous treatment was administered six times a day, and it was kept up for thirty-one days. Then the missionaries were put back into the jail. Here they remained for another eight months.[179]

The authorities, having determined that nothing would shake the faith of these prisoners, sentenced these missionaries to death. "On September 3, 1632, they were brought to the usual place of execution [the Hill of Martyrs], near the shore, were tied to stakes, and slowly burned alive."[180] "The firewood was arranged in a wide circle. In the midst were six columns to which one of their fingers was tied with a light string. Many people witnessed the martyrdom. The Christians formed processions and sang psalms."[181] With the five foreigners was martyred a native Japanese priest, from the region of Nagasaki.

*For further information, contact*
Convento de Santa Monica
Peña Pobre – 83
Col. Toriello
Guerra de Tlalpan
14050 México D.F. México

## 3. ✠ Saint Katharine Drexel

*Places: Philadelphia and Cornwell Heights,*
*Pennsylvania; Omaha, Nebraska*
*Fame: Devotion to the Blessed Sacrament. Founded Sisters of the*
*Blessed Sacrament for Indians and Colored People.*

Katharine Drexel (1858-1955) gave up millions of dollars, a life of comfort, and seemingly limitless freedom in order to gaze upon the Lord and serve Him and his beloved poor according to the vows of poverty, chastity, and obedience.[182] The newspapers in Philadelphia, Pennsylvania, heralded this news with the following headlines, "Miss Drexel Enters a Catholic Convent," and "Gives Up Seven Million."[183] Katharine writes,

KATHARINE DREXEL

How good beyond all measure, and entirely and utterly beyond all that we deserve, God has been in calling us to be His in the religious life. People think we have done a great thing in giving ourselves to the service of our Lord. They do not know, as we do, that it is our Lord who has done us the greatest possible favor in calling us into His service and to dwell with Him in His own house.[184]

Katharine grew up as the second of three daughters of the financier Francis A. Drexel. The family's fortune had originated with Katharine's grandfather, who had founded the Drexel investment and banking company. Because of the family's wealth, Katharine enjoyed great comfort at the family's center-city mansion, at their suburban home, on summer vacation at Cape May, and in frequent trips to Europe. She, nevertheless, grew up exposed to the harsh realities of life. Five weeks after Katharine's birth, her mother died. Katharine's stepmother taught the three girls how to cook, sew, and manage the household and estate. Their stepmother also introduced the girls to the city's less fortunate people. She required the girls to assist her in distributing food, shoes, clothing, and rent to the poor who queued up at the back room of the mansion three days each week.

Katharine lived in a faith-filled home. Each evening, her father came home from the office, and prayed for half an hour. At the children's bedtime, both parents gathered the girls into the family's private oratory, knelt down and said night prayers. Sometimes the family assisted at Mass in the oratory, when the local pastor, Father James O'Connor, visited the home. Both parents donated time, talent, and treasure to numerous charities and institutions. After Katharine's stepmother died in January 1883, it was discovered that she had paid the rent for one hundred fifty families, for over twenty years, totaling over a half-million dollars in charity.[185]

When Katharine's father died in February 1885, his will stipulated that one-tenth of the inherited fifteen million dollars was to be distributed to nineteen charities, that nine-tenths was to be placed in trust for his grandchildren, and that his three daughters would receive the interest from the trust. Within one year beginning in January 1889, all three Drexel daughters chose the direction of their lives: Louise married; Katharine entered religious life; and Elizabeth married. Since neither married daughter bore any children, nine-tenths of the inheritance reverted to the stipulated charities Francis Drexel had listed in his will. Since the will had been written in 1885, and Katherine's community was not founded until 1891, her community was not included among the beneficiaries.

After her father's death, Katharine's frail health worsened. The family physician recommended that the three daughters take an extended vacation. In July 1886, the girls sailed to Western Europe. At Rome, during a private audience with Pope Leo XIII, Katharine requested from the pope that he might send more missionaries to the U.S. frontier. The pope replied, "Why not, my child, you yourself become a missionary?"[186]

Three months after returning home, the Drexel women visited the Indian missions, which they had been supporting by generous donations. In September 1887, the trio left Philadelphia and traveled by train, wagon, and horseback throughout the Dakotas. They took a similar journey the following year, to the Upper Great Lakes region. The Indians' primitive living conditions struck the women forcibly.

Katharine increased her donations to these missions; by the time Katharine entered the convent, she had already financed the construction of dozens of mission schools for poor Indians and Negroes.

For many years, Katharine had been thinking about becoming a nun. When her stepmother was dying with cancer, Katharine pondered further this vocational possibility as she cared for almost two years for her terminally ill stepmother. Katharine discussed this vocational choice with the family friend and her spiritual director whom she had known for over twenty years, James O'Connor, who was now Bishop of Omaha.

O'Connor discouraged Katharine about religious vocation because of her weak health and accustomed comfort. He wrote in August of 1885 that, "The conclusion to which I have come in your case is, that your vocation is not to enter a religious order."[187] Two years later, he writes that he has "no doubt" that her vocation was to be in the world and not in religious life.[188] Finally, she writes in 1888, "How I wish to spend my entire life entirely given to Him by the three vows which would consecrate me to Jesus Christ! . . . It appears to me that the Lord gives me the right to choose the better part, and I shall try to draw as near to his heart as possible. . . . Are you afraid to give me to Jesus Christ?"[189] The bishop immediately abandoned his opposition and gave his full support to her. Three months later, in February 1889, he suggested that Katharine found a religious community to serve the Indian and Colored People.

In February 1891, Katharine took vows as the first member of the Sisters of the Blessed Sacrament. Shortly thereafter, thirteen women joined her as postulants and novices. In 1892, the community moved its motherhouse to Cornwell Heights (now Bensalem, Pennsylvania).

For forty-four years, Katharine served as superior general of the congregation. She administered the construction and staffing of schools for Indian or Colored children. The threat of violence against the sisters was real both on the reservations from Indians angry at the white man's having broken almost all of the three hundred seventy peace treaties, and from white racists angry at the nuns' assisting blacks. In Nashville, Tennessee, when it was discovered that the sisters had purchased property for a school for black children, the original owner tried to buy back the land, and after that attempt failed, the town council suggested building a highway through the property. Katharine remained undaunted. She writes:

It seems so appropriate for a Convent of the Blessed Sacrament — Christ dwelling with us — and the School of the Immaculate Mother to have people of the city [say that they] have no room for our precious charge. They say, "There is another place on the city's outskirts" for our educational work. How truly was the Cave of Bethlehem the great educator of the world! This was indeed the School of the Immaculate Mother.... My God! How much light can be wasted when the darkness does not comprehend it![190]

Mother Katharine proved indefatigable. Before suffering a serious heart attack in 1935, she had founded fifty schools. Twenty years later, when she died, her community was serving in twenty-one states and the District of Columbia, in over seventy institutions. The community had grown to almost five hundred members.

Katharine's sickness at seventy-six provided her with time to pray until she died at ninety-six. She never once interfered in the administration of the community after she had left the position of superior general. She entered into deep prayer. She writes, "However high and holy our occupation, external activity has the power to distract, to cloud the soul. It is only by entering into oneself in prayer and meditation that the soul can be restored to its true poise, the mind clarified and the value of unimportant things be seen in its true light.[191]

*For further information, contact*
Saint Katharine Drexel Shrine
1663 Bristol Pike
Bensalem, PA 19020 U.S.A.

## 3. ✠ Venerable Concepción Cabrera de Armida

*Places: San Luis Potosi, San Luis Potosi; and México City, D.F.*
*Fame: Mystic. Originator of the Five Works of the Cross.*

Unbeknownst to her husband, their nine children and her friends, Concepción Cabrera de Armida (1862-1937), familiarly called

Conchita, enjoyed profound mystical experiences.[192] The archbishop of México, a revered spiritual writer and theologian, reportedly commented, "Conchita is among the greatest mystics in the Church."[193] The priest founder of the Missionaries of the Holy Spirit, Father Félix Rougier, writes, "Conchita was an extraordinary saint, one of the greatest saints of the Church."[194] The testimonies of the archbishop and the priest-founder are significant since the Church currently is considering both of these men for canonization.

CONCEPCIÓN CABRERA DE ARMIDA

While growing up, Conchita took part in the usual activities of childhood. At nineteen, she experienced a conscious deepening of her spiritual life. She married at twenty-two. While making a retreat at twenty-seven, she experienced the Lord saying to her, "Your mission will be to save souls."[195]

Conchita shared with her spiritual director the insights gained during her prayers. She felt that God was calling her to promote the "works of the cross." Eventually, she assisted in founding five organizations, whose fundamental charism was related to the cross of Christ. The five organizations are identified hereafter. The Apostleship of the Cross, founded in 1895, calls all baptized persons to offer their activities, especially their sufferings, for the salvation of all people. The Religious of the Cross of the Sacred Heart of Jesus, founded in 1887, consists of contemplative nuns who pray for the sanctification of priests. A dozen years later, Conchita established the Covenant of Love with the Sacred Heart of Jesus, a lay group whose members offer themselves with Christ on behalf of priests. In 1912, she began the Fraternity of Christ the Priest to unite priests and bishops in the ministry in seeking their and others' sanctification through the spirituality of the cross. And two years later, Conchita witnessed the foundation of the men's community, The Missionaries of the Holy Spirit, who work for the sanctification of the laity, priests, plus all religious men and women.

As Conchita's continuing impact spread in ever-widening circles, her and her works became investigated by the Church. "Two commissions of theologians, first in México, and later at Rome, examined her person, papers and writings. She notes in her diary, "I spoke five times, alone, to Pius X."[196] She produced over two hundred volumes of spiritual writings, with her diary alone amounting to sixty-six volumes. The essential grace which she experienced is described as "mystical incarnation."[197] Christ entered her soul.

Mystic and mother, on her twenty-fifth wedding anniversary, she writes to her children.

> If I die, if God should call me, I would have you remain valiant Christians, with ardent faith, without human respect, practicing it [the faith] with sturdy fidelity, proud of being members of the Catholic Church. Take care to carry out what the Church requires. Be generous with Jesus, who so loves you, to whom you owe so many good things, and who wills to save you. I beg you to pass on your Faith to your children, both by teaching and by example, never hesitating at any sacrifice their Christian education requires, taking special care of the spiritual formation and their religious instruction. Above all, I recommend that you be one, union, union, union![198]

As her children entered upon major moments in their lives, Conchita wrote to each individual child. On the wedding day of her oldest son, she writes, "Never speak harshly to Elise, your wife, never be offensive. If you feel you temper rising, from the first moment, keep silence."[199] To her eldest daughter, as she entered religious life, Conchita, writes, "Be faithful, absolutely faithful to this Jesus who so loves you. Never resist his inspirations, cost what it may to leave yourself aside and whatever else could be a drag in your climb heavenward.[200] To her son the Jesuit priest, Conchita writes, "The world regards love as enjoyment. In its selfishness, it supposes love to be receiving, to be consoled and pampered, it supposes love to be self-satisfaction, ... when love is really nourished by the gift of self and by immolation."[201]

At the conclusion of the book on her Eucharistic meditations, she reflects on the phrase, "Who do you say that I am?" She writes, first from the perspective of Jesus, and then, from her perspective.

> Today, in this day of intimacy with Me, you hear My lips repeating in your ears this same question: And you, *Who do you*

*say that I am?* Speak, I want to listen. I want to hear and know what you think of Me. Give Me your impressions. One thing only is necessary for Me: *love, love and only love*. If you love Me, be not afraid, empty your heart into Mine. If you love Me, you would have known, studied and reproduced Me in your heart. You would have drunk and fed on the Eucharist. . . .

Lord, Who do I say that You are? The God of my heart and my eternal inheritance, the Infinite, the Word made Flesh, the Savoir of my life. Jesus my beloved, my joy, my hope and the only treasure of my heart. You are, Lord, the warmth of my existence, the light of my eyes, the breath of my mouth, the fire of my heart, the palpitations of all my being. You are my realized ideal, the One I love with all the titles of tenderness that can exist such as father, mother, brother, spouse, friend, all mothers to their children. [202]

*For further information, contact*
Missionaries of the Holy Spirit
Christ the Priest Province
9792 Oma Place
Garden Grove, CA 92841 U.S.A.

## 7. ✠ Georges-Philias Vanier

***Place:** Montréal, Québec*
***Fame:** Exemplary Catholic layman, lawyer, military hero, diplomat, and governor-general of Canada. Loving husband and father of five children.*

Georges Vanier (1888-1967) performed outstandingly in all his endeavors.[203] When World War I erupted in 1914, this Montréal native left his budding law practice, and volunteered for the military. He served as a founding member of 22$^{nd}$ Battalion of the Canadian Expeditionary Force, an entirely French Canadian battalion. Having demonstrated much bravery and skill, he was awarded the Military Cross in 1916. Two years later, while leading his troops at Cherisy, France, he was shot in the chest and both legs, and the next day, had his right leg amputated. For his valor in battle, he received, in 1919, the Distinguished Service Order and the Bar to the Military Cross.

GEORGES-PHILIAS AND PAULINE VANIER

After the war, he returned to Montréal, where he rejoined the law firm, and married. He and his wife Pauline gave birth to five children. All of their children in adulthood took up careers dedicated to serving others. The daughter became a medical doctor, and their sons became a Trappist monk, an artist-painter, a translator, and perhaps most famous of all, founder of the international *L'Arche Community* for mentally handicapped adults.

In 1921, Georges was named aide-de-camp to the Governor-General, which necessitated that Vanier live in Ottawa at Rideau Hall. In 1925, after being named Commander of the famous 22nd Battalion, he moved to The Citadel in Québec City.

His diplomatic career began in 1928, when he was appointed Canada's military advisor to the League of Nations. Two years later, the government promoted him assistant to the Canadian High Commissioner in London. In 1938, he was appointed Ambassador to France. In 1939, when the Nazis overran France, he fled with his family to London, where he served as Canada's representative to France's government-in-exile. In 1940, the Canadian government called him home to oversee the military protection of Canada's Atlantic seacoast from German submarine attacks, and to recruit men for the military. In 1944, within days of the U.S.A.'s liberating France, he returned as ambassador to France. In 1953, at sixty-five, having reached the mandatory age of retirement, he resigned his post of ambassador, and returned home to Montréal.

During and following World War II, at London, Paris, and Montréal, Georges Vanier's spiritual life had deepened significantly. He attended Mass and received Communion daily. He meditated for half-an-hour most days. The "little way" promoted by Saint Thérèse of Lisieux inspired him, and he tried to live that way. He writes movingly about his devotion to the Blessed Virgin Mary, and reveals mystical appreciation of his relationship with her. He and his wife transformed their prayer into action by assisting refugees, especially Jews fleeing Nazism, to begin new lives in Canada. Back in Montréal, Georges and Pauline dedicated their retirement years to aiding the poorest of the city by prayer and practical service.

At seventy-one, Vanier was invited to come out of retirement to serve his country again. Prime Minister John Diefenbaker asked Georges to accept the position of Governor-General of Canada. His wife kidded Georges by telling the septuagenarian that the first thing he ought to consider is getting a physical, especially since he earlier had suffered a mild heart attack. Georges replied, "As a French Canadian, I must accept this function even at the expense of my health. If I must fulfill this function, God will give me the strength to do it."[204] This excerpt from Vanier's Inaugural Address reveals his spirituality:

> My first words are a prayer. May Almighty God in his infinite wisdom and mercy bless the sacred mission which has been entrusted to me by Her Majesty the Queen and help me to fulfill it in all humility. In exchange for his strength, I offer him my weakness. May he give peace to this beloved land of ours and, to those who live in it, the grace of mutual understanding, respect and love.[205]

In 1959, Georges was sworn in as Governor-General, which position he held until his death in 1967. Georges spent those years encountering, encouraging, and inspiring the Canadian populace. He traveled coast to coast, meeting Canadians of every class and walk of life. He spoke repeatedly on the need for spiritual values among Canadians, the need for national unity between the two major linguistic and cultural factions, and the foundational role of family in society. The last theme developed into a National Congress on the Family, organized by the Vaniers, which attracted three hundred scholars to Rideau Hall. This theme was also continued in the still vibrant Vanier Institute of the Family.

*For further information, contact*
Roger Quesnel
175, rue Main
Ottawa, Ontario K1S 1C3, Canada

## 14. ✠ Vasco de Quiroga

*Place: Morelia, Michoacán*
*Fame: Lay leader, lawyer, and administrator. First bishop of Michoacán.*

This lay diplomat for the Spanish Crown was ordained a bishop about 1538. In one day, it seems, he received all of the Church's minor and major orders. His professional and private life in México, originally as a layman and later as a bishop, centered on creating a just situation for the Native Americans.

Young Vasco de Quiroga (c. 1470-1565), after earning the licentiate in canon law, entered royal service as an ambassador for the King of Spain. In 1525, he began serving as judge in the Mediterranean city of Ortan (now in Algeria). In 1530, the king appointed Vasco one of five *oidores* (hearers) of the second *audiencia* of New Spain. The king wanted to right the wrongs of the first *audiencia*, whose corrupt and cruel leader, Nuñoz Beltran de Gúzman, had oppressed New Spain's native people. To the second *audiencia*, the king appointed only persons of proven highest quality. Vasco de Quiroga, who enjoyed a reputation for impeccable integrity, was named one of the *oidores*.

An avid devotee of St. Thomas More, who had written *Utopia* in 1516, Quiroga wished to implement his lawyer-colleague's vision in the New World.

> In 1532, out of commiseration for the plights of the Indians, he established near México City a hospital-town, called Santa Fe, to care for the sick and needy, and to instruct the Indians in the Catholic faith. It was patterned after the plan of society presented in Thomas More's *Utopia*. In 1533-34, he was sent to the province of Michoacán to visit the area and correct abuses. There he established another hospital of Santa Fe on the model of his previous foundation.[206]

This virtuous layman used his own money to build these hospital-towns.

Quiroga's plan, which he implemented with outstanding success, was to create communities in the vicinity of Lake Patzcuaro, the heart of the Tarascan counry, where Indians would receive instruction not only in religion, but also in arts and crafts, and in the fundamentals of self-government.[207]

Shortly after the diocese of Michoacán was created in 1536, Vasco de Quiroga was named and was ordained as the diocese's first bishop. Already he had constructed an apostolic school to provide native-speaking priests for the Indians. These institutions namely, the hospital-towns and the apostolic school, enjoyed the bishop's special attention both in his life, and in his beneficence at this death. Initially as *oidor* and later as bishop, Vasco de Quiroga sat as judge in numerous legal suits. In cases pertaining to the enslavement of the Indians, he regularly decided in favor of the natives.[208]

When the ecumenical Council of Trent was convened, Bishop Vasco de Quiroga attempted to attend this august meeting. In 1545, he was forced to return to México, however, when his ship almost suffered shipwreck. Two years later, he tried again. En route, he spent time at the royal court in Spain. The *oidor*-turned-bishop shared with the king firsthand observations about life in the New World, and brought to the court numerous Indians for the court personnel to experience firsthand.

Bishop Vasco de Quiroga returned to México in 1554. The next year, he convened and led the First Provincial Council of the Mexican Bishops. This council discussed the bishop's desire to build hospitals in every town, and to transfer the responsibility of parishes from the communities of missionary religious priests to the growing number of diocesan priests.

*For further information, contact*
Anexo Cathedral
Centro
Apartado Postal #17
58000 Morelia, Michoacán, México

# 15. ✠ Eusebio Francisco Kino

*Places: Northern Sonora and southern Arizona*
*Fame: Apostle and defender of the Pima Indians.*
*Renaissance man: expert in arts,*
*sciences, and spirituality.*

"Extraordinary" is the only word to describe the person and achievement of Father Eusebio Francisco Kino (1645-1711). The states of both Sonora in México and Arizona in the U.S.A. have honored his memory.

Eusebio was born at Segno, in Tyrol (now in Italy). He attended the local primary school, and studied with the Jesuits both at Trent and Hall (now Innsbruck). Shortly after graduation, Eusebio became very ill. The young man promised God that if he regained his health, he would model his life after the great Jesuit missionary St. Francis Xavier. Eusebio recovered. He kept his promise.

In 1665, Eusebio entered the German province of the Jesuits. After completing the customary formation and education programs, "he distinguished himself in the study of mathematics, cartography, and astronomy and taught mathematics for a time at the University of Ingolstadt."[209] After being ordained a priest in 1677, he was assigned to teach. He longed, however, to labor in the missions. In 1678, his wish was answered, and while waiting at Genoa to depart, he and another Jesuit selected by lot where each would go: México or China. Kino selected México. Nearing the port of Cadiz, however, the ship from Genoa became shipwrecked, which delayed for two years Eusebio's departure from Cadiz. In the interim, he studied at Seville.

In January 1681, he sailed from Cadiz for Veracruz. The voyage lasted three months. The priest made his way from the coast to the capital at México City, where, he was assigned to teach. In 1683, while he was sent on mission to Baja California, Kino applied his knowledge of mathematics, geography, and astronomy to observe the land. Although scholars of the day were teaching that Baja California was an island, Kino observed the land, waters, and seashells, and after extensive research, drew maps indicating that Baja California was not an island, but a peninsula. In 1685, when the mission to Baja California had to be abandoned, Kino returned to México City.

In 1687, Kino undertook the ministry that would occupy him until his death two dozen years later. He was missioned to Pimería Alta, where lived the Pima Indians, whose territories extended over northern Sonora and southern Arizona. Making his headquarters at the mission *Nuestra Señora de los Dolores*, he established communities and *rancherias* which extended from southern California, through southern Arizona, over to southern New México. Kino focused his concerns on the Indians' spiritual and socioeconomic life. He is credited with having baptized four thousand five hundred Pimas. Many present-day roads, towns, villages, and cities owe their foundations to him.

> He was at the same time a man of God and a defender of the Indians. Placed between God and Creation, he was pioneer-explorer, historiographer, cartographer, cowboy, rancher, and peacemaker. He taught the Indians how to cultivate fruits and vegetables unknown in these lands; he introduced cattle breeding, carpentry, and iron working. He valiantly protected the dignity and interests of his Indian neophytes against the overbearing schemes of the Spanish *hacendados*. Fearlessly, he enforced a royal decree that exempted Indians from hard labor in the mines and from paying tribute. He fashioned a whole new economy in the harsh, sun-baked land.[210]

Kino published many books, three of which are especially famous. He published *Exposicion Astronómica de el Cometa* in 1681, shortly after his arrival at México City. He had gathered the material in Spain, during his delay at Seville, where he had observed and studied a current comet. In the New World, after more than forty expeditions in the Pimería Alta region, which took him along the Rio Grande, the Colorado River, and the Gila River, he produced in 1705 a map which covered an expanse two hundred miles east-to-west, and two hundred fifty miles north-to-south. This map served as the standard for the region for more than a century. Reflecting on his priestly ministry among the Pimas, he wrote in 1708, the two-volume work: *Favores Celestiales de Jesus y Maria*. An excerpt from *Favores Celestiales*, from his entry for April 1, 1701, describes some of his multi-faceted ministries.

I remained [at the village] for some small matters of business, and to await some replies from the interior and for the building of a little church, almost a chapel, of Nuestra Señora de Loreto, in which I was able to say Mass on three days.... I left very solid and well-established peace-agreements between these Pimas and those Quiquimas [from California], who promised that they would come to meet one another and to confer in a very friendly way and in great numbers at a half-way point, as was done.... Orders were given to clear land to plant maize which in sufficient quantity the captain of El Coma had brought us from Tucubabia. At the nightfall the governor came bringing the messages and presents from the Quiquimas, especially some blue shells from the opposite coast, saying that with very friendly anxiety they had been waiting for us, greatly desiring friendship, in order to be converted to our holy faith.[211]

*For further information, contact*
Arquidiócesis de Hermosillo
Catedral de la Asunción
Plaza Zaragoza
C.P. 83000
Hermosillo, Sonora, México

⚮

## 23. ☩ Pauline Vanier

*Place: Montréal, Québec*
*Fame: Exemplary Catholic laywoman. Wife of the*
*governor-general, mother, national heroine.*

The roots planted in her youth provided a firm foundation for the life-long challenges which Pauline Archer Vanier (1898-1991) encountered, and for the achievements which she made.[212] The only child of an aristocratic family, her father served as chief justice for the Superior Court at Québec, and her mother traced her Canadian roots to a prominent scigneurial family in 1730. Even before Pauline started school, her mother took the daughter to the homes of the poor in the slums of Montréal. Her mother instructed Pauline that the blessings of life were to be shared among all, and not to be regarded as a privilege for oneself alone. Pauline took her elementary education at Sacred Heart Convent in Montréal, and continued studies at home with a governess and tutor in English and French literature. When WW I broke out, she wanted to join the army, but her attempt was foiled. Next, "she secretly enrolled in a nursing course and to her parents' dismay accepted a job at a military convalescent hospital, where she laboured long hours until the war's end."[213]

GEORGES-PHILIAS AND PAULINE VANIER

In her early twenties, mutual friends introduced her to Georges-Philias Vanier. She liked him immediately. They shared common values. They married in 1921, and within the next seven years, gave birth to four children, and a fifth child in 1942.

"Pauline's life was not without trials and tribulations. During the 1930s, she lapsed into a state of chronic depression [about which she comments]: 'It was a bad period and I'm ashamed to say it went on for almost seven years.' At another time she went through a dark night of the soul for about two years."[214]

During World War II, Pauline demonstrated an extraordinary degree of courage, compassion, and faith. After living in Paris with Georges and their four children, Pauline and the children fled when the Nazis overran French defenses. Seemingly, all of Paris poured onto the roadways leading south. At that same time, German warplanes arrived, machine-gunning the fleeing civilians. Pauline and her children arrived at Bordeaux, where they found refuge on a tramp steamer that carried them to Britain after harrowing five-day sea voyage. She later endured the thirty-days blitzkrieg bombing of London.

When U.S. troops liberated Paris in August 1944, her husband, now Canada's ambassador to France, became the first diplomat to arrive in the city. She persuaded the Red Cross to designate her as their representative in France and became the first wife of a diplomat to enter Paris.

Once there, she set to work to help handle the daily flood of returning refugees. She organized the wives of [some of] the diplomatic community to set up welcoming centers at the main railway station, she established an information network to reunite refugees with their families, and she helped French priest Abbé Pierre set up housing and workshops for the homeless. It was sixteen months of consuming, exhausting work before she could return to the normal life of ambassador's wife. A grateful French government awarded her the Legion d'Honneur for her Herculean efforts.[215]

During WWII, the ambassador and his wife began attending Mass and receiving Holy Communion daily, and meditating for a half-hour each day. Weekly, Pauline visited and prayed at a Carmelite Monastery, in order to "recharge her spiritual batteries."[216]

When her husband died in 1967, Pauline returned to Montréal and continued her charitable works of visiting the sick, poor, and imprisoned. She was appointed chancellor of the University of Ottawa. At the investiture, she said, "The realm of justice and gentleness should prevail. . . . The true Christian spirit looks upon all spiritual values . . . as part of the divine treasure entrusted to mankind by the Creator. . . . Faith, far from being outmoded or old-fashioned, imparts a beauty, a richness, and a radiance that can be found in no other source."[217]

Desiring to involve herself in more meaningful enterprises, she resigned as university chancellor in 1972 and joined her son Jean, who had founded near Paris a community of mentally handicapped men and women. Pauline separated herself from all worldly attachments, and dedicated herself to the care of the poorest. Quickly, she became the live-in grandmother-figure for the guests, and mother-figure for the counselors. Guests numbered two hundred, as did the counselors.

She died in 1991, a few days short of her ninety-third birthday. Prime Minister Pearson observed, "She was one-half of a perfect partnership in the service of Canada."[218]

*For further information, contact*

Roger Quesnel
175, rue Main
Ottawa, ON K1S 1C3 Canada

# 24. ✠ Oscar Arnulfo Romero

*Place:* San Salvador, El Salvador
*Fame:* Martyr for social justice; archbishop of San Salvador.

In the middle of Mass, while Archbishop Oscar Arnulfo Romero (1917-80) was preparing the bread and wine for the sacramental representation of Jesus' sacrifice, a lone gunman burst through the doors of the chapel at Hospital de la Divina Providencia, in downtown El Salvador. From the rear of the chapel, the marksman killed the archbishop. Just minutes before, the archbishop had preached the following words:

> Those who surrender to the service of the poor through the love of Christ, will live like the grain of wheat that dies. It only apparently dies. If it were not to die, it would remain a solitary grain. The harvest comes because of the grain that dies. We know that every effort to improve society, above all when society is so full of injustice and sin, is an effort that God blesses, that God wants; that God demands of us.[219]

The archbishop's life has been threatened many times. Just three weeks after his appointment as archbishop in February 1977, one of his youngest priests, Rutilio Grande, had been killed by the government's "death squad." The young cleric's defense of the poor occasioned the violent outburst by hired gunmen, who were defending the wealthy. At that time, the new archbishop took up the banner of the poor. The archbishop complimented Father Grande and other recently assassinated priests, saying, "They grasped reality with great clarity and saw that the common enemy of our people is the oligarchy."[220]

In El Salvador, with a population of over five million people, all economic and political power lay in the hands of twelve families primarily, and no more than two hundred families totally. These families controlled the military and its death squads. In three years, over seventy-five thousand Salvadorans were killed, one-million fled the country, and another million were left homeless.[221] The archbishop kept pleading for justice and its resultant peace. He preached:

> The Church is obliged by its evangelical mission to demand structural changes that favor the reign of God and a more just and comradely way of life. Unjust social structures are the roots of all violence and disturbances. How hard and conflicting are the results of evangelical duty! Those who benefit from obsolete structures react selfishly to any kind of change.[222]

The oppression continued. From 1968 until the archbishop's death in 1980, the United States government provided the Salvadoran military with over one-and-a-half million dollars each day.[223] "In 1980 the war claimed the lives of three thousand per month, with cadavers clogging the streams, and tortured bodies thrown in garbage dumps and the streets of the capital weekly."[224] In February 1980, Archbishop Salvador wrote to the president of the United States, Jimmy Carter, imploring him to cease sending military aid that was tearing apart the country of El Salvador. The archbishop writes,

> The present junta government, and especially the army and security forces, unfortunately have not shown themselves capable of solving the country's problems, either by political moves or by creating adequate structures. In general they have only resorted to repressive violence, amassing a total of dead and wounded far higher than in the previous military regimes, whose systematic violation of human rights was denounced by the Interamerican Human Rights Commission. . . . Political power is in the hands of the armed forces. They use their power unscrupulously. They know only how to repress the people and defend the interests of the Salvadoran oligarchy.[225]

The next day, and in following days, the archbishop received death threats. On February 28, 1980, he testified in an interview about his faith, hope, and love of God and of the Salvadoran people. He speaks:

> I have to confess that, as a Christian, I don't believe in death without resurrection. If they kill me, I will rise in the Salvadoran people. I'm not boasting or saying this out of pride, but rather as

humbly as I can. As a shepherd, I am obliged by divine law to give my life for those I love, for the entire Salvadoran people, including those Salvadorans who threaten to assassinate me. If they should go as far as to carry out their threats, I want you to know that I now offer my blood to God for justice and the resurrection of El Salvador.[226]

About the archbishop's death, the United Nations Truth Commission in 1992 made the following report: 1. There is full evidence that… Former Major Robert D'Aubuisson gave the order to assassinate the archbishop and gave precise instructions to members of his security service, acting as a "death squad, to organize and supervise the assassination."[227]

Oscar Arnulfo Romero was an unlikely hero. He had grown up in Ciudad Barrios, about ten miles from El Salvador's border with Honduras, in a wooden home without electricity, and without enough beds for the family. His education began at the local public school, where he studied for three years, before continuing his education at home for the next four years. Next, he studied at the Seminary at San Miguel, in the National Seminary at San Salvador, and in the Gregorian University at Rome, where he was ordained a priest in April 1942. The scholarly priest wished to pursue doctoral studies, but pastoral needs in El Salvador demanded the young priest's return in August 1943. Back home, he served in various positions, including secretary of the diocese and pastor of the cathedral parish. He was named a monsignor in 1967, was appointed editor of the archdiocesan newspaper *Orientación* in 1971, and was ordained bishop in 1974. In 1977, Rome appointed Romero archbishop. "He was a compromise candidate elected to head the bishops' episcopacy by conservative fellow bishops. He was predictable, an orthodox, pious bookworm who was known to criticize the progressive liberation theology clergy so aligned with the impoverished farmers seeking land reform."[228]

Archbishop Romero, however, surprised many people. The reality of the sufferings of the people, the Church, and the country had inspired and encouraged him to risk his own life for his people. In a homily which the archbishop preached half-a-year before his assassination, he declared his opposition to violence. An excerpt follows:

The only violence that the gospel admits is violence to oneself. When Christ lets himself be killed, that is violence — letting himself be killed. Violence to oneself is more effective than violence against others. It is very easy to kill, especially when one has weapons, but how hard it is to let oneself be killed for love of the people![229]

*For further information, contact*
Arzobispado, Urbanizacion Menendez
Calle San José y Avenida Las Americas
San Salvador, El Salvador

# APRIL

## 1. ✠ Anacleto González Flores and Companions

*Place: Guadalajara, Jalisco*
*Fame: Lay martyr, lawyer, youth organizer, husband, and father*

When government officials who had murdered Anacleto González Flores (1888-1927) returned the corpse to his young wife, she turned to her oldest son, and urged him, "This is your father. He was murdered for confessing the faith. Promise me over his body that you will do the same when you are older, if God wills it."[230] This response demonstrated the depth of faith which motivated the Mexican martyrs.

Anacleto had served as one of the principal leaders of the Associación Católica de la Juventud Mexicana (ACJM). He had been involved in coordinating Catholic youth for many years. At twenty, he had entered the apostolic seminary, not to advance to priesthood, but to expose himself to excellent religious education. Five years later, he left the seminary and entered the university, where he studied law. Graduating in 1922, he forewent a law practice in order to dedicate himself to Catholic causes. He coordinated the first National Congress of Catholic Workers, and a few years later, he served as the president of the Party of the Popular Union; and worked closely with the women's group, the Society of Joan of Arc. He originated the weekly Catholic newspaper *Gladium*. He was arrested for his Catholic activities and was shot to death by government officials on April 1, 1927.[231]

Also arrested on April 1 were three brothers: Jorge, Florencio, and Ramon Vargas González. Florencio was released later in the day because the generals investigating the case thought he was a minor. Ironically, Ramon was a minor, but he was detained and killed. The brothers' family had moved from Ahualulco de Mercado to Guadalajara, but the father had continued to return to Ahualulco, where he maintained his medical practice. Jorge (1899-1927) worked in a hydroelectric plant, and Ramon (1905-27) was a medical student, just one-year away from earning his medical license. The family home provided a refuge for priests and Cristeros fleeing authorities during the persecution.

Because the brothers were active, along with Anacleto, in the ACJM, they were arrested. At the jail, the police kept asking the brothers to give information pertaining to the whereabouts of Anacleto. When the brothers refused to provide the desired information, the general in charge ordered that the brothers be beaten and tortured. The general himself kept cutting with a knife the soles of the bare feet of the two arrested men. After many hours, the general summarily announced that the brothers would be killed. The pair prayed together, and then they were shot dead.

The final martyr to meet his death that day was Luis Padilla Gómez (1899-1927). A native of Guadalajara, one of four children, from his youth he had been involved in Church affairs. At sixteen, he joined a Jesuit-led Marian youth group. The next year, he entered the seminary, where he remained for five years. Upon leaving the seminary, he joined the ACJM, of which he became the archdiocesan president; the Union Popular de Jalisco, of which he became secretary; and the Liga Nacional Defensora de la Libertad Religiosa. "In 1926, in charge of ACJM, he supported an economic boycott against the governmental services, and worked with Anacleto González in the activities of the Liga."[232] He also conducted classes in his home for schoolchildren, whom the archbishop had forbidden to attend state schools where atheistic socialism was being taught.

Arrested in the early hours of April 1, Luis was placed in the same jail as Anacleto and the three Vargas González brothers. After being beaten and tortured, he was allowed to pray with his friends before being shot to death.

The next day, two more brothers were arrested. Ezequiel (1876-1927) and Salvador (1880-1927) Huerta Gutiérrez, who were known associates of Anacleto. Salvador was a mechanics teacher, and Ezequiel was a church cantor. Both belonged to the Ejército Nacional Libertador de los Cristeros. After being arrested, beaten, and placed in a cold and dirty jail cell, they thought for a moment that their situation might improve when two guards arrived, and suggested they move to another place. The brothers followed the guards who led the pair directly to a cemetery. Perceiving the inevitable, Ezequiel turned to Salvador, and said, "We are forgiving them, right?"[233] Immediately shots rang out, killing Ezequiel. The trio kept walking. Salvador reached for a candle atop a grave, and said to the soldiers, "I am putting this candle right on my chest so that you don't miss my heart, and because I want to die for Christ."[234]

The companions of Anacleto profited from the teachings of this faith-filled orator and organizer. Anacleto's writings inspired many followers to stand up for their faith. An excerpt follows:

> Until all or almost all Catholics do something more than pray to God that He act, that He labor, that He make things happen, that He alone might do something or everything for the benefit of the Church in our country, [little or nothing will change]. . . . His Holiness Pius XI has said to us clearly and categorically that we are in grave error when we hope that by God's action alone, even with our abstaining from doing something, [that something good will happen] for the sake of God and the Church. In his Apostolic Letter, he has said that Catholic Action is necessary, and therefore, Catholics must act.[235]

*For further information, contact*
Arquidiócesis de Guadalajara
Liceo 17 Centro – Apartado Postal 1-331
C.P. 44100
Guadalajara, Jalisco, México

## 3. ✠ José María Vilaseca Aguilera

*Place:* México City, D.F.
**Fame:** *"God's will first, despite the difficulties that may follow."*
*Founder of Hermanas Josefinas and Misioneros de San José.*

"God's will first, despite the difficulties that may follow," describes the maxim that guided the highly talented and zealous priest José María Vilaseca (1831-1910).[236] His father wanted the son to pursue a well-paying position in a factory, but José opted instead to become a priest. The Mexican government wanted his work stopped, and him exiled; but the persevering priest returned to continue his mission. His religious community, the Vincentians, asked him to stop associating with the women's community he had founded; but José instead separated from the Vincentians and joined the men's community he had founded.

The centrality of doing God's will was confirmed for José, when, at thirty-one, he fell seriously ill with typhoid. Rushed to the hospital, the doctors tried and failed various remedies, and informed him that death was imminent. Years later, he shared his reflections on the experience:

> I confessed my sins; I helped myself; and on this afternoon, I saw and felt an immense emptiness and I was pondering that I was going to die, and I was feeling a loneliness of which you could have no idea. At that time, whatever people are saying matters for nothing, whether it be your father, mother, or the doctor; nothing matters because everything is external, and in the presence of God, everything else is nothing. I experienced in this one moment an emptiness of all human aid, and a complete aloneness.[237]

Born at Igualada, forty miles from Barcelona, he was the second of six children. José's tailor-father and dressmaker-mother sent him to the local primary and secondary schools. In 1843, the family moved to Barcelona, where José worked in a tire factory, then a sacristy before joining the seminary.

At the seminary in 1849, a visiting Vincentian spoke inspiringly about the missions in México, and young José's heart and soul became set afire for this mission. He asked to transfer from the diocesan life to the Vincentian community. After three years of praying and waiting, the young man was permitted to join the Congregation of the Mission. After a three-month transatlantic voyage, José arrived at México City in March 1853. He later writes about his prayer before entering the novitiate, "When I finished the holy exercises, I formed the intention to consecrate myself to God, whatever it may cost me, and with that resolution, I sought to be admitted to the novitiate."[238] During his first three years in México, two of his sisters and his mother died, prior to his ordination to priesthood in December 1856.

The accomplishments of this priest, despite the government's anticlerical persecution, are extraordinary. Even a partial list of the innovative achievements of this priest is exhausting. After having preached popular missions for ten years throughout central and northern México, José began a publishing house called *Biblioteca Religiosa*, which printed the finest works being produced in Europe; and disseminated countless articles which he wrote in opposition to Protestantism and Freemasonry. He founded the first and now the oldest magazine in México, *El Propagandor*, to proclaim and explain the Catholic faith, and he began a newsletter called *Boletin El Sacerdocio Católico* to promote support for priests in their vocations. To collect funds for the education of seminarians, and for the promotion of devotion to St. Joseph, he organized *La Associación Universal de los Devotos de San José*. Because anticlerical laws prohibited religious from administering or teaching in church-related schools, he opened schools and staffed them with young laywomen members of the *Hijas de María*; these schools did not last due to lack of funds and persecution by the government. After the Vincentian seminaries had been closed at Saltillo and Monterrey, he opened at México City, the seminary *Colegio Clerical del San José*, which during its twenty-year existence educated over two thousand students and ordained over two hundred priests.

He founded in 1872, México's first community of women religious, the *Hermanas Josefinas*. This community of native women served heroically when all other religious communities had been forbidden to operate at all. When the political climate improved for the Church under the years of Porfirio Diaz, this community grew rapidly in members, plus number of schools and hospitals. The Hermanas missed Father José, however, when in 1873, the government arrested and jailed him, and exiled him and nineteen other foreign-born priests. Father José spent the next two years communicating with the Hermanas Josefinas from Paris, where he lived with the Vincentians, and from Rome, where for some weeks, the pope interviewed Father José about the conditions of the Church in México. In 1875, a change in government provided him with the opportunity to return to his adopted country.

Two years after his return, however, his religious community required his decision, whether he would remain with or separate from the Vincentians. The previous superior general had supported his ministry. A new superior general, however, took a different point of view. In 1877, the superior general ordered José to separate himself from either the Hermanas Josephinas or the Vincentians. Many people in México, including the archbishop and Vincentians, sent pleas to Paris for compromise. These pleas, however, fell on deaf ears. The bishop advised José to leave his community.

After separating from the Vincentians, Father José joined the *Misioneros de San José*, which he had founded in 1876, to evangelize the remote Indian tribes especially in the regions of the Tarahumaras, the Yaquis, the Huicholes, and the Lacandones.[239] In 1903, the Vatican granted approval to the community of Misioneros.

His body began to wear down. In 1904, he showed symptoms of emphysema. Two years later, he relinquished leadership of the communities, and received the last rites. On the first day of April 1910, an artery burst, to which injury he succumbed on April 3.

*For further information, contact*
Hermanas Josefinas
Condor 336
Col. las Aguilas
Delg. Alvarado Obregon
01710 México D.F. México

❧

## 5. ✠ Élisabeth Bruyère

*Place: Ottawa, Ontario*
*Fame: Educator and innovator. Foundress of the*
*Sisters of Charity of Ottawa.*

Bytown, whose name was changed to Ottawa in 1854, was described by a contemporary pastor as a "Babylon" because of the town's "marked hostilities among the citizens of different ethnic, linguistic, and cultural backgrounds."[240] Early on, French fur traders had settled in this Ottawa River region, and they were followed by English soldiers who received free land grants in 1815.[241] In 1826, the descendants of Frenchmen who had

ÉLISABETH BRUYÈRE

settled along the St. Lawrence River region came to Bytown in order to build the Rideau Canal and to develop lumber camps nearby. Soon, Irish and Scot settlers came in their wake, and developed the town to a population of six thousand citizens. Fights occurred regularly between the French-speaking and English-speaking, between Catholics and Protestants, and between the lumberjacks and townspeople. In this bilingual, multicultural, volatile environment, twenty-six year old Sister Élisabeth Bruyère (1818-76) began her assignment as religious superior. She initiated numerous faith-based social services. At her death, thirty-one years later, the townspeople hailed her as the locale's great benefactress. The obituary from the local newspaper reads,

> Since then [Élisabeth's arrival at Bytown in 1845], she has not ceased to consecrate all her time, all her health, all her fine intelligence and all her indefatigable energy to the service of the community; that is to say, at the service of God, at the service of the poor and the sick to help and to care for them, at the service of infants and young children, to instruct and to form them.[242]

Élisabeth was born and raised in the village of L'Assomption, twenty-four miles north of Montréal. Her widowed father, already with four daughters, married Élisabeth's birth-mother when he was fifty-three, and she, twenty. Six years after Élisabeth was born, her father died.

After the father's death in 1824, Élisabeth's mother moved the family many times. In 1827, Elisabeth resided at the rectory in Saint-Esprit, where her cousin was the parish priest; his sister, the housekeeper; and their cousin, Émilie Caron, the teacher and friend of the poor. The latter played a prominent role in young Élisabeth's life for, later in life, Elisabeth would say, "She reared me in part; she was my teacher and mother."[243] At approximately sixteen, Élisabeth began teaching in the parish school at Saint-Esprit.

Having been under the influence of religious persons for many years at home, the rectory, school, and work, Élisabeth felt called to religious life. At twenty-one, she entered the Sisters of Charity at Montréal. After taking her religious vows on Pentecost 1841, she was given responsibility for managing forty-one adolescent orphans, with the help of three employees. Élisabeth's superior writes to the bishop about the newly professed sister's duty: "She is obliged to teach these children their catechism, their prayers, reading, writing, composition, mathematics and different types of sewing; she is further obliged to give them good work habits, to make, wash, and mend their clothes."[244]

For the next thirty-one years, Élisabeth remained at Ottawa. After the Oblate Fathers of Mary Immaculate moved to Bytown in early 1844, they recognized the need for religious sisters to deal effectively with "children without schools, the sick without hospitals, and the poor without assistance."[245] The Oblates asked the bishop to seek sisters for Bytown. The bishop sought and received agreement from the Sisters of Charity of Montréal. Six women were sent. Twenty-six-year-old Élisabeth went as superior. The sisters departed on their one-hundred-twenty-five-mile journey from Montréal, on the morning of February 19, on sleigh across the frozen Ottawa River, and snow-covered fields and forest paths, and arrived the next evening, after an overnight at Petite Nation.

Immediately, Élisabeth involved herself and the other sisters in responding to the needs at Bytown. On their first day in town, Élisabeth and the other sisters visited the sick and the poor. Within a couple of weeks, they opened the village's first school for both French-speaking and English-speaking young girls. Two months later, they opened the town's first hospital. Although cramped into a two-story convent measuring twenty-four feet by sixteen feet, the four sisters found room to house orphans. Father Adrien Telmon, O.M.I. and Élisabeth formed an association of the Ladies of Charity to assist the poor. The sisters too lived poorly. Élisabeth comments in the community's *Chronicle*, "Our sisters suffered much from poverty to the point of having only dark bread to eat for a long time, and for beverage, barley coffee at breakfast and water at supper."[246] To serve the poor and to live poorly, remained an essential virtue for the community; Élisabeth teaches her sisters, "If we lose the love of the poor, we lose our very spirit."[247]

Over the next thirty years, Élisabeth and the Sisters of Charity responded to the basic needs of the Church in and around Ottawa. For the education of girls, the sisters opened primary and secondary schools in the Province of Ontario at Ottawa, Cornwall, Eganville and Pembroke; in the Province of Québec at Hull, Buckingham, Maniwaki, Montebello, Aylmer, Gatineau, Témiscaminque, and Saint-François-du-Lac,; and after French Canadians moved to New York State in search of jobs, the sisters opened schools at Buffalo, Plattsburg, Ogdensburg, Montebello, Hudson, and Medina. At Ottawa, the Sisters of Charity offered night classes in home economics. For the sick, the sisters' original ten-bed hospital founded in 1845 evolved into the Ottawa General Hospital in 1860. The sisters nursed the sick during a typhus epidemic in 1847, and during a smallpox epidemic in 1871. In the midst of these multiple services, the sisters responded positively to a request that an English-speaking sister be sent to Montréal during the 1847 epidemic; and that sister missionaries be sent to the Indians at Winnipeg, beginning in 1851.

When Élisabeth completed her first three-year term as superior, she was prepared to return to Montréal. Many people implored her, however, to remain at Bytown. Her sisters and Oblate Father Telmon pleaded that Élisabeth might remain at Bytown; they wrote to the bishop of Montréal, and the superiors of the Sisters of Charity at Montréal. Their efforts proved successful. Élisabeth stayed. Five more successive times, the sisters re-elected Élisabeth. And the number of recruits for the community kept increasing.

Élisabeth asserted herself firmly in discussions with her many critics. At the beginning of 1849, she submitted to Bishop Guigues her plans to build a larger and more sturdy house. She requested a three-story building, but the bishop wanted only two; she wanted the structure be of stone, but he wanted wood. Interestingly, in 1850, the sisters moved into their three-story stone house! When a priest retreat director preached with more passion than purpose, she informed the chaplain that the priests were to give the sisters substantive teaching and preaching. After Élisabeth asked Father Aubin to review the community's *Constitutions*, she too reviewed them herself. When the Sisters of Charity of Montréal expressed surprise about the sisters teaching in Ottawa, since their Rule specified that the Institute's purpose was service of the poor, Élisabeth replied that she had enhanced the Rule by adding the work of education. Regarding sending sisters to study, the superior explains, "It is not to make erudites of them that we ask the sisters to study; but that they may be more useful to the Congregation and to their neighbor; and to work efficaciously to the glory of God and to the good of souls."[248]

Beginning in 1872, Élisabeth suffered from an enlarged tumor. Continuing as superior, she communicated with the sisters by correspondence instead of on-site visits. In May 1875, although in great pain, she visited the houses in the United States. Upon her return to Ottawa, doctors discovered an enlargement of the heart. From September of that year, until April of the following year when she died, she received the Sacrament of the Sick oftentimes. Kidding with her sisters who kept praying fervently for her recovery, she says, "You make me languish with all your prayers for my healing; I long to go to heaven."[249] On Christmas Eve 1875, Élisabeth wrote a circular letter, encouraging her sisters to practice the "spirit of simplicity, of charity, of fidelity to the Church; virtues which should characterize the Congregation."[250] In early April, she shared her last recommendation to her sisters, "Greater mortification... Greater humility... With a lot of good will, we can accomplish much."[251]

*For further information, contact*
Centre Cause Élisabeth Bruyère
9 rue Bruyère
Ottawa, ON K1N 5C9 Canada

# 5. ✠ Rosalie Cadron-Jetté

*Places: Montréal, Québec*
*Fame: Christlike caregiver for pregnant, unwed women.*
*Foundress of Sisters of Miséricorde.*

Who would take care of unwed pregnant
women: shelter them, feed them, and provide
medical attention before, during, and after the
births of their children?[252] Who would do this
despite the negative views of the populace, who
hurled sticks, stones, and insults at single women
who gave birth out of wedlock? Bishop Ignace
Bourget, the second bishop of Montréal, in 1845,
asked Rosalie Cadron-Jetté (1794-1864) to con-

ROSALIE CADRON-
JETTÉ

sider not only caring for these women, but also establishing a community of religious women to perpetuate this care.

Rosalie hesitated and pondered the bishop's invitation in prayer during the month of May and then responded, "Yes, God wills it."[253]
Already for over a decade, she had been sheltering these women, feeding them, and serving as their midwife. She had welcomed prostitutes
and unwed pregnant women into her own home. Besides caring for
them, she encouraged them to change their ways. She prayed with and
for these women.

As a child, Rosalie had grown up on the family farm at Lavaltrie, in
Lanaudière County, Québec. Her father earned a comfortable living as
a farmer, while the mother served the area as a midwife. Rosalie had two
siblings: a younger brother who died in childbirth, and a sister Sophie, a
dozen years younger than Rosalie.

Rosalie manifested a sensitivity towards all suffering persons.
Orphaned and abandoned children found shelter with her. Job seekers on
their way to Montréal received food, clothing, and shelter at her home.
Children preparing for their First Communion had their clothing mend-
ed by her. Rosalie's sister Sophie reports that she saw her sister "taking
homemade cookies fresh out of the oven and giving them to someone
passing by, bringing chickens and eggs to a poor sick woman, keeping in
her house an Indian family for a whole week because of the severe cold."[254]

According to the custom of the time and place, Rosalie married a man much older than herself: she was almost seventeen, and he, thirty-three. Having married in 1811, Rosalie and her husband Jean-Marie gave birth to eleven children over the next twenty-one years, until 1832, when Jean-Marie died during a cholera epidemic. At thirty-eight, Rosalie became widowed with seven living children between the ages of twenty and one-month. Four of the children had died already between infancy and four years of age.

Life in Lavaltrie was prosperous, but as their sons were growing older and Jean-Marie could not give them farm space, the couple decided to leave Lavaltrie. Within a space of five years, 1822-27, financial realities forced them to move three times: in 1822, from the donated property at Lavaltrie, to Vercheres; in 1824 from Vercheres to Saint-Hyacinthe, where they lost their land because the alleged owner sold them land he did not own; and in 1827 from Saint-Hyacinthe to Montréal.

The Providence of God led Rosalie to her eventual ministry. One night, a frantic knock shook the front door of Rosalie's home. Her husband went to the door, without opening it. Urgently, almost hysterically, a woman begged to be allowed inside. She blurted out that two sailors were chasing her with a hatchet, with which they intended to kill her. Jean-Marie asked her name. She pleaded just to be allowed inside, and she would explain the next day, who she was. Jean-Marie opened the door, and the woman burst into the room. A few minutes later, two sailors knocked. They asked if a woman had just entered. Jean-Marie replied, "No." The men forced their way in, insisting on looking for themselves. Fortunately, Jean-Marie had hidden the surprise visitor in the cellar. The two intruders left. The female stranger emerged from the basement and profusely thanked Jean-Marie and Rosalie. The next morning, Rosalie chatted with the woman. Seeing that the woman was a working member of the world's oldest profession, Rosalie urged this woman to change her life. Rosalie fed and provided her with a clean change of clothing. The woman departed safely. Later, the woman emigrated to the United States, married and settled down, and wrote to Rosalie to assure her that she had changed her life.

For years, Rosalie unselfishly dedicated her time and energies to assisting single pregnant women and prostitutes. Being single and pregnant in that cultural context created a great stigma, morally and socially. Word spread that all persons in need were welcomed into the home of Rosalie Cadron-Jetté. Once, Bishop Bourget brought to Rosalie six young brother and sister orphans. Within a few days, Rosalie found homes for each one, and all were adopted into the families who had offered assistance.

As Montréal's metropolitan population kept growing, up to two hundred thousand by 1827, and the social problems of unmarried single mothers kept mounting; Bishop Bourget observed that the situation called for more than Rosalie's individual efforts. He suggested in May 1845 that Rosalie might found a religious community of women to achieve for perpetuity and more widely what Rosalie had been doing individually and locally. Rosalie agreed.

In May 1845, Rosalie expanded her church service. Her son rented a house, and let his mother occupy the attic, where she gave hospitality to women in need. A first, Rosalie gave her bed to overnight guests, while she insisted on sleeping on a plank with bed coverings. A wealthy benefactor visited the shelter, saw the deprivations, and provided furniture for the bedroom and kitchen, and a stove and utensils with which to cook. By July, a widow joined Rosalie. Some of Rosalie's children, embarrassed by their mother's companions and living conditions, confronted her saying, "You are dishonoring our family. What will people in the world say? You should not do this. Think of your reputation. It makes us feel bad to hear the things that people are saying about you."[255] On another occasion, two of her children approached her, and said, "Mother, enough is enough. You are going to die in this miserable place. People ridicule you. You are going to come home with us."[256] They picked up their mother's belongings, and waited for their mother to rise and leave with them. Instead, Rosalie said, "Take everything I own, if you want; but as for me, I'm staying here."[257] After all, she was doing God's will; she was doing what the bishop had asked. In the first year of operation, at any given time, seven or eight young pregnant women were living in Rosalie's Hospice.

The next year, Rosalie moved the hospice to a larger house. During the second year of operation, thirty-three pregnant women, at one time or another, lived at the Hospice; and twenty-five babies had been born there.[258] Rosalie never refused entrance to any woman in need of shelter.

At the end of April 1846, women began entering the nascent community's postulant program. On January 16, 1848, Rosalie and seven women took religious vows in the community. This date became regarded as the foundation date of the Institute of the Sisters of Miséricorde. At their profession they received from Bishop Bourget the veil, cross, cincture, and their religious names. Rosalie was named Sister of the Nativity, in honor of the Blessed Mother's birthing of her son Jesus, and in recognition of Rosalie's role in birthing the children of so many women in need.

More and more women, inspired by Mother Jetté's treatment of unwed mothers, joined the Sisters of Miséricorde. The candidates commented, "Mother Jetté possessed a great maternal tenderness for these young mothers. She called them, 'her heart'."[259] Mother advised the sister-candidates to have a similar attitude, saying, "These dear children have a good heart, and we want to be available for them in their greatest need."[260] When one novice expressed fear about sleeping in the same dormitory as the girls, Rosalie replied, "Those poor girls are better than you think; go, and don't be afraid."[261] Repeatedly, Rosalie advised the sister-candidates, "Do not stay here if you are not able to love these women."[262]

Five years before she died, Mother contracted an acute kidney disease. Her health worsened. She passed her time praying for her unwed mothers. She advised her sisters, "When I had a sick child, I did not count the hours I spent with the child. I preferred to forego my sleep in order to watch, relieve their sufferings, and comfort them. I have done the same with my dear abandoned women of the street. Love endures all things."[263] In 1864, the bishop made a canonical visit, reviewed the *Constitutions and Rules* with his co-founder, then administered the last rites of the Church, giving Rosalie the Eucharist and praying over her. He said, "My dear girl, you may die now; go and receive your crown in heaven which God has lovingly prepared for you to reward you for all the sacrifices and works which you have so generously undertaken for His glory."[264] The next day, Rosalie died. Throughout her sickness, her countenance radiated calm and kindness.

A few years later, the bishop gathered together the sisters to reflect on Rosalie's life. One of the nuns observed, "She (Rosalie) placed herself beyond caring about the judgments of the world, when she placed before herself only conforming to the holy will of God."[265]

*For further information, contact*
Centre Rosalie-Cadron-Jetté
12435, avenue de la Miséricorde
Montréal, QC H4J 2G3 Canada

## 9. ✢ Marcelle Mallet

*Place: Québec City, Québec*
*Fame: "In all our pains, let us console ourselves in the divine Heart of Jesus." Foundress of Sisters of Charity of Québec.*

Good Mother Mallet (1805-71)! At nineteen, Marcelle entered the religious community of the Congregation of the Sisters of Charity at Montréal, which Marguerite d'Youville had founded in 1737. After twenty-five years in religious life, when the Coadjutor Bishop of Québec Pierre Flavien Turgeon requested that the Sisters of Charity might send sisters to his diocese, Sister Marcelle volunteered.[266] In August 1849, she, who just had been elected superior of the mission, four newly professed sisters, and one novice left Montréal to establish an autonomous community at Québec. This assignment required Marcelle to leave family and friends, to found a new community in another city, and to depend on God ultimately for providing vocations and financial support for the community. Mother Marcelle would serve in this challenging mission for the next twenty-two years, until the moment she died.

Upon arriving at Québec on August 22, 1849, Mother Mallet encountered a city being ravaged by cholera. "From June to September [1849], Québec recorded the deaths of 1185 of its people."[267] Immediately, Mother responded to the people's needs. The widespread sickness left many children orphaned. Mother gathered these waifs, and welcomed them into the Glacis Street Orphanage, which the Catholic Women's Charitable Society of Québec had founded in 1831. By the end of Mother's first two weeks in the city, the original group of thirty children had doubled.[268] Part of the reason the Sisters had come to Québec was, at the Catholic Women's request, to take over responsibility for the institution, which transfer was completed in April 1850. Mother accepted the responsibility, and revived the vitality of the orphanage. In the next two decades, she and her religious sisters would serve over eleven hundred orphans here.

In the capital city, when fathers became desperately ill or injured, and could not work, families fell into dire poverty. To serve these poor families, Mother Marcelle organized centers to receive and distribute food. For the sick and the dying, Mother Mallet opened a dispensary to provide medicines. Noting the pauperous condition of many elderly women, she opened in the sisters' home a ward wherein they cared for aged and infirm women. Home visitation became one of the hallmarks of the sisters' apostolate; "every month the Sisters made six hundred visits to the poor and to the sick."[269]

Inexorable waves of immigrants kept arriving at the city's port. Unwittingly, these immigrants brought with them germs of the epidemic, which exposed the resident population to disease against which they had no immunity. Year after year, the epidemic besieged Québec City: not only in 1849, but also in 1851, 1852, 1854, 1855, and 1866.

Throughout the crowded city, another threat lurked among the rows of wood-frame houses, mills, stores and churches. "Fire" was waiting to extend its far-reaching flames. When residents became burned out of their homes, Mother found shelter for them, either in the convent or with generous townspeople. Fires and epidemics impacted the city not only physically but also economically, politically and socially.

Another reason why the Sisters of Charity came to Québec was to provide religious instruction to children, especially girls. During the sisters' first year in the city, "on the eighth day of October [1849], some two hundred fifty girls, besides the orphans, invaded the first school opened by the Sisters of Charity of Québec."[270] Also, when Mother discovered that many poor boys wished to become priests, she sought and found donations and scholarships for them.

One year after the sisters' arrival, the bishop arranged that a large chapel was constructed for the sisters and their guests. The chapel was completed in 1850, but burned to the ground four years later. Another fire in 1869, consumed the second chapel, which was rebuilt immediately. As Mother Marcelle's community grew in vocations, and in requests for the sisters' services, she opened, between 1857 and 1862, five convents and accompanying boarding schools, at Cacouna, Lévis, Deschambault, Plessisville, and La Pocatière. The sisters in these new houses applied themselves to instructing the children, caring for the poor, and visiting the homebound sick. The establishment of new houses occasioned the separation of sisters from their motherhouse at Québec. Mother movingly writes to the first group just after they left the motherhouse:

> My dear Sisters, I experienced such great desire to console you for having made the sacrifice of being the first to leave the Mother House, that I felt ready to endure much more fatigue in order to help you. Now, I sense that the great consolation I experienced being with you, there, was surpassed by far by the sadness I felt having to leave you. I left you, but now my motherly heart is heavy and broken. God wanted this to happen, let us be resigned to His holy will.[271]

The God-given personality and spirituality that Marcelle brought to Québec, she had developed through her experiences in her youth, and in the convent at Montréal. Having been born in the Montréal suburb of Côte-des-Neiges, she moved with her family to l'Assomption before she celebrated her first birthday. At five, she returned with her family to Montréal, where she received her First Communion. By five, she already had suffered the deaths of her father and maternal grandmother. By ten, six of her seven siblings had passed away. Her mother survived until Mother Marcelle celebrated her forty-eighth birthday. Because of the young family's poverty, they had moved four times in twelve years. Reduced to a penniless state, her mother was forced to sell the family's possessions at public auction. When the mother could no longer provide a home for Marcelle and her brother Narcisse, her senior by three years, her mother's childless sister and husband at Lachine offered to adopt the pair. The birth mother allowed the adoptions, and the adoptive parents provided a welcoming and warm environment for the children. Marcelle, who had received her initial education at home from her mother and maternal grandfather, continued her studies with the Sisters of the Congregation of Notre Dame at Montréal in spring 1817.

In 1822, when seventeen-year-old Marcelle received the sacrament of confirmation, she resolved to assist poor people. Having regularly performed charitable works with the Sisters of Charity in Montréal, she entered on May 6, 1824, the convent of that community popularly known as the Grey Nuns. One year later, she put on the habit of the Grey Nuns, and on May 18, 1826, she professed her vows. Her duties in the convent at Montréal consisted of being cook, sacristan, assistant general, and overseeing a medical ward. "In the summer of 1832, a terrible epidemic of cholera struck Montréal and took the lives of six hundred thirty-two persons in ten days. . . . The sisters, young and old, were obliged to work day and night during this emergency, at which time, Sister Marcelle was initiated to the nursing profession."[272] Inside and outside the convent, Marcelle's God-given compassion for the suffering and the poor, was manifested in her gentle way with everybody. In the midst of the greatest difficulties, Mother Marcelle conducted herself with great stability; "her gentleness conditioned her firmness."[273]

Mother Mallet's spirituality hinged on two devotions: the Sacred Heart of Jesus, and the Blessed Virgin Mary. On one of some of the small pieces of paper found in her room, she had written, "In our sorrows, let us go to the Heart of Jesus, fountain of all virtues. If I love the Heart of Jesus, nothing will be difficult. I beg Him to embrace my heart with His love and to give me gentleness, patience, humility and resignation."[274] The joy of her devotion moved her to promote devotion by others to the Sacred Heart.

Mother possessed a deep devotion also to the Blessed Mother. In 1847, Mother Marcelle participated enthusiastically in the pilgrimage to the shrine of Our Lady of Good Help to which Bishop Ignace Bourget of Montréal had asked the city's population to visit to beseech the aid of the Blessed Virgin Mary in lessening the impact of the epidemic afflicting the city. As superior at Québec, "She introduced the custom that required the new superior of the community, after each election, to go to the statue of Our Lady and acclaim her as the true superior of the community."[275]

After seventeen years as superior of the community, the foundress chose to step away from the position of leadership. Mother's assigned task became caring for the food garden, which provided sustenance for the sisters, orphans, and elderly women. Mother continued to work in the garden until two years before her death. At that time, in 1869, she was diagnosed with cancer. Two years later, on Easter Sunday, she died.

*For further information, contact*
Centre Marcelle-Mallet
2655, rue Le Pelletier
Beauport, QC G1C 3X7 Canada

❧

## 17. ✠ Blessed Kateri Tekakwitha

*Places: Auriesville and Fonda, New York;*
*La Prairie de la Madeleine, Québec*
*Fame: She prayed always. Lily of the Mohawks.*

Despite growing up in a society that promoted promiscuity and physical violence, Kateri (1656-80), dedicated her life to God as a virgin and person of prayer.[276] Because of her counter-cultural attitude and behavior, she suffered much ridicule and ostracism from her family, friends and fellow villagers.

Born in the same village, where ten years previously her Mohawk tribesmen had tomahawked to death Isaac Jogues and Jean de Lalande, Kateri

KATERI TEKAKWITHA

was the daughter of an Algonquin woman and Mohawk chief. Kateri's mother was a baptized Catholic, who prior to marriage had practiced her faith among the French at Trois-Rivières, but whose unbelieving husband subsequently prohibited her from practicing her faith. Observers suggest that the mother nonetheless introduced Kateri to the rudiments of the Catholic faith through the mother's words, prayers, and actions. When Kateri was four, a smallpox epidemic swept through the village, leaving dead her mother, father, and younger brother. Kateri suffered disfigurement for life by the disease, which left her half-blind and pock-marked over her face. A new chief was elected, and this man and his wife, Kateri's aunt, adopted Kateri and another abandoned young girl. The chief moved the village a little farther west of the site of the sickness. Initially the new chief was indifferent to the religion of the Blackrobes. After dozens of villagers over the years, however, converted to the "Prayer" and moved to the Catholic mission four miles south of Montréal, the chief grew increasingly hostile to the Catholic religion.

As a young girl, Kateri learned sewing and embroidery, and became outstanding in her sewing of beads, belts, leggings, and moccasins. At eight, she ran outside the house when her adoptive parents brought into their home a boy her age, who as an infant had been betrothed to Kateri. The boy's ritual visit and sharing of food was to confirm the original betrothal, which Kateri refused to accept. With her girl friends, she shied away from their games, perhaps because of her poor eyesight, and she walked away from the group's gossiping. Instead, she would go off by herself and pray. She evidenced a spiritual dimension, unusual in anyone, especially in someone so young. In 1667, she met priests for the first time when her father gave hospitality for three days to three Jesuits.

As a teen, she continued her singular behavior. Girls her age were expected to enter into sexual experiences. She refused. Once, her father arranged that some drunken friends would initiate his stepdaughter into sexual experience. Kateri fled from the men's grasp. She wanted to give herself over to God, penance, and prayer.

The Jesuit priest James de Lamberville began ministering in Kateri's village in 1675. Lamberville enjoyed a particularly profound relationship with Kateri. One day, he passed by her longhouse wherein she was recovering from an ankle injury. He visited her.

> In spite of the fact that there were several of her townspeople with her, she poured out to the blackrobe the pent up desires she had of learning more of the "Prayer" and of being baptized.... He was wise enough to sense that here was an exceptionally delicate soul. He proposed difficulties to her and told her of the heroism required for Christian living in a village teeming with temptation. She answered only that she had made her decision, and nothing, not even exile or flight, would change her. He

promised to instruct her and invited her to the catechism classes.[277]

While most catechumens underwent a two-year period of instruction and probation prior to baptism, Lamberville conferred the sacrament on Easter Sunday 1676, just one month after Kateri had requested baptism. Lamberville had perceived that Kateri "was of a sweet and peaceable nature, inclined towards good and with an extreme aversion to all sorts of evil."[278] Kateri's formal entrance into Catholicism, however, set her apart even more. She refused to marry, and to work on Sundays. A young brave, with tomahawk in hand, threatened her with death if she did not apostasize from her new faith. Children threw stones at her, and mockingly called her "Christian." One of her aunts reported to Lamberville that she suspected Kateri kept going to the woods, not to pray, but to meet a secret lover. Distressed over others' opposition to her way, Kateri sought out Lamberville for advice. He suggested that she might want to flee this village and go to the Catholic mission of St. Francis Xavier at Sault St. Louis, near La Prairie de Madeleine, on the way to Montréal. Kateri accepted this suggestion.

One day three Catholic catechists from the mission St. Francis Xavier visited Fonda, when Kateri's chieftain stepfather was absent. Kateri fled with two Catholic men, a Huron and the Mohawk. As soon as Kateri's father arrived back home, he loaded his gun and took off in pursuit of Kateri. Twice, this threesome had close calls in which they eluded Kateri's father. Completing the three-hundred mile and three-month journey, they arrived at St. Francis Xavier mission in October 1677. Kateri carried with her a letter from Lamberville for the Jesuit Father Cholonec. Kateri, who cold not read or write, handed the letter to the priest. The letter reads, "Katherine Tekakwitha is going to live at the Sault. Will you kindly undertake to direct her? You will soon know what a treasure we have sent you. Guard it well! May it profit in your hands, for the glory of God and the salvation of a soul that is certainly very dear to Him"[279]

The villagers at Kateri's new home recognized her as a saint. She arrived at the chapel each morning by four o'clock, and remained there for several hours, praying without movement of her lips, but with sighs of the heart and tears in her eyes. She spent an hour in preparation for confession, which she made every eight days. At the Canadian mission, two of Kateri's closest friends were Anastasia, her birth mother's sister, and Teresa Tegaiaguenta, a recovering alcoholic. Kateri communicated openly with both of these women, especially the latter. When Teresa pointed out to Kateri the new chapel that was under construction, Kateri replied, "A chapel of wood is not what God wants; He wants our souls to make a temple of them."[280] On her first Christmas at St. Francis Xavier, Kateri received her First Communion, eighteen months after her baptism. As at Auriesville and Fonda, the Indians at St. Francis Xavier, encouraged Kateri to marry. Her aunt Anastasia kept urging this. Her adopted sister questioned Kateri, thus:

> Have you thought seriously about what you are doing? Have you ever heard tell of such a thing among the Iroquois girls? Where did you get this strange idea? Can you not see that you expose yourself to the derision of men and the temptations of the devil? Can you expect to accomplish what no girl among us has ever done? Forget these thoughts, my dear sister; do not trust your own strength, but follow the custom of the other girls.[281]

Kateri knew her own intentions. She approached Father Cholonec in March 1679, and requested that she might dedicate her virginity to God. The priest replied that this was a solemn step and that she ought to think about this momentous step. He suggested that she think and pray for three days, and then return to him. Kateri left, and returned in ten minutes. She replied, "I do not need any more time. This has been the desire of my whole life."[282] From that point on, Kateri identified her position by wearing the simple braids of the unmarried Iroquois maidens.

At Sault St. Francis Xavier, Kateri became ill, and one year later, she died. On Tuesday of Holy Week 1680, she confided to her friend Teresa that death was near. Kateri urged Teresa, "Keep up your courage. Don't mind the sneers of those who have no faith. Listen to the Fathers. . . . I will love you in heaven. I will pray for you. I will help you."[283] That evening, some Sodality friends, with the approval of the priest went into the forest and performed penances for Kateri. The next morning, Kateri thanked her friends, saying, "You are very pleasing to God, and I shall pray for you in heaven. I know where you have been and what you have done. Keep up your courage. I know you are pleasing to God and I will help you when I am with Him."[284] Within hours, she died.

*For further information, contact*
National Shrine of Blessed Tekakwitha
P. O. Box 627
Fonda, New York 12068 U.S.A.

## 17. ✣ Mother Maria Kaupas

*Places: Chicago, Illinois; Scranton and Mt. Carmel, Pennsylvania; and Clovis, New Mexico*
*Fame: "Chicago's Second Cabrini," and foundress of the Sisters of Saint Casimir of Chicago.*

Persecution provided the cultural context in which Casimira Kaupas (1880-1940) was born and raised in the village of Gudeliai, Lithuania.[285] Since 1795, when Empress Catherine II had confiscated two-thirds of the territory of Lithuania, and declared Russian Orthodoxy the state religion, successive Russian czars persecuted the Lithuanian people. Churches, monasteries, convents, and parish schools were closed. Religious orders were expelled. Printing houses no longer were permitted to publish works using

MARIA KAUPAS

the Latin alphabet; henceforth, all private prayer books, ecclesiastical sacred texts, and general literature had to employ the Russian Cyrillic alphabet. When Casimira, or Kaze, which her family affectionately called her, was a young girl, the ethnic persecution had become intensified in response to the Lithuanian people's rebellion of 1863.

Lithuanian Catholics went underground. "They formed bands of smugglers known as 'legitimates,'who used secret routes to Tilzit, Prussia, where printers ran stocks of newspapers and books, all ready to be smuggled into Lithuania. Risks were great: arrest, confiscation of one's entire homestead, and exile to Siberia."[286] Casimira Kaupas's father participated in this movement and, seventeen-year-old Casimira also carried a forbidden manuscript upon herself while she was being smuggled out of Lithuania to the United States. Under the leadership of the heroic bishop Matthew Valancius, priests and laity participated courageously in the underground movement.

At the same time that Catholics were suffering for the faith in Lithuania, their compatriots were rejoicing over their newly found religious freedom in the United States. The immigrants in the New World kept writing home to relatives and friends to share their good news and to invite their loved ones to come to America. Maria Kaupas's brother Anthony left the fatherland in 1892 to become a priest for the Lithuanian people in the U.S.A. After ordination in 1896, and assignment to St. Joseph Lithuanian church in Scranton, Pennsylvania, he wrote to his parents to inquire if Casimira might want to come to the U.S.A. to serve as his housekeeper.

Accepting her brother's invitation, seventeen-year-old Casimira traveled to the United States in 1897. For the next four years, she lived with and worked for her brother, until, having become homesick, she returned to Lithuania. "In 1905, back in Lithuania, she resolved to become a teaching religious to help the Lithuanian Americans concerning matters of faith, since it was impossible to do so in her native land."[287] With financial help from a priest friend of her brother, Casmira studied at Ingenbohl, Switzerland, where the Sisters of Mercy of the Holy Cross for three years provided her religious formation. In preparation for her return to the U.S.A., Casmira asked her brother to identify a spiritual advisor for herself and her intended community. Her brother suggested Father Anthony Staniukynas, who then sought and received the support of his bishop, John W. Shanahan of Harrisburg, to sponsor the new congregation. Bishop Shanahan enlisted the aid of the Sisters of the Immaculate Heart of Mary of Scranton to provide further spiritual formation to Casimira and her two companions. Lithuanian Catholics immigrants generously supported this endeavor.

In Scranton, on August 29, 1907, the new congregation, the Sisters of St. Casimir was founded. Bishop Shanahan gave Casimira the religious name of Maria, in honor of the novice's devotion to the Immaculate Conception of Mary. Four months later, the sisters of the new congregation founded their first school in the United States at Mount Carmel, Pennsylvania, located sixty miles southwest of Scranton. Other foundations and ministries quickly followed. The burgeoning community located and built its motherhouse in Chicago, where the largest concentration of Lithuanian immigrants had settled. The sisters quickly opened schools in Chicago and Waukegan, Illinois; and in Philadelphia and Newtown, Pennsylvania. Twenty years later, Mother Maria accepted Bishop Mundelein's request that she take over responsibility for Holy Cross Hospital in Chicago since the financially strapped Lithuanian Catholic Charities was unable to do so. In 1937, the community started schools in New Mexico. And Mother laid the groundwork for expanding to Argentina, which occurred one year after her death.

After making her perpetual vows in 1913, Sister Maria was elected superior general of the community, and, thereafter, was called "Mother." She retained leadership of the community for twenty-seven years, until her death. When she died in 1940, the community had grown to over three hundred forty sisters, living in over thirty houses.

At the conclusion of World War I, the Lithuanian people gained freedom from Russian oppression and declared their political independence in 1920. The bishops of Lithuania implored Mother Maria to return to her homeland to establish her congregation to educate the youth there. Mother Maria traveled with four sisters to Lithuania, where she opened a convent and school at Pazaislis. Fourteen years later, because the local bishop desired to make the sisters a diocesan community, the Lithuanian branch separated from the American community. With a heavy heart, Mother Maria yielded to the desires of the bishop. Following the separation, until her death she sent heartfelt letters, supporting the sisters, spiritually and financially. She writes:

> What a paradise life would be if each and every one, forgetting self, were to strive to manifest love for others by first cultivating it within one's own heart, and then expressing this in word and deed. Strive not to judge the thoughts and intentions of others, for external actions and words are not always an indication of what is truly present in their minds and hearts. Leave judging and

fault-finding to small and mean minds; let our concern be this noble desire and aim: to love as the Savior taught."[288]

Mother Maria's health began to fail at fifty-three, when she was diagnosed with breast cancer, which advanced into bone cancer. On her sixtieth birthday, she told her sisters, "It will be my last with you."[289] After suffering excruciating pain for the last three weeks of her life, she died in peace. Her prayer had been answered that her last three hours might be like those of Our Lord's last three hours on earth.

Mother Maria Kaupas, who for over three decades had led the Sisters of St. Casimir, always communicated clearly her love to her sisters. She signed all her letters to her sisters, "Loving you. Mother Maria."[290]

*For further information, contact*
Sisters of St. Casimir Motherhouse and Museum
2601 W. Marquette Road
Chicago, IL 60629 U.S.A.

❧

## 18. ✠ Blessed Marie Anne Blondin

*Places: Vaudreuil, Saint-Jacques, and Lachine, Québec*
*Fame: Attaining sanctity while suffering mistreatment.*
*Foundress of the Congregation of Sisters of St. Ann.*

Church history is replete with saintly founders and foundresses whose religious communities literally or nearly banished those holy persons from the communities which they had founded.[291] Among that list are included: St. Francis of Assisi, St. Alphonsus Liguori, St. Joseph Calasanctius, Blessed Teresa Couderc, Blessed Teresa de Soubiran, St. John of the Cross, and St. Benedict of Nursia.[292] Blessed Marie Anne

MARIE ANNE BLONDIN

Blondin (1809-90) deserves to be added to that list. Her life in religious community was simultaneously heroic and tragic.

Four years after Esther Blondin had founded the Congregation of the Sisters of Saint Anne, the bishop, acting on the advice of a controlling priest-chaplain, removed her as superior general. Four years later, her successor removed Mother as superior of a convent school when Mother failed to send to the new superior general as much revenue as she wanted. This same superior sent Mother to an isolated mission for a year, erased her name from the community's list of personnel assignments, forbade the sisters to communicate with her, and required anyone with letters from Mother to send these to the motherhouse for burning. The superior general forbade the sisters to call Marie Anne by any honorific titles such as Mother, Superior, or Foundress.

After her "zero year," as Mother calls it, she was brought back to the motherhouse, where for the next thirty-two years, until she died, the foundress worked at menial tasks, namely, as sacristan, dressmaker and laundress. Twice, in 1872 and 1878, the sisters elected the foundress as general assistant to the general superior, but each time the superior ignored Mother's presence at meetings, and refused to inform her about issues to be decided. In 1863, the community sent to Rome a document seeking recognition of the establishment of the community. The Vatican returned a Decree of Praise, which identified the site of the foundation of the community not as Vaudreuil, where Mother had founded the community, but as Saint-Jacques, where the bishop and Mother's successor usurped the administration of the community.[293]

Although the bishop, a few clergy and sister-administrators of the community repeatedly mistreated Mother, witnesses declared that she never complained about any of these malefactors. She spoke honestly and forthrightly, but always she followed the Scriptural command to "speak the truth with love."[294] Decades after her assigned disappearance to the basement of the motherhouse, a novice expressed to Mother shock that the foundress of the community was assigned to the hidden task of ironing clothes. Marie Anne replied, "Our Lord planted the root in manure; that's why the tree grew so fast."[295]

Born in rural Terrebonne, eighteen miles north of Montréal, Marie-Esther Sureau-Blondin first applied for and was accepted by the Congregation of Notre Dame. Some months later, however, she was sent home because of her poor health. Beginning in 1833, she began assisting another former novice of the Congregation of Notre Dame, Suzanne

Pineault, at a parochial school at Vaudreuil. Within five years, Pineault left the school, and Esther was named director. After the school year 1846-47, Esther became seriously ill. While recuperating, Esther prayed for guidance as to God's will for her life.

Esther Blondin felt called to found a community of religious sisters dedicated to the education of poor country children, both boys and girls in the same classroom. This approach was viewed as "subversive, and contrary to the principles of sound morality" because the customs of the day allowed that only men would teach boys, only women would teach girls, and boys and girls studying in the same classroom was forbidden.[296] In 1848, Esther took her idea to the pastor at Terrebonne, and afterwards to Bishop Ignace Bourget of Montréal. The two clergymen accepted Esther's plan.

Within the next few months, Esther sought out women whom she thought might make good nuns. In 1848, under Esther's leadership and authority, she and six other women entered their novitiate. The next year, the same seven took the religious habit, and religious names, with Esther taking the name Sister Marie Anne. In 1850, Marie Anne, now called Mother, along with four companions, officially founded the religious community of The Daughters of Saint Anne.

The community grew fast: by 1853, there were eighteen professed sisters, six novices, and six postulants.[297] More space was needed both to house the sisters, and to board and teach the students. The bishop found the sisters space at St. Jacques, thirty miles north of Montréal. In August 1853, the nuns arrived there, and one week later arrived Father Adolphe Maréchal, who had asked the bishop to assign the priest as the sisters' chaplain. This twenty-nine-year-old priest already had been assigned to six different places. One pastor writes of him, "He has caused me much suffering, the dear child. He sowed discord all along my path"[298]

Maréchal involved himself excessively in the affairs of the community. Mother Marie Anne wrote to the bishop about the chaplain's transgressions of his authority. The difficult priest also wrote to the bishop, demanding, in effect, "remove her or remove me."[299] The young priest did much good, but he could not refrain from overstepping boundaries. "He desired the good immoderately, forgetting that a community has its customs, its *Rule*, its canonical legislation, its administrative autonomy, and that a chaplain is but a chaplain and not a general superior."[300] In August

1854, the bishop ordered Mother to remove herself as superior general of the diocesan religious community. The bishop writes to Mother, "You will resign willingly, and you will tell your Sisters that you are authorized never again to accept the superiorship even if they wish you to assume it."[301]

Mother Marie Anne's successor in 1854, assigned the foundress to Sainte-Geneviève, located on the outskirts of Montréal, as the religious superior and directress of the convent school. In 1858, the superior general summarily removed Marie Anne from Sainte-Geneviève, recalled her to Saint-Jacques to the motherhouse, to perform the task of sacristan. At this time, the community was opening a mission at Vancouver Island in the far western part of Canada, for which Mother volunteered. The bishop, however, refused her permission to volunteer. Instead, her community sent her to the isolated wilderness mission at Saint-Ambroise-de-Kildare, about seventy-five miles north of Montréal. She received no assignment; she was simply removed to a remote place. When the motherhouse was moved to Lachine, near Montréal, in 1864, Mother was assigned there. Again, she performed menial tasks.

Sister lived her hidden life in humility, obedience, and graciousness. She rejoiced with the sisters over the rapid growth of the community. By the time of her death, the community had expanded in Canada from Montréal to Vancouver Island; and in the United States, from Oswego, New York State to Juneau, Alaska.

Throughout all these difficulties, witnesses testify that Mother always spoke the truth without rancor. She trusted the bishop, even though he had withdrawn his trust of her. She recognized the disdain in which Father Adolphe Maréchal held her, and she repeatedly tried to bring reconciliation to their relationship. She held her ground in stating her opinions, but she never held any animosity towards him. She always openly and honestly, truthfully and faithfully, despite the cost, desired to do God's will, as it was manifested through her superiors, not with a blind obedience, but with a mature obedience after she had voiced her perception of the truth.

*For further information, contact*
Marie Anne Blondin Center
1950 Provost Street
Lachine, QC H8S 1P7 Canada

## 18. ✠ Venerable Cornelia Connelly

*Places: Philadelphia, Pennsylvania; Natchez, Mississippi;
and Grand Coteau. Louisiana
Fame: To do God's will at any cost.
Foundress of the Society of the Holy Child Jesus.*

Cornelia Peacock was born and raised in Philadephia, the youngest of seven children, who joined two step-sisters from her birth-mother's first marriage.[302] The Peacock family enjoyed financial comfort, but suffered significant instability. By the time Cornelia "was fourteen years old, (she) had resided in at least seven different houses."[303] Within a space of five years, 1818 to 1823, her real-estate broker father and mother died. The adolescent was adopted by her step-sister, Isabella Bowen Montgomery.

At twenty-two, Cornelia changed her religious affiliation from the Presbyterian Church to the Episcopal High Church. Nine months later, she married twenty-seven-year-old Pierce Connelly, a University of Pennsylvania graduate, who had been raised Presbyterian, but became Episcopalian, and was serving as assistant rector in Philadelphia. Cornelia's

CORNELIA CONNELLY

step-sister had forbade the wedding; why, remains unknown. Within a couple of months, early in 1832, Pierce received his own rectorship, at Natchez, Mississippi, where his family had numerous real estate investments. The newlyweds lived at Natchez for three years, and their first two children, Mercer and Adeline, were born there.

During rabid anti-Catholic uprisings, Pierce investigated the historical and theological accuracy of the criticisms. His investigation resulted in resigning his rectorship, and traveling to Rome to inquire about conversion to and ordination in the Catholic Church. Cornelia, perceiving that Pierce's ordination might end their marriage, writes, "I am ready at once to submit to whatever my loved husband believes to be the path of duty."[304] At Rome, she pleaded, "Is it necessary for Pierce to make this sacrifice and sacrifice me?"[305] After receiving instructions, Cornelia was received into the Church in January 1836, and her husband was two months later. Pope Gregory XVI supported Pierce's conversion, but suggested that the neophyte take more time before seeking ordination in the Church.

Beginning in fall 1837, Pierce found employment at the Jesuit College of St. Charles at Grand Coteau, Louisiana, one hundred sixty miles west of New Orleans. Living arrangements were found at the Sacred Heart Sisters Convent School, where the young family moved into the comfortable cottage Gracemere. Cornelia gave private piano and guitar lessons, and taught singing in the school. In September 1839, Cornelia suffered the death of her seven-week-old fourth child, Mary Magdalen. In early January 1840, her two-and-a-half year-old son John Henry was knocked over by a Newfoundland dog; and the boy fell into a sugar-cane boiler, which scalded him severely. He died in his mother's arms two days later. On October 13, her husband Pierce asked Cornelia if she would be willing to live a celibate life. At that time, pregnant with her fifth child, she replied, "Great as is the sacrifice, if God asks it of me, I am ready to make it to Him and with all my heart."[306]

With Cornelia's agreement to live celibately, Pierce left for Rome in spring 1842. He took their oldest child, eight-year-old Mercer, and enrolled him in a London boarding school. He discovered a source of income in serving as the traveling tutor for a young student; aristocratic Pierce was able to gain entrée for the student into the elite social circles of Europe. Cornelia, meanwhile, with children Adeline and Frank, remained at Grand Coteau. For fourteen months, Pierce, in his own words, enjoyed "a delightful time," traveled through the major cities of Europe, and did not contact Cornelia.[307] At Rome, the itinerant husband, learned that the pope would make no decision about the proposed ordination, with its requirement of celibacy, without speaking directly with Cornelia. Pierce returned home, gathered Cornelia and the children, and headed back to Rome. The pope met with the couple, and encouraged Pierce to spend each week "a joyful hour or two with

Cornelia and the children."[308] Cornelia considered entering a convent. Feeling ambivalent about her husband's ordination, Cornelia offered Pierce the opportunity to return to their married life, if he wished. Pierce, however, remained firm in his convictions. That being the case, she took a vow of perpetual chastity on June 18, 1845; and, three days later, he was ordained a priest.

What might she and the children do? After consulting her spiritual director, Jesuit Father John Grassi, she envisioned founding a congregation of religious women, the Society of the Holy Child Jesus, thus allowing her to keep her children, while devoting the remainder of her life to God as a celibate sister. Mercer was already in a boarding school at London, and, on the advice of Bishop Wiseman of Westminster, Cornelia enrolled Adeline at a similar school in Rome, and Frank, at Hampstead. Feeling profoundly sad at the separation from husband and children, Cornelia "did not yield to despair. Under the impact of these harsh blows, she grew ever more spiritually mature."[309]

Bishop Wiseman imagined that Cornelia could do for women what John Henry Newman had done for men. He suggested that Cornelia and her three candidates might go to Derby, where they could staff a newly opened Catholic school.

Arriving at Derby in September 1846, Cornelia, now called Mother since she had been elected superior, was moved with pity at the plight and poverty of the English working poor, and the recent Irish immigrants fleeing the Potato Famine. The religious women offered at their Poor School a day-school for children, a night-school for their mothers, and Sunday-school for women and children. "The Poor School had about two hundred girls on the register, but there would rarely be more than sixty or seventy present; the rest were working in the factories, especially in the silk mills."[310] The night school enrollment stood at one hundred older girls and women. The new school was architecturally breath-taking, but the inside was unfurnished, and huge debt remained to be paid for its construction. The bishop offered, "I will take the whole convent and its liabilities on myself," but he was transferred to another diocese, and became unable to keep his promise.[311] The sisters lived extremely poor lives in the convent. They had little money, little food, and patched their shoes and religious habit. Cornelia maintained a joyful spirit among the sisters, and during the first two years of their existence at St. Mary's, twenty-one postulants joined the society. In school, Cornelia developed a comprehensive curriculum unheard of in the public schools: music, dance, art, drama, plus the liberal arts and sciences.[312] Just before Christmas 1847, Cornelia renewed her vow of chastity, and took too the vows of poverty and obedience.

Pierce became restless, if not deranged. Upon completing his first year at Rome, he sought and received a three-year leave of absence from Rome to work in England. He became an assistant at the parish near Derby, where Cornelia was living. In March 1847, Pierce showed up unannounced at the convent's front door. Cornelia was horrified. She feared that gossips would misinterpret every chance meeting of the couple. She insisted that Pierce leave immediately. He became enraged, and oscillated between bursts of anger and tear-filled depression.

Pierce, in January 1848, kidnapped the three children from their respective schools. A half-year later, he appeared again at the convent's doorstep, as if nothing had happened. Cornelia met him and explained that she would speak with him, only if he released their daughter to the mother's care. In England, at that time, wife and children were viewed as the property of the husband and father; he alone determined their fortunes. Cornelia also informed Pierce that he was not to interfere with her religious community. "When Pierce heard this, he threw himself in a 'passion of tears' on the sofa . . . for six hours in the convent parlor, while Cornelia prayed in her room."[313] One year later, he sued in the court of the Church of England for restoration of his conjugal rights, and he won. It took Cornelia two-and-a-half years to win an appeal. Finally, she paid his court costs, on the agreement that he could never re-open the case. Pierce renounced his priesthood, rejected his religion, turned the children from their Catholic faith, and enrolled them in foreign schools, far removed from their mother. In 1868, he found a job in Florence as rector of the American Episcopal Church.

What became of the couple's remaining children? In 1852, the eldest child, Mercer, died in New Orleans of yellow fever. Adeline remained with her father until he died in 1883, and saw her mother only once or twice after that. She returned to the Church through her continuing conversations with one of the Sisters of the Holy Child Jesus. Frank succeeded as an artist, and "maintained sporadic contact with his mother. . . . He loved her but hated the Church, which he blamed for ruining his childhood home and his parents' lives.[314]

The Society of he Holy Child Jesus continued to expand: in England, at Mayfield and Sussex; in France, at Toul and Neuilly; and in the United States, at Towanda, Pennsylvania, initially; but after a small enrollment and bitter winter, in Philadelphia and at Sharon Hill, Pennsylvania.

By the time of her death, the Society of the Holy Child Jesus had grown to one hundred fifty-five sisters, working in seven houses, located throughout England, France and the United States. Philadelphia-born Mother Cornelia had spent exactly half of her seventy years in the U.S.A., and the other half outside of her native country. Clearly, she had spent her married and religious life trying to discern and to do God's will. "God alone" is what mattered to her.[315] As she neared death, she told her sisters, "Let us all pray for each other, not forgetting that we have a community in heaven waiting for us to join them there."[316]

*For further information, contact*
Society of the Holy Child Jesus
460 Shadeland Avenue
Drexel Hill, PA 19026 U.S.A.

# 24. ☩ María del Refugio Aguilar y Torres

*Place: México City, D.F.*
*Fame: Continued her ministry despite the dangers of persecution.*
*Foundress of the Mercedarian Sisters of the Blessed Sacrament.*
*Apostle of the Eucharist for the New Millenium.*

Wife and mother, foundress and innovator, teacher of school children and defender of the faith, this oldest of eight children was a natural-born teacher and leader.[317] As a child at home, Refugio (1866-1937) played school, teaching her siblings and friends. In professional life, she led a community of nuns who dedicated their lives to God by teaching children. The apostolate of Catholic education at this time required great

courage because of the current anti-Catholic persecutions plaguing México.

Refugio married, at her father's request, at
twenty, a man who was thirty-six. Because her
husband was a tax collector and friend of the
reigning dictator Porfirio Díaz, María's father
expected that this marriage in 1886, would give
security to his daughter. After a son and daughter were born, however, the husband died "from a
severe bout of pneumonia" in1889; and the son
died in 1891.[318]

MARÍA DEL REFUGIO
AGUILAR Y TORRES

At twenty-two, a widow and single mother, Refugio found solace in
her faith. In 1895, she joined the Third Order of the Franciscans, in
which group she heightened her devotion to the Blessed Sacrament,
served as novice mistress and catechist, and provided hands-on service
to the poor and needy.

> One of the characteristic missions of the Franciscan tertiaries
> at that time was to teach the catechism in preparation for First
> Holy Communion. As a catechist, Maria del Refugio realized
> that, in order to be able to instill effectively in children the truths
> of the Catholic faith, particularly those relating to theEucharist,
> she should make these teachings her own if she wished to find a
> means of capturing something of the grandeur of the Mystery.[319]

In 1904, while visiting her daughter, whom Refugio had enrolled in
a *colegio* at Morelia, in Michoacán, the mother stopped into the cathedral. Praying before the statue of the Virgin of Guadalupe, Refugio felt
inspired to found a religious community whose devotion to the Blessed
Sacrament would permeate all their apostolic work, and whose primary
work would be the education of children. To prepare spiritually and
practically for establishing a new order within the Church, Refugio and
her daughter entered in 1908 at México City, the boarding house run by
the Company of Mary. Refugio's daughter, who had graduated with a
degree in education, joined her mother in the teaching apostolate in
1908. Two years later, Refugio founded the Apostolate of the
Eucharistic Jesus. One month after the community was founded,

Refugio established her first school, the Institute of the Blessed Sacrament. Refugio describes the goal of the Institute:

> The premise of this educational endeavor is that God rests at the center of all the sciences, and that participation in Jesus' Eucharist and the protection of Mary authenticate the Christian life. In other words, to go beyond academic activity, making the learning experienced a mystical experience which discovers for us and moves us to enjoy and thank God for the presence and the grandeur of God.[320]

At her Institute, Refugio not only educated students, but also distributed food and clothing, and housed orphaned girls. To assist poor students to attend her school, she initiated with the help of wealthy donors a scholarship fund. Meanwhile, her religious community kept growing in vocations and school sites.

A perilous time arose with the presidency of Plutarco Elias Calles (r. 1924-1928). He initiated a merciless war against the Church. His infamous Calles Laws effectively subjected all religious authorities to political authorities. In February 1926, he ordered religious schools and seminaries closed, thereby shutting down Refugio's school. In late April, the bishops achieved an accommodation with the president whereby the schools were reopened. Refugio opened her schools, but insisted that the crucifixes and other religious images be displayed as symbols of the faith and an essential means to fulfill the school's mission. In May of that same year, two government agents arrived at the convent, with pistols in hand, to search for and to shoot on sight any priests who might be hiding there. Refugio led the agents through the rooms of the convent, hiding the Eucharist under her habit, in case the government officials might desecrate the chapel. These unannounced searches became a regular occurrence during the next three years. In early July 1926, Calles promulgated the infamous "Calles Law" whereby the government asserted the authority to expel foreign clergy, close the houses and monasteries where priests and nuns lived, confiscate properties owned by religious for their schools and social services, censor correspondence, outlaw the Catholic media, "and even made the practicing of religion in private punishable by law."[321]

Not being able to minister openly, Refugio expanded the community overseas. Already in 1925, she had started a house in Cuba. That convent served as the gateway for sisters to immigrate to other countries. Beginning in August 1926, Refugio opened in one year, five houses: in El Salvador, the United States, Chile, Spain, plus a second house in Cuba. Within a few more years, she opened houses in Colombia and Italy. "The superior general [Refugio] and her council of advisors remained in México, leaving temporarily their convent and taking refuge in the basement of a nearby house."[322]

The continuing governmental persecution of the Church occasioned the bishops to shut down all schools and religious activities. The sisters continued their ministry in an abbreviated fashion in secret in the homes of courageous Catholics.

> She [Refugio] remained in México with a reduced number of sisters, changing residences constantly due to the dangers and threats, hiding herself in house basements and cellars. During all this time she continued the adoration of the Blessed Sacrament which was hidden among the dishes and silverware. In addition, she provided refuge and shelter to bishops, priests, and seminarians, in spite of the risks that this implicated. She established clandestine groups in order to continue the education of the children and youth. She fought in favor of the Christian education of children, defying the authorities. She tried everything possible to defend the Congregation's patrimony, denouncing injustice and confronting the government agents.[323]

Fearing the worst, Refugio left the capital in favor of Coyoacán. Even here, however, the sisters frequently had to flee for safety from one residence to another. Refugio instructed the sisters never to speak ill of those who confiscated the community's property. She taught, "Ultimately, the Lord had permitted that we be deprived of our motherhouse, for which we had made so many sacrifices, and in which we had placed so much hope. Blessed be the Lord in his gifts, and may his will be done."[324]

Refugio kept pursuing canonical recognition of her community of religious women. In 1922, the sisters received approval from the Holy See as a diocesan community. The Sacred Congregation for Religious recommended changing the name from the Apostolate of the Eucharistic Jesus to the Apostolate of the Blessed Sacrament. In 1925, the sisters aggregated their community to the Order of Mercy.

Refugio's already poor health began deteriorating in the mid-1930s. Twice before, she had tried to resign from the position which she had occupied ever since she had founded the community in 1910. Each time she tried to resign, her term was extended. In September 1936, she contracted pneumonia, and within the next six months, she developed typhoid fever, bronchial pneumonia, and kidney failure. In April, a blood transfusion worsened Refugio's condition. She died the next day. Upon her death, the sisters of the community voted for her successor, and elected as their new superior general Refugio's daughter, who had joined the community in 1920. More than a decade after Refugio's death, the pope in 1948, recognized the Apostolate of the Eucharistic Jesus as the Mercedarian Sisters of the Blessed Sacrament

*For further information, contact*
Causa Maria del Refugio
Fernandez Leal 130
04330 Coyoacán, D. F. México

⚭

## 26.  ✠  José Antonio Plancarte y Labastida

*Place: Jacona, Michoacán, and México City, D.F.*
*Fame: Victim of calumny. Builder of churches, schools, an orphanage,*
*and railroad branch. Founder of the Congregation of Religious*
*Daughters of Mary Immaculate of Guadalupe.*

Father José Antonio Plancarte y Labastida (1840-98) spent fifteen years at a parish in Jacona in the state of Michoacán, and another sixteen years at a parish in México City. In both places, he demonstrated vision, initiative, and determination to build for his people institutions to serve their needs. At Jacona, he built a school for middle-class girls, a preparatory seminary for boys, and a free school for all children. To educate these youth, he founded in 1878, a congregation of religious women called the Daughters of Mary Immaculate of Guadalupe. When he noticed that the parish cemetery had fallen into disrepair, he organized a clean-up of the cemetery to restore it to its deserved dignity. Because Jacona was isolated, he conceived the idea, and organized the construction of a railroad from Jacona to Zamora. In México City, in the wake of the destruction of churches during the Juárez-led persecution, he and some outstanding laymen proposed and persevered in constructing the National Expiation Church of Saint Philip, in reparation for the violations which politicians and their enforcers had wreaked against many churches. Commentators observe that the Church of Saint Philip, which Father José Antonio had designed, was his greatest architectural achievement. Young José Antonio had studied engineering and commerce before changing his course of studies to the liberal arts in preparation for priesthood.

The many construction projects which the talented priest undertook cost considerable dollars. He organized and oversaw the fund-raising for these projects. In the anti-clerical, anti-Catholic atmosphere that permeated México at that time, rumors surfaced about what the priest was doing with all the money he had collected. Accusations arose that he was hoarding the money, and using some of it for his personal gain. A formal ecclesiastical investigation was conducted. No evidence appeared of any wrongdoing on the priest's part; instead, evidence arose of jealousy and envy among his critics who doubted he could have achieved what he had set out to accomplish.

The priest's reputation, however, had been tainted. Twice the bishop removed Father José Antonio from his assignments. The priest's last assignment was to serve as abbot at the shrine of Our Lady of Guadalupe. He undertook the task with his usual vision, vigor, and determination. Again, he brought physical improvements to the buildings which he oversaw.

All that he did, he performed with grace and humility. Offended and upset terribly by the calumnious accusations, he continued to dedicate himself and his efforts to the good of his people, the Church in México, and the Kingdom of God on earth.

In his family life, he had experienced sorrows which had prepared him for his life in ministry. He was the tenth of eleven children, all of whom were born at Zamora except himself, who was born in México City, where his mother had gone to seek medical assistance. During his elementary school years, the family moved to Morelia. After completing grade school in 1851, the boy entered the apostolic school at Morelia, and in 1854, he continued his studies at the seminary at Puebla, where his uncle was bishop. In 1855, his uncle, who was exiled to Cuba, suggested that José might want to study in England, where he remained until 1862, after which he studied at Rome for the next three years. On the occasion of each of his parents' deaths, the boy was away at school: his father died in 1854; and his mother, in 1861. After his mother's death, José Antonio, who had been studying abroad, changed his major from business commerce at Saint Maria de Oscott at Birmingham in England, to philosophy and theology at the seminary located next door. After being ordained in 1865 at Rome, he returned to México. For a few months, he worked at a parish in Zamora, but after his health failed him, the bishop re-assigned the young priest. Father José Antonio ministered at Jacona from 1867 to 1882, and at México City from 1882 until he died in 1898.

*For further information, contact*
Curia Diocesana
Apartado Postal #18
C.P. 59600
Zamora, Michoacán, México

❧

## 28. ✠ Adolphe Chatillon

*Place: Montréal, Québec*
*Fame: "Make students happy to make them learn better."*
*Extraordinary teacher.*

Born at Nicolet, Québec; the middle of nine children, four of whom died in infancy, Adolphe Chatillon (1871-1929), like two of his brothers, entered Church service. The brothers became priests, and Adolphe became a Christian Brother. Adolphe's parents participated actively in

their parish as musicians, and as members of the
St. Vincent de Paul Society.

After his mother died when he was nine,
Adolphe was placed in two successive local
boarding schools operated by the Christian
Brothers: first, at Baie-du-Febvre, and later, at
Yamachiche. At thirteen, he entered the junior
novitiate of the Christian Brothers at Montréal;
and three years later, he entered the senior novitiate. At seventeen, he received the religious
habit of the community, and took for his religious name Brother Théophanius-Léo:
Théophanius signifies "one who shows forth God", and Leo means "one
who possesses the courage of a lion."

ADOLPHE CHATILLON

After completing in 1889, the two-year senior novitiate, and college
studies, Théophanius-Leo spent the next forty years in the ministry of
formation and education. In the early years of his ministry, he taught in
parish schools at Iberville (1890), Québec City (1891), Lachine (1904),
and Montréal (1907), with a six-year stint interspersed as assistant
novice director in the junior novitiate (1898). The remainder of his
career he spent ministering in seminary formation and education: a total
of twenty-two years at the junior and senior novitiates. The last six years
of his professional career, he was assigned as the international Visitor
General for formation, which position took him to Montréal, Québec,
and Toronto in Canada; and to Baltimore, New York City, New Orleans,
Saint Louis, San Francisco, and Santa Fe in the United States.

Théophanius-Léo was blessed with an excellent mind, heart, and
soul for the teaching profession. *Mind*: students enjoyed his lectures
because he explained matters in a concise and precise way. *Heart*: he
engaged people easily by his warmth, simplicity, and ability to listen.
"Audiences found him a captivating speaker."[325] *Soul*: he possessed a profound love of God, the Mother of God, and God's people. Because he
practiced the love that he preached, his teaching possessed great credibility.

Two of Brother's keys to living well his vocation were the Scriptural
exhortation, "Learn from me; for I am gentle and lowly in heart" (Mt

11:29), and the motto, "Make them happy in order to make them better."[326]

While participating in the Christian Brother's General Assembly in Belgium, in fall 1928, Théophanius-Léo was diagnosed with intestinal cancer. He struggled to meet all his responsibilities, but the sickness sapped his strength. At the beginning of March 1929, he crossed the Atlantic Ocean one last time, to return to the novitiate located at Mont-de-La-Salle. There, he transformed his bedroom into a prayer-room, where he prayed quietly throughout his final days. After one year at the Mont, he was transferred to the motherhouse, at Laval-des-Rapides. A month later, on April 29, 1929, he died.

In 1908, Brother formally had consecrated himself to the Blessed Virgin Mary, according to the way of Saint Louis de Montfort. Brother, a lifelong devotee of Mary, rejoiced at opportunities to speak of the Blessed Mother. Because students knew that Brother would deliver an inspiring talk, they would burst out into wild applause whenever Théophanius-Léo announced that he was going to give an instruction on Mary. His profound love for the Blessed Mother permeated his words and manner when he spoke about Mary. As Marian feasts occurred throughout the year, Théophanius-Léo would renew his commitment to the Lord and his mother. Across the top of his personal notes and letters to others, Leo would write the name of Mary. In his private journal, he writes,

> Always desire to please Our Lord, and to be more successful in this work, unite yourself to the most holy Virgin. It is the most direct way, the easiest means to arrive at a greater perfection... How my heart desires that our good Mother be loved, honored, and imitated more and more. How I wish I had the talent to make people love her and pray to her.[327]

*For further information, contact*
Cause du Frère Théophanius-Léo
300, chemin du Bord-de-l'Eau
Laval, QC H7X 1S9 Canada

# 29. ✠ Venerable Élisabeth Bergeron

*Place: Saint-Hyacinthe, Québec*
*Fame: Availability to the needs of the Church.*
*Foundress of Sisters of St. Joseph of Saint-Hyacinthe.*

Simple, humble, joyful service in praise of God and God's people, especially the poorest, typified the life of Élisabeth Bergeron (1851-1936).[328] Although she desired to found a religious community of contemplative nuns, she yielded to her bishop's request that she would begin a community of active nuns who would educate children in rural areas. In 1877, the bishop appointed this foundress to be the first superior of the community, but startlingly, two years later, he removed

ÉLISABETH BERGERON

her, and appointed a younger, more educated sister as superior. At this latter time, Élisabeth was asked to accept the number two position in the community. Simply, humbly, joyfully, Élisabeth accepted this change, because what mattered most to her, was to do God's will, as it was manifested through the bishop, and to serve as a stabilizing and inspiring force for the new community.

As a child, Élisabeth conducted herself precociously in practicing and promoting the faith. At eight, accompanying her older brother to his First Communion classes, she behaved so well, learned the catechism so thoroughly, and prayed so fervently that the parish priest invited her to receive Communion four years ahead of the minimum age. At thirteen, when Élisabeth was left home alone in charge of her youngest sibling, a beggar knocked at the door of the family home, and asked for some bread. Élisabeth invited the gentleman inside, fed him an entire meal, and lent a set of her father's clothes to the man while she washed and sewed the visitor's clothes. At fifteen, Élisabeth conducted catechism classes for children in her neighborhood.

In 1865, because of financial difficulties on their farm, Élisabeth's father moved the family from La Présentation to the United States. The Bergerons moved, first, to Brunswick, New Hampshire, where family members including Élisabeth worked for one year, in the local cotton mill until it burned to the ground. The family then moved to Salem, Massachusetts, where they worked at another mill for the next four years. In 1870, having made and saved enough money, the family returned to Canada. Five years later, the parents gave the farm at La Présentation to their three oldest sons, and with the remainder of the family, moved to Casavant Village in Saint-Hyacinthe.

When the family returned to La Présentation in 1870, Élisabeth decided to pursue her vocation to the religious life. She applied successively to four congregations, namely, the Sisters of Charity of Saint-Hyacinthe, the Sisters of the Precious Blood, the Mercy Sisters, and the Présentation-de-Marie, but they all refused her admission. Finally, in July 1877, Élisabeth sought out Bishop Louis-Zéphyrin Moreau, and explained that she would like to found a contemplative community. On their third meeting, the bishop reported that he needed not a contemplative order, but an active one to educate Catholic children, especially in the Eastern Townships, where the Protestant majority was trying to convert Catholic children. Élisabeth replied that she could not assist in that project since she herself was so poorly educated. The bishop listened, and asked her to think and pray about his request, in light of the fact that Jesus had chosen the Twelve Apostles, even though they too were not well educated. Two months later, she yielded to the bishop's request. On September 12, 1877, twenty-six-year-old Élisabeth, with three companions, founded the Sisters of Saint Joseph of Saint Hyacinthe. Almost one year later, the sisters put on the religious habit, and took religious names. Élisabeth received from the bishop the name Mother Saint Joseph. In March 1880, the sisters took permanent vows.

The nascent community suffered greatly from poverty, sickness, and gossip. The first community house doubled as a school and convent at La Providence (now part of the City of Saint-Hyacinthe). The first day of class, eighty students arrived to attend the school. But the poor student could pay very little for their education. The sisters were forced to beg for their necessities. Severe sickness struck the sisters, the students, and their families. Elisabeth became ill within four months of opening the community's first school, and she had to be hospitalized. The next year, one of the sisters died during a scarlet fever epidemic. Four years later, Élisabeth again contracted the flu; and another sister died, during an epidemic of typhoid fever. In the midst of these sufferings, some citizens waged a war of gossip against the sisters, reporting that the sisters drank a lot, and that good-intentioned people ought to discourage girls from joining this community.

In the midst of these turbulent events, Bishop Moreau, with no fore-warning, announced that he was removing Élisabeth as superior, and was replacing her with a younger, more educated sister who more effectively could oversee the school, and interact with the school board. The sisters were shocked. Elisabeth remained serene. The foundress commented, "It is God who has decided on this change and it is not our place to question his wishes."[329] Élisabeth instructed her sisters, "The day you will have abandoned everything, God alone will be enough for you."[330] In her new role, Élisabeth enjoyed greater availability than ever before to be present to the sisters and students.

Mother St. Joseph remained in her position of first assistant to the general superior for forty-six years, until she retired from that post in 1925. "She was unquestionably a wise and experienced advisor, and the community always recognized and venerated her as the founder."[331] Throughout these years, young women kept joining the Sisters of Saint Joseph. Larger residences, and more apostolic sites, kept being added to meet the needs and availability of the sisters. For almost half a century, Élisabeth traveled to the community's convents and schools: speaking with the students in their classrooms, visiting the sick and aging sisters, listening to the individual sisters, encouraging them, praying with them, and by her presence, inspiring them. Mother instructed the nuns, "Sisters, be very kind to your dear pupils, especially the poorest and the less talented; through kindness you shall win their hearts and do good to them. See Our Lord in each of them."[332]

After celebrating her and the community's golden jubilees, the octogenarian began to express readiness for death. She contracted pneumonia twice in the last two years before she died. She often said, "I long to see God,"[333] Mother spent increasingly long hours in front of the Blessed Sacrament, recalling Bishop Moreau's promise to her long ago, when he insisted on her forming an active community, and assured her that, "Later you will devote yourself to contemplation."[334] Élisabeth Bergeron died on April 29, 1936, one month shy of her eight-fifth birthday. At the time of her death, the community had grown to five hundred thirty-four sisters, who were working in four dozen schools, which were located mostly in the province of Québec, with six schools in Western Canada, one in Ontario, and another one at Salmon Falls, Vermont, in the United States.

*For further information, contact,*
Centre Élisabeth-Bergeron
805 Raymond
Saint-Hyacinthe, QC J2S 5T9 Canada

✤

## 30. ✠ Blessed Marie Guyart de l'Incarnation

*Place: Québec City, Québec*
*Fame: First woman missionary to the Amerindians*
*in the New World. Wife, mother, and Ursuline mystic.*

The spiritual writer Jacques-Bénigne Bossuet describes Marie Guyart (1599-1672) as "the Teresa of Ávila of the New World."[335] She was practical and mystical, focused simultaneously on heaven and earth, dealt successfully with the mundane matters, and enjoyed mystical experiences of God's presence and gifts of revelations.[336]

MARIE GUYART DE L'INCARNATION

Born at Tours, France, Marie was the fourth child of middle-class parents; her bourgeois father owned a bakery, and her mother claimed a noble lineage. As early as seven years, Marie experienced dreams of Our Lord calling her to dedicate her life to him. She memorized and recited homilies, and expressed interest in becoming a nun. At seventeen, however, she acquiesced to her parents' desire that she marry. According to custom, the parents chose the husband, who was a silk merchant named Claude Martin. Two years after her wedding, Marie was left a widow with a six-month old son and a bankrupt business. She moved back to her parents' home, and worked as an embroiderer.

An extraordinary spiritual event occurred to her on March 25, 1620. In a vision, she glimpsed Christ's Incarnation, his Sacred Heart, and the Trinity; and she saw all her faults revealed, with herself swimming in the blood of Christ, and being saved by his divine mercy. "This event changed her completely, and her desire to be involved in religious life translated to prayer, liturgical devotion, and charity."[337]

After three years at her parents' home, Marie moved in with her sister and her husband. Marie began working as a bookkeeper for her brother-in-law's transport business. After she demonstrated excellent administrative skills, the brother-in-law appointed her manager of the firm.

Continuing to experience the call to religious life, Marie consulted with her spiritual director. With his approval, she decided to enter the convent. Marie's sister accepted the responsibility of raising twelve-year-old Claude. Marie entered the Ursuline Sisters at Tours on January 25, 1631, and took for her religious name, Marie of the Incarnation. Her son, initially resented his mother's decision, but in 1641, he became a Benedictine priest, and five years after his mother's death, he authored a biography about his extraordinary mother.

Two years after entering the convent, Marie was named director of novices, which position she retained for six years, until 1639. Beginning in late 1633, Marie had begun experiencing a series of dreams in which Jesus was calling her to a missionary vocation. By 1635, it became clear that her destination consisted of a "huge country of mountains and forests, and the message that it was Canada, and that she must go there to build a house for Christ."[338] She made preparations by collecting funds. She met in France with some Jesuits, who had ministered in New France. These Jesuits invited her and the Ursuline Sisters to join the Jesuit mission among the Huron.

Marie and two other Ursuline Sisters and their benefactress Madame de la Peltrie left Tours on January 25, 1639. From Dieppe, they sailed on April 3, 1639, and arrived at New France three months later. The four lived in a small home until 1642, when the convent was completed. Eight years later, the convent burned down, and Marie oversaw its reconstruction. These first women religious came to the New World to catechize the female children of both the settlers and the Indians. Their convent school was the first institution in the New World dedicated to educating girls.

Marie applied herself diligently to the task at hand. She became proficient in the Native American languages; she produced a catechism in Iroquois, and dictionaries in four languages: Algonquin, Iroquois,

Montagnais, and Ouendat. Also, she authored a catechism, and a collection of the lives of the saints for her novices. Marie served as the superior of the Ursuline Sisters for all thirty-three years that she labored at Québec. She endured the deprivation of food, clothing, shelter, medicine, and books; and the ever-present danger of Iroquois attacks.

Perhaps her most famous contribution lay in her mysticism. The works, which provide the best insights into her transcendental experiences include the following. The *Relation of 1633*, which she wrote, in obedience to her spiritual director, shortly after she joined the Ursulines, outlines her spiritual life. The *Relation of 1654*, which she wrote at the request of her son, describes her mystical life. The *Retreat*, written in 1636, presents her mystical prayer on the scriptural *Song of Songs*.

Mother Marie de l'Incarnation possessed a strong personality and profound spirituality. In the midst of almost overwhelming sufferings and trials, she maintained a heart and soul that were full of faith, hope, and love. She writes about the sisters' living quarters, "The house is so poor that at night, we see the stars gleaming through our ceiling; and only with great difficulty can someone keep a candle lit because of the wind."[339] During various epidemics, school was closed because the building was transformed into a hospital. When the convent burned down, Marie writes, "The fire took everything we had, and reduced us to standing on the snow as the good Job stood on his dung-heap. There is this difference, however: our good friends, the French and the Indians, were moved to a great compassion, which Job did not receive."[340] Perhaps Marie's greatest suffering came from the constant fear and frequent losses of life and property because of Iroquois attacks. She writes one night:

> My God, my dear Love, you abandoned me this evening. This is of little importance since you have filled me with so many graces and I am sufficiently strong to endure it. But, God of kindness, do not abandon New France, which already is so red with the blood of martyrs that it seems to blaze up like autumn! Today we had to convert our convent into a fort because, since the beginning of 1660, the attacks by the Agnieurs have been repeated. We live with a fear that will never leave us. People don't feel

secure; everyone remains on the alert! My God of Love, remove the Agniers, the Onontagues, and the Tsonnontouans.[341]

When others suggested abandoning the mission at Québec and returning to Europe, she refused to hear such talk. She reiterated that New France was a treasure, which, although the king and his court failed to appreciate it, would one day prove its worth.

*For further information, contact*
Centre Marie-de-l'Incarnation
10, rue Donnacona
Québec, QC G1R 4T1 Canada

# MAY

## 4. ✠ Blessed Marie-Léonie Paradis

*Place: Memramcook, New Brunswick; and Sherbrooke, Québec*
*Fame: Fidelity to vision and vocation. Foundress of the*
*Little Sisters of the Holy Family.*

Marie-Léonie Paradis (1840-1912) manifested great focus: as a child, in her pattern of praying to God; as a teenager, in her invincible desire to be a nun; as a nun, in persevering in her vocation to serve priests.[342] She maintained her focus against great odds.

As a child, Élodie, which her family called her although she had been baptized Alodie Virginia, would seek out a quiet place and pray. In the midst of family need, she would pray to the Blessed Mother; or when some item was lost, she would pray to St. Anthony. Years later,

MARIE-LÉONIE
PARADIS

Léonie writes, "I did this willingly. On my knees, with my hands folded, I prayed fervently. But, after a certain time, if they forgot to call me, I would interrupt my prayers and cry out, "Maman (sic), have you found your needle? or, "Have you obtained your favor?"[343]

When Élodie was five, her family moved from L'Acadie to Laprairie, where her father hoped to provide a better living by opening a mill where he "sawed timber, ground grain, and carded wool."[344] In 1848, Élodie entered the local boarding school operated by the Congrégation de Notre-Dame. Élodie's mother thought the only girl in the family, with five brothers, needed more feminine socialization. Her father, however, missed his only daughter, and repeatedly offered to bring her home for weekends. In 1849, with the mill not prospering, Élodie's father caught the Gold Rush fever, moved the family to Napierville, and he moved to California. The next year, with the father still in California, the mother sent the daughter back to Laprairie to continue her schooling with the Sisters.

At thirteen, in 1854, Élodie entered the Sisters of the Holy Cross. She desired to dedicate her life to the domestic service of priests. She entered at Saint-Laurent, and served as a novice at Sainte-Scolastique. At sixteen, when she was on the verge of taking vows in the community, her father came back from California, went to the convent, and literally tried to drag her home.

> Discreet protests from the superiors, the tears and supplications of the young novice, and her assurance that she would not want to leave the convent for anything in the world, all were to no avail. The father was indomitable. Exhausted, frustrated and depleted of her strength and arguments, Sister Marie of Saint-Léonie ran to the statue of the Blessed Virgin and in tears asked Mary to make her die rather than allow her to be torn away from her dear novitiate. Hardly had she completed her anguish-filled prayer than she suffered a pulmonary hemorrhage. Frightened by what he believed was divine intervention, the unhappy father immediately abandoned his plan and returned home alone, leaving his Marianite to God.[345]

At seventeen, Élodie professed her vows. Within the next five years, she was assigned to teach at three different missions: Varennes, Saint-

Laurent, and Saint-Martin. In 1862, she was missioned to New York City, where she administered an orphanage and a school for French-speaking Catholics. During Élodie's stay in New York City, the Holy Cross congregation experienced much internal turmoil: in terms of divisions and directions. "Feeling at a loss, Sister Léonie returned to Saint-Laurent, where she lived through two months in the darkness of doubt and moral agony. Finally, she caught a glimpse of hope. To be faithful to her first vocation, she would turn to the American Province of the Sisters of Holy Cross.[346]

The Superior General of Holy Cross assigned her to St. Joseph's College at Memramcook, New Brunswick, founded by the Holy Cross Fathers, to train young Acadian women how to perform domestic services. Arriving in 1874, she discovered that the region was rich in vocations to the sisterhood. The next year, 1875, while bringing some Acadian recruits to the American province's novitiate at Notre Dame, Indiana, Élodie traveled through Montréal, where the archbishop suggested to Léonie that she might found a community of sisters to do domestic work at Catholic Colleges. So unsettling was the continuing dispute within the Holy Cross community that in 1880, Léonie founded a new community, namely, the Little Sisters of the Holy Family. The community had for its stated purpose, the service of Christ's priests, and to provide sisters as domestic workers at Canadian colleges administered by priests of the Holy Cross community. As time went on, the sites expanded to include seminaries, bishops' residences and rectories, for all priests.

Léonie's community grew rapidly. As early as 1877, Léonie had assigned her "auxiliaries" to colleges. By 1880, Élodie's "auxiliaries" were working at three foundations: Notre Dame de Côte-des-Nieges; Saint-Cesaire of Rouville, and Farnham.

Although the Holy Cross Fathers approved of Léonie's community as early as 1880, the bishop of New Brunswick was moving slowly to approve the Little Sisters. The community kept growing in vocations and sites: at Sorel, Québec in 1887; Van Buren, Maine in 1893. A controversy arose when the archbishop of Montréal instructed the Little Sisters to stop wearing the religious habit, because the Little Sisters had not yet been approved as a congregation, and were not yet Sisters in the eyes of the Church.

How might the Little Sisters receive Church approval? The bishop of New Brunswick had not acted on their requests, which the community had repeated oftentimes since 1880. Finally, in 1895, the bishop of Sherbrooke invited the Little Sisters to reside in his diocese, and he promised to provide diocesan approval. Léonie happily transferred the mother-house, all its personnel and possessions, the five-hundred-mile distance. In less than four months, the bishop approved the new community.

Léonie, however, was still a member of her original Holy Cross community. In 1904, the bishop of Montréal and her host bishop of Sherbrooke urged her to adopt the religious habit of the Little Sisters, and to transfer communities. This entailed great sacrifice for Léonie. She had worn the Holy Cross habit and been a member of the community for forty-nine years. In 1905, Pope Pius X approved the transfer from the Sisters of the Holy Cross to the Little Sisters of the Holy Family.

The spirituality of Léonie focused on devotion to Jesus in the Eucharist, to Mary his mother, and Joseph his foster-father. She promoted among the sisters devotion to Our Lady of Sorrows, and Our Lady of the Holy Rosary. Regarding the community's mission of performing domestic duties for priests, Léonie writes to her sisters, "Think of Jesus when you see a priest; he is Christ on earth."[347] A zealous worker herself, she encouraged her sisters, "Let us work, my dear daughters, while we are on earth because this is all God asks of us. There is no better prayer that we could offer Him than our dedication to work. We will all rest in heaven."[348] Eventually, Léonie's sisters would devote themselves "to the humble duties of housekeeping in the Apostolic Delegations at Ottawa and Washington, D.C; in Cardinals' Residences; Residences of Archbishops and Bishops in various cities; in Seminaries; Communities of Religious Orders; Homes for Retired Priests and in Rectories."[349]

The sisters' life was simple and poor. Each day, the sisters rose at four-thirty, said their morning prayers, and meditated in their community room with Sister Léonie presiding. One of the sisters recalls the early days, writing, "There were but a few chairs that were carried from one room to another as needed, but most of the time, we sat on the floor around Sister Léonie. This way of doing reminded us of the holy house of Nazareth."[350]

The community of the Little Sisters grew rapidly. After its origin in 1880, the community had grown to ninety sisters fifteen years later. At Léonie's death in 1912, six hundred sisters had joined the community, serving in thirty-eight missions, in thirteen dioceses in Canada and the United States. At the time of her death, Léonie, who had remained a member of the Holy Cross community from 1854 to 1905, lived only the last seven years as a Little Sister, although she had led the community for thirty-two years.

*For further information, contact*
Le Centre Marie-Léonie-Paradis
1820 West Galt Street
Sherbrooke, QC J1K 1H9 Canada

⚮

## 6. ✠ Blessed François de Montmorency Laval

*Place: Québec City, Québec*
*Fame: A much beloved pastor, innovator, and administrator.*
*First bishop of Québec, Canada*

After twenty years of knowing Bishop François de Laval (1623-1708), Mother Marie de l'Incarnation, the superior of the Ursuline Sisters at Québec writes about the bishop, "He is a saint, a father to the poor and to the whole population. The king loves him very much on account of his merits and qualities. The queen wishes that he would remain in France. But the love that this good prelate bears for his new church [in New France] will make him return."[351] Bishop Laval, pastor and administrator *extraordinaire*, dedicat-

FRANÇOIS DE
MONTMORENCY LAVAL

ed his episcopal energies and worldly possessions to laying a firm foundation for the Church in Canada.[352]

Laval, who was born into a family of French nobility, forsook his family inheritance, and entered the seminary. He dedicated himself the "vocation within a vocation," i.e., to serve as a priest in the foreign missions. He was ordained a priest in 1647.

Laval volunteered to serve in the Far East, and six years after ordination, he was named vicar general for Tonkin, Vietnam. The Portuguese Royal Court, however, successfully blocked the appointment of a Frenchman to a position which might have been occupied by a Portuguese. For the next three years, beginning in 1655, Laval stayed at the revered "Hermitage of Caen," at Normandy, where he practiced prayer and asceticism. In 1658, the Papal Nuncio ordained Laval the bishop of the ancient see of Petra, and Apostolic Vicar of Québec. Rome chose not to name Laval the bishop of Québec for two reasons. First, Québec as an ecclesiastical foundation was too new and small; and second, the Vatican did not wish to upset the Bishop of Rouen, whose see, for fifty years, had administered the region, whose citizens had come principally from the Diocese of Rouen.

Laval embarked from La Rochelle on April 13, 1659. After stopping at Percé, at the eastern mouth of the St. Lawrence River, to confirm one hundred forty people, the bishop arrived at Québec in mid-June. In the town of Québec lived approximately five hundred colonists, and in the rest of Canada, another approximately seventeen hundred. Laval set about organizing the jurisdiction, which "was undoubtedly the largest ecclesiastical circumscription in the world."[353] The diocese extended through all North America except the narrow strip of British settlements in New England and along the Atlantic Coast, and the Spanish settlements in Florida and the Southwest. Laval's jurisdictional territory is administered today by over one hundred dioceses. In good weather and bad weather, by foot, snowshoes, or canoe, the bishop traversed the four hundred fifty miles distance from Gaspé to Montréal in order to meet and serve the colonists and the Amerindians. Québec remained a vicariate for five years, until Rome established it as an independent diocese in 1764.

Valuing education and desiring to establish a native clergy, the bishop built at his own expense various academic institutions. He founded the Major Seminary of Québec in 1663, and built the city's minor seminary five years later. Numerous other primary schools and the vocational School of Arts and Sciences at Saint-Joachim arose from his largesse. These schools were opened to colonists and Amerindians alike.

Pastorally, the bishop promoted spiritual devotions, and opposed the sale of alcohol to the Indians. He fostered devotion to the Blessed Virgin Mary as the Immaculate Conception three hundred years before the formal declaration of this Marian dogma, and promoted devotion to St. Anne, at Beaupré, rebuilding in 1673 the shrine which had burned to the ground in 1661. He introduced devotions to the Holy Angels and the Holy Family. When colonists treated the Indians unfairly, Laval interceded on the Natives' behalf. Four times the bishop sailed to France to protest directly to the king the ill treatment received by the Indians at the hands of the king's governor and councilors, and French traders. Although the bishop consistently opposed the sale of alcohol to the Natives, the commercial interests of his contemporaries won out. Laval himself baptized the Iroquois Indian Chief Garakontié as an expression of the importance, which the bishop placed upon evangelization of the Indians.

Administratively, the bishop asked the Jesuits to continue their missionary ministry among the Indians, and to teach in the seminaries; and he encouraged the Sulpicians, Recollects, Ursuline Sisters and Sisters of the Congrégation de Notre-Dame to continue their ministry of education. The Augustinian Hospitaller Sisters, he asked, to continue their hospital ministry at the Hôtel-Dieu. Laval received into New France many priests of the Paris Foreign Missionary Society. The innovative bishop created a viable structure of parishes and communal living for his diocesan priests. Since no parish could provide the necessities of life for even one priest, the bishop arranged that all the priests would live at the major seminary. From their common living place, the priests would radiate out to serve the clusters of Catholic faithful. The seminary was to serve as a home for these secular priests during ministry, in sickness, and in old age. Financially, the faithful paid tithes to the seminary. The bishop through the treasurer of the seminary then provided monies to the priests according to the parishes' and priests' needs. When the bishop retired from administration in 1688, there were "twenty-four parishes, one hundred and two priests (thirteen Canadian-born), and ninety-seven sisters."[354]

After a quarter century of exhausting service as a frontier bishop, Laval thought it best that a younger man might replace him. Laval retired to the seminary to pray, and to minister in whatever way his successor might ask. In a matter of months, after his successor arrived at Québec, he proved to be abrasive and antagonistic. The new bishop had run-ins with each of the religious communities, the colonists and Indians, and the governor. Laval maintained an admirable distance and profound humility, as he witnessed first-hand the destruction of many of his policies and programs, and much of the young diocese's progress. When the new bishop was absent from the diocese for thirteen continuous years, 1700-1713, due to his nine-year house custody at Paris, and his four-year imprisonment in England, Laval performed the essential episcopal duties for the diocese. By the time of his death, the people called the eighty-five-year-old bishop *Monseigneur l'ancien*, i.e., affectionately and respectfully, "the old bishop".

Laval served for thirty years, at the king's request, as a charter member of the Sovereign Council, which advised the governor of Québec. While doing all that he could for the political and economic development of the colony, Laval acted to inspire and implement policies to aid the moral life of the colonists and Indians. He focused his energies on promoting justice for the Indians by trying to protect them from unscrupulous fur traders and sellers of alcohol.

The bishop's spirituality focused on the Eucharist, devotions, prayer and asceticism. He rose each day at two o'clock in the morning, until in his retirement, he delayed his rising until three o'clock, on doctor's orders. At home, in his private chapel, he prayed for an hour in front of the Blessed Sacrament, then walked to the cathedral, even in the cold of winter with lantern in hand. He opened the church doors, lit the candles throughout the nave, and prepared the accoutrements and altar for Mass, which he celebrated every day at 4:30 A.M. for the working class. He remained praying in the sacristy until 7:00 A.M. The rest of the working day, he passed in administrative and sacramental duties. At night, he would say the Rosary, complete the Liturgy of the Hours, and do spiritual reading. Throughout the day, he practiced mortifications typical of the era. His daily devotions included a special affection for the Blessed Mother, the Holy Angels, and the Holy Family. In 1684, he created a diocesan Confraternity of the Holy Family, and a liturgical feast day on which to celebrate this purpose. Many years later, this feast would become celebrated on the Church's universal liturgical calendar. "Pope Leo XIII [heralded Laval] as one of the main initiators of this devotion in the world."[355]

In his lifetime, many critics opposed Laval. Political authorities resisted his alleged encroachments on their temporal jurisdictions. Religious community leaders resented his attempts to control their congregations. While some authorities opposed his authoritative stances, none criticized his sanctity.

*For further information, contact*
Le centre Francois-de-Laval
20, rue De Buade
Québec, QC G1R 4A1 Canada

## 6. ✠ Demetrius Augustine Gallitzin

*Place: Loretto, Pennsylvania*
*Fame: Russian Prince who became a pioneer priest.*
*Apostle of the Alleghenies of Western Pennsylvania.*

Born to politically prestigious and religiously indifferent parents, Demetrius Gallitzin (1770-1840) followed in their footsteps, until he was seventeen.[356] He inherited from his father the aristocratic title of prince. "The father's branch of the Golitsyns, known in Russian history as the Great Golitsyns, included great statesmen, prominent diplomats and highly educated humanists of Western European culture."[357] His mother was the Countess Amalia, daughter of Field Marshall von Schmettau, who commanded

DEMETRIUS
AUGUSTINE GALLITZIN

Frederick the Great's troops. Demetrius's best friend in his youth was Frederick William, who became the first King of the United Netherlands.

When Demetrius was sixteen, his mother became seriously sick, and promised God that if she recovered, she would return to the Catholic faith. Amalia discovered that the Catholic system of philosophy and theology provided a depth of meaning, which the contemporary secular philosophies could not match. In 1787, in the midst of her conversion, she led her son and daughter from the Russian Orthodox Church to Roman Catholicism.

Demetrius was born and raised at The Hague in Holland. Authors dispute whether he was baptized at infancy, or at two, when Czarina Catherine the Great, his godmother, visited The Hague. After receiving at home an education "as extensive and demanding as possible," ten-year-old Demetrius was sent to Munster, Germany, where he received his formal education.[358] He played at least three musical instruments, and spoke at least three foreign languages. On Trinity Sunday, in June 1787, Demetrius and his sister received their First Holy Communion, and five years later, Confirmation. At Confirmation, he took the name Augustine.

At twenty-two, Prince Gallitzin hoped to pursue a military career. For religious and political reasons respectively he was prohibited from joining the Russian and Austrian armies. Because the customary continent-crossing "Grand Tour" was unsafe due to the European wars, his parents sent him on a tour of North America. Accompanying the young man would be his tutor, the Catholic priest Felix Brosius. The pair sailed from Rotterdam in August 1792, and arrived at Baltimore ten weeks later. To avoid drawing unwanted attention to his aristocratic status, Prince Gallitzin adopted the name Smith.

Having observed Father Brosius in transit, and having heard about the extensive needs of the Church in the United States, Demetrius felt called to priesthood. Shortly after meeting Bishop John Carroll, Demetrius expressed to the bishop the desire to become a priest. Against the objections of his family the young man entered St. Mary's Seminary at Baltimore in 1792, and was ordained on March 18, 1795, becoming the first priest to be ordained in the United States who had made full theological studies in this country.[359]

Given the young man's prestigious background and excellent education, the seminary faculty hoped that he might join them. The young priest, however, preferred the frontier. The diocese of Baltimore, at that time, "extended westward from the Atlantic to the Mississippi and northward from the Gulf of Mexico to Canada."[360] The bishop, acceding to the wishes of the newly ordained, assigned him to celebrate Mass on Sunday with the German-speaking community of Baltimore, and to work with three other priests in the twenty-thousand-mile triangle that extended from Winchester, Virginia, to Port Tobacco, Maryland, and to Conewago, Pennsylvania. In December 1798, Father Demetrius was assigned as resident priest at Taneytown, Maryland.

The priest's life changed forever in 1796, when he was summoned on a sick call for a Protestant woman, who wished to make a death-bed conversion to Catholicism. She lay one hundred thirty miles west: Father Demetrius was residing at Conewago (ten miles east of Harrisburg), and she lived at McGuire's Settlement (twenty-eight miles west of Loretto). Upon returning to Baltimore, Father Demetrius requested of Bishop Carroll that the priest receive a permanent assignment in that westward region. The bishop agreed, but delayed appointing the young priest to McGuire's Settlement until March 1799.

In spring 1799, using his own money, Father Demetrius purchased three hundred acres at four-dollars-an-acre contingent to the four hundred acres which Michael McGuire in 1788, had donated to Bishop Carroll. In July 1799, Gallitzin and Catholic settlers from Conewago and Western Maryland set out for the site, which he named Loretto, in honor of Our Lady of Loretto. Loretto became his home-base from which he reached out to people in a hundred miles radius.

At that same time, his mother wrote, urging her son to return to Europe, where culture and comfort awaited him. The son writes in reply, "You can be fully assured that I have no other will in life, and wish to have no other, than that of fulfilling God's will. I have no other will than to please God, to make myself and my neighbors eternally happy. To attain this purpose, I am ready to renounce all that can please me in this world."[361]

Loretto became "the cradle of Christianity in Western Pennsylvania."[362] The territory served by Demetrius in his original single-man parish is served now by the entire territory of the dioceses of Pittsburgh, Erie, and a large part of Harrisburg. On February 9, 1800, writing to Bishop Carroll, Demetrius describes his church as "the only house of God from the Susquehanna to the Mississippi."[363]

With the westward movement of peoples across the Alleghenies, and some settling out at McGuire's Settlement, the log church built in 1800 was doubled in size in 1808, and ten years later, was replaced by a larger church. By 1839, the parish had mushroomed to five thousand Catholic families.[364] In other nearby settlements, camps had matured to towns, and cities; footpaths and horse trails evolved into roads; and mission chapels grew into parish churches. The diocese of Baltimore was elevated in 1808 to an archdiocese, and in 1810, the area served by Gallitzin was assigned to the new diocese of Philadelphia.

Repeatedly, beginning in 1800, Demetrius sought the assistance of another priest. Not until 1834, except for a brief period in 1830, was a priest sent to assist him. Church officials recognized Demetrius's unusual talents, and wished to promote him at various times. While he accepted in about 1823, the title and responsibility of Vicar General for Western Pennsylvania, he turned down the bishopric when it was offered him for Cincinnati around 1816, for Detroit in 1821, and for Philadelphia in 1833. In addition, he had been considered for the episcopacy for Philadelphia in 1814, for Bardstown in 1816, for Pittsburgh, and for sees in Germany.

In his early ministry, Demetrius suffered, from 1804 to 1807, much vilification from his congregation. A golden-tongued Irishman E. V. James, originally from Lancaster, Pennsylvania, purchased four hundred acres of land, five miles from Loretto, but had difficulty in attracting people to his new town of Munster. James went on a campaign against Father Demetrius. James publicized that the priest had allowed a woman teacher to remain overnight at the chapel-house for months on end; James failed to mention that it was a bitterly cold winter, and that a housekeeper and numerous orphans were living in the same house at the same time. James wondered aloud what dark secrets motivated the priest to change his surname. The trouble-maker urged the priest's servant to run for political office, and to secure the backing of the priest, so that James might accuse the priest of meddling in politics. Father Demetrius, however, maintained a neutrality, which frustrated James, and which angered the servant. James circulated a petition against the priest, but added the names of people who had never signed the document. Father Demetrius, having failed at normal communications with James, took the case to court, and won. Animosities have a long life, and in 1809, a group of drunken men appeared at the church to beat up the priest. Providentially, a giant of a man, John Weakland, passed by, and pounced upon the ruffians, who scattered immediately.

The prince-priest had begun his ministry as an extraordinarily wealthy man, but over the years, spent his own money on constructing and furnishing his church, orphanage, and rectory. To create jobs for his people, he built a grist-mill, a saw-mill, and a tannery.[365] He lent his personal money to farmers, businessmen, and passing pioneers, which monies were almost never repaid. "It is estimated that he expended $150,000 (as valued in 1800) of his inheritance, a small portion of the amount that should rightly have come to him, but an immense sum for the times in which he lived."[366] The larger portion of money was inherited by his sister, and was claimed by the Russian government.

Father Demetrius Gallitzin made lasting contributions in his groundbreaking evangelization, and defense of the faith, in the face of majority opposition. He discovered that by putting his teaching and preaching into pamphlets, he could evangelize a much broader audience, with a more permanent effect. He authored *Defense of Catholic Principles* (1816), *An Appeal to the Protestant Public* (1819), *A Letter to a Protestant Friend on the Holy Scriptures* (1820), and *The Bible: Truth and Charity* (1836).

As Father Demetrius was growing older, decades of difficult conditions were taking its toll. Added to the effects of aging, in 1834, he was thrown from his horse, which accident seriously injured his leg. Soon, he developed a hernia, which further limited his activities. He resorted to using a sleigh in the winters. He died on May 6, 1840. The prince-priest had become the pioneer-priest, for the sake of Christ, and for the benefit of the people of Western Pennsylvania.

*For further information, contact*
The Prince Gallitzin Chapel House
357 St. Mary Street
P.O. Box 99
Loretto, Pennsylvania 15940 U.S.A.

⚭

## 8. ✠ Blessed Catherine-de-Saint-Augustin

*Place: Québec City, Québec*
*Fame: Nun and nurse. Co-foundress of the Church in Canada.*

In 1648, sixteen-year-old Sister Marie-Catherine-de-Saint-Augustin (1632-68) sailed from Dieppe, France and traveled to Québec, in New France.[367] She had volunteered to serve across the Atlantic Ocean in response a plea, which her fellow Augustinian Hospitaller Sisters of the Mercy of Jesus at Québec City had written. For two years, she had been reading about the North American missionaries in the Jesuit *Relations*. Three weeks after celebrating her sixteenth birthday, Catherine embarked on a disease-filled transatlantic ship. On board, she and other nurse-sisters cared untiringly for sick passengers during the nearly three-month-long voyage. Twenty years later, Catherine died in her adopted country, where she had served practically and piously.

Born at Saint-Saveur-le-Viconte at Normandy, Catherine de Longpré, the third child among ten, was placed by her mother early on under the care of her maternal grandparents. The grandmother operated a hospital, in which she cared kindly and capably for the patients. The grandfather earned a living as a well-respected lawyer. From the grandparents, the child learned compassion, patience, justice and practice of the Catholic faith. At three and four years of age, Catherine expressed the desire to know and do God's will. At ten, and again at sixteen, she consecrated herself to the Virgin Mary.

Eager to accompany her older sister, Catherine begged her parents for permission to enter the convent. They resisted. She persisted. At twelve and a half years of age, Catherine and her sister entered the convent of the Augustinian Hôtel-Dieu de Bayeux. At fourteen, Catherine began the postulancy program, and two years later, entered the novitiate, wherein she received her religious habit and religious name. Upon completing the two-year novitiate, she took vows, and three weeks later sailed for Québec.

Upon arriving at Québec on August 19, 1648, Catherine lived in the monastery of the Hotel-Dieu. At first, she nursed the sick. Three years later, she was appointed treasurer for the debt-ridden convent. She managed the funds so effectively that she achieved a balance, and even undertook a fundraising campaign to construct a new hospital, which was completed and blessed three years later, in 1657. Soon, she was named mistress of novices. In all of these positions, Catherine manifested great intellect, common sense, and compassion. Constantly, she sacrificed herself so that others might have good health and comfort. Joy and humility characterized the manner with which she served others. The classical phrase *fortiter et suaviter* (firm but gentle) describes her character.

Catherine's spiritual life consisted in trying to do God's will. At ten, she consecrated her life to the Virgin Mary, and six years later, reaffirmed this consecration. As a teen, she desired to imitate the sanctity and sacrifices of the North American martyrs. As a nun, she prayed faithfully, reflected on God's Word, read the lives of the saints, and received regularly the Sacraments of the Eucharist and Reconciliation. Throughout her twenty years as a missionary, she experienced extraordinary phenomena. Jean de Brébeuf, her fellow Normandy native, who was martyred at Ontario, seven months after Catherine had arrived at Québec, appeared to her beginning in 1662, and increasingly so from 1664 on. On a few occasions, Our Lord appeared to her and made revelations about impending dangers. In her lifetime, miracles were attributed to her. Despite these experiences of the marvels of the spiritual life, she kept experiencing temptations to evil.

Indian attacks were occurring oftentimes when Catherine arrived at Québec in 1648. The intensity and frequency of these attacks crescendoed during the first fifteen years of Catherine's two decades in New France. Not only Jesuit missionaries who lived nine hundred miles inland among the natives had been killed, but also French settlers along the St. Lawrence River had been attacked, and since 1660, attacked on a virtually daily basis. After learning of Jean de Brébeuf's martyrdom at Sault-Sainte-Marie, Catherine added his name to her list of intercessors in heaven. Soon after Brébeuf's death in 1649, the young nun writes to her superiors at Bayeux, "I am willing to do and to suffer everything that is asked of me, by my God who has sent me."[368] Catherine studied diligently and learned proficiently the Huron language, and the fundamentals of many other Indian dialects, including that of the hostile Iroquois.

Health problems affected Catherine her entire life. Beginning at five, and continuing into her teen years, she suffered severe headaches. This affliction worsened when she was at Québec. In 1657, her religious community invited her to return to France to receive medical attention. Catherine, however, chose to remain at Canada. Beginning in 1660, the physical suffering intensified. Other sisters observed that Catherine never complained, and never absented herself from spiritual exercises or community life activities. In 1665, she prayed that she might take on the spiritual sufferings of Québec's governor who was approaching death but was not at peace. The governor's spirit changed, as did Catherine's. She claimed she inherited his *esprit de mal*. Exhausted from her physical and spiritual combats, she died on May 8, at thirty-six.

The sister superior alerted all the Augustinian Hospitaller Sisters about the death of Catherine. The superioress writes:

> Her outward bearing had a charm that was the most attractive and winning in the world: it was impossible to see her and not love her. Her nature was one of the most perfect that could have been desired: prudent, with simplicity, keen of perception, without curiosity; sweet and gracious, without flattery; invincible in her patience; tireless in her charity; amiable to all, without undue attachment to any any; humble, without being mean-spirited; courageous, without any haughtiness.[369]

For Catherine's wake and funeral, the village of Québec turned out *en force* to pay their respects. The famous Sister Marie de l'Incarnation comments about Catherine, who had welcomed Marie into the Hospitallers' home when the Ursuline convent burned down in 1650, "The graces which God had bestowed upon her were founded on three virtues: humility, charity and patience."[370] Bishop François de Laval says about Catherine, she was "the holiest person he had ever known."[371] Preaching about her at the funeral Mass, he consoled mourners by saying, "if she had cared for us so powerfully during the time that she spent on earth among us, . . . [imagine] what she will do now that she knows all of our needs, like the pastor knows his sheep?"[372]

Because Catherine had dedicated her life to the evangelization and service of her Canadian countrymen, in its earliest and most perilous days, Canadian Church leaders have named her as one of the six co-founders of the Church in Canada.

*For further information, contact*
Centre Catherine-de-Saint-Augustin
32, rue Charlevoix
Québec, QC G1R 5C4, Canada

∝

## 8. ☩ Miriam Teresa Demjanovich

*Place: Bayonne, New Jersey*
*Fame: "Jesus, my well-beloved . . . have mercy on us."*
*Young contemplative in an active community.*

By personality, a serious-minded and reflective child, Teresa Demjanovich (1901-27) in her relatively brief life developed, by the grace of God, a profound contemplative relationship with Our Lord.[373]

MIRIAM TERESA
DEMJANOVICH

Teresa's parents emigrated from Bardejov, Slovakia in the Carpathian Mountains in 1884, and settled in New York City. The parents, however, missed the religious support of their Ruthenian-Greek Catholic Church. In 1885, the family moved across the Hudson River to Bayonne, New Jersey. Teresa was born in 1901, the last of seven children, five of whom survived infancy. Her father was a master craftsman, but not a successful businessman; his soft heart resulted in more outstanding bills than income. He gave up the shoemaker business and worked instead as a barrel cooper, which paid him an adequate salary and freed him from the risks of self-employment.

In the Bayonne public elementary and secondary schools, Teresa studied diligently. After graduating at sixteen, she dedicated herself for the next two and a half years to caring for her sick mother. After her mother died in November 1918, Teresa, at the encouragement of her siblings, enrolled in September 1919, at the College of St. Elizabeth in Morristown, New Jersey. The college was administered and operated by the New Jersey Sisters of Charity. Although her college teachers described her as "studious but not brilliant," she, nevertheless, was one of only two students who graduated that year *summa cum laude*.[374] This reflective student composed poetry, and wrote for her school newspapers both in high school and college. Although she never revealed any literary genius, she always revealed depth of soul and lighthearted humor in her writings.

After graduation in June 1923, she taught at the Academy of St. Aloysius in Jersey City, administered by the Sisters of Charity. She taught English and Latin. Some students complained that "Miss Demjanovich treated them as if they were Ph.D's."[375] Other students complimented the young teacher on her patience in the classroom. After one year, she left the Academy, recognizing that teaching high school students was not her God-given gift.

Vocation to religious life had appealed to her since her youth. During summer and autumn of 1924, Teresa prayed that she might discern God's will in knowing which religious community to enter. She visited the Carmelite community in the Bronx to learn more about them. Concerned about her poor eyesight, caused by oscillating pupils and resultant headaches, the Carmelites suggested that she wait a few years before applying. In the interim, she busied herself in the St. Vincent de Paul Parish choir, the Blessed Virgin Sodality and the parochial arm of the National Catholic Welfare Conference. In 1924, she made a novena for the feast of the Immaculate Conception. Within a couple of days after the December 8 feast, Teresa applied to the Sisters of Charity at Convent Station. Entrance was planned for February 2. Meanwhile, her father caught a cold, which developed into pneumonia, and led to his death on January 30. Teresa's entrance was delayed until February 11. Teresa's priest-brother and two sisters took her to the convent. Teresa "ran up the stairs ahead of them (her siblings), so eager was she to begin her religious life. She retired to her room to change into the dress of the postulants, and it was thus that she bade her brother and sisters good-bye."[376]

After three months of postulancy, Teresa donned the novice's habit and took as her religious name, Miriam, which she prefixed to her baptismal name Teresa. Father Benedict Bradley, O.S.B., who had been serving as the community's spiritual director for the past five months, recognized that Teresa was blessed with an exalted spirituality. He encouraged Teresa to write what God had inspired within her. In time, with the approval of the Mother Superior, he requested that Teresa might write conferences which he would deliver as his own. Teresa agreed. Father Bradley appreciated that Teresa's spirituality was more profound than his own. Mother Superior granted Teresa time and space to write a conference each week for Father Bradley.

In a little more than two years after Teresa had entered the convent, she died. Within days, Father Bradley informed the community that the conferences, which he had been giving had come from the pen of Sister Miriam Teresa. Immediately, the community hailed her as a saintly person. One year later, in 1928, the community published her conference writings, titled, *Greater Perfection*. These writings have been heralded as theologically accurate and spiritually insightful. A central element of her spirituality is this, "God's purpose in my life is this in general: To teach men that Our Lord's promise: 'If any man love Me, he will keep my word; and my Father will love him, and we will come to him, and make our abode with him,' is held out to every single soul regardless of calling; and is the perfect realization of his prayer and ours: Thy kingdom come."[377] A litany which the young nun composed follows.

*Litany of Love*
Lord, have mercy on us;
Christ, have mercy on us;
Lord, have mercy on us;
Jesus, hear us;
Jesus, lovingly hear us.
God, the Father of heaven, have mercy on us.
God, the Son, Redeemer of the world, have mercy on us.
God, the Holy Ghost, have mercy on us.
Holy Trinity, one God, have mercy on us.
Jesus, my Well-Beloved
Jesus, my Strength
Jesus, Light of my mind
Jesus, Power of my will
Jesus, Fire of my Love
Jesus, Life of my life
Jesus, Life of my soul
Jesus, Soul of my life
Jesus, Soul of my soul

Jesus, my Ceaseless Delight

Jesus, my Rapturous Bliss

Jesus, my infinite Joy

Jesus, True Peace of my soul

Jesus, my only Existence

Jesus, my Own

Jesus, my Heaven

Jesus, my Magnificent Love

Jesus, my Eternal Repose

Jesus, my Vehement Desire

Jesus, my Crucified Spouse

Jesus, my King

Jesus, my God

Glory be to the Father and to the Son and to the Holy Ghost; as it was in the beginning, is now, and ever shall be, world without end. Amen.[378]

In November 1926, this novice complained of illness. The novice mistress found it hard to believe that "a quinsy sore throat" would make someone so young, so sick [379]. Teresa underwent a minor operation for removal of her tonsils and returned home from St. Joseph Hospital at Paterson on the last day of 1926. She could hardly walk upstairs to her room, she felt so weak. A few days later, she requested again that she might be allowed to go to the infirmary. The mother superior, who was very caring and supportive of Teresa during the writing of the conferences and her illness, visited Teresa and instructed the novice, "Pull yourself together."[380] After mother superior left the room, Father Bradley entered. Teresa related to the priest the superior's comments, and added with a wry sense of humor, "Father, for a long time there has been nothing to pull."[381] The priest telephoned Teresa's priest-brother, who telephoned Teresa's nurse-sister. When the sister arrived at the convent infirmary, she took Teresa immediately to the hospital. Her condition noted on the medical chart reads: "Physical and nervous exhaustion, with myocarditis and acute appendicitis."[382] Because of her general weakness, the urgent operation was delayed until May 6. All the while, her condition worsened. Fearing her death, her brother requested and received permission from the Sisters of Charity to allow Teresa to take her vows at once. She professed vows of poverty, chastity and obedience on April 2, 1927. About a month later, May 8, she died. Post-mortem miracles were alleged to have occurred both at the hospital and at her funeral.

*For further information, contact*
Sisters of Charity
P.O. Box 476
Convent Station, NJ 07961 U.S.A.

☙

## 10.  ✠  Blessed Damien de Veuster

*Place: Molokai, Honolulu, Hawaii*
*Fame: Damien the Leper. Apostle among those afflicted with leprosy.*

Shortly after the death of Father Damien de Veuster (1846-89) at the Kalawao Settlement for those afflicted with leprosy, admirers inscribed on his tombstone the encomium, "Greater love has no man than this, that a man lay down his life for his friends" (John 15:13).[383]

DAMIEN DE VEUSTER

Damien was the name he received when he professed vows at twenty, in the Congregation of the Sacred Hearts of Jesus and Mary. He had been baptized Joseph, the seventh of eight children. On his parents' small farm at Tremelo, Belgium, located six miles from Louvain, Joseph became a jack of all trades, knowledgeable about agriculture, carpentry, and plumbing. Joseph's initial education stopped at the elementary school level, because his skills and labor were needed on the family farm. When Joseph was twelve, his father sent his son to Louvain to the College of Braine-le-Comte, where he was to study the commercial aspects of operating a farm. At the college, a Redemptorist preached a retreat which inspired Joseph to become a priest. Three of his children, two daughters and one son, had already joined religious orders. Like his older brother Auguste, called Pamphile in religious life, Joseph joined the Congregation of the Sacred Hearts. On his thirteenth birthday, the boy entered the seminary, and a month later, as a novice, he received the name Damien. He studied diligently, and after taking vows of poverty, chastity, and obedience on October 7, 1860, he began philosophical and theological studies.

In spring 1863, the provincial of the Congregation of the Sacred Hearts asked for volunteers to evangelize the inhabitants of the Sandwich Islands, now called the Hawaiian Islands. Both Pamphile and Damien, among others, volunteered. The provincial selected Pamphile, but when he became ill while ministering to victims of a typhoid epidemic at Louvain, Damien was selected to replace his brother. After briefly visiting his parents, Damien left Bremerhaven on October 23, 1863, and, after an uncomfortable five months on the high seas, arrived at Honolulu on March 19, 1864.

Two months after his arrival, Damien was ordained a priest at the Cathedral of Our Lady of Peace. His superiors assigned him to the eastern part of the big island of Hawaii, the largest of the islands. For eight months, he ministered at Puna, and for the next eight years, he ministered in the neighboring districts of Kohala and Hamakua. Catholics made up approximately a third of the district's inhabitants, which numbered in the thousands. Damien became a circuit-riding missionary, with each circuit taking approximately six weeks. His nine-year ministry consisted of sacramental, pastoral, and administrative duties.

In spring 1873, Bishop Louis Maigret of the diocese of Honolulu requested priest-volunteers to serve the population afflicted with leprosy, whom the government in 1865, had gathered and segregated at the colony of Kalaupapa on the island of Molokai.

> The Kalaupapa peninsula is located at the northern end of the Island of Molokai. It measures approximately three miles at its base and three miles north to south. Separated from the rest of the island by a wall of cliffs 1500 to 2,000 feet high and on the remaining boundary by a relentless ocean — the peninsula was made for exile.... Geographically, the Kalaupapa peninsula was made for isolation; no avenue of escape [was] possible. It was to this forsaken spot that the Hawaiian government sent shiploads of people diagnosed with leprosy.[384]

Four priests volunteered in response to the bishop's appeal. It was decided that the individuals would rotate turns every few months. Damien took the first rotation, arriving on May 10, 1873. At the end of his first week, Damien wrote to his provincial that the young priest would be happy to remain forever among those suffering from leprosy. The provincial, replied, "You may stay as long as your devotion dictates."[385] Sixteen years later, Damien died at Molokai.

Damien received instructions on how to preserve himself from contracting Hansen's Disease. He was not to breathe the air emitted by the lepers. He was not touch anything used by the afflicted ones. He would have to wash his hands repeatedly in the course of every day. To implement these procedures, however, proved to be impossible. How could the priest visit people's homes, sit down and talk with them, without breathing their same air? How could he eat their food but not touch what his hosts had prepared with their leprous hands; how could this priest anoint his people but not touch them? How could he wash frequently when the community's only water source lay many hundreds of yards away?

Damien busied himself not only in succoring for the people's spiritual life but also in improving their quality of life. Among the colony's six hundred inhabitants, he ministered to two hundred Catholics by baptizing them, confessing them, catechizing and counseling them, celebrating Eucharist for them, and providing Benediction and Adoration of the Eucharist for them. For all the citizens of Kalawao Settlement, Damien repaired or built homes, constructed streets, developed a sanitary system, and constructed a pipeline to bring water into the middle of the community. The former farm boy taught his new companions how to raise chickens and cows. "[For the sick] he washed their bodies, bandaged their wounds, tidied their rooms and made them as comfortable as possible."[386] Out of respect for the deceased, Damien created a space for a cemetery, built coffins for the dead, ritualized the funerals with formal prayers for the dead, and a formal procession to the cemetery in which a band he organized played on musical instruments. During his sixteen years at the Kalawao Settlement, in the midst of flagrant drinking, stealing, and sexual attacks, Damien instituted separate quarters for women, an orphanage for children, and devised a security force for the protection of all inhabitants. "To the lepers of Molokai, Father Damien was priest and doctor, carpenter and plumber, but above all he was the tangible evidence of God's love among them."[387]

Throughout his ministry, Damien longed for the companionship of another priest. Finally, a confrere arrived in 1868. Damien and he split the territory, and approximately every three or four months, the pair met and enjoyed each other's company. While on the island of Molokai, Damien writes to his provincial, "Being deprived of the companionship of my colleagues of our dear Congregation is more painful to bear than leprosy."[388] In late July 1886, after Damien had spent thirteen years without peer companionship, a Civil War veteran from Vermont arrived unannounced at Kalawao. Ira Barnes Dutton, who in 1883 had converted to Catholicism and took the name Joseph, wished to serve as a lay volunteer. Damien welcomed the volunteer. "They labored marvelously together, and Joseph, now dubbed 'Brother Joseph,' became Father Damien's closest and most cherished associate."[389] In November 1883, Mother Marianne Cope and four sisters of the Third Order of St. Francis came from Syracuse, New York in response to the government's worldwide request for religious women with professional training in medicine. Five years later, in November 1888, Mother Marianne transferred from Oahu to Molokai to assist Father Damien.

Ever since the end of 1873, his first year at Molokai, Damien had experienced the burning sensations symptomatic of the onset of Hansen's Disease. Five years later, the symptoms disappeared, and Damien rejoiced that perhaps a miracle had occurred. Two years later, however, in 1881, some symptoms resurfaced, and in 1884, he noticed while bathing his feet, that although he felt no heat, his feet had blistered because of the very hot water. In 1885, he was diagnosed medically with Hansen's Disease. To his provincial's invitation to be transferred and to receive treatment, Damien replied, "I would not be cured if the price of my cure was that I must leave the island and give up my work."[390] In July 1886, he traveled to Honolulu to receive treatment from a renowned Japanese doctor, but the salutary effects lasted only a few months. At this same time, Damien's eighty-three-year-old mother discovered for the first time, while reading the newspaper in Belgium, that her son had contracted leprosy, and was suffering the disease in its advanced stages. The mother died shortly thereafter, of a broken heart, clutching to her heart her son's photograph. On March 19, 1889, Father Damien celebrated twenty-five years of service in the Hawaiian Islands. On March 27, he became bedridden at home, and on April 15, 1889,

Monday of Holy Week, he died. Shortly before his death, Damien had commented with a smile on his face, "The good Lord is calling me to celebrate Easter with him."[391]

As a public figure, Damien was subject to both praise and criticism. Beginning in 1873, and up to the time of his death, the secular newspapers at Honolulu lauded his humanitarian work. In September 1881, Princess Liliuokalani, sister of the reigning King David Kalakaua visited the settlement, and profusely thanked Damien in the name of the Hawaiian people for his selfless contribution to the people. She bestowed a public honor upon him. Critics too stepped forward. Some claimed, and blamed, that Father Damien's failure to take adequate medical precautions led to his contracting the dreaded Hansen's Disease.

*For further information, contact*

Damien Museum
130 Ohua Avenue
Honolulu, HI 96815 U.S.A.

❧

## 14.  ✠  Eugenio Balmori Martínez

*Places: Coatzacoalcos and Acayucán, Veracruz*
*Fame: Apostolic lay leader. Husband and father.*

Catechists and church activists Eugenio Balmori (1900-46) and Marina Francisca Cinta Sarrelangue (1909-88) met in 1931, became engaged five years later, and married in 1937. They were blessed with five children. Throughout their lives, these two exemplary Catholics had dedicated themselves to church service, especially to the education of young people in their faith.

Eugenio was the oldest of eleven children. His birth mother died after the sixth child was born, and the father remarried in 1937. Because of the father's employment in the burgeoning oil industry, the family moved many times. Eugenio was born in the city of San Luis Potosi.

During the late 1920s, when the most intense persecution of the century-long persecution against the Church occurred, Eugenio courageously founded eighteen catechetical centers, hid priests in his home, and wrote in defense of the faith and clergy. Because of his illegal activities, he changed his residences frequently.

When, in 1931, the place of Eugenio's work as a draftsman changed to Coatzacoalcos in Veracruz, Eugenio went with his work. At Coatzacoalcos, he continued his clandestine ministry. Under special permission of the local bishop, Eugenio was permitted to keep at his home the consecrated Eucharist, which he then carried door to door to the sick, at great risk.

At Coatzacoalcos, Eugenio first met Marina Francisca Cinta Sarrelangue. Nine years younger than Eugenio, she was working as an instructor for Singer sewing machines. In their off-hours, they both catechized youth at the same time that the Calles government had prohibited public worship. They dated for five years.

In May 1936, Eugenio and Marina became engaged. Shortly after, his work required him to move to México City. The couple continued their romance by letters. In one letter Marina writes to Eugenio, "It seems that life has become more beautiful for me in knowing that I love you, and that you love me, and that the good God blesses and approves of our affection."[392] Eugenio writes, "Later when we are united, my mission will be to love you and to see that both of us encounter the true joy that will never terminate, because it will be prolonged in heaven. We will live in one love, with one goal: to form a Christian home."[393]

Half a year after becoming engaged, Eugenio moved back to Coatzaocoalcos. Marina, however, had to go to Acayucán to assist her parents. Finally in November 1937, the couple married at Acayucán. As the church and government recently had signed the *arreglo*, their wedding was the first religious service conducted in the reopened parish church.

This itinerant pair was forced by Eugenio's loss of his job to move to México City. There, within the next four years, their first three children were born. In 1942, again because of Eugenio's employment, the family moved back to Coatzacoalcos. There, the couple gave birth to their fourth and fifth children. Again, the pair became separated for months at a time because of Eugenio's job. Eugenio writes home to Marina, "My only goal is that while we are in this world, I always will love you, as I always have loved you. God desires that we be very happy. Believe me that our home will be a chapel of love, where no other ideal will reign other than to thank God and to love each other very much."[394]

When he came home to Coatzacoalcos, Eugenio assisted the parish priest in building the church of San José. Twice in 1946, Eugenio returned to this church: the first time, to have his fifth child baptized; and the second time, one month later, to be buried after he was killed on May 14, in an auto accident at forty-six.

Decades after his father's death, the priest-son of Eugenio and Marina observes about his parents: "Like two roads that converge, Eugenio and Marina met in God, to form a marriage united in faith and love, based in the Eucharist, illuminated by their apostolic experience as catechists, and sustained by the desire to gain all souls for Christ."[395] He adds that his parents kept seeking to know and to do God's will in all of life's circumstances. They followed Christ by embracing the cross. They lived the Christian life by being faithful to and active in the Church.

This same son describes his parents' spirituality.

> The spirituality which Eugenio and Marina lived as lay Christians, as catechists and as a married couple is seen now as a message of faith and love for the entire Christian community. All those who knew this couple testify to their union with God, and the great example they gave in their daily lives to all whom they met. Faith in God, love and fidelity in their married life, responsible parenthood, Christian education of their children, a Eucharistic homelife, participation in the catechetical apostolate, participation in the apostolate of the Catholic publications, devotion to Mary and St. Joseph, union with the Church and a spirit of collaboration, are the overall characteristics which one sees in the life of this couple, these servants of God.[396]

After Eugenio's death, Marina moved many times. She worked for CEISMA stores for twenty-six years, and for Cineteca Nacional for another nine years. Eventually, all the children graduated from universities and entered careers as professionals: the two daughters pursued careers in business education, and the three boys became an engineer, architect and priest respectively.

Eugenio was laid to rest initially at Minatitlan, Veracruz. In 1954, Eugenio's remains were transferred from the public cemetery to the parish church, which is now the cathedral, at Coatzacoalcos.

*For further information, contact*
Diócesis de Coatzacoalcos
Aldama 502
Coatzacoalcos, Veracruz, México

## 21. ✠ Saints Cristobal Magallanes and Companions

*Places: States of Chihuahua, Colima, Durango, Guanajuato, Guerrero, Jalisco, Michoacán, Morelos, and Zacatecas*
*Fame: "I am innocent, and I die innocent." Martyrs.*

CRISTOBAL
MAGALLANES

Twenty-five martyrs, including twenty-two priests and three laymen, were canonized together for the heroic deaths which they suffered during the anticlerical persecution in México. All except two of these men died between 1926 and 1928; one died in 1915, and the other, in 1937. These deaths took place in twenty separate incidents. On one occasion, three lay youth leaders along with their priest chaplain were killed at Zacatecas. In a second incident, a pastor and curate were captured and killed together at Jalisco. Again at Jalisco, a parish priest and the diocesan vicar were captured separately and killed jointly. Altogether, fifteen of the murders occurred within the state of Jalisco, four at Zacatecas, and one in each of six other states, namely, Chihuahua, Colima, Durango, Guanajuato, Guerrero, and Morelos. Geographically, these states are located mostly in the western and northern regions of México.

All of the martyrs belonged to the Catholic Action Movement. Those members were searched for, hunted down, and killed outright. The priests ranged in age from twenty-six to sixty-eight. These twenty-two priests represented the gamut of socioeconomic classes: from the very wealthy and well-educated to the extraordinarily poor with only the requisite education. Most were pastors; some were curates; one was a diocesan official, and another, a professor. The three laymen included a youth director aged twenty-eight, and two youths nineteen and twenty-one.

These murders were dictated by the laws of the Mexican government. Military officers ordered the specific killings, and ordinary soldiers generally followed out the orders. In three places, the appointed soldiers refused to kill the priests, and consequently those soldiers too were killed on the spot.

Father Cristobal Magallanes (1869-1927) exemplifies the spirit of the martyrs. Born to a farming family who lived in humble surroundings, he grew up working as a shepherd. At nineteen, he left home to study in the seminary at Guadalajara, where "he was distinguished for his piety, honesty, and sense of responsibility."[397] When the political authorities closed the seminary, Cristobal gathered his classmates and found another location where his fellow students could study. The government soon shut down this site too. Subsequent sites that Cristobal and the other boys arranged, the government closed as well. After continuing his seminary education in private homes at some risk, Cristobal in 1899 was ordained a priest at the Church of Santa Teresa at Guadalajara.

His first assignment took him to the Holy Spirit School of the Arts and Sciences in Guadalajara, where he served as chaplain and assistant director. After eight years, he was transferred to a parish at Totatiche, where he served for seventeen years, until he died. He focused his energies on not only developing the people's spiritual life, but also improving the townsfolk's educational and economic opportunities, especially for the poor. He founded a school and a catechetical center. He built carpentry shops and helped to construct a dam to provide electrical power for mills, and water for an irrigation system. For poor and abandoned children, he established an orphanage. For the indigenous Indians, he developed a modest land-sharing system.

The priest's services to the parish and parishioners came to an abrupt end on May 25, 1927. While walking to a farm to celebrate Mass, Father Cristobal was caught in the middle of a gun battle between the Cristeros and the government's forces. The government's soldiers captured, arrested, and jailed Father Cristobal. In jail at Totatiche, the priest discovered his parochial vicar too had been taken captive and brought there. The pair was soon transferred to Momax in Zacatecas. While being moved again, instead of going to México City as they had been told, the two prisoners were taken instead to Colotitlan. There, inside the Municipal Palace, without a trial having been conducted, the sentence was given to kill the two priests. General Goni admitted, "they would have taken no part in the Cristero movement, but it is sufficient grounds that they are priests to make them responsible for the rebellion."[398] Father Cristobal gave away his possessions to the men assigned to kill him. A by-stander recorded Cristobal's last words: "I am innocent and I die innocent. I forgive with all my heart those responsible for my death, and I ask God that the shedding of my blood serves towards the peace of our divided México."[399]

Soldiers removed from the yard of the Municipal Building the limp bodies of the two victims, and tossed the corpses into an alley. Six years later, at the conclusion of the persecution, the remains of the two priests were removed to the cemetery of the parish of Totatiche.

*For further information, contact*
Arquidiócesis de Guadalajara
Apartado 1-331, Liceo 17
C.P. 44100 Guadalajara, Jalisco, México

♣

## 24.  ✠  Blessed Louis-Zéphirin Moreau

*Place: Saint-Hyacinthe, Québec*
*Fame: Kindness. He was known popularly as "Good Bishop Moreau."*

Rich and poor alike in the dioceses of Montréal and Saint-Hyacinthe called the young priest Louis-Zéphirin Moreau (1824-1901), "Good Father Moreau."[400] As Moreau received more responsibility and more exposure, and was advanced to the episcopacy, the popular epithet was changed to "Good Bishop Moreau." Even before his death, people began referring to the kind and self-sacrificing bishop as "saintly Bishop Moreau."[401]

LOUIS-ZÉPHIRIN MOREAU

Louis Zéphirin Moreau almost never became a priest. One year before ordination, the bishop of Québec informed the young man that because of his frail health, the bishop had to send the young man home. The bishop explained that he could not ordain any "weaklings."[402] Young Moreau went home, accepting the bishop's decision as a sign from God. The local pastor and priests of the seminary faculty, however, argued that if the bishop of Québec City would not ordain Zéphirin, perhaps the bishop of Montréal would ordain the seminarian. After interviewing Zéphirin, Bishop Ignace Bourget of Montréal accepted the candidate, and a few months later, ordained him a priest.

The bishop assigned Zéphirin to the chancery and cathedral parish. During his first six years, the priest served admirably as assistant chancellor, curate of the cathedral parish, chaplain to the recently founded Sisters of Providence, and overseer of direct services to the poor in the downtown parish. Zéphirin's kindness in administering the sacraments, preaching and teaching, distributing food and clothing to the needy, and assisting in finding shelter for the homeless won for him the sobriquet, "Good Father Moreau."

In 1852, the pope divided the burgeoning diocese of Montréal, which resulted in the erection of the diocese of Saint-Hyacinthe. Bourget's coadjutor Jean-Charles Prince was chosen to lead the new diocese. When Bishop Prince moved, he took with him the kind and capable Moreau, whom the bishop appointed as his chancellor. Moreau's responsibilities included serving as secretary to the bishop, chancellor of the diocese, treasurer of the diocese, and director of various diocesan religious communities. Moreau served not only Prince but also his two successors. Moreau's durability and flexibility were manifested in his having served well the different personalities of three successive bishops. After twenty-three years of serving in the diocese of Saint-Hyacinthe, Moreau was named the fourth bishop of that see.

For the next twenty-five years, from 1876 to 1901, Moreau served as bishop of one of Canada's busiest sees. He oversaw the construction of the cathedral, the convocation of synods, and the creation of programs of ongoing education and formation for his clergy. Also, he consolidated various men's and women's communities, co-founded two women's communities, namely, the Sisters of Saint Joseph and Sisters of Saint Martha; and facilitated bringing to his diocese two men's communities, namely, the Marist Brothers and Dominican Fathers. In the midst of these milestone achievements, Moreau continued the daily overseeing of the rural diocese. His correspondence consisted of over eighteen thousand letters, which included pastoral letters to the faithful, circular letters to the clergy, administrative letters dealing with developing new parishes, and the development of schools. In the midst of this busy-ness, Moreau prayed daily and assiduously; he was known for his "constant and intense prayer."[403] Moreau lived as both a man of God and a man of his times.

In his seventy-sixth year, Bishop Moreau, frail in health, but energetic in his work, and kind in his manner, succumbed to illness. He was "the first bishop, of both Canadian birth and residence, to be beatified."[404] His episcopal motto, "I can do all things in him who strengthens me" (Phil 4:13), reveals a sense of his personal deficiency and dependence on the power of Jesus.

The kindness of Bishop Moreau is made manifest in a few vignettes. "One day, he recommended a rich industrialist to help out a poor woman who was also blamed for her bad behavior. A good number of people were shocked and criticized him discreetly. He merely answered: And if we do not give her anything, will she be any better for all that?"[405] Another time, Protestants reneged on a financial commitment they had made publicly to a village. Some Catholics wanted to take legal action against them, to which the bishop responded that he would be "intensely repelled" by such a distasteful avenue. The bishop writes, "Precisely because they are Protestants, we have to show more patience and tolerance in order not to increase their prejudice against our holy religion."[406] Moreau "was even a precursor, using in all likelihood for the first time with regard to the Protestants, the expression 'separated brothers' so commonly heard nowadays."[407] Moreau desired frankness in all his dealings. "He would readily say that he was more fearful of a liar than of a thief for . . . 'one can protect himself better from the latter than the former'."[408] In another instance, he writes to a priest, "We will not put on any diplomacy in the settling of our matters, we will tell each other the truth, the plain truth. This way, we will constantly know where we stand, and there will never be any ambiguity."[409]

Moreau's family roots in colonial Canada originated at Trois-Rivières, where his family had settled on both banks of the St. Lawrence, especially at Batiscan and Becancour. He was the fifth of thirteen children born to faith-filled Catholic parents who worked as farmers. When he was a youth, people observed that Louis possessed a bright mind, a pleasant disposition, and a sociable personality. He excelled at school and seminary, and as priest and bishop. From his youth until his dying days, Moreau manifested a unique harmony of virtues: "prudence, strength and gentleness, greatness of soul and simplicity, tireless zeal and trust in Providence."[410]

For further information, contact,
Éveché de Saint-Hyacinthe
1900, rue Girouard Ouest
Saint-Hyacinthe, QC J2S 7B4 Canada

## 30. ✠ Éléonore Potvin

*Place: Hull, Québec*
*Fame: Housekeeper who became a contemplative.*
*Foundress of the Servants of Jesus and Mary.*

Éléonore Potvin (1865-1903) was born and raised at Angers, Québec, twenty miles northeast of Hull.[411] Her parents observed that their sixth of seven children conducted herself uniquely. She possessed a reserved and reflective personality. At play, sometimes, she would gather other children into a make-believe procession in honor of the Blessed Virgin, with the group singing hymns as they processed reverently. Overall, "exteriorly, there appeared nothing remarkable about this

ÉLÉONORE POTVIN

child, either at home or at school. But interiorly, her heart beat entirely open to the love of God and the tenderness of the Virgin Mary."[412] At ten, her father died, occasioning the mother's moving the family to her husband's brother's farm at Masson, five miles to the northeast. Three months later, Éléonore made her First Communion, which simultaneously consoled her after her father's death, and intensified her spiritual life. Beginning in her teen years. She began walking six miles daily to Mass and Communion. In the parish church, oftentimes she would make a prolonged thanksgiving, and not return home until the dinner hour.

At fifteen, she prayed before a statue of the Blessed Mother, "I consecrate myself entirely to you. In order that I better belong to Jesus, give me your heart in order that I may love as you love."[413] Her education consisted of learning from her mother the four R's: religion, reading, 'riting, and 'rithemetic; and she received some little formal schooling. Also at home, she learned dressmaking. Moving out of the family home at twenty, she went to Hull, across the river from Ottawa, to make her living as a seamstress. Away from home, she continued to go to daily Mass and Communion. For two years, she attended Mass with the Sisters, Adorers of the Precious Blood at Ottawa. At twenty-four, she applied for admission to that community. Because this cloistered community had no spaces available, they referred her to their sister community at Toronto, where, she entered. Three of the first four weeks, however, she lay sick in bed. The sister superior recommended that. Éléonore return home, since her health appeared quite fragile. Back at Masson, Éléonore confided to her mother that the young woman still wished to dedicate her life to God, even if it could not be in the community of the Sisters Adorers.

The move back to Masson affected forever Éléonore's life. In April 1890, Éléonore introduced herself at the rectory, and inquired if she might find employment there. She had not known that the pastor, Father Alexis-Louis Mangin, who had arrived only eight months previously, had been praying a novena asking for a housekeeper. Within a few weeks, the brother noted that Éléonore was an exceptional employee. Not only did she cook and clean in the rectory in a meticulous way, but also she prayed for long hours before the Blessed Sacrament in the parish church.

Three years passed. Early on during that period, another young woman Sophie Chauvin arrived in town, and explained to the pastor that she wanted to dedicate her life to God. The pastor pointed her in the direction of Éléonore. The two discovered that they were soul mates: seeking to know and do only what God might ask of them. The pair joined a newly inaugurated Third Order of St. Francis, with. Éléonore taking the name Sister Zita, and Sophie calling herself Sister Delphine. Sister Zita, as part of her promise to live the vow of poverty, refused to accept pay for her labor at the rectory; room and board was all she required.

After three years, Sister Zita reported to Father Mangin that, while she had been praying in the church, extraordinary spiritual events had happened between April 20 and 27, 1893. The Blessed Virgin appeared to her, saying, "I have taken care of my divine Son, and you will take care of priests who are representatives of my Son."[414] By the end of that week, Jesus appeared to her, placed a crown of thorns upon her head, and asked her to begin an apostolate of praying for priests. Father Mangin was delighted. He shared with his housekeeper that a similar idea had been germinating within himself, i.e., of forming a religious community of women whose mission would be to pray for priests.

Father Mangin and Sister Zita discussed these providential events. He asked if she might make a prolonged retreat to try to test the depth of her virtue. She agreed. After weeks of praying, she commented that she wanted to do whatever God might ask of her. "She really cherished God's will more than anything else."[415]

Father Mangin and Sister Zita of Jesus discussed their proposed new apostolate. They agreed that the members of the community would live as cloistered contemplatives. Their work would consist of praying before the Blessed Sacrament, in perpetual adoration, i.e., day and night, in praise of Jesus in the Eucharist, and in his priests. Father Mangin offered that he might serve as spiritual director for the community.

Sister Zita founded the apostolate December 10, 1894. Sister Delphine also committed herself to this work, therefore, becoming Zita's first companion in this ministry. By spring 1895, two more women joined. With the religious community in its gestation stage, Father Mangin asked the archbishop for his blessing. The archbishop was both supportive and skeptical. He appreciated that the goal was noble, but advised that the achievement would be difficult. He nevertheless allowed the community to begin. On May 23, 1895, Sister Zita of Jesus and Father Mangin officially co-founded the Congregation of the Servants of Jesus and Mary. On that same day, Sister Zita and three other women, for the first time, put on the religious habit of the Congregation of the Servants of Jesus-Mary. The next month, Father Mangin appointed Sister Zita as superior. Because she preferred not to accept this symbol of authority, Sister Zita suggested, "Permit me to be simply the servant of my sisters, and Mary Immaculate will our true Mother and superior."[416] Ever since that time, the chief administrator of the community calls herself "mother-servant."[417]

The community grew quickly. Recruits kept coming. The pastor gave to the women the use of a small stable which was located on the edge of the parish's property. By December 1894, the women converted this stable into a four-bedroom home, with space for a chapel. This "little stable" became in effect the congregation's first monastery. Needing space, the following year, the sisters moved across the Ottawa River to the convent of Notre-Dame-des-Neiges. By 1898, the community, having swelled to twenty-five members, was forced to move again, this time to Aylmer, ten miles southwest of Ottawa, in the province of Québec, not far from Hull. That house proved unsatisfactory because of its remoteness from resources. Four years later, in May 1902, the sisters moved again, this time to Hull, which remains to this day the site of the motherhouse. The site at Hull provided the sisters with a physical environment conducive to their life of contemplation, i.e., river front property surrounded by forests. The sisters supported themselves by making altar breads.

Right from the start, the sisters had desired to have in their convent the Eucharist exposed day and night. Special permission was required, however, since canon law prohibits without permission the exposition of the Eucharist outside of a diocesan church. Permission was granted, but only in stages, and over time. Wishing that the sisters might create an atmosphere of continuous prayer even without enjoying the continuous presence of the Eucharist, Sister Zita suggested that they spiritually unite themselves with Masses being said throughout the whole world. In March 1897, the archbishop permitted Mass to be said daily in the chapel. In June of the following year, he approved that the Blessed

Sacrament be exposed every day after Mass, and on the entire day of the Feast of the Sacred Heart. At Christmas of that year, he granted that the Eucharist might remain in the tabernacle. At Easter 1902, he gave permission for the perpetual adoration of the Eucharist, day and night.

Mother-servant Zita of Jesus labored diligently for the community since its inception. She shared with the sisters the community's original vision, goals and means. For the sisters she provided exemplary service, and oversaw the development of the community. She became physically fatigued by all this labor, praying and caring not only for priests, but also for the sisters of the community. Despite being tired, she pressed on to write a *Constitution and Rules* for the community. In June 1902, she became quite ill with tuberculosis. The following May, she received the sacrament of the dying. On May 30, 1903, she expired. Mother Zita was thirty-eight years old, and had lived a total of eight years in religious life.

In the weeks before she died, Mother Zita and Father Mangin prepared the community's *Constitutions*. This document was distributed to the sisters, and the Vatican approved it many years later.

The Servants of Jesus and Mary are inserted in the heart of the Church, the People of God, as a contemplative and cloistered congregation, of pontifical right. The Sisters consecrate themselves totally to the Lord by their religious vows.

The special end is to honor the Sacred Heart of Jesus in the Eucharist and the priesthood, and to collaborate, in union with Mary, to the realization of the eternal Plan of Union: "that all might be one."

By their life of prayer and self-sacrifice centered on Jesus, Priest and Victim, whom they adore day and night, in the exposed Blessed Sacrament, they pray for priests, in a spiritual apostolate, which pours out benefits on the entire Church.[418]

*For further information, contact*
Les Servantes de Jésus-Marie
210, rue Laurier
Hull, QC J8X 3W1 Canada

# JUNE

### 3. ✠ Blessed Vital Grandin

*Place: Northwest Territories of Canada*
*Fame: First Bishop of St. Albert, Alberta.*
*Evangelizer and defender of the Native Peoples.*

Ironically, Vital Grandin (1829-1902), as a seminarian, had been sent home not only by the Brothers of the Holy Cross on account of his poor health, but also by the Paris Foreign Mission Society because of his inability to communicate in a foreign language.[419] Later, he served heroically for half a century in one of the world's most difficult and demanding mission territories, i.e. Canada's Northwest. There he traveled by snowshoes, dogsled, and canoe the distance equivalent to seven or eight times

VITAL GRANDIN

around the world, and communicated regularly with the Dene and Cree tribes in their native languages. The shy, sensitive, and self-effacing youth became eventually an out-reaching, outgoing, and outstanding missionary. Members of the Metis tribe called Grandin their "Indian bishop" on account of his protecting them from invaders, providing them with food and clothing during harsh winters, and preaching to them about Jesus in a way that touched their hearts and inspired them to convert to the Catholic faith.

The ability to endure deprivation, Grandin had learned as a boy. He, his eight living siblings, and their parents survived a hurricane, which destroyed all the buildings on their farm near Valois. The family tried their hand by opening a wayside inn, but when the father disallowed drunkenness and visits by women of ill repute, the business failed. The impoverished family was forced to move. Ten-year-old Vital was sent to an uncle's home, where Vital worked as a shepherd and field hand. After a few months, Vital returned home to his family, whom he loved dearly and had missed sorely.

Becoming a priest proved challenging for the boy. His family could not afford to send a second son to the seminary, where one of Vital's older brothers already was studying. Forsaking the idea of becoming a priest, Vital chose to become instead, a lay brother, and was accepted by the Brothers of the Holy Cross. During his first year in the seminary, however, his health failed, and the community sent him home. His mother, perceiving her son's disappointment, enlisted other people to aid him. The parish priest and soon Vital's seminarian brother instructed Vital in Latin. A Carmelite nun arranged that Vital could live in a boarding house near the seminary, so as to consult the seminarians regarding the subjects needed for priesthood. A Visitation nun implored the bishop to meet with the boy, after which meeting, the bishop's secretary served as benefactor for Vital's studies. At seventeen, Vital entered the college seminary. He met all the goals of the seminary faculty. "The teachers were very fond of him and repeatedly went on record with praise for him. He had, they declared, a reasonable disposition, was sensitive, very shy, extremely well-behaved and exceptionally good in religious studies."[420] After four years of college studies, he advanced to the major seminary in 1850. Yearning to pursue the missionary vocation, he entered in 1851, into the seminary program of the Paris Foreign Missionary Society. After a few months, however, the seminary refused him admission because he spoke with a lisp. Recalling that a former classmate had joined the newly founded missionary Order of Mary Immaculate, Vital entered the OMI novitiate in November 1851, and on April 23, 1854, he was ordained a priest.

The newly ordained priest's first assignment was the Red River district of western Canada. His family and friends bade him farewell at the dock at Le Havre. The separation was emotionally painful for him. He writes,

> On the night before leaving, the pain in my heart was boundless. God wanted me to feel the extent of my weakness. Yet, He was my help in this troubling circumstance. What gave me strength was the thoughts of so many people praying for me, especially my brother [the priest]. Fortunately, no one realized my heart was suffering to the breaking point."[421]

After arriving at Québec in late June 1854, Vital reached in early November to Saint-Boniface Mission (now Winnipeg), where Bishop Taché mentored the new priest for one year. The next year, Vital was assigned to the most distant part of the expansive territory, the shores of Lake Athabasca, located seventeen hundred miles northwest of Saint-Boniface. The assignment proved to be lonely, and dangerous. Vital, asking himself if he was happy, replies, "Humanly speaking, I am not happy; but I submit myself to whatsoever my superior will command. I am happy since I am where the Lord wants me; and here, there is a possibility of making Him known and loved."[422]

In July 1858, a letter to Vital arrived, announcing that he had been named coadjutor bishop of the Diocese of Saint-Boniface. Vital was shocked. He knew his limitations: the brevity of his three-years' experience as a priest, his weak health, his difficulty in speaking the native languages, his spiritual unworthiness. He wrote to his community's founder Bishop Eugène de Mazenod, and respectfully declined the appointment. Mazenod reaffirmed the selection, and required Vital to comply. Reluctantly, Vital traveled to Marseille, France, where on November 30, 1859, he was ordained bishop. Vital chose as his motto, "I will boast of the things that show my weakness" (2 Cor 11:30).

Upon returning to the diocese of Saint-Boniface, Vital experienced some of the worst years of his life. He almost died: once while traveling by dog sled he suffered so egregiously in the snow and wind that he and his traveling companion prepared for death. He suffered extreme privation: he lacked proper clothing , food, and fuel for his shelter. He lacked the consolation of satisfying conversation: the Indians were primitive, the Protestants were bigoted and blocked his efforts to provide churches and schools for the natives. He even lacked writing paper for correspondence. Fire destroyed the mission at Ile-a-la-Crosse, and Bishop Vital had to beg for funds to continue the Lord's work.

Upon returning to Saint-Boniface, Bishop Grandin learned that he had been appointed the first bishop of the new diocese of Alberta, in the newly opened western provinces of Canada. The diocese, at its incorporation in 1871, encompassed all of the present political province of Alberta and a great part of Saskatchewan, which territory measured almost two-million square miles, in which lived and labored only five priests. Adding Alberta to the Dominion allowed thousands of immigrants to pour into the region. In this wave came not only good-living hard-working immigrants in search of a better life, but also some malefactors wanting to make a living off the reputed alcoholism of the natives, and the loneliness of the miners and hunters. On the one hand, winter brought trials of cold, hunger and thirst; and on the other hand, summer oppressed the frontiersmen with high heat, humidity, and swarms of mosquitoes. With no money for the mission, and few priests and nuns to evangelize among the Indians, Bishop Grandin went searching for monies and personnel. The bishop attracted numerous women and men's religious communities to serve the mission in the Canadian wilderness. When Grandin died, there were sixty-five missions, fifty schools, three hospitals and two seminaries.

The missionary bishop traveled extensively to visit the far-reaching limits of his diocese. One visitation lasted three years, so remote were the parishes, one from another. In a letter, Grandin describes the typical travel in winter:

> One of the men goes ahead, axe in hand. I follow. Then come the dogs, drawing our provisions and theirs. And the second Indian trudges behind the sled, so as to push when necessary. My clothes are far from episcopal. They are not even clerical. Except for a flannel shirt, they are all made of leather. My trousers are moose-skin, my outer shirt is caribou-hide with the hair on the inside, and over it I wear a large moose-skin blouse. My cross and my episcopal ring hang from a cord around my neck. My finger would be frozen in no time, were I to wear my ring on it. From another cord hang two large sacks, made of white bear skin: they are my mitts and I have to keep my hands in them all the time. I wear a beaver-skin hat, over which is a shawl to cover my neck, ears and parts of my face. All this peculiar headdress is enveloped with a huge hood. Within half an hour of my putting it on, all the clothing near my face is covered with ice, due to my breathing.[423]

Worn out, Grandin felt the need of a coadjutor bishop to assist him in his duties. His oft-repeated request was satisfied in June 1897, when he ordained his successor. In early 1902, Bishop Vital became seriously ill, and in June, he died peacefully. In his customary simplicity, he had requested, "If I happen to die while on the road, my wish is that in order to continue preaching the mystery of the Redemption even after my death, a large wooden cross [is to] be erected at the camp where I die. No expense is to be incurred to have my remains transferred: my body is to be buried at the foot of the cross."[424] Grandin died, at home in his rectory, and his remains rest in the simple frontier cathedral, which he began building at Saint-Albert, Alberta, two years before he died.

*For further information, contact*
Archivist
5, avenue Saint-Vital
Saint Albert, AL T8N 1K1 Canada

## 3. ☩ Juan de Zumárraga

*Place: México City, D.F.*
*Fame: Protector of the Indians, devotee of Our Lady of Guadalupe.*
*First bishop and archbishop of México.*

Administrator, evangelizer, protector of the Indians, and devotee of Our Lady of Guadalupe, Juan de Zumárraga (c. 1468-1548) excelled in all of these roles and responsibilities.

From his earliest years in priesthood, until his dying day as archbishop, Juan served in leadership positions in the Church. As a young priest, he was named guardian of the Franciscan friary at Abroxo near Valladolid. From 1520 to 1523, he served his religious community as provincial. When a crisis arose in New Spain, and Emperor Charles V needed a bishop with proven exceptional judgment, the emperor in 1527 selected Juan and sent him as bishop-elect to the New World. At his see, after four years of suffering calumnies from many accusers, Juan was recalled by the emperor to face accusations at Madrid. Given the opportunity to explain himself, Juan satisfactorily responded to the emperor, who then permitted the ordination of Juan as bishop.

Returning in 1534 to the New World, Juan ministered in his diocese which stretched as far south as, and including, Guatemala; and as far north as, and including, Jalisco. When the colony's first Viceroy arrived in 1535, he and Zumárraga worked together to develop the faith and social life of the Indians. Juan founded schools for the Indians. In 1536, he opened the first seminary and high school in the Americas. The following year, he laid the groundwork for the prestigious University of México, which opened five years after his death. Juan was one of the first persons to introduce the printing press to the New World. "He published the first catechisms in the Castilian and Mexican languages, as well as ascetic and liturgical works for the benefit of his diocese. He himself wrote some of these works, e.g., *Doctrina Breve Muy Provehosa* (México City, 1544) and *Regla Christiana* (México City, 1544)."[425] He convened councils of bishops to deal with ecclesiastical and social issues including the situation of Native American husbands taking multiple wives. In accord with the *Nuevas Leyes* which Bartolomé de las Casas had won at Spain which forbade that Indian territories be distributed as land grants, the bishop suggested that no *new* land grants should be permitted. Zumárraga's compromise "undoubtedly saved [New Spain] from a bloody civil struggle such as engulfed Peru on account of the enforcement of these same laws and from which the Indians emerged worse off than they were before."[426]

When Juan arrived at New Spain in 1528, the good care with which the discoverer Hernando Cortes had treated the Indians was not continued by his successors. Gúzman and other *auditores* were abusing the Indians. "They impoverished the Indians by taxes, sold them into slavery, branded them with hot irons, sent shiploads to the Antilles, offered violence to Indian girls, and persecuted with incredible fury the followers of Cortes."[427] Juan, after having called repeatedly for an end to the *auditores's* abusive treatment of the Indians, excommunicated in 1530 the incorrigible leaders. Although Juan had written repeatedly to the emperor, describing the abuses, his letters never traveled very far as Gúzman and his henchmen intercepted the letters before they left the New World. Eventually, Juan and a fellow Basque sailor devised a way to conceal the letters among the cargo being shipped from Veracruz to Cadiz; the sailor concealed the letter inside a ball of wax which was submerged in a barrel of oil. Unfortunately, this famed evangelizer of the Indians oversaw the destruction rather than the preservation of the Native Americans' temples, idols and writings. This archival material is not available to scholars to study. Juan described in a letter to the

Franciscans' general chapter meeting at Toulouse the success of the evangelization. In summary, the successes include:

> More than a million Indians baptized; over five hundred pagan temples deserted; and whereas formerly twenty thousand children were sacrificed to the devil every year by having their living hearts torn out of their bodies and burnt before the idol, now there were just as many children being reared in a Christian way, and they in turn were leading their parents to the Christian religion.[428]

Many people remember Juan Zumárraga as the bishop of México City to whom Juan Diego revealed the sign of Our Lady of Guadalupe. The sign was not only the gift of the roses growing in the middle of winter, but also the image of Our Lady of Guadalupe emblazoned on Juan Diego's *tilma*. A few days previously, the bishop had responded openly, but cautiously to Juan Diego's initial statement and request. After Juan Zumárraga saw the image, however, the saintly bishop fell to his knees in prayer in wonderment. Within two years, he had laid the foundation for the church which the Lady had requested. News of these events spread rapidly among the native population. "According to Fray Toribio de Motolinia the number of baptized Indians in México in 1536 numbered five million."[429]

*For further information, contact*
Arquidiócesis Primada de México
Curia: Durango # 90
Col. Roma – Apartado Postal #24-433
06070 México, D. F. México

## 6. ✠ Blessed Rafael Guizar y Valencia

*Place: States of Veracruz, Puebla, and Morelos; México City, D.F.*
*Fame: Fugitive from persecution. Bishop of Veracruz.*

Three times, Rafael Guizar y Valencia (1878-1938) fled for his life from the anticlerical persecutions conducted by the government in México.

For twenty-four years of his thirty-seven total years as priest and bishop, he spent ministering in exile, either abroad or in hiding outside of his diocese.

Rafael grew up as the fifth child in a family of ten children. After Rafael's mother died when he was nine, the boy began manifesting a clear sensitivity to the sufferings of others. At twelve, he entered a Jesuit school, and one year later, he was admitted to the local seminary in his hometown of Cotija, Michoacán. For the next ten years, he studied for the priesthood, although he took one year off from studies, worked on a farm, and returned to the seminary even more dedicated to his vocation.

In 1901, the bishop of the diocese of Zamora ordained Rafael a priest. Immediately, Father Rafael demonstrated great zeal for the salvation of souls. In 1905, the pope named Rafael missionary apostolic for México, and the bishop appointed him spiritual director for the diocesan seminary. Outstanding in holiness and outgoing in personality, he was named, in 1913, a canon of the cathedral, in which position he served also as chaplain to the military forces in the district of México City, plus the states of Puebla and Morelos. Shortly thereafter, however, the government instituted anticlerical persecution, and Father Rafael fled for his life. He sought refuge in the United States of America, Guatemala, and Cuba.

In August 1919, the pope named Rafael the bishop of Veracruz. After receiving ordination at Cuba, Bishop Rafael returned to México. While the bishop was busy caring for the victims devastated by a recent earthquake, and re-establishing the seminary at Jalapa, the government officials made life difficult for him. They kept disrupting life at the seminary, which forced Bishop Rafael to transfer the seminary program to México City, where the seminary continued successfully for fifteen years until the persecution ended. A new persecution of the Church was underway, this time led by President Pultarco Elias Calles. Again, the bishop left the country. He returned to the United States, Guatemala, and Cuba, and visited Colombia. Only in 1929, did he return after hundreds of clergy and thousands of lay persons had been killed by the government. Upon his return, the bishop encountered the wily strategy of the governor of Veracruz, who had declared falsely that the entire diocese had converted to the schismatic religion which the government's department of religion had established. In light of this abuse of human and civil rights, the bishop suspended all religious services, and he fled again, this time to México City.

In the capital, the bishop disguised himself as a junk dealer, which ruse allowed him to make his rounds of the city, visit many homes, and talk with the faithful. "At the same time, he was suffering from cardiac problems, diabetes, obesity, and phlebitis."[430] Exhausted from a lifetime of service and thirty-seven years in ministry, he died at México City, and his body was transported to Jalapa, Veracruz for burial.

*For further information, contact*
Obispado
Insurgentes Veracruzanos, #470
C.P. 91700
Veracruz, Veracruz, México

⤝⤞

## 24. ✝ Venerable María Guadalupe García Zavala

*Places: States of Jalisco and Sonora*
*Fame: "The heart of Mother Lupita has no limits in doing good." Co-founder of the Servants of St. Margaret Mary and of the Poor.*

Anastasia Guadalupe García Zavala (1878-1963) was born in the village of Zapopan, on the out-skirts of Guadalajara, in Jalisco.[431] "Lupe," as she was called affectionately, was one of eight chil-dren, of whom the two youngest died as infants. Lupe's aunt, who was a nun, educated the child at home. Her parents lived until Lupe reached mid-life: her merchant father died in 1926, and her mother, five years later.

In her childhood and teen years, as throughout her life, Lupe demonstrated a degree of compas-sion for the sick and poor, well beyond her years

MARÍA GUADALUPE
GARCÍA ZAVALA

and peers. As a young member of the St. Vincent de Paul Society, she vis-ited a local hospital and treated the sick with unusual kindness and ten-derness. When she was performing volunteer service in the Conference of

St. Margaret Mary, she stood out above the others. At twenty-three, feeling called to give her life to God as a vowed religious, she approached the parish priest and director of the Conference, Father Cipriano Iñiguez Martín del Campo. The priest applauded her decision. He then shared with her that he felt called to found a religious community of women whose mission would be to care for the sick and the poor in the hospital. He invited her to consider co-founding with him this diocesan community of women religious dedicated to serving the sick and poor. Already, she had been doing that work. In humility, she hesitated; in fidelity to discerning and doing the will of God, she accepted the call.

In October 1901, Lupe took vows and repeated them in 1903, after which she renewed them every five years, until 1924, when she took perpetual vows. When Father Cipriano died in 1931, Sister Lupe was assigned the role previously filled by him, namely, Director of the Conference of St. Margaret Mary, and spiritual guide for the sisters. One month later, she was named superior general of the community.

Simplicity and sincerity characterized her religious life. She acted as a caring mother toward her sisters in religious life, and treated their families with the greatest kindness. The elderly she treated with special solicitude, doing for them whatever small tasks and favors might be needed to provide them with greater comfort, rest, and the best possible health. In the hospital, she was alert as to how to improve the patients' lives: medically, emotionally, and spiritually. To the poor on the streets, she bestowed food and clothing as generously as possible. Recipients of her kindness commented, that you felt as if you were in the presence of your own mother. So genuine was her care that the nuns and those she met and served called her spontaneously Madre Lupita. One sister reports the following firsthand anecdote:

> One afternoon, it happened that Madre Lupita was walking with another sister.... Upon seeing me, Mother asked me if I would substitute, in place of the other sister. We passed by a place filled with much agitation, in front of a house. Some people were crying over a sick person. Mother approached them, spoke to them with so much tenderness, that she calmed them and these poor people received a certain peace.

We continued walking, and the topic of conversation turned to me. We arrived at chairs, and sitting down, Mother looked at me and said: "Humanity suffers. And God has chosen us precisely to alleviate in any way possible humanity's sufferings. Do not remain hard of heart to the misfortune of another person; suffer with those who suffer, console those who are crying, heal those who are ill. This is the purpose to which God has called us and what we, in good conscience, have to do. . . . Forget yourself and surrender yourself to those sacrifices to which God calls you. It does not matter what it costs you; at the end, God will repay you. Soon we will pass to the other life, and no more will we be doing these good deeds."

Reverend Mother Lupe, in an extraordinary way, put herself at the service of everybody including her enemies and persecutors, whom she treated with so much amiability even in giving them food, and in excusing them like Jesus in these words: Poor fellows have been ordered, and they are hungry. It is necessary for us to do what the Lord asks. Now is the time.[432]

One of her guiding principles was that "God is the only good for every person."[433] With that she spent her life following God's will, and leading other people to God, by her childlike simplicity, and mother-like caring.

In the next sixty years, she and her sisters established eight works: five hospitals, two senior citizen homes, and domestic assistance at the bishop's residence. Five of the houses were located at or near Guadalajara, and three more were located at Navojoa, Sonora.

As Mother lay dying in her final days, her physician asked her, "How are you doing, Mother Lupe?" She replied, "I'm walking towards heaven."[434] The doctor then took her hand and, with tears in his eyes, reverently kissed it. After the death of the foundress, the sisters opened twenty-five more institutions.

*For further information, contact*
Casa Generalicia de las
Siervas de Santa Margarita María de los Pobres
Reform 1440 S.H.
Guadalajara, Jalisco, México

## 29. ✢ James A. Walsh

*Places: Boston, Massachusetts; and Ossining, New York*
*Fame: "Seek first the kingdom of God."*
*Co-founder of Maryknoll Fathers and Brothers.*

James Anthony Walsh (1891-1981) was a faith-filled visionary, and practical-minded missionary.[435] Faith formed his vision to take the gospel of Jesus beyond the United States to unchurched foreign lands. He writes, "There is for Catholics no real distinction between home and foreign missions, since the Church of Christ simply has *a mission*, and that is to 'preach the gospel to every creature,' and to 'teach all nations'."[436] His practical sense enabled him to consider all

JAMES A. WALSH

details, to envision likely consequences, and to focus his and others' energies on clear goals and objectives. He thought big; he writes, "Be big: bigger than your mission — bigger then your Society, as big as the Church. Mindful of your own place do not forget that it is only a small portion of a great body which calls for the cooperation of all its parts so that it may function strongly for the greater good, and incidentally for your own."[437]

James Walsh's parents had left County Cork as children. The two met and married in Boston. James studied and graduated from Boston College High, and in 1884, he continued studies at Boston College. In the summer of 1885, James left BC, attended Harvard as a non-matriculating student, and in September 1886, entered the Seminary of St. John at Brighton.

Two events especially affected James during his youth. First, in elementary school, going door-to-door in his neighborhood, he collected pennies for the Holy Childhood Association to ransom Chinese babies. Second, in the seminary, he and a mission-minded Sulpician priest Gabriel Andre edited weekly *Mission Notes* for a parish publication.

Father Andre shared with Walsh a letter from one of his classmates who was ministering in Japan. In a 1924 talk to the novices of the Maryknoll Sisters, Walsh recalled the gist of the letter.

> I am writing to you, my classmate. It is sixteen years since I left the seminary, with the fervor of youth and a strong desire to shed my blood for Christ. These sixteen years have passed in hard work, with very poor results. I have accomplished little and have come to the conclusion that nothing can be done in this district until some man's blood has been spilled; and I tell you in all sincerity, as friend to friend, coldly — far from that fervor of the young apostle — that if tomorrow I were called upon to meet death for Christ and souls, I should be the happiest of men.[438]

After ordination in May 1892, and serving for eleven years at St. Patrick's in Roxbury, Walsh was assigned as archdiocesan director of the Society for the Propagation of the Faith. In 1904, at a meeting in Washington, D.C., for priests working in home missions in the United States, Walsh presented a paper suggesting that home missions in the U.S.A. would prosper if American Catholics would develop an international vision of mission. In the audience, Father Thomas F. Price, became intrigued with the idea. The two clerics spoke after the presentation. Two years later, Walsh established the Foreign Mission Bureau to inform Catholics about the activities of overseas missionaries. The next year, he began publishing a mission magazine *The Field Afar*.

By chance in 1910, Walsh and Price were attending the Eucharistic Congress at Montréal. Renewing their previous discussion, the pair agreed to found a mission-sending society. The next year, they presented and gained approval for their proposal from the United States Bishops, and two months later from the Propagation of the Faith at Rome. The next day, June 30, 1911, Pope Pius X gave his blessing to the two priests, and their new Catholic Foreign Missionary Society of America. Walsh became the chief administrator of the society, overseeing the education and formation of the seminarians. Walsh, who had purchased property near Ossining, New York, thirty-five miles north of New York City, named the hilltop, Maryknoll, in honor of the Blessed Virgin Mary.

In 1917, just before Walsh witnessed the ordination and departure of Maryknoll's first missionaries, he traveled to the Far East to identify an area of mission responsibility for the new community. He accepted an area in China. Within the next seventeen years, Walsh received from the Vatican Congregation for the Propagation of the Faith responsibility for additional missions in China, Japan, Korea, the Philippines, and Hawaii. Part of Walsh's vision is included in his directives to his missioners:

> The hallmark of a sterling missioner is his willingness to forget the customs of his own country and to enter sympathetically into the lives of those whom he would shepherd for Christ.... The Son of God took upon Himself the nature of man, so the missioner should unite to the people whom he would evangelize — becoming one with them in all things but sin. Marked success has followed those missioners who have pursued this line of conduct, while no single influence has injured the cause of worldwide evangelization so much as the attempts to force the habits of the West on the people of the East.... Our missioners should aim not to destroy what is good in pagan life and culture. Rather they should perfect what is good with the spirit of Christ, instilling his sublime teachings in season and out of season.[439]

Walsh encouraged the Maryknoll Fathers, Brothers, and Sisters to live simply, to develop native vocations, and to involve laity in the Maryknoll ministry. In 1930, he writes to the Maryknoll Sisters, "I hope to God that neither your community nor ours [Maryknoll Fathers and Brothers], will ever be wealthy. We don't know how we are going to live from day to day, what we are going to do. It's good we don't because we throw ourselves more on almighty God."[440] To promote native vocations, Walsh writes to his confreres, "We look forward to a native clergy, to a self-supporting Catholic body, to a day when the appointment of native bishops will mean the assignment of future Maryknollers to other fields."[441] Decades ahead of his time, he advocated for lay volunteers. He writes in 1922, "Surely there will be generous souls, in numbers proportionate to the grace of God, who may not feel called to devote their entire lives to a religious work, but who would gladly spend a certain time, say five years or more, in teaching on the missions."[442]

To promote information about, and inspiration for the missions, he publicized in *The Field Afar*, and in three books, the realities, challenges and possibilities facing missionaries and the Church. Candidates for membership in the men's community founded in 1911, and the women's community founded the next year, responded generously to the challenge and invitation.

In April 1933, in recognition of Walsh's efforts to launch a spirit of world mission in the U.S. Church, Pope Pius XI named Walsh titular bishop of Siene. The motto the bishop chose for his coat of arms was the same motto he had chosen twenty-two years earlier for the Maryknoll community, "Seek first his kingdom" (Mt 6:33). Two months later, in Rome, at the ceremony of episcopal ordination, Walsh felt fatigued. He brushed aside any concern for serious sickness, and continued his usual busy pace. His experience of general weakness worsened. Walsh died at Maryknoll on April 14, 1936.

Twenty-five years after its origin, Maryknoll had grown to over two hundred fifty members, working in five countries, on two continents. The society's magazine had grown to one hundred twenty thousand subscribers.

*For further information, contact*
Maryknoll Fathers and Brothers
P.O, Box 304
Maryknoll, New York 10545 U.S.A.

෴

# 29. ✠ Thomas F. Price

*Places: Wilmington and Raleigh, North Carolina;*
*and Ossining, New York*
*Fame: Mystical relationship with the Blessed Virgin Mary.*
*Co-founder of Maryknoll Fathers and Brothers.*

A broad faith-vision, deep spirituality, and end-less energy guided Father Thomas Frederick Price (1860-1919) in his ministry for home missions initially, and foreign missions eventually.[443]

THOMAS F. PRICE

Thomas Price's parents were born Protestants: his father was Episcopalian, and his mother, Methodist. At eighteen, the mother converted to Catholicism. Shortly before he died, the father converted. Thomas Price grew up as the youngest of ten children. Two of his three sisters became Sisters of Mercy, and three of his six brothers entered the seminary, with one of them advancing to priest-hood. His father worked as editor of the *Wilmington [N.C.] Daily Journal.* Young Thomas inherited his father's gift for writing. Thomas was educated at the local Catholic grade school, where his older sisters taught him. His pastor, James Gibbons, who later became Cardinal Gibbons of Baltimore, encouraged Thomas to enter St. Charles Seminary at Ellicott City, Maryland, and later St. Mary's Seminary in Baltimore. As a seminarian, a passenger ship on which he was sailing, crashed in a storm; the young man believed the Blessed Virgin Mary protected him by leading him to a piece of floating debris. Ordained in 1886, young Price was assigned to Bern, North Carolina, near Asheville.

In North Carolina, there were fewer than five thousand Catholics among the state's two-million people. For Price's first ten years of priest-hood, he used New Bern as his base of operations, and traveled by horse and buggy to minister to Catholics in seventeen surrounding settle-ments. In 1896, Price requested and received permission from his bish-op to work as an itinerant missionary for the conversion of non-Catholics throughout the entire state. Choosing the state capital, Raleigh, as his base, the priest introduced in 1897 the monthly magazine *Truth*, which soon achieved a national circulation of seventeen thousand subscribers. Two years later, the zealous clergyman founded an orphanage. Two more years passed, and he opened a missionary training center, *Regina Apostolorum*, which he hoped would attract and develop priests to assist him in his mission. In 1903, he began publishing the magazine *The Orphan Boy* to earn income for the orphanage. Price's two magazines continued in publication long after his departure from North Carolina, but the orphanage and the apostolic school eventually closed.

While attending a national meeting of the Catholic Missionary Union in 1904, Price listened to a lecture given by James A. Walsh, a priest of the archdiocese of Boston. Walsh was working in Boston for the U.S. Bishops' Office of the Propagation of the Faith. Walsh suggested that interest in home missions would develop, if the United States developed a greater interest in the foreign missions. In the *Truth*, Price wrote editorials about the mutual benefits of home and foreign missions. Price and Walsh exchanged correspondence, in which Price expressed support for Walsh's idea.

On the last day of the Eucharistic Congress at Montréal in 1910, Price and Walsh met again. They agreed to establish a mission-sending society of priests and brothers. Price enjoyed great contacts. His former pastor, for whom Price oftentimes had served daily Mass, was James Gibbons, who later became the Cardinal Archbishop of Baltimore. Gibbons agreed to support the missionary proposal. Price contacted too a former classmate from St. Charles Seminary in Catonsville, Maryland; William O'Connell, the Archbishop of Boston. Price requested that Walsh might be released from the archdiocese to develop the foreign missionary society. Price, who already enjoyed a national reputation as editor and publisher, gained the support of the U.S. bishops, who on April 27, 1911, approved Price and Walsh's proposal. Price and Walsh traveled to Rome, where on June 29, 1911, the Congregation for the Propagation of the Faith approved the U.S. Bishops' recommendation for the foreign mission society, and the next day Pope Pius X met with the co-founders, and blessed them in their new work.

The enterprise between Price and Walsh in founding Maryknoll suffered a difficult gestation. Price wanted his North Carolina missions, or national home missions included in the scope of the new society, whereas Walsh and Gibbons preferred to limit the focus to foreign missions.

Price wanted the Philippines and Latin America to be included in the society's field of labors, whereas Walsh preferred to limit the area to places already under the auspices of the Propagation of the Faith. Walsh's view prevailed both times.

During the community's early years, Price's primary responsibility consisted of promoting interest in the foreign missions, and to recruit candidates and raise funds for the new society. He traveled mainly along the East Coast and throughout the Midwest.

One biographer describes Price's spirituality as Christocentric, Marian, and based in humility.[444] Price frequently quoted the Pauline declaration, "It is no longer I who live, but Christ who lives in me" (Gal 2:20).[445] Price sought no glory for or attention to himself but only for the Master. The Blessed Mother played a key role in Price's spirituality. Four times, he visited the shrine of Our Lady at Lourdes. His Marian devotion developed a mystical depth. Beginning on August 21, 1908, until the day he died in 1919, he wrote daily letters to Mother Mary, totaling three thousand eighty-seven. He practiced humility to heroic degrees, by readily accepting personal humiliations, and actively seeking to live simply.

In 1918, when Walsh asked Price if he would serve as superior of Maryknoll's first missionaries to China, Price readily accepted. He labored in Yeungkong, China for nine months, until he became ill with an infected appendicitis. He died on September 12, 1919, in Hong Kong, and there was buried. People at Yeoungong described Price, named P'o Shan Foo, as "he was virtue."[446] In 1936, his remains were brought to Maryknoll, and lain beside James A. Walsh, his colleague in co-founding the missionary society.

*For further information, contact*
Maryknoll Fathers And Brothers
P. O. Box 304
Maryknoll, New York 10545 U.S.A.

☙

## 29. ✠ Venerable Pablo Anda y Padilla

*Places: San Luis Potosi, San Luis Potosi; and León, Guanajuato*
*Fame: Zealous pastor. Founder of the Minim Daughters*
*of Mary Immaculate.*

A man of action! Having been educated by the priests of the religious community founded by Saint Vincent de Paul, Father Pablo Anda y Padilla (1830-1904) mirrored in his priesthood the vision and virtues learned from that saint.[447] As Vincent became renowned as the patron of charity in Paris, so too Pablo became renowned as patron of charity in San Luis Potosi and León.

PABLO ANDA Y PADILLA

At seventeen, this kind and capable youth left home to enter the seminary at León, in the neighboring state of Guanajuato. The priests there, he had met already when he was traveling on one of his father's business trips. For nine years at León, Pablo studied the liberal arts, philosophy, and theology. An additional year of study was spent at the seminary in San Luis Potosi, where he served as secretary to the bishop of San Luis Potosi, and as member of the town council. Upon completing his studies, Pablo was ordained in 1856. The new priest traveled back to León to offer his first Mass at the parish administered by the Vincentians. "His gratitude for the Paulinos [known as the Vincentians in the U.S.A.], his teachers, undoubtedly obligated him to return to León in 1856 to celebrate his First Solemn Mass."[448] After Mass, he returned right away to San Luis Potosi.

At San Luis Potosi, Father Pablo distinguished himself by his creativity and charity. The region was engulfed in the longstanding war between pro-Catholic and anti-Catholic political factions. The wounded from both sides lay on the battlefields. Father Pablo took it upon himself to aid all those in need, regardless of their political party; he heard confessions, said Mass, and assisted in wrapping bandages as needs arose. In the midst of the fighting, when the local hospital could not care for the high number of wounded, Father Pablo opened a small hospital to offer medical treatment to all those who sought it.

The war devastated the local economy, and many noncombatants suffered privations of food, clothing, and shelter. In 1864, he established in his parish a Saint Vincent de Paul Society, whose members sought out and assisted the most needy persons in the area. To educate children, who were attending no school, he founded an elementary school. To prepare unemployed workers for future work, he opened a trade school.

When the pope established in 1863, a new diocese in the nearby region of León, the bishop-elect asked Father Pablo if he might join the new bishop. Father Pablo spoke with his bishop of San Luis Potosi, who approved the priest's disassociation from San Luis Potosi, and incardination in the diocese of León.

Father Pablo, in 1865, entered enthusiastically into his new mission area. The next year, the bishop appointed him chaplain of the cathedral choir and master of ceremonies for all services held at the cathedral. In 1870, Father Pablo initiated as an annex to the cathedral the construction of the Sanctuario de Nuestra Señora de Guadalupe. The priest rolled up his sleeves, and joined the workers in this labor of love. Four years later, he added to the Sanctuario by developing a house of spiritual exercises for those who wished to advance further in the spiritual life.

The government's warring against the Church and its religious orders led in 1875, to the eventual exile of the beloved Daughters of Charity, who were famous for their charities and social services. Who would provide these services to the people? Father Pablo called upon the *Hijas de María* to assist him. The *Hijas de María* helped both in the clinic which he had created in his own home to serve wounded soldiers, and in the school which he had founded to educate abandoned children. In 1886, he wondered aloud to some members of the *Hijas de María*, if they might consider forming under his direction a new religious community. Four took up the invitation, and as director, Father Pablo named them the Minim Daughters of Mary Immaculate. In 1887, the first seven novices took permanent vows. The community devoted itself to ministries in hospitals, schools, and homes for the elderly. The motto of the community was, and remains, "Love and sacrifice for God and others."

Countless activities occupied Father Pablo's time and energy. In almost fifty years as a priest, he had founded hospitals and clinics, schools and vocational training programs, which aided children, elderly, soldiers, and workers. In doing these things, he pursued the goal of

Christlike charity, through the means of innovative programming, in a manner of humility. He trusted in the Providence of God to assist him to accomplish all that needed to be done. Once, the sister in charge of feeding the children at the Casa de Niñas de San Vicente, told him in the morning that she had no money to feed the children that afternoon. Pablo responded by saying, "I will go say Mass; the Lady will provide."[449] During Mass, an anonymous benefactress knocked on the door of the school, and handed the sister the exact amount of money which she had just told Father that she needed.

Pablo loved to sing, and to write poetry. An excerpt from a poem and prayer in honor of Our Lady of Guadalupe follows. Unfortunately, this author's translation fails to communicate the mellifluous rhyme and rhythm of the original author.

> Arouse in our suffering hearts, O Mother, your great zeal.
> Did not you, O Virgin, descend from heaven to México to fill us
>     with your blessings.
> Will you permit an enemy, bloated with anger and impiety,
> To blind the eyes which the Lord has entrusted to his poor priests?
> Impossible! Purest Maiden!
> Our eyes are always upon you, imploring your aid
> Because in heaven, you are our Star; and in México, you are our
>     Queen and Protectress.[450]

Exhausted by almost a half century of labors, Father Pablo's health began to deteriorate. In 1903, he voluntarily resigned from his position as chaplain to the cathedral choir. The next year, the bishop regretfully asked for Father Pablo's resignation as director of the Minims, and of houses of mercy. Father Pablo acquiesced humbly. In June of that same year, the elderly priest collapsed at the altar at the end of Mass. He was carried to bed, where the sisters visited him, thanked him, and prayed with him. The next day, June 29, 1904, he died.

*For further information, contact*
Hijas Minimas de María Inmaculada
Calle Hermosillo 425
Apartado Postal 93
84040 Nogales, Sonora, México

## 30. ✠ Venerable Pierre Toussaint

*Places: Haiti; and New York City, New York*
*Fame: Proud to be black. Proud to be Catholic.*
*Slave, husband, father, hairstylist, philanthropist.*

Among the cardinal archbishops buried at St. Patrick's Cathedral lies only one layman, Pierre Toussaint (c. 1766-1853).[451] His contemporaries regarded him as a saint.

PIERRE TOUSSAINT

Pierre practiced his Catholic faith in exemplary fashion. Every morning at six o'clock, he attended daily Mass and said the rosary at the only Catholic Church in New York City, namely, St. Peter's on Barclay Street, eight blocks north of Wall Street. He assisted Elizabeth Ann Seton at her home at Battery Park in raising funds for orphaned children. After she became a Daughter of Charity, Pierre supported that religious community's charities for decades. When the city's orphanage would not accept black children, he opened an orphanage in his own home, and contributed generously to the construction of a private orphanage. To teach Negro boys a skill, when it was illegal to educate Negroes, he started the first school for black children in the city. To the nascent religious community of Negro nuns, the Oblate Sisters of Providence, he donated generously. For fellow refugees from Haiti, he provided food, clothing, and shelter. For French aristocrats, who had fallen on hard times after the collapse of their fortunes in Haiti, he discreetly aided those who were too proud to beg. When a yellow fever epidemic struck New York City, and approximately half of the population of two hundred thousand fled from the city, he remained behind to nurse the sick, and twice, he brought sick men into his home, one, a priest with typhus, and another, a white man, sick with yellow fever.

Pierre was born in Saint Dominique (now Haiti), into a third generation slave family on the plantation L'Artibonite, which the Frenchman

Jean Jacques Berard owned. Because Pierre worked as a domestic servant rather than a field hand, he was taught to read, write, play the violin, and exercise the etiquette of the elite class.

In Haiti in 1791, unrest was boiling among slaves who numbered four hundred fifty thousand of the island's five hundred twenty thousand people.[452] Slaves suffered the inhumanity of the economic system, and many of them suffered brutal physical conditions. Anticipating a bloody rebellion, Monsieur Berard moved his family to New York City. He took his wife Marie, whom he had married the previous year after his first wife had died of tuberculosis, Marie's two sisters, plus five domestic slaves including Pierre and his sister Rosalie, with the permission of their mother and grandmother, who were trusted employees of the Berards. In 1791, rebellion arose, and escalated into full-scale revolution. In the fighting, both the French and the slaves committed atrocities. In 1801, Berard returned to the island, investigated the situation, and wrote to his wife, that the family's property had been "irretrievably lost."[453] A little while later, a second letter arrived for Madame Berard, informing her that Jean Jacques had contracted pleurisy and died.

Madame Marie Berard was heartbroken. She was also penniless, and creditors kept knocking at her door. Her brother moved in, but neither he nor she had marketable skills. She married Gabriel Nicholas, but he too was dependent. She became depressed. Pierre rescued her and the situation. He provided the income for the entire household. At the earlier suggestion of Monsieur Berard, Pierre had become apprenticed to a hairdresser in New York City, and acquired that skill. He become popular with the wealthiest women in the city, "many of whom spent as much as a thousand dollars a year on their tresses."[454] Madame Berard wanted to grant Pierre manumission, but he refused. He felt a Christian duty to assist the struggling Berard family. He accumulated some money and used this to assist the Berards, to purchase manumission for other slaves, and to aid the poor.

In 1807, at thirty-two, Madame contracted tubercular laryngitis. Soon, unable to speak, she grasped the hands of Pierre, and with her eyes expressed profound gratitude to him. The two had arranged that upon her death, Pierre would receive manumission.

Pierre's business prospered. He inherited the Berard home, and married in 1811, a former slave from Haiti, Juliette Gaston, who had lived in New York City for many years. The couple, unable to conceive, adopted the six-month-old orphan of Pierre's sister, whose husband had abandoned her and their infant. Eventually, Pierre purchased a home at 144 Franklin Street, from where he walked to his shop at 141 Canal Street. The orphan Euphemia was quite sickly, and succumbed to tuberculosis at fourteen.

Customers appreciated Pierre's skill in hairdressing, but over time people appreciated more his closeness to God, and good counsel. He readily quoted the Sermon on the Mount, the Beatitudes, *The Imitation of Christ*, and the French spiritual writer Bossuet. When a customer would ask for some news about another client, prudently Pierre would reply in broken English, "Toussaint dresses hair; he no news journal."[455] Clients sought him for the opportunity to speak at meaningful levels with him. "Many [of his customers] called him 'Our Saint Pierre'."[456] The hairdresser spoke comfortably and confidently spoke about his faith, and the wisdom he had gained in church.

> He explained the teachings of the Church with a simplicity so intelligent and so courageous that everyone honored him as a Catholic. He would explain our devotion to the Mother of God with the utmost clearness, or show the union of natural and supernatural gift in the priest, or quote our great spiritual writers in a way to account best for the faith that was in him. . . . He had a strong sense of the dignity of being a creature of God, and no outward circumstances of birth, of station or even of bondage could lessen his interior contentment.[457]

Juliette and Pierre enjoyed forty years of marriage. "She proved a perfect helpmate: happy, fun-loving, kindness itself. She was as interested in Pierre's charities as he was."[458] He writes of her, "I would not change her for all the ladies in the world! She is beautiful in my eyes."[459] Shortly after their fortieth anniversary, Juliette died. Pierre buried his wife next to their daughter Euphemia. Pierre missed Juliette terribly; after her death and before his, he spent two lonely years.

Four days before Pierre died, one of his wealthy longstanding customers, Eliza Hamilton Schuyler visited him at home. Their conversation began this way, she writes, "When I entered, he revived a little, and looking up, said, '*Dieu avec moi* — God is with me'." When I asked him if he wanted anything, he replied with a smile, "*Rien sur la terre* — Nothing on earth."[460] Poetically and prophetically, one admirer has described this candidate for sainthood, as "God's reflection in ebony."[461]

*For further information, contact*
Pierre Toussaint Guild
P. O. Box 98
Bronx, New York 10471 U.S.A.

# JULY

## 1. ✝ Blessed Junípero Serra

*Places: San Diego to San Francisco, California*
*Fame: "Always go forward, and never turn back."*
*Founder of nine missions.*

Already well into his fifties, Junípero Serra (1713-84) was selected by his superiors to establish missions in the territory now known as California.[462] Traveling with the Spanish military, Serra, with a half-dozen friars, founded missions at San Diego (1760), San Carlos Borromeo at Monterey-Carmel, (1770), San Antonio (1771), San Gabriel (1771), San Luis Obispo (1772), San Francisco (1776), San Juan Capistrano (1776), Santa Clara (1777), and San Buenaventura (1782). In all these

JUNÍPERO SERRA

sites, Serra took action to protect, proselytize, and instruct the Native Americans. He regarded them as the "children of God." For contributing to the foundation and civilization of California, Serra's likeness was placed in Statuary Hall in the foyer of the United States Capitol.

Miguel José Serra, the third of his parents' five children, was born at Petra on the island of Mallorca, Spain. He received his education from the Franciscan friars at Petra and Palma. At sixteen, he entered the Franciscan novitiate, where he took as his religious name Junípero, and modeled himself after his Andalusian neighbor, the sixteenth century Franciscan missionary to America, Francisco Solano, who in 1726 had just been canonized. After six years of studying philosophy and theology, he was ordained a priest in 1738. He earned a doctorate degree in philosophy at Lullian University in 1742, and soon he was appointed to the Duns Scotus chair of philosophy. His first love, however, lay in preaching.

On Palm Sunday 1749, he learned from a former student, Francisco Palou, that the two had been assigned to the American missions. Serra departed Mallorca on April 13, 1749, and arrived at San Juan, Puerto Rico, where he preached his first mission in America. The ship continued on to the Mexican port of Veracruz, from where Serra traveled overland to México City, which he reached on New Year's Day 1750.

In México, he labored for the next thirty-four years. He journeyed to the Sierra Gorda Mountains, where he served approximately thirty-five hundred Pame Indians who lived "at the conjunction of the modern Mexican states of Tamaulipas, Hidalgo, San Luis Potosi, and Querétaro."[463] Serra so well formed the faith of the natives during his evangelization from 1750 to 1758, that in 1770 the bishop of the area removed these Native Americans from mission status and incorporated the tribe into the diocese.

Serra was re-assigned to the San Saba River region in central Texas. Attacks by Apache Indians, however, forced the Franciscans to leave that region. While waiting for further assignment, Serra was assigned to the College of San Fernando, from where he preached in the dioceses of México City, Puebla, Oaxaca, Valladolid, and Guadalajara. Later, Serra was sent to Baja California. "Texas's loss became California's gain."[464]

After the Spanish Crown expelled the Jesuit community in 1767, Baja California stood in need of missionaries. Franciscan authorities asked Serra to lead the mission in Baja California, which lies within current-day México. On April 1, 1768, Serra, plus twelve other friars, including Palou, moved to Baja California at San Fernando de Vilicatá.

Less than one year after Serra's entrance into Baja California, the Crown decided to enter Upper California as well. Again, Serra was chosen to head this mission. During the next fifteen years, from 1769 to 1784, Serra established the first nine of the famous California missions. He worked indefatigably, founding farms, rancherias, and schools. He learned six languages. Sufferings were enormous: hunger, stormy seas and a near shipwreck, and violent attacks and threats of attack from enemy Indians. He baptized over six thousand Native Americans, and confirmed over five thousand. He traveled on foot or by pack animal approximately four thousand three hundred miles.

Frequently he found himself at odds with the local Spanish military leaders. Captain Pedro Fages bullied his soldiers and disparaged the friars. This military man permitted his horsemen to chase Indian women, lasso them, rape them, and shoot dead the Indian men who rushed forth to defend their women. In 1773, Serra undertook an arduous two-thousand-mile journey from San Diego to México City to request directly to the viceroy that, among other things, Fages be removed. Of Serra's thirty-two recommendations, the viceroy accepted all but three, and Fages was removed.

Fages's successor was Captain Fernando de Rivera. Repeatedly, he refused to send soldiers with the friars to protect them as they advanced the extent of the mission. "Indecisive and dilatory, Rivera was inclined to find fault with plans that had not originated with himself and was immutable in the decisions at which he finally arrived."[465] The fearful captain watched from the safety of his presidio and ordered his soldiers not to leave the compound when Indians burned to the ground the San Diego mission and killed one of the friars. For this and similar inactions, Rivera was recalled in disgrace for having shamed the Spanish government.

Rivera's replacement was Captain Felipe de Neve, who attempted to transform Serra's missions into municipalities with native mayors. Serra, with his quarter-century experience with the Indians, regarded the transition as premature. The missions, as he intended, were to develop the natives from hunters into farmers, from illiteracy to learning to read and write the native language and Spanish, and from using primitive tools to working as carpenters, tanners, and blacksmiths.

When the Crown expressed interest in reorganizing the California missions and taking responsibility for administration from the Franciscans and handing it over to the Dominicans, Serra humbly agreed to surrender his ministry. He replied, "Let the most holy will of God be done for this vineyard of His, and since He so orders it, doubtless these workmen are more suitable."[466] Serra died before this decree was canceled.

In mid-August 1884, the frail but indefatigable friar, who had suffered for decades from a leg injury and asthma, contacted his friend Palou. Serra asked if his student might assist his teacher in dying. Palou rushed to Serra's side. For ten days, the two prayed together, until Serra's health no longer permitted that. On August 28, surrounded by his beloved Native Americans, Junípero Serra died. This philosopher-turned-missionary had fulfilled his personal motto throughout his ministry: "Always forward."

*For further information, contact*
The Cause of Padre Serra
The Old Mission
2201 Laguna Street
Santa Barbara, CA 93105 U.S.A.

## 5. ✠ Gérard Raymond

*Place: Québec City, Québec*
*Fame: "What now, Christ?" Boy saint.*

How profound a spirituality might a teenager have?[467] Gérard Raymond (1912-32) appeared normal in his academic, athletic, and social activities; however, in his spirituality, he was extraordinary. At fifteen, he received his priest spiritual director's approval to keep a journal, which he described as a "long conversation" with God.[468] His writings reveal a depth of union with God that canonized saints, even those much older than him, never wrote down.

Gérard's parents were exemplary in their practice of the faith. His father assured his children that each day, as he drove his trolley, he prayed. He explained, "In making my circuit in the downtown area, I pass before such and such a church, at such and such a time, and before each church and each time, I unite myself with the holy sacrifice of the Mass that is being offered inside."[469] Gérard's mother stayed at home on the farm, where she raised her eight children, of whom Gérard was the fourth. She prayed the rosary daily with her children, then weaned them so that each one would say the prayer on his/her own. She instructed the children in the faith long before

GÉRARD RAYMOND

they started school. When Gérard was five and a half years old, the parish priest visited the home and happened to question Gérard about the faith. So clear was the lad's understanding of the Eucharist, that the priest let the boy begin to receive Communion. From that moment on, Gérard received the Eucharist virtually every day of his life. A visiting priest, having witnessed the home life of the Raymond family writes the following for his Chemin parish bulletin in 1919:

> I know a family, a truly patriarchal family, poor in the material goods of this world, but rich in the spiritual blessings of heaven. After the mother is able to balance her humble weekly budget, she puts aside the remainder of the family's income for the poor. The children from an early age are formed in charity towards those who suffer. Each child has a little bank where he or she deposits money received, and all of this is intended for the poor; never does one of those children purchase a candy for him- or herself. The little Gérard (age seven) never accepts presents except for the poor. With what admirable joy he gives to the poor the savings from his little bank. How the angels of heaven ought to bless this precocious charity.[470]

Eventually, five of the eight children entered the seminary or convent. Two sisters entered the Congregation of Notre Dame. Another sister entered the White Sisters of Africa, but left for health reasons. Gérard hoped to become a missionary, but he had not yet decided which community to enter. A younger brother became a diocesan priest.

Gérard entered the Minor Seminary of Québec in 1924, at twelve. He writes in his journal in 1929, "Ever since my childhood, I have never thought about choosing any vocation other than being a priest."[471] He wished to live like Christ, become a missionary, and if it were God's will, die a martyr.

In the seminary, he earned a reputation for hard work and holiness. Natively intelligent, he always finished first or second in academic rank among his classmates. In his journal, he admits his achievement in the classroom, but never boasts of it; simply, he thanks God for his gifts. Devoted to the Eucharist, Gérard suggested to a classmate that the two would visit the Eucharist in every church they might pass as they walked. Gérard comments, "Jesus, our best friend, is there. Most often, he is alone. He invites us to enter. Why would we refuse? Some people might treat us like fools. So be it! "[472] He writes in his journal, "I have not found in my past life any grave sin."[473] On May 6, 1928, Gérard enters into his journal his commitment to pursue holiness.

> I am going to force myself to see in my hands, the hands of a future priest; in my feet, the feet of a future priest; in my eyes, the eyes of a future priest; in my senses, the senses of a future priest. I will work at seeing in my hands the hands which one day will hold the sacred Host, "the chalice of salvation." I hope to avoid also many faults. I wish to form in myself a soul worthy to receive the holy oil, a man worthy of carrying Jesus in my hands, of making Him descend upon the altar.[474]

At his annual retreat in September 1930, Gérard notes that he felt some discomfort on the right side of his stomach. He wondered what it might be, but offered it up: "As you wish, O God, do with me as you would wish. I accept with joy any suffering that you might send me."[475] In June 1931, with the discomfort still present, he confides that he is ready to die and to meet God, if that is what God wishes. He writes, "I wish to follow you, I wish to help you to win back sinners. . . . You gave your life, I will give mine."[476]

During the Christmas – New Year's holiday of 1931-1932, Gérard's sickness worsened. He returned to school, but attended only two days of classes. While in the infirmary, he suffered a hemorrhage on January 22. In mid-February, he was transferred to Laval Hospital. As he was being taken there, he said to his parents, "It is the will of God. Not a word more."[477] In mid-June, he received the sacrament of the sick. On the night of July 5, holding his rosary, nineteen-year-old Gerard, just six weeks shy of his twentieth birthday, died peacefully.

A week after the funeral, his mother discovered the journal. . . . It was written innocently, honestly, spontaneously. Considering that the journal would be an inspiration for all people and especially young people, extracts from the work were published in November 1932, and a month later, the journal was published as a small book. "Printed in French, twenty thousand copies were made. Then, the book was translated into several languages."[478] Gérard's short life made him a model for all youth who seek to know and do God's will.

*For further information, contact*
La Cause de Gérard Raymond
1, rue des Remparts
Québec, QC G1R 5L7 Canada

⌘

## 6. ✠ Catherine-Aurélie Caouette

*Place: Saint–Hyacinthe, Québec*
***Fame:*** *Author of "Sitio," her mystical meditation of Jesus on the Cross.*
*Foundress of Sisters Adorers of the Precious Blood, the first contemplative religious community founded in Canada.*

"Heaven has given you a highly favored child. Give thanks to God, and watch over your precious treasure," so advised the parish priest to the parents of eight- or nine-year-old Catherine-Aurélie Caouette (1833-1905).[479]

Catherine was not your ordinary child.[480] Many witnesses observed her experiencing mystical phenomena. At four or five, outside her home, as if in a trance, she would carry over her shoulder and drag on the ground a heavy piece of wood. When her father asked what she was

CATHERINE-AURÉLIE
CAOUETTE

doing, she explained that the wood symbolized the cross which Jesus carried. At six, she walked half a mile to attend daily Mass and remained in church praying, getting home at ten or eleven. Catherine's mother witnessed her daughter at age seven levitating as she came downstairs from the second to the first floor. The mother asked if Catherine were afraid of falling. The child replied, "No Mama, I have come down the stairs like that before ... since the time I went up the steps saying the Hail Mary at each step."[481] During First Communion classes, "her precocious intellect and her well-thought-out answers to his [the priest's] questions on sound doctrine" occasioned the priest to allow her to receive Communion immediately, at nine, instead of after the usual two or three years of instruction.[482] "When she received Communion for the first time, she developed a passion for the Eucharist. Her entire life would bear the imprint of it."[483] Catherine, the seventh of nine children, grew up at Saint-Hyacinthe, about fifty miles east of Montréal.

She received her formal education, from twelve to seventeen, at the boarding school of the Congregation of Notre Dame at Saint-Hyacinthe. "When it was time for recreation, everybody sought to draw her into their own little group, wishing to enjoy her conversation. A joyous geniality was her shining virtue, the one with which she clothed all her other virtues. This made her the favorite classmate, the closest friend of each of her companions."[484] At school, Catherine attended Mass daily, and joined the Children of Mary. Before the end of her first year, the school's priest-spiritual director, perceiving that Catherine was extraordinarily blessed, suggested that she write him a letter describing her spiritual experiences. After writing to the priest for the first time in 1846, she wrote five hundred seventy-seven more letters to him, who remained her spiritual director until his death in 1887.[485] One day in class, twelve-year-old Catherine declared that she was unable to finish a composition assignment. The sister-teacher, noticing that Catherine was red, apparently with a fever, said, "You are sick. Tell me about it, just as you would tell your Mama."[486] Catherine began to cry and said: "I am not sick, but I...I can't think of anything except what Our Lord told me this morning during Mass."[487]

The Passion of Christ attracted Catherine throughout her life. She writes, "O my God, I wish to return you love for love. I am ready to sacrifice for you in order to demonstrate how much I love you, how much I desire that you be loved."[488] At twenty, she made a private vow of virginity. The following year, she made profession as a Third Order

Dominican, and took the name Aurélie. She holds the distinction of being the first lay tertiary in Canada. Sensing that God might be calling her to institutionalize and publicize love for the Precious Blood, she approached her bishop at Saint-Hyacinthe, the Bishop of Montréal, and her spiritual director; then, in 1861, she founded the first contemplative community in Canada.

The number of community members increased rapidly. From the original four sisters in 1861, the community grew to seventeen by 1863, and to twenty-seven, within another three years. Besides the "cradle," at Saint-Hyacinthe, Mother opened houses in Toronto (1869), Montréal (1874), Ottawa (1887), Three Rivers (1889), Brooklyn, New York (1890), Portland, Oregon (1892), Sherbrooke (1897), Manchester, New Hampshire (1898), and Santa Cruz, Cuba (1902). The community received its dual motto in 1881, when, on the occasion of Bishop Moreau's approving the community's *Constitutions*, he and Mother Catherine wrote, each on an opposite side of a prayer card: he, "Fidelity, constancy, generosity"; and she, "*Sitio*, to adore, to repair, to suffer."[489]

Rapid growth brought dissension and dissipation of the founding spirit. Beginning in the mid-1880s, some sisters complained that Mother Catherine had become lax in following the "order of the day," and in applying the community rules to certain sisters. Mother, in fact, excused herself from community prayer when she was distributing food to the poor, providing spiritual counsel to souls, or resting because of her weak constitution. Some complained that she kept medicines in her own room, and that she received an excessive number of visitors. Regarding the *Rule*, she relaxed the *Rule* towards some sisters, whose health seemed unable to bear the community's severe fasts and disciplines. The critical sisters wrote to Bishop Louis-Zéphirin Moreau. After he received many complaints, he deposed Mother in 1882. He replaced Mother Catherine and her council with a new administration. Subsequently, he said on many occasions, "I have caused this poor Mother great sorrow, and I wonder how I can make her forget it."[490] Mother Catherine describes this period as her Calvary. Another sister, observing Mother, writes, "Our Mother is strong and sublime. She is bearing her suffering heroically."[491]

Moreau's newly appointed administrators did not satisfy the complaining sisters, so he called for new elections in December 1887. Over two-thirds of the sisters chose Mother Catherine as their superior. After serving two consecutive five-year terms, she could not be re-elected according to the *Constitutions* approved by the Vatican in 1896. Eligible for election again in 1902, Mother and another sister tied in the number of votes received. Mother withdrew her name, saying to the community, "I have no doubt of your filial affection and devotion. However, believe me, I would not finish my five-year term as superior."[492]

Dissipation of the founding spirit arose from the independence demanded by bishops into whose territory the community had expanded. Different bishops and diocesan-appointed spiritual directors unconsciously applied their diverse spiritualities to shape the sisters. During a visit to the house at Montréal, Mother was "wounded to the very depths" of her being after experiencing the sisters' "coldness of heart" towards her.[493] At that house, the local priest-spiritual director, a very reserved man, was forming the sisters according to his personality. The sisters did not want the local independence required by the bishops. Mother writes to the Bishop of Toronto, "What grieves me... is the prospect of complete independence among the various houses of the Institute."[494]

Catherine's spirituality focused on suffering with, in, and for Christ, in reparation for the sins of others, in adoration of the Eucharist and Precious Blood, and in honor of the Immaculate Mary. She suffered for Christ, in order to identify more with Christ. She fasted regularly, performed disciplines, suffered the dark night of the soul, and experienced, like Catherine of Siena, the invisible stigmata, which was received in Catherine-Aurélie when she was nineteen. Our Lord consoled her with classical spiritual phenomena: frequent visions, pervading sense of His presence, ecstasies, levitation, a physically burning heart, the wound of love, transfixion of the heart, and mystical marriage. Yet Catherine oftentimes tried to resist these consolations in order to experience more of Jesus' suffering. Her inspiration is summed up in her *Sitio*, which she composed, according to tradition, "during a night of exposition of the Blessed Sacrament leaning upon the little altar conserved at the Monastery at Saint-Hyacinthe."[495] Probably, she wrote the *Sitio* ("I thirst.") shortly before November 25, 1865.

Yes, our Jesus is all charity, He is the perfect model of love. Our souls, ravished by the charms of this Spouse of love, burn with the desire of resembling Him and of walking in His foot-steps; they choose the mountain of myrrh and the hill of incense for the abode of their exile. The way is short, the route is all traced: let us tread it, my friends, my sisters, in the train of the Spouse of Blood made victim for us, and desiring to continue in us, with us, and for us, that life of immolation and praise to the glory of His Father and for the greater good of souls. Our Love has been crucified, let us be crucified with Him; He has given us all His Blood, let us give Him all our love; let us bathe in His sacred wounds with tears of love. Upon the altar of the new Cavalry, let us daily immolate a thousand victims of love; let us, by our strains of love, repair the outrages He there receives.... I thirst to be, in turn, a victim with Thee; I thirst to share Thy sor-rows, to weep over the outrages and forgetfulness of sinners.[496]

Throughout Catherine's life, she received extraordinary spiritual phenomena. Bishops, priests, sisters, laity, and medical professionals attested to seeing effusions of blood flow from her forehead, hands, side, and feet, reminiscent of the wounds of Jesus Christ. A crucifix that she wore suspended near her heart emanated heat sufficient to melt wax and to burn the hand of anyone who touched it. These phenomena occurred especially at the moments that she received Holy Communion.[497] On Fridays, Mother Catherine-Aurélie remained in her room at the convent because on that day, "the Foundress endured some of the torments of the Passion."[498] Accounts abound about these and other singular phenome-na experienced by Mother Catherine-Aurelie.[499]

In March 1905, Mother's chronic bronchitis worsened. An inch-long cross began pulsating through the back of her left hand. Mother com-mented, "I want only the will of God."[500] In June, Mother suffered a series of heart attacks. On July 6, "holy Mother Caouette," as she was popularly known, died.

*For further information, contact*
Centre Aurélie-Caouette
2520, rue Girouard Ouest
C.P. 401
Saint-Hyacinthe, QC J2S 7B8 Canada

## 7. ✠ Blessed María Romero Meneses

*Place: Granada, Nicaragua; and San José, Costa Rica*
*Fame: Salesian nun — the female Don Bosco.*
*Social Apostle of Costa Rica.*

Just twenty-five years after her death, Sister María Romero Meneses (1902-77) was declared Blessed by Pope John Paul II. The rapidity of the process of beatification testifies to the unusual character, blessings, and achievement of her life.

María was the sixth of eight children born to Félix Romero Arana and his second wife Ana Meneses Blandon, after Félix's first wife had died childless. The family enjoyed great wealth and comfort from the father's position of Minister of Finance in the Nicaraguan government.

As a child, María manifested an affection for Our Lord and his Blessed Mother, and solicitude for the poor. Anecdotes from her childhood include her offering gifts to the infant Jesus in the Christmas crib, and to his statue in the family's kitchen. She gave to the poor her almost-brand-new clothes, which occasioned her mother to caution the daughter to be more selective in what she donated, to which the child replied, "But, mama, we're not supposed to give the worst things to the poor, but nice things, yes, to make them happy?"[501] At eight, she received her First Communion, about which she writes, "It was a day from heaven.... I felt Jesus' grace of predilection take hold of me."[502] At twelve, she contracted rheumatic fever, and lay paralyzed for six months, during which time her heart suffered permanent damage. Later, however, Maria experienced a miraculous healing. She writes about the incident, "I know that the Virgin takes care of me."[503] The next year, María joined the lay Daughters of Mary, in which sodality girls dedicated themselves to Jesus through Mary. María describes her entrance into the sodality as "one of the happiest days of my life; ... I felt I was in heaven."[504] At fourteen, she took a private vow of chastity, with the approval of her priest-confessor.

María's parents provided their daughter with a fine education. At home, tutors instructed the pre-school child. Paternal aunts then provided the elementary education in the private school which they operated. For secondary education, María studied with the Salesian Sisters at Colegio María Auxiliadora, where she learned the violin and piano, art appreciation and application, and the basic liberal arts.

At eighteen, she entered the religious Institute of the Daughters of Mary Help of Christians. Her spiritual director supported her entrance, but warned her of inevitable "pricklings" which one should expect in religious life.[505] She traveled to San Salvador, El Salvador, where she began postulancy, followed on January 6, 1920, when she entered the novitiate. When the novices were urged to meditate on the theme, "Lord, who am I," María heard the Lord say twice to her, "You are the chosen of my Mother and the dear one of my Father."[506] In preparation for her first vows, María writes, "Jesus, teach me to speak, work, and to live only in your love and by your love."[507] Upon completing the novitiate, María served as assistant to the novice mistress, which position she retained until 1925.

From 1925 to 1931, María worked in her home village of Granada. At the Colegio Maria Auxiliadora, María taught music and painting. During her stay at Granada, on the occasion of her final vows on January 6, 1926, María writes, "The Virgin wished of me a total and absolute dedication to live only by God and for God, promoting her devotion and giving me the means to do good for my neighbors. Such delicate treatment by the Virgin was truly for me a call to sanctity."[508] Others too began to notice her high degree of piety. Her spiritual director observed, "Sister María is an intelligent religious, and not yet a saint, but she lacks just a little to become one."[509]

For the next forty-six years, beginning in 1931, Sister María labored at San José, Costa Rica, where she taught girls of financial means. She instructed her students, "Religion is the science of the truth, the divine science which brings us the knowledge and the love of God. As Christians, we have the obligation to study our religion so that we might be able to keep burning the lamp of faith."[510] Having dedicated already much of her free time to teaching poor children, Maria organized her wealthy students to serve as catechists for the poor. She also directed skilled laborers to instruct the unskilled. Beginning in 1941, she formed

the school's alumnae and students into Catholic Action groups to perform service projects for the poor. In 1944, the archbishop suggested to
Sister María that she establish oratories throughout the *barrios* of the
poor. By the end of the next year, María had founded nine oratories.
Soon, the total number burgeoned to thirty. In 1945, the religious community asked Sister María to serve as their fund-raiser, at which she
excelled. Simultaneously, she approached the poor and asked for their
prayers for the rich. In 1953, she founded the first of her many food dis-
tribution centers. In 1961, she started a school to teach poor girls marketable skills. Five years later, she opened a medical clinic, where doctors and nurses volunteered services for the care of the poor. Next, she
opened The House of Mary Help of Christians to assist poor youth. In
her early seventies, in 1973, she organized lay volunteers to construct
homes for the homeless. Instead of seeking bank loans for the construction project, she involved the rich: "the women were to be employed in
the administrative work and the men, lawyers, engineers and other
industrialists would see to the actual construction."[511]

For almost half a century, Salesian Sister María Romero responded
affectively and effectively to the needs of the poor. In recognition of her
contributions, the hemispheric Union of American Women named her
in 1968 the "Woman of the Year." Popularly, this sister of the double
family of Saint Don Bosco was called the female Don Bosco, so closely
did her ministry reflect the founder's charism and achievements.
Seemingly indefatigable, one year before she died, María founded the
*Associación de Ayuda a los Necessitados*. She referred to this organization as
"the jewel of gold of my life," wherein other people would continue the
vision and work she had been performing.[512]

Like many saints, she had great trust in the Providence of God. One
day, after she had ordered bread for five hundred children, the baker
arrived with the bread, and the bill for five hundred *colones*. Sister María,
however, had no money. The story continues:

> María without getting agitated asked him [the baker] to wait
> a moment. Then she prayed to Our Lady asking her simply to
> "put your hand in here [the money box] before mine!" The door
> opened and a cooperator walked in saying to her joyfully, "I have

been able to sell that land... this is for you." She handed Sister María an envelope. It contained exactly five hundred *colones*.[513]

Sister María was admired and loved by many, especially the poor. Some people, however, in her religious community, the parish churches, and society at large criticized her efforts. A sister-biographer of María's community writes, "God alone knows the sacrifices, the number of prayers and tears that Sister María paid. Many times upsetment occurred because of misunderstandings, lack of appreciation, murmuring, and rejection which she suffered."[514] Undaunted, Sister María moved forward, whispering the prayer of St. Teresa of Ávila: "Let nothing disturb you. Let nothing frighten you. All things are passing. God alone remains constant. Whoever has God lacks nothing."[515]

On the fiftieth anniversary of her religious profession, seventy-five-year-old Sister María writes to God in her journal, reflecting on her vocation:

O happy exchange. In place of my father, you have given me yourself; in place of my mother, the Blessed Mother; in place of my brothers and sisters, the saints; in place of my friends, the angels; in place of my country, the whole world, and after that, heaven; in place of my will, your will; in place of my comforts, rest and peace in your heart; in place of my material riches, spiritual riches; in place of my earthly satisfactions, spiritual delights. Embracing the cross, I have encountered you, and live and die with you, to praise you eternally.[516]

Two years later, at seventy-seven, Sister María Romero was resting on vacation at Léon, Nicaragua. Looking out at the sea, she mused, "I see God in every drop of water in this sea. How beautiful it would be to die facing the ocean!"[517] A few hours later, she suffered a heart attack.

*For further information, contact*
Casa Provincial
Nuestra Senora de los Angeles
Apartado 664
2300 Curridabat, Costa Rica

## 9. ✠ Rose Hawthorne Lathrop

*Place: Hawthorne, New York*
*Fame: Poet, author, convert, wife, widow. Foundress of the Servants for Relief of Incurable Cancer.*

Rose Hawthorne Lathrop (1851-1926), a descendant of a blueblood Mayflower family, changed from being a socialite in New York City to being a religious sister serving poor outcast cancer patients in Manhattan's Lower East Side.[518] An acclaimed poet and short-story author, she had written *Along the Shore* (1888), *Memories of Hawthorne* (1923), and had co-authored with her husband *A Story of Courage: Annals of Georgetown Convent of the Visitation of the Blessed Virgin Mary* (1894).

ROSE HAWTHORNE LATHROP

At twenty-nine, this mother suffered the death of her only child, a four-year-old boy. At forty, she and her husband converted to the Catholic faith. Four years later, after short-lived separations from her alcoholic husband, she signed formal separation papers from this man, whom she loved even up to his death, three years later.

Searching for deeper meaning in life, Rose Hawthorne Lathrop made a private retreat with the Sisters of Charity of Halifax at Wellesley Hills. At the conclusion of this prayerful respite, she left with a gift implanted in her heart and soul, the maxim of St. Vincent de Paul, "I am for God and for the poor."[519] Her parents had blessed her with exemplary compassion for the "brotherhood" of all humanity. Father Damien of Molokai inspired her by his dedication to leprosy patients. The final impetus arose from her having about a young seamstress, who contracted cancer, but lacked funds to purchase medical care, and had to admit herself to the New York City almshouse on Blackwell's Island. There in the middle of the East River, were gathered hardened prisoners, the insane, and the incurably ill; all inmates on their journey to death. Rose writes, "A fire was then lighted in my heart, where it still burns. I set my whole being to endeavor to bring consolation to the cancerous poor."[520]

The medical profession and public citizens in the late nineteenth century viewed cancer as a contagious disease. Patients diagnosed with cancer had to leave their hospitals in order not to expose other patients to the dreaded disease. If a cancer patient possessed sufficient funds, then a nurse might come to that person's home. If a cancer patient were poor, then the sick person had to leave one's home and fend for oneself.

Profoundly moved by the plight of the cancerous poor, and desiring deeply to do God's will, Rose enrolled in a three-month nursing course at New York Cancer Hospital. After completing her studies, she gathered a few belongings and found lodging at One Scammel Street, in New York City's Lower East Side. Rose's home was a three-room tenement flat. From these quarters, she visited the poor, wrapped their bandages, cook their meals, cleaned their homes, and returned home each night to pray. Within one month, she began to receive the poor into her hovel. Initially, the experience was frightening. Eventually, the experience was lovely. Recalling her earliest days in this work, she says, "No description had given me a real knowledge of how dark the passages are in the daytime, how miserably inadequate the water supply, how impossible that the masses of the poor in tenements should keep themselves or their quarters clean."[521] She describes her purpose as "to take the lowest class we know both in poverty and suffering and put them in such a condition, that if our Lord knocked at the door we should not be ashamed to show what we have done."[522]

Rose needed assistance in caring for her patients. In the local newspapers, she appealed for basic material necessities and someone to join her in caring for the cancerous poor. The appeal concludes, "Let the poor, the patient, the destitute, and the hopeless receive from our compassion what we would give to our own families.... This is all, yet it requires the sacrifice of your life. But that is why Christ asked it and blesses with unending reward the simple choice.[523]

Alice Huber, thirty-six, read the appeal. She became intrigued. On December 15, 1897, she visited Rose on site. Both women might have seemed out of place in the Lower East Side. Rose's father had been the nation's beloved novelist, and had served as Consulate to England. Rose's mother Sophie Peabody traced her lineage to the Mayflower at Plymouth Rock. Rose' husband had worked as editor for the *Atlantic Monthly*. And Alice had studied and taught art for fifteen years. Her father was a prominent medical doctor in Lexington, Kentucky. Alice describes the context and conversation of the first meeting between her and Rose Hawthorne Lathrop:

> I had never been in the very poor part of any city before and I must confess that I hesitated going down Water Street after catching a glimpse of it from the corner. I came to a rickety frame building. I looked for a bell, but could find none; some children who were playing in the hall said, "If you are looking for Mrs. Lathrop, go to that door. . . . A fair, bright-faced woman, who was bending over an old woman bandaging up her leg rose from her work and came forward to meet me. . . . Mrs. Lathrop was youthful looking with a mass of reddish hair; she wore a nurse's dress and was simple and cheerful in her manner of dealing with the old woman . . . Everything about the place and neighborhood seemed perfectly repulsive to me. . . . As I looked at her, a great feeling of affection and pity came into my heart for her. . . . So, at last I mustered up courage and offered to help her one afternoon of each week.[524]

Three months later, March 1898, Alice moved into the Water Street home. One month later, Rose's husband George Parson Lathrop died at Roosevelt Hospital. The cause of death was liver disease. Elizabeth writes in her diary, "As I stood beside his body soon after death, the beauty, the nobility and exquisite gentleness of his life . . . spoke plainly to me of his virtues, and the welcome our Lord had given him into His rest. My own soul was trembling in the dark uncertainty of all unworthiness."[525]

In February 1899, a Dominican priest visited Rose's home at Water Street. He admired the charitable work being done by Rose and Alice. Noticing a statue of St. Rose of Lima, who was Rose Hawthorne's name saint, the priest suggested that the two ladies might want to become Dominican tertiaries like St. Rose of Lima. In September, with the approval of the archbishop, Rose and Alice became novice tertiaries, with Rose taking for her religious name Sister Alphonsa; and Alice, Sister Rose. In November 1900, the archbishop gave them permission to wear the Dominican habit, pronounce vows, and to form a community, which they called, The Servants of Relief for Incurable Cancer.

During the previous year, a wealthy non-Catholic benefactor whose Catholic wife had died of cancer, provided a new home two blocks away from the Water Street home, at 426 Cherry Street. The Cherry St. home sufficed for the women patients, but the men patients had to be located in surrounding tenements.

In 1901, a French Dominican informed Mother Alphonsa about a large property available for purchase, and perfect for her purposes. The French Dominicans, who had decided to return to France, owned nine hilltop acres on the Hudson River at Sherman Park (now Hawthorne), thirty miles north of New York City. On the property was situated a sixty-room building ready for occupancy by her patients. The sisters had little money, but lots of friends. Mother Alphonsa purchased the property for her new congregation. She named the place Rosary Hill Home. The next year, the townspeople changed the name of the village to Hawthorne in honor of the woman who brought the sisters to Westchester County. Thanks to the donated services of medical professionals, the work flourished. In 1912, the old St. Rose's Home was razed and a new St. Rose's Home was completed. In 1922, a Christmas holiday fire burnt down the home, and required a fund-raising campaign to build anew. For that project, Mother raised almost a quarter-million dollars.

In all her charitable work, Mother Alphonsa sought and accepted no monies from the sick. She feared that the poor might be neglected if money became a factor in caring for the patients. Donations were sought from the public and from wealthy benefactors, but no monies were accepted from the poor, their relatives, or the government. Mother Alphonsa begged for monies instead through her publication, *Christ's Poor*.

After thirty years of caring for the cancerous poor, and twenty-six years of leading her religious community, the ever energetic Mother Alphonsa began slowing down. One night, six weeks past her seventy-fifth birthday, she passed away peacefully in her sleep. At the time of her death, the community had grown to thirty-one members.

*For further information, contact*
Rosary Hill Home
600 Linda Avenue
Hawthorne, New York 10532 U.S.A.

## 10. ✠ Anthony Kowalczyk

*Places: Lac La Biche, St. Paul, and Edmonton, Alberta*
*Fame: Piety. Lay brother.*

Simplicity and piety characterized Anthony Kowalczyk (1866-1947), lay brother of the missionary Order of Mary Immaculate.[526] "Brother Anthony," as people affectionately called him since they had difficulty pronouncing his surname, manifested deep devotion to the Blessed Mother, and dedication to the menial tasks to which he was assigned.

ANTHONY KOWALCZYK

Born and raised in the village of Dzierzanow, near Poznan, Poland, Anthony was the sixth of a dozen children, of whom half survived into adulthood. His local parish was a regional shrine dedicated to Mary, Our Lady of Consolation. In this village, at home, and at the Marian shrine, originated Anthony's lifelong devotion to the Blessed Mother.

Anthony's formal education began at age seven and lasted six years. At thirteen, he went to work to help to provide for the family. Three years later, he became apprenticed to a blacksmith at Krotoszyn. At nineteen, hoping for better employment, he moved to the seaport city of Hamburg, in generally Protestant northern Germany. There his co-workers ridiculed his Catholic faith, religion, and pious practices.

> They abused him with vulgar language; at the least annoyance at work they uttered scandalous blasphemies and gloated over immorality. When Anthony blessed himself, they laughed him to scorn and humiliated him. Confused, angry and helpless, he was afraid that he would be tainted with this godlessness. He fell to his knees in a public place and shouted to heaven his faith in God.[527]

The tension and pressure he felt at work seemed to have contributed to a relentlessly burning and blinding pain in his eyes. A physician confirmed the physical nature of the condition but could not lessen the pain. In dire need of relief, Anthony stopped in a church and prayed before the altar dedicated to the Blessed Mother. As he prayed the Stations of the Cross, halfway through he felt a physical change in his eyes, removed the bandage, and marveled that he could see. Leaving Hamburg in favor of predominately Catholic southern Germany, he found work across the river from Cologne, at Mulheim. In his boarding house, the owner, a Mrs. Prunnenbaum, observed her pious houseguest, and suggested that he might join the same community of missionaries to which her son belonged, namely, the Oblates of Mary Immaculate. Twenty-four-year-old Anthony replied that he was too old. Mrs. Prunnenbaum kept encouraging Anthony to apply.

After being accepted into the religious order, Anthony traveled to Limburg, Holland, where he entered St. Gulach Novitiate in September 1891. After one year, one of his evaluators observes, "He is intelligent enough, and his education meets the requirements for the life of a coadjutor brother. His energy and virtues point towards a life of piety, with every promise that he will become a good religious. He appears to be devout and seems well suited for community life."[528] At the conclusion of the two-year novitiate, Anthony renewed his vows. At this time, 1893, he volunteered to minister overseas, but he was refused. The next year, he volunteered for Ceylon (now Sri Lanka). and his request was approved, but three days later, was withdrawn. Within a few days, he was assigned to St. Albert, in western Canada (now the province of Alberta). "His superior wrote this to Brother's new superior in Canada: 'He is the best among our coadjutor brothers, a saint in the making.'"[529]

Departing Holland on May 20, 1896, Brother Anthony arrived at Edmonton on June 11. He worked in the sawmill operated by the Oblates. Within weeks of his arrival, his hand became trapped in a conveyor belt, which crushed his right arm and fingers. He was "rushed" one hundred twenty miles over four days from Lac La Biche to Edmonton. The horse and wagon trip over bumpy roads, surrounded by stinging flies and mosquitoes in the boiling summer sun, exhausted the patient. By the time he arrived at the hospital, gangrene had set in, necessitating that the arm be amputated. No anesthesia was available, and medical personnel wanted to strap him to the operating table. He asked instead that they hand him his vow cross, which he grasped tightly throughout the operation without a word of complaint. Not until 1912 could doctors provide him with a prosthesis with a metal hook attached in place of his hand. In the intervening years, Anthony learned to live and work with one arm.

Anthony's superiors transferred him to nearby St. Paul, where he remained from 1896 for fifteen years, working with the Metis Indians, and white settlers. After fire destroyed that mission, he was assigned to St. John's College at St. Albert, where he remained from 1911 until he died in 1947. At St. Paul, he and two confreres built a rectory, convent, and boarding school for one hundred students; plus Anthony raised a couple of hundred pigs to help feed the students. At St. Albert, Anthony worked as blacksmith, handyman, gardener, chicken farmer, bell ringer and sacristan, all of which he performed well. At St. John's College, Anthony assisted countless boys; "he was always ready to help them: to repair a watch, cut a key for the locker, sharpen skates, or mend the frame of eyeglasses."[530]

Anthony was blessed with a deep devotion to the Blessed Virgin Mary. At the time of his work accident, he was clutching the rosary. At St. John's College, he built a Lourdes-like grotto in honor of Mary. Constantly, he was lighting vigil candles to Mary. Whenever a difficult task was given to him, he would fall to his knees, pray a Hail Mary, rise, and complete the task. He even gained the reputation of working minor miracles, by falling to his knees, praying to Mary, rising to find lost articles, and fixing apparently irreparable machinery. When the students asked Brother to pray for them before an exam, he responded, "Say an Ave."[531] Witnesses assert that he was "always praying" to the Blessed Virgin.[532] No doubt his devotion to the Blessed Mother sustained him when, in 1897, a harsh superior forbade him to receive Holy Communion except on Sundays for a period of three months, after Brother had asked to be relieved of some of his workload.

On September 17, 1945, Anthony missed morning prayers. Someone went to check on the almost octogenarian brother. They discovered him bloodied and bruised, with his eye badly swollen. Someone inquired, "Who did this to you, Brother?" He responded, "I don't know. I think it was the devil. He fought with me all night."[533] The community took the living saint to the hospital, where they healed his physical wounds, but the elderly man never recovered fully from this event. In less than two years, he died. After having spent his final days at St. John's College, "on his hands and knees weeding the garden," he went on annual retreat at nearby St. Albert, where two days later, he died.[534]

*For further information, contact*
Cause of Anthony Kowalczyk
Rev. Zygmunt Musielski, O.M.I.
71, Indian Trail
Toronto, ON M6R 2A1 Canada

## 13. ✠ Blessed Carlos Manuel Rodríguez

*Place: San Juan, Puerto Rico*
*Fame: Lay apostle of the liturgical movement. The second Latin American layperson after Juan Diego to be beatified.*

The cause for the canonization of Carlos Manuel Rodríguez (1918-63) stands unique in the modern annals of the *Index and Status of the Causes of the Saints*: the promoters for Carlos Manuel Rodríguez are the laity. All other causes are promoted by dioceses, archdioceses, or religious communities.

Carlos, who was called "Charlie," was the second of five children. When he was six, the family's store and home burned to the ground, and the young family moved in with the maternal grandmother who lived in Caguas, a suburb south of San Juan. At nine, Carlos heroically rescued an infant cousin who had been snatched up by a rabid dog; Carlos suffered bites and injuries in the process of freeing the child. At eleven, Carlos would pretend to celebrate Mass at home at a make-believe altar, with his two younger sisters playing as "altar boys."

At thirteen, he was diagnosed with ulcerated cancer. He lost his appetite, weight, and energy. Because of his weakened condition, his high school studies progressed at a slower pace than that of his peers. He graduated, and at thirty went to the University of Puerto Rico, but after one year his health required him to withdraw. At the time of his departure from the university, his grade point average was the highest possible grade: 4.0. Subsequently, after some initial lessons, he taught himself to play the piano and organ.

For many years, he worked as an office clerk, first at a business at Caguas, and later at the University of Puerto Rico in the Agricultural Experiments Station. In both places he started Liturgy Circles, whereby he instructed fellow employees in the liturgical changes that scholars were discussing, and which would be promoted after Vatican II. To prepare himself for this apostolate, Charlie read voraciously, and prayed constantly. His favorite encyclicals included Pope Pius XII's *Mystici Corporis* (1943) on the unity of all peoples in God, *Divino Afflante Spiritu* (1943) on the desired use of archeology, history, linguistics, and other sciences in the study of the Scriptures, and *Mediator Dei* (1947) on the liturgical movement. Some of his most admired and most quoted spiritual authors included St. John of the Cross, St. Teresa of Ávila, and Ven. Charles de Foucauld. Theologians whom this layman regularly read included Jean Danielou, Henri de Lubac, Ives Congar, and Karl Rahner. In front of his typically Puerto Rican home-altar, he prayed daily a shortened form of the Divine Office.

As he saw the Liturgy Circles enjoying success, he perceived a growing number of students and adults losing their faith in an increasingly secular society. He resigned his university position, and devoted himself full-time to the evangelization of the Puerto Rican people.

To evangelize youth, he formed youth groups and taught high school students the basics of their faith. So that his students would better understand better the Mass, he translated the common parts of the Mass from Latin into Spanish. He suggested to priests that the Mass should be celebrated in the vernacular, with the priest facing the people, in order to encourage lay participation in the Mass. He emphasized that the apex of the church's liturgical year was the celebration of the Easter Vigil, about which he used to teach, "We live for that night."[535]

To reach a wider audience with permanent impact, he published his teachings. He wrote *Christian Life Days* so that students might better understand the Church's liturgical year. Using his own money, he started the magazine *Liturgy and Christian Culture*. Active in his parish, he belonged to various societies, including the Brotherhood of Christian Doctrine, the Holy Name Society, and the Knights of Columbus.

Companions loved to hear Charlie's many wisdom-sayings:

"There are no easy ways to do difficult things."

"Shallow are the souls that have not suffered in their lifetimes."

"Great men inevitably have to endure great misfortunes."

"Whoever is embarrassed to ask questions will never arrive at the truth."

"The best philosophy is that which best prepares us for death."

"There is only one sadness, that is, not becoming a saint."

"Whoever wishes to do great things only, and not to do little things, exposes himself to doing nothing."

"Whoever has not loved cannot be good."

"Passion is neither good nor evil; it depends on you. The saints were almost always people of great passion, but so were evil-doers. Be careful."

"Sanctity is not the negation of human life. Saints have lived as kings, artisans, preachers, doctors, priests, painters, and poets."[536]

One of the professors who participated in the Liturgy Circle at the University of Puerto Rico writes about Charlie:

Charlie was an extraordinary person: simple, a good communicator, generous, with an unquenchable faith in the Lord, and a good sense of humor. He lived for the Lord. He possessed an incredible capacity for work. . . . He seemed always to be contented, desirous of sharing with others his love and his surrender to the Lord. His faith was translucent. He possessed a generosity — all his money went to buying books and materials for disseminating the word of the Lord.[537]

*For further information, contact*
El Circulo Carlos M. Rodríguez
Centro Universitario Católico
Mariana Bracetti #10
Río Piedras, Puerto Rico 00925

## 22. ✠ Venerable Anna Bentivoglio

*Place: Evansville, Indiana; Omaha, Nebraska;*
*and New Orleans, Louisiana*
*Fame: "I will God's will." Foundress of the Poor Clares*
*in the United States.*

Extraordinary perseverance in doing God's will characterized Mother Mary Magdalen Bentivoglio (1834-1905).[538] Mother Magdalen and her older sister, both by blood and in religion, Sister Constanza, were selected by their Poor Clare community to establish a cloister of strict observance in the United States. This expansion had been requested by Pope Pius IX, was supported by the Franciscan Minister General, and a Third Order convent in Minnesota had requested the presence of the Poor Clares. The process of starting the monastery, however, occasioned for the foundress rejections, misunderstandings, dire poverty, false accusations, and even temporary banishment from the convent which she had founded and in which she was serving as abbess.

Born the twelfth of sixteen children, and baptized Annetta, she was called Countess because her aristocratic father was a Count. Annetta followed by four months her older sister Constanza into the monastery at San Lorenzo. While Constanza kept her secular name as her religious name, Annetta took the name Mary Magdalen of the Sacred Heart of Jesus. After ten years at San Lorenzo, Magdalena and Constanza transferred from the Poor Clares of the Urbanist Rule to the stricter Sisters of the Primitive Observance of San Damiano. The Minister General approved their transfer. At the same time, the pair traveled, under obedience, from Rome to New York City. A Franciscan priest, Paolino of Castellaro, traveled with the two sisters as their chaplain.

Upon arriving in the New World in October 1875, the sisters encountered a series of rejections. The supposedly host Franciscans at Minnesota communicated that they were expecting an active and not contemplative community, i.e., teaching sisters, not cloistered nuns. At New York , their chaplain announced that he opposed the sisters'going to Minnesota, and recommended that they remain in New York City. Mother Magdalen, who had been named abbess, before she and her sister left Rome, approached the cardinal of the Archdiocese of New York. The Cardinal had no time for the sisters, telling them "their form of life was contrary to the spirit of the country."[539]

The pair moved on to Philadelphia, where the archbishop welcomed them with open arms. Two months later, however, the archbishop, whom the cardinal of New York had contacted and influenced, withdrew his approval for the proposed monastery. The archbishop explained that the sisters' kind of community was contrary to the apostolic direction of the United States. The archbishop added that since the sisters' chaplain was no longer acting as their director, the two sisters would have to leave his archdiocese.

Mother Magdalena and her sister, on the advice of other women religious, traveled to Cincinnati, which had the reputation of being the "Rome of America."[540] The sisters went there without invitation, and discovered there that the view current in the archdioceses of New York and Philadelphia, prevailed in Cincinnati too. "The bishops sought to recruit these cultured ladies as teachers, nurses, social workers, and catechists, but these ministries were not part of the vocation of a Poor Clare."[541]

Archbishop Perche of New Orleans personally invited the sisters to his archdiocese. They arrived in March 1877, and their first postulant joined them there. Soon the sisters received a visit from the German Franciscan Provincial of the Holy Cross, who was visiting his houses in middle America and had been delegated authority over Mother Magdalena. The visitor found the monastic life in Mother's convent to be exemplary, but he considered them too removed geographically from other Franciscan houses, thereby not providing the sisters with ample Franciscan direction. This provincial ordered the sisters to leave New Orleans. The provincial suggested that the women consider Cleveland, where he was hoping to consolidate two communities: Mother Magdalen and her group from Italy and another Franciscan group from Holland.

Mother Magdalen, her sister, and the postulant arrived at Cleveland in August 1877. "The convent was a converted cigar factory."[542] Five months later, the Italian sisters welcomed into their home the Carmelite

Sisters from the Netherlands. The two communities did not mix well; they differed in languages, *Constitutions*, traditions, and habits. The bishop and priest-provincial could not understand how these things mattered. Most basically, the two visions differed: the Collettine Poor Clares followed a relaxed rule, whereas the Poor Clares of the Primitive Observance adhered to St. Clare's strict rule. Five months after the Dutch sisters arrived, Magdalena and her sisters left. They returned to New Orleans, where they knew people wanted them.

Shortly after their arrival at New Orleans in May 1878, the bishop of Omaha invited the sisters to establish themselves in his diocese, which in those pioneer days included the entire state of Nebraska. The philanthropic Creighton family offered to build a home for the sisters. The first construction collapsed during a tornado in 1878, and by 1882 the Poor Clares moved into their monastery. At Omaha, the sisters achieved their first foundation after attempts in four cities over seven years. At Omaha, "several postulants were admitted and two sisters transferred from an active religious community."[543]

New Orleans developed a second community of Poor Clares of the Primitive Observance. That burgeoning community sought the presence and advice of Mother Magdalen. The Minister General advised Mother to travel to New Orleans, but not to share with the host bishop in Omaha that she would be absent. When the bishop in Omaha discovered Mother's absence, he became insulted at her lack of communication, and, as he perceived it, lack of respect. Mother begged forgiveness, which the bishop accepted.

Suddenly, at Omaha in 1888, a controversy erupted among the sisters, who had circulated rumors inside and outside the convent about the behavior of the abbess and her sister, the vicar-abbess. "Mother Maddalena and her sister, Constanza, were shamefully denounced by an emotionally unstable sister as guilty of irregular personal conduct, alcoholic intemperance, financial mismanagement, and acting without due deference to the bishop.[544]

The bishop was inclined to believe the rumors. In June 1888, he called for a formal canonical investigation into the charges. When no substance was found to support the accusations, he asked for another investigation, which was undertaken in November. The same results occurred. The Bishop of Omaha asked the Bishop of Cleveland for his opinion of the Poor Clares. The bishop wrote from Cleveland: "My present conclusion is — there is no place in the American Church for drones and non-workers such as are the Poor Clares."[545] The bishop of Omaha called for a third trial in February 1889. The accused pair were never told the charges against them and were never interviewed. The Minister General in Rome criticized the unjust manner in which the trial had been conducted. "He denounced it in the strongest terms and designated it as 'pharisaic'."[546] Again, the results supported none of the accusations. All the same, the bishop ordered a formal interdict upon the cloister: no Masses were to be celebrated, no communions were to be distributed, no Eucharist was to be reserved, and no postulants were to be accepted. In the midst of this turmoil, Rome intervened. In September, three priests visited the convent, asked Mother Magdalen and Sister Constanza to leave the convent for the two-week duration of the investigation. The pair received hospitality from the local Sisters of Mercy. On the final day of the investigation, the two sisters who had initiated the charges failed to show up to present their case; they had skipped town the previous night. All charges were dropped. About their return to their faction-ridden convent, Mother Magdalen writes, "Our hearts were filled with sorrow together with joy. We did not know why; it seemed that the very air we breathed was cause of sorrows."[547] In January 1890, the bishop received a letter exonerating from all guilt the Bentivoglio sisters.

Throughout this nineteen-month ordeal and two-week banishment from the convent, Mother Magdalen remained prayerful, peaceful, never angry, even humorous on occasion, and always solicitous for the troubled sisters who had fanned the flames of hatred and calumny.

A third foundation developed in Evansville, Indiana. A young candidate whose father owned and operated a lumber yard offered to use her eventual inheritance to build a Poor Clare monastery in Evansville. Four years later, when the father died, Mother Magdalen and three other sisters headed there. The sisters lived there literally on bread and water; they suffered near-starvation. The townspeople, having heard that the two sisters were countesses, imagined incorrectly that the sisters were wealthy. A fourth foundation was begun in Boston, but was not yet completed when Mother became deathly ill.

Death loomed for the aging sisters. In 1902, Constanza passed to the Lord. Three years later, Mother became deathly ill. She asked that the sisters lay her on a mat on the floor in imitation of St. Francis of Assisi. The sisters did so, and kept praying for her restoration. Finally, Mother asked the sisters no longer to pray that her good health be restored. She wanted to "be allowed to go home."[548]

*For further information, contact*
Monastery of St. Clare
6825 Nurrenbern Road
Evansville, Indiana 47712 U.S.A.

## 25. ✠ Dario Acosta Zurita

*Place: Veracruz, Veracruz*
*Fame: Ordained three months. Martyr.*

After a crazed former seminarian attacked him, the Governor of Veracruz, Colonel Adalbert Tejada, retaliated by terrorizing Church leaders and destroying church buildings. He ordered his henchmen to intimidate priests into stop saying Mass. Ironically, the anticlerical murders by the government galvanized the people into demonstrating in support of the Church and her priests. The reaction of the faithful masses confirmed Tertullian's dictum: "the blood of martyrs is the seed of Christians."

The details of the murder were gathered in depositions taken at an ecclesiastical court between April 15, 1994, and October 23, 1996. The court concluded that Father Dario Acosta Zurita (1908-31) had been killed out of hatred for the faith and that sufficient grounds existed, based on his life of heroic virtues and reputation for sanctity, to advance the cause for the beatification of the priest.

On the morning of July 25, 1931, after the fanatical former seminarian had attempted to assassinate Governor Tejada, he vented his fury against other clerics. He ordered his henchmen to strike out against the Church in various towns and villages. In Veracruz, the priests had heard no news of these events and were unsuspecting of trouble.

In the Church of Our Lady's Assumption, which now serves as the Cathedral of Veracruz since the relatively recent erection of the diocese in 1962, three priests were busy in their ministries at approximately six o'clock in the evening. Father Rosas was in the pulpit instructing fifteen catechists. Father Dario, a twenty-three-year-old priest who had been ordained two months previously, was standing at the baptismal font, having just baptized an infant. Father Landa was standing at the front of the far nave. An anonymous man entered the church and said to Father Landa, "We are coming to attack you." The priest walked to the sacristy to look for the pastor, who was sitting there quietly. When the one priest relayed the threat to the other, the pastor asked the sacristan to see if anything unusual was happening in the church. The sacristan looked out into the church and reported that he saw nothing. Ten minutes later, with the three assistant pastors in their aforesaid locations within the church, between five to ten men according to different eyewitness, entered the church. They walked to the communion railing, stopped, and began shooting. Father Rosas ducked down and hid inside the pulpit. A bullet grazed his leg. Standing two or three yards in front of the attackers was Father Dario. A witness states that she heard the priest say to the gunmen, "If you have business with me, accompany me to the sacristy."[549] Before he reached the sacristy, however, the thugs shot him in the back. The young priest, riddled with bullets, fell into a pool of his blood, and exclaimed, "Jesus."[550] Father Landa froze. He neither ran nor defended himself. A gunman shot him in the face.

Panic erupted. People screamed. Some other adults and children had been shot, and some of the injured lay dying. Teachers instructed the children to lie down on the floor. Two of the Catholic Action boys, one of whom had been shot, were seized by the attackers. These youths were taken immediately to the police station and later were allowed to escape from there. The parish pastor ran to the scene of the murders, and shouted to the assassins, "Kill me too."[551]

An ambulance arrived quickly. Father Landa was rushed to the hospital. The bullet had entered his cheek, and exited through his throat. He survived. Father Dario, however, lay dead on the floor of the church. The murderers picked up his body and carried it away. Very early the next morning, they attempted to bury the corpse secretly. Some Catholics who had been observing the activities noted the location of the cemetery and the exact place of the corpse. The conspirators who deposited the body left no identifying name or number at the cemetery, only a rock to identify the place. Just as secretly, friends of Father Dario kept a careful, cautious watch over the location, lest enemies come and try to remove the body.

On the evening of the same day on which the murders had taken place, Bishop Guizar sent a letter to Governor Tejada. The shepherd writes, "Today Veracruz was watered with the blood of martyrs. The city will bear fruit from truth and justice, and from religion which instead of being extinguished in my beloved diocese will, like a well-pruned sprout, despite the force of bullets, shine brilliantly before the rock of God."[552]

The Secret Police, according to the testimony of one of the participating members, namely, Angel Ojeda Luna, received from the grateful governor within a few days after having committed the atrocity a gift of new pistols marked, "Star."

In order not to expose other priests and parishioners to state-sanctioned murder, the bishop ordered all churches to be closed until further notice. Six years, from 1931 to 1937, passed without public services. Shortly after the priest's death, the governor offered some token financial compensation. The bishop rejected the offering. Instead, the bishop visited the governor and challenged him. "You have given the orders to your troops to kill me whenever and wherever they might find me. You say that I do not wish that any of my diocesan flock be stained with my blood. Take your pistol and kill me. You have given that order."[553] The governor turned pale. He kept silent. Gathering himself, he took the bishop's hand and said to him, "Calm yourself. I take back the order."[554]

The people of the city committed themselves to keeping alive the memory of Father Dario. Privately and publicly, people prayed for his soul, shared memories of him, popularized him as a martyr. His mother who was a member of the parish, and had spoken with her son briefly after that morning's Mass, suggested that miracles might be sought in his name. People prayed regularly at his gravesite, adorning it with flowers and lit candles. Monthly, the faithful paraded with songs and prayers in procession to the church where Father Dario had been martyred. The crowd proclaimed proudly and loudly, "We are going to have a saint."[555] The people appreciated that their famous martyr originated from the insignificant town of Naolinco. In 1947, the Church transferred the priest's body from the cemetery, and placed it inside the parish church where the priest had been martyred. A translation of a hymn composed to memorialize Father Dario follows:

O Father Dario, you are in heaven. I hope in you. Bless your people.

You are the first light of Naolinco, having died for Christ in Veracruz.

From your youth, Jesus had called you to follow in his steps to the foot of the cross.

In the seminary, you modeled faith and other virtues as one sent from above.

Bishop Guizar y Valencia consecrated your hands so that you might bless all humanity.

By divine order, God charged you with teaching his teachings in your apostolate.

With great zeal, you converted souls and opened the gates of heaven.

You preached to the people with humble voice and sweet comfort for the glory of God.

Cruelly you were persecuted for following Christ, which was your choice.

Your mission of shedding light has ended, but the divine light now shines at Veracruz.

Your example of faith and courage in dying in the church of our Redeemer teaches those in search of teaching, even after the assassin's bullet silenced your voice.

O Father Dario, you are in heaven. I hope in you. Bless your people.[556]

*For further information, contact*
Arzodiócesis de Veracruz
Insurgentes Veracruzanos #74
C.P. 91700 Veracruz, Veracrua México

## 29. ✠ Nelson Baker

*Place: Buffalo and Lackawanna, New York*
*Fame: Businessman who became a priest. Founder of Our Lady*
*of Victory Homes of Charity.*

Successful businessman Nelson H. Baker (1842-1936), at the age of twenty-eight, gave up a promising career in booming Buffalo.[557] Feeling called to an "intangible more," he dedicated his life to praising God, and caring for tens of thousands of people. A few days after he died, the city newspaper printed this encomium about Nelson Baker.

NELSON BAKER

To have known Father Baker was to marvel at his energy and at the works that flowed from it.... To the hungry during his ministry he fed fifty million meals. During the depression at one time he was serving more than a million meals a year. He gave away a million loaves of bread. He clothed the naked to the number of a half million. He gave medical care to two hundred and fifty thousand and supplied medicines to two hundred thousand more. Three hundred thousand men, women, and children received some sort of education or training at his hands. A hundred thousand boys were trained for trades. Six hundred unmarried mothers in their distress knocked at his door and did not knock in vain. More than six thousand destitute and abandoned babies were placed in foster homes.... Men will give thanks that he lived and bless his memory.[558]

After ordination in 1876, Father Baker was assigned as assistant pastor to Limestone Hill in West Seneca, where St. Patrick's Parish oversaw both St. Joseph's Orphanage and St. John's Protectory. The young priest remained there for five years and observed the institutions sinking deeper into debt. When he arrived in 1876, the debt stood at $27,000. Five years later, the debt doubled to $56,000. Nothing that the pastor attempted reduced the debt. Assistant pastor Baker was frustrated; he asked for a transfer. He said to his bishop, Stephen Ryan, C.M., "St.

Joseph's and St. John's are doomed, ... and I cannot continue."[559] The bishop sent Baker to St. Mary's Parish in Corning. After one year, the bishop asked the priest to return to St. Patrick's and restore it to firm financial position.

Within a few hours of Father Baker's arrival, angry creditors were knocking at his door. Some of them recognized the former businessman, and took him on his word that he would pay what was owed them. Other less patient creditors, he paid out of his own pocket from savings earned while he had been in business.

Penniless, where would he turn? In prayer, he sought the assistance of Our Lady of Victory. Shortly thereafter, he founded a coast-to-coast mail-order fund-raising campaign. He wrote to U.S. postmasters across the country, asking each for the names of a few Catholic women who might donate to his orphanage and boys' home. Baker sent these women invitations to join the Association of Our Lady of Victory, at a cost of twenty-five cents a year. To keep the donors informed, he founded a newsletter called, *The Appeal for Homeless and Destitute Children*. Donations poured in, and within two years Baker paid off the institutions' entire debt. As donations kept coming in, he expanded the orphanage, and built a trade school. "They [orphan boys] learned tailoring, barbering, carpenter work, glazing, laundering, plumbing, electrical work, shoemaking, photography, sign-painting, painting and printing."[560] In the orphanage's chapel, he placed a statue of Our Lady of Victory. To publicize to donors the benefits that they had made possible, Baker started a magazine, *The Annals of Our Lady of Victory*.

Running low on money, he wondered if natural gas might be discovered on his property, as gas had been discovered a few miles away, across the Niagara River in Canada. After much prayer and consideration, Baker asked the bishop for money to dig a well. The bishop hesitated, then relented, and gave the priest two thousand dollars. The drilling crew arrived and inquired about the location of the drilling site. Father Baker replied that he would point out the site that afternoon.

At exactly four p.m., the doors of St. Patrick's flew open and a religious procession emerged. Scores of altar boys clad in cassocks and surplices, the Sisters of St. Joseph, the Brothers of the Holy Infancy, all in full habit, walked solemnly in procession behind the cross. At the end of the group, leading the rosary, was Father Baker. The procession moved slowly along [Father Baker's] prayer path; finishing the rosary, the assembly sang joyous hymns in honor of Our Lady. Reaching the end of the path, the procession halted and Father Baker sprinkled the ground with holy water. Then, taking a small statue of Our Lady of Victory from his pocket, he buried it about a foot into the ground. The drilling crew observed all this with a sense of wonderment.... "That is where you put down your drill, as close to that statue as you can." And, he added, "Don't touch the statue with the drill."[561]

Many months passed. The crew drilled deeper: six hundred, seven hundred, eight hundred feet. No gas was discovered. Tongues wagged about "Father Baker's Folly." Two thousand more dollars were poured into the well. A novena was prayed. No gas was discovered. Another novena, and still, no gas. Drilling continued: nine hundred, one thousand feet. Finally, on August 21, 1891, a stream of gas shot upward, from eleven hundred thirty-seven feet. The gas lit an open forge, and the subsequent explosion knocked down people in the vicinity and rocketed an eighty-foot flame into the sky. That well produced for many years beyond the experts' expectations. When that well dried up, other successful wells were drilled nearby. To this day, many of Our Lady of Victory's building are fueled, in part, from on-site gas wells.

With money in his pocket, Father Baker went on a building spree. In 1893, he expanded the protectory to include a gymnasium and recreation hall. In 1901, he started a Working Boys Home in order to give his vocational school graduates a place to live. Seven years later, he broke ground for an infants home, since Baker recently had discovered in a two-year-old sewer the bodies of two hundred abandoned babies. To provide pre-natal care for infants, in 1915, he started a Maternity Hospital for unwed mothers. Five years later, he transformed that hospital into a general hospital. In the foyer of the Infants Home, stood a bassinet where anyone at any time without any explanation could leave a baby. "His prodigious activity continued. He added new trade schools, built an orphan home for abandoned and neglected babies, and established a large hospital and nursing home."[562] In all, he built two dozen major buildings, and housed and educated each year, in his heyday, almost four hundred young boys, and almost one hundred working boys. To feed his boys, Baker purchased a two-hundred-seventy-five-acre farm. Assisting Father Baker in his orphanages, homes, schools, and hospital were the Sisters of St. Joseph, without whom little of his good works could have been performed.

In 1921, at seventy-nine, he developed plans to build a shrine to Our Lady of Victory. Five years later, as he was celebrating his golden jubilee of priesthood, Father Baker assisted Cardinal Patrick Hayes of New York and Bishop William Turner of Buffalo in dedicating the completely-paid-for Basilica of Our Lady of Victory.

During the early 1930s, with the Great Depression was rearing its ugly head, Baker fed one thousand people daily in his soup kitchen and clothed thousands more. "He turned his attention particularly to Buffalo's black population, which had suffered so much in the Depression. He worked with such energy and zeal among them, that many, moved by his faith, embraced the Catholic religion."[563]

In early 1936, Father Baker became ill, and never fully recovered. On July 29, he died of cardiac exhaustion and dehydration. It is estimated that up to a half-million people attended his wake and funeral. Seven hundred priests, four bishops, and one archbishop prayed for the saintly priest at his funeral Mass. Baker had received many ecclesiastical honors: he had been named monsignor, appointed diocesan vicar general at the end of his silver jubilee, honored as domestic prelate three years later, and in 1926, during his golden jubilee, he was named prothonotary apostolic. Regardless of the honorific titles, he remained publicly and popularly "Father Baker."

Many experiences from Baker's home, church, and schools prepared him for his ministry. His German-Lutheran father, a grocer, exemplified good common sense and good business sense. His Irish-Catholic mother passed on her deep faith in Jesus and the Church. The four Baker boys participated in various boyhood pranks. On one occasion, late one night, Nelson woke up a younger brother and the two slipped outside. On the second floor of the Baker home was located the office of the local Republican Party. The young Bakers lowered the Republican flag, ran up the street to the offices of the Democratic Party, where they lowered that flag, and replaced it with that of the Republicans. They raced back home, and hoisted the Democrats' flag on the Republican flagpole. In the morning, the boys watched gleefully as members of the two parties almost started a fist-fight.

Church provided Baker with opportunity to pray and serve. St. Patrick's Church was located a few blocks from the Baker home. The mother and two boys would walk there each Sunday for Mass. Nelson joined the St. Vincent de Paul Society, through which he assisted people in their material needs.

Schools provided Nelson with a good education. He graduated from high school in 1859. For a decade he interrupted his education in favor of military service and a business adventure. Military duty took him for seven weeks to Gettysburg, where he saw limited action in the Civil War, and on to New York City to deal with the draft riots. Returning to Buffalo, he and a partner began a grain and feed business. Thinking of becoming priests, he and two other men in 1868, took Latin classes three nights a week with a Jesuit priest at St. Michael's Parish in downtown Buffalo. These classes served as the forerunner of Canisius College, which opened in 1870. In summer 1869, needing time to think and pray, Baker took a Great Lakes steamer cruise. Back home, he entered the Seminary and College of Our Lady of Angels, above Niagara Falls, New York, where the Vincentian Fathers instructed Baker. Nelson Baker fully embraced St. Vincent de Paul's charism of seeking out and serving the poorest of the poor. After ordination in 1876, Baker returned to the seminary to celebrate his First Mass, and returned every year thereafter to participate in the annual reunion, until his health failed in old age. In 1883, the college became known as Niagara University.

Father Baker's dedication to Our Lady of Victory originated in 1874, during a pilgrimage to Rome. The pilgrims visited Marian shrines along their route to Rome. At Paris, the group celebrated Mass at the shrine of Notre Dame des Victoires. "No one knows what went on in the heart of the seminarian during that Mass, but a lifelong devotion to the Blessed Mother under her title Our Lady of Victory was begun. The relationship was to influence his whole life."[564] Later, Baker writes about the experience, "As I knelt there praying, a great light seemed to fall upon me. . . . I could both feel and understand it."[565] On the way home from Rome, Baker stopped again at the same shrine. "While there he promised Mary he would take advantage of every opportunity to further devotion to her under that special title."[566] Father Baker kept his promise.

*For further information, contact*
Our Lady of Victory Homes of Charity
780 Ridge Road
Lackawanna, New York 14218 U.S.A.

✧

## 30. ✠ Saint Pedro de San José Betancur

*Place: Guatemala City, Guatemala*
*Fame: First saint from Central America. Founded the world's first hospital for convalescents. Founded the Bethlemite Order.*

At twenty-three, the layman Pedro de San José Betancur (1626-67) left his native Tenerife Island, the largest among Spain's Canary Islands, and headed for Honduras, where he hoped to serve as a priest among the Native Americans.[567] Although Pedro's widowed mother preferred that Pedro might marry and remain at home, Pedro sought counsel from an aunt who possessed a reputation for holiness. She encouraged him, saying, "The service of God waits for you in the West Indies. Your calling, Pedro, is not that of

PEDRO DE SAN JOSÉ BETANCUR

flesh and blood. Like St. Peter, you must go across the waters to encounter God."[568] Pedro left behind his significant ancestral fame and his labor as a shepherd. In the process, he began to confront his moral weaknesses: "pride, arrogance, and the instinct to win and dominate," which he knew needed to be replaced with "the opposite virtues of humility, obedience, and making himself 'ever small before the eyes of God and man'."[569]

On September 18, 1649, Pedro sailed from Santa Cruz, Tenerife, and headed for Honduras. The ship, however, encountered difficulties, and landed at Havana, Cuba. There Pedro passed many months, helping to repair the ship. Embarking again for Honduras, he became deathly ill while at sea, which occasioned the sailors' abandoning him on a beach with minimal food and drink. He walked for days to the nearest town. Arriving on February 18, 1651, at Santiago de los Caballeros (now Old Guatemala City), and wanting to thank God for having preserved his life during the sea journeys and sickness, Pedro knelt down, kissed the earth, and prayed, "I want to live and die here."[570]

For a few years, he worked as a shepherd, during which time, he met Jesuit and Franciscan priests. The Jesuits invited Pedro to attend their College of San Borgia, to study for the priesthood. In school, however, some professors treated the twenty-five-year-old Pedro just like the younger students, which caused him much embarrassment. After two years of study, Pedro was asked by the Jesuits to leave their apostolic school. A year later, Pedro pondered becoming a hermit. While praying in the Dominican hermitage at Petapa, he sensed the Blessed Mother saying to him, "Return to Guatemala City. There, God desires that you live, and that you busy yourself in a life of service to others."[571]

Wishing to dedicate the remainder of his life to God, Pedro joined the Third Order Franciscans. In January 1655, Pedro put on the Order's religious habit, and eighteen months later professed the vows of poverty, chastity, and obedience. At the time of profession, he was given the names of Peter, his name saint, and Joseph, his patron saint; thus, he became known as Brother Pedro de San José. For his ministry, he was assigned as sacristan at the Church of Calvary at Petapa, at Old Guatemala City.

The humble tertiary lived the rest of his life in Guatemala. Daily, he prayed for hours in the church. Regularly, he ate and drank sparsely, even trying to kill the taste of savory foods by adding excessive amounts of chilies. This contemplative committed himself to serving the poorest of the city.

In 1658, Pedro began the social works for which he is hailed as a hero. He converted the palm-branch hut in which he lived into a school for children, a hospice for foreign students, and a convalescent home for the sick. Interestingly and ironically, the minimally educated Pedro taught children the basics of religion, reading, and writing; and in doing so, founded the first free school in Central America. At the same time, his home-turned-hospital is recognized as the first-ever convalescent home in all the Americas. Pedro named his home-for-social services: Casita de la Virgen.

At the start of his missionary endeavors, Pedro opened an oratory called the House of Our Lady of Bethlehem. His lay volunteers and other Third Order Franciscans prayed with him before the Blessed Sacrament. He prepared the church for Forty Hours devotion and participated in the annual procession in honor of the Blessed Sacrament. From this original circle of faith-filled friends arose the community of the Hosptialler Bethlemites, for whom Pedro would write the *Constitution and Rule*. Not until twenty years after Pedro's death did the Vatican officials allow the community members to profess vows, and not until forty-three years after his death did the Vatican recognize the Order of the Bethlemites as a religious community with full canonical status in the Church.

Word of Pedro's kindness spread rapidly. Many sick and homeless persons appeared at his doorstep. As his guests increased, so did his desire to assist them. Daily, he walked through the streets of the city, begging food and clothing for those whom he was helping. When the convalescents' needs outgrew his resources, he approached local leaders of the Church, government, and business and sought their assistance in constructing and outfitting a hospital. These leaders generously supported his social services. Volunteers joined him in his ministries. During Christmas 1661, Pedro purchased property on which to build a convalescent home for the poor, which charitable work he placed under the patronage of Our Lady of Bethlehem.

The community accepted an increasing number of school-age children who had been either abandoned or orphaned. Pedro opened a home to provide the children with food, clothing, shelter, education, and security. Community members began visiting prisoners on a regular basis. When ruthless people verbally or physically attacked the local Native Americans, Pedro defended them in word and deed.

Besides his devotions to the Blessed Sacrament and the Virgin Mary, Pedro promoted among his disciples and townspeople a devotion of praying for the poor souls in purgatory. He walked throughout the town at night, ringing a bell and crying out, "Remember brothers and sisters, that we have only one soul, and if we lose it, we will not regain it."[572] Walking without shoes and without head covering, in all kinds of weather, he dedicated himself to praying for the poor souls. At the beginning of each month, he would go door-to-door, offering to pray for the deceased members of each home. Daily, he performed his charities for the intention of the poor souls in purgatory. From the poor whom he helped materially, he asked their help spiritually by their praying for the souls in purgatory.

Pedro enjoyed a particular devotion to the Feast of the Presentation of Our Lord, for which he prepared by nine days of fasting and praying the rosary at midnight with arms extended in the form of a cross. "In 1654, two hundred years before it would be proclaimed a dogma of the Church by Pope Pius XI, he made a vow to defend the Immaculate Conception even at the peril of his life."[573] Two other devotions which Pedro promoted, and which continue to be practiced in contemporary times, are the *posada* in Advent, and the processional Way of the Cross in Lent. Historians regard Pedro as the creator of the practice of the *posada*.

Years of selfless service took their toll on Pedro's health. On April 21, 1667, four days before dying, Brother Pedro wrote his last will and testament. In that document, he begins with a profession of faith, "I offer and commend my soul to God, Our Savior who created and redeemed my soul by the infinite price of his own blood, passion, and death through which my soul might receive God's mercy." After sixteen years in Guatemala, Brother Pedro died from bronchial pneumonia, at the age of forty-one. In his final hours, Pedro kept repeating ardently, "Who would like to be able to see God?"[574] In the final minutes of his approaching death, he said, "Rejoice, let us see God."[575]

Thousands of mourners from the city, including religious and political leaders, participated in the funeral procession and Mass. Pedro was buried among other Third Order Franciscans at the Church of St. Francis in Old Guatemala City. To this day, thousands of faithful believers annually stream to this church to pay their respects, and request the intercession of Brother Pedro. Pedro had gained a reputation for sanctity. It was said of him, "He personifies charity. He was charity."[576] He is known simply as "the man who was charity."[577]

Currently, plans call for a statue of Brother Pedro to overlook the entire region of Guatemala City. The statue, composed of materials from both Guatemala and Tenerife, is expected to stand approximately thirty-five feet high on a base of seven feet, with the inscription, "Remember brothers and sisters, that we have only one soul, and if we lose it, we will not regain it."

*For further information, contact*
Frailes Franciscanos OFM
El Museo del Santo Hermano Pedro de Batancur
Iglesia San Francisco El Grande
Antigua Guatemala Sacatepequez, Guatemala

∝

## 30. ✠ Saint María de Jesus Sacramentado Venegas

*Places: Guadalajara, Jalisco*
*Fame: Prayerful and practical religious nurse and administrator.*
*First female saint of México.*

María Natividad (1868-1959), affectionately called Nati by her family, friends, and religious community members, was the twelfth and final child born to a farming family at Zapotlanejo, Jalisco. The family fell on hard economic times because the father generously had made loans and accepted IOUs, but did not have the heart to collect from the poor the debts which they owed to him. The family moved to the neighboring state of Nyarit, where the father hoped to find better employment in order to provide the fami-

MARÍA DE JESUS
SACRAMENTADO
VENEGAS

ly with a better living situation. At Nyarit, Nati's mother died and Nati and an older sister were placed in an orphanage. Eventually, her father permitted Nati and the older sister to move back to Zapotlanejo, where they took up residence with relatives. At nineteen, Nati lost her father too. Nati, who had suffered so much, felt a great sympathy for others in their sufferings. This young lady expressed her *sympatico* for the poor and needy in her profession as teacher, and in her church activities as catechist and member of the *Hijas de María* (Daughters of Mary).

In 1887, Nati made an eight-day retreat according to the spiritual exercises of St. Ignatius of Loyola. Having always desired to become a religious sister, and blessed already with a deep devotion to the Blessed Sacrament and the Virgin Mary, she heard again Jesus' call, "Come, follow me." In prayer, she decided to enter religious life. In 1905, she joined a group of nurses at Guadalajara in the recently founded religious community of the Daughters of the Sacred Heart of Jesus. Five years later, she pronounced her first vows of poverty, chastity, and obedience. The community, having been founded under the auspices of the local archbishop, had for its mission the serving of the sick, especially the poor among the sick. Sister Nati, in the way that she cared for her patients at Sacred Heart Hospital in Guadalajara, gained the reputation of a self-sacrificing and gentle nurse.

In 1921, she was elected superior of the community, which position Mother Nati held for the next thirty-three years. Also in 1921, the local bishop assisted the sisters in writing the *Constitution and Statutes* of the young diocesan community. Nine years later, the Holy See approved these same documents, which approbation established as a religious community the *Congregación de las Hijas de María del Sagrado Corazón de Jesus*. At this time, Mother Nati chose as her name in religion Sister Maria de Jesus Sacramentado. Prayerful, prudent, and practical, Mother Nati advised her sisters, "Every devotion which delays our duties is a useless activity."[578] During that time, she oversaw the apostolic expansion of the community into sixteen hospitals in eight states. During the period of the bloody anti-Catholic persecution, which worsened especially between 1910 and 1934, Mother Nati held together the religious community, and accepted into the community sisters whose original communities had been closed by the government. After a lifetime of service, she died at ninety-one.

Less than half a century after she died, she was canonized. Mother María de Jesus Sacramentado Venegas is México's first woman saint.

*For further information, contact*
Sanatorio Licano, S.A. de C.V.
Jesús García y Luis Donaldo Colosio
83000 Hermosillo, Sonora, México

# 30. ✠ Blessed María Vicenta Chavez Orózco

*Places: Mexicaltzingo, Michoacán; and Guadalajara, Jalisco; México*
*Fame: Having been healed, she healed others. Foundress of the*
*Servants of the Holy Trinity and the Poor.*

On February 20, 1892, family members brought twenty-five-year-old Vicenta Chavez-Orózco (1867-1949) to Holy Trinity Hospital in Mexicaltzingo, Michoacán, where she was treated for pleurisy.[579] She, who had spent her entire life in the Mexicaltzingo district of poor unskilled workers, benefited from the services which she received at the hospital. A few years previously, the local parish priest Augustin Beas had founded Holy Trinity Hospital in order to provide at least minimal medical care for the people of the neighborhood. Father Augustin had transformed one room of the rectory into a hospital ward-room. He placed six beds into one room, organized the women of the St. Vincent de Paul Society to care for the sick, and named the place: Holy Trinity Hospital.

MARÍA VICENTA
CHAVEZ ORÓZCO

On July 10, 1892, five months after Vicenta had experienced a full recovery, she returned to the same hospital, and volunteered her services in gratitude for the care she had received. Poor as Vicenta was, she wished to assist her neighbors.

The priest, appreciating the capable and kind assistance of Vicenta and other women volunteers like her, recommended that they might consider taking private vows to dedicate themselves to the sick poor. On Christmas Day 1805, three women pronounced their private vows, namely, Vicenta, Catalina Velasco, and Juana Martin del Campo. Ten years later, the archbishop of Guadalajara, delighted with the women's continuing contribution to the diocese, recognized and named their group the Servants of the Poor. That date of episcopal recognition, May 12, 1905, is regarded as the foundation day of the community. Within the next few years the women decided that they would wear religious habits and take religious names. Vicenta selected Sister Maria Vicenta of Santa Dorothea. In 1911, Sister Dorothea professed her permanent vows. At this same time, Sister Dorothea was selected as the mistress of novices. Her personal motto became, "The love of Christ controls us" (2 Cor 5:14).

At the community's first general assembly in 1913, the community members elected Sister Dorothea as their superior general. She was re-elected in 1919, 1925, 1929, and 1936; altogether she served thirty years as leader of the community which she had co-founded.

In 1914, early in the Mexican Revolution, as part of the revolution's anti-Catholic expression, Sister was ordered to close her hospital and the community's half-dozen other health-care facilities. She refused. She continued to serve the poor and sick. In 1926, when the revolution and its persecution was approaching its denouement, the military claimed the nuns' St. Vincent Hospital in Zapotlan and made this building their military headquarters in the city. Daily, the soldiers taunted Sister María and other Servants with insults and occasional death threats. Nonetheless, the women of God courageously continued to nurse the sick. When a commandant arrived at the hospital and witnessed the soldiers' mistreatment of the good nuns, the commandant severely reprimanded the officer in charge for permitting this misconduct.

By 1942, the Servants of the Holy Trinity and the Poor were operating seventeen health care facilities: hospitals, clinics, and dispensaries.

In 1948, just one year before this octogenarian died, Sister Dorothea developed a severe eye ailment. When she lay dying, the archbishop of Guadalajara, who later became México's first cardinal, José Garibi Rivera, celebrated Mass in the sister's room. She who had consoled so many sick people at the times of their deaths, received the consolation of prayers and Masses as she lay dying.

In 1987, the sisters changed the name of the community to its current title: the Servants of the Holy Trinity and the Poor.

*For further information, contact*

Hermanas de la Trinidad y de los Pobres
Calle Miguel Blanco 1225
C.P. 44100
Guadalajara, Jalisco, México

# 31. ✠ Venerable Solanus Casey

*Places: Superior and Milwaukee, Wisconsin; Yonkers, Manhattan,
Harlem, and Brooklyn, New York; Huntington, Indiana;
and Detroit, Michigan*
*Fame: Equanimous and magnanimous.
Wonder-worker, counselor of souls.*

Although he was ordained *sacerdos simplex* (i. e.,
a priest who is permitted to say Mass but not
allowed to preach or to hear confessions) because
of concern about his grasp of the intellectual
aspects of theology, Father Solanus Casey (1870-
1956) became, in the words of his provincial, "the
greatest man that the [Capuchin] Province of St.
Joseph ever produced."[580] The farmboy from
western Wisconsin, who had experienced difficulty in the seminary with Latin and German

SOLANUS CASEY

declensions and conjugations, found ease in the parishes listening to
people, praying for them, and obtaining wondrous cures.[581]

Father Solanus, whose baptismal name was Bernard Francis, had been
born to Bernard James Casey and Ellen Elizabeth Murphy, who in the
1850s had emigrated from famine-struck Ireland to Boston,
Massachusetts. The couple met at a Fourth of July picnic in 1860 and
married three years later. After the Civil War, the Union Army shoemaker moved his family from Philadelphia, Pennsylvania, to Wisconsin, where
he took up farming, first at Prescott, then Trimbelle, and eventually
Burkhardt. Bernard, nicknamed Barney, was the sixth child among ten
boys and six girls. Rural Wisconsin suited his reflective and prayerful way,
where the burgeoning family prayed the rosary daily and assisted at Mass
on alternating Sundays, when one parent and half the children would use
the family's horse and buggy to travel the nine miles to the parish church.
The Caseys experienced the usual vicissitudes of farm life.

Upon completing elementary school at the advanced age of seventeen, Barney worked as a logger, brick-maker, hospital orderly, and
prison guard before moving to Superior, Wisconsin, where he found
employment as a trolley car motorman. Once, in his job as a motorman,

Barney rounded a corner in his trolley and happened upon a crowd of bystanders encircling a drunken sailor standing with a knife poised over a young girl. Barney was aghast at this threat of evil. Police arrived and spirited away the would-be attacker. Two days after this dramatic event, Barney visited his pastor and expressed the desire to become a priest.

In the diocesan seminary, the twenty-one-year-old man was assigned to study with thirteen-year-old boys in freshman-year high school. For the next five years, he tried his best at St. Francis de Sales Seminary in Milwaukee. "His mediocre grades, and an inadequate grasp of German and Latin resulted in his dismissal."[582] Although the faculty had recommended that Barney leave the seminary for academic reasons, they appreciated that he might have a vocation. The faculty suggested that Barney might try to enter a religious order. Barney's Franciscan spiritual director suggested that Barney investigate joining a variety of religious congregations, among them the Capuchins. While making a novena to the Blessed Virgin Mary to seek inspiration, he heard directly in prayer, which he revealed years later, "Go to Detroit."[583] Detroit was the location of the Capuchins' motherhouse and novitiate.

On Christmas Eve 1896, Barney was admitted to the Capuchin monastery at Detroit. Three weeks later, he entered the novitiate, wherein he received the religious name Francis Solanus in honor of the sainted Franciscan missionary (1549-1610) who had evangelized in Peru, Paraguay, and Argentina. Although Francis Solanus was his formal name in religion, he soon became known simply as Solanus. In July 1898, Solanus pronounced his vows, and undertook the formal study of philosophy and theology at the Capuchin seminary in Milwaukee. Again, he did not fare well academically; German and Latin texts and lectures confounded him. The director of studies for the seminarians recommended that Solanus be ordained, saying, "He will be to the people something like the Curé of Ars."[584]

For the first twenty years, beginning in 1904, Father Solanus ministered in and around New York City: in Yonkers at Sacred Heart Friary, in Manhattan at Our Lady of Sorrows, and in Harlem at Our Lady of Angels. His main assignments consisted of being sacristan and doorkeeper. At Harlem, people began noticing a special power and sanctity emanating from Father Solanus. He was becoming known as a "miracle-worker."[585] While he had encouraged many people to enroll in the

Seraphic Mass Association in order to receive spiritual benefits from the Masses celebrated by the Capuchins, members whom Father Solanus personally enrolled and for whom he prayed seemed to receive the cures they had sought. Father Solanus seemed to know who would receive cures. People viewed his prayers as particularly powerful. Petitioners came to him from New York, New Jersey, and Connecticut. In 1923, at the request of his religious provincial, Father Solanus began to keep a record of alleged cures and prayers answered. By the end of his life, these brief daily entries filled seven notebooks.

In August 1924, the beloved priest was transferred from New York to St. Bonaventure Friary at Detroit, where for the next twenty-one years he continued his responsibility as doorkeeper and his role as won-der-worker. Generously, he made himself available to people every wak-ing hour. When the stock market crashed in 1929, and the Capuchins expanded their soup kitchen, Father Solanus was charged with begging for the hungry. He enlisted volunteers to work in the soup kitchen, espe-cially among those who had benefited from his intercessory prayers. An example of Father Solanus's hand-chosen volunteers was a Detroit fire-fighter. The fireman, just as he was being wheeled on a hospital litter to the operating room for removal of a stomach tumor, bumped into Father Solanus in the corridor. The two renewed their acquaintance. Before leaving the sick man, Father Solanus patted the sick man's affected area, and Father suggested that another x-ray be performed before operating. The new x-ray revealed that the tumor had disappeared. The jubilant and grateful firefighter happily responded when Father Solanus later asked if the cured man might volunteer at the soup kitchen.

An example of one person being cured and another not being cured occurred at St. Joseph Mercy Hospital in Detroit in 1935. The person cured was Sister Mary Joseph.

> A severe streptococcus infection on the right side of her throat had sent her temperature to 105 degrees, and her neck became rigid. She began to slide into a coma, with heavy choking spells. Her doctor informed Sister Mary Philippa, a hospital supervisor, that the infection was spreading to the other side of the patient's throat. He ordered a tray set up, preparatory to doing a quick tra-cheotomy if needed.

At this point Sister Mary Philippa telephoned Father Solanus. He said he would come at once. When he entered the sick sister's room, he went directly to stand at her bedside, seemingly oblivious of others. Taking a book from his pocket, he started reading prayers, slowly and quietly, though the sister was in the midst of a choking spell. Almost immediately, Sister Mary Joseph's choking stopped.

While reading the passion and death of Christ from the Gospels, he several times blessed the sister with a relic of the True Cross and placed it to her lips and throat. Thus for two hours he read and prayed, while three sisters, kneeling, joined their prayers to his. Then he closed the book and said, "Sisters, it won't be necessary for me to return. Sister Mary Joseph will soon recover and join her community.[586]

A few minutes later, while walking down the hospital corridor, Father Solanus met an acquaintance. The man asked him to bless his wife. Father Solanus visited the woman and blessed her. As the husband thanked Father Solanus, the priest advised the man to be resigned to his wife's imminent death. The man was shocked: "Father, her operation wasn't serious — why do you say this?"[587] Father Solanus consoled the man and again urged him to prepare for imminent death. The woman died a few minutes after Father Solanus left the hospital.

The years were flying by. In July 1945, religious authorities transferred Father Solanus from Detroit to St. Michael's Friary in Brooklyn. Even though his health was failing, people kept seeking Father Solanus' counsel and healing. The next year, in April 1946, the superiors transferred him again — from bustling and accessible New York to the bucolic and remote setting of St. Felix Monastery in Huntington, Indiana. For ten years, Father Solanus enjoyed the prayerfulness of semi-retirement. Still, busloads of faithful traveled to see and speak with him. He maintained an extensive correspondence with many of these petitioners. The Capuchin community provided him with correspondence secretaries to assist the octogenarian. Many times, he revealed in his letters his life's message: that confidence in God provides the foundation of and condition for God's supernatural intervention in our lives. Oftentimes, Solanus quoted from a poem written by his brother, Monsignor Edward

Casey: "God condescends to use our powers, if we don't spoil his plans by ours."[588]

When, in May 1956, Father Solanus' chronic eczema flared up and became exacerbated by phlebitis, his superiors transferred him again to Detroit, a location which would provide accessibility to the city hospitals. To give the old man more rest, his religious superiors restricted the number of visitors and phone calls allowed. Shortly thereafter, Father Solanus's skin condition deteriorated into severe erysipelas. After more than a year-long illness, and a one-month stay in the hospital, the day before he died, Father Solanus told his provincial, "I looked on my whole life as giving, and I want to give until there is nothing left of me to give. So I prayed that when I come to die I might be perfectly conscious, so that with a deliberate act I can give my last breath to God."[589] The next day, he whispered as he died, "I give my soul to Jesus Christ."[590] Father Solanus had enjoyed sixty years in the Capuchin community, and fifty-three years as a priest.

*For further information, contact*
The Father Solanus Guild
1780 Mt. Elliott Avenue
Detroit, MI 48207 U.S.A.

# AUGUST

⚜

## 5. ☩ Frédéric Jansoone

*Place: Trois-Rivières and Cap-de-Madeleine, Québec*
*Fame: Radiated the presence of God. Apostle of the Holy Land.*

During his twenty-eight-year stay in Canada, beginning in 1888, Franciscan Father Frédéric Jansoone (1838-1916) communicated his profound presence of God through retreats, parish missions, books, and magazine articles.[591]

Many people perceived Father Frédéric to be especially holy. As a young retreat preacher in Egypt in 1876, he gained the reputation as "the holy father."[592] Within one month of his arrival at Québec City in 1881, the congregation and journalists described him as a "holy man."[593] Three months later, the parish priest who was hosting Frédéric at Cap-de-la-Madeleine, writes to the Minister General at Rome, "You have sent us a holy man, a saintly religious, of

FRÉDÉRIC JANSOONE

extraordinary influence. . . . It is a fact that many surprising cures have occurred, but no one is surprised when one considers his life."[594] Three years later, his blood brother, a missionary priest in India, writes to his sister after his visit to Frédéric at Jerusalem, "My very dear brother Frédéric is a real saint, a great and lovable saint, like those we read about with admiration, a saint who works miracles. The sight of him so struck me that the memory of his face haunts my mind continually."[595]

Frédéric's stay in Canada consisted of two parts. The first visit lasted eight months, from August 1881 until April 1882, during which he intended to raise funds for the Holy Land, and to revive the Third Order Franciscans, which organization had become largely defunct in Canada since the suppression of the Franciscan Recollects in 1796. His second visit began in 1888 and lasted until his death in 1916. Continuing to raise funds for the Holy Land, he also spent fourteen years as director of Cap-de-la-Madeleine and another fourteen years as promoter and preacher of pilgrimages to the Cap, to Sainte-Anne-de-Beaupré, and after 1912, to Saint Joseph's Oratory on Mount Royal.

He began his first visit to Canada, preaching in Québec, until he committed a political *faux pas*. In some sermons, he preached that Liberalism "has caused much harm in France and must be combated here."[596] Liberalism in Canada, however, lacked the anti-religious bias which characterized it in France. The Canadian Liberal political party reacted with furor. The archbishop asked the well-intentioned but misinterpreted preacher to leave the archdiocese. Frédéric was received immediately in neighboring Trois Rivières, where he resided at Cap-de-la-Madeleine and continued his preaching with extraordinary results. During this time, he revised and published the *Manual of the Third*

*Order*. At the end of April, he was called back to the Holy Land because of the outbreak of war in Egypt. He, as Assistant Custos (Guardian), needed to oversee two sites: the Basilica of the Holy Sepulchre and the Church of the Nativity at Bethlehem.

Frédéric's second missioning to Canada originated in mid-1887, when the pope re-instituted a worldwide collection for the benefit of the Holy Land sites. Frederic and two other Franciscans were asked to develop in Canada a commissariate to collect funds for the Holy Land. The bishop of Trois-Rivières, priests, and faithful welcomed with opened arms the famed "holy man" back to Cap-de-la-Madeleine.

On June 22, 1888, two weeks after his return to Canada, an extraordinary event occurred to Father Frédéric. After celebrating the rededication of the shrine of Our Lady of the Rosary, a trio of persons, including Frédéric, another priest, and a sick man, witnessed the "prodigy of the eyes." The three were praying quietly in front of the main altar, on which stood the statue of Our Lady of the Rosary. "Suddenly, the statue came to life; the lowered eyes of the statue opened to gaze far off over the heads of the three men. All three asked each other: 'Do you see it?' . . . For five or ten minutes, he (Frédéric) saw the face of a living person, with a serious, severe expression marked with sadness."[597]

Frédéric's ministry at Cap-de-la-Madeleine continued for fourteen years. He preached retreats and missions, and led pilgrimages to Canadian shrines. "He was ever the same ardent preacher, the man of intense interior life, the guide whose special interest was the individual soul of the pilgrim"[598] Also, from 1892 to 1895, he directly cared for Italian immigrants who had flooded into Montréal. His work with the Franciscan Third Order flourished, and in 1895 over eight thousand Tertiaries gathered at Cap-de-la-Madeleine. He continued to write: in 1892, he founded the shrine magazine, *The Annals of the Holy Rosary*, for which he served as editor for the next decade.

Administratively, he planned and implemented many improvements to the shrine. He developed greater railroad access, constructed outdoor Stations of the Cross, gained permission for a plenary indulgence for shrine pilgrims, created an approved liturgical text for the Mass of the Holy Rosary, and produced a jeweled crown for the statue of Mary. Frédéric left the shrine in 1902, when the Oblates of Mary Immaculate took over its administration as he had suggested. He returned briefly in

1904, when the pope's Apostolic Delegate celebrated the public crowning of Mary, with fifteen thousand people participating. In 1909, the First Plenary Council of Québec declared Cap-de-la-Madeleine a national shrine.

This man of great prayer and apostolic zeal practiced great pastoral compassion. Among his regular activities, he included visiting the sick. A companion of Frédéric writes,

> One day, I was taking him to see my cousin. On our way, we had to pass by the house of a sick man whose face had been eaten away by a cankerous growth. Father Frederic asked if we could stop by and visit this man, When he entered the man's house, he went straight to his sick-bed. Kissing his sores, he blessed and consoled him. I found the whole thing deeply moving and edifying.[599]

During his two six-year terms as Assistant Custos beginning in 1876, Frédéric proved to be a capable administrator. He codified the extremely complex rules regulating the relationships and responsibilities in the sites of the Holy Land among five competing religious groups: the Greeks, Latins, Copts, Armenians, and Ethiopians. Frédéric's work remains operative today; his *Status quo* became civil law in 1900. He re-established the ancient but three-hundred-year-defunct tradition of praying the Stations of the Cross along the *Via Dolorosa* on Good Friday, and later, he arranged that this pilgrim activity be practiced every Friday. "He was involved in the planning and founding of the pilgrim hostelry of Notre Dame de France," located outside of Joppa Gate of the walled Old City of Jerusalem.[600] After he volunteered to raise funds to construct the poverty-stricken parish church in Bethlehem, he providentially met the Canadian priest Léon Provencher, who invited the friar to come to Québec to seek donations from the laity.

In June 1916, the health of the septuagenarian broke down. Ever since 1884, he had experienced intermittently acute digestive problems. But now, the suffering did not abate; the pain persisted fifty days. He repeatedly cried out, "Come, Lord Jesus. Come. Don't delay."[601]

In the course of his life, he wrote one hundred thirty-one books, articles, and pamphlets. After his *Manual* sold over five thousand copies, he condensed the material into a smaller book and sold over ten thousand copies. His magazine, the *Annals of Our Lady of the Cape,* attracted ten thousand subscribers. The *Life of Jesus Christ,* which was regarded in Canada as a best-seller, sold forty-two thousand copies. He published a book of interest to all Holy Land pilgrims: *The Life of the Blessed Virgin Mary according to Sister Mary of Agreda.* His articles included lives of St. Joseph, St. Anne, St. Francis of Assisi, and St. Anthony of Padua. He traveled to over one hundred fifty parishes throughout the dioceses of the Province of Quebec, and the New England states to promote devotion to Our Lady of the Rosary.

Frédéric had been born and raised at Ghyvelbe, France, near Dunkerque. The youngest of nine surviving children, he studied formally from age twelve to seventeen, at which time he found employment at a textile plant. The owner, observing how sociable and efficient the youth was, rapidly promoted him to the front counter, and then to traveling salesman, which position he held from age nineteen to twenty-five. After his mother died in 1861, Frédéric applied to the Franciscans, which community he entered in June 1864. Six years later, he was ordained. With the outbreak of the Franco-Prussian War in 1870, he was assigned as chaplain to a military hospital. The next year, he was appointed assistant novice director, and later, superior. In 1876, in response to his repeated requests to labor in the Holy Land, his community missioned him to the Basilica of the Holy Sepulchre in Jerusalem. His mission in Jerusalem led to his apostolate in Canada.

*For further information, contact*
Musée Père Frederic
890 Saint-Maurice
Trois-Rivières, QC G9A 3P8 Canada

## 6. ✠ Venerable Antonio Margil

*Places: Querétaro, México; and San Antonio, Texas*
*Fame: Indefatigable missionary. Apostle of México and Texas.*

Two dozen Franciscan missionaries left Cadiz, Spain, in March 1683 and disembarked at Veracruz, México, three months later.[602] Their mission consisted in evangelizing the indigenous population in New Spain. One among these missionaries stands out for his extraordinary zeal and sanctity: Antonio Margil (1657-1726). He has become known as the Apostle of México and Texas. Only Our Lady of Guadalupe, when she appeared to Juan Diego in 1531, did more than Antonio Margil to spread the gospel in the New World.[603]

ANTONIO MARGIL

In the course of his forty-three-year ministry in the New World, this zealous friar walked barefooted from his original assignment at Querétaro, México, as far south as Panama, and as far north as Texas and Louisiana. Traveling lightly, he carried only his breviary and articles for Mass, along with a gourd of water, a walking staff, and a sombrero. Normally he covered forty to fifty miles a day, which warranted him the nickname of "the flying Father."[604] Despite the difficulties of nearly impassable paths, the dangers of wild animals, opprobrious weather, and sometimes hostile Indians, he continued undaunted on his mission. Occasionally, his preaching in favor of Christian behavior aroused the enmity of some members of his audience, who consequently beat and tortured him. Along the way, he established missions and apostolic colleges, wrote a dictionary of various Indian dialects, served as superior in his religious community three times, and baptized tens of thousands of Indians. His goal was to bring Christ to all people, and all people to Christ. As he walked, he sang the hymn taken from the poem *Alabado*, which he had written:

> Whoever seeks to follow God
> And strives to enter into his glory,
> *One thing he has to do*

And from his heart to say:
"Die rather than sin.
Rather than sin, die."[605]

After having entered the Franciscan community in 1673 and being ordained to priesthood nine years later, young Father Antonio volunteered for the missions across the Atlantic. He arrived at the Mexican port city of Veracruz and walked to his mission at the College of the Holy Cross at Querétaro. From 1684 to 1688, he evangelized in the areas of Yucatan, Tabasco, and Soconusco in México; and he preached throughout Guatemala, Honduras, Nicaragua, and Costa Rica. For the next three years, he remained at Talamanca in Costa Rica. In 1691, he undertook a five-year program of evangelization at Verapaz in Guatemala. After serving as religious superior at Querétaro from 1697 to 1700, and at Guatemala from 1702 to 1705, he returned to the mission he had founded at Talamanca. Two years later, he established the apostolic college of Our Lady of Guadalupe at Zacatecas, México, just as he had founded in 1701 the college of Christo Crucificado at Guatemala.

Beginning in 1711, he headed northward. He evangelized in the area of what is known now as the states of Nayarit, Coahuila, and Nuevo León. In 1716, he led five other Franciscans into East Texas, where, under his leadership, they established six missions, including Nacogdoches. Three years later, when the French from Louisiana invaded East Texas and destroyed the Spanish missions, Margil went to Bejar, Texas, and founded in 1720 Mission San José near Mission San Antonio. After one year, when the French left the region, Margil restored these missions and continued eastward as far as current-day Naquadoshish, Louisiana, where he established another mission.

In 1722, Father Antonio was appointed once again as a Franciscan superior, this time at the apostolic college at Zacatecas, México. In obedience, he left his beloved Indians and the mission ministry at Texas. He returned to Zacatecas to give himself wholeheartedly to his community responsibility. Five years later, he lay dying after preaching a mission at México City. "A huge crowd gathered outside to hold vigil for the dying man of God. When an image of Our Lady of Remedies was placed before him, he prayed, 'Good-bye, Lady, till tomorrow.' The next afternoon, August 6, 1726, Antonio Margil de Jesus died."[606]

*For further information, contact*
Margil House of Studies
2321 Peckham
Houston, Texas 77019 U.S.A.

## 9. ✠ Venerable Marianne Cope

*Places: Syracuse, New York; and Molokai, Hawaii*
*Fame: Co-worker with Blessed Damien of Molokai. Missionary to patients with Hansen's Disease on the Hawaiian Islands.*

When the Vicar Apostolic of Hawaii in 1873 requested a priest to serve persons afflicted with leprosy on a remote peninsula on the island of Molokai, Damien de Veuster, now known as Blessed Damien of Molokai, stepped forward.[607] Ten years later, when a new Vicar Apostolic of Hawaii sought a community of nuns to nursing the sick poor, especially those afflicted with leprosy; Mother Marianne Cope (1838-1918) volunteered.

MARIANNE COPE

A priest emissary representing both the government and Vicar Apostolic had sent letters to over fifty religious congregations, seeking sisters to work at Molokai. The priest received only one promising response. Mother Marianne, provincial of the Sisters of the Third Order of St. Francis in Syracuse, New York, replies, "I hardly know what to say. . . . Shall I regard your kind invitation to join you in your missionary labors, as coming from God? This is a question that has been constantly on my mind. . . . My interest is awakened and I feel an irresistible force drawing me to follow this call."[608]

The priest immediately traveled to Syracuse. He had not yet revealed that the hospitals were leprosariums. As Mother Marianne and the other sisters whom she had invited to the meeting listened to the emissary's description of the needs of those afflicted with leprosy, interest soared among them. Their final decision would lay with the Father Provincial of the Franciscan community. Mother writes expectedly about him, "I hope his good heart will approve my desire to accept the work in the name of the great St. Francis."[609] When the provincial approved of the mission in Hawaii, Mother Marianne writes to the emissary, "I am hungry for the work and I wish with all my heart to be one of the chosen ones whose privilege it will be to sacrifice themselves for the salvation of souls of the poor Islanders. . . . I am not afraid of any disease, hence it would be my greatest delight to minister to the abandoned lepers."[610] The community agreed to provide six sisters initially, and possibly additional sisters in the future. The community was fairly new, having been founded only in 1860, and its eighty sisters were already teaching in a dozen elementary schools, and sponsoring two hospitals.

Seven sisters arrived at Honolulu in November 1883. Mother accompanied the sisters to help establish the new ministry, but she was expected to return to Syracuse to continue her administrative responsibilities as provincial. In Hawaii, however, it became clearer at every stage of planning, implementing, and gaining governmental approvals that the superior intellect and interpersonal skills of Mother were needed to give firm foundation to this new work. She wrote to Syracuse that the greater need required her to remain at Hawaii at this time. After Father Damien was diagnosed with terminal leprosy in 1884, all likelihood of Mother's returning to Syracuse vanished.

Within two months of their arrival in Honolulu, the sisters began working at Kakaako Branch Hospital, where two hundred patients lived in a space built for one hundred. "No task was too menial for the small group of sisters, and with their scrubbing, cleaning, and just plain caring, they gave the patients an uplift in morale beyond measuring."[611] Mother insisted on strict sanitary procedures, and no sister to this day has ever suffered from the highly contagious Hansen's disease. By 1888, Mother had opened three medical facilities: Malulani's first General Hospital at Maui, the Kapiolani Home on Oahu Island for healthy female children of leprous parents; and the C.R. Bishop Home for homeless women and girls with leprosy, on the Kalaupapa peninsula at Molokai

When in 1888 a new coalition of political leaders and the Board of Health required all those with leprosy to be transferred to and treated at Molokai, the greater need shifted to that peninsula. Thereafter, on average, about seven hundred persons suffering from Hansen's Disease resided there annually. "The desolate island [peninsula] was surrounded on all sides by imposing rock cliffs and rough seas. It was considered the last stop from which no one returned."[612]

Mother looked forward to moving from Oahu to Molokai, but she insisted on the sisters' spiritual needs being provided before she as superior would commit the sisters. She knew the sisters needed a chapel and a priest who would provide the sacraments and counsel. She writes to the bishop, "Our spiritual wants are of the greatest importance. . . . I cannot accept the mission until I have assurance from Your Lordship that you will kindly supply this want, as you alone can."[613]

After Father Damien died in 1889, Mother kept her promise to him to care for his boys. She took charge of the boys' home at Kalawao, just two miles from the C.R. Bishop Home for females, where she and two other sisters were already at work. Mother kept nuns on Oahu to care for the children at Kapiolani Home and at the receiving station for leprosy patients. Mother writes to the bishop about her care for the boys:

> We visited the boys' establishment for he first time on the 28th of November '88 — and ever since that day, my heart has bled for them, and I am anxious and hungry to help to put a little more sunshine into their dreary hearts. Sympathy for these poor little ones prompted me to say to [the chaplain replacing Father Damien] Father Wendelin that Sisters were needed there to improve the condition of things.[614]

Mother expressed similar care for the girls. In the first days of the sisters' presence at Molokai, Mother insisted that the women have security and be protected from drunken men who came in groups at night to attack those who had no police to guard them. She also obtained safety rules to protect the incoming children, girls and boys, from predators who awaited their arrival at the settlement shore.

The ministry at Molokai took its toll on Mother Marianne. In 1902, at sixty-four, she writes to her nephew Paul Cope in Chicago,

I am wondering how many more [years] our dear Sweet Lord will allow me to spend for Him. I do not think of reward, I am working for God, and do so cheerfully. How many graces did He not shower down on me, from my birth till now. Should I live a thousand years, I could not in ever so small a degree thank Him for His gifts and blessings. I do not expect a high place in heaven. I shall be thankful for a little corner where I may love God for all eternity.[615]

After thirty-five years of service to the victims of Hansen's Disease in the Hawaiian Islands, Mother died at Kalaupapa. The obituary about her in the local newspaper reads in part:

Throughout the islands the memory of Mother Marianne is revered, particularly among the Hawaiians, in whose cause she has shown such martyr-like devotion. Those who have met the sweet, delicate little woman, whose face was almost spirituelle (sic), have always been impressed with her intellectual qualities, for she was a woman of splendid accomplishments, and had fine executive ability. She has impressed everyone as a real "mother" to those who stood so sorely in need of mothering.[616]

Who could have written the script for this woman's life? Born at Heppenheim, north of Heidelberg, Germany, the fifth child and third daughter of her father's second marriage, Barbara Cope, when she was one-year old, sailed with her family to New York City. The father led the family to upstate Utica, where they joined St. Joseph's parish and Marianne attended the parish school. As a teen, she desired to enter religious life, which entrance she delayed nine years because her factory salary and helping hands were needed at home. In 1862, one month after her father died, she joined the two-year-old Central New York branch of the religious community founded by Bishop John Neumann. During her first eight years in religious life, she served as teacher and later principal at three Catholic elementary schools in Syracuse, Oswego, and Rome, New York. Despite her youth, she served on the governing board of her religious community, thereby participating in the decision to open hospitals in cities which had none: St. Elizabeth's in Utica (1866) and St. Joseph's at Syracuse (1869). In 1870, she was appointed chief administrator of St. Joseph's Hospital, and seven years later, she was elected the second provincial of her community. During her second term as provincial, she received the letter seeking help in Hawaii. Mother Marianne Cope responded in a saintly fashion, and throughout her days, she met herculean challenges in an heroic way.

*For further information, contact*
Cause of Mother Marianne Cope
St. Anthony Convent and Motherhouse
1024 Court St,
Syracuse, New York 13208 U.S.A.

# 14. ✠ Michael J. McGivney

*Places: Waterbury and New Haven, Connecticut*
*Fame: Apostle of Christian Family Life. Founder of the Knights of Columbus.*

Barely four years after ordination, Father Michael J. McGivney (1852-90) founded the Knights of Columbus to provide identity, inspiration, and insurance to Catholic men.[617] The Knights of Columbus struck a need and nerve in the Catholic Church. By the time of its centennial anniversary, the Knights of Columbus had grown from one parish council with twenty-four members in downstate Connecticut to over nine thousand councils with almost a million-and-a-half members in twelve countries.

MICHAEL J.
McGIVNEY

Michael McGivney grew up with the pain, poverty, and outcast position of first-generation immigrants. His parents fled County Cavan and the Irish potato famine, and emigrated to the United States. They married at Waterbury, Connecticut, in 1850, and proceeded to have thirteen children, six of whom died in infancy or early childhood. The first-born, Michael, attended school for six years before leaving at thirteen to work in a brass factory where he remained for three years. His teachers write that he conducted himself with "excellent deportment and proficiency in his studies."[618] Desiring to become a priest, he studied at the College of Saint-Hyacinthe at Québec, the Seminary of Our Lady of Angels at Niagara University, New York, St. Mary's College in Montréal, and St. Mary's Seminary in Baltimore, Maryland. Archbishop and later Cardinal James Gibbons ordained Michael at Baltimore's famed Cathedral of the Assumption on Dec. 22, 1877. After celebrating his First Mass with his widowed mother and siblings at the family's Waterbury parish of the Immaculate Conception, Father McGivney headed to his assignment at St. Mary's Church, the oldest parish in New Haven.

Beginning his ministry on Christmas Day, Father McGivney applied himself to the usual priestly responsibilities: Masses and public devotions, visiting the sick and imprisoned, and organizing youth activities. Father McGivney's downtown church made news in *The New York Times* in 1879, when the newspaper's headlines reported, "How An Aristocratic Avenue Was Blemished By A Roman Church Edifice."[619]

In October 1881, the twenty-nine-year-old parish priest gathered a group of sixty men into the basement of St. Mary's Church. McGivney envisioned forming a Catholic organization to provide both fraternity in faith and financial assistance to families in times of sickness, death, and burial.[620] At this time in United States history no federal social security system existed and numerous banks and insurance companies had suffered financial losses, and some had collapsed. Before approaching his parishioners with his idea, the young priest had discussed the idea with his bishop and had traveled to Boston and Brooklyn to learn about Catholic benevolent societies in those dioceses.

The men at St. Mary's in Hartford responded optimistically. The priest suggested that they call their organization the Sons of Columbus, to remind blue-blooded Connecticut Protestants that long before the Puritans arrived Columbus had discovered the New World. The men preferred Knights to Sons, believing knights indicated a more noble status.

After months of discussion and detailed work about insurance factors, maximum ages for entrance, minimum initiation fees, and the disbursement of benefits, the first Knights of Columbus council was founded in the basement at St. Mary's Church in New Haven in May 1882.

To enlarge the base of membership, McGivney mailed letters to all the parishes in the diocese. Months passed. Not even one parish expressed interest. McGivney writes to a priest friend in Massachusetts, "Our beginning is extremely slow, but I think that when our by-laws are distributed we will advance more rapidly."[621]

By the summer of 1882, the Knights at Hartford were complaining loudly. Members' interest and attendance had fallen sharply. Criticisms were surfacing about their lay leaders. Questions were raised about having a priest as financial officer. Suggestions circulated that the group either ought to disband or assimilate into other existing fraternities. Father McGivney held the dissident group intact by the very strength of his vision, optimism, and perseverance. To lend greater clarity to roles, rules, and expectations, the priest submitted to the council a clear statement of purpose, structure, and conduct for the Supreme Knight, the Supreme Council, the Supreme Committee, the Supreme Chaplain, and the Knights themselves. McGivney possessed an innate sense for organization and business.

In March 1883, a priest at nearby Meridien expressed interest in the Knights. Two months later, the second council of the Knights of Columbus came into existence. In the next month, three more councils were added: at Middletown, Wallingford, and another at Meridien. By the end of 1884, a dozen councils had arisen. The bishop joined, in part, to demonstrate his support for McGivney's society. And by year's end in 1885, a total of thirty-one councils had been founded. Part of the Knights' success may be attributed to Pope Leo XIII, who in April 1884, published the encyclical *Humanum Genes*, in which he condemned Freemasonry, and encouraged Church leaders to form Catholic societies to combat the secret societies, and to offer social and financial benefits to members. The *Connecticut Catholic* provided an unsolicited endorsement for the Knights on May 10, 1884: "The Holy Father has recommended the formation and fostering of societies which will counteract the effect and ward off the dangers of those secret societies which are [proscribed] by the Church. For these great purposes the Knights of Columbus, as an organization, is eminently fitted."[622]

In April 1884, at the society's second convention, Father McGivney removed himself as Supreme Secretary and suggested that he serve, not in the position of financial overseer, but as supreme chaplain. In November of that same year, Father McGivney was transferred to St. Thomas's Church at Tomaston, where a poor parish in a poor factory town awaited his holiness and genius.

The farewell from St. Mary's Church proved to be emotionally moving for both the priest and congregation. The *Connecticut Catholic* reports on the priest's departing speech:

> He said that, like St. Paul, he has been called upon to depart. He was before them to say those sad words "good bye." . . . If he had ever been seemingly severe or austere he asked forgiveness. Whatever he had done had been in the interests of morality, in justice to religion, and for the people's spiritual welfare. He prayed that they would meet in heaven, where there are no partings, and where no one is called upon to say "good-bye."[623]

Father McGivney's second assignment, like his first, required McGivney to serve his people liturgically, sacramentally, and pastorally. He focused on promoting the faith and family life. As pastor, he not only served the spiritual needs of his flock but also acted as administrator, overseeing the maintenance and development of the physical plant and fundraising the necessary resources. Remaining active in the Knights as chaplain, he rejoiced in gratitude to God that the Knights flourished. By June 1889, the organization had blossomed to over five thousand members, in fifty-one councils.

Just as the Knights of Columbus were beginning to flourish, death approached for the beloved pastor. In January 1890, he contracted pneumonia which evolved into tuberculosis. His health deteriorated until in March he traveled to Virginia to enjoy a region unaffected by the epidemic. After returning to his parish for Holy Week services, he suffered a relapse in July and died on August 14, just two days after his thirty-eighth birthday

The bishop celebrated the funeral Mass, along with seventy priests, hundreds of parishioners, and over two hundred fifty Knights who represented almost all the fifty-six councils. Shop-owners in Thomaston shut their doors so that they too might attend the Mass. Extra railroad cars were added to the trains bringing mourners into the city, and virtually all the horse-drawn taxis throughout Waterbury and neighboring towns were occupied by funeral-goers.

The Knights of Columbus succeeded whereas dozens of other death-benefit societies failed. The Knights provided spiritual, social, and financial benefits, which satisfied the range of the men's needs. The Knights organization focused on the future, rather than trying to hold onto the past. They proudly identified themselves as Catholics and Americans, when it was dangerous to be the former, and doubted by their fellow citizens to claim to be the latter. Father McGivney's vision of an organization of Catholic men rather than a canonically approved Catholic Church organization permitted the group proper flexibility and freedom. Of all the fraternal and financial societies founded at that time, "only the Knights of Columbus evolved as a broad movement grounded in a burgeoning American-Catholic culture."[624] Within two years of McGivney's death, the Knights expanded beyond Connecticut into Massachusetts and New York, and after another dozen years, all across the country. Other fraternal societies have come and gone, but the Knights have survived and thrived.

*For further information, contact*
The Father McGivney Guild
One Columbus Plaza
New Haven, CT 06510 U.S.A.

❦

## 17. ✠ Blessed Bartolomé Laurel Díaz

*Place: Acapulco, Guerrero; and Querétero*
*Fame: Franciscan brother who learned limited medical skills.*
*Marytr in Japan.*

Between 1597 and 1632, the shoguns of Japan led three major persecutions against the Christians. In the first two onslaughts, many hundreds of laity were killed. In the last wave of persecution, many hundreds of clergy were martyred. The shoguns wished to exterminate Christianity from Japan.

Bartolomé Laurel Diaz (c. 1598-1627) was born at Cadiz, Spain. When he was still an infant, his parents brought him to New Spain. Historians report that Bartolomé's younger brother was born and baptized at Acapulco in 1599.

Bartolomé wished to become a Franciscan. In 1615, he applied for, and entered the religious community, but he soon left. The reason for the quick departure remains unknown. The very next year, however, he entered again, and after one year in the novitiate, he took vows at the Franciscan house at Querétaro.

Yearning to be a missionary, he was missioned to the Far East in 1618. He sailed to and stayed for five years at Manila, where his work in a hospital occasioned his learning some medical treatments from the hospital staff and learning some of the Japanese language from native Japanese patients.

Brother Bartolomé and three Spanish Franciscan priests sailed for Japan in 1632. Brother Bartolomé's responsibility was to assist Father Francis, the leader of the mission. The Franciscans ministered in the hills surrounding Nagasaki. Interestingly, Brother Bartolomé's skills in medicine gained entrée for the cleric to do his ministry in the homes of the peasants. For four years, the Franciscans carried on their hidden ministry. Finally, an informer reported their whereabouts. When soldiers came and arrested the Christians, the soldiers took into custody eleven people: Brother Bartolomé, three Franciscan priests, the lay catechist, the host couple who had hid the clergy, and six other laity. All the laity belonged to the Third Order Franciscans.

The eleven were discovered on the Tuesday after Pentecost, but they were not killed until August 17. The method of killing the Christians was determined according to their dignity in the Christian community. Most of the laity were beheaded. The leaders, both lay and clerical, suffered the more excruciating death of being burned slowly to death. According to Japanese tradition, those to be killed were tied to stakes erected in the ground. Soldiers lit fires at the rim of a twenty-five foot semi-circle of firewood strewn at the base of the stakes. When the fires grew too hot too quickly, which meant the victims would die too soon, and not suffer further, the flames were doused. Over the course of many days, all the martyrs succumbed to the flames, but none succumbed to the temptation to deny their faith.

*For further information, contact*
Franciscan Friars
Provincial Curia
Caballocalco 11
Coyoacán, México D.F. 04000 México

## 17. ✠ Élisabeth Turgeon

*Place: Rimouski, Québec*
*Fame: Educator, despite many adversities. Foundress of the Sisters of the
Little Schools (now Sisters of Our Lady of the Holy Rosary).*

As a young woman, Élisabeth Turgeon (1840-81) dreamed of serving children as a vowed religious.[625] Time after time, however, circumstances delayed her plans: her poor health, her father's death, and her helping to raise younger siblings at home. Eventually, she founded a religious congregation when she was thirty-nine. Two years later, she died.

ÉLISABETH TURGEON

In 1861, Élisabeth left home to study for her teaching degree at Laval Normal School. She returned home, however, before completing studies because of her poor health. At home, she continued to study, took her final exams with her classmates, and graduated on time. Between 1863 and 1874, she taught at three successive schools, during which time she took numerous sick leaves. While teaching in Québec, twice she lay at death's doorstep and received the Church's last rites. Despite poor health, she continued in her teaching profession.

The bishop of Rimouski knew Élisabeth Turgeon well. He had taught her at Laval Normal School, where he had served as priest-principal. He remembered her as "having a brilliant intellect, and a mature personality; being a diligent worker, and kind and strong in character."[626] After his episcopal ordination in 1867, the bishop invited Élisabeth in 1871 to direct a school for the Catholic education and formation of boys. She expressed genuine interest, but declined the offer on account of her currently poor health. Three years later, the bishop repeated his invitation. He added that she might want to join an existing "small society" of teachers for rural schools. Again, Élisabeth declined; she was teaching already at Sainte-Anne-de-Beaupré. Privately, she was focusing on becoming a nun. She had maintained correspondence with a community of women religious who were operating an orphanage in the U.S.A. In 1875, when the bishop invited her a third time, Élisabeth envisioned that in the "small society" she could achieve both of her desires: teaching children and living religious life. Already, the women of the "small society" of Rimouski were living in community and were calling themselves sisters. Élisabeth's oldest sister Louise belonged to the group and was serving as their superior.

On April 3, 1875, Élisabeth arrived at Rimouski. The next day, she and the bishop discussed their respective visions. A few weeks later she was appointed directress of novices in charge of studies and manual works. She also taught in the local school from 1876 to 1878.

Élisabeth's sister Louise served the small society of the Sisters of the Little Schools not only as the superior but also as the recruiter of candidates. Unfortunately, she recruited indiscriminately. The first few years proved difficult for Élisabeth and the other sisters as numerous unqualified candidates arrived at the convent's doorstep. "No one was ever refused admission no matter what her state of health, character, age, or aptitudes."[627] While the superior had the task of admitting candidates, the novice directress had the task of discerning their vocations. Tensions arose.

Throughout this time, the sisters suffered terrible poverty. They lacked adequate food, shelter, and furniture. Cold and hunger were constant companions in the convent. The community of fourteen women owned only six chairs, which had to be transported from the chapel to the kitchen or living room, as needed.

Existing poverty and insecurity about the future of the community led to verbal explosions within the convent. Townsfolk referred to the sisters as, "the crazy old maids."[628] In January 1879, six novices left the community, none of whom left quietly. At the end of February, Élisabeth, suggested to the sisters, "My dear sisters, we will have to separate from each other, you are perishing here from hunger and cold, return to your families, . . . leave discreetly in order to spare us from the pain of a final farewell. I will be the last to leave, I will remain a few more days near the tabernacle."[629] The sisters assured Élisabeth that they were willing to endure the deprivations and would remain.

Élisabeth's oldest sister Louise left the small society in July 1879, which departure caused Élisabeth great personal pain. In August, the bishop made a canonical visitation to the society, and during the visit he gave permission for the sisters to take religious vows the following month. He urged the sisters to persevere in vocation; he did not want to see the society disbanded. In September, thirteen women of the society formally dedicated their lives to God and to the education of children, especially those living in rural and poor areas. That same day, the bishop named Élisabeth superior, after which the sisters called her Mother Mary Élisabeth.

The young community flourished. Young women continued to join, although some older women from time to time decided to leave the congregation. Many parishes sent requests for the services of the sisters. Soon the demand exceeded the supply. In her letters, Elizabeth prayed that her sisters would be Christlike among the poor whom they served.

> Let us always remember that our work is among the poor in rural areas, and that these children are the very purpose of our foundation as a religious institute. Let us therefore, cherish our vocation because it is the work of Christ. Let us be generous in the service of the poor for his sake, let us strive for the education of the poor with all our hearts and until our death.[630]

Mother instructed her daughters to foster a deep devotion to the Blessed Virgin Mary. "Invoke Mary, and her powerful intercession will guide you in the path which will lead you most assuredly to her Divine Son."[631]

In September 1880, Elizabeth, although feeling ill and acting contrary to her doctor's orders, left Rimouski to visit the sisters' missions at Saint-Godefroi and Port Daniel on the Gaspé coast. Upon her return home, she was exhausted and quite ill. Indefatigable, she set out to visit other missions. Once back home, her condition worsened. On March 23, the priest and doctor were called to her bedside and the sisters gathered around her. It was thought that she would not survive the night.

She assures those surrounding her, "God is calling me. I am resigned to His Holy will. However, I would not refuse to live if He were to cure me."[632] She begged forgiveness of all those whom she had offended in any way whatever. In the annals of the congregation, it is reported that Mother Élisabeth spoke the following to her sisters:

> I recommend to you all, the faithful practice of fraternal charity and union among yourselves. Remember that the essential thing is devotion to the accomplishment of your daily duties however painful they may be. We will only realize in heaven what it is to be a religious. How great it is to be a spouse of Christ.[633]

Mother Élisabeth survived a few more months. In the meantime, the major seminary of the diocese burned to the ground in April 1881. Élisabeth, appreciating the need for the education of the seminarians, offered from her deathbed the convent in which she and the other sisters were living. The bishop accepted the offer and in exchange offered that the sisters might move a few blocks away into a home belonging to his family. Mother's health improved slightly in June, but that upturn did not last long. On August 17, she died peacefully, surrounded by her sisters and priest confessor.

At the time of her death, the community consisted of fourteen professed sisters, plus one novice, and two postulants. Ten years after Élisabeth's death, the community changed its name to Sisters of Our Lady of the Holy Rosary, as the bishop had suggested, and as the general council of the congregation accepted.

*For further information, contact*
Centre Élisabeth-Turgeon
300, allée du Rosaire
Rimouski, QC G5L 3E3 Canada

# 19. ✠ Blessed Pedro Manrique de Zuñiga

*Place: México City, D.F.*
*Fame: Mexican colonial, son of the Spanish Viceroy. Martyr in Japan.*

Although the death sentence was the penalty for any Christian missionary discovered within Japan, the young priest Pedro Manrique (1685-1722) ventured twice into this forbidden land.[634] Capturing him the first time in 1618, the Japanese governor, fearing a diplomatic controversy over killing Father Pedro, whose father was the Spanish Viceroy at México, expelled the priest. Two years later, the priest reentered Japan. Captured again, he was held prisoner for almost two and a half years before being killed.

Father Pedro's second attempt to enter Japan occurred when he discovered a Japanese Christian sea captain and crew who were willing to risk their lives to further the evangelization of their countrymen. These sailors agreed to smuggle the priest into Japan. A Dominican priest, Louis Flores, joined the Augustinian priest Pedro Manrique in this attempt. The pair disguised themselves as merchants in search of new markets.

As the ship sailed from Manila towards Japan, a storm arose and blew the ship off course. When the ship entered the waters of Formosa, the English, who controlled this region, rescued the adrift voyagers. Viewing suspiciously the pair of supposed merchants, the English handed over the Japanese captain and crew, and two passengers to Dutch sailors who were heading for Japan. "The Protestant English and the Calvinist Dutch were the enemies of the Catholic Spaniards; and they cooperated with the Japanese authorities in their persecution of the Catholics in Japan. In 1609, the Dutch had been allowed to establish a trading center in the Japanese port of Hirado, and when the first English ship arrived four years later, they too were permitted to set up a similar center at the same place."[635] Neither the Dutch nor the English wished to jeopardize their lucrative trading arrangement with the Japanese.

Having docked at Hirado, the Dutch captain placed in prison all ten captives. For a year and a half, local Japanese authorities tortured the two priests in an attempt to have them identify themselves as priests. The clergymen did not yield. If they had given in and identified themselves, they would have placed the captain and crew at great risk.

Two attempts to rescue the priests and the Christian sailors failed. A Franciscan priest from Belgium, Richard Trouvé of St. Ann, tried on October 18, 1620, but he was captured and later killed. In late October 1620, five Japanese lay Christians attempted to free the prisoners, but they too were captured, and were tossed into the same prison as the men whom they had been trying to rescue.

Eventually, on December 8, 1621, Father Pedro Manrique admitted he was a priest. Immediately, he was separated from the other prisoners, and was transported to an island where again he was imprisoned. After three months Father Louis Flores too admitted he was a priest. He also was taken to the prison where Father Pedro was being held captive. Historians surmise that the captain and crew plus the would-be rescuers, were placed in the same island prison. On August 15, 1622, all these prisoners left their familiar prison, and were transferred to a prison at Nagasaki. On August 19, they were led to the place of execution. The two priests and captain were burned to death, and the twelve lay Christians were beheaded.

Pedro had lived in México for approximately a dozen years: eleven years as a child, and another half-year as a priest. His father had served as Viceroy from 1585 to 1590, and chose to remain in the country with his family for another five years. After Pedro was ordained a priest at Spain, he volunteered to serve in the Philippines. En route to his mission field, he traveled from Spain, and stayed in México for six months before continuing from Acapulco to Manila. After laboring in the Philippines for six years, Father Pedro learned that his priest-confrere Fernando Ayala Fernández had been martyred in Japan. After Father Pedro volunteered to take the place of the slain priest, Father Pedro received a place beside his confrere in the annals of the martyrs.

*For further information, contact*

Augustinians
Convento de Santa Monica
Peña Pobre 83
Col. Toriello Guerra – Del. Tlalpan
14050 México D.F. México

# 19. ✠ Blessed Louis Flores

*Place: México City, D.F.*
*Fame: Zealous missionary. Martyr in Japan.*

"A native of Belgium, a national of Spain, a colonial of México (New Spain), a Dominican friar and priest, a missionary in the Philippines, and a martyr of Japan," Louis Flores (c. 1570-1622) experienced a cosmopolitan life four hundred years ago. [636]

Joining his father in a transatlantic shipping business, Louis moved with his parents from his birthplace in Belgium back to their native Spain and then to México in search of further business opportunities.

In México, however, Louis made the first of two life-changing decisions. Feeling called to the religious life, he forsook a business career and instead joined the Dominicans. He studied for the priesthood and became ordained. His community, recognizing Louis' character and capabilities, appointed him director of novices.

In 1602, Father Louis left México to work as an itinerant missionary in the Philippines. He labored zealously there, especially in the area of the islands around Ogachon. Again, his talents were appreciated, and his religious community appointed him one of the provincial councilors who would render advice on the development of the mission in the Philippines. After seventeen years of generous service in this mission area, he was assigned to Manila to recuperate.

While recuperating in the Philippines' capital city, Louis learned about the devastating persecution being conducted in Japan. Missionaries were losing their lives, and the mission was desperate for more priests. Father Louis made his second life-changing decision: he heroically volunteered for the Japanese mission.

In 1619, Father Louis set sail for Japan with Pedro Manrique de Zuñiga, an Augustinian priest. The ship's captain was a Japanese Catholic layman, Joachim Firayama-Díaz. Great risk was involved for all aboard; identity as Christian and smuggling Christians into Japan were offenses punishable by death. After a storm arose at sea, the ship was blown off-course. English sailors saved the lives of the crew and passengers but handed them over to Dutch traders. The Dutch, wishing to maintain good business relations with the Japanese, in turn handed over the beleagured sailors to the Japanese at Firando. Both the English and the Dutch, being anti-Catholic Protestants, had no desire to assist the papists, and being shrewd businessmen, they wished to maintain good business relations with the Japanese.

The government imprisoned the men and interrogated them frequently. After almost two years' captivity, on December 8, 1620, Father Pedro admitted he was a priest. Three months later, Father Louis did the same. As soon as the priests admitted their identities, the captain and crew were charged with having smuggled into Japan outlawed priests. The crimes bore sentences of capital punishment. The two priests, captain and crew, were transferred to another prison.

On August 15, 1622, Louis and the other Christian prisoners were marched to Nagasaki. On August 19, the soldiers slowly burned to death Louis, the other priest, and the captain, and decapitated the laymen.

*For further information, contact*
Convento de San Alberto Magno
Odontologia #35
Col. Copilco Universidad
04360 México, D.F., México

# 25. ✠ Blessed Louis Sasada

*Place: México City, D.F.*
**Fame:** *Japanese native, student at México for four years.*
*Martyr at Nagasaki, Japan.*

The Japanese youth Louis Sasada (1600-24) spent four years in México, 1613-17, before being martyred at Nagasaki, Japan in 1624. During his time in México, Louis had entered the Franciscan Order and had begun studies for priesthood.

Louis Sasada had come to México with the Franciscan Father Louis Sotelo and members of Father's entourage. Father Sotelo was most respected: he had spent ten years on the missions in Japan, 1603-1613; and had developed great proficiency in the Japanese language.

Accompanying Father Sotelo as his personal servant was Louis Baba, a Japanese layman. The entourage included the northern Honshu ambassadors to Madrid and Rome, the Spanish ambassador to Japan, and thirty Japanese noblemen. The group traveled from Japan through Manila, via México, to Madrid, and eventually to Rome. The entourage embarked from the northern Honshu port of Uraga. The trans-Pacific trip had taken three months over stormy seas. Before leaving Japan, Father Sotelo had befriended young Louis Sasada, whose "father Michael, a pious and esteemed Japanese nobleman, had died a Christian martyr with seven others a short time before, when they were beheaded on August 16, 1613."[637] Louis Sasada was the only member of the traveling party who remained in México. Years later, Father Sotelo returned from Europe and stayed five months in México, before setting out for the Asian ports. In Rome, Father Sotelo had been named bishop-elect of Oshu, in northern Honshu. Father Sotelo asked Louis Sasada to serve as the bishop's secretary.

On April 2, 1617, Louis Sasada embarked from Acapulco with Father Sotelo and other Franciscan missionaries, and arrived at Manila three months later. In Manila, precocious Louis completed his studies for the priesthood, and with special permission because of his young age, he was ordained. Father Sotelo himself provided most of the instruction in the faith and in theology.

In the Philippines, Father Sotelo was desirous of returning as soon as possible to Japan, where he wished to continue his ministry. The Japanese ambassador to Rome, Rokuemon Hasekura, however, was not anxious to return to northern Honshu.

In autumn 1622, Father Sotelo, Louis Sasada, Louis Baba, and others disguised themselves and at Nueva Segovi boarded a ship bound for Japan. As the ship neared the Japanese port of Satsuma, the captain refused to let his passengers disembark. He had suspected that they were priests, and not long before, on August 19, the captain Joachim Díaz-Hiroyama and crew had been decapitated by the Japanese government for smuggling priests onto the island. This captain, instead of risking his life and that of his crew, handed over his suspected Catholics to the Japanese governmental authorities at Nagasaki. There, the three men were imprisoned, and within six months they had been transferred to a new prison at Omura. Soon, two more priests, the Dominican Pedro

Vasquez and Jesuit Miguel Carvalho, joined them in jail. Father Sotelo describes the opportunity to say Mass.

> Though there are four priests here in jail, we have all that is required to perform our religious exercises and even to celebrate Mass. The Christians at the risk of their lives procure for us all that we need. Therefore, we partake daily of the Table of the Lord, which gives us wonderful consolation and helps us in our privations. The prison is for us, not a prison, but a real palace or delightful garden.[638]

Nearly two years after having been arrested, the prisoners received news on August 25, 1624, that their sentences had been decided, namely, death; and that the penalty would be applied immediately. At midmorning, the five prisoners were taken to the place of execution. On the mound of a hill, five crosses had been erected in a semicircle. Father Louis Sasada was positioned at one end, Louis Baba on the other end, and Father Sotelo in the middle of the five. The fire was lit to burn quickest at the ends of the semicircle and longest in the middle. A Franciscan brother who had disguised himself as a stable boy witnessed the events. He reported that when the fire lapped at the ropes which tied the hands of Louis Sasada and Louis Baba, these two were freed from their crosses. "Both of them went over to Father Sotelo and, kneeling before him, asked for his blessing. 'I bless you,' said Father Sotelo, 'and may God bless you and give you the fortitude which will obtain for you the crown of eternal life which has been prepared for you'."[639] The pair returned to the places of their stakes, and were soon consumed by the fire. The other three priests died soon, with Father Sotelo suffering the longest. The martyrs collapsed from their stakes into the fire. The soldiers then tossed on top of the bodies the prayer books, vestments, and sacred vessels which the priests had used to say Mass.

*For further information, contact*
Franciscan Friars
Provincial Curia
Caballocalco 11
Coyoacan, México D.F. 04000 México

# SEPTEMBER

❧

### 1. ☩ Marie Fitzbach

*Place: Québec City, Québec*
*Fame: Wife, mother, and widow. Foundress of the*
*Good Shepherd Sisters of Québec.*
*First native Québecois to found a religious congregation.*

"What do you expect? When we leave prison, we're disgraced and penniless, and no one wants us around, except in evil places. That's why you so often see us back behind bars!"[640] So spoke a woman inmate to a lawyer visiting the women's prison in Québec City.[641] The lawyer, a member of the St. Vincent de Paul Society, reported this exchange to the bishop. The churchman approached Mrs. Marie Fitzbach-Roy (1806-1885) and asked her to oversee St. Magdalen's

MARIE FITZBACH

Refuge, which the Society was planning as a shelter for women ex-prisoners and prostitutes. Maria was shocked by the bishop's request. She was forty-three, widowed, and living in a convent.

Marie-Josephe Fitzbach had left her rural home at her mother's suggestion, at thirteen, to find work in Québec City as a domestic servant. François-Xavier Roy hired Marie to care for his dying wife. Marie also taught the couple's two children basic reading, writing, and religion. In her free time, Marie visited the sick at the Hôtel-Dieu hospital, "where the nuns entrusted the most derelict women to her care"[642] After his wife died in 1827, Mr. Roy sold his business and moved to Cap-Santé, forty-five miles southwest of Québec. Some months later, François proposed marriage to Marie; he was thirty-seven, and she twenty-three. After consulting with her spiritual director, Marie married François in 1828.

The couple gave birth to three girls within the next five years. In 1833, François died.

Marie possessed great faith and compassion. When she had made her First Communion at eleven, Marie experienced the desire to love God and to love Him in her neighbors. "Marie's first contact with the Eucharist seems to have brought her a special grace of union with the Lord, one that marked her prayer-life forever afterwards."[643] Away from home, as a teenager and twenty-something, she rose daily at four o'clock, and attended Mass. She learned compassion from dealing with her father's death when she was two, her mother's remarrying four years later, the family's moving from Saint-Vallier to Saint-Charles; the departures from home of her six older siblings, and burying her husband. Upon her husband's death, his family took his two children from the first marriage and most of his income, and left Marie with her three girls. The youngest of the three died at fourteen. In these sufferings, Marie's faith brought her closer to Jesus Christ and to all fellow sufferers.

After praying about the bishop's request, and discussing it with her daughters and spiritual director, Marie replied, "Your Grace, I am your humble servant. Do with me as you please. I shall consider your will as God's own Will"[644]

Marie loved assisting these women. Within ten years, they numbered sixty at any one time. Some of the women had been imprisoned and came to the Refuge after their release. Some were brought to Marie by their family members; some arrived alone, pleading to be admitted. Still others, Marie found in brothels and invited to the Refuge. At the Refuge, Marie cooked, sewed, did the laundry, cleaned the house, and at times begged for food.

Pursuing preventative as well as rehabilitative measures, Marie and companions opened a school for girls. Marie advised her companions, "If there is only one space in your school, and if two pupils — one rich and one poor — ask to be admitted, give your preference to the latter "[645] As the years passed, more classrooms were added and hundreds more students enrolled.

Other works, too, were added to the original double mission of providing shelter to troubled women and educating children. In 1870, the community opened a Reform House for girls and, four years later, the House of Mercy for young unwed mothers.

On February 2, 1856, Marie and six collaborators founded the Congregation of the Servants of the Immaculate Heart of Mary Refuge of Sinners. Despite the community's name, the townspeople called them the Good Shepherd Sisters of Québec, because their work resembled that of the Good Shepherd Sisters in France. Within thirty-five years, one hundred seventy-two women joined the community, living in fifteen convents, all in the Province of Québec except for one house in Biddeford, Maine, two hundred fifty miles south of Québec City.

As a religious, Marie, now called Mother Mary of the Sacred Heart, preferred direct service to administration. "She found her ideal and the dream of her life not in giving orders to others or being in authority, but in one impressive realization alone: I am a religious sister!"[646] In 1856, the sisters elected her the first superior of the congregation. Three years later, she resigned that position. The sisters then elected her the first assistant. After six years in that role, she received permission from the bishop to refuse any further elected position. Beginning in 1865, she sat on the Council, without formal position, but as an advisor. "No important decision was taken without her being informed or consulted"[647] In her freedom from administration, Mother Marie asked her spiritual director what rule of conduct he might suggest to her. He replies in part,

"Love to be ignored and counted as nothing"; this first recommendation is from the *Imitation* [*of Christ,* by Thomas à Kempis], and you will find it bitter. Here is the second one, which will produce the same effects but is coated with the sweetness of divine love: "Learn from Me that I am meek and humble of heart."[648]

As she aged, her asthma worsened. Two months before she died, she writes to the wife of her stepson, "It is really necessary for the machine to break down so that the soul may soar to the eternal mansions. And that is where I hope to see all my loved ones."[649]

Towards the end of her life, Mother Marie spoke the following to her sisters in religious community, "Tell them [the novices] that I entreat them to become holy religious women. May they love the good Lord well! I'm not saying that I myself have been a holy religious, but I can say that I have always loved God and that my greatest happiness was to help others love Him too"[650]

Marie Fitzbach had faced many challenges in her life, which resulted in her identifying easily with the homeless, the jobless, all suffering souls. Twice, as a child and in marriage, she was a member of a "blended family." Twice, as an adolescent and a widow, circumstances forced her to look for work. Twice she retired, at forty-three and fifty-nine, only to come out of retirement because the needs of those around her called her into action.[651]

*For further information, contact*
Centre Marie-Fitzbach
2550, rue Marie-Fitzbach
Sainte-Foy, QC G1V 2J2 Canada

## 2. ✠ Blessed André Grasset de Saint-Sauveur

*Place: Montréal, Québec*
*Fame: First native-born Canadian to be beatified.*
*Martyred in Paris during the French Revolution.*

Born and raised in Montréal until six, young André (1758-92) benefited from the religious atmosphere of the city.[652] The day after he was born, he was baptized at the old church of Notre-Dame, which was replaced by the new cathedral in 1827. When the boy was five, the father bought a home very near the chapel of Bon Secours, where Marguerite Bourgeoys had served.

The Grasset family moved to France in 1763. Fourteen years before, in 1749, the father had moved from France to New France. The father, a lawyer by profession, had found a position with the new governor of New France. In 1752, when the governor lost his position, Grasset opened a private practice in the city. Soon after his arrival in Canada, he got married and fathered two daughters, one of whom died in infancy along with his wife. That same year, he married again and soon had five sons, the second of whom was André. When France, according to the Treaty of 1763, handed over to England the claim on the Canadian territory, the father returned to France with his family. The family moved to Calais first, then to Sens after the father was named consul at Trieste in 1772, and again to Venice when he became consul there in 1780.

By this time, André had established himself in the seminary for the diocese of Sens. At twenty-one, he received a benefice as chaplain at Saint-Europe in Sens; two years later, he was named a canon of the cathedral of Sens with responsibility for safeguarding the cathedral's art treasures; and at twenty-five, in 1783, he was ordained a priest.

The French Revolution erupted in 1789. The next year, the Constituent Assembly attempted to erect a schismatic Church in France: independent of the pope's authority, and dependent only on the French people who would vote for their bishops and priests. The assembly suppressed the cathedral chapter, and all religious orders and congregations. In 1791, the assembly declared that all clergy had to sign an oath supporting the Civil Constitution of the clergy. The pope condemned this document, and most bishops and priests refused to sign it. By the end of the year, the new Legislative Assembly threatened all non-complying priests to leave the country or to face either ten years in jail, or exile to the state colony at Guyana in South America. Father André, rather than comply with the assembly's demands or succumb to their threats, took refuge in the house of the Eudist Fathers in Paris, where about sixty priests had gathered to maintain their priestly way of life. Having moved to the Eudist House in early 1792, Father André was arrested in August of that same year, when a mob entered the house and removed the priests to the Carmelite monastery in Paris. On September 2, 1792, the revolution's leaders announced that those held as prisoners at the Carmelite house had been declared guilty.

> Led by [Stanislas] Maillard, a mob armed with guns, pikes, and clubs rushed to the monastery-prison and began to massacre the priests in cold blood. In the midst of the carnage Maillard bethought himself of giving it some semblance of judicial procedure. He set up a makeshift tribunal, and the prisoners who were still alive were brought before him. "Are you willing to take the oath of allegiance?" he asked them. One and all replied: "No! My conscience forbids me to do so." The leader gave a sign, and they were hustled to the outer stairway near the entrance. Here they were pierced with bayonets, sabers, and pikes until all of them

were dead. The bodies of some of the martyrs were thrown into a well at one end of the monastery garden; the others were cast into trenches at the four corners of the city. In this way, three bishops and one hundred eighty-eight priests — and one of them Blessed Andrew Grasset de St. Sauveur — won the martyr's crown. Pope Pius VI spoke of them as "a choir of martyrs."[653]

In Paris, in the crypt of the Carmelite Monastery where the horrific slaughter took place and where the remains of the martyrs now are encased, a plaque was put in place after Pope Pius XI in 1926 beatified the one hundred ninety-one martyrs. Included on the list of names is "Blessed André of Montréal."[654]

In Montréal, in the entrance to the Cathedral of Notre-Dame, stands an altar dedicated to the Martyrs of the French Revolution, one of whom was Montréal's native son: Blessed André Grasset de Saint-Sauveur.

*For further information, contact*
La Catedral de Notre-Dame
424 St. Sulpice
Montréal, QC H2Y 2V5 Canada

⚭

## 4. ✠ Blessed Dina Bélanger

*Place: Sillery, Québec; and New York City, New York*
*Fame: Desired not to commit a single sin. Mystic and Concert Pianist.*

At eight, in response to her teacher's statement that the Church had no Saint Dina, Dina Bélanger (1897-1929) said to herself, "Very well, I will be a saint. I will provide a patron for those who bear my name."[655] As a postulant, Dina believed that each religious was to be "a great saint."[656] As a novice, she writes, "I want to be a saint."[657] Her classmates nicknamed her, "Saint Dina."

When her pastor heard that Dina was about to be beatified, he commented, "Her mother is the one who ought to be beatified first."[658] Dina's mother says of her daughter, "Before she was born, I asked God that this child, soon to come into this world, accomplish something good in its life, and not by halves, that this child become a religious, man or woman, if such was his will. Every time I went to Mass, I renewed this request."[659] The father earned a comfortable living as an accountant. Dina accompanied her parents on visits to the sick and the poor. She observes, "Their joy always was to give silently and discreetly."[660]

DINA BÉLANGER

Seventeen months after Dina's birth, a son was born, but he survived only three months. Dina grew up an only child.

Dina began taking piano lessons at eight, and studied "with a passion."[661] After graduating from boarding school at Québec, she studied piano for two years at the Conservatory of Music in New York City. Upon returning home to Québec, she performed and gained acclaim for the next three years as a concert pianist.

From her childhood, Dina developed a personal relationship with God. She learned the usual prayers, and sensitivity towards those in need. After declaring at eight, that she wanted to be a saint; she began the next year to discipline her senses, and to perform "little sacrifices of love for Jesus."[662] About her First Communion at ten, she writes, "External things were of no concern to me, I was thinking of the One who was to become my sacred Guest."[663] She did not allow herself to be distracted by a new silver wristwatch she had received; instead she rejoiced that, "Jesus was mine, and I was his."[664] At ten, she was absorbed for half an hour by these mere words from her prayer book: "Lord, my God."[665]

At eleven, Dina deepened her relationship with Jesus. She writes that on Holy Thursday 1908, "During my act of thanksgiving after communion, Our Lord spoke to my soul by means of a new light. This was the first time I heard his voice so well, interiorly, of course, a soft melodious voice that filled me with happiness."[666] In her *Autobiography*, Dina offers a clarification: "I want to explain once and for all the expressions that I shall use, such as: 'I saw' . . . 'Jesus said to me'. . . and other similar expressions. They mean 'I saw in my imagination', 'Jesus told me by that interior voice which every soul hears in the depths of the heart in moments of divine consolation.'"[667] At the same age, Dina delighted in looking at herself in the mirror and fought against the temptation to vanity. As a teenager, she avoided gossip; she writes, "In my thoughts, I attributed the best intentions to everyone, whether the deeds were good or reprehensible. If their guilt seemed obvious, I found excuses. I would defend those who were not present; how I suffered when of necessity I had to remain silent! ... I cannot remember having deliberately judged anyone."[668]

At boarding school homesickness afflicted Dina. She notes, "I cried tears fourteen consecutive nights; after that, for several weeks, it was every two or three evenings; in the end, my will grew stronger and I was comforted."[669] This shy young girl gradually overcame her reserve. Mimicry came easily to her, and she amused others with this gift. At this same time, she continued to grow in union with God: denying her senses, and developing a "cheerful exterior and interior self-denial."[670] At fourteen, she offered God her virginity, and expressed the willingness to die a martyr.

Upon completing studies at sixteen, Dina wanted to enter the convent, but her parents, pastor, and spiritual director, advised her to wait a few years. She busied herself, participating in parish societies, visiting the sick, and assisting the poor. While she enjoyed family and friends, the material attractions of the world bored her. She writes, "Bright colours, excessive jewelry were distasteful to me, and yet I often wore all kinds. I found it torture to wear jewelry so often, yet opportunities were not lacking."[671] What interested her were the things of God.

At the New York Conservatory of Music, Dina advanced quickly through the degrees of licentiate, master, and professor. She and another student from Québec became best friends. Dina writes, "Our intimate and communal life in a strange country, our shared joys and setbacks, our frequent fits of mutually incited laughter, as well as our soothed tears, in a word, our fraternal life, the abandonment and trust of two sisters, was to tie the bond of a noble, tender and precious friendship. Jesus himself was already the link which united our two souls."[672] Dina continues, "The greatest advantage [of residing in the sisters' hostel] was to have access to a chapel where the Master lived and kept constant vigil, where Holy Mass was celebrated every morning, where the liturgical ceremonies were held. I could never enter or leave the house without passing by Jesus, without greeting him."[673]

After completing studies at the Conservatory in 1913, Dina returned to Québec. She performed at concerts and taught music. She writes of her concert play, "Before playing in public ... I would invite him [Jesus] to hear the pieces I was to perform, with the Blessed Virgin, and the angels and saints."[674] "At first, it seemed he was at my side, that he was walking close by me. Then I found he was within me."[675]

While praying about her vocation, Dina heard Jesus say to her, "I want you in the Congregation of Jesus and Mary."[676] She replied that she had little interest in teaching, to which Jesus replied, "You will not teach long."[677] One year later, August 1921, Dina entered that congregation, whose stated purpose was, "To make Jesus and Mary known and loved by means of Christian education, with a predilection for the young and among them, the poor."[678]

Life in the convent supported Dina's spiritual growth. As a postulant preparing for the novitiate, she writes about the extraordinary grace she experienced of the Lord substituting the hearts of Jesus and Mary in place of Dina's heart.

> I felt overwhelmed with sheer delight, all was peace and love. Then my good Master took hold of my poor heart, just as one picks up an object from a particular place, and replaced it with, — O gift of infinite love! — his Sacred Heart and the Immaculate Heart of Mary! Again, it was an image; but there certainly took place within me a divine transaction that no pen could describe.... From that moment, I have acted and loved, with the Heart of Our Lord and that of his Blessed Mother."[679]

At prayer, Dina played games with Jesus. The pair competed as to which one loved more or suffered more. Dina responded to Jesus' claims of endless love and suffering that he and she were tied in the competition because she had united her heart to his. In February 1922, she took the religious habit and religious name, Mary Saint Cecile of Rome: Mary in honor of the Blessed Mother; and Saint Cecile of Rome because of her martyrdom, i.e., her giving her all to Jesus.

One of her favorite devotions was the Eucharistic Heart of Jesus. She reported that Jesus had invited her to "console" him for the thoughtless transgressions of priests, plus men and women religious.[680] Her mission was to be "an apostle of love, a victim of love, a martyr of love, a victim of love, an apostle of love."[681] Although Dina enjoyed extraordinary graces, she suffered also from "aridity, dryness, aversion, temptation to discouragement and despair,"[682] Also, she suffered significant temptations against chastity.[683]

After taking vows in August 1923, Dina was missioned to Saint Michel School at Bellechasse. Three times in that first school year she became sick and was transferred to the community's infirmary. During this year of oscillating good and poor health, Dina experienced Jesus ever more intimately. She describes Jesus' promise: "From now on, I am giving you the awareness of my presence within you, that is, you will enjoy the felt presence of God.[684]

In March 1924, the sister superior asked Dina to write her autobiography. Obediently, Dina wrote from March until the end of June, about her childhood to the present moment. In November, under obedience, she continued to write her *Autobiography* covering the period July 1 to the end of November. In December, she began to share her spiritual diary. On her deathbed in September 1929, she proclaimed, "I am going to God to work for my (Congregation of) Jesus and Mary until the end of the world ... (and) for other souls too."[685]

*For further information, contact*
Religious of Jesus and Mary
Dina-Belanger Centre
2049, St. Louis Road
Sillery, QC G1T 1P2 Canada

⚮

## 10. ✠ Blessed Vicente Ramírez de San José

*Places: México, D.F.*
**Fame:** *Lay brother assigned to assist elderly priest.*
*Mexican colonial martyred at Nagasaki, Japan.*

The child Vicente Ramírez de San José (1597-1622) emigrated with his parents from Ayamonte, Spain, to México City, México. At eighteen, he entered the Mexican province of the Franciscan order, and the next year, professed his religious vows. In 1618, this Mexican colonial was missioned to Japan.

In November 1617, two Franciscan missionaries to Japan had disembarked at Veracruz on their way from Rome back home to Japan. Louis Sotelo had just been named the bishop-elect of Oshu, Japan; and the priest Pedro de Avila was accompanying him. Sotelo had been laboring in Japan since 1603 and "had a perfect command of the Japanese language."[686] The bishop and fifty-five-year-old priest traveled overland to México City, where they remained for five months. When the spring weather provided good sailing conditions, they prepared to depart from Acapulco for the Orient. In México, several Franciscans, including Vicente Ramírez, joined the charismatic Sotelo.

Departing in early April 1618, the missionaries arrived at Manila in early July. Although Bishop Sotelo would be delayed another four years before departing from Manila for Japan, five of the Franciscans including Vicente disguised themselves as merchants and in 1619 attempted to enter Japan. At that time, being a Christian inside Japan presented a real danger. In 1614, the *daimyo* Ieyasu Tokugawa had decreed that Christianity was to be abolished, and that it was illegal, under penalty of death, to practice and promote Christianity. For the mission in Japan, the Franciscan superior of the apostolate assigned young Brother Vicente Ramírez to assist the elderly Father Pedro de Ávila.

The evangelization proceeded well until December 18, 1620, when the identities of Father Pedro and Brother Vicente were discovered. A Christian apostate named Ochoso approached the pair and inquired if they were priests. When Father Pedro replied affirmatively, the supposed Christian requested time to prepare for confession and assured the men of his prompt return. When he came back, he brought soldiers with him.

When the soldiers arrived, Father Pedro opened the door, treated them courteously, and shared a little Spanish Mass wine with them. Father Pedro and Brother Vicente put on their Franciscan habits along with their rosaries. Then they were tightly bound and brought to the jail at Nagasaki. Here they languished for almost a year until Father Richard Trouvé, another victim of Ochoso, joined them. Soon, the three were transferred to Omura.

At Omura, Father Pedro and Brother Vicente were tried and convicted. Like many other Christian prisoners incarcerated at Nagasaki, they were marched back there. On September 10, 1622, Father Pedro and Brother Vicente were among the Spanish and Mexican lay and clerical missionaries, and Japanese clergy and laity, including men, women, and children, who suffered martyrdom. The laity generally were decapitated, and the clergy and lay leaders were burned slowly over an open pit fire. These martyrs are included among the two hundred five persons whom Pope Pius XI beatified in 1867 as the Martyrs of Japan.

*For further information, contact*
Franciscan Friars
Provincial Curia
Caballocalco 11
Coyoacán, México D.F. 04000 México

∞

## 10.  ✠  Blessed Richard Trouvé of St. Ann

*Place: México City, D.F.*
*Fame: Ministered for four years under the threat of death,*
*if captured. Martyred at Nagasaki, Japan.*

As a youth, Lambert Trouvé of St. Ann (1585-1917) frequented houses of prostitution. One evening, he accompanied a friend to one of their haunts. At their destination, for some unclear reason, Lambert decided to return home, whereupon his friend chose to remain. That same night, as Lambert lay sleeping, a terrible noise awoke him. The ghost of his friend stood at Lambert's bedside and said, "Woe is mine. Stay away from that house where we were a little while ago. Out in the street you'll find my dead body. My soul has been damned. The same would have happened to you if the Holy Virgin had not protected you because of those three Hail Marys you say on awakening and retiring. Happy will you be if you heed this warning."[687] Startled, Lambert jumped out of bed and ran outside, where lay his friend's body. Just then, Lambert heard the church bells of the nearby Franciscan Friary. He ran there, knocked frantically on the door, and begged admission into the order. On the spot, after hearing his story, the friars admitted Lambert. Fact or fiction? Credible witnesses testify to the veracity of the story.[688]

After his formation for religious life, Lambert took vows in 1604, and took Richard as his name in religion. He served as a porter in the local monastery at Nivelles, Belgium. Two years later, while visiting the Arcoli Friary at Rome, he encountered a former missionary. This confrere inspired Richard by regaling him with stories of the missionaries' endeavors and sufferings in Japan. Richard responded, "How happy I would be if I could lay down my life for the salvation of souls, and so atone for my past sins."[689]

Richard transferred from his native Belgian province to the mission-sending province of Alcantira, Spain. Assigned to the Orient, he traveled to México, where he studied, before reaching Manila in 1609. Before long, his superiors sent him back to México, where he continued his studies and was ordained a priest in 1611. After serving as director of novices for a few years, Richard sailed from México to Manila and Japan. No sooner had he arrived than Emperor Ieyasu issued an edict in 1614 banning from Japan all foreign missionaries. Richard returned to Manila. Three years later, Richard and other missionaries risked their lives to re-enter the country. Richard used various disguises to travel about, accompanying and encouraging the dozens of Catholics condemned to death for their faith. For four years, he successfully hid out among the caves and mountains, while ministering to the people in and around Nagasaki.

In 1621, Richard was arrested, and the next year, he was martyred. After the Japanese informant Ochoso had handed over to governmental authorities both Father Pedro de Ávila and Brother Vicente Ramírez, Richard castigated that fellow. A few days later, the same informant told authorities about Richard too. Richard was arrested and was dragged from the home of a Belgian family who had been sheltering him; the husband, wife, and daughter were captured as well. At Nagasaki, Richard was imprisoned with his confreres Father Pedro and Brother Vicente, who were part of the group of thirty-one people arrested for practicing the Catholic faith; sixteen of these were laity, and the remainder were Dominican, Franciscan, and Jesuit missionaries. All thirty-one prisoners were marched to Omura, about five miles from Nagasaki, where they joined the other martyrs in the making.

On September 10, the prisoners from Nagasaki were marched back there. Other Christian prisoners from other cities were delivered there as well. Forty thousand onlookers witnessed the execution. Before Richard left Omura, he penned a letter to the Franciscan guardian at the friary back home at Nivelles. An excerpt reads:

> I have been for nearly a year in this wretched prison, where are with me nine religious of our order (Franciscan), eight Dominicans, and six Jesuits. The others are native Christians who have helped us in our ministry. Some have been here for five years. Our food is a little rice and water. The road to martyrdom has been paved for us by more than three hundred martyrs, all Japanese, on whom all kinds of tortures were inflicted. As for us survivors, we also are all doomed to death. We religious and those who have helped us are to be burnt at a slow fire; the others will be beheaded. . . . If my mother is still alive, I beg you to be so kind as to tell her of God's mercy to me in allowing me to suffer and die for Him. I have no time left to write to her myself.[690]

*For further information, contact*
Franciscan Friars
Provincial Curia
Caballocalco 11
Coyoacán, México D.F. 04000 México

✜

# 14. ✜ Martyrs of Georgia

*Place: Golden Isles, Georgia*
*Fame: Defenders of monogamy. Martyred by opponents*
*of the Church's teaching on monogamy.*

In mid-September 1597, a band of Guale Indians went on the warpath against the Franciscan missionaries in the Georgian coastal area. The mission stretched fifty miles from St. Catherine's Island in the north to Cumberland Island in the south.[691]

The incident which triggered the rampage occurred after the chief's nephew Juanillo married a second wife, while remaining married to his first wife.[692] Father Pedro de Corpa (c. 1560-1597), the regional superior of the missions, conferred about the situation with

MARTYRS OF GEORGIA

Father Blas de Rodríguez (c. 1555-1597), who lived at the mission at Tupiqui (now near Eulonia). The two experienced missionaries — Father de Corpa who had arrived at the Golden Isles ten years previously, in 1587, and Father Rodríguez, who arrived in 1590 — had become familiar with the Indian language, customs, and receptivity to Christianity. This pair decided that they could not permit Juanillo to succeed his uncle as chief. "His example in practicing bigamy would have undermined the faith in these small mission settlements."[693] When Father Pedro appointed as successor the elderly Indian named Francisco, the young Juanillo became enraged. He withdrew from the village, and joined up with other opponents of the new religion. "Some dissatisfied Christians, including chiefs of several neighboring villages, joined them and the unbaptized pagan natives.[694]

During the next few weeks, martyrs' blood ran freely in Georgia. The rebels snuck under cover of darkness into the mainland village of Tolomato (now near Darien, opposite Sapelo Island). At daybreak on September 14, they found Father Pedro de Corpa praying quietly at the Mission Nuestra Señora de Guadalupe. The rebels smashed a tomahawk into his head, killing him immediately. They decapitated him, and placed the head atop a lance, which they placed at the canoe landing area. As if in defiance of the priest's teaching on monogamous marriage, "other Indians raped Christian women, and the mission itself was looted."[695] At a formal governmental investigation conducted at St. Augustine, Florida, ten months later, various Indians remembered Juanillo having delivered this speech, after murdering Father Pedro:

Now the friar is dead.... He would not have been killed had he let us live as we did before we became Christians. Let us return to our ancient customs.... They take away our women, leaving us only the one and perpetual, forbidding us to exchange her. They prevent our dancing, banquets, feasts, celebrations, games, and warfare, so that by disuse we shall lose our ancient courage and skill inherited from our ancestors. They persecute our old folks, calling them witches. Even our work annoys them, and they want us to cease on certain days.[696]

Before leaving for the mainland village of Tupiquí, the raiders sent a message to the chief at St. Catherines Island, asking him to kill the two friars there: Father Miguel de Añon and Brother Antonio de Badajoz.

After arriving at the Mission Santa Clara at Tupiquí, the Indians informed Father Blas de Rodríguez that they had come to kill him. He requested, and they permitted, that he would say Mass before dying. At the end of the Mass, he distributed his belongings to some Indian women. His would-be attackers allowed him to live for two days. During that time, the priest mentioned to his attackers,

My sons, for me it is not difficult to die. Even if you should not cause it, the death of this body is inevitable. We have to be ready at all times, for we, all of us, have to die some day. But what does pain me is that the Evil one has persuaded you to do this offensive thing against your God and Creator.[697]

On September 16, Father Blas was tomahawked to death. His murderers threw the corpse in a place where the dogs might consume it. Faithful Indian Catholics, however, recovered the body, and gave it a proper burial.

At St. Catherine's Island, the chief who had received Juanillo's message to kill the two Spaniards, alerted the pair that their lives were endangered. For whatever reason, the chief's warnings went unheeded. Finally, the chief himself went to Mission Santa Catalina. The chief offered a canoe and a team of rowers to take the priests to San Pedro Island (now Cumberland Island). Again, the advice was not acted upon. The priest and lay brother celebrated Mass. The attackers arrived and went directly for Brother Antonio, hit him once in the head with a tomahawk, killing him outright. At first, the Indians hesitated in attacking Father Miguel de Añon, whose demeanor evoked much respect. Suddenly, one Indian lunged forward and with a blow to the head, knocked the priest unconscious. Another brave, with a swift blow, split open the priest's skull and killed him instantly.

Two missionaries remained alive. The rebels rowed to Asao (now St. Simons Island). Father de Veráscola had left Mission Santo Domingo for St. Augustine to acquire supplies. The Indians waited patiently for him. On an uncertain date, but before October 4, he returned in his canoe. The Indians went to the shore and pretended to greet him. They surrounded him and sprang upon him. The attackers outnumbered the physically powerful priest, known affectionately to his confreres as "the giant from Cantabria."[698] The Indians tied him a tree, beat him, and bound him in an animal's cage. After three days of beatings and starvation, they decided to burn him to death. A huge rainstorm washed out that plan. They set upon him with an axe and hacked him to death.

By this time, Father Francisco de Ávila had learned of the killings. He hid in the forest near his mission at Ospo (now Jekyl Island). The rebels came looking for him. For a while, he watched the braves loot the mission. Then he ran deeper into the thick forest. Spotting him, the Indians chased after him and captured him. "Taken prisoner, he was at first condemned to die until it was decided to keep him alive as a slave. He became servant to all, abused by his captors and jeered at by children. The Indians urged him to give up his religion, get married, and serve in their spirit house."[699] He refused. For the next nine months, Father Francisco remained enslaved. Because he did not die at the hand of these attackers, Father de Ávila is not included among the Martyrs of Georgia.

Word of the attacks reached the Spanish governor at St. Augustine. He sent one hundred fifty soldiers north to find the rebels. The Spanish soldiers took out reprisals against various villages en route. In the area of the priest-murders, the Spaniards burned several towns and crops. The already short food supply was worsened.

After the winter, the governor sent an envoy to Santa Elena (now Parris Island, South Carolina) to request the aid of loyal Guale Indians against the rebels. Within a few months, the counterattack proved successful. The Gualean leaders captured seven rebels and negotiated for the release of Father de Ávila, who was returned to St. Augustine.

Juanillo had escaped to Yfusinique, but there the loyalists caught up with him, killed him, and sent his scalp to the governor as a sign of his death.

At St. Augustine, governmental and ecclesiastical authorities expected Father de Ávila to testify against the attackers. The priest refused, however, on grounds of clerical immunity: he did not want his testimony to lead to the death of anyone, not even these murderers. Later, he was sent to Cuba, where under the vow of obedience he wrote down the events as he knew them.

In July 1598, the government held an official hearing. One brave was condemned to die. The others were released. In 1603, Governor Gonzalo Méndez de Canzo toured the affected areas. He sought and received the Indians' assistance in rebuilding the towns, including the burnt-out mission churches. By December 1605, the missions were operating again, with the help of recently arrived Franciscans. New missions were established, namely, Mission San Buenaventura at St. Simons, Mission San José de Zapala on Sapelo Island, and Mission Santiago de Ocone at Jekyl Island. "A total of 1,652 were confirmed in the area which is now called Georgia."[700]

The next five decades of peace was disrupted, however, by the arrival of the English in 1670. The English invited the Yamassee Indians to ally themselves with the newest colonizers. The English and Yamassee Indians attacked the Guale Indians and drove them farther south, eventually into Florida and out of existence. The Battle of Bloody Marsh in 1742, which the English won on St. Simon's Island, signaled the last gasp of the Spanish settlements in Georgia.

*For further information, contact*
Vice Postulator
The Cause of the Georgia Martyrs
Franciscan University of Steubenville
Steubenville, OH 43952 U.S.A.

## 16. ✣ Blessed Martyrs of Oaxaca: Juan Bautista and Jacinto de los Angeles

*Place: Cajonos, Oaxaca*
*Fame: Lay leaders. Martyrs.*

At San Francisco Cajonos, in the state of Oaxaca, two indigenous lay leaders, Juan Bautista and Jacinto de los Angeles, died for the Catholic faith in 1700. Both men were beatified.

When the pair refused to participate in the idolatrous ceremonies of the local community, the crowd of pagan believers grew angry. The mob rushed the monastery in which the pair was hiding. Angrily the mob threatened that if the two did not surrender, or if the monks did not hand them over to the crowd, then the mob would burn them out, and the monks with them.

Anticipating the inevitable, Juan Bautista (c. 1660-1700) presented himself to the mob and said, "We are going to die for the law of God, and since I have no fear of God's divine majesty, I need no weapons."[701] One of the priests heard Juan's confession, and then the soon-to-be martyr spoke again to the crowd, "Here I am, if you have plans to kill me tomorrow, kill me now."[702] While the crowd angrily beat him, he said nothing other than to cry out for the help of God and the Blessed Virgin. His final prayer was for the observing friars to remember him in their prayers before God. "Jacinto de los Angeles (c. 1660-1700) was taken along the route named Zempoalatengo, where the crowd hanged him, slit his throat, opened his chest, and ripped out his heart, which they threw to the dogs, and tossed the corpse off a mountain near Xagacia."[703]

According to baptismal and marriage records of the church at Cajonos, both men were husbands and fathers. Juan had married Josefa de la Cruz, and the couple gave birth to a daughter Rosa. Jacinto had married Petrona, and they were blessed with the daughter Incolaza.

*For further information, contact*
Arquidiócesis de Antewquerra [Oaxaca]
Curia Vigil #600
Centro Apartado Postal #31
68000 Oaxaca, Oaxaca, México

## 20. ✠ Saint José María de Yermo y Parres

*Places: León, Guanajuato, and Puebla, Puebla*
**Fame:** *The Giant of Charity, Founder of the Servants
of the Sacred Heart of Jesus and the Poor.*

Born into wealth, José María de Yermo y Parres
(1851-1904) experienced at thirty-four a conversion to serve the poor.[704]

José had always been a good student and a
good priest. As a youth, he was educated first at
home by private tutors and later at a private
school where he won an academic award from
Emperor Maximilian himself. At sixteen, José
entered the Vincentian seminary, completed the
novitiate, and took vows in that religious community in 1869, after which he was sent to Paris

JOSÉ MARÍA DE
YERMO Y PARRES

to study theology. Upon returning from Paris, he became quite ill and
lived with his family instead of returning to the seminary.

The young man experienced a vocation crisis. He left the Vincentian
community in 1877, and transferred to the Archdiocese of León. Two
years later, the bishop of León ordained José to priesthood at the
Cathedral of Our Lady of Light. Despite his frail health, young Father
José worked diligently in his parish assignment. He devoted special
attention to the religious education of children and to the Catholic
newspaper, *El Pueblo Católico*, for which he wrote a regular column
advising mothers how to raise their children in the faith. In addition to
parish work, Father José held various posts in the chancery.

Interior conflicts arose for Father José when a new bishop arrived at
León in 1885 and missioned the priest from the city parish to serve as
chaplain to two extremely poor communities on the outskirts of the city.
The communities were El Calvario and Santo Niño. José confessed
years later that he had considered refusing the assignment. He and his

friends thought it was humiliating for someone of José's sophisticated background to serve among the least sophisticated. Nevertheless, the young priest accepted the new ministry. As pastor, Father José strengthened the spiritual life of the parish by promoting devotions to the Eucharist, the Sacred Heart of Jesus, and Our Lady of Light. The learned priest also completed two construction projects which the previous pastor had begun but left unfinished; namely, a new church and a retreat center for priests.

A life-changing event occurred to Father José María in 1885. While walking to the church at *El Calvario*, the priest looked along the riverbank and saw pigs eating the bodies of two newborn infants. Shocked, he ordered that the building planned as a retreat house for priests ought to be converted into a shelter for the poor. Needing help to serve the poor, he invited into the parish the Paris-based Little Sisters of the Poor, but the anti-Catholic atmosphere under President Benito Juarez dissuaded these nuns from coming to México. Father José asked for local volunteers. Four women stepped forward. They called themselves the Mothers of the Poor. In December 1885, the priest and women opened the Sacred Heart of Jesus Home, which had a capacity of sixty poor people: the hungry, homeless, orphans, and elderly. In four years, these lay women founded the sisters of the Servants of the Sacred Heart of Jesus and the Poor. For this community, José provided the founding vision, administrative structure, draft of the *Constitution*, plus he prepared the paperwork needed for diocesan approval and papal approbation, which occurred three years after his death.

Although his ministry in the poor parishes on the outskirts of León was proceeding marvelously for the young pastor, the bishop in 1889 transferred Father José to Puebla. There he continued the same ministry he had performed at his previous assignments: feeding the hungry, clothing the naked, instructing the youth in their faith, absolving adults of their sins, and assisting the elderly.

At Puebla, prostitution was commonplace. Feeling compelled to help the women, he provided them with spiritual guidance, emotional support, medical attention, and vocational instruction. He opened a center called Christian Mercy, whose volunteers assisted the women in learning a new trade.

*For further information, contact*
General House
3 Poniente # 1512
72000 Puebla, Puebla, México

## 20. ✠ Venerable Mother Mary Theresa Dudzik

*Place: Chicago, Illinois*
*Fame: Faith-based service to the poor. Foundress of the Franciscan Sisters*
*of Chicago, the first religious sisterhood founded in Chicago,*
*and the first Polish sisterhood founded in the United States.*

In a the remote village near Kamien, Poland, approximately one hundred seventy-five miles west of Warsaw, Josephine Dudzik (1860-1918) was born.[705] This third child of six children demonstrated great charity in her youth. Years after Josephine's death, her oldest sister testifies:

MARY THERESA
DUDZIK

> From her early childhood, Josephine was characterized by piety and love. As many times as there were opportunities to come to the aid of a neighbor, she willingly did so. She always shared what she had with others.

Josephine could not bear to see people in need without coming to their aid. She would share her supper with a poor girl; she took food to a sick neighbor; she aided another by sitting with her children so that the neighbor could attend Mass; with money she saved, she bought medicine for others; she aided those in sorrow; there was not a week when she did not perform some good deed.[706]

The two oldest Dudzik children emigrated to Chicago in 1873. They settled on the northwest side of the city near St. Stanislaus Kostka

Church. The two sisters prepared the way for the remainder of the family, who would join them eight years later.

In 1881, at twenty-one, Josephine arrived in Chicago. The city was still recovering from the Chicago Fire of 1871 and the financial panic of 1873. In the wake of these two disasters, the cost of food escalated, adequate housing deteriorated, and the average workingman's salary fell to about nine dollars a week. Upon her arrival, Josephine saw the city's poor, sick, homeless, and others living in crowded, unsanitary conditions. Cholera, scarlet fever and diphtheria spread throughout the area.

St. Stanislaus Kostka Parish, which had survived the Chicago Fire, became known as the cradle of the Polish Colony in Chicago and served as the center of religious and community life for Polish immigrants. Father Vincent Barzynski, a Resurrectionist priest, assumed the pastorate in 1874. A dozen years later, this parish had grown from four hundred to eight thousand families, totaling over forty thousand people. The parish property grew from a church, rectory, and school building valued at twenty thousand dollars to a complex worth half a million dollars, including the school which held three thousand students, a convent for forty teaching sisters, and meeting rooms for the parish's fifty-one societies. "Under his guidance, St. Stanislaus Kostka Church emerged as the largest parish in the United States."[707]

Father Barzynski served as Josephine's spiritual director. He guided her as she brought the homeless, aged, and sick from the streets into the apartment which she and her mother shared. The priest depended on her, referred needy people to her, and trusted her to solve many of the problems that people brought to him. Her peers elected Josephine to leadership roles in the parish's spiritual and social societies.

Josephine happily served the needy. She explains, "I felt the misery and suffering of others, and it seemed to me that I could not love Jesus, or even expect heaven if I were concerned only about myself, . . . not suffering any inconvenience, but simply living in comfort."[708] Using skills taught her by the Congregation of the Sisters of St. Elizabeth in Kamien Krajenski, Poland, Josephine sewed to earn money to feed her mother, the people she took in, and herself. The situation was becoming increasingly difficult.

Trusting in Divine Providence, she writes in her journal: "Once while at prayer, a thought suddenly occurred to me to rent or purchase a home in the vicinity of St. Stanislaus Kostka Church and assemble all the [Franciscan] tertiaries from this parish who would desire to join me in a common life of prayer, labor, and service."[709] In 1893, aided by her friend and associate Rosalie Wysinski, who later would be known as Sister Anna, Josephine Dudzik began to build a religious community of women.

Knowing Josephine's devotion to the Blessed Virgin Mary, Father Barzynski suggested that the sisterhood might be placed under the patronage of the Immaculate Conception. The community's date of foundation was December 8, 1894.

By December 20, 1894, the group settled into Josephine's flat at 11 Chapin Street, and she changed later to 1341 Hudson Avenue. Josephine was unanimously elected superior. Since all the women were tertiaries, they called themselves by the names they had received at the time of their profession. Josephine was now called Sister Mary Theresa. Their life of prayer and service required self-denial, and the courage to bear the burdens, insecurities, and stresses of establishing a new community of religious women. The Franciscan Sisters of Chicago were the first sisterhood founded in that city, and the first Polish sisterhood in the United States.

By 1896, Sister Mary Theresa and the sisters moved to larger quarters at 1368 Ingram Street (now Evergreen Street) in Chicago. The sisters occupied the first and second floors. Soon this residence became crowded because of the increasing numbers of needy persons. To support themselves and the usually penniless residents, the sisters sewed and did laundry.

Father Barzynski advised Sisters Theresa and Anna that they and their colleagues should consider living in the developing area of Avondale, located five miles northwest of Chicago. Following the priest's suggestion, the seven vowed tertiaries, plus Theresa's mother and another sister's mother, lived together. This living arrangement created great stresses. These Polish immigrants had come from different geographical, social, and educational backgrounds. The tertiaries were independent women in their thirties and forties. Some were extremely critical, and others were moody. When the nuns assigned to laundry duty complained that Sister Theresa's work as a seamstress was easier than their work, she switched jobs with them just to make peace. At the end of three years, four of the original seven sisters had left.

Sister Theresa depended on the continuing direction of Father Barzynski even if his counsel occasionally caused her suffering.[710] At times, he reprimanded her. On one occasion, he reversed a decision that she had given to one of the sisters. Pressed by need and eager to build a home for the aged and infirm, Sister Theresa felt that the pastor's Planning Commission was moving too slowly. Finally, in 1897, a loan was obtained to begin construction of St. Joseph Home for the Aged and Crippled. At the signing of the documents for the loan, Father Barzynski's signature was affixed to the document because unmarried women, let alone vowed religious women, were unable to secure loans.

Through all these challenges, Sister Theresa persevered and grew in holiness. Repeatedly she reflects on this theme: "In spite of any adversity, I maintained my happy disposition since I saw the Will of God in all life's events. I remembered the promise I had made freely to Father Barzynski to preserve the community. I resolved not to lose heart in adversity, but to labor all the more energetically for the survival of the community."[711]

The doors to St. Joseph Home opened in 1898. In that year, Father Barzynski, without any explanation, removed Theresa as religious superior. Some observers suspected that the pastor acted to quell rumors that Theresa's fundraising was intended for her or her family's benefit. Regarding removal from office, Theresa writes that she felt "as if a heavy stone had fallen from around my neck, and I perceived unusual happiness."[712] She remained, however, as administrator of St. Joseph Home until she died.

In 1899 the Community, expanding from its original apostolate of St. Joseph Home for the Aged and Crippled, accepted into their care the children of St. Vincent Orphanage Asylum. Two years later, the Sisters accepted their first ministry in education.

In March 1918, Sister Theresa was diagnosed with cancer. She suffered unbearable pain. At fifty-eight, on September 20, 1918 she died. One witness writes, "Sister M. Theresa bore her illness amid the humiliations associated with it with her characteristic benevolent smile and gracious nature. She edified the sisters by her abandonment to the Divine Will and bore her pain heroically."[713] At the time of Sister

Theresa's death, the community had grown to one hundred and twenty-five sisters, serving at St. Joseph Home, St. Vincent Orphan Asylum, three day care centers, and thirty-one elementary schools in seven states.

Much later in the community's history, the sisters recognized the role of foundress that Sister Theresa had played. In respect for all that she had done, the community gave her posthumously the honorific title, "Mother."

*For further information, contact*
Franciscan Sisters of Chicago
Our Lady of Victory Motherhouse
11400 Theresa Dr.
Lemont, IL 60439 U.S.A.

## 23. ✠ Blessed Teen Martyrs of Tlaxcala

*Place: Tlaxcala, Puebla*
*Fame: Avid evangelists. Martyrs.*

Soon after the Spanish Franciscans arrived in 1524, at Tlaxcala, México, Father Martin de Valencia established a school to teach the Catholic faith to Indian children. Three of the boys, all of whom were approximately twelve years old, soon defended and died for the faith they had been taught.

TEEN MARTYRS OF TLAXCALA

In the first incident, General Acxotecatl and his wife Tlapaxilotzin allowed their son, whom the bishops later called Cristobalito, (c. 1515-27) to attend the mission school. One night when the Tlaxcaltean general had been drinking, his son offered to teach him the Catholic faith. The general resisted, declaring that he believed in the pagan gods. With that the boy broke some of the father's clay idols, and some containers of pulque, which is the alcoholic drink produced from the maguey cactus plant.

The father became enraged, beat his son, and threw him into the home's fireplace. The boy, although rescued by his mother, suffered severe burns and died the next day. The general buried his son's body in the patio of the home, and murdered his wife in order to eliminate witnesses. Before long, suspicious authorities investigated the disappearance of Axcotecatl's wife and son. The general's deeds were discovered, and he was hanged until he died.

In a second incident, two boys, Antonio (c. 1517-29) and Juan (c. 1517-29), accompanied two Dominican priests on a mission about thirty miles from Tlaxcala, to the towns of Tepcyacac and Cuauhtinchan, in the current state of Puebla. The missionaries evangelized the Indians, and inspired them to abandon their idolatrous cults. Not all the Indians, however, accepted the teaching. After spending three or four days on the mission and finding no idols to destroy, the boys grew bored. Soon, Antonio walked into an unoccupied home, and there discovered some idols. Leaving his companion posted at the front door, Antonio destroyed the idols. Neighbors heard the commotion, and alerted the residents of the house. When two of the men arrived home, they spotted Juan at the front door. Each man, holding an oak log in his hands, threw the boy to the ground, and beat him furiously and repeatedly. Antonio heard the commotion, ran outside, and saw his friend lying dead. Antonio asked the men why they had attacked an innocent person since it was Antonio who had entered the house. Antonio began to instruct the men about their erroneous beliefs in the idols. The men, however, quickly grew tired of the boy's speech. They rushed directly at Antonio, and beat him to death. The Indians took the dead bodies, and hurled them over a cliff.

What is the historical accuracy of these stories? The oldest extant document of these stories is included in the *History of the Indians of New Spain*, written by Friar Toribio de Benavente, known popularly as Motolinia, one of the original twelve Franciscans who came to México. Motolinia in 1601 translated the account of the stories from the original Nahuatl language into Spanish, and included both texts side by side in his book. A copy of this document can be found at the National Library of Paris. Almost two centuries later, i. e. in 1791, the Viceroy of New Spain ordered an investigation into the accuracy of Motolinia's translation. The investigation verified the accuracy of the translation, without attempting to verify the accuracy of the stories, which continue to be regarded as true unless and until proof demands otherwise.

*For further information, contact*
Diocese of Tlaxcala
Lardizabal #45, Centro
Apartado Postal #84
90000 Tlaxcala, México

## 24. ✠ Blessed Émilie Tavernier-Gamelin

*Place: Montréal, Québec*
*Fame: Spent her life taking care of others: as child, housekeeper,*
*wife, mother, widow, laywoman, and mother-foundress.*
*Foundress of Sisters of Providence.*

Nature and grace moved Émilie Tavernier (1800-51) to reach out compassionately to the poorest of the poor.[714] Contemporaries claimed that she was a living saint. Bishop Bourget, who perhaps knew her best and worked most closely with Émilie in founding and developing the Sisters of Providence, writes that he has "taken on as a real obligation to reveal, after her [Émilie's] death, the staunch virtues concealed in this beautiful soul."[715]

ÉMILIE TAVERNIER-
GAMELIN

As a child, Émilie developed the habit of focusing on others instead of herself. In her teen years, Émilie regularly joined her adoptive mother in distributing food and clothing to the poor who came to the family's doorstep. She grew up giving.

She grew up grieving also. Her mother died when Émilie was four, and a decade later, her father passed away. By this time, all but five of her fourteen siblings had died. In 1818, Émilie's brother's wife died, and he invited Émilie to keep house for him and his child. Émilie agreed, on one condition: "their table would always be open to the hungry who came to the door."[716] This table, she called the "Table of the King."

When Émilie was twenty-three, fifty-year-old Jean-Baptiste Gamelin, owner of a prospering apple orchard, proposed to her. The couple married at Montréal's only Catholic church and established a home at Côte Saint-Antoine, "which was the most fashionable area in Montréal at that time."[717] Jean-Baptiste joined Émilie in her pious practices and practical service of the poor. The couple gave birth to three boys. This paradisiacal time was shattered, however, by the successive deaths, within a space of four years, of each of her boys and her husband. She writes, "The most difficult of all [her sufferings] was the loss of my husband and [my last] child; I shed tears every day, my heart is pierced by a painful sword; my only source of consolation was to meditate on the sorrows of Mary and contemplate her picture."[718] Widowed and without children at twenty-seven, what would she do?.

> [Émilie] took Mary, Mother of Sorrows, as her guide for dealing with these losses, and during her time in prayer, she came to see all the poor and needy as her new family. She turned her home and inheritance into a shelter for the poor, for orphaned, abandoned, or runaway children, the mentally ill, homeless, handicapped, immigrants, and destitute in any form. People began to refer to her home as the House of Providence.[719]

Just after her husband's death, Émilie assured others that she would continue Jean-Baptiste's support of the mentally retarded man Dodais and his elderly mother, whom her husband had been helping the last few years. Within weeks of her last son's death, Émilie joined the parish's Confraternity of the Holy Family, whose members visited the poor. "In her [Émilie's] regular visits to the poor in their homes, she became aware that such occasional help did not meet the needs of the aged and infirm women. She welcomed several of them into her own home."[720] In 1830, Émilie opened a home for elderly women. Twice daily, she visited these guests, sixteen of whom were charter members, read to them from spiritual books, explained the catechism, and prayed with them the Stations of the Cross. Years later, when a novice referred disparagingly to one of the women as, "Old So and So," Émilie immediately advised the young girl, "Can you not refer to her as Mrs.? . . . Go to the chapel and ask pardon of Our Lord, for it is He whom you have offended in the person of that poor woman."[721] Virtually every day from 1828 until her death in 1851 Émilie visited these elderly women.

A dozen years later, in November 1841, Bishop Bourget, the second bishop of Montréal, invited the Daughters of Charity to take over from Émilie the work among elderly women. Bourget wanted to assure "the permanence of the Christian work which our faithful sister, Émilie Gamelin, began a long time ago."[722] At the last minute, the sisters were prohibited from coming to Montréal. Deciding to start his own diocesan community, the bishop, in February 1843, invited lay women to become nuns. Seven women stepped forward. Four months later, Émilie too volunteered for the religious life. The bishop rejoiced at Émilie's decision. In March 1844, the religious community called the "Daughters of Charity, Servants of the Poor," was founded when Émilie and six others took vows and put on religious garb. The sisters' dress and *Rule* were modeled after those of the Daughters of Charity. The sisters became known popularly as the Sisters of Providence after the names of two of their houses: the House of Providence, and Providence.

The religious community thrived. Seven years after the founding, the original seven sisters had grown to more than fifty. The founding house for the elderly had grown to seven more houses including an orphanage for boys, a home for women boarders, a soup kitchen, a home for aged and infirm priests, a house for handicapped women, an elementary school for girls, and a school for the deaf.

The patron chosen for the religious community and its works was Our Lady of Sorrows. This devotion had guided Émilie since her childhood, and Bishop Bourget advised that "the devotion to Our Lady of Seven Dolors is essential to your institute."[723] Sorrows abounded for the young community: in finances, fires, and disease. Financially, the community lived from day to day. Countless stories are told in the community's lore about the privations which the sisters suffered for the benefit of the poor. Fire was a constant threat and frequent reality. The home for elderly women burned to the ground in 1844, and at LaPrairie fire destroyed three hundred homes plus the rectory and part of the sisters' hospice. Typhus and cholera decimated the general population and the ranks of the sisters. In 1846-1847, cholera took the lives of over six thousand Irish immigrants, and a new wave of cholera epidemic in 1849, claimed hundreds more. When Bishop Bourget in 1847 approached the fifty sisters and candidates to seek volunteers to nurse the Irish sick, who were lying and dying in sheds at the river's edge, every woman in the community volunteered, proclaiming, "I am ready."[724]

Twice, Émilie traveled to the United States to visit with and learn from the Daughters of Charity. In 1843, Émilie traveled, to New York and Baltimore; and again in 1850, she spent five weeks visiting at Albany, New York City, Baltimore, and Emmitsburg, Maryland.

In early September 1851, while visiting her sisters in the village of Sainte-Élisabeth, Émilie became ill. Out of breath, she sat down, and observed, "The atmosphere is heavy; it is cholera weather."[725] She continued her labors as best she could for the next few days. She confided to her sisters, "I see you now for the last time, I have prayed to St. Elizabeth [of Hungary] that you may always love the poor, and that peace and union may be ever preserved among you."[726] She returned to the motherhouse, continued her prayer and work, but worsened in health. On September 22, she died.

An interesting tangent is offered. A phenomenon which occurs in the lives of many saints is demonstrated in the life of Émilie: community life proves to be very difficult for many saints. The cross of community life is rarely spoken of, yet rarely escaped.

> Accustomed to the praises showered upon her, she [Émilie] suffered agony at seeing herself the butt of constant mutterings against her, of which she was well aware. With a straightforward nature such as hers, she could not get used to the roundabouts and under-handed ways which prevailed in the house. She was always on edge, for she noticed that everything she did was falsely interpreted and mercilessly judged. She deeply felt that she was not loved and trusted by her community.[727]

One of the original seven novices believed that she and not Mother, who joined the community six months after its initiation, should have been elected the first superior of the congregation. This sister and some others complained about Mother's manner and methods. Bishop Bourget gathered these complaints into twenty-two paragraphs of criticism. One day after receiving the letter, Mother responded, without excuses, without self-defense, humbly:

I am grateful to you for the advice you so kindly gave me in writing. My first reaction was one of discouragement, believing it was impossible for me to correct so many faults. After some reflection, I decided that I must try, come what may, regardless of the great sacrifices, since this is what God asks of me. All I can say is that there has never been any ill will, and it is due to lack of close scrutiny that I have so grievously disedified my daughters. Forget the past; I have resolved, once and for all, to grieve you no longer. ... This community is in its infancy, and it is imperfect; however, God's designs will be realized, in spite of our unworthiness. As for myself, I recognize how unworthy I am to govern it.[728]

Émilie spent her lifetime taking care of others, as a child at home, as housekeeper for her brother, as wife and mother, as widow and laywoman for fifteen years, and for seven years as a vowed religious. In all that she did, she desired to know and to do God's will, and to serve God's people compassionately.

*For further information, contact*
Émilie Tavernier-Gamelin Center
12055, rue Grenet
Montréal, QC H4J 2J5 Canada

## 26. ✠ Saint Jean de Brébeuf

*Place: Midland, Ontario*
*Fame: Apostle of the Hurons. Martyr extraordinaire.*

The horrific martyrdoms suffered by the Jesuit priests Jean de Brébeuf (1597-1649) and Gabriel Lalement exceeded in cruelty what other martyrs endured throughout the two-thousand-year history of the Church.[729] The Iroquois wished to eliminate the Blackrobes on account of the priests' gospel of forgiveness, their association with the enemy Huron, and the murderous disease which the white men had brought into the Indians' villages. The site of Brébeuf's martyrdom was Saint-Ignace, which lay six miles from the mission at Saint-Louis, where he and Lalement were captured just two miles west of Midland, Ontario. Brébeuf's religious superior writes the account of the martyrdom which eye-witnesses reported.

JEAN DE BRÉBEUF AND THE NORTH AMERICAN MARTYRS

> As soon as they [Brébeuf and Lalement] were taken captive, they were stripped naked, and some of their nails were torn out; and the welcome which they received upon entering the village of St. Ignace was a hail-storm of blows with sticks upon their shoulders, their loins, their legs, their breasts, their bellies, and their faces — there being no part of their bodies which did not then endure the torment." [730]

Brébeuf and Lalement were tied to separate stakes, whereupon Jean kissed his stake. The captors slashed the priests' bodies with knives, and cut off the captives' hands. Kindling wood at the base of the stakes was set ablaze. The flames leaped at the lower parts of the victims' bodies. A necklace of red-hot tomahawk blades was draped around their shoulders so that the skin burned. Red-hot tomahawks were pressed against the victims' armpits and loins. A belt of tree bark and pitch was wrapped around the priests' waists, and the belts were set on fire. Jean de Brébeuf preached to his attackers and onlookers:

> "My children, let us lift our eyes to heaven at the height of our afflictions; let us remember that God is the witness of our sufferings, and will soon be our exceeding great reward. Let us die in this faith; and let us hope from his goodness the fulfillment of his promises. I have more pity for you than for myself; but sustain with courage the few remaining torments. They will end with our lives; the glory which follows them will never have an end." [731]

To stop Jean's preaching, his torturers thrust a red-hot iron rod into his mouth and down his throat, then cut off his nose, and ripped off his lips. They stuffed a cloth inside his mouth. With a flaming rod, they poked out his and his companion's eyes. Mocking the baptism administered by priests, the Iroquois poured boiling water over the two captives' heads. Their burning skin was cut off in large pieces and was eaten in front of them by their persecutors. Jean endured all this without complaint. He had raised his eyes to heaven at the beginning of his torture, and some suggest that he may have been in ecstasy throughout the ordeal. While the victims were still alive, the torturers cut open their chests, ripped out their hearts, and drank the warm blood. Three hours after the torture had commenced, Jean died. Gabriel survived for fifteen hours before he succumbed.

Jean had been blessed with extraordinary spiritual gifts. Many times, he had experienced visions of Christ and of the Blessed Virgin, especially during his annual retreat in 1630, his return to New France in 1633, his annual retreat in 1640, and later that same year, in a vision which "consisted merely of a cross of tremendous proportions spread out against the southern sky, large enough . . . to hold not only some one person but every one of the Jesuits who were laboring on that mission. Significantly, it appeared over the territory of the Iroquois."[732] Jean writes in his diary in 1640.

> For the two days past I have felt within me a great desire to be a martyr and to endure all the torments the martyrs suffered. Jesus, my Lord and Savior, what can I give you in return for all the favors you have first conferred on me? I will take from your hand the cup of your sufferings and call on your name. I vow before your eternal Father and the Holy Spirit, before your most holy Mother and her most chaste spouse, before the angels, apostles and martyrs, before my blessed fathers Saint Ignatius and Saint Francis Xavier — in truth I vow to you, Jesus my Savior, that as far as I have the strength I will never fail to accept the grace of martyrdom, if some day you in your infinite mercy should offer it to me, your most unworthy servant.[733]

Having been born and raised near Lisieux, in Normandy, Jean expressed interest in priesthood ever since his childhood. Educated by the Jesuits, he entered their novitiate at Rouen in 1617. Four years later, he contracted tuberculosis and completed his theological studies privately. Because he had covered only the fundamental subjects, but not the full course of theological studies, he was not sent to teach during his student years. At thirty, he was ordained, and at thirty-two, he and two other Jesuit priests became the first members of their society to be missioned to Québec.

Jean served two tenures with the Indians, from 1625 to 1629 and 1633 to 1649. After arriving at Québec in mid-June 1625, Jean established his wigwam at the same site on the St. Charles River, where Champlain had lived a dozen years previously. He wintered voluntarily among the Algonquin Montagnais Indians for five months. The next year, he was missioned to Huronia at Ihonatria (currently near Penetanguishene), which lay nine hundred miles west of Québec. The Indians named Jean, who was a giant of a man, *Echon*, which means load-bearer. Jean learned the Huron language and customs and remained with this tribe until 1629, just before England seized New France and expelled the French missionaries. Back in France, Jean worked at his former job as bursar for the College of Rouen.

After England restored New France to the French in 1632, Jean returned there the following year. Father Anthony Daniel joined Jean, and the two journeyed for thirty days up the St. Lawrence River, the Ottawa River, the Mattawa River, across Lake Nipissing, down the French River, and across Georgian Bay, to Huronia. About seven years later, Jean and Father Chaumonot traveled to northern Lake Erie to evangelize the Neutral tribe. The long winter yielded no converts. In summer 1641, when the survival of the French colony was doubtful because of the Iroquois-Huron wars, Jean's superiors recalled him to Québec. There he recovered from a broken collarbone which he had sustained in a fall, and he worked on the reservation near Sillery. In 1643, Jean was assigned with Father Noel Chabanel to lead another mission among the Huron, at Sainte-Marie on the Wye, where Jean established the Jesuit's central mission house for Huronia. In 1647, the Iroquois made peace with the French but maintained their hostilities toward the Huron. Experiences of his twenty years of ministry among the Huron are recorded in the *Huron Relations*, which is part of the much larger *Jesuit Relations*, which records the order's worldwide missionary activities.

Ministry among the Indians was challenging. Jean describes the challenges he faced: diet, climate, mosquitoes, portages, disease, death by tomahawk, perilous travel, plus accidental or intentional burning of the priests' cabin. He offers practical advice to Jesuits who might be considering missionary ministry in North America:

When you come to us, we will receive you with open arms into the vilest dwelling imaginable. A mat, or at best a skin, will be your bed and often enough you will not sleep at all because of the vermin that will swarm over you. If you have been a great theologian in France, you will have to be a humble scholar here and taught by an unlearned person, or by children, while you furnish them no end of amusement. The Huron tongue will be St. Thomas and Aristotle, and you will be happy if after a great deal of hard study you are able to stammer out a few words.

The winter is almost unendurable. As for leisure time, the Hurons will give you no rest night or day. You may expect to be killed at any moment, and your cabin, which is highly inflammable, may often take fires through carelessness or malice. You are responsible for the weather, be it foul or fair, and if you don't bring rain when it's needed you may be tomahawked for your lack of luck. And there are foes from without to reckon with. On the thirteenth of this month a dozen Hurons were killed at Contarea, which is only a few days' distance from here; and a short time ago a number of Iroquois were discovered in ambush quite close to the other village.

In France, you are surrounded by splendid examples of virtue. Here, all are astonished when you speak of God. Blasphemy and obscenity are common things on their lips. Often you are without your Mass, and when you do succeed in saying it the cabin is full of smoke or snow. Your neighbors never leave you alone and are continually shouting at the top of their voices.[734]

On March 16, 1649, the Iroquois attacked Saint-Louis Mission. Lalement had the opportunity to escape, but remained and baptized the natives who begged him for the sacrament, welcoming them into the Catholic faith. One year later, the continuing attacks of the Iroquois resulted in the extinction of the remnant Huron. Jean de Brébeuf had achieved seven thousand converts among the Huron, and authored both a Huron catechism and a Huron-French dictionary.

*For further information, contact*
Martyrs' Shrine
Midland, Ontario L4R 4K5 Canada

## 26. ✠ Saint Antoine Daniel

*Place: Teanaustayé, near Midland, Ontario*
*Fame: "Today, we shall be in heaven." Martyr of North America.*

A band of typically ferocious Iroquois attacked the mission of Saint-Joseph, just south of the mission Sainte-Marie, near Midland, Ontario, at the same time that Jesuit priest Antoine Daniel (1601-48) was completing Mass.[735] Still wearing the Mass vestments, Antoine encouraged his terrified Huron flock to be strong in the faith. "There were so many who cried to him that he was constrained to dip his handkerchief in water and baptize them by aspersion."[736] Ignoring his people's pleas to flee for his life, the priest chose instead to seek out and encourage the sick and elderly who would be left behind in the panic. He encouraged them, saying, "Brother, today we shall be in heaven."[737]

ANTOINE DANIEL

Because the invaders had the greater number, the relatively few Hurons could not possibly defend their village and so they ran to the church thinking that would be the best place in which to die. Father Daniel joined them, and when the Iroquois came he fearlessly faced them and forbade them to enter. Though at first amazed at the priest's courage and valor, they responded by raining upon him a shower of arrows and directing a bullet into his heart. As soon as he fell to the ground the assassins stripped his body and further violated it. When the chapel was fully ablaze, they tossed it [Antoine's body] into the flames.[738]

Antoine had been born at Dieppe, was ordained in 1629, and taught the classics at the College at Eu, before being assigned in 1632 to the mission at Québec. In 1635, he was assigned to start at Québec a school for Native American candidates for priesthood. This institution is recognized as North America's first college for men. After seven years' dedication to this academic institution, Antoine was assigned to the mission fields in Huronia. After making his annual retreat at Sainte-Marie, he traversed the twelve mile journey to Mission Saint-Joseph. Two days later, the Iroquois attack occurred, and Anthony experienced martyrdom.

*For further information, contact*
Martyrs' Shrine
Midland, Ontario L4R 4K5 Canada

☙

## 26. ✠ Saint Charles Garnier

*Place: Near Midland, Ontario*
*Fame: Although wounded, he continued assisting others. Martyr.*

"Father Charles Garnier seemed an unlikely candidate for the Jesuit missions in New France."[739] He was born and raised in Paris, France, in a wealthy family, and received an excellent education.[740] At eighteen, he entered the Jesuit formation and education program and eleven years later was ordained a priest. He requested immediately to go to the missions among the Native Americans in North American. His request was denied, when his father protested to the Jesuit

CHARLES GARNIER

authorities. The next year, Charles repeated his request, the father relented, and the Jesuits assigned the young priest to the Huron mission under the tutelage of Father Jean de Brébeuf, the superior of the mission.

Charles Garnier (1606-49) left his native Paris, sailed from Dieppe on April 8, 1636, and arrived at Québec two months later. By July 1, Father Garnier left Québec, traveled to Trois-Rivières, continued up the St. Lawrence River, and arrived at Huronia on August 13. As he began his thirteen-year ministry among the Huron and Puten tribes, he writes to his father, "There is no place on earth where I could be happier."[741] Father Garnier labored in the interior of the country, as far west as

Saint-Ignace, and as far south as Ossernenon, never returning to Québec during his entire ministry among the Native Americans.

One day when the Huron warriors were far from the village of Etarita, the Iroquois attacked the defenseless village of women, children and elders. "An orgy of incredible cruelty followed, in the midst of which Garnier, the only priest in the mission, hastened from person to person, giving absolution to the Christians and baptizing the children and catechumens, totally unmindful of his own fate."[742] As he ministered rapidly to those in need, he was shot twice, and although wounded, continued to minister the sacraments, until he was tomahawked to death. The site of his martyrdom lay thirty miles from the mission Sainte-Marie.

*For further information, contact*
Martyrs' Shrine
Midland, Ontario L4R 4K5 Canada

## 26. ✠ Saint Gabriel Lalement

*Place: Midland, Ontario*
*Fame: His long-desired mission ended in a*
*long-suffering martyrdom. Martyr.*

Gabriel Lalement (1610-49) arrived last among the eventually eight Martyrs of North America.[743] He teamed up with Jean de Brébeuf, who had come first among this same group of martyrs. Gabriel lived for two years at Québec and another six months in Huronia before he was captured and killed in his adopted country by those whom he had come to serve.

GABRIEL LALEMENT

Having been born at Paris, and although of delicate constitution, Gabriel excelled as a Jesuit student, was ordained in 1637, and was assigned to educational institutions in France, until he departed for New France in 1646. This former professor, researcher, and college administrator had promised God in

1632, when the young man first professed the vows of poverty, chastity, and obedience, that he vowed too "to die among the Indians."[744] At ordination, and every year thereafter, he repeated to his superiors his desire to minister among the Native Americans in North America. Finally, fourteen years after having his private vow, Gabriel followed in the footsteps of his two paternal uncles, Charles and Jerome, who had worked many years in these missions, and of whom the latter had just been named superior of the mission. Gabriel Lalement was about to experience one of the harshest martyrdoms ever suffered in the history of the Church.

After a thirteen-week voyage from La Rochelle to Québec, Gabriel remained at the Jesuit house at Sillery, where for two years, he assiduously studied the Huron language. He departed for Huronia in August 1648, and joined Jean de Brébeuf in September. The two worked well together, converting hundreds of Huron to the Catholic religion.

On the morning of March 16, 1649, however, Jean and Gabriel were seized at their mission at Saint Louis, four miles north of the mission at Saint Ignace. The Iroquois swooped upon the mission, climbed its palisades and slaughtered all its defenders. The two priests were taken as prisoners. The two were tortured for long hours before they were killed: Jean endured the torture for three hours, and Gabriel held on overnight for a total of fifteen hours. Their tortures and deaths, as reported by Huron eyewitnesses to the Jesuit superior, are regarded as among the most brutal martyrdoms ever suffered in the two-millenia history of the Roman Catholic Church. The martyrdom is described in detail in the biography of Jean de Brébeuf.

*For further information, contact*
Martyrs' Shrine
Midland, Ontario L4R 4K5 Canada

☙

# 26. ✠ Saint Noel Chabanel

*Place: Near Midland, Ontario*
*Fame: Persevered in primitive surroundings, for the sake*
*of the gospel. Martyr of North America.*

Although comfortable as the son of a wealthy
wine merchant and respected as a brilliant scholar, Noel Chabanel (1613-49) exchanged life in
native France for life of a Jesuit missionary in
New France.[745] His experience proved difficult
for him. He never adjusted to the new culture: he
never learned the native language, never liked
their food, and detested their coarseness.
Nevertheless, he vowed, in the presence of the
Blessed Sacrament, to remain with and die
among the Indians.

NOEL CHABANEL

Noel Chabanal had entered the Jesuit seminary when he was seventeen. After the usual course of studies, and ordination, he taught "for
several years in the Jesuit college at Toulouse."[746]

Upon his arrival at Québec in 1643, he was assigned to assist Father
Charles Garnier in the ministry among the Huron tribe. Danger, however, became all too real: nine months previously, Jean de Brébeuf and
Gabriel Lalement had been killed at Sainte-Marie; and nine months
before that, Antoine Daniel had been killed at Teanaustayé. Garnier
advised young Chabanel to return to the safety of Québec. Chabanel left
Garnier on December 5th, and stayed overnight with Jesuit confreres on
December 5th and 6th at Saint-Mathias mission. As they drew near to
the mission of Saint-Jean, they decided to rest.

On the 7th he [Chabanel] walked with his Huron companions a difficult eighteen miles through thick woodland, and when
night came the party rested. His companions soon fell asleep, but
he stayed awake and prayed. Towards midnight he heard noises
in the distance, and as the sounds came nearer he recognized the
victory songs of the Iroquois mixed with the sad cries of their
captives. Unknown to him [the mission at] Etarita had been

attacked that afternoon and Father Garnier massacred by these same Iroquois.[747]

Chabanel awoke his companions, and they tried to race back to Saint-Matthias. Chabanel was too exhausted from the past day's journey; he could not keep up with his companions. They ran ahead; he walked behind. He came to a swollen river, and waited on its shore. A Huron Indian, passing by in his canoe, offered to take the priest to the other side. Chabanel accepted, but his would-be rescuer, "formerly a Christian but now an apostate, robbed him of his belongings, tomahawked him, and threw his body into the river."[748]

*For further information, contact*
Martyrs' Shrine
Midland, Ontario L4R 4K5 Canada

☞

## 26. ✠ Louis Émond

*Place: Québec City, Québec*
*Fame: Exemplary lay leader. Companion of Père Victor Lelievre.*

Many hundreds of saints provided mutually good influences on each other.[749] One wonders whether some persons would have become saints if their companion also had not been saintly; e.g., Vincent de Paul and Louise de Marillac, John Bosco and Dominic Savio, Rose of Lima and Martin de Porres. The same question applies to two candidates for canonization: priest Victor Lelièvre and layman Louis Émond. These two complimented each other in style, and supported each other in vision and values.[750]

As a youth, having worked assiduously in the unhealthy fetid basement of a saddle-tanning establishment, Louis (1876-1949) appreciated the conditions that the working class had to endure. Having married at twenty-six, and having fathered three children, he knew first-hand the situations of Catholic married couples and parents. Having been raised in a good Catholic home, he loved his faith, and wished to support the faith of other people. He devoted himself to daily prayer, and to service of disadvantaged youth through his membership and service in the St. Vincent de Paul Society.

In 1902, he got married and moved into Saint-Sauveur Parish. The next year, Father Victor Lelièvre arrived at the parish as vicar. The two men discovered their mutual interests and became mutually beneficial in fulfilling their dreams for service and sanctity. They enjoyed a great complimentarity.

> At the side of the impulsive and unrealistic Oblate [Father Victor Lelièvre], Louis was a thermostat, regulating and balancing with a consummate prudence and tact. The all-consuming flame, which easily engulfed the one, was preserved by the patience and the solid good sense of the other. Pious, sincere, generous, Louis was the providential complement of Father Victor in all their works. Similar souls, who possessed the greatest respect for each other, they mutually counterbalanced the other and became sanctified together. They were seen as not being able to function, one without the other. During twenty-seven years, Louis Émond, a brightly burning lamp in his own right, gave a talk at the closure of each retreat at Jesus the Worker Retreat House.[751]

Louis Émond played an indispensable role in Father Lelièvre's retreats. As one retreatant described Louis's role, "Father Lelièvre prepared me for confession; another priest heard my confession, but it was Louis Émond, who assisted me in persevering to go to confession."[752] And Father Lelièvre said of this church volunteer, companion, and good friend, "Discovering Louis was one of the greatest graces of my life."[753]

On his deathbed, Louis whispered to the attending Oblate, "In my intimacy with the Lord, I am celebrating my fiftieth anniversary of being in the state of grace."[754]

*For further information, contact*

Maison Jésus-Ouvrier
475, boulevard Pere Lelièvre
Ville de Vanier, QC G1M 1M9 Canada

## 29. ✠ Marina Francisca Cinta Sarrelangue

*Places: Coatzacoalcos and Acayucán, Veracruz*
*Fame: Apostolic lay leader. Exemplary wife and mother.*

Catechists and church activists Eugenio Balmori Martinez (1900-46) and Marina Francisca Cinta Sarrelangue (1909-88) met in 1931, became engaged five years later, and married in 1937. They were blessed with five children. Throughout their lives, i.e., in their youth, young adulthood, married life, and widowhood, Eugenio and Marina dedicated themselves to Church service, especially to catechizing youth.

Marina had originated from Acayucán, Veracruz. She was the third of twelve children. During her childhood, she had moved many times because of her father's employment as a supervisor of a plantation and activities of the revolutionaries. Her parents sent her and two of her sisters to study together at México City at a *colegio* operated by the Madres Guadalupanas. Upon completing her studies in 1924, Marina returned to Acayucán, where she found work in nearby Coatzacoalcos, selling Singer sewing machines, and teaching dress-making. Class enrollment climbed to as many as sixty students. In her free time, she voluntarily taught Christian doctrine to children.

At Coatzacoalcos, Marina met Eugenio. Both were involved in catechetical work, at great risk to their own safety. The anti-Catholic Calles government was persecuting the Church by expelling bishops, priests, and religious; confiscating convents, closing churches and church-related institutions. Public worship was forbidden. These two courageous young people, were not only keeping the faith, but also were passing it on to others.

In May 1936, Eugenio and Marina became engaged. A few months later, Eugenio's work as a draftsman required him to move to México City. The couple continued the romance by exchanging letters through the mail. In one letter Marina writes to Eugenio, "It seems that life has become more beautiful for me in knowing that I love you, and that you love me, and that the good God blesses and approves of our affection."[755] In November, Eugenio moved back to Coatzaocoalcos, but by that time, Marina had to return to Acayucán to assist her parents. She writes him a poem, titled, "The Joy of my soul," to express her love, even though they are separated by many miles.[756]

Life for me is a sweet dream
From which I never wish to wake up,
For when I look at you, my one-and-only,
My heart is comforted completely.

The future appears to be bright,
About that I yearn to sing.
Nothing else in the world matters
When your eyes look at me.

I am happy in loving you, Gene.
I am conscious of nothing else in the world
When for any moment, we two are together.

Therefore, I feel profoundly
That a love greater than my life
Is protecting you from within my soul.[757]

The couple married at Acayucán in November 1937. Because Eugenio lost his job, this itinerant pair moved to México City, where within the next four years, their first three children were born. In 1942, because of Eugenio's employment, the family moved back to Coatzacoalcos, where were born the fourth and fifth children. Again, the couple were separated for months at a time because of Eugenio's job requirements. When he was at Coatzacoalcos, Eugenio assisted the parish priest in building the church of San José. Four years later, Eugenio returned to this church, the first time for the baptism of his fifth child, and the second time, one month later, to be buried after he was killed on May 14, in an auto accident at forty-six.

After Eugenio died, Marina moved to the Mixcoac section of México City, but her twenty-six years of employment with the Mexican Exporting and Importing Company CEISMA required her and the children to move many more times. During this time, in her life at work and with the family, she lived intensely her faith and union with Christ through prayer and participation in the Eucharist, consecrating to God her widowhood, and communicating to everyone peace and serenity. In

1973, Marina took a job with Cineteca Nacional, where she remained employed until a fire destroyed the operations in 1982.

Eventually, all the children finished their schooling. They graduated from universities, and entered careers as professionals: the two daughters pursued careers in business education, and the three boys became respectively an engineer, architect, and priest.

For more than forty years, Marina attended with her family the parish church of San Juan at Mixcoac, served by the *Misioneros Josefinos*. In September 1987, Marina became ill, which resulted in her being hospitalized two months later. The next year, on September 29, 1988, she died.

A year before her death, her children had compiled and published the letters which their parents had exchanged for years. Included in the publication were copies of the seventy-five poems which Marina had composed for her husband and children at significant moments throughout their lives. Many other of Marina's writings have been saved. One of her hand-written prayers reads, "My Jesus, I love you. I offer to you my soul, my heart, and my life in proof of the love which I profess. Give me your love, so that I might be able to love you in the way that you desire."[758]

At Eugenio's death, he had been laid to rest initially at Minatitlan, Veracruz, and in 1954, his remains were transferred from the public cemetery to the parish church, which is now the cathedral, at Coatzacoalcos. When Marina died forty-two years later, she was buried initially at México City, and her remains were transferred later to the cathedral at Coatzocoalcos, where she was laid to rest beside her husband.

*For further information, contact*
Diocesis de Coatzacoalcos
Aldama 502
Coatzacoalcos, Veracruz, México

## 30. ✣ Venerable Alfred Pampalon

*Place: Levis and Sainte-Anne-de-Beaupré, Québec*
*Fame: Devotee of the Virgin Mary and St. Anne;*
*long-suffering without complaint.*

Alfred Pampalon's parents gave birth to twelve children in fifteen years.[759] Four offspring died shortly after birth, and the mother died in childbirth. Alfred was the ninth in birth order. The father worked as a stone mason who specialized in building churches. The family lived in Levis, across the St. Lawrence River from the thriving capital city of Québec. From her deathbed, Alfred's mother spoke to her children:

ALFRED PAMPALON

> My children, my dear little ones, your mother must leave you.... But, I entrust you to a better mother still. ... She is the best of mothers! I entrust you to your heavenly Mother.... The Virgin Mary welcomes you.... She will watch over every one of you. Love her the best you can! Pray to her a lot! She will take good care of you.[760]

One year after his wife's death, Alfred's father remarried. The stepmother happily cared for the eight Pampalon children and bore her new husband two more children.

As for education, Alfred was tutored at home until almost nine, when he entered the College of Levis. An average student academically, he excelled in virtue and amiability. He was a good organizer and a leader in sports.

Alfred suffered from poor health. During his teen years, twice he almost died. At fourteen, as he recalls in his autobiography, "By an act of Divine Providence, I fell seriously ill. God gave me to understand that I did not belong to the world, but to him."[761] Observers perceived that Alfred aged physically, emotionally, and spiritually by this near-death experience. Three years later, Alfred suffered inflammation of the lungs, which condition deteriorated into pneumonia. The parish priest administered the last rites. Family and friends begged the Blessed Mother and her mother St. Anne to spare Alfred's life. The youth survived. In the novitiate, he writes, "What made it irrevocable [his consecration to God] was my second illness. God was there to inspire me with the idea to strengthen my purpose with a vow. I did that, hoping to recover my health."[762]

Alfred kept his vow. A neighbor reports, "he [Alfred] started a great novena for his vocation. . . . he was resolved to take on religious life."[763] He asked people to pray for his vocation, and thanked them for praying for him. In June 1886, he made a pilgrimage, walking twenty-one miles from his home to the two-hundred-year-old Shrine of St. Anne de Beaupré. After renewing his private vow to become a priest, he went to the Redemptorist monastery next door, and sought admission into the community. Despite his poor health, evident in his wan complexion and diminished energy, the priests accepted the candidate, whose older brother was already a seminarian in the community. In July 1886, Alfred sailed for Belgium, where the Redemptorists seminary was located. At Beauplateau, Belgium, Alfred spent six years studying philosophy and theology. On October 2, 1892, he was ordained a priest.

In preparation for ordination, Alfred writes, "I promised my good Mother I would become a saint."[764] He copied from another text, "O priest, you are not yourself any longer. . . . You do not belong to yourself, for you are the servant and minister of Christ. You do not belong to yourself, for you are the Spouse of the Church. You do not belong to yourself, because you are a mediator between God and humankind."[765] His private prayer resulted in the following resolution: "Better die than become a tepid priest."[766]

The Redemptorist superiors assigned newly ordained Alfred Pampalon to the monastery of Mons at Hainaut, Belgium. On August 31, 1893, he began his ministry. The Redemptorists looked forward to hearing him speak, and commented, "His lectures always seem too short."[767] By standards of rhetoric, Alfred, who suffered from a minor speech impediment, "which interferes with his enunciation and makes him hesitate," was not an outstanding preacher; however, "those who hear him have no doubt. This young priest is a saint. The Word of God pours out from the heart of this apostle. He lives what he preaches. He is on fire with the love of God."[768]

In April 1894, Alfred, according to community *Rules*, had to make a second novitiate. During the five months at Beauplateau, his tuberculosis returned. Back at Mons, at the end of September, he entered wholeheartedly into giving parish missions. By December, however, he began coughing, experiencing difficulty in breathing, suffering a stabbing pain in the back, and spitting up blood. Community authorities sent him from the coal-mining town of Mons back to the clean-air environment of Beauplateau village. He writes humorously to his confreres at Mons, "I am in Beauplateau. When I am asked what am I doing, I answer: I am here to recover my health. When someone wants to know how long I will stay, I say: that depends on the cook."[769]

The moral life, Alfred lived in exemplary fashion. His confessor testifies, "During all the four years, I heard his confession, I never found matter for absolution."[770] Alfred set out to avoid even the slightest venial sin, or transgression of the community *Rule*. A confrere observes, "One word characterizes his conduct: innocence."[771] His spiritual director writes,

> His (Alfred Pampalon's) life is a model for all Redemptorists and especially for our youth. You will find there no visions, no ecstasies, no miracles worked while he was living, no extraordinary mortifications. His life demonstrates what degree of perfection one can attain in an ordinary life, just by the exact observance of the *Rule*, and, most of all, by interior life, a life hidden in God. The merit of Father Alfred's life rests in this intimate union with Jesus Christ, through faith, hope and love. There lies the secret of his present glory in heaven.[772]

Alfred spent long hours in prayer to the Blessed Mother, and her mother, St. Anne, and before the Eucharist. One day, the seminary director challenged Alfred, "I think you love Mary more than God." "No," he [Alfred] replies, "but after God, I love Mary most."[773] Each day, upon waking, Alfred prostrated himself in his room, and offered the day to the honor of the Blessed Mother, whom he beseeched to keep him pure. He read and re-read many times two Marian classics: St. Alphonsus Liguori's *Glories of Mary*, and St. Louis de Montfort's *True Devotion to the Blessed Virgin*. Describing his relationship with Mary, Alfred writes, "I am like a young child who cannot be separated from his mother."[774] In preaching, his favorite topic was Mary. He composed over two thousand verses in honor of the Blessed Virgin. An excerpt follows:

You love me, Mary, and I love you.
The measure of your love, I cannot appraise.
To my own love I set no limits.
Can you love me more than I love you?

Mother of Beautiful Love, if I loved you
As much as a child can love his mother,
As much as all children love their mothers,
Would my love then equal your love for me?
No, I find no words to express your love.
There are no scales to weigh your affection.[775]

Alfred's life was cut short; he died two months before his twenty-ninth birthday. For the previous fifteen years, he had suffered ill health. In September 1895, on the advice of his superiors, he sailed home to Canada. After visiting his family, and the graves of his father and two sisters who had died during his nine years abroad, Alfred went to live at the Basilica of St. Anne. On New Year's Day 1896, he writes to his mother, "As for me, well, I am sick: I cough day and night and perspire tremendously. I am afraid that, without a special intervention from Good Saint Anne, I will go Emma's way. [His older sister Emma, who had became a nun, died in 1889, at twenty-five.] May the sacred will of God be done!"[776] By August, dropsy affected his feet, his legs, and eventually his whole body. His biographer describes Alfred's condition: "He aches all over. He can find no comfortable position. He cannot even lie on his bed. He is hungry and cannot digest anything. He is always thirsty. No relief during the day, no rest during the endless nights. It is pure and simple suffering. Yet the patient continues to refuse morphine that would alleviate his pain."[777] On the twenty-second [of September], wracked with pain, Alfred cries out: "I wish to suffer everything for Jesus." Asked when he wants to go to heaven, he answers: "When God so desires."[778]

On the last day of September, with the crucifix of Our Lord lying on his chest, the chaplet of the Seven Sorrows hanging around his neck, and his community *Rule*, rosary, pictures of the Blessed Mother and St. Joseph clutched in his hands, Alfred left earthly life, and entered into eternal life.

*For further information, contact*
Postulator of the Cause of Father Pampalon
Basilica of Sainte-Anne-de-Beaupré
Beaupré, QC G0A 3C0 Canada

# OCTOBER

❧

### 1. ✙ Venerable Juan de Palafox y Mendoza

*Places: Puebla, Puebla, México*
*Fame: Broad-minded and wise administrator.*
*Archbishop of Puebla, México.*

A broad background enabled Juan de Palafox (1600-59) to function as a broad-minded bishop. This illegitimate son of the nobleman Jaime Palafox, the Marqués de Ariza, received an excellent education at the prestigious universities of Alcalá and Salamanca. At twenty-seven, he was appointed the treasurer of the Council on War, and the Council of the Indies.

Upon completing studies for the priesthood, Juan was ordained, and was named immediately the abbot of the monastery of Cintra, chaplain to and chief almoner for María Infanta of Spain. When she traveled to Germany to marry her cousin Emperor Ferdinand III, thus becoming the Empress of the Holy Roman Empire, Father Juan accompanied her.

Upon returning from Germany, Juan was named bishop of Puebla, México. In 1640, he was ordained bishop in the cathedral of Madrid by the cardinal of Compostela. In going to his assignment in New Spain, the new bishop traveled in the company of the new viceroy. Part of the bishop's responsibility at Puebla would be to serve as Visitor to the *Audiencia*, which oversaw New Spain, and to serve as Visitor to the University of México. Shortly after Juan's arrival, the viceroy, who was a first cousin to a Portuguese duke, was recalled to Spain under suspicion of seditious cooperation with the Portuguese. During the viceroy's absence in Madrid, Juan was given the responsibility of acting-viceroy. After a few months later, Juan abdicated the position as soon as the viceroy was vindicated and returned to New Spain.

Bishop Juan de Palafox developed the diocese in a significant way. He completed the construction of the cathedral at Puebla de los Angeles. He promulgated rules and regulations for religious communities, and a new constitution for the University of México. This highly educated bishop fostered education by expanding the Tridentine College of Saint Peter, founding the theological school of Saint Paul, and instituting the girls' school Niñas Virgenes de la Concepción, to which he donated his personal library of six thousand books.

Controversy with religious communities occupied this pro-active bishop. The religious rebelled when the bishop excluded religious order priests from holding the position of rector of the University of México. When the bishop withdrew the Jesuit community's ecclesiastical faculties to preach and hear confessions, the irate Jesuits sued the bishop. The suit lasted several years until the pope eventually settled the case, in favor of the bishop.

Bishop Palafox, in 1649, returned to Spain, where he was named Bishop of Osma. There, he similarly served his people pastorally, and wrote professionally. Posthumously his works were gathered into fifteen volumes, representing works on a variety of topics: canonical, religious, moral, literary, political, and historical.

> His political writings reflect a great concern for the decline of Spanish power, and . . . he analyzed the foreign and national policies that contributed to the decline. Although he was essentially a Hispanist, Palafox was able to see the importance of the various nations, that is, of the multiple nationality of the monarchy. He pleaded for the recognition of the individuality of each group and its equality with Castile and decried the distrust that prevented the full use of the monarchy's resources and energy.[779]

The bishop was renowned for his boundless dedication to God and God's people. Whatever he undertook, he did with greatest enthusiasm and self-sacrifice. His tombstone reads: "Indefatigable defender of ecclesiastical rights, and compassionate towards all."[780]

*For further information, contact*
Arzodiócesis de Puebla de los Angeles
2 Sur #305
Centro – Apartado Postal #235
72000 Puebla, Puebla, México

✣

## 2. ✠ Charles Nerinckx

*Places: Kentucky*
*Fame: Apostle of Kentucky, Founder of Sisters of Loretto*
*at the Foot of the Cross.*

Before coming in 1804 to the United States, where he ministered for twenty years, Father Charles Nerinckx (1761-1824) had served as priest for nineteen years in Belgium.[781]

Born and raised at Herffelingen, Belgium, Charles studied philosophy at the University of Louvain, and theology at the Major Seminary of Mechlin, before being ordained a priest in 1795. In priesthood, he labored eight years as vicar at the cathedral of Mechlin, and eleven years as pastor at Everberg-Meerbeke. His zeal and effective manner were limited, however, by the French Directory's restrictions on priests. The French Revolution's famed promise of "liberty, fraternity, and equality" applied only to those who supported the Revolution, who looked for the day, when "the last nobleman [will be] hung with the entrails of the last Catholic priest."[782] In this antinomian atmosphere, the Belgian government in 1797, legislated that all priests had to sign an oath of hatred against the royalty. In conscience, Father Charles and many other priests refused to sign this document. For seven years, Father Charles secretly ministered to his flock. During daylight, he hid on the property of the hospital administered by his aunt, a Benedictine nun: his usual hiding places were upstairs in the attic and outside in the chicken coop. Beginning at midnight, he visited people, instructing them in the sacraments, hearing confessions, and teaching the Scriptures. At two o'clock each morning, he celebrated Mass for as many as two hundred people at a time.

Wishing to be more effective, and lamenting "the almost utter uselessness of my presence in Belgium," Father Charles volunteered for ministry in the United States.[783] In 1803, while he and his bishop were meeting secretly to discuss Father Charles's desire to do missionary work, soldiers spied on them. They arrested the bishop, and chased after but could not catch the fleet-footed priest. Charles wrote to a friend, asking that benefit from the intervention of the mother of Demetrius Gallitzin, who was already ministering in the U.S. The wealthy noblewoman wrote to Bishop John Carroll, who in May 1804, invited Charles to come to the U.S. Without informing his family, he walked for ten days from Mechlin to Amsterdam. In mid-August, he sailed on what he described as "a floating hell," because of the irreligion, immorality, disease and danger experienced on ship.[784] Three months to the day, the forty-three year old priest disembarked at Baltimore. After four months of studying English at Georgetown University, and one-month of living with Bishop Carroll, Father Charles was assigned by the bishop to the Kentucky Territory.

Father Charles's pastoral area extended two hundred miles north-to-south, and an equal distance east-to-west; at that time, "Father Nerinckx' district [was] embracing nearly half of the state [of Kentucky]."[785] The number of Catholics in Kentucky had swelled from seven hundred to seven thousand, and some sources would say even double that number in the twelve-year period prior to Father Charles' arrival in the territory in 1805.[786] The priest rode on horseback to serve these Catholics; the circuit ride required six weeks. Almost every year, he added another parish community, and built another church. The need for priests kept growing, and in 1815 and 1820, Father Charles traveled to Europe, seeking men and money for the mission. When abroad, he purchased and carried to the U.S. numerous crucifixes, chalices, vestments, paintings, and other religious articles, many of which possessed extraordinary value. Many of these religious artifacts are housed now either at the motherhouse of the Sisters of Loretto or the chancery office of the Archdiocese of Louisville.

His achievements and energy attracted the admiration of John Carroll, whose see was raised to an archepiscopacy on April 8, 1808. Carroll suggested to the pope that he might appoint Nerinckx a bishop. The pope in 1808, nominated Nerinckx as bishop of New Orleans. Father Charles, however, responded to the news, by praying aloud the psalm, "Having myself to be taught goodness and discipline and knowledge, I am unable to teach these things to others."[787] Father Charles wrote to the pope, thanking him for the consideration, but refusing to accept the nomination.

Pastorally, much needed to be done in Kentucky. Because children needed to be educated, Father Charles began in 1812, near Hardin's Creek, Kentucky the first community of religious women founded in the United States. This community is known formally as the Friends Of Mary At The Foot Of The Cross, and is known popularly as the Sisters of Loretto. The sisters founded schools for girls, especially for those who were poor, slaves, and Indians. By the time of Father Charles's death, a dozen years after their founding, the sisters had increased to over a hundred members.[788] Nerinckx instructed the sisters in the following ways, "Never forsake Providence, and Providence will never forsake you;" and "I know not what to say to impress you sufficiently with the sacredness of your calling."[789] The priest taught the sisters the following morning prayer, which he called their *Morning Manna*:

Love your Jesus dying with love for you on the cross.
Love Mary, your loving mother, sorrowing at the foot of the cross.
Love one another, have only one heart, one soul, one mind.
Love the Institute, love the *Rules*, love Jesus' darling humility.[790]

Throughout his ministry, Father Charles felt the pangs of petty persecution. Priests who replaced him in one of the parishes he had founded publicized themselves as "easy," and discarded the piety, practices, disciplines, and advice, which Charles had preached from the pulpit and had taught to married couples. Regarding the direction of the sisters, his successor complained bitterly to the bishop about Father Charles' allegedly excessive rigor and austerity. Not wishing to confront his detractors, Father Charles suggested to the bishop that the sexagenarian priest might move farther west. His bishop agreed, and Bishop Rosati of Bardstown, Kentucky assigned the priest to the Upper Louisiana Territory, now as Missouri. Father Charles intended to develop missions among the Indians there.

Father Charles Nerinckx left Loretto on June 16, 1824. Less than two months later, he died at St. Genevieve, Missouri. Ten years later, his bodily remains were transported back to Loretto. In his will written in 1820, the ever-zealous pastor leaves this prayerful instruction to his beloved sisters:

> Zeal for souls — your own and that of so many desolate orphans and scholars — burning zeal of Jesus and Mary! Gain souls, hunt souls, catch souls, court souls, draw souls, pull souls, carry souls, deliver souls, shelter souls, buy souls! . . . Souls! Souls! And nothing but souls, for the love of Jesus, the owner of all souls![791]

*For further information, contact*
Nerinx News
Loretto Motherhouse
515 Nerinx Road
Nerinx, Kentucky 40049 U.S.A.

## 3. ✠ Blessed Mother Theodore Guerin

*Place: St. Mary-of-the-Woods, Indiana*
*Fame: "My dear daughters, if you lean with all your weight*
*upon Providence, you will find yourself well supported."*
*Foundress of the Sisters of Providence of St. Mary-of-the-Woods.*

Born during the French Revolution, when churches and schools were forced to close, Anne-Thérèse Guerin (1798-1856) received most of her Catholic elementary education at home.[792] In the fishing village of Etables-sur-Mer on the Normandy Coast, both of Anne-Thérèse's brothers died as infants in separate fires, and in 1814, robbers killed her father. Because these losses overwhelmed Anne-Thérèse's mother, the care of the mother and the younger sister fell to fifteen-year old Anne-Thérèse.

THEODORE GUERIN

In 1823, Anne-Thérèse joined the Sisters of Providence of Ruille-sur-Loir. Two years later, she pronounced vows, received the religious habit and the name Sister St. Theodore. In Sister Theodore's early days in the convent, she received a medicine which saved her life, but which "worked havoc with her digestive system. For the remainder of her life, she was unable to digest solid food and suffered much from impaired health until her death."[793] In 1824, young Sister Theodore was sent as superior to the industrial town of Rennes, which was "the community's largest and most difficult mission."[794] There, she gained the reputation of an excellent teacher, and much-loved leader. After eight years, she was transferred to the country parish of Soulaines, where she administered and taught in the school, and studied medicine and pharmacy so that she might render medical service.

In 1839, the Normandy-native priest Celestine de la Hailandière traveled from Vincennes, Indiana, to recruit sisters in France for the American frontier. While de la Hailandiere was in France, his bishop died. De la Hailandiere was named the successor; and was ordained bishop before he left France. In response to de la Hailandière's request for assistance, the Sisters of Providence asked Sister Theodore if she would go to America. Sister Theodore accepted the assignment.

Sister Theodore, two other professed nuns, and three novices, left Ruille in mid-July 1840. Two weeks later, they sailed for New York City, which voyage lasted six weeks. After passing a few days in New York as guests of the wealthy Parmentier family, the sisters traveled by train through Philadelphia to Frederick, Maryland, where they transferred to a stagecoach, which carried them through the Cumberland Pass to Wheeling. At the Ohio River, they caught a steamboat to Madison, Indiana, and another boat to Evansville. At Madison, the sisters met Bishop de la Hailandière, who explained to the sisters that their destination would not be Vincennes, but Saint Mary-of-the-Woods, seventy miles north of Vincennes. The sisters continued by stagecoach to Terre

Haute, crossed the Wabash River on a ferryboat, and arrived at their wilderness destination on October 22.[795]

For the next sixteen years, until she died, Sister Theodore and her sisters served in the diocese of Vincennes, which at that time included the state of Indiana plus the eastern third of Illinois, and measured three hundred miles both north-to-south and east-to-west. The bishop and approximately three dozen priests were serving this region.[796] Schools and teachers were needed desperately: "In 1840, of the more than 250,000 children in Indiana, less than 50,000 regularly attended school."[797] Nine months after their arrival, the sisters opened St. Mary's Female Institute, later called St. Mary's Academy. Within a few years, they opened other schools in Indiana at Jasper, Terre Haute, Fort Wayne, St. Mary-of-the-Woods; and St. Francisville, Illinois, They opened also two orphanages, one for boys at Highland, and one for girls at Vincennes, which was later moved to Terre Haute.

The missionary sisters suffered from weather and opponents. Extreme cold and heat, hurricanes, hail storms, and locust plagues resulted in improper diet and inadequate housing. A divisive novice had to be dismissed. In 1842, an arsonist's fire consumed the nuns' barn, which was filled with recently harvested crops and the community's farm tools. The sisters' community in the U.S.A. suffered not only geographical separation, but eventual legal separation from its French foundation due to differences in culture and difficulties in communication. Mother Theodore's worst suffering, however, occurred with Bishop de la Hailandière. He regularly would make promises but revoke them a few weeks later. He felt easily threatened by capable people. Mother Theodore, in a letter of late 1844 to Bishop Bouvier in France, describes her frustration: "It would be better not to have the congregation at all than to have one that would have no other rule than the caprices of a disordered imagination, which will condemn tomorrow what it commands today." [798] The bishop wished absolute control over the sisters.

While Mother Theodore was in France on a fund-raising tour from April 1843 until March 1844, the bishop far exceeded his authority. Upon her return from Europe to Vincennes, Mother, "grieved, but calm and submissive," approached Bishop de la Hailandière.[799] For two hours, the bishop hurled accusations at her. He demanded that she return the next day for more of the same. The next day, however, the bishop's ill mood had passed, and the two held a cordial discussion about the Sisters of Providence.

To his credit, Bishop de la Hailandière recognized his shortcomings. A little more than three years after his episcopal ordination, he wrote to Rome, requesting that the pope might relieve de la Hailandière of his episcopal duties: "I fear to lose my soul. That is why I beg his Eminence to examine before the good God whether it would not be expedient that I cease to occupy the See of Vincennes."[800] In January 1845, while visiting Europe, de la Hailandière traveled to Rome, where he personally repeated his offer of resignation. Pope Gregory XVI refused the resignation. One year later, the bishop writes to the pope, "The mission confided to me has always seemed a charge much beyond my strength."[801]

Conflicts between the bishop and the sisters continued. Mother Theodore, on the advice of Bishop Bouvier, saw that leaving the diocese was her only way to escape from the anguished bishop. Many priests already had left the diocese, after their letters to the metropolitan bishop of Baltimore proved ineffective in removing de la Hailandière. Mother and the sisters made one last effort to gain the bishop's "approbation of our holy *Rule* and [the sisters' possession of] the property of Saint Mary's."[802] The bishop agreed, on the condition that the sisters would sign an *Act of Reparation* for the alleged slander he suspected that they had spoken about him. The sisters signed the document, and committed themselves to remaining at Vincennes. A few months later, in spring, the bishop called in Mother Theodore, and reprimanded her for four hours, at the end of which he asked her to write a letter seeking his permission for her to return to France.

On May 20, 1847, "the seven years of sorrow," between the sisters and the bishop reached its culmination.[803] While planning to depart Vincennes for St. Mary-of-the-Woods the next day, and having purchased already a stagecoach ticket, Mother Theodore visited the bishop in the afternoon. During the meeting he accused her of conniving to remain as superior. She denied the charge. Frustrated, the bishop locked Mother in the reception room, and went to dinner. When Mother failed to return home, the sisters went to the bishop's residence to inquire of her whereabouts. The bishop answered the door, and then went directly to another door behind which Mother was locked. As he opened the door, Mother fell to her knees and asked for his blessing. He gave her his blessing, and motioned silently for her to leave. That evening, the bishop appeared at the convent.

The bishop declared to our Mother that not only was she no longer the superior but that she was not now even a Sister of Providence, for he released her from her vows; that she had to leave the diocese immediately and go elsewhere to hide her disgrace; that he forbade her to write to the sisters at St. Mary's.[804]

The bishop threatened that any sister who left with Mother would be excommunicated. He warned that any sister who dared to take anything belonging to the diocese, would have the police pursuing her. Despite the threats, all the sisters agreed to follow Mother Theodore. The workmen too at St. Mary's agreed to go with Mother Theodore.

In late May 1847, a letter from Rome arrived at the bishop's residence, indicating that his resignation had been accepted. Mother prayed for the resigned bishop. She writes to Mother Mary at Ruille-sur-Loir, "We pray for him daily. . . . He will be much higher in heaven, I am convinced, than if he had remained bishop."[805] Throughout these tribulations, Mother Theodore never spoke ill of the man; she treated him instead with respect and compassion. "She obeyed his wishes until he began interfering with the internal governance of the Congregation and demanding procedures that opposed the Sisters of Providence *Rule*.[806]

Mother Theodore's health began worsening. The intestinal ailments from which she had suffered in childhood had continued to plague her. In her last year of life, she traveled seven hundred miles in a five-week period, in order to visit with and to serve the sisters. Over time, Mother's energy became sapped.

Despite tribulations, Mother Guerin's congregation grew rapidly during the sixteen years of her service in the U.S.A. The original six sisters increased to sixty-seven professed susters, nine novices, and seven postulants. The teaching apostolate expanded from the Academy at St. Mary-of-the-Woods to a dozen schools and two orphanages serving twelve hundred students. Mother's pedagogy, which she inculcated in her sisters, began with the exhortation: "love the children first, and then teach them."[807]

*For further information, contact*
Cause of Blessed Mother Theodore Guerin
Providence Hall
Saint Mary-of-the-Woods, IN 47876 U.S.A.

## 3. ✠ Jeanne LeBer

*Place: Montréal, Québec*
*Fame: Prayer-filled contemplative recluse.*
*Heiress who renounced her wealth.*

The only daughter of the wealthiest man in Montréal gave up all her riches, comfort, and the possibility of marriage in order to fulfill Jesus' invitation to "Go, sell what you posess and... come, follow me" (Mt 19:21).[808] At eighteen, Jeanne (1662-1714) informed her parents and four brothers, that she desired to dedicate her life to God as a recluse. The family then provided in their home a room to which she confined herself the entire day except for a one-block walk to the

JEANNE LEBER

parish church for morning Mass. At thirty-three, she left home, and entered a three-story, fifteen-by-eight foot cell attached to the chapel of the Sisters of the Congregation of Notre Dame. From then until her death at fifty-two, she remained in her cloister.

This only daughter was raised in the most comfortable circumstances available in the frontier village of Montréal. She received an excellent spiritual formation and academic education, relative to that time and place. When Jeanne was two and a half years old, her paternal aunt came to live with the family, until she entered the convent four years later. At six, Jeanne began attending the school run by Marguerite Bourgeoys, who probably taught Jeanne at some point. In 1674, Jeanne studied in Québec at the Ursuline Sisters' Convent School, where most likely she met Sister Marie de l'Incarnation. Jeanne studied "catechism, grammar, and arithmetic,... history and literature... sewing and knitting and began fancy work."[809] She became highly skilled at embroidery.

After completing her schooling in 1677, Jeanne returned home. Many suitors asked for her hand, but she refused all offers. People wondered if Jeanne were to enter the convent, would she follow her aunt and become an Ursuline nun at Québec, or join Marguerite Bourgeoy's congregation at Montréal. Jeanne surprised everyone by announcing that she wished to be a recluse.

Jeanne, like St. Catherine of Siena, lived the cloistered life at home. She undertook this vocation for a probationary period of five years. After taking private vows of chastity and reclusion, she spent her day in prayer, Scriptural reading, spiritual reading, and manual labor. When she left home each morning for the five o'clock Mass, she walked silently with her eyes downcast. Jeanne maintained this lifestyle for fifteen years, from 1680 to 1695.

In 1694, just after the convent of the Congregation of Notre Dame burned to the ground, Jeanne offered to pay for the reconstruction of the chapel, if the sisters would add onto the apse a three-story cell wherein Jeanne would live as a recluse with exposure to the Blessed Sacrament. Jeanne requested too that her nun-cousin of the same congregation might bring to Jeanne food, fuel, and sewing materials as needed. The superior agreed.

The transition from her home to her chapel cell took place on August 5, 1695. A religious procession marked the event. Participants included altar servers, parishioners, political leaders, the Sisters of the Congrégation-de-Notre-Dame, and the clergy, all of whom were singing psalms and reciting prayers, as they led Jeanne's relatives, siblings, parents, and the recluse herself to her new quarters. Reaching the chapel, the father broke out in tears, and excused himself. Sister Marguerite Bourgeoys commented, "I was overjoyed the day Mademoiselle LeBer entered this house as a recluse."[810]

Jeanne spent from 1695 to 1714 in her chapel cell. Everyday, she prayed the Divine Office at dawn, midday, and in the middle of the night, when she would descend from her sleeping quarters, enter the chapel, and prostrate herself before the Blessed Sacrament. She attended daily Mass and received Communion through a small turnstyle inserted into the wall between her quarters and the chapel. Her daily prayers consisted of the offices of the Holy Virgin, the Holy Cross, and the litany of the saints. Three times weekly, she prayed the Office of the Dead. Daily, she read the Sacred Scriptures and spiritual writers. She dressed in "a worn dress of coarse serge, with an apron of the same material, and wearing shoes of corn straw which she had made herself."[811] She slept on "a straw mattress, . . . a straw pillow, and a simple blanket."[812]

To the poor, Jeanne gave much of her inherited wealth, clothing which she no longer needed, and clothing which she had made. For poor students, she supplied funds for the Congregation to build a boarding school for the country girls, and seven scholarships for girls too poor to pay their own tuition, room, and board. For poor parishes, she purchased sacred vessels and donated hand-made sacred vestments and church linens, whose exquisiteness can be admired still in the museum of the Congregation in old Montréal.

Because the citizens of Ville-Marie recognized Jeanne as a living saint, they besought her to pray for their particular needs. In 1711, when the nascent colony appeared about to be overrun by the opposing British army, people rushed to her and begged her intercession for divine intervention. An army of three thousand British soldiers was marching towards Montréal, and a fleet of many ships with full complements of sailors was advancing up the St. Lawrence River towards Québec. The meager French and colonial forces were outmatched. Local citizens begged Jeanne to pray on their behalf. She responded, "The Blessed Virgin will look after this country. She is the guardian of Ville-Marie. We should fear nothing."[813] When Jeanne was warned about the imminent danger, she wrote a prayer; the handwritten prayer was then placed on the Congregation's barn door to protect the wheat stored therein. Another cousin, the commander of the Canadian troops, begged for her help. She sent him a banner of the Blessed Virgin Mary, with this handwritten prayer attached, "Our enemies place full confidence in their weapons, but we place ours in the name of the Queen of Angels whom we invoke. She is as strong as an army in battle array. Under her protection, we hope to conquer our enemies."[814] In fact, the expected battle never materialized. Seven ships of the British fleet were wrecked on the reefs approaching Québec, which resulted in the army's cancellation of its planned attack.

Before she died, Jeanne dispersed all of her inheritance. Since 1711, she had been urging the Sisters of the Congregation of Notre Dame to build a boarding school, and in 1713, when the sisters agreed to do so, Jeanne signed over to them a sizeable endowment. A few days later, the benefactress became sick. One year later, she died.

*For further information, contact*
Centre Jeanne-LeBer
4873, avenue Westmount
Westmount, QC H3Y 1X9 Canada

✂

## 5. ✠ Blessed Francis Xavier Seelos

*Places: Pittsburgh, Pennsylvania; Baltimore, Cumberland,
and Annapolis, Maryland*
*Fame: John Neumann and he ministered together in Pittsburgh.
Confessor, preacher, and parish priest.*

Upon completing elementary school at Füssen, in the foothills of the German Alps, and secondary education at Augsburg, Francis Xavier Seelos (1819-67) entered the University of Munich.[815] Intending to become a priest, he felt unsure whether his vocation was to the diocesan or missionary ministry. After two years in Munich, having completed philosophical studies, Francis confided to his father, that "he wished to follow the example of his namesake by becoming a missionary priest in a foreign land."[816]

The Redemptorist community in the U.S.A. disseminated throughout Western Europe requests for assistance in the United States. Francis learned about the request, and communicated his desire to serve as a missionary, especially among the German-speaking immigrants in the United States.

During his first year in theological studies, Francis felt the influence of the Blessed Virgin Mary. "His brother Adam later reported, 'One Sunday, when I came to him for my writing lesson [Francis was tutoring Adam], he said to me: 'Today we will not write. Last night the Blessed Mother appeared to me. I have to become a missionary'."[817] In spring 1842, he left the university and applied to the Redemptorist community. Francis waited for a reply throughout spring, summer, and fall. Half a year passed. Still, no reply arrived from the Redemptorists. Deciding he could wait no longer, he entered the diocesan seminary of Augsburg on November 3. The letter of acceptance from the Redemptorists arrived three weeks later. The very next morning, Francis began the process of withdrawal from the seminary, which he left on December 9.

On St. Patrick's Day in March 1843, Francis' ship sailed from Le Havre, France, and arrived on April 20, at New York City. The seminarian was received by, and lived with the Redemptorists, who had been stationed in the city for a few years already. One month later, he traveled to Baltimore, where he entered the novitiate at St. James Parish, and where, one year later, he took his vows. Another eight months later, he was ordained a priest, on December 22, 1844. During this time, he wrote to his family that he loved the ministry with the German immigrants and the American blacks, but that he found the U.S. citizenry somewhat uncultured.

His first assignment as a priest took him to St. Philomena's Church at Pittsburgh, Pennsylvania. Here the oft-recurring phenomenon of two saints living together occurred again: Francis' religious superior and pastor was John Neumann, whom the church canonized in 1977. John Neumann mentored Francis Seelos. At Pittsburgh, where Francis preached in German, French, and English, he became renowned for his humorous style of preaching, compassionate manner in the confessional, and warm welcome to all children. He was named pastor in 1851. The Catholic people perceived him to be a saint. Not everyone, however, liked Catholics. The anti-religious political party whose members shamelessly called themselves "Know Nothings" actively persecuted the Catholic Church and its members. On one occasion, after Francis responded to a feigned urgent plea for help at a home, the residents locked him inside and beat him up.

After nine years at Pittsburgh, Francis was assigned to the Redemptorist missions in Maryland, where he served for almost a dozen years. In 1854, he arrived at the parish of St. Alphonsus in downtown Baltimore, where he met the people with his usual generosity and openness. He received with equality and equanimity all people: men and women, religious and laity, young and elderly, white and black, rich and poor. The story is told that Father Francis, who had been summoned in the middle of the night to assist a young woman dying in a local brothel, rushed to her aid and remained at the prostitute's bedside the whole night. He did this act of Christian charity and justice, regardless of the gossip that he knew would circulate in the morning. His zeal adversely affected his health. After his superiors discovered him spitting up blood one morning, they transferred this active pastor to a less demanding position. He was assigned in May 1862, to parochial and seminary ministry at the church of Sts. Peter and Paul at Cumberland. The seminarians grew to love Father Francis. They found him approachable for counseling, flexible in applying seminary rules, and exemplary in prayer. When the Civil War battles began threatening the security of the seminary, Father Francis and others moved the seminary to Annapolis, approximately twenty miles southeast of the capital city. At Annapolis, he ministered to soldiers and prisoners of both sides. Before leaving Cumberland, Francis traveled to Washington, D.C., to try to thwart attempts to conscript seminarians. The priest met with President Abraham Lincoln, who assured Father Francis that the president would do what he could. The seminarians were not drafted.

While Francis was loved by those whom he served, he was not loved as much by some with whom he lived in religious community. In the parish, fellow priests criticized him for spending twelve-hour days in the confessional, listening to and not rushing penitents. His confreres chided him for his allegedly inefficient method of passing so much time with so few people when so much work needed to be done. In the seminary, fellow priests complained that he was lax in his job, which resulted in his being removed from his position as director of the seminary.

A few influential Redemptorists began spending unbelievable amounts of time and energy filing official complaints about his personal defects. One confrere complained to local and Roman superiors that Father Seelos lacked experience, insight, and firmness as a superior and — the ultimate jab — he could not speak Latin well. Others complained that he was "an old mother" and "a blockhead." He was accused of being a pushover and criticized for allowing the students to play music after night prayers, to go swimming, and to put on school plays.[818]

After religious superiors removed Father Francis from his position at the seminary, he rejoiced at being freed from administrative responsibilities. In 1860, when the bishop of Pittsburgh recommended Father Francis as a candidate for a vacant bishopric, the Redemptorist frantically acted to remove his name from consideration. Father Francis wrote directly to Pope Pius IX, and provided reasons why not to be ordained a bishop.

In August 1863, the Redemptorist superiors named Father Francis the superior of the community's preaching band. During the next three years, he preached annually more than twenty-one two-week missions in over a dozen states within the Midwestern, Mid-Atlantic and New England regions. In autumn 1865, he delighted in no longer being superior of a Redemptorist house. He was named assistant pastor for St. Mary's parish in Detroit, where he served for ten months.

Beginning on September 27, 1866, Father Francis began his ministry at St. Mary's Assumption Parish in New Orleans. The next year, the Delta City was hit by a yellow fever epidemic. On September 17, the priest, who had been busy ministering to victims, contracted the disease. In less than three weeks, he succumbed to the fatal effects of the illness.

*For further information, contact*
Seelos Center
2030 Constance St.,
New Orleans, LA 70130 U.S.A.

☙

## 6. ✠ Blessed Marie-Rose Durocher

*Place: Longueuil, Québec*
*Fame: Special care for the least significant, the poorest, the youngest students. Foundress of Sisters of the Holy Names of Jesus and Mary.*

Mother Marie-Rose Durocher (1811-49), who was baptized Eulalie-Mélanie, responded throughout her life, for the love of God and in devotion to Jesus and Mary, to people's real needs.[819]

Eulalie grew up as the youngest of ten surviving siblings, living at Saint-Antoine-sur-Richelieu on the outskirts of Montréal. Despite suffering from poor health throughout her youth, she manifested great joy. She studied at a local boarding school run by the Congrégation de Notre-Dame, but two years later, she returned home because of repeated sicknesses at school. At sixteen, Eulalie's parents sent her to another of the sisters' boarding schools, and she remained there for two years, but she attended classes for only seven months because of her recurring sicknesses. At home, after Eulalie received from her father the gift of a horse, her health improved with her outdoor recreation and maturity in caring for the horse.

MARIE-ROSE
DUROCHER

After Eulalie's brother Théophile was ordained a priest in 1828, he asked Eulalie if she might live as his housekeeper at the rectory at Saint-Benoit-des-Deux-Montagnes. She happily managed the household. After only a few months, Théophile was transferred to Boleil, twenty miles outside of Montréal, and Eulalie followed him in 1831. In the rectory, Eulalie cared for the priest guests, and nursed the elderly priests who oftentimes took up residence in the eight-bedroom rectory. Early in Eulalie's employment, her brother hired Mélodie Dufresne to share the workload with his sister. The two women developed a lifelong friendship. They worked together not only in decorating the altars, and making or mending church vestments, but also in organizing women's retreats, instructing the youth in religious education, and visiting the poor.

When the newly ordained Bishop Ignace Bourget came to the diocese of Montréal in 1840, he invited the missionary Oblates of Mary Immaculate to help the local clergy. One of these Oblates, Pierre-Adrien Telmon, made a positive impact on Eulalie, and through her, on the Church in Canada. Telmon sought Eulalie's help in founding parish-based sodalities called the Daughters of Mary Immaculate. This group was to provide religious inspiration and social support for young women. As the sodality's first president, Eulalie provided organizational and spiritual leadership, which enabled the sodality to expand from one parish in 1842 to over fifty parishes by 1849. Her spirituality originated from Jesus' words, "I came to cast fire upon the earth" (Lk 12:49).

Eulalie's interest in instructing the young in their faith led her to found a religious community. As a laywoman, she already had been providing religious education to children. After Bishop Bourget failed to bring from France to Canada the Sisters des Saints Noms de Jésus et de Marie of Marseille to instruct the young, he suggested to Eulalie that she might found a community of nuns to educate the young.

Shocked at first, Eulalie pondered the suggestion, and soon responded affirmatively. At thirty-two, Eulalie with her friend Mélodie Dufresne, and a teacher Henriette Cere, under the guidance of Father Telmon, founded the Sisters of the Holy Name of Jesus and Mary at Longueuil, Québec. The trio entered their postulancy in late 1843, with rules sent by the Sisters of Marseille. A few months later, the three entered the novitiate, took religious garb and religious names. Eulalie received for her name Sister Marie-Rose. She wrote to her sister, "I wish to be a rose of agreeable odor for Jesus Christ."[820] Before the first year had concluded, nine recruits joined the new community. At first, the founding trio administered the community, but in September 1844, Bishop Bourget realized that one sister ought to be in charge, and for that position he recommended Sister Marie-Rose. In December 1844, Bishop Bourget formally recognized the Sisters as a religious congregation. Three months later, the civil authorities gave legal status to the sisters. By the sixth year, the community had received sixty-six candidates, of whom forty-four persevered and became community members.

The nuns' first mission was to build a school at Longueuil. In 1844, Mother Marie-Rose sent sisters to Montréal to learn from the recently arrived Brothers of the Christian Schools the most current methods of instruction. At Longueuil, the pupils studied religion, music, art, design, painting, theater, home economics, as well as reading, writing, and English. The enrollment for the first year of operation at Longueuil in 1843, consisted of thirteen resident-students, and forty day-students. In 1846, the nuns opened another school at Beloeil, and two years later, they opened two more schools at Saint-Timothée and Saint-Lin. By 1849, the community was teaching four hundred forty-eight students.

Throughout these years, Mother Marie-Rose grew in her experience of the presence of God. Entering the chapel each day at 4:30 A.M., this woman of faith and woman of the Church delighted in the love of the Lord at Eucharist, and in her devotions to the Sacred Heart and the

Virgin Mary. A contemplative in action, she carried beyond the chapel the benefit of her prayer by seeing God's goodness in each person, and perceiving God's will in everyday events. Strong and tender in personality and behavior, she asserted herself as needed, especially with those few clergy who obstructed her serving the most needy. As an innovator, she implemented programs that her contemporaries could not begin to imagine. Joyfully, she served as superior of the sisters, the animator of the community, and administrator of schools. She respected all children as God's children regardless of their cultural, economic or religious backgrounds; all the while, she possessed a special "solicitude for the least significant, the poorest, the youngest."[821] She urged the children of different language groups to communicate with and try to understand each other. "She recommended without ceasing that the sisters practice unity and peace amongst themselves."[822]

In early February 1849, Marie-Rose caught a bad cold while traveling to Beloeil. She never recover her good health. In August, she offered to resign her position as superior because of an unfortunate division among the sisters. In September, she received the last rites of the Church. During one of her sleepless nights she composed for her sisters a farewell, which demonstrates her gentleness, while asking pardon for her transgressions. The letter reads in part:

> I beg pardon, my sisters, for lacking sweetness and kindness in your regard. I beg pardon for having hurt anyone in conversation at recreation, for having spoken harsh or offensive words. I beg pardon for having lacked charity in not having towards you the heart of a mother. I beg pardon for my irregularities in spiritual exercises. I beg pardon for my shortcomings.[823]

On October 6, 1849, her thirty-eighth birthday, and after fewer than six years in religious life, Mother Marie-Rose died. Her legacy continues among the Sisters of the Holy Names of Jesus and Mary, and among those affected inside and outside the classroom by the charism embodied by Mother Marie Rose in the community which she founded.

*For further information, contact*
Centre Marie-Rose
80, St. Charles Street, East
Longueuil, QC J4H 1A9 Canada

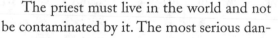

## 6. ✛ Terence J. Cooke

*Place:* New York, New York
*Fame:* "Thy will be done." Cardinal of New York.

Terence Cooke (1921-83), for as long as family members could remember, always wanted to be a priest.[824] Throughout his seminary studies, and rapid rise in the ranks of Church hierarchy, the call to priesthood inspired him, grounded him, and guided him. Personal notes, handwritten by him when he was a young priest, and discovered after his death, reveal his vision:

TERENCE J. COOKE

> The priest must live in the world and not be contaminated by it. The most serious danger of the parish priest is worldliness. The priest must have a cloistered heart faithful to Christ. Each priest is a rock on which many souls will rest. Each priest is a fisher of men, a shepherd of the flock, a laborer in the vineyard, a reaper in the fields. We are to be the leaven of society, to be a delegate of God. We must then be at the side of God to be a light to the world in reflecting Christ. Christ has chosen me to be with him until I die. This means close union with him and continual independence of the world. Wherever Christ needs me I will go. I will be his mediator, his instrument, ever seeking souls.[825]

About a quarter-century later, in 1977, Terence Cooke, then Cardinal Archbishop of New York, again in handwritten notes, describes his vocation as priest. "These glowing words sum up how Terence Cooke saw himself and his vocation as priest. His whole life, and especially his work as the shepherd of the Church of New York, are concentrated in these words."[826] Cardinal Cooke's words follow:

From the day of his ordination, a priest can never forget that he has been called by God himself. The priest is called to be a *servant*, giving up a family of his own, so that he can minister to those who need him more. The priest is called to be a *victim*, ready to share the sufferings of his people and not hide from them, and even ready to bear their sufferings in their place if God asks him to do so. A priest is called to be a *brother*, who shares the worries and fears and the frailty of the people around him, and who brings to them not any great strength and invulnerability of his own, but his joyful trust in the Father who loves him in Jesus whose priesthood he shares. The priest is called to be a *listener*, to learn prayerfully from the way in which God has worked in the lives of His people, and full of faith to carry that message to others. A priest is called to be a *friend*, conscious of the need of justice and brotherly concern in our society, a friend to people who have few friends in their hour of need. The anointing that Jesus gives us is to help us bring Him into our world, not to carry us out of it.[827]

The gifts of personality and spirituality which Terence Cooke received from God were nurtured at home with great care by his faith-filled parents. Michael and Margaret Gannon Cooke had emigrated from County Galway, Ireland, and moved to Morningside Heights in Upper Manhattan, wher they raised their three children, the youngest of whom was Terence. At home, the boy first learned the importance of daily prayer, adoration of the Eucharist, and devotion to the Blessed Virgin Mary. The parents named their son in honor of Terence MacSwiney, an Irishman who six weeks before Terence's birth, had died in a hunger strike while protesting the British occupation in Ireland. When Terence Cooke was five, the family moved to the spacious and green area of the Bronx. At nine, Terence lost his mother, probably to peritonitis. To care for the family, his mother's single sister Mary, moved into the home. After Terence graduated from St. Benedict's Elementary School, he entered the archdiocesan minor seminary, first attending Cathedral College, and six years later, advancing to St. Joseph's Seminary at Dunwoodie. On December 1, 1945, in St. Patrick's Cathedral, Francis Cardinal Spellman ordained Terence Cooke a priest.

After ordination, Cardinal Spellman assigned Father Cooke to pursue graduate studies in social work. The new priest attended the University of Chicago for a couple of weeks, until a longstanding eye ailment forced him to withdraw. Twenty months later, he began studies at the National Catholic School of Social Service at the Catholic University of America, where he received a master's degree in 1949. Returning to New York City, he was assigned to the Youth Division of Catholic Charities. In 1954, he was named procurator of St. Joseph's Seminary, and three years later, the cardinal's secretary. In rapid succession, Cooke was named vice chancellor of the archdiocese (1958), chancellor (1961), vicar general and auxiliary bishop (1965). After Cardinal Spellman died in December 1967, Bishop Cooke was named, probably on the cardinal's recommendation, the seventh archbishop of New York, despite being the youngest of the archdiocese's ten auxiliary bishops. Shortly after Archbishop Cooke was inaugurated, he was named the Military Vicar for the United States Armed Forces. In 1969, at forty-seven, Terence J. Cooke was named Cardinal of the Church.

Near the end of August 1983, it became known publicly that Cardinal Cooke had contracted cancer, and had little time to live. Doctors in 1964, had diagnosed cancer, and treated the dreaded disease in an on-going way. In November 1975, however, the cancer was diagnosed as having evolved into a terminal condition. For years, Terence Cooke had taken chemotherapy, and blood transfusions which only a handful of people knew about. His sickness did not reduce his working hours or workload. By August 1983, however, he could no longer work as he had been accustomed. Doctors informed him that his time was short.

The cardinal wrote a letter to the people of the archdiocese. His last letter to the faithful was read on October 8-9, which propitiously happened to be Pro-Life Sunday. The cardinal had died on October 6, 1983. The cardinal, who had led the U.S. Bishops Pro-Life Campaign since his appointment in 1995, writes with personal conviction, supported by personal experience.

The "gift of life," God's special gift, is no less beautiful when it is accompanied by illness or weakness, hunger or poverty, mental or physical handicaps, loneliness or old age. Indeed, at these times, human life gains extra splendor as it requires our special care, concern and reverence. It is in and through the weakest of human vessels that the Lord continues to reveal the power of His love.... At this grace-filled time of my life, as I experience suffering in union with Jesus Our Lord and Redeemer, I offer gratitude to Almighty God for giving me the opportunity to continue my apostolate on behalf of life.[828]

Two anecdotes demonstrate the saintly kindness and compassion of Cardinal Cooke. First, during the Vietnam War era, at an ordination service at Fordham University, while the oils were still wet on their hands, two newly ordained priests refused to give the sign of peace to the cardinal. Instead, one marched to the lectern, where he declared that he would not offer peace to the Cardinal until he resigned as Military Vicar. The other newly ordained said something akin to, "I too have difficulty making peace with war."[829] At this point, the Cardinal paused. He explained to the congregation his viewpoints on the war. "After that he walked towards the two newly ordained men with his hands extended to offer the peace to them."[830]

A second incident reveals a similarly profound interior and exterior peace possessed by Cardinal Cooke. At a Priests' Senate meeting in 1970, a young priest from a religious community, publicly criticized the Cardinal,

> for not moving fast enough and not giving enough leadership in social action. Among other things, he took it upon himself to represent all of the clergy when he said, "We are ashamed of you as our bishop." The cardinal never lost his composure, but responded to the young priest, telling him he was doing the best he could, taking into consideration all the factors concerning this complex situation. Cardinal Cooke almost seemed to apologize for making this man ashamed.[831]

Terence Cardinal Cooke had practiced throughout his priesthood a Christ-like kindness. He respected each person as a child of God, listening attentively, and responding gently to every person, in every situation. His motivation was to do God's will, to live according to God's way, as Jesus had manifested the Father's will, the Father's way.

∽∞

## 9. ✠ Cipriano Iñiguez Martin del Campo

*Place: Guadalajara, Jalisco*
*Fame: "Charity, even to the point of sacrifice; and constancy, even to death."*
*Founder of the Servants of St. Margaret Mary and of the Poor.*

Cipriano Iñiguez (1873-1931) grew up the third of ten children, in Jalisco's state capital of Guadalajara.[832] As a child, he attended the local school conducted by two male lay teachers, who taught him catechism, and other subjects. At fifteen, Cipriano entered the city's Conciliar Seminary. Life in the seminary proved challenging for Cipriano: not the studies, but the strictness. The boy was full of life, a prankster, a mischief-maker. Twice, he was almost expelled, once for having taken and hidden the seminary bell

CIPRIANO IÑIGUEZ
MARTIN DEL CAMPO

which the priests used to call the boys to rise, wash, eat, study, play, and pray. His classmates loved his pranks, but the authorities perceived them as a sign of lack of vocation. After ten years of seminary formation and education, Cipriano was ordained a priest on November 30, 1898.

Young Father Cipriano rolled up his shirtsleeves. In February 1899, he succeeded the priest-founder of the ten-bed hospital, Blessed Margaret.[833] The hospital stood in dire need of physical repair and enhancing medical services. Father Cipriano applied all his energy and skill to this work. Through the Saint Vincent de Paul Society, whose members already were visiting the patients, Father Cipriano met Maria Guadalupe García Zavala. He asked her assistance to found for women a Conference of Saint Margaret, and an auxiliary conference for young girls, the Holy Innocents.

The two conferences would help him in improving the hospital, and providing a Holy Thursday banquet for the poor. For the women and girls, he would provide weekly conferences, and an annual retreat. In the first year, over four hundred women joined the Conference of Saint Margaret. Father Cipriano was a marvelous pastor and preacher. Through his conferences, he promoted devotion to the Blessed Sacrament, Our Lady of Guadalupe, and Our Lady of Sorrows.

In early 1901, María Guadalupe approached Father Cipriano to let him know that she was preparing to enter the Franciscan community as a nun. He listened patiently. He replied that he was in the process of asking the diocese for permission to start a religious community of women, and he believed that Our Lord had chosen her, María Guadalupe, to be the first member and leader of this religious community. The congregation would be called Servants of Saint Margaret Mary and of the Poor. Its motto would be, "Charity, even to the point of sacrifice; and constancy, even to death." Its apostolate would be to care for the suffering sick and poor of Jesus Christ. María Guadalupe accepted on the spot. She explained, however, that she would seek the approval of her parents. Her parents resisted, claiming, the hospital had no money, no guarantee of security, and not only could the hospital not provide for their daughter, but *a fortiori* for the other young women who might join the new community. Father Cipriano responded that life provides few guarantees, and that hope too is part of life. Father Cipriano added, "It is necessary not only to hope, but also to do something for others."[834] On October 13, 1901, María Guadalupe left her parents' home, entered the hospital as superior general, and thereafter was called affectionately, Madre Lupe.

Numerous young women rushed to the community: one or two every week, for the first year at least. The community grew in membership and in works. Father Cipriano visited the convent twice a week, giving conferences, offering Masses, and instructing the sisters in the way and wisdom of living religious life. Madre Lupe's father, however, had been proven right: the community had very little money.

In January 1908, Father Cipriano founded a men's group, The Society of Thomas à Kempis. The group's purpose was to follow Christ in word and deed, by learning their faith, and caring for their neighbors. As Father Cipriano had provided for the women, Father provided for the men, weekly conferences and an annual retreat. The group grew to eighteen hundred men. Each Holy Thursday, these men would feed over one thousand poor people.

Throughout these years, Father Cipriano kept expanding the size and services of the hospital. In 1919, the bishop gave him charge of another hospital, Saint Joseph.

Trouble was brewing. Many people in government resented that the Catholic Church, in its positive leadership of the masses, might become more powerful than the civil government. Anti-Catholic measures were legislated by the federal government. These were enforced to different degrees according to various cities and states. Between 1910 to 1918 in Guadalajara, Father Cipriano, like many other priests, was arrested many times. His life was endangered at these moments; many priests lost their lives while under arrest, without the benefit of trial or jury. One time, he was imprisoned up to eight days.[835] Despite the difficulties he kept experiencing, he celebrated in 1923, his silver jubilee as a priest. On the invitation, Father Cipriano writes, "the Lord, in his infinite mercy, has raised me to the ineffable dignity of priesthood, [and] desiring to express my gratitude for this incomparable blessing, I will celebrate a solemn Mass in the Sanctuary of Our Lady of Guadalupe, in Guadalajara."[836] Three years later, however, the political-religious situation worsened with the ascendancy of Plutarco Elias Calles as president. Priests and laity were murdered by the thousands. Father Cipriano sought refuge, like many priests, in the crowded streets of the capital, México City. He lived with his sister from 1926 to 1929. These years proved very difficult not only for Father Cipriano in his absence from his active ministry, but also for the sisters of the new community, and for the vibrancy of their apostolic works. Father's leadership was missed. During his absence, letters, money and goods were smuggled oftentimes between Father's hiding place in México City, and the sisters' houses in Guadalajara.

In August 1929, Father Cipriano returned to Guadalajara. The next month, he preached for the sisters his first Holy Hour after his return. The sisters recorded his words:

> To be a saint is to have the intention of doing all things for God. How rich and easy is the spiritual life! Why do you eat? To

have the strength to serve God. Why do you sleep? Why do you obey? Not because my superior has a notebook in her hand, but to serve God. Why do you rise early each morning? To serve God. Why do you obey a superior who is difficult and quarrelsome? Because I have subjected myself to serve God. Why do you sweep? To serve God. . . . Daughters, if all that you do, you do for God, how can you do anything evil? Avoid wondering if what you are doing is the will of God, and make sure your intention is right and pure.[837]

Physically, Father Cipriano was ailing. A month before his return from México City to Guadalajara, the priest had undergone medical surgery for a throat ailment. Nonetheless, Father continued preaching; in 1930, he preached one hundred thirteen sermons, and delivered one hundred fifty-six conferences.[838] The next year, his failing health brought him to a hospital bed. On October 9, 1931, after having prayed with the sisters, and having received absolution from the attending priest, and a blessing from four other visiting priests, Father Cipriano breathed his last breath, and gave up his soul to God.

*For further information, contact*
Siervas de Santa Margarita María y de los Pobres
Reforma #1440
Z.C.
C.P. 44680
Guadalajara, Jalisco México

❧

# 11. ✠ Elias del Socorro Nieves

*Places: Yuriria, and La Cañada de Caracheo, Guanajuato*
*Fame: Peasant priest who forgave and blessed his assassins. Martyr.*

Elias (1882-1928) suffered poverty at home, school, and in his parish life; but he enjoyed a wealth of faith, courage, and mercy. When this poor peasant priest was discovered breaking Mexican law by saying Mass for his people, he forgave and prayed for the soldiers who knelt before him to receive his blessing, before they stood erect and shot him to death on orders of their captain.

Life had never been easy for Elias. He grew up the son of poor peasant farmers at San Pedro in Yuriria, in the state of Guanajuato. From his early years, he expressed the desire to become a priest, but an almost fatal bout with tuberculosis at twelve, and the death of the boy's father shortly thereafter, prohibited him from entering the seminary in his early teen years. Not until he was twenty-two, was he freed from the responsibility of helping to provide for his family. In 1904, he entered the Augustinian apostolic college at Yuriria, where this experienced farmer studied with seminarians who were ten years younger than himself. Success at studies, and finding financial support for his education, always presented a problem for him. But he always found a solution, through his faith in the Providence of God, and his perseverance in bringing to completion the tasks he had begun. At twenty-nine, he took vows in the Augustinian Order, at which time he exchanged his birth name of Mateo Elias for the religious name of Elias del Socorro, since he had sought and received the assistance of so many people in his journey towards priesthood.

After ordination to priesthood in 1916, he served in various localities of Bajio, until in 1921, when he was assigned to the extremely poor and isolated village of La Cañada de Caracheo. When the Juárez government at the end of 1926, imposed the anti-Catholic laws, Elias continued to serve his flock but under the cover of darkness lest he be discovered. Instead of moving to the city as the government required of priests so that governmental leaders could control every movement of the priests, Elias fled to and hid out in the hillside caves at La Gavia. For fourteen months, the courageous priest performed nocturnally his pastoral duties, assisted by brave lay persons.

Early one morning, however, Elias's active ministry came to an abrupt end. The priest and two ranchers, namely, the Serra brothers, happened to cross the path of a posse of soldiers. As soon as the military men noticed the priest's vestments under Elias' peasant garb, they arrested Elias and his companions, and took the trio to the jail at La Cañada. Some lay persons offered to ransom Elias, but he refused to accept their generous offer. At dawn on March 10, soldiers led the three captives from La Cañada in the direction of the capital at Cortazar.

Before long, the captain halted the party. He ordered the soldiers to shoot and kill the two ranchers. A little farther on, the captain stopped again. He said to Elias, "Now, it is your turn; let us see if dying is like saying Mass."[839] Elias replied, "You have spoken the truth, because to die for the faith is a sacrifice pleasing to God."[840] The priest requested a few minutes to recollect himself before experiencing the inevitable. Elias prayed quietly, handed his watch to the captain, and gave his blessing to the soldiers who had knelt down to be blessed by him. As the priest began to recite the Creed, he was shot to death. His last words were, "*¡Viva Cristo Rey!* [Long live Christ the King!]"[841]

*For further information, contact*
Convento de Santa Monica
Peña Pobre 83
Col. Toriello Guerra - Del. Tlalpan
14050 México D.F, México

## 12. ✠ Walter Ciszek

*Place: Shenandoah, Pennsylvania*
*Fame: Faith-filled long-sufferer. Spent twenty-two years*
*in captivity in Siberia.*

The parents of Walter Ciszek (1904-84) emigrated from Poland in the 1890's, to Shenandoah, Pennsylvania, which lay about one hundred miles northwest of Philadelphia.[842] The father earned a living first as a coal miner and then as a saloon owner, while the mother dedicated herself as homemaker for the couple's thirteen children. Walter was the seventh child.

WALTER CISZEK

In his autobiography, *With God In Russia*, Walter describes himself as an unlikely candidate for priesthood. As a youth, he had taken pride in being "tough, . . . stubborn, . . . a bully, the leader of a gang, a street fighter."[843] He played hooky so often from St. Casimir's Grade School that he had to repeat an academic year. His exasperated father begged the police to send his eighth-grade son to reform school. At the conclusion of eighth grade, Walter announced that he wanted to become a priest. He entered Saints Cyril and Methodius Seminary at Orchard Lake, Michigan. There, he alone rose daily at 4:30, ran five miles, swam in the near-frozen lake in November, ate nothing one Lent except bread and water, ate no meat for another year, and quit playing baseball to prove that he could give up this sport which he loved. One summer, he remained at the seminary to endure the loneliness of separation from family and friends. He always wanted to do "the hardest thing."[844]

After hearing a priest speak about the toughness of the young Jesuit Saint Stanislaus Kostka, who had walked from Warsaw to Rome to become a priest, Walter decided that he too wanted to become a Jesuit. He entered St. Andrew's Novitiate at Poughkeepsie, New York, and a few months later, Pope Pius XI addressed a letter "To all seminarians, especially our Jesuit sons," seeking volunteers to minister to the persecuted Church in Communist-controlled Soviet Union.[845] Immediately, Walter volunteered. He writes, "I knew I had come to the end of a long search."[846] After completing seminary studies at Wernersville, Pennsylvania; and Woodstock, Maryland, Walter sailed for Rome, where at the Gregorian University and the Collegio Russico, he and another Jesuit seminarian, Nestrov, read everything they could about Russia: its geography, history, language, culture, and its Oriental liturgical rite. After ordination to priesthood at the Basilica of St. Paul Outside the Walls on June 24, 1937, Father Walter was assigned to a parish in Albertyn, Poland, where he waited for the opportunity to minister in Russia.

In September 1939, Germany and the Soviet Union invaded Poland. Father Walter and his friend Nestrov obtained false working permits for the Ural Mountain region, and hopped a railroad boxcar going to Russia. At Tepkaya-Gora, due east of Moscow, using the alias Wladimir Lypinski, Father Walter began work as a laborer hauling logs from the river, and piling them ashore. He and Nestrov would periodically walk into the woods, where one said Mass while the other stood guard. They used a tree stump for the altar, and repeated from memory the prayers of the Mass. Gradually, believers learned of the priests' presence, and asked to be baptized or instructed, which services took place under the cover of night.

In June 1941, Germany invaded the Soviet Union. Within weeks, the NKVD (which soon would become known as the KGB) arrested hundreds of people, including Father Walter. Father Walter was surprised to learn that the KGB knew his real name, national origin, status as a priest, and possession of false documents. For the next two months, the KGB beat Father Walter with rubber clubs. Imagining that Father Walter was a German spy, the KGB transferred their prisoner to the dreaded Lubianka Prison in Moscow. For the next four years, he lived in a cell measuring six feet by ten feet, outfitted with a bed and a toilet-bucket, lit by a single light bulb, and ventilated by a barred and shuttered window. Guards watched their prisoner through a one-way peephole. The priest-prisoner was allowed out of his cell twenty minutes daily for an exercise. He prayed daily the Morning Offering , the Mass prayers, the Angelus, an examination of conscience, and three rosaries. He also created his own prayers, begging God for help, and expressing trust in God's providence.[847]

At Lubianka, Father Walter's initial nine months consisted of "relentless questioning."[848] When he explained his activity as "priestly work," the guards "had no understanding at all of spiritual motives, and argued that he must have had some political reason, either sabotage or espionage."[849] Under the influence of drug-laced tea, he confessed that he was a Vatican spy. Months passed in conversation. When officials asked the prisoner to sign an agreement to work as a spy, he refused, and guards removed him roughly.

In July 1942, Father Walter was sentenced to fifteen years of hard labor. He remained at Lubianka and Butirka for a combined four years, before being transferred to the Siberian slave-labor camps. Meanwhile, his community and family had received no news from or about him since June 1941. The Jesuits in 1947, declared him officially dead, and had memorial Masses said for the repose of his soul. Over the course of the next decade and a half, the "undernourished and overworked" priest labored above the Artic Circle at Dudinka and its neighboring Norilsk, in a succession of jobs: coal heaver, log-retriever, construction worker, and coal miner. In both camps, he worked also as a priest.[850] At Dudinka, he said Mass for the first time in five years. At Norilsk, he met a dozen priests from the Baltic region and Poland, and these men of God encouraged each other, and served the laity among them.

Three months shy of completing his fifteen-year sentence, he was released from prison in April 1955. He was told that he had to live in Norilsk, and had to register with local governmental officials; he could not leave Siberia, let alone the country. In the city, Father Walter and two priest friends shared a small apartment, whose ten-foot-square living room doubled as a chapel. Laity came cautiously to the apartment, where the priests began celebrating Sunday Masses. Masses were followed oftentimes by baptisms, weddings, and visits to the sick. In order to avoid detection, Mass sites were rotated among the homes of the laity. Informers were everywhere.

At times, officials warned Father Walter not to engage in "missionary work," and "subversive activities."[851] Father Walter replied that the Soviet Constitution guaranteed the freedoms of religion and conscience, and that he was only responding to people's requests that he pray for them. Later on, he was warned again to "watch out" and to avoid "unwarranted activities."[852] During Easter Week 1958, governmental officials, intending to silence him, gave him ten days to leave Norilsk. He traveled seven hundred miles south to Krasnoyarsk, where he replaced the former priest who had mysteriously "disappeared."[853] Soon, authorities ordered him to live at nearby Abakan.

In September 1963, the KGB called him to their offices. Without telling him why, they took him to Moscow, where they wined and dined him for a few days. On October 11, 1963, Father Walter and another American citizen were exchanged for a Russian couple who had been convicted of spying in the United States. The next day, Father Walter arrived at Idlewild Airport (now Kennedy Airport) in New York City. He had left the U.S.A. in 1935, when he studied at Rome, then ministered in Poland for two years, before entering the Soviet Union in 1939, when he began his twenty years of imprisonment, which was followed by two years of a restricted prison-release program.

Father Walter spent his next two decades in public ministry. Having returned to Wernersville, Pennsylvania, he produced a manuscript which led to two books: his autobiography, *With God in Russia* (1964) and his spiritual journal, *He Leadeth Me* (1973). In 1964, he was assigned to the John XXIII Center for Eastern Studies at Fordham University in the

Bronx, where he taught, counseled, and gave retreats until he died at Fordham on December 8, 1984.

How did he survive? "Providence," he answers. He continues, "God has a special purpose, a special love, a special providence for all those he has created. God cares for each of us individually, watches over us, provides for us."[854] In the perspective of Father Walter, with God watching over us, no moment is insignificant, no action is trivial.

Adapted from Father Walter's manuscript is the following Prayer of Surrender:

> Lord Jesus Christ, I ask the grace to accept the sadness in my heart, as Your will for me, in this moment. I offer it up in union with your sufferings, for those who are in deepest need of your redeeming grace. I surrender myself to your Father's will and I ask you to help me to move on the next task that you have set for me.
>
> Spirit of Christ, help me to enter into a deeper union with you. Lead me away from dwelling on the hurt I feel: to thoughts of charity for those who need my love, to thoughts of compassion for those who need my care, and to thoughts of giving to those who need my help.
>
> As I give myself to you, help me to provide for the salvation of those who come to me in need. May I find my healing in this giving. May I always accept God's will. May I find my true self by living for others in a spirit of sacrifice and suffering. May I die more fully to myself, and live more fully in you.
>
> As I seek to surrender to the Father's will, may I come to trust that He will do everything for me.[855]

*For further information, contact*
The Father Walter Ciszek Prayer League
231 North Jardin Street
Shenandoah, PA 17976 U.S.A.

# 14. ✠ Francisco Aguilar y Seijas

*Places: Michoacán and México City. D.F.*
*Fame: Defender of morality and builder of churches, hospitals, and the*
*seminary. Bishop of Michoacán and Archbishop of México City.*

From the Old World of Galicia in Spain, to the New World of Michoacán in México, came bishop-elect Francisco Aguilar y Seijas (d. 1698) in 1679. Three years after his arrival and service as Bishop of Michoacán, Aguilar was appointed Archbishop of México City.

The archbishop became renowned for his zeal and charity. He laid the cornerstone for the Basilica of Our Lady of Guadalupe, oversaw the construction of numerous churches and convents, founded the Colegio of Saint Michael of Bethlehem, and established two hospitals for women, including one for mentally ill patients. When the king of Spain failed to erect a seminary as the Council of Trent (1545-60) had required, Archbishop Aguilar himself set out with great determination to see this project concluded, finishing the construction in 1691. "He waged an unceasing fight against gambling, cockfighting, bullfighting, and the theater; . . . and made visitations of his entire [arch]diocese in 1684 and in 1696."[856]

*For further information, contact*
Arquidiócesis Primada de México
Curia: Durango # 90
Col. Roma - Apartado Postal #24-443
06700 México, D.F. México

✦

# 15. ✛ Venerable Felix De Andreis

*Places: Bardstown, Kentucky; and St. Louis, Missouri*
*Fame: Seminary professor who longed to become a missionary.*
*Laid the foundation for the Vincentian mission in the U.S.A.*

Having died at forty-two, Vincentian Father
Felix De Andreis (1778-1820) left many tasks
undone except his having lived well his vocation
as a Vincentian priest.[857] After eighteen years of
educating seminarians and priests, and preaching
missions to the laity, he attained the *fama sancti-*
*tatis*. At his death, cures were attributed to his
intercession.

FELIX DE ANDREIS

Felix grew up in a middle-class family at
Demonte in northern Italy. Like his brothers
who were a doctor and a lawyer, he received an
excellent education. At fifteen, he expressed interest in joining the
Congregation of the Mission, which St. Vincent de Paul had founded in
France in 1625. The Vincentian superior advised the candidate that it
might be difficult for someone of Felix's comfortable background to
minister to the poor and to prepare clergy for this simple service: "Its
duties (the Vincentian vocation), therefore, do not require brilliancy of
thought... but serious study, and discourses without pomp and orna-
ment. How difficult it would be for a young man like yourself to become
accustomed to such things."[858] After praying, Felix writes,

> I entered into myself and endeavored to correct whatever I
> knew to be reprehensible in my conduct... and I traced out a
> plan of a more serious life, having resolved to become a mission-
> ary, in order to atone for my sins, give glory to God, work out my
> own salvation, and by the aid of Divine Grace promote that of
> others; such was my intention, and I acknowledge it to be from
> Thee alone, O my God.[859]

One year later, in November 1797, Felix entered the Congregation of the Mission. After two interruptions of his seminary studies due to governmental interference, he was ordained a priest in August 1802.

Felix spent fourteen years of priesthood in Italy. At Piacenza, from 1802 to 1806, the newly ordained priest preached parish missions to the laity, and substituted occasionally for the seminary professors at his alma mater Collegio Alberoni. When Felix's health suffered, his superiors transferred him from the northern climate of the Piedmont region to the more southern climate of Rome. In the Eternal City, for ten years, Felix taught seminarians for both the Vincentian community and for Propaganda Fide. In his spare time, the zealous priest gave missions to the laity, preached retreats, and provided continuing formation for priests.

During one of Felix's conferences to priests, the bishop of the Louisiana Territory, Louis William DuBourg, overheard Felix preaching. The bishop was impressed. DuBourg, who was visiting Rome to recruit priests for his see in the New World, spoke with Felix to inquire if he had any interest in coming to the New World, and possibly in starting a seminary there. After the priest responded enthusiastically, the bishop asked the Vincentian superior if Felix might be made available for the American mission. The superior replied that Felix lacked the robust health necessary for the missions, and that he was serving well already in the apostolate of the education and formation of seminarians. Undaunted, DuBourg took his case to the pope. The pope listened to both sides, and recommended that two cardinals make the decision. The cardinals sided with DuBourg.

DuBourg, De Andreis, and the Vincentian superior signed a contract outlining mutual responsibilities and expectations for this first Vincentian venture into the United States. Among many matters, the contract stipulated that the Vincentians were to live a common life, that the Vincentian style of missions would be maintained, that the bishop would erect a seminary as soon as possible, and that DeAndreis would recruit in Italy five or more Vincentians to assist him.

By the time of embarkation, De Andreis and DuBourg had gathered thirteen volunteers: priests, lay brothers and seminarians, four or five of whom were Vincentians. De Andreis' first recruit was Joseph Rosati, whom DeAndreis had taught in the seminary from 1808-1811. De

Andreis knew that Rosati, who had come from a noble Neapolitan family, possessed traits desirable in a missionary. The story is told of these two teacher-student friends that De Andreis one day passed by Rosati's room, where the latter was working diligently, and the former asked the latter what he was studying. The student answered, "Hebrew." De Andreis replied, "Leave Hebrew aside. It is not what you need. Learn English."[860]

De Andreis and the other volunteers departed in two groups from Rome: Rosati led one group by sea, and De Andreis led the other group overland. The two groups planned to meet at Bordeaux, which they did in late January, in order to spend four months studying French. Halfway through their studies, however, a letter arrived from DuBourg saying that he had changed their destination, from New Orleans to St. Louis. On June 13, 1816, De Andreis with Rosati and the other volunteers sailed from Bordeaux on the American ship, "The Ranger."

On board, De Andreis conducted a seminary schedule for the students: morning and evening prayers, morning meditation, daily Mass, spiritual reading, theology classes, English classes, and study periods. The priests studied English on board. After disembarking at Baltimore on July 26, the missionaries traveled in two groups and a week apart, overland from Baltimore to Pittsburgh, on flatboats down the Ohio River to Louisville, Kentucky, then thirty miles to St. Thomas Seminary, beyond Bardstown, Kentucky. De Andreis and one brother arrived there on November 21. "It had taken them nine days to cover two hundred forty miles."[861] The remainder of the group arrived on December 4.

At St. Thomas Seminary in Bardstown, where De Andreis remained for about one year, he taught theology, and studied English. Soon, he was able to speak and preach spontaneously in English.

In October 1817, De Andreis, Rosati, a Vincentian brother, and Bishop Benedict Joseph Flaget of Bardstown set out westward from Bardstown and arrived nine days later at Kaskaskia, about sixty miles from St. Louis. "The village was almost entirely Catholic and, in years gone by, had been the center of the Jesuit missions among the Indians."[862] After a respite of four days at Sainte Genevieve, the missionaries traveled for two more days before arriving at St. Louis. "Thus ended a long journey that had begun in Rome in October 1815 and came to a happy conclusion in October 1817."[863]

Bishop Flaget recommended that De Andreis, after four days at St. Louis, might exchange assignments temporarily with the parish priest at Sainte Genevieve. Flaget wanted the parish priest to serve as architect for the final stages of the renovation of the lodgings, and the preparation for the new cathedral at St. Louis. De Andreis's parish assignment lasted two months. "On Holy Days he celebrated two Masses and preached; during the week he busied himself instructing the children, hearing confessions, and visiting the sick."[864]

On January 6, 1818, De Andreis returned to St. Louis. De Andreis, whom DuBourg had named vicar general of the Upper Louisiana [Territory], zealously assisted the bishop in administrative and pastoral duties. In accordance with the contract signed by DuBourg and the Vincentian superiors in Rome, a seminary was erected at Perryville, Missouri, for the training of local clergy. In December 1818, De Andreis started at St. Louis the first novitiate of the Vincentians in the United States. Two priests and a seminarian, who had accompanied De Andreis on the transatlantic journey, were the first three novices.

> In the midst of his [De Andreis's] many occupations there, two things stood out. One was his interest in helping and evangelizing the blacks, both slave and free. It caused some surprise among the local population that a man of culture and gentility would do such work. Equally notable was his concern for the Indians. De Andreis was fascinated by the possibility of being a missionary to the Indians and apparently achieved some mastery of the local dialect. He translated the Our Father [which remains extant] and intended to begin a catechism, but he never had sufficient time.[865]

Four years after his arrival in the United States, Felix De Andreis died. He had described, in over three dozen letters, the hardships of travel, food, and repeated sicknesses. At the same time, he wrote with great joy and enthusiasm about his ministry among the Indians, and the great possibilities he envisioned for conversions, and for vocations including two young Native Americans, whom he wished to send to Rome for seminary studies. His stomach ailments, however, kept worsening. His fragile health failed when a doctor treated him with toxic mercury. The missionary died on October 15, 1820. So significant was his role and abilities, that many wondered if the Vincentian mission in America could survive without him. De Andreis, however, already had appointed his friend and former student Joseph Rosati as his successor. The Vincentian mission flourished, having received a firm foundation from Felix De Andreis. "Out of these activities on the part of Felix De Andreis arose . . . a program of Vincentian activities which has grown from a single mission into a network of five American provinces serving from the east to the west coasts.[866]

*For further information, contact*
De Andreis-Rosati Memorial Archives/Special Collections and Archives
John T. Richardson Library
DePaul University
2350 North Kenmore Avenue
Chicago, IL 60614 U.S.A.

&

## 16. ✝ Saint Marguerite d'Youville

*Place: Montréal, Québec*
*Fame: Canada's first native-born saint. Foundress of the*
*Sisters of Charity of Montréal, the "Grey Nuns."*

Marguerite d'Youville (1701-71) experienced an enormous degree of both suffering and success.[867] She suffered at every stage of her life: in her birth family, married life, religious life, and church life. She succeeded as a wife, mother, widow, businesswoman, foundress of a religious community, servant of the poor, and saint.

In her birth family, her father died when Marguerite was seven, and she, the oldest of the six children, helped to raise her siblings. She attended school for the first time when she was

MARGUERITE
D'YOUVILLE

eleven, when she left her native Varennes, outside of Montréal, and resided at the Ursuline Sisters Convent School at Québec. At eighteen, she became engaged to the man of her dreams, but two years later, just after her widowed mother married beneath her class, her fiancé abruptly broke off the engagement. At twenty, she married a prosperous businessman with political ties. Early in the marriage, she discovered, however, that her husband's lucrative business consisted of selling liquor illegally to Indians. And his political ties were based in a bribe paid to the governor for overlooking illegal liquor sales. Her mother-in-law lived in the home, and this "avaricious and domineering woman . . . made life miserable for Marguerite."[868] After eight years of marriage, and five children, with Marguerite pregnant again, her husband died, as did four of their babies by age two.

This widow with two young sons opened a little shop in Montréal wherein she sold her handmade clothes and other accoutrements for the home. She paid off her husband's substantial debts, to educate her two boys, who both would become priests. As early as 1730, with the local Sulpician Fathers as her spiritual directors, she began doing volunteer work as a member of the Confraternity of the Holy Family. At the local hospital, which in those days took in the homeless, helpless, indigent, insane, aged, as well as the sick, she gave her time and talents by mending clothing, and cleaning rooms. "She begged for funds to bury criminals who had been hung in the marketplace. Anybody in need of food, clothing, shelter, or love struck a responsive chord in her generous heart."[869] She took the poor into her home. Three women joined her in this ministry. On December 31, 1737, the four women consecrated themselves to God to serve the poor. This decisive moment would one day be considered the founding date of the Sisters of Charity of Montréal, the "Grey Nuns."

While Marguerite and her three companions dedicated their lives to serving the poor, some citizens wondered aloud why she took in unsavory characters and where she obtained the money to provide for these guests. Some questioned if she were operating the liquor business which her husband had begun. Even the local parish priest doubted her motives and means, and once refused Holy Communion to Marguerite and her sisters as they knelt at the altar railing. People mocked the sisters by calling them, "*les soeurs grises*;" playing on the word *grise's* double meaning: gray, and tipsy from excessive drinking. Seventeen years later, wanting to adopt a modest, simple dress of the day and possibly accepting the name *grise*, Marguerite designed for her sisters a gray religious habit. When the number of guests outgrew the space available in

Marguerite's home, the four women built a larger home. When the crowd of poor outgrew that residence, the sisters rented space in another home, until they were evicted shortly by the landlord.

In 1747, when the owner-operator of the general hospital of Montréal could no longer financially manage the institution, the city offered to give the hospital to Marguerite, provided she accept too the hospital's debt of forty-nine thousand pounds. Marguerite, who had already paid off her deceased husband's debt of eleven thousand pounds, accepted the offer. Her first action was to incur additional debt by repairing the institution so that it could better serve its clientele. She bought farms whereby she might feed the one hundred eighteen people dependent on her. Her main revenue sources consisted of selling her handmade goods, taking in boarders, and receiving reimbursements from the local bishop and the French king for expenditures. In her new quarters she welcomed every kind of poor, fed the hungry, and opened an orphanage.

Having sought civil and ecclesiastical approval of their community, the sisters were filled with gratitude when, in 1753, King Louis XV of France signed the "Letters Patent" which established the new institute of the Sisters of Charity, "Grey Nuns." Canonical approval by Bishop de Pontbriand came two years later.

The bishop of Montréal, having listened to the usual public complainers about Marguerite, sent a letter to her in which he challenged her undertaking new construction, new responsibilities, and new debt. She writes back, expressing directly her intentions, and defending her integrity, after which the bishop retreated from his position and wished her the best. She writes:

> I am sincere, upright, and incapable of any subterfuge or reservation which could disguise the truth or give a double meaning. I have really borrowed 9,550 pounds for the benefit and restoration of the farms of this hospital. I owe this money and there remains to me no other way of paying it back except through the reimbursement which I am awaiting from Your Excellency and the other administrators. What I have the honor to tell you is the absolute truth, and I would not tell the least lie for all the riches in the world.[870]

In Europe, France and England were engaged in the Seven Years War (1755-63), which conflict in the New World was called the French and Indian War. At Montréal, with the war raging in its environs, Marguerite and her sisters cared for civilian and military victims on both sides of the battle, without regard for the political affiliation of the wounded. In 1759, her younger priest-son and some of his parishioners were captured by the English, and were taken as prisoners to a brig, whence they were not released until four months after the end of the war. At the Treaty of Paris in 1763, the victorious English agreed to permit to the Canadian Catholics the freedom of religion, in so far as the practice of Catholicism did not transgress the laws of England.

A horrific fire in 1766 destroyed much of Montréal, and the General Hospital. When the conflagration began blocks away from the hospital, Marguerite sent some of her sisters to assist the victims. When the winds shifted, the fire raced through other homes to the roof of the hospital. With the upper floors ablaze, volunteers rushed in to carry out what they could. Before long, Marguerite's twenty-year hospital project went up in smoke. Her sisters and guests swarmed about her, and wondered what they might do in the aftermath of this tragedy. She said, "My children, we are going to say a *Te Deum* on our knees to thank God for the cross that He has just sent us."[871] Having completed the prayer, and standing upright, Marguerite said, "Take courage, my children, our home will never burn again!"[872] And to this day, almost two hundred fifty years later, the rebuilt hospital has never suffered another fire.

Five years after the fire, in the autumn of 1771, Marguerite's health failed her. In early December of that year, she suffered a stroke. Just before Christmas, on December 23, she died. In the midst of lifelong suffering, she habitually had looked beyond herself and her situation, to the Providence of God. In the midst of her and others' suffering, she succeeded in conveying God's love for each one of His children, especially the most needy. Marguerite's vision of caring for the poor continues beyond her life through her daughters, the "Grey Nuns."

*For further information, contact*
La Maison de Mère d'Youville
138, rue Saint Pierre
Montréal, QC H2Y 2L7 Canada

## 19. ✣ Saint Isaac Jogues

*Place: Auriesville, New York*
*Fame: Suffered torture and mutilation, without rancor.*
*One of the Martyrs of North America.*

At Ossernenon (now Auriesville, N.Y), Jesuit Father Isaac Jogues (1607-46) suffered a martyrdom unparalleled in the history of the United States.[873] The story of Jogues is reported in *The Jesuit Relations*, which provides spell-binding reading.

ST. ISAAC JOGUES

Isaac Jogues was born and raised at Orleans, France. His well-to-do parents sent him, the fifth of nine children, to the local Jesuit school. Upon graduation, at seventeen, he joined the Society of Jesus, and was ordained a priest in January 1636. Three months later, he departed for the New World. The new missionary arrived at the mouth of the St. Lawrence River in June, made his way to Québec by July, and in August arrived at Three Rivers.

From Three Rivers, began the long journey to Georgian Bay. Traveling in a Huron flotilla of canoes, Jogues departed Three Rivers on August 24, 1636, and reached his destination nineteen days later, after traversing water routes and dozens of overland portages. Living among the Tobacco and later the Huron Indians, Jogues learned the natives' languages and customs. In mid-June 1642, the Indians had become desperate for supplies: "harvests were poor, sickness abounded, and clothing was scarce. Quebec was the only source of supplies, and Jogues was chosen to lead an expedition."[874]

> Some time before his departure from the Hurons in order to come to Kebec (sic), finding himself alone before the Blessed Sacrament, he prostrated himself to the ground, beseeching Our Lord to grant him the favor and grace of suffering for his glory. The answer was engraved in the depth of his soul, with a certainty similar to that which Faith gives us: "Your prayer is heard;

what you have asked of me is granted you. Be courageous and steadfast."[875]

In the next four years, Jogues encountered three times the feared Mohawk tribe at Ossernenon. In August 1642, he was captured on the St. Lawrence River, and was taken to Ossernenon, where he was greeted with barbaric torture and mutilation, and enslavement for one year, until he escaped. In spring 1646, he served as ambassador for the French government, which was formulating a peace treaty with the Mohawks at Ossernenon. In mid-October 1646, he returned as missionary to the hilltop village, where he was martyred.

During the first trip to Ossernenon, while he was returning with supplies from Québec, the Huron flotilla was intercepted on August 2, 1642, by a Mohawk war party. Seventy Mohawks surprised the forty Hurons, about half of whom escaped. Along with the braves were captured a Huron woman named Teresa, and three Frenchmen: Jogues, and two lay *donnés* (a seventeenth century form of Jesuit lay volunteers), René Goupil and William Couture. The warriors gathered their captives, and paddled up the St. Lawrence River, into the Richelieu River, to Lake Champlain, and into Lake George. Along the way, the Mohawks encountered some fellow tribesmen, for whose entertainment the captors forced their prisoners to strip, and run a gauntlet of one hundred people on each side, while being beaten with knotted clubs.[876] After this diversion, the Mohawks forced the Hurons and Frenchmen back into the canoes to complete the journey.

Two hundred miles and twelve days later, the war party arrived at Ossernenon. Again, the captives were forced to run through a gauntlet as they climbed the two-hundred-foot hill from the Mohawk River bank to the hilltop village. Jogues, Goupil, and Couture were singled out for special mistreatment. The trio were exposed naked on a platform. Men and women approached and stabbed the captives. Indian squaws ripped out the men's fingernails, sawed off their left thumbs with an oyster-shell, and mangled their fingers by chewing on them. One woman bit off Jogues' left index finger, leaving him only a stub in its place. At the end of the day, as the victims lay severely wounded, Indian children approached the Frenchmen, and "delighted in throwing hot coals and burning cinders on their tortured flesh, in tearing open their wounds and in inflicting other senseless barbarities."[877] Later, Jogues would write in obedience to his superiors:

> What seemed to me to be the cruelest of all their torments was that, when we were exhausted after five or six days of traveling, they came up to us with no semblance of anger and in cold blood tore out our hair and our beards, and scratched us deeply with their fingernails which they keep sharply pointed, in the most tender and sensitive parts of our bodies. All these sufferings were external, however. My interior sufferings were much more intense when I saw that sad procession of Hurons, now slaves of the Iroquois. Among them were many Christians, five of them converts of long standing and pillars of the infant Huron church. I will admit naively that from time to time I could not restrain my tears, deploring their lot and that of all my companions, but even more filled with anxiety for the future.[878]

For the next three months, the enslaved men performed menial tasks for villagers. Couture was removed to a neighboring village. Jogues was assigned to a longhouse, under the supervision of an elderly woman, who had been the daughter, wife, and mother of chiefs. Treating the missionary kindly, she gave him back his copy of *The Imitation of Christ*. Jogues called her "aunt," and she called him "nephew." Dutchmen from Fort Orange (now Albany) arrived, and attempted to ransom the Frenchmen, but the Mohawks refused to release their captives.

On September 29, René Goupil spontaneously made the sign of the Cross over some children. The grandfather of one of the children rushed to Goupil, "kicked him aside, and seized his grandson."[879] As soon as Jogues heard about the incident, he sought out Goupil. "Together they went into the nearby forest, where they frequently went to pray, and prepared themselves for death."[880] Before long, two braves appeared, and ordered the Jesuits to return to the village. While walking, and just after completing the fourth decade of the rosary, the pair stopped at the entrance to the village. With that, one of the Iroquois swung a hatchet onto Goupil's head. He fell, motionless. Jogues knelt down over Goupil's body, absolved him of his sins, and waited to receive the same treatment. Instead, the braves walked away. The next day, intending to give Goupil's body a Christian burial, Jogues searched for the corpse, which he found "in a ravine, in shallow water."[881] Taking the body, Jogues "put it beneath the water, weighted with large stones."[882] He intended to return to give the corpse a proper burial. Two days later, when the priest returned, he was unable to find the body. Whether the body was carried away by water, animals, or Indians remains unknown.

In autumn 1643, the Indians brought along Jogues on a fishing trip down the Hudson River, probably around Catskill Creek. Some Dutchmen offered Jogues the means to escape. The priest pondered the consequences for the captive Hurons. He explains to his rescuer, "The affair seems to me of such importance that I cannot answer you at once; give me, if you please, the night to think of it. I will commend it to our Lord; I will examine the arguments on both sides; and tomorrow morning I will tell you my final resolution."[883] The next day, Jogues agreed to escape. The Dutch hid him in a boat along the Hudson River. The Mohawks searched furiously for their missing slave, and after six weeks, gave up, and returned home. The Dutch smuggled the missionary down the Hudson River to New Amsterdam (now New York City), where, on November 5, he received free passage on a ship sailing to La Rochelle, France.

Arriving at the Breton Coast on Christmas Day, the priest attended Mass. He continued on to Rennes, arriving there on January 5, 1644. At the local house of the Jesuit community, he received a hero's welcome. One confrere describes Jogues this way: "He is as cheerful as if he had suffered nothing; and as zealous to return among the Hurons, amid all those dangers, as if perils were to him securities."[884] With his disfigured fingers and absent thumb, Jogues needed a dispensation to celebrate Mass, which the pope granted, writing, "It would be shameful that a martyr of Christ be not allowed to drink the blood of Christ."[885] Jogues visited his mother at Orleans in April 1644, and the next month, embarked for New France.

Sailing with Jogues across the Atlantic Ocean was the governor of New France, who invited Jogues to assist in formulating a peace treaty with the Mohawks. Jogues knew the natives' languages, customs, and tribal leaders. After arriving at Québec in June, Jogues served the residents of the recently established colony at Montréal until 1646, when the governor implored Jogues to go to Ossernenon as ambassador for the French Government. The priest, with the approval of his superiors, accepted the request.

For his second visit to Ossernenon, Jogues left Three Rivers on May 16, and arrived at his destination on June 5. The Mohawks readily agreed to the terms of the peace treaty. Before leaving the village, Jogues visited the Huron captives, heard their confessions, and baptized some elderly Mohawks. With his "aunt" Jogues left a small box, which contained his vestments, prayerbooks, and beads, as a sign that he expected to return.

A few months later, in September 1646, some Hurons approached Jogues, and asked him to go with them to Ossernenon to clarify details of the treaty. Jogues accepted the invitation. He writes to his superiors at France, "My heart tells me that, if I am the one to be sent on this mission, I shall go, but I shall not return. But I would be happy if our Lord wished to complete the sacrifice where he began it."[886] On September 24, 1646, Jogues, a lay volunteer Jean de Lalande, the Huron ambassador Otrihoure, and a few Huron braves departed from Québec for Ossernenon. Within a few days, some Iroquois warned the travelers that some dissident Mohawks were on the war-path. Hearing that news, the Huron braves abandoned the mission. Only Jogues, de Lalande, and Otrihoure remained. The trio paddled towards their destination.

Meanwhile, at Ossernenon, crops had failed, and an epidemic had arisen. The medicine men of the village calculated that evil spirits must have emanated from the box that Jogues had left behind. Braves took to the river in search of any Frenchman to kill. Lo and behold, who was paddling towards them: Jogues himself. The Mohawks captured the three foreigners, stripped them, beat them, and led them back to the village; the date was October 17. The next day, a brave entered the longhouse where Jogues and de Lalande were being kept captive. The brave announced that Jogues was invited to a dinner. Jogues pondered the situation: acceptance or rejection of the invitation could mean death. The priest left with the brave, and as Jogues entered another longhouse where the banquet was promised, a brave, reached out and tomahawked him to death. The next day, de Lalande, although having been ordered by friendly Mohawks to remain in the longhouse, peeked outside to see if he might find Jogues. As soon as the layman exposed his head, a tomahawk came crashing down on him. Both men were decapitated, their bodies were rolled down the hill, and into the river. Their skulls were thrust atop wooden poles of the palisades guarding the village.

*For further information, contact*
Shrine of Our Lady of Martyrs
136 Shrine Road
Auriesville, N.Y. 12016 U.S.A.

## 19. ✠ Saint Jean de Lalande

*Place: Auriesville, New York*
*Fame: Lay volunteer. Martyr.*

When the Hurons asked Father Isaac Jogues to accompany them on a peace-making trip to Ossernenon, he agreed readily.[887] The priest in turn asked his superiors if they might assign someone to accompany and assist him on the journey. The Jesuit superior recommended young Jean de Lalande (d. 1646). "Jean was an experienced woodsman, intelligent, and brave. He was born in Dieppe, and came to New France as a settler sometime before 1642. There he offered himself to the Jesuits as a *donné*, desiring to devote his life to the service of God and to work with the missionaries."[888]

JEAN DE LALANDE
AND RENÉ GOUPIL

In September 1646, Jean de Lalande stepped forward to accompany Jogues. The priest warned the lay volunteer that the trip would be arduous, and perhaps even dangerous. "The missionary's description of possible privation could not undo Jean's determination. He took the missionary's mutilated hands into his own and professed his desire to share his future with him, even if it meant martyrdom."[889]

The party departed on September 24, 1646. "After twenty days of paddling, portages, and hiking, the party was almost within sight of Ossernenon when a screaming band of Mohawks surrounded them and took them prisoner."[890] The chiefs of the village placed them in the custody of the respected elderly woman whom Jogues, on his first trip to

Ossernenon in 1642, had "adopted" as his Indian "aunt." She provided hospitality, but explained that the box of religious articles which Jogues had left with her when he departed from his second visit in spring 1646, was being blamed as the source of evil spirits which had caused a crop failure and a smallpox epidemic.

The chiefs left the village the next day, October 18, in order to confer with chiefs in a neighboring village, as to what to do with the prisoners. In the absence of the chiefs, some of the braves grew impatient and importunate. They created the ruse that Jogues was invited to a banquet in one of the longhouses. Jogues knew if he went with the braves, or if he remained where he was, either action could be interpreted as justification for killing him. The experienced missionary chose to go with the braves. He no sooner entered the designated longhouse, then another brave leaped at him, and killed him with one swift blow of a tomahawk.

Jean de Lalande had been warned not to leave the house of the "aunt" under any circumstances. Concerned about Jogues' long absence, de Lalande peeked his head outside the house, and immediately, he was tomahawked to death.

Both men's heads were decapitated, and placed on stakes of the palisades surrounding the village. Their bodies were rolled down the steep hill into the Mohawk River.

*For further information, contact*
Shrine of Our Lady of Martyrs
136 Shrine Road
Auriesville, N.Y. 12016 U.S.A.

## 19.  ✠  Saint René Goupil

*Place: Auriesville, New York*
*Fame: Layman, surgeon, martyr.*

René Goupil (1606-42), a native of Anjou, France, entered the Jesuit seminary, but left because of ill health.[891] He studied medicine, and advanced to become a surgeon. Desiring to give his life to God and others, this layman volunteered to go to New France. After arriving at Quebec in 1638, he worked there at a hospital. Two years later, he became a *donné*, a Jesuit lay missioner.

In June 1642, Father Isaac Jogues visited Québec in search of supplies for his mission at the Georgian Bay. Jogues asked Goupil if he would want to join the priest in the mission work with the Hurons nine hundred miles to the west. The lay volunteer responded affirmatively. The pair traveled upriver to Three Rivers, where they made further preparations, and gained the services of another French lay volunteer, William Couture.

On August 1, Isaac Jogues, the two laymen, a Catholic Huron named Teresa, and forty Huron braves set out in a dozen canoes onto the St. Lawrence River, heading west for the Georgian Bay. Early on the morning of the second day, shortly after the group again had entered the river, a flotilla of enemy Mohawks attacked them. The seven canoes in the rear of the Huron flotilla escaped. The five canoes up front were trapped. The Huron braves paddled for shore. Jogues, Couture, and Teresa ran into the woods. Goupil, however, was caught on shore. Soon, Teresa too was captured. Jogues gave himself up, because he as leader could not abandon those who were assisting him.

Five days after the capture, the war party brought the captives as far south as Lake Champlain. The captives were forced to run the gauntlet, during which they were beaten with knotted clubs, and afterwards branded.[892] After this brief visit, the Mohawks and their captives continued for a few more days on the journey to Ossernenon (now Auriesville, New York). During this voyage, Goupil asked Jogues if the layman might become a vowed brother in the Jesuit order. Jogues rejoiced, and Goupil pronounced the vows of poverty, chastity, and obedience, thus becoming a professed Jesuit. Upon their arrival at Ossernenon, the captives again ran a gauntlet up a two-hundred-foot hill from the bank of the Mohawk River to the village.[893] Once in the village, the three Frenchmen were tied to a post. Women proceeded to chew on Jogues and Goupil's fingers, and sawed off with a seashell the left thumbs of each man.

On September 29, René Goupil, blessed some children with the sign of the cross on their foreheads. One of the grandfathers, who had been told by the non-Catholic Dutch that that gesture signaled an invocation of evil spirits, quickly seized his grandson. Jogues heard about the incident, and sought out Goupil. The two went to into the forest to pray, and to prepare for death. Two braves searched for the Jesuits, found them, and ordered to return to the village. Jogues reports:

> Having stopped near the gate of the village, to see what they might say to us, one of those two Iroquois draws a hatchet, which he held concealed under his blanket, and deals a blow with it on the head of René, who was before him. He falls motionless, his face to the ground, pronouncing the holy name of Jesus (often we admonished each other that this holy name should end both our voices and our lives.) At the blow, I turn around and see a hatchet all bloody; I kneel down, to receive the blow which was to unite me with my dear companion; but, as they hesitate, I rise again, and run to the dying man, who was quite near. They dealt him two other blows with the hatchet, on the head, and dispatched him, — but not until I had first given him absolution, which I had been wont to give him every two days, since our captivity, and this was a day on which he had already confessed.[894]

The next day, intending to bury Goupil's body, Jogues went in search of the corpse. He found the body in the shallow water of a ravine. Jogues weighted the body with rocks, and hid it in deeper water. Two days later, he returned, but the body was gone. Whether the water carried it away, or animals took it, or if Indians claimed it, remains unknown.

*For further information, contact*
Shrine of Our Lady of Martyrs
136 Shrine Road
Auriesville, N.Y. 12016 U.S.A.

## 24.  ✠  Saint Anthony Mary Claret

*Place: Havana, Cuba*
*Fame: Archbishop, popular preacher, prolific author.*
*Founded the Missionary Sons of the Immaculate Heart of Mary,*
*and Religious Sisters of Mary Immaculate.*

Zeal for souls consumed Anthony Mary Claret (1807-70).[895] Eschewing serving in one parish in order to preach in hundreds of parishes, he devoted his life to doing the most good for the most people. He published one hundred forty-four books, and hundreds of pamphlets to make his message more widespread and more permanent. He preached twenty-five thousand sermons, which many thousands of people heard. His prodigious achievements were rooted in zeal for souls. He writes near the beginning of his

ANTHONY MARY
CLARET

*Autobiography*, which his religious superiors ordered him to write for the benefit of younger community members:

> The first ideas I can remember date back to when I was five years old. When I went to bed, instead of sleeping — I have never been much of a sleeper — I used to think about eternity. I would think, "forever, forever, forever." I would try to imagine enormous distances and pile still more distances on these and realized that they wold never come to an end. Then I would shudder and ask myself if those who were so unhappy as to go to an eternity of pain would ever see an end to their suffering. Would they have to go on suffering? Yes, forever, and forever they will have to bear their pain. This troubled me deeply. ... The power of this idea made me work, and will make me work as long as I live, in converting sinners, in preaching, in hearing confessions, in writing books, in distributing holy cards and pamphlets, and in having familiar conversations.[896]

Growing up at Sallent in northern Spain, he enjoyed praying and helping people. With his father, the lad attended two Masses on holy days, and practiced devotions to the Blessed Sacrament, especially in Benediction; and to the Blessed Virgin Mary, especially in the rosary. About receiving his First Communion at ten, he writes, "Words cannot tell what I felt on that day when I had the unequalled joy of receiving my good Jesus into my heart for the first time."[897] Once, his nearly blind grandfather needed help fleeing the advancing French armies during the war for independence (1808-1814). Although Anthony's older brothers and cousins fled for their lives, Anthony took his grandfather's hand and carefully led the elderly man to safety.

Anthony excelled in both school and business. As a young man, he attained the status of master weaver. In Barcelona, at twenty-one, he was distracted at Mass with ideas of whirling machines. As he says, "there seemed to be more machines in my head than saints on the altar," and he recalled the gospel passage, "What does it profit a man, to gain the whole world and forfeit his life?" (Mk 8:36). The elderly Anthony recalls, "This phrase impressed me deeply, and went like an arrow to my heart."[898] That summer, he felt protected twice by the Blessed Mother: once, when he nearly drowned; and second, when a woman attempted to seduce him. He decided to pursue his long-standing on-again off-again desire to be a priest. In 1829, he entered the seminary at Vich, and was ordained a priest in June 1835.

The newly ordained priest was assigned to his home parish as assistant pastor. Within eight months, he began, with the permission of his bishop, to preach missions in other parishes of the diocese. Thousands turned out to hear him. In 1839, he offered his services to the Office of the Propagation of the Faith to minister in any mission worldwide. In 1842, Rome named Anthony an Apostolic Missionary, which freed him to preach throughout Catalonia. There, Anthony earned the reputation as "the greatest preacher of his day."[899] From 1840 to 1847, he labored zealously in this ministry.

> He spent long hours in the confessional, ate very little, slept only a few hours, never accepted any remuneration, and always traveled on foot. At Olot, in 1844, he preached for a whole month, some of his sermons lasting three hours. Twenty-five priests were needed to hear confessions, and every morning three

priests were kept busy distributing Holy Communion. Most of the night he spent praying and writing.[900]

His preaching in Catalonia was interrupted by the revolution sweeping across Spain in 1848. His bishop sent him to preach at the Canary Islands. The next year, on July 16, he founded with five priest friends the Congregation of the Missionary Sons of Immaculate Mary. The ideal of each Missionary, Anthony describes in the following way:

> A son of the Immaculate Heart of Mary is a man on fire with love, who spreads its flames wherever he goes. He desires mightily and strives by all means possible to set the whole world on fire with Christ's love. Nothing daunts him: he delights in privations, welcomes work, embraces sacrifices, smiles at slander, and rejoices in suffering. His only concern is how he can best follow Jesus Christ and imitate Him in working, suffering, and striving constantly and single-mindedly for the greater glory of God and the salvation of souls.[901]

On August 11, the bishop hand-delivered to Anthony an urgent letter, dated August 4. The news: less than three weeks after Anthony had founded his religious community, the pope nominated him Archbishop of Santiago de Cuba. Anthony was torn: "on the one hand, I didn't dare accept; on the other hand, I wanted to obey."[902] He adds, "I considered myself unworthy and incapable of such a dignity, for which I lacked both the necessary knowledge and virtue."[903] Accepting the nomination, Anthony was ordained bishop on October 6, 1850; and arrived at Cuba on February 16, the following year.

Cuba presented a challenge. Corruption among the island's leaders, and malaise among the populace prevailed. The new archbishop preached in virtually every parish of the diocese within two years of his arrival. To lay a foundation for the reform, Anthony sent informational and inspirational circular letters to his priests, required his clergy to make a ten-day annual retreat and to attend ongoing education conferences three times weekly. To catechize the people, the archbishop sent pastoral letters to be read to congregations, and he founded the Religious Sisters of Mary Immaculate, and established the Confraternity of Christian Doctrine to instruct children and adults.

Routinely, he visited jails and hospitals. He bought a ranch where he sheltered and educated street children. For the working class, he created cooperatives and credit unions. During a devastating earthquake, and a subsequent four-month cholera epidemic, he oversaw the diocesan pastoral response. Despite all these efforts, he suffered much persecution, including fourteen assassination attempts, an arson attempt, and actual arrest for blessing interracial marriages.

Having been recalled to Spain, he left Havana in April 1857. The queen had appointed him her personal confessor and spiritual director, and tutor to her five-year old daughter. This position was a veritable cross for the always active Anthony. He writes, "I can't settle down or become accustomed to staying in Madrid. I have no inclination or disposition to be a courtier or palace retainer. . . . I feel like a caged bird that keeps looking through the bars of its cage for a way to escape."[904] In 1867, he resigned his position.

During the Spanish revolution, which began in 1868, he was exiled from Spain, and found refuge in France. He assisted at Rome in the preparatory work for Vatican I. At the Council, he spoke firmly in favor of papal infallibility. At the Council's conclusion, he returned to France. The the anti-clerical Spanish government attempted to capture him and bring him to Spain for trial. He fled to a Cistercian monastery for sanctuary, and there he died in exile. The following words are on his tombstone, "I have loved justice and hated iniquity; therefore, I die in exile."[905]

At his death, in 1870, the Missionary Sons of the Immaculate Heart of Mary had grown significantly in vocations and works. One of his books, *Camino Recto* (The Right Road) sold in his lifetime over half a million copies. Two publishing companies, which he had founded, continued to promote and distribute quality works of Catholic authors. Anthony Mary Claret's own words in his Autobiography sum up his life's purpose: "my only aim was to glorify God and save souls."[906]

*For further information, contact*
Claretian Missionaries Archives
205 W. Monroe St., 3rd Floor
Chicago, IL 60606 U.S.A.

## 27. ✠ Blessed María Encarnación Rosal

*Place: Quezaltenango, Guatemala*
*Fame: Reformer of the Bethlemite Institute.*
*First native Guatemalan to be beatified.*

Vicenta Rosal (1820-86), at seventeen, felt attracted to the cloistered life of the Bethlemite Sisters. During Christmas week 1937, she traveled one hundred fifty miles from her native town of Quezaltenango to the city of Santiago de los Caballeros to visit the convent of Bethlehem. On New Year's Day 1838, she entered the convent, and later that same year, received the religious habit. On January 26, 1840, she professed her first vows, and took as her religious name, María Encarnación of the Sacred Heart.

María Encarnación Rosal

Soon after Vicenta entered the convent, she observed that many sisters lacked dedication to the charism, with which Saint Pedro de San José Betancur had founded the community in 1658. The passage of almost two centuries had occasioned a lessening of the fervor of the community. The cloister had become busy and noisy, where silence and prayer gave way to idle conversation between the sisters and secular visitors and schoolgirls who repeatedly dropped by to chat. Externs had virtually free access to the cloister.

Although disheartened by the sisters' laxity, Encarnación kept hoping and working that the situation might change. On January 26, 1840, she professed her first vows in the community. Added to the dwindling of the religious spirit was the Cortes of Cadiz decree in 1820, that abolished the Bethlemite Order in America. The Bethlemite Order of Brothers had guided the sisters and served as their chaplains since the founding. Without the direction of the Brothers, the sisters were becoming more apostolic and less contemplative.

Realistic enough not to expect radical changes in the community, Encarnación received permission to live outside of the Bethlemite Order in order to experience the fervently cloistered community of Catalina nuns. Encarnación enjoyed the Catalinas, but still felt a commitment to the Bethlemites. She resolved that she would return to the Bethlemites, and try to apply in her own life the best aspects of the cloistered life of the Catalinas.

The Bethlemite Sisters welcomed back Encarnación with open arms. They placed her in various positions, which enabled her to make the changes, which she envisioned for the community. In 1843, she was appointed principal of a girls school where she provided formation for the students. In 1849, the community elected her assistant superior of the convent, and the mistress of novices. Six years later, she was named the superior. A biographer comments, "Wherever she is placed, she leaves an imprint of organization, fervor, energy and activity."[907] In 1857, she rewrote the *Constitution* of the community. Many younger sisters whom Mother Encarnación had formed embraced Mother's way, although many older sisters refused to follow Mother's direction.

Mother Encarnación decided to make a new foundation in a new house. She and some younger sisters went to Antigua, where the Bethlemites had made their original foundation. The site had symbolic value but "due to insurmountable circumstances, the foundation crumbled."[908] On October 21, 1861, she and others traveled to her native Quezaltenango, where she made a new foundation, which soon flourished. Here, many women pursued the cloistered vocation, and its apostolic works. The numbers of nuns and works grew rapidly. Unfortunately, an anticlerical storm erupted in Guatemala, and the government ordered the expulsion of religious orders. Mother Encarnación and her sisters prayed at great length for the wisdom to know what to do. At last, all twenty-four professed sisters formulated and signed the *Protesta* (an affirmation.). An excerpt follows:

> We protest that no human force would be able to change our vocation, and if we are forced to abandon the sacred cloister, we have no intention to alter anything concerning our promises and vows made to the Lord, Our God.
>
> We protest that if the tyrannical violence of civil authorities effects a disunity among us, our will is to serve God always and never to separate ourselves from this holy community, living united in the spirit and religious charity, exactly keeping our vows and rules. . . .

We protest that, in fact, we are subjects to Our Reverend Mother Superior, living in the world as true religious, doing the will of God until we are reunited. . . .

Finally, we protest to pray every day the Divine Office, seeking to live and die in its spirit of purity and integrity of our holy religion Bethlemita.[909]

Providentially, when Mother and her sisters closed the ministry at Guatemala, they were freed to establish institutions in other places. In December 1877, Mother and the sisters traveled to Costa Rica, and founded two schools, at Cartago and Heredia. At Pasto, Colombia, the sisters opened a school, and months later, founded an orphanage for girls. Later, Mother traveled to Tulcan, Ecuador, to investigate the possibility of establishing a new apostolate. Ten days after her arrival, however, she died.

Mother Encarnación believed in herself, her abilities, and her vision for the community. She had the strength to stand alone in the face of opposition. Everyone liked her, and she never spoke ill of anyone. "From the testimonies we conclude that Mother possessed a rich and balanced personality: intuitive, constant, tenacious having power to will, ardent in her purpose, humble and with great human qualities. She was happy and agreeable, sensitive, enthusiastic, and gifted with flexible wisdom that took her from one style of life to another."[910]

*For further information, contact*
Bethlemite Sisters
Saint Joseph's Convent
330 West Pembroke
Dallas, Texas 75208 U.S.A.

# NOVEMBER

## 3. ✠ Victor Lelièvre

*Place:* Québec City, Québec
*Fame: Charismatic preacher, innovator, and organizer.*
*Apostle of the Sacred Heart.*

Born in the village of Vitre, in Brittany, France,
Victor Lelièvre (1876-1956) was his parent's
sixth and final child, and the only one who survived past infancy.[911] From his parents, he learned
to pray, "My God, I give you my heart, close it to
sin, and open it to grace."[912] At eighteen, Victor
entered the seminary of the Oblates of Mary
Immaculate. Eight years later, he was ordained a
priest, and was missioned to a parish at Angers,
France.

VICTOR LELIÈVRE

In 1903, after the Conseil d'État suppressed the teaching and
preaching religious congregations throughout France, the Oblate superiors assigned Father Victor to Québec City. Arriving there in August
1903, the young priest began his ministry which would consist of two
assignments: Saint-Sauveur Church, for twenty years; and Jesus-Worker
Retreat House, for thirty-three years.

At Saint-Sauveur Church, which had thirteen thousand parishioners, the young priest was very busy: in his first ten years, he presided
at five hundred fifty baptisms, one hundred ninety-nine weddings, and
eight hundred forty-two funerals. [913] His responsibilities included overseeing youth ministry, publishing the parish newsletter *The Spark*, leading the St. Vincent de Paul Society, and reviving First Friday devotions.

Father Victor was extraordinarily zealous and effective. To revive the
First Friday devotion, he called a meeting of those interested in praying
the Holy Hour. To the fifty women who came, he asked them to recruit
other Catholics to participate in this devotion. The next First Friday,

over five hundred people prayed the Holy Hour. Within a short time, that number increased to over eighteen hundred devotees.

The next year, he founded the society Royal Service, which consisted initially of seventy-two disciples, and eventually of more than two hundred men, whose task was to recruit men for the First Friday Holy Hour. Father Victor visited factories, where he personally invited men, "My good friends, all of you have brave hearts. I invite you to come to understand the Sacred Heart. We meet every First Friday evening at six o'clock, immediately after your work ends. Come as you are, in your work clothes. It is not clean hands that I want, but your hearts."[914] At the first Holy Hour, nine hundred men attended. The next month, nearly two thousand participated. Within a couple of years, Father Victor returned to the factories, and took with him statues of the Sacred Heart to be enshrined in each workplace. These statues soon were found in many village squares, and one hundred thirty-eight churches. Victor explained, "For distinguished men, we erect monuments. The Sacred Heart deserves its own monument, because it represents the most distinguished of men, namely, the God-Man."[915]

Father Victor introduced public processions in honor of the Sacred Heart. In 1910, he led his first procession of devotees. By 1934, over twenty thousand people marched in the procession. By 1949, over one hundred thousand took part in the procession.

Jesus-Worker retreats were initiated by Father Victor at Saint-Augustin de Portneuf in 1913. The village school served as the retreat house. Ten years later, his Committee of the Sacred Heart purchased property and built a suitable retreat house. In forty years, more than twenty thousand persons made retreats with Father Victor.

Victor was a prodigious preacher. He regularly preached four or five times daily at the Jesus-Worker Retreat House. In the cathedral at Moncton, he preached once, for two and a half hours; and another time for almost six hours. At seventy-six years old, he preached seven sermons on the same day at the Oratory of Saint Joseph in Montréal. At Gravelbourg, he preached nine sermons in one day. He traveled and preached throughout Canada, New England, and France. For any special occasion in the province of Québec, fellow priests called upon Father Victor to preach. He held people spellbound. At the cathedral at Moncton, the parish priest was lamenting to other priests about Father

Victor's long sermon, "This is a disaster; the retreat is ruined. I know my people, they will not come back."[916] The next day, however, the crowd was larger than the first night. Each night the crowd grew until it spilled outside the church. Whenever Father Victor preached on the Feast of the Sacred Heart, local bars, dance halls, and theaters shut down; most of their clientele preferred to pray with and listen to the priest.

All Father Victor's retreats, Holy Hours, First Friday services, and preaching led to countless conversions. Thousands of people came to church through the charism of Father Victor. People would say, "He preaches the good God to us, that God loves us, consoles us, and draws us close; that the Sacred Heart with his arms extended calls poor sinners and says, 'Come to me'."[917]

Father Victor made a great impact on young people discerning vocation to priesthood and/or religious life. He directed approximately two hundred youth to enter the seminary or convent. With each young person, he discerned which diocese or religious community seemed most appropriate for the individual.

The holy priest did not escape suffering. For nine years, from 1923 to 1932, his local religious superior held a personal animosity against Victor, and subjected him to frequent criticisms, restrictions, and humiliations. Father Victor suffered too when, after having worked indefatigably for half a century, his arteries hardened and dementia set in. Interiorly, he suffered from scruples and fear of eternal damnation; this sensitive and holy man perceived his sins as more and worse than they appeared to others.

A vibrant spirituality sustained Father Victor throughout his life. His love of the gospels and devotion to the Sacred Heart inspired him to put into action an extraordinary zeal for souls. Known popularly as the Apostle of the Sacred Heart, Father Victor's devotion to the Sacred Heart provided the purpose for his Committee, First Friday services, Holy Hour, and Jesus-Worker Retreat House.

*For further information, contact*
Maison Jésus-Ouvrier
475, boul. Père-Lelièvre
Vanier, Qué G1M 1M9 Canada

## 6. ✠ Jérôme Le Royer de la Dauversière

*Place:* La Flèche, France
*Fame:* Promoter of the founding of Montréal.
Founder of Daughters Hospitallers of St. Joseph.

The lay visionary Jérôme Le Royer de la Dauversière (1597-1659) never set foot on Canadian soil, but he is regarded as a co-founder of the city.[918] This tax collector from La Flèche, located about one hundred miles southwest of Paris, suggested in the early 1630s that a colony be established on the island now called Montréal. The colony, to be called Ville-Marie in honor of the Blessed Virgin Mary, he proposed would serve as a center for ministering to the French colonists in the region, and evangelizing Native Americans.

JÉRÔME LE ROYER DE LA DAUVERSIÈRE

Jérôme Le Royer, on at least three occasions between 1630 and 1635, experienced spiritual events whereby he believed God was calling him to a special mission. First, he felt called to found a community of Daughters Hospitallers to serve the sick-poor in La Flèche's hospital. Second, he felt inspired to found a center for evangelization on an island to be called Ville-Marie, and to establish a hospital there. Within thirty years, all his extraordinary missions had been accomplished.

Jérôme lived an apostolic spirituality. Although most of his writings were destroyed just before his death, the extant *Constitutions and Statutes* of the Confraternity of the Holy Family, which he established, reveal part of his soul. The confraternity was to be guided, "under the name of the Glorious St. Joseph, to honor in perpetuity the Holy Family of Jesus Christ, of whom this great saint [Joseph] is the head by virtue of his humility, in order that by his patronage and intercession, having access to the holy Virgin and by both Joseph and Mary's access to Our Lord Jesus Christ, ... [the confraternity] might become a perfect adoration and glorification of the august Trinity."[919] All that Le Royer did, he did for the glory of God; as he said, "God is the Master."[920]

The first of the three spiritual events occurred on February 2, 1630. In the small pilgrim sanctuary at Notre Dame du Chef du Pont at La Flèche, Jérôme was praying with his wife and three of their eventual five children. Kneeling after Communion, Jerome heard an interior voice ask him to found a community of women religious, who would provide medical care for the sick poor. He consulted with his priest spiritual director, who told the layman to drop such a "pious fancy."[921] This man of faith nonetheless, began repairing the dilapidated hospital Hôtel-Dieu, and therein constructed a chapel to his patron St. Joseph.

A few years later, the second spiritual event took place. "Jérôme Le Royer believed that he was called to a humanly impossible mission, that of founding a center of evangelization on the island of Ville-Marie and of opening a hospital there served by the future Daughters of St. Joseph"[922] Some influential persons labeled Jérôme's idea as "an extravagant project, . . . a mission humanly impossible."[923]

In February 1635, Jérôme experienced a spiritual locution. While praying at the foot of the statue of the Virgin Mary in the Cathedral of Notre-Dame at Paris, "Mr. Le Royer saw himself in the presence of the Holy Family and heard the Lord tell him: "You will be my faithful servant. . . . Fulfill my mission. . . . My grace is sufficient for you."[924] Feeling confirmed in his call to found Ville-Marie, the layman reported this experience to his Jesuit counselors, who encouraged him to do what God had commanded.

The first of Jérôme's objectives, the founding of a religious community to serve the sick poor at La Flèche, was accomplished in May 1636. Marie de la Ferre and a friend moved into the Hôtel-Dieu, and joined their service to that being done by three servants who already were working there. This group became known as the Daughters Hospitallers of St. Joseph, who fifty years later, became the Religious Hospitallers of St. Joseph.

The second objective, namely, the founding of Ville-Marie, proved very challenging. Devotees of the Holy Family prayed for the success of the mission. Benefactors provided funding. Volunteers sailed to New France to inhabit the island where dangers and deprivations awaited them.

Jérôme contacted the Catholic philanthropist Pierre Chevrier, the baron de Fancamp. After Pierre replied with interest in Jérôme's plan, the pair contacted Jean-Jacques Olier, who supported Jérôme's action. These three men, plus four others, gathered one day in February 1641, at the statue of the Virgin Mary at Notre Dame Cathedral at Paris. After discussing Jérôme's vision and ideas, they formed the Society of Men and Women of Our Lady of Montréal. In time, other persons joined this Society, but their numbers, after an initial growth, plummeted so that in 1663 the few remaining members donated the island to the Sulpician Fathers.

Jérôme persuaded Pierre Chevrier to give financial support to this project. Olier gained the support of his wealthy friends. Jeanne Mance, at the initiative of some influential persons and the Jesuit Father Lalement, was introduced to Madame de la Bullion, who for decades would donate generously to the mission. These wealthy persons, in turn, contacted their wealthy friends, and received additional donations.

Mr. Jean de Lauson, a former member of the Company of One Hundred Associates, owned the island of Montréal. Jérôme and Pierre Chevrier approached Mr. de Lauson, and in December 1640, negotiated the donation by Lauson, whereby Jérôme and Pierre became lords of a part of the island, and obtained the title to the property.

The Society of Nôtre-Dame de Montréal estimated that forty volunteers would be needed to found the village. They found forty-five men and four women. Jérôme chose twenty-nine year old Paul de Chomedy de Maisonneuve as the leader of the future colony. At La Rochelle, Jérôme met Jeanne Mance, and invited her to join the first group of colonists and to build a hospital at Ville-Marie. Jérôme confided to Jeanne, "I am certain this is God's work and He will do it, but I have no idea how."[925]

The first settlers, in two ships, departed on May 8, 1641, from La Rochelle, and after wintering at Québec, arrived on May 17, 1642, at the island which they named Ville-Marie. Coming ashore, the colonists celebrated Mass, and built palisades, houses and shelters for food and military supplies. At first, the small colony lived an idyllic existence: "The nature of the colony was recorded in 1643: 'The inhabitants live for the most part communally, as in a sort of inn; others live on their private means, but all live in Jesus Christ, with one heart and soul.'"[926] After a few months, however, the Iroquois began attacking the colonists, sometimes in small roving bands, killing single settlers who had wandered too far from the fort; and at other times in war parties, numbering in the hundreds. These constant attacks depleted the population, and depressed the morale of the colonists. The very existence of Ville-Marie was threatened. By 1649, Jérôme Le Royer had become nearly bankrupt, and liens had been placed against his property and possessions. Beginning in 1649, Mance, Maisonneuve and other colonists traveled to France and pleaded the case that the colony needed more manpower and money. Their efforts proved successful.

Maissoneuve recognized the need for schools and seminaries for colonization and evangelization. On one of his trips to France, he persuaded Marguerite Bourgeoys to come to Ville-Marie to start a school for girls, which she did, departing Troyes in February 1653. Five years later, Jérôme Le Royer convinced Mr. Olier to send some priests of Saint Sulpice, to open a boys' school, which later became a seminary.

Two years after her arrival in 1642, Jeanne Mance opened the first hospital in Montréal, the Hôtel Dieu. Fifteen years later, in June 1659, this hospital was placed on even firmer foundation, when Jeanne recruited three Daughters Hospitallers of St. Joseph. These Hospitallers eventually took over the administration of the hospital.

Jérôme had achieved all three objectives assigned to him in his spiritual experiences. A few months before he died, he stood at the harbor at La Rochelle in June 1659, and waved farewell to Jeanne Mance, Marguerite Bourgeoys, and the three Daughters Hospitallers of St. Joseph. They were sailing to Ville-Marie, where they would contribute to the work already begun by Jeanne at the Hôtel Dieu. Jérôme returned home, where he became seriously ill, and died on November 6. His God-given mission had been completed.

*For further information, contact*
Bureau des Fondateurs des Religieuses Hospitalieres
2450, chemin de la Cote Sainte-Catherine
Montreal, QC H3T 1B1 Canada

## 11. ✠ José de Jesús López y González

*Place: Aguascalientes, Aguascalientes*
*Fame: Exemplary Bishop of Aguascalientes.*
*Founder of the Congregation of the Catholic Sisters-Teachers*
*of the Sacred Heart of Jesus.*

José de Jesús López y González (1872-1950) and his four sisters grew up in a poor adobe home on the ranch "El Coton," where his father worked as a *campesino*, about four miles east of the city of Aguascalientes.[927] At the age of four, José lost his father. His widowed mother moved the family to Aguascalientes. At seven, he made his First Communion, which he, like many saints, experienced as "the happiest day of his life."[928]

JOSÉ DE JESÚS LÓPEZ Y
GONZÁLEZ

Feeling called by God, he entered the seminary at fourteen. He studied at Aguascalientes, Zacatecas, and Guadalajara. On the last day of November 1897, he was ordained a priest for the Diocese of Aguascalientes.

The bishop assigned this new priest to the parish of Jesús-Maria at Aguascalientes. In 1903, Father López erected a school, the Escuela Libre de Derecho, for the benefit of studious youth. Two years later, the bishop asked the young priest to teach in the seminary at Aguascalientes. In 1913, he was named pastor of the parish of Jesús-Maria, where he had begun his ministry, and in his second tenure, remained there until 1921. In May 1927, he was appointed the vicar general of the diocese, and the next year, he was ordained the auxiliary bishop of Aguascalientes. His episcopal ordination took place at San Antonio, Texas, where the bishop of Aguascalientes was residing in exile during the Mexican government's religious persecution. The bishop hastened the episcopal ordination of López, when the bishop discovered that the Holy See was considering ordaining López for the see at Zacatecas. Six weeks after López's ordination as auxiliary bishop, the bishop of Aguascalientes died, and López was promoted to the position of apostolic administrator of his home diocese. Because of the ongoing political persecution of the Church, Bishop López could not take possession of his see until January 30, 1930.

This pastoral-minded bishop excelled in three areas: the institutions he established, the programs he developed, and the sanctity he manifested. Regarding institutions, Bishop López founded the Nazaret Orphanage, dispensaries and social service agencies, labor organizations for factory and farm workers, plus catechetical schools for youth and adults in cities and rural areas. To enhance liturgical music, he began the diocesan School of Sacred Music. To instruct the young, he founded the Congregation of the Catholic Sister-Teachers of the Sacred Heart of Jesus, who flourish to this day.

Among the programs he initiated were the diocese's first Eucharistic Congress, the diocese's second synod, and two diocesan-wide catechetical congresses. A good administrator, he reorganized the diocesan Curía, and founded the Liga de Reciprocos Auxilios to encourage vocations and to funnel financial support to the seminary.

Spiritually, he promoted devotions to the Sacred Heart, the Eucharist, and Our Lady of Guadalupe. To counter the official atheism of the liberal government, he called for a "campaign of prayers" and instituted a diocesan Apostolate of Prayer to intercede for the needs of the Church. He authored sixteen pastoral letters. In his preaching and teaching, he conscientized the laity to issues of social justice, and asked that every parish establish a Catholic Action society. He conducted himself with gentleness, and kindness in the midst of personal suffering and public oppression. His flock described his demeanor as "the smile of God."[929]

In times of crisis, his gentle manner and deep wisdom won for him many responsibilities and plaudits. When the federal government forbade the opening of any seminaries, he traveled with almost two dozen seminarians to Montezuma, New Mexico, where the Mexican bishops founded a seminary under the leadership of Bishop López. In his home diocese, he visited the seminarians on a weekly basis, and personally ordained seventy-six priests. When the government closed and refused to reopen the Escuela Libre de Derecho, he replied, "Forget the matter; leave it in the hands of God."[930] To the sisters' community which he had founded, he said:

My daughters, those who have suffered during the persecution have had the good luck of proving their love for God by suffering.... These are the ones who have drawn closer to Jesus, becoming more holy and more loving. They didn't find sweetness in this life, but sufferings. God wants, and I, with all my soul, beg it from Him, in view of the interest that I have in forming a sure and firm community, that you all will know how to resist and to overcome the circumstances of afflictions and hardships.[931]

After the revolution, he advised members of the Catholic flock, "Have much prudence, ... and ask God for moderation in your judgments and opinions."[932] On his golden jubilee as a priest, he received many honors from lay organizations, schools, and social service institutions, and from political and business leaders in the capital city, and throughout the diocese. At this time, he received too one of the highest honors a churchman can receive when Pope Pius XII honored the bishop as a *Conde* (i.e., one of very few papal advisers).

Bishop José de Jésus López y González was blessed by God with great abilities: spiritual, pastoral, intellectual, organizational, and administrative. When he died of complications following a cancer operation, the entire diocese mourned his death. Just three years previously, the entire city of Aguascalientes, including governmental offices, businesses, and schools, had shut down in order to celebrate his golden jubilee. Throughout his life, José de Jesús López y González had affected profoundly the lives of countless persons by his personality, spirituality, programs, and institutions.

*For further information, contact*

Causa de Canonización de José de Jesús López y González
Columbus # 637
C.P. 20240
Aguascalientes, Ags., México

# 12. ✢ Jeanne Mance

*Place: Montréal, Québec*
*Fame: First lay nurse in North America. Co-founder of Montréal.*

Jeanne Mance (1606-73) is celebrated as one of five co-founders of Montréal, and the first lay nurse in North America.[933] At thirty-six, she left the comforts of France, and took on the challenges of New France.

JEANNE MANCE

Born at Langres, in the province of Champagne, Jeanne was the second oldest of a dozen children of a middle-class family. She helped to raise her siblings after her mother died in 1627, and her father, in 1635. When a plague ravaged Langres, taking five thousand lives in 1637, Jeanne nursed the sick and dying. A pious person, she belonged to her parish's Confraternity of the Blessed Sacrament. While wondering how she best might serve God, she heard a priest-cousin speak in early 1640, about New France and the Church's presence there. Possessing a "spirituality of events," Jeanne felt called by God to serve as a lay missionary in New France.[934]

Leaving Langres at the end of May 1640, she traveled to Paris, where she read copies of *The Jesuit Relations*, describing the society's evangelization efforts in the New World. In Paris, she learned about the recently established Society of Notre Dame of Montréal, and about Jérôme Le Royer's visionary project of founding a colony called Ville-Marie. Probably the Recollect priest Charles Rapine, although no one knows for sure, introduced Jeanne Mance to wealthy Madame Claude de Bullion, who offered to provide the funding to build a hospital in New France.

After almost one year in Paris, Jeanne Mance left for La Rochelle, where preparations were in process for the first expedition to Montréal. She joined the Society of Notre Dame of Montréal, and accepted Jérôme Le Royer's invitation to go to Ville-Marie.

Two ships left La Rochelle on May 9, 1641. Jeanne, another woman, a priest, and a dozen laymen traveled on one ship. On the second ship sailed Paul de Chomedey de Maisonneuve, whom the Society had appointed as governor, and twenty-five men and the crew. A third ship left from Dieppe. All three ships arrived safely at Québec, where the colonists spent the winter. In all situations, Jeanne demonstrated innate leadership, and unwavering faith in God. In springtime, the colonists embarked on a three-hundred-mile journey to their distant island, where they arrived on May 17, 1642. For Mass, Jeanne decorated a makeshift altar. In the next few weeks, whenever Native Americans stepped forward to be baptized, Jeanne stood as each one's godmother. Jeanne described this early period as "idyllic," and noted that "no doors were ever locked; [and] everybody attended Mass before going to work in the morning."[935]

From the very beginning at Ville-Marie, Jeanne cared for the sick. She had experience, but no training in nursing, since no formal training programs existed in the seventeenth century. She was an organizer, who took charge. Her patients included settlers, friendly Hurons, and hostile but wounded Iroquois. Jeanne welcomed the sick into her home until about 1645, when the colonists completed building the island's first hospital, the Hotel-Dieu.

> The Hôtel-Dieu was built of wood and stone in roughly equal proportions. The men's ward contained six beds and the women's two. There was a large fireplace at the end of the men's section that did for both wards. All the cooking was done in this fireplace, and the druggist had a corner there for his work. Here also the linen and dressings were washing and, more often than, not, there were too many sick for the provisions available. The winter cold was a terrible hardship, which was compounded by a simple, Spartan menu. As this was the only hospital west of Quebec City, it had a wide territory to draw from.[936]

After the first few months, the colonists became subject to attacks from Iroquois. Sometimes roving bands of braves, and at other times a war parties of hundreds of Iroquois attacked the village, killed and scalped men, and captured and carried off the women. Jeanne on two occasions narrowly escaped capture. By 1650, the colony's population faced near extinction. Jeanne gave money donated by Madame Buillion so that Governor Maisonnevue might sail to France to recruit men to man this mission. He departed on November 5, 1651, and returned on September 22, 1653, bringing with him one hundred four men. Jeanne was relieved, and renewed her hope that Ville Marie might survive.

After seventeen years of being the sole person rendering medical aid on the island, Jeanne, in 1658, accompanied by Marguerite Bourgeoys, traveled to France to seek assistance. "She [Jeanne] was of an attractive enough exterior, and she spoke of God as none could do better."[937] She successfully recruited for the hospital at Ville-Marie three Sisters of St. Joseph whose community Jérôme Le Royer recently had founded.

Although Ville-Marie's population continued to increase, reaching fifteen hundred by 1671, financial support remained a problem. Funding from the Society of Notre Dame lessened as did their membership, which plummeted from its original one hundred members in 1640, to five members by 1663. Jeanne suggested that the responsibility for the project might be transferred to the Sulpician Fathers, who possessed both the necessary funds and the practical interest in New France, since their missionaries had been at Montréal since 1652. The transfer of the deed from the Society to the Sulpicians was completed in 1663. The Sulpician Fathers, in turn, immediately donated the property to the apostolic seminary, so that the school could help both to educate lay and clerical students, and to assist the island colony in perpetuity.

In June 1672, the townsfolk honored Jeanne Mance by inscribing her name along with the names of four other co-founders on the cornerstone of the new Notre Dame church, which the citizens were building.

Worn out, Jeanne succumbed to sickness in June 1673. The prologue to her last will and testament reveals the rock-firm faith, which sustained her courageous actions to serve the Church and to evangelize the Amerindians in the holy endeavor of Ville-Marie.

> I proclaim that I live and die in the true faith of the holy Church, catholic, apostolic, and Roman, that I hold and recognize as the only true Church, outside of which there is no salvation. I believe and approve all that it approves, and I renounce that which it renounces. I revere and honor and recognize the Church as my one true Mother, vowing an entire and perfect obedience as its true daughter for my whole life and all eternity.[938]

*For further information, contact*

Musée des Hospitalieres de l'Hotel-Dieu de Montréal
201, avenue des Pins Ouest
Montréal, QC H2W 1R5 Canada

## 13. ✠ Mother Frances Xavier Cabrini

*Places: Chicago, Illinois; Denver, Colorado; Los Angeles, California; Newark, New Jersey; New York City, New York; New Orleans, Louisiana; Philadelphia, Pennsylvania; Seattle, Washington*
*Fame: Tremendous trust in God. First United States citizen to be canonized a saint.*

So many Italians, exiles far from home, found in the heart, the affection, and the generosity of Mother Cabrini and her companions the renewed sense that life was worth living, and were imbued with the hope and joy that gradually they would be assimilated by the American society, for this was the goal of Mother Cabrini and her sisters. And if the Sisters were happy in the gift of themselves in the service of their poor compatriots, the immigrants themselves were even happier.[939]

FRANCES XAVIER CABRINI

Francesca Cabrini (1850-1917), less than five feet tall and of poor health throughout her life, founded in 1880 a religious community of women who, before she died in 1917, numbered over one thousand sisters who were serving in sixty-seven institutions in eight countries on three continents.[940]

Francesca was the youngest of ten children, of whom all but four died before adulthood. Her parents' farm at Sant' Angelo, twenty miles south of Milan, provided the family with a comfortable living. As the father would regularly read to the children from the *Annals of the Propagation of the Faith,* "Frances became enthralled by the adventures of the saints, and even before she was thirteen years old, she expressed a burning desire to share her faith as many of them had done in far-off China."[941] She attended the Sant' Angelo School and, at thirteen, studied at Sacred Heart Academy run by the Daughters of the Sacred Heart at Arluno, west of Milan. She graduated at eighteen with a government license to teach elementary school in the province of Milan.

Shortly after graduation Francesca applied to the Daughters of the Sacred Heart, but they refused her admission because of her poor health. For the next two years, Francesca taught in her hometown Sant'Angelo school and nursed her aging parents, both of whom died when Francesca was twenty. In 1872, Francesca began teaching in the public school nearby at Vidardo, where the curate Antonio Serrati met her. When Francesca applied to the Canossian Sisters at Crema, Serrati and two other priests implored the sisters not to accept Francesca because the priests were concerned for her health and the valuable services she was rendering to them.

Serrati recommended to his bishop that Francesca could improve the "deplorable" management of a local orphanage for girls, the House of Providence.[942] There pious women were trying to establish a religious community called the Sisters of Providence, but their efforts were hampered by an ill-suited superior, Antonia Tondini, and her companion, Teresa Calza. Three years later, after Francesca had taken vows, a religious name, and put on the religious habit, the bishop named her superior. Immediately, trouble erupted from the displaced superior and her companion. The annals of the House of Providence report: "Enemies began to appear both within and without the convent. . . . Mother Superior has become the object of serious calumny . . . and threats."[943] Within a few months, Francesca's health broke. At Christmas 1878, Francesca alerted that bishop that the situation kept worsening. She writes:

> Your Excellency, I do not want to be the cause of the slightest disturbance to you. I want to talk with my heart in my hand as if I were before you at this moment, in which I strongly feel the weight of my difficult position. . . . Pray, Most Reverend Father . . . that I may be granted, at least for now, the strength that is necessary to hide my sufferings so that I may be able to give comfort to the Sisters who depend so much on me.[944]

Frustrated, the bishop closed the house in 1880. The bishop then asked Francesca to start a new community. Francesca and six other women founded the Institute of the Salesian Missionaries of the Sacred

Heart. Mother Francesca designed a simple habit appropriate for the sisters' work: a flat cap without a starched headdress, and rosaries were kept inside one's pocket. In 1881, the community's *Rule* was approved by the bishop.

Mother Cabrini's community grew quickly. Within the first seven years, Mother opened seven houses in the diocese: schools, social-service agencies, a residence for women students, and an orphanage. Mother, meanwhile, insisted that the community include "missionary" in its title. Some clerical authorities objected to the word since, up to that time, all missionary societies had been male. Mother Francesca retorted, "If the mission of announcing the Lord's resurrection to the apostles had been entrusted to Mary Magdalene, it would seem a very good thing to confide to other women an evangelizing mission."[945]

Mother Cabrini sought Vatican approval of her community, and to open a religious house in Rome itself. Four months after Mother Cabrini's arrival at Rome, she obtained the desired approbation. In response to her request to evangelize in China, Pope Leo XIII advised her, "Not to the Orient, but to the West."[946] The pope had become aware of the pressing needs of the Italians in the United States, and he knew the fledgling community would need the firm financial footing that could be found more likely in the United States than in China.

At the end of 1887, Archbishop Michael Corrigan of New York requested from Bishop Scalabrini of Piacenza to send priests from the Institute he recently had founded. Scalabrini replied positively, and suggested that the archbishop invite Mother Cabrini too to assist Italian immigrants in New York City. Mother conferred with the sisters, and reported, "Everyone ardently desires that this great work be undertaken." [947] At the end of March 1889, the seven sisters arrived at New York Harbor.

The sisters proceeded to visit the immigrants in their homes, hospitals, workplaces, and jails. The sisters trained children for baptism, confession, and First Communion. The zealous women formed sodalities and societies for both religious and social purposes. For the adults, the sisters offered evening classes to learn English, and to prepare for reception of the sacraments. The sisters identified for the priests various couples whose marriages needed to be regularized. For poor families, the sisters found food, clothing, and jobs. The sisters made God's love visible. The Italian families, some of whom were being wooed by Protestant churches, flocked to the Church of their origin.

The Missionary Sisters of the Sacred Heart were so effective in serving the Church in the Italian community, that various dioceses inside and outside the United States begged Mother for her assistance. Before the turn of the century, Mother Cabrini's sisters were serving in schools and orphanages in the dioceses of New York, Brooklyn, Newark, Scranton, Chicago, and New Orleans. Early in the new century, Mother expanded her services to the dioceses of Denver, Nesqually (which became Seattle in 1907), Los Angeles, and Philadelphia. The famous Columbus Hospitals were begun in Manhattan (1892), Chicago (1905), and Seattle (1915). Between 1891 and 1915, Mother's community founded numerous schools, orphanages, residences for women, and other services in, besides a dozen sites in Italy, Nicaragua (1891), Panama (1895), Argentina (1895), France (1898), Spain (1899), England (1902), and Brazil (1902).

Mother Cabrini personally oversaw the establishment of each foreign mission, and decided the assignment of each sister. She sailed across the Atlantic Ocean twenty-three times in order to meet personally each novice. In 1909, at fifty-nine, she became a naturalized citizen of the United States.

Mother Cabrini made these extraordinary achievements despite extraordinary obstacles. Poor health afflicted her throughout her life: she was born two months premature, almost drowned in a swift current of the Venera River at seven, contracted smallpox at twenty, faced the possibility of death at thirty, and suffered a series of illnesses, namely, bronchitis, fevers, flu, and chest colds throughout her adulthood. Regarding religious life, she was refused admission to two religious communities, and after she was accepted into a third community, the superior there made life miserable for her. After that community was dissolved, Francesca founded her own community. Priests also sometimes hindered her. A few priests thwarted her admission to the Canossian Sisters, another failed to assert himself in correcting abuses among the Sisters of Providence, and many ridiculed her use of the phrase "missionary" to describe her new community. Shortage of money in her missionary ministry plagued her constantly, as she and the other sisters begged to keep their people and themselves fed and clothed, and their institutions solvent. She remained undaunted. She firmly believed she was doing God's work, and that God would provide. She writes to her sisters, from New York's Columbus Hospital at the start of World War I:

> You will have it [Jesus' peace] by accepting all that happens — great and small — as gifts of God and placing all your joy in pleasing Him. This full conformity to the will of God, this abandonment of self in the bosom of the infinite bounty renders the soul a participant in two attributes of God: impeccability and infallibility. As two liquefy and become one, so the soul by conformity to the will of God becomes one with Him.[948]

*For further information, contact*
Saint Frances Cabrini Shrine
701 Fort Washington Avenue
New York, New York 10040

## 16. ✠ Henriette Delille

*Place: New Orleans, Louisiana*
*Fame: Servant of slaves. Foundress of the Sisters of the Holy Family.*

Henriette Delille (1812-62) grew up as a free woman of color in antebellum New Orleans.[949] Dedicated to the sufferings of "her people," as she called persons of African descent, she spent her life assisting the sick and dying, and evangelizing and catechizing persons in the Catholic faith. The prayer that she wrote in her diary at twenty-four, guided her whole life: "I believe in God. I hope in God. I love God. I want to live and die for God."[950]

HENRIETTE DELILLE

Henriette is the first U.S. born African-American whose cause for canonization has been opened officially by the Catholic Church.

Henriette's great-great-grandmother had been brought as a slave from Africa to Louisiana. Shortly after her arrival, a French colonist named Claude Dubruiel purchased her and had her baptized Marie Ann in 1745. Claude was married to a white woman, but proceeded to beget with Marie four more children. One of Claude's legitimate sons freed his step-siblings and their children more than a decade after his father's death. One of Claude's grandchildren was Henriette's great grandmother.

At home in New Orleans, Henriette, lived with her mother, brother, older sister Cecile, and her sister's four children. Cecile had entered into a liaison with a white Austrian businessman. The practice of white married men having black mistresses had become institutionalized in the quadroon system. Contributing to the situation were the limited choices available to free women of color: free men of color were few in number, and free women of color were prohibited by law from marrying whites. The quadroon system flourished, especially in New Orleans. Even though the Catholic Church officially preached against this institution, otherwise observant Catholics continued to practice it. Henriette herself was approached by white suitors, but she refused to involve herself this way.

At seventeen, Henriette gathered three other free women of color to join her in catechizing people of color, whether slave or free. Seven years later, under Henriette's leadership, these women formed a pious confraternity called the Congregation of the Sisters of the Presentation of the Blessed Virgin Mary. The members lived at home, vowed themselves privately to poverty, chastity, and obedience; and dedicated their lives to helping people of color. Each sister was to "seek to bring back the Glory of God and the salvation of their neighbor by a charitable and edifying behavior."[951] The sisters were to work together; "each woman alone could do little to evangelize or care for others."[952] The people for whom they cared were "the sick, the infirm, and the poor." [953] The sisters visited the needy in their homes, assisted them in practical ways, and taught "the principal mysteries of religion and the most important points of Christian morality."[954] The community views its foundation date as 1842, when the women left their individual homes and entered into community living in a house purchased for them by their cathedral pastor. At this time, the community received affiliation with the international Sodality of the Blessed Virgin Mary. An early account of the community's origin reads:

It was during the existence of slavery, in the year 1842, that this humble Institution was founded. Four young ladies, natives of this city, and descendants of some of our most respectable families of color (free), burning with zeal for the salvation of souls, commenced by teaching catechism and preparing colored girls and women for their First Communion. For years they persevered in this arduous work, devoting all their time, talents and dowries, doing much good and giving promise of much more when organized into a Religious Community.[955]

The sisters' manner and ministry attracted admirers and persons in need. Not only a proven innovator, but also an able administrator, Henriette expanded the numbers of people serving and persons served. She formed in 1847, the lay-led Association of the Holy Family, whose members assisted the sisters' ministry by prayer, money, and administering a home for elderly women. Three years later, Henriette used her own money and borrowed an equal amount to purchase a home wherein the sisters provided religious instruction for young girls during the day, and for women at night.

The sisters lived simply. They depended on friends who supplied the sisters with used clothing, basic foods, and wood for their fireplace. Still, the sisters shared the little they possessed with the poor. After Henriette's death, one of the founding sisters recalls the poverty-stricken experience of the early days.

Many were the times that the foundresses had nothing to eat but cold hominy that had been left from some rich family's table. It is not necessary to say a few words about their clothing, for it was more like Joseph's coat that was of many pieces and colors, darned until darn was not the word. In spite of the charity of their many kind friends, they suffered much owing to the strickness [sic] of the times.[956]

Since Henriette and her sisters had never received formal instruction in religious life, the bishop arranged that the Religious of the Sacred Heart would provide them that experience and instruction. Henriette and some of her sisters traveled in 1851 to Convent, Louisiana, north of New Orleans, where they lived for some months. A year later, Henriette and two other sisters took private vows to dedicate their lives in Jesus' name "for the education of young ladies of color, and the success and relief of poor old colored people and orphan girls."[957] Seven years after Henriette died, the community received from Rome formal recognition as a religious community. At that same time, the sisters adopted a religious habit.

The obituary for Henriette reads in part:

> Miss Henriette Delille had for long years consecrated herself totally to God without reservation to the instruction of the ignorant and principally to the slave. To perpetuate this kind of apostolate, so different yet so necessary, she had founded with the help of certain pious persons the House of the Holy Family, a house poor and little known except by the poor and the young, and which for the past ten or twelve years has produced quietly a considerable good which will continue. Having never heard of philanthropy, this poor maid has done more than the great philanthropists with their systems so brilliant yet so vain. Worn out by work she died at the age of fifty years after a long and painful illness borne with the most edifying resignation. The crowd gathered for her funeral testified by its sorrow how keenly felt was the loss of her who for the love of Jesus Christ had made herself the humble servant of slaves.[958]

*For further information, contact*
Henriette Delille Commission Office
6901 Chef Menteur Highway
New Orleans, LA 70127 U.S.A.

# 17. ✠ Saint Rose Philippine Duchesne

*Places: St. Charles, Missouri*
*Fame: "Woman who prays always." Frontier Foundress*
*of the Religious of the Sacred Heart in the U.S.A.*

A deep personality and spirituality guided Rose Philippine Duchesne (1769-1852) through endless challenges.[959] People of significant depth appreciated her, but people of superficial personality had difficulty relating to her. Born into a prestigious middle class family at Grenoble, in southern France, Philippine forsook comfort and status in order to bring Jesus' message to the United States. She committed her life to discerning and doing God's will, and persevering in that.

> Her name has been associated through more than a century with strength, endurance, austerity, a burning zeal for souls, patience under trial and failure, a certain severity of manner and outlook, and complete detachment from the things people generally cling to so tenaciously. Yet in this apostle of the Sacred Heart there were sweetness and sympathy, as well as strength, and hand in hand with endurance went a sensitiveness that made it all the more heroic. Her austerity was not born of any natural relish for suffering, nor was her patience the flowering of innate self-control. Hers was a vigorous personality, an intensely affectionate nature not ashamed to give expression to its inmost sentiments, a will fired with ambition to do big things and motivated from her teens by the single, dominating urge of love for the Sacred Heart.[960]

Mother Duchesne, at forty-nine, was missioned by her superiors to the frontier of the Louisiana Territory. Mother Duchesne, whom Mother Madeleine Sophie Barat, the superior general, had named the superior of four other religious, left Bordeaux on March 14 and arrived at New Orleans on May 29. After having traveled by steamboat seven hundred miles up the Mississippi River to St. Louis, they boarded a springless wagon and rode over rough roads to St. Charles. After a bitter winter in their log cabin, the bishop moved the sisters closer to St. Louis, at Florissant. There Philippine and her companions opened in

1819, the first free school west of the Mississippi River, an orphanage, a short-lived school for Indian children, and the first novitiate of the Religious of the Sacred Heart in the New World, where Philippine, in the next twenty years, received sixty-four candidates. Philippine remained at Florissant from 1819 until 1827, when she was assigned to open a house at St. Louis. The City of St. Louis, the gateway to the West, expressed the city's gratitude for Mother Rose Philippine Duchesne and other pioneers by inscribing their names on a bronze plaque for the Pioneer Roll of Fame. The plaque reads, "Some names must not wither," Mother Rose Philippine Duchesne heads the list.

In the next several years, this frontier foundress opened five more convents: at Grand Coteau in 1821; at St. Michael's in 1826; at St. Louis in 1828; at St. Charles in 1828; and at Bayou la Fourche in 1828. Mother Duchesne investigated each new site. The one-way journey from St. Louis to Grand Coteau lasted thirteen weeks. On the return voyage, yellow fever broke out. Having become quite ill, Philippine asked to be put off the boat at Natchez, where she found no bed except that belonging to a woman who had just died from yellow fever.

For twenty-two years, Philippine served as superior. She endured much criticism from the sisters, and from others to whom the sisters spoke about Philippine's degree of austerity, poverty, and alleged inflexibility. She bore it all with fortitude. Finally, in 1840, a young visiting assistant to Mother Barat listened to the complaining sisters, and immediately removed Philippine as superior.

Philippine, now seventy-one, volunteered to work with the Native Americans. After twenty-two years' service in the Mississippi River valley, she was looking forward to ministering at Sugar Creek, Kansas. Some sisters opposed Philippine's going. The Jesuit priest who was seeking the sisters' assistance in the mission replied, "She must come. . . . Why, if we have to carry her all the way on our shoulders, she is coming with us. She may not be able to do much work, . . . but she will assure success to the mission by praying for us."[961] When Philippine and three other sisters arrived at Sugar Creek, seven hundred Potawatomi, Kickapoo, Wabash, and Osage Indians welcomed them.

Septuagenarian Philippine could neither read nor write the natives' language; nor could she teach or cook. Within a few weeks, however, the

Indian people loved her, and frequently brought gifts to the "good old lady."[962] One of the nuns writes about Philippine:

> She stayed all morning in the church.... After dinner she went again for three or four hours of prayer. The Indians had the greatest admiration for her, recommended themselves to her prayers, and called her Woman-who-prays-always.... Her incapacity for active work brought her loneliness of heart which she admitted and accepted with love, but not without pain. The solitude at Sugar Creek was not merely a physical remoteness, but also a spiritual aloneness that grew out of the sensed fact that she was a burden on those who cared for her, an anxiety for them. Borne in close union with the mystery of Christ's loneliness, this suffering only drew her closer to his Sacred Heart, where she buried the pain by renewed and more loving surrender.[963]

After Philippine's first year at Sugar Creek, the bishop wrote to Mother Barat, and suggested that Philippine return to St. Charles on account of her deteriorating health. The Potawatomi held a farewell celebration for her. "She [had] learned to live at peace with disappointment, yet eagerly to press forward."[964] Philippine departed Sugar Creek on June 19, 1842, and after a four-day wagon ride to Westport, and a six-day boat ride on the Missouri River, arrived at St. Louis. After a brief stay, Philippine rode to St. Charles, where she took up her position in the chapel. Two days later, she writes to a fellow sister at France, "I cannot forget the savages.... Many of the children had learned to read, knit, card wool, and spin.... With the help of the prayers offered to God and the perseverance of the nuns in caring for them, they will make progress in virtue and knowledge."[965] Without bitterness, and with great peace, she resumed her usual activities: praying, reading, sewing.

Ten years passed. She corresponded regularly with other Sacred Heart sisters, and with many relatives. Continuing her prayer-filled ways, "she seldom left the chapel on days of Exposition of the Blessed Sacrament."[966] Her room, measuring eight feet by sixteen feet, was situated next to the chapel. "Her bed was a mattress two inches thick, laid on the ground by night and put away in the day in a cupboard."[967] Three months before she died, she writes to her dearest friend, Madeleine Sophie Barat, "Yesterday, I received the last sacraments, but God may still keep me waiting for the happiness of seeing him," and to her sole-surviving sister, "I am leaving you with sorrow because you are so alone.... I carry into eternity with me the memory of them [her sister's children] and you. *Adieu*, loving and dear sister."[968]

Philippine had been born and raised in Grenoble, at the foot of the French Alps. Her father was a prominent, politically active lawyer. Her mother came from one of the region's most respected families. Philippine's mother educated the girl at home, until she went at twelve to the convent school of the Visitation Nuns. As a young girl, Philippine developed a desire to work with the American Indians. She explains,

> My first enthusiasm for missionary life was roused by the tales of a good Jesuit Father who had been on the missions in Louisiana and who told us stories about the Indians. I was just eight or ten years old, but already I considered it a great privilege to be a missionary. I envied their labors without being frightened by the dangers to which they were exposed, for I was at this time reading stories [the *Jesuit Relations*] of the martyrs, in which I was keenly interested.[969]

When she was seventeen, her father tried to interest Philippine in marrying a certain young man. Philippine, however, had her mind set on entering the convent. At eighteen, Philippine invited an aunt to accompany her to the Visitation Sisters' Convent of Sainte-Marie d'en Haut. Once there, however, Philippine decided to remain, and the aunt had to walk home alone. The next day, Philippine's parents arrived, and the father pleaded unsuccessfully with his daughter to return home.

Four years later, the Reign of Terror in France closed the houses of all religious communities, with the exception of houses belonging to the famed Daughters of Charity, who insisted that their brother community of Vincentians remain open in order to serve the Daughters. Philippine returned home, and for the next ten years she instructed children in the Catholic faith, visited the sick, and assisted priests who were risking their lives to serve the faithful. In 1801, when the Holy See and Napoleon signed the Concordat allowing the Church some restoration of its authority, Philippine attempted to reopen the Convent of Sainte-Marie, but few nuns remained ready to return to their former way of life. Philippine and four other nuns lived at the convent.

In November 1804, Mother Madeleine Sophie Barat, who had founded the Society of the Sacred Heart four years earlier, invited Philippine to join the Society. Philippine entered their novitiate in late December 1804, and took vows on November 21, 1805. For the next ten years, Philippine served well. In 1815, Mother Barat charged Philippine with establishing the mother-house in Paris. When the bishop of Louisiana, requested in 1817, that Mother Barat might send sisters to his territory, Mother Barat remembered Philippine's long-standing desire to live among the Indians, and assigned Philippine to that mission. In living among the Potawatomis, Philippine fulfilled her childhood dreams of dedicating her life to God, and of working directly with the Native Americans.

*For further information, contact*
Society of the Sacred Heart Archives
4537 West Pine Blvd.
801 S. Spoede Road
St. Louis, MO 63108 U.S.A.

⧢

## 20. ✠ Ovide Charlebois

*Place: Upper Manitoba and Saskatchewan*
*Fame: Zeal for souls. Missionary priest and First Bishop of Keewatin.*

As a college student, Ovide (1862–1933) felt a romantic attraction to missionary ministry. His heart and soul were captured by the stories of Oblate bishop Vital Grandin, who oftentimes visited and regaled the students at L'Assomption College about his missionary experiences in the diocese of St. Albert's in Western Canada (now the Province of Alberta). Years later, Ovide remembered Grandin's exhortation, "If you wish to come to the Northwest, love God a lot. Do not come out of love for me; but out of love for the

OVIDE CHARLEBOIS

good Lord."[970] After his own forty-six years as a missionary, Ovide writes, "When you have spent ten to fifteen years in suffering all sorts of miseries, when harassed with fatigue, you have to sleep under the open sky, being bitten by mosquitoes or by lice, or else shivering from the cold on a few spruce branches, all this fine poetry will become prosaic."[971] A fellow missionary priest describes the way Ovide occupied his time:

> Teaching, preaching, instructing, hearing confessions. He never lost an opportunity to have souls hear the word of God. For the little ones, the catechism; for the grown-ups, three or four instructions a day. I remember, among others, that one time when he was on the way to Beauval, he was held up at Delmas. He profited by the delay to preach a three-day retreat in English and French. Another delay at Meadow Lake, another retreat of four days in Cree [language]; held up again at Green Lake, eight days this time. Finally, getting to Beauval, he preached the eight-day retreat he had come for.[972]

Ovide estimates that he spent one-third of his time on the road. The roads in Northern Manitoba and Northern Saskatchewan, however, consisted of footpaths, river routes, and portage treks through thick forests. His first mission, which lasted sixteen years, extended in a hundred mile radius from St. Joseph's Mission at Cumberland House on the Saskatchewan River. From 1903 to 1910, he administered and taught at the Indian School at Duck Lake. When in 1911, he was named Bishop of Keewatin, his see extended south to the fifty-third latitude, north to the North Pole, embracing the eastern boundary of the province of Manitoba, and the western boundary of the province of Saskatchewan, which see he administered for twenty-three years.

Two missionary trips: his first as bishop in 1911, and his last, in 1932, exemplify the burdens and benefits of his missionary journeys. He writes of his first journey:

> During this trip [which lasted five months], I covered about three miles by railroad, eighty miles in big wagons without springs over terrible roads, two thousand miles by canoe, forty to fifty miles on foot in the portages through the forest. I slept sixty times on the ground, sheltered by a little canvas tent. I celebrated Holy

Mass as often under the same tent. I visited fourteen missions comprising a population of four thousand five hundred Catholic Indians: six of these missions had never been visited by a bishop. I preached seven retreats of four to six days. I confirmed eleven hundred savages whose good dispositions greatly edified me.[973]

His final missionary journey, which he undertook at seventy, he describes in this fashion, "I traveled more than one thousand miles by canoe. I made eighty portages with my luggage on my back, through the forest, sometimes on the rocks, sometimes in floating swamps. And the mosquitoes! You understand, there were lots of them!"[974]

Ovide had grown up on a farm, first at Saint-Benoit, and then at Sainte-Marguerite, about twenty-five miles north of Saint-Jérôme. When Ovide was sixteen, the family moved to L'Assomption College, where his father had obtained work as overseer of the college's farm and instructor in agriculture. Ovide, the seventh of the family's fourteen children, received his education initially at home and, beginning at twelve, at L'Assomption College.

At L'Assomption College, Ovide demonstrated a level-headedness. "He was very pious . . . he was obedience personified, respectful to his professors; he liked to study and aimed to succeed. Towards his fellow students, he was good and charitable; he never had enemies."[975] Upon completing his classical studies at twenty, he entered the Oblate Fathers of Mary Immaculate in 1882 and was ordained a priest in 1887.

Superiors assigned Ovide to St. Joseph's Mission at Cumberland House in Saskatchewan. He visited the Native Americans' settlements, learned their language, hunted and fished with them, conferred the sacraments upon them, built schools and more than a dozen chapels and priest-living quarters throughout the territory. Many Indians converted to the Catholic Church. He rose daily at four o'clock, and meditated for two hours on Jesus' gospel and the Oblates' *Rule*. He carried with him two favorite books: the *New Testament*, and *The Imitation Of Christ*. At the end of his first year of priesthood, he committed himself to becoming a saint. He writes in his retreat notebook, "We are all first-class dunces if we don't become saints."[976]

Ovide chose adherence to the community's *Rule* as his means to attain sanctity. He resolved, "To do only religious acts. That is to say, to make all my actions conformable to our only *Rule* and to the spirit of our *Rule*."[977]

The years in Cumberland proved challenging and satisfying. Ministry among the Indians had been Ovide's dream, and at the end of his third year, he writes, "Strangers who pass through here all keep repeating: 'What a poor country. I would not live here for all the money in the world!' They are quite right; you have to be crazy to live here for the sake of mere money; but when it concerns the salvation of souls, it isn't the same. Isn't the salvation of a single soul worth more than all the money in the world!"[978]

In November 1910, the pope appointed Ovide bishop and the first Vicar Apostolic of Keewatin. In 1911, Ovide assigned a priest to start missions among the Eskimos at remote Hudson Bay. A dozen years later, he himself visited there. He built two hospitals: at Le Pas and La Crosse. At Keewatin, he built a cathedral for the newly erected diocese. He admired, respected, and tried to imitate the Indians in many of their virtues. When white-men abused the Indians, Bishop Ovide defended the natives. "He was always able to discern, respect and encourage the legitimate traditions and customs of the Indians, as well as their admirable ingeniousness."[979]

Ovide's humor served him well along his difficult journeys. On one occasion, he reports, "For my part, my shoulders and my [bare] feet complain of treatment they have received. The former found the burden too heavy and the latter miss the pieces of skin left on roots and stones."[980]

This Oblate of Mary Immaculate had "two inseparable loves": the Sacred Heart of Jesus, and Mary Immaculate.[981] About the great aloneness, which he suffered in priesthood, he writes, "Here I am alone in my modest house; I have no other companion than Our Lord in the Blessed Sacrament, but He is sufficient for me. He knows how to strengthen me, console me, guide me, make me happy."[982] When he was endangered on stormy seas or in dense forests, he trusted in the Blessed Mother; he writes, "It seemed to me that the Blessed Virgin held my beads herself and that she led me."[983] Of the two loves, he writes,

> It is very difficult, not to say impossible, to separate Jesus from His divine Mother. Devotion to the Sacred Heart goes hand in hand with that of the Blessed Virgin. We go to Jesus only

through Mary: *Ad Jesum per Mariam*. Thus, while preaching love towards the Sacred Heart, also preach that of our kind Heavenly Mother. These two loves make only one.[984]

In 1925, a long-time lay friend approached Ovide and requested that he sign a letter from the Canadian bishops to the pope, thanking him for having canonized St. Thérèse of Lisieux. Ovide refused. The visitor asked why. Ovide replied that if he was going to write to the pope, he would ask for something, and suggested that Thérèse ought to considered the Patroness of Missions and Missionaries. The visitor shared Ovide's vision with other bishops, and they responded enthusiastically. Seven months later, two hundred thirty-two bishops from Canada and around the world submitted to Vatican officials the request which Ovide had originated. A contemporary declares, "This idea was really born in his heart. It comes from him alone."[985] In December 1926, the pope declared St. Thérèse of Lisieux the Universal Patroness of the Missions.

In spring 1933, Bishop Ovide ordained his successor the coadjutor bishop. That November, the septuagenarian Ovide died, as he had lived, in love with the Sacred Heart, the Immaculate Mary, his religious community, and the Indians whom he had served so generously and simply for almost half a century.

*For further information, contact*
Archeveché de Keewatin-Le Pas
Chancery Office
108, First Street, West, P. O. Box 270
Le Pas, MN R9A 1K4 Canada

# 21. ✠ Venerable Julia Navarette Guerrero

*Places: Oaxaca and Aguascalientes in México, and Texas in U.S.A.*
*Fame: Long-suffering contemplative mystic and active religious.*
*Foundress of the Congregation of Missionary Daughters*
*of the Most Pure Virgin Mary.*

Julia Navarette Guerrero (1881-1974) served God as an active religious and a contemplative mystic, while suffering greatly throughout her religious life.[986]

At seventeen, she entered the Congregation of the Cross. Five years later, on the advice of her spiritual director, she left that community and founded at Aguascalientes the Institute of the Most Pure Immaculate Virgin Mary. Six other professed sisters and six candidates left the Congregation with Julia to form the new community. The stated aim of the congregation was for the sister's "individual and communal sanctification, through giving comfort and reparation to the Sacred Heart of Jesus."

For the next seventeen years, Julia served as superior general of the community. After the sisters elected Julia to her third consecutive term, the local bishop suggested that she step down from the position. She did so, and immediately the sisters elected her as the assistant, or vicar general. Off and on, she served another thirty-four years as either superior general (elected in 1935, 1941, 1947, and 1959) or vicar general (elected in 1953, and 1965). In 1947, 1953, and 1969, she petitioned the Holy See that she might refuse the position of superior general. The Holy See accepted her renunciation only in 1969, and honored her with the title Superior General Emerita, at which time, the foundress was eighty-eight. During the more than half-century in which Julia served as superior general or vicar general, she opened thirty-two institutions, mostly schools, and mostly in México; she opened three foundations in Texas as well.

Throughout her religious life, Julia suffered accusations and mistreatment from opponents. Shortly after she left the community which she had joined as a teenager, a priest and lay woman allegedly obstructed the institutional progress of the community which Julia then founded. In the community which she founded, after Julia voluntarily stepped down as superior general, her successor introduced steps to remove Julia geographically and emotionally from other sisters. Julia was transferred eight times in the next fourteen years, mostly to missions in remote Sonora and Texas; and the sisters were forbidden to write or to visit her. In 1927, the Bishop of Corpus Christi encouraged her to leave the congregation, but she refused, having decided to remain faithful to her congregation.

How did Julia respond to mistreatment? She went to chapel, and prayed, "Oh my God! You alone know what I suffer."[987] She writes, "Only God can fathom the cruel bitterness in which my soul saw itself submerged.... I felt hurt, offended, and profoundly resentful."[988] She prayed in the words of Saint John of the Cross,

> To come from everything to Everything,
> You have to leave everything for Everything.
> And when you have Everything,
> You have to seek to not seek anything.
> Because if you seek to have something in anything,
> You will not have God in his entirety.[989]

Over the decades, Julia grew in intimacy with the Lord. She writes in her autobiography:

> I believe that I can say that from 1953 to 1960 my spirit over-came a special difficulty. The circumstances that used to surround me, used to upset and annoy me, no longer did so. Sometimes in the silence and quiet the Lord used to communicate to me the pro-found conviction of his good, of his mercy and his infinite love. I used to feel immersed in this atmosphere of the perfection of God, which would awaken in my soul an immense confidence, an absolute certainty of his good towards me. I used to approach Jesus frequently, saying, "What do you wish from me?" He would reply, "that you die to yourself, that you rise above your worldly interests; die to everything, even to those affections that seem to be holy, live at a level where life's contradictions don't disturb you, where atten-tions don't flatter you. Seek only God and his interests.[990]

When Julia died on November 21, 1974, at Toluca, México, the community had burgeoned to over five hundred sisters, who were labor-ing in forty-eight convents, mostly in México and some in the United States.

Julia had been born in Oaxaca, the second of six children, whose five brothers would include a priest, and an archbishop. Her father worked as a professor. Her mother taught Julia at home until she began school at nine. Early in life, Julia developed devotions to the Sacred Heart of Jesus, the Holy Spirit, and the Virgin Mary. Beginning at six, Julia attended daily Mass, and at seven, she made her First Communion, at which time she dedicated her life to God. At fifteen, she felt some anxieties about purity, which her spiritual director treated as growing pains. The next year, a young man proposed marriage to her, which she declined because she wanted to become a nun. From her Jesuit spiritual directors she learned the Ignatian method of prayer, which she followed from fifteen until her death at ninety-three.

Biographers describe Julia as intelligent, mature, zealous, and an excellent teacher. She possessed a deep degree of *smypatico* which perhaps resulted from her own sufferings, which included severe headaches when she was a child, and a stomach ulcer and bronchitis in adulthood. Five times, a priest was called to anoint her in mid-life as she appeared near-death. A member of the congregation describes Julia in the following way:

> Very feminine, . . . [with] exquisite taste, . . . rich and strong, the spirit of a leader, a singular sympathy, and a gift that which open doors and win over hearts, an eloquent and persuasive speaker, perspicacious and observant, . . . firm, energetic, decisive, courageous. . . When by the light of reason or faith, she discerned God's will, neither anything nor anybody could dissuade her. She was not intimidated by dangers, privations, sufferings, humiliations. Never would she be idle, and nothing appeared difficult, if she understood that God desired it.[991]

*For further information, contact*
Causa de Madre Julia Navarette Guerrero
Héroe de Nacozari, #721 sur
Apartado Postal #221
20240 Aguascalientes, Ags., México

∽

# 22. ✠ Magin Catalá

*Places: Santa Clara, California*
*Fame: "Holy man of Santa Clara." Mystical missionary.*

Magin Catalá (1761-1830) was born and raised in Montblanch, in the Catalonia region of northeastern Spain. He and his twin brother benefited from the example of Christian living demonstrated by their pious parents, from the educational opportunities provided by their physician-father, and from their maternal grandfather who had been a successful merchant. In April 1777, at sixteen, Magin and his twin entered the Franciscan seminary at Barcelona, where, in the next year, they took vows and put on religious habits. After ordination in February 1785, Magin volunteered to labor in the New World missions. His brother spent his religious life ministering in Catalonia.

In fall 1786, Father Magin sailed from Cadiz and probably by the end of the year, arrived at México City. For eight years, he remained at the College of San Fernando, where he studied mission methodologies and Indian languages. In 1793, his superiors sent Magin to Monterey, California, where he worked as chaplain on the Spanish ship Aranzazu, which sailed regularly between México and Nootka Sound (now Vancouver Island). At the end of his one-year chaplaincy, the governor requested that Magin might remain for an additional term. "But since he had been appointed to serve the Indians, Fray [Friar] Magin thought he could no longer postpone his primary duty, and thus, he respectfully declined the governor's invitation."[992] Magin spent August 1794 at Mission San Francisco, and in the next month, journeyed forty miles south to Mission Santa Clara, where he labored until he died thirty-six years later. Mission Santa Clara had been founded in 1777, the eighth of the twenty-one California Missions. It would be secularizd in 1836, by the Mexican government, which confiscated the property, sold the assets, and kept the income for itself.

Already living in Mission Santa Clara were over one thousand Indians, and living in ten outlying settlements were thousands more. Father Magin traveled "as far as San Jacinto Valley, some hundred miles distant, to search out unconverted Indians to attract them to reside in the Christian mission or in one of the Indian villages or rancherias that surrounded it."[993] After three years at the mission, Catalá was named senior priest, giving him responsibility for the spiritual well-being of the congregation. A recently arrived junior priest was assigned responsibility for the material well-being of the mission: overseeing the farms, livestock, facilities, and tradesmen. Catalá served the Indians in the mission and its surrounding settlements by instructing them in the Catholic faith through hymns and prayers; in Lent, by leading the Indians along the Way of the Cross, and in May, by reciting with them the rosary. He preached from a pulpit until he became too aged and infirm to climb it, at which time, he stood preaching from the altar rail, and eventually sitting in a chair at the altar rail. He spoke to the natives in their native tongues and Spanish. In 1818 and 1825, he built new churches for the mission. His teaching and preaching, he continued until the day before he died.

Father Magin Catalá always traveled by foot, even though he suffered constant pain from inflammatory rheumatism, which he had contracted early on at Mission Santa Clara. "In 1794, his rheumatism became more inflamed, so that he could only limp along with pain when he went to the outlying Indian rancherias. Fray Magin's dedication to the Indians at Santa Clara was but the outward expression of his dedication to God."[994] About his sickness, he never complained, but he felt incapable of fulfilling his task, he asked on three occasions to return to Spain. He asked in 1797, 1798, and 1801. The first time, his superiors refused in the hope that the sickness would pass; the second and third times, his superiors agreed to the transfer, but he chose to remain in California because of the shortage of missionaries. Magin Catalá worked indefatigably.

> From early morning until late at night he labored for his neophytes. No labor was too great, no journey too difficult for the salvation of souls. Often, he made perilous journeys to distant tribes and invariably returned accompanied by large numbers of pagan Indians whom his sweet charity had induced to abandon their wild life for the happy Christian community at Santa Clara.[995]

During Father Magin Catalá's tenure at Mission Santa Clara, "there were 5,471 baptisms (infants, children, and adults), 1,905 marriages and over 5,000 burials."[996] Conversions to the Catholic faith occurred because of the strength of the Christian message and the kindness of the missionary's manner.

The priest practiced a high degree of asceticism. He fasted every day of the year, never ate anything until noontime. His evening meal consisted of gruel, made from corn and milk. "He never used meat, fish, eggs, or wine."[997] He practiced daily disciplines in accord with the contemporary spirituality in order to diminish the temptations of the flesh.

Father Magin experienced the mystical life in some of its rarest expressions. Each day, he prayed for many hours before a life-size crucifix which was hanging in the chapel at Mission Santa Clara, and each night, he spent additional hours in contemplation. When giving testimony about the holiness of Catalá's life, "two witnesses declared under oath that they had seen the holy missionary raised from the floor while he was praying before this crucifix, and that while so elevated, Christ embraced him."[998] The gifts of miracles, prophecies, revelations, and locutions were also attributed to him. The Indians reverently called Magin Catalá "the holy man of Santa Clara."[999]

*For further information, contact*
Archives of Archdiocese of San Francisco
320 Middlefield Road
Menlo Park, CA 94025 U.S.A.

⚬⫯⚬

## 23. ✠ Blessed Miguel Pro

*Place: México City, D.F.*
*Fame:* "¡Viva Cristo Rey!" *Prototypical priest-martyr for México.*

From his earliest days in childhood, Miguel Pro (1891-1927) exhibited a personality rich in happiness, laughter, and playful mischieviousness.[1000] Frequently he entertained his family and friends with storytelling, cartoon-drawing, and music-playing on his guitar and violin. Family and friends described him as a jokester, prankster, and mimic.

Miguel was born the third child and first son among eight children. As a toddler, Miguel was deathly ill, when his father in desperation lift-ed up his son and cried out to the Blessed Virgin, "My mother, give me back my son."[1001] With that the child spit out bloody phlegm which, for over a year, had limited his breathing and had plagued him with fevers and convulsions. As a youngster, Miguel visited with his mother the homes of the poor, and distributed to them food and clothing. In his teen years, the boy worked alongside his engineer-father in the administration of governmental mines, from which experience he developed a respect for workers.

MIGUEL PRO

The family moved many times because of the father's work. Miguel grew up at Gaudalupe, in Zacatecas; and at Monterrey. At ten, he went to boarding school at México City, but left after a few months when anti-Catholic administrators forced him to say Protestant prayers and prohibited him from attending Sunday Mass. Miguel, at sixteen, went with the family to Concepción to assist his father. On one occasion, labor riots broke out, and Miguel protected the family by bracing the door against the threatening mob. Mounted policemen arrived, and Miguel watched horrified as protesting workers were crushed under the hooves of horses.

A humorous story is told about Miguel in his teen years. Naturally, he took an interest in girls, and enjoyed the evening *paseo* (stroll) during which the girls walked in one direction around the town square, while the boys walked in the opposite direction. He once mailed two letters, but accidentally inserted the letter to his mother in the envelope addressed to his girlfriend, and the letter to his girlfriend in the envelope addressed to his mother! The relationship with the girlfriend soon ended.

After two of his sisters entered the convent in 1910, Miguel was moved the next year to enter the Jesuit seminary at El Llano, Michoacán, southwest of México City. His professors and peers teasingly called him, "the brother who is convinced God wants him to be a saint."[1002] When the four-year-old Mexican revolution reached remote Zacatecas in 1914, the seminary authorities sought refuge in the United States for their fifteen students. In small groups and in disguises, the seminarians traveled for two months through Zamora, Guadalajara, Laredo, San Antonio, and El

Paso, for Los Gatos, California. After one year, the Jesuits transferred their seminarians to Spain. In 1925, Miguel was ordained a priest at Charlerois, Belgium, where he had spent summers ministering to miners. None of his family was able to attend the ordination.

After ordination, Miguel's ever-present stomach pains worsened. He lost sleep and weight. Within four months, he underwent three operations, but his health still worsened. In the meantime, his mother died. Jesuit authorities sent home to México the sick and broken-hearted Father Miguel. Before leaving Europe, he visited Lourdes, France. He writes, "I was at the feet of my Mother and . . . I felt very deeply within myself her blessed presence and action. . . . for me, going to Lourdes meant finding my heavenly Mother, speaking to her, praying to her."[1003]

Father Miguel arrived in mid-July 1926, at Veracruz, and made his way to México City. Twenty-three days later, the Mexican Government unleashed a virulent anti-Catholic persecution. The government prohibited all public worship outside of churches, secularized all education, dissolved religious communities, and confiscated as state property the Catholic churches, monasteries, and convents. The bishops of México replied in a pastoral letter, claiming prophetically, "Beloved children, the church in México is today delivered up, persecuted, imprisoned, reduced to a state resembling death. But the Mexican Church will also, after a short period, rise again full of life and strength, more vigorous than ever. Hold fast to this hope."[1004] For any priest to minister during this time meant risk of arrest, torture, and execution.

For the next fifteen months, Father Miguel, like thousands of other Mexican priests, heroically served his congregation. Fortunately, because Father Miguel had arrived only recently in the country, he was not well known as a priest. His family had moved to México City, where he joined them. Because of the persecution, the Vatican had granted priests permission to say Mass wearing no vestments, praying only the essential parts, using any bread, and using any glass as a chalice as long as it was broken and never used again. Disguising himself at times as a garage mechanic, a wealthy gentleman, taxi driver, beggar, street sweeper, and several times as a policeman, he bicycled around the city. A couple of times he passed policemen, chatted with them, and continued on his way to bring Communion. Father Miguel rotated Communion stations, where he distributed Communion to three hundred people daily, and to over a thousand on First Fridays. To multiply his efforts, he organized one hundred fifty youth who catechized children. To serve the poor, he collected and distributed food and clothing. Baptisms, weddings, the last rites, and counseling he performed regularly. Part of the message he preached was: "We ought to speak, shout out against the injustices, with confidence and without fear. We proclaim the principles of the Church, the reign of love, without forgetting that it is also a reign of justice."[1005]

He narrowly escaped from the police many times. One time, with the police walking less than fifty yards behind him, he took the arm of a young woman, introduced himself as a priest, and walked with her in romantic embrace. Another time, the taxi in which he was riding sped away from the police, turned a corner, enabling Father Miguel to roll out past the open door, hit the curbside, light a cigar, and lean calmly against a light pole as if waiting for a bus, as the police cars rounded the corner, chasing after their suspect in the fleeing taxi. After the Defense of Religious Liberty group had distributed thousands of flyers around México City via six hundred airborne balloons, he was arrested in a round-up of suspects. In jail, Father Pro, in a humorous voice, laughingly explained to the jailer that the word "*Pbro*" at the end of his name was not the abbreviation for priest, i.e., *presbítero*, but a misspelling for Pro, which was his surname. With both men now laughing at the supposedly typographical error, the guard mistakenly released the priest.

The level of violence kept escalating. In the first week of September 1927, México suffered over three hundred political assassinations. On November 13, someone attempted to assassinate General Alvaro Obregón, who had arranged with Calles that they would alternate presidencies. The car which the assassins used had belonged originally to the Pro brothers. Although the car had been sold twice by successive owners, Calles arrested the Pro brothers: Humberto and Roberto, who belonged to the propaganda arm of the Defense, and Miguel. On November 17, the three Pro brothers were whisked away in a dawn raid. The brothers were interrogated many times. Three other suspects were rounded up, and confessed to the crime. The general in charge of the investigation reported to Calles the innocence of the Pros. Calles refused to listen to the facts. He ordered the brothers to be executed by a firing squad.

On the morning of November 23, despite the arrival of an *amparo* which legally required a stay of execution, the general, on the orders of

Calles, marched the prisoners to the bullet-riddled wall behind the police station. Calles, wanting to use the execution as a message to his opponents, had invited the press, photographers, and distinguished guests to the "big show."[1006] Miguel walked with his crucifix in his right hand, and the rosary in his left hand. He requested two minutes to kneel and pray. Standing up, he refused the customary blindfold, and extended his arms in the form of a cross. Bravely facing the firing squad, he said, "May God have mercy on you. May God bless you. Lord, you know that I am innocent. With all my heart I forgive my enemies."[1007] As the twelve soldiers took aim with their rifles, Father Pro shouted aloud, "*¡Viva Cristo Rey!* [Long live Christ the King!]" Shots rang out. The priest lay mortally wounded, but not yet dead. A soldier approached him, and point-blank shot the priest in the head. Calles proudly had the photos and accounts of the execution distributed. The "show" backfired on Calles. The populace became enraged. Calles quickly reversed himself and declared the possession of the photos to be a crime. Humberto too was executed. Roberto's life was spared by the last-minute arrival of a plea from the ambassador of Argentina.

Although Calles had forbidden any public display of support for the Pro brothers, thousands of supporters filed past the casket at the Pro home. The next day, the funeral procession, consisting of over five hundred cars, filed past an estimated twenty thousand well-wishers along the funeral route. As the coffins passed by, the crowds knelt down, sang hymns, and prayed aloud the rosary.

Ever since his return to México in 1926, Father Miguel prayed that God might permit him to suffer martyrdom. After his fifteen-month ministry in his native land, and ten days before his execution, he wrote a prayer to Our Lady of Sorrows, in which he prays that he might identify with her sufferings. He concludes the prayer with the following words:

> For my life, I covet the jeers and mockery of Calvary; the slow agony of your Son, the contempt, the ignominy, the infamy of His Cross. I wish to stand at your side, most sorrowful Virgin, strengthening my spirit with your tears, consummating my sacrifice with your martyrdom, sustaining my heart with your soli-

tude, loving my God and your God with the immolation of my being.[1008]

*For further information, contact*
Iglesia La Sagrada Familia
Puebla 144
Colonia Roma,
06700 México, D.F. México

⚮

## 23. ✠ Marie-Clément Staub

*Places: Worcester, Massachusetts; and Sillery, Québec*
*Fame: Lifelong devotee of the Sacred Heart.*
*Founder of Sisters of St. Joan of Arc.*

"I want to be a saint," writes young Joseph Staub as a teenager in the seminary at Alumnat de Taitegnies, in his native Alsace.[1009] "And the way to sanctity is through prayer and study, writes Staub, as a student in the major seminary at Rome, "I will be able to do good only to the extent that I shall be saintly and learned: now is the time to become both."[1010] At Rome, he earned two doctorates, in philosophy and theology.[1011]

MARIE-CLÉMENT
STAUB

As a novice in the Assumptionists in1896, Joseph took as his religious name Marie Clément, in honor of the Blessed Mother Mary, and his father Clément. He did his seminary studies at Louvain and Rome, where he was ordained a priest in March 1904. His first two assignments were two-year terms as novice director, first at Louvain, and then at Gempe. After preaching in England for one year, he went to the United States in late 1909.

In 1908, Father Staub met Edith and his life changed forever. Edith was the recognized leader of the Archconfraternity of Prayer and Penance in honor of the Sacred Heart of Jesus. For over forty years, beginning in 1870, Edith allegedly had been receiving visions and messages from the Blessed Mother. With thousands of people already participating in this devotion, Staub envisioned propagating this religious expression to widespread places.

Devotion to the Sacred Heart of Jesus had been a part of Staub's spirituality since his youth. A few years before his birth, church leaders had dedicated France to the Sacred Heart. The Basilica at Montmartre was begun as the expression of the French people's dedication to the Sacred Heart. In his family's home at Kaysersberg hung a picture of the Sacred Heart. The seminary, which Staub attended, was dedicated to the Sacred Heart. As novice director, Staub placed the internal seminary under the patronage of the Sacred Heart. In his early priesthood, he wrote articles about the benefits of devotion to the Sacred Heart.

The young priest received permission from his religious community's authorities that, in addition to his regular assignments, he might preach on devotion to the Sacred Heart of Jesus. This he did as superior of a high school seminary near London, England, and as chaplain at an orphanage near Worcester, Massachusetts. Despite his lack of fluency in English, and a throat ailment which made preaching difficult for him, he looked for every opportunity to propagate this devotion. He wrote and disseminated brochures, and saw that medals were struck and distributed. Thousands joined the movement. "He spoke with such conviction, such enthusiasm and love. His one desire was to spread love like a blazing fire, that the whole world might be plunged into the burning, loving Heart of Jesus.[1012] In March 1914, when he had occasion to visit Pope Pius X, Staub brought with him lists identifying seventy-seven thousand devotees of the devotion. The pope requested membership for himself too. Back in the U.S.A., Staub approached various bishops and priests for the opportunity to preach about the Archconfraternity. The Archconfraternity aimed to enthrone the Sacred Heart in Catholic homes, schools, and workplaces. Members were to perform prayer and penances weekly, if possible, and monthly, certainly, in reparation for sins, and in praise of the Sacred Heart. By 1919, over one hundred thousand persons joined the Archconfraternity.[1013]

Another devotion which Staub held dearly was honoring Saint Joan of Arc. This fifteenth-century Maid of Orléans had rescued France from relentless English advances, but for political reasons and on charges of alleged heresy, she was burned at the stake in 1431. She had been canonized in 1920, which canonization he attended while a student in Rome. Joan hailed from Lorraine, which bordered on his native Alsace. At the canonization, he promised, "Joan, I will do something for you someday."[1014]

One day in spring 1913, when Staub was preaching and seeking donations in order to build an altar in honor of Joan of Arc at Assumption College, a woman in Fitchburg, Massachusetts, commented, "Joan of Arc wants more than an altar from you. She wants you to provide a community of Sisters, who will offer themselves as victims of love to the Sacred Heart for the benefit of priests."[1015] The woman was Alice Caron, a forty-year-old rectory housekeeper.

Staub met with Alice Caron and two other women on Christmas Eve 1914, when the foursome prayed a Holy Hour, and celebrated Midnight Mass. The following week, on New Year's Eve, Staub met with the same three women, plus four more women, who prayed a Holy Hour, and moved to an on-campus cottage, which is regarded as the birthplace of the Sisters of St. Joan of Arc. Here the future founder and charter members of the community discussed the vision and mission of the Sisters of St. Joan of Arc. Staub generously provided direction and inspiration to the nascent community. One of the sisters took shorthand notes of his conferences, homilies, addresses, and instructions, which were collated into two books, *Life of Union with the Sacred Heart*, and *My Mission as a Sister of St. Joan of Arc.*

The founder suggested that the community might expand into Canada. Beginning in 1915, Staub, while preaching throughout Canada, met with numerous men's and women's religious communities, and with priests, bishops, archbishops, and the Cardinal of Québec. Staub inquired if a need existed for his proposed Sisters of St. Joan of Arc. All groups answered affirmatively. Bergerville, which borders on Québec, was selected as the foundational site. Thus, three years after establishing the community in the U.S.A., Staub expanded the community into Canada. Formal episcopal and papal approval of the Sisters of Saint Joan of Arc was received three years later, in 1920. Eight years later, Staub established foundations in France. The community became known popularly as the Lorraines, in reference to Joan of Arc's birthplace. The sisters acquired the castle at Beaulieu-les-Fontaines, where Joan had been imprisoned for nine days, and transformed the dungeon into a shrine in her honor.

By 1936, Staub began feeling the effects of his exhaustive service. Although ill with "general fatigue and dropsy in the legs", he continued to plan.[1016] He wrote in February to the superior general of the Assumptionists that the current novitiate, which had accommodations for twenty-five women, was bursting at the seams with the current class of forty-five novices. Three years ahead of schedule, the construction was completed.

On May 10, 1936, the Father Founder preached at the community's Mass celebrating the silver anniversary of the canonization of St. Joan. On the morning of May 16, he said to the novices, "Only the valiant become saints! So you must become holy and valiant souls! I desire so much that you become like Saint Joan.... I shall speak to her for you."[1017] Later that evening, he died. At the time of his death, the community had grown to two hundred thirty-nine members, operating in thirty-four houses in three countries.

*For further information, contact,*
Secrétariat Père Marie-Clément Staub
Soeurs de Sainte-Jeanne d'Arc
505, rue de l'Assomption
Sillery, QC G1S 4T3 Canada

☙

## 29. ✠ Dorothy Day

*Place: New York City, New York*
*Fame: Radical lay pacifist and promoter of human rights.*
*Co-founder of the Catholic Worker Movement.*

Dorothy Day (1897-1980) possessed compassion for the poor and vision for a new world order.[1018] In early 1933, she co-founded with Peter Maurin the Catholic Worker movement, in May of 1933 *The Catholic Worker* newspaper, at the end of 1933 Hospitality Houses, and in 1935 Catholic Worker Farms. Dorothy Day anticipated by decades the call for an end to war, the role of laity in the Church, and liberation theology. Her compassion for all people motivated her to write, "The heart hungers for that new social order wherein justice dwells."[1019]

Dorothy was born and raised the third of five children. Although Dorothy and her parents rarely attended their Episcopalian church, she daily prayed the Lord's Prayer in public school, and each evening whispered night prayers at her bedside. When Dorothy was six, her family moved from Brooklyn to San Francisco, then later to Chicago, where she won a full scholarship to the University of Illinois at Urbana. There, she joined the Socialist Party, and two years later, in 1916, when her parents returned to New York, Dorothy quit school, moved back east, and wrote for, in turn, *The Call*, *The Masses*, and *The Liberator*, all Socialist publications. Eventually, she became a free-lance writer.

In New York, Dorothy pursued a bohemian lifestyle among artists and social radicals in Greenwich Village. Opposing all organized government and religion, she writes, "I wavered between my allegiance to socialism, snydicalism [workers' unions] . . . and anarchism."[1020] Although many of her friends belonged to the Communist Party, she never joined "because the Communist Party approved of violence in labor confrontations, . . . and because the Communist Party adhered to Lenin's atheist, anti-religious line."[1021] In 1917, she protested in front of the White House on behalf of the women's suffrage, and received a jail sentence of thirty days, ten of which she spent in a hunger strike. This act of civil disobedience was the first of her many arrests and five imprisonments.

With the advent of the World War, Dorothy studied nursing in 1918, and worked at Kings County Hospital in Brooklyn. Although, she writes, "I had been a good and sympathetic nurse," Dorothy realized that her genuine vocation was writing.[1022] After many romantic affairs, she moved to Europe, where she lived for a year with her husband Barkeley Tobey in London, Paris, and throughout Italy, writing as she traveled. Having moved back to Chicago, and no longer married, Dorothy worked successively as a sales clerk, waitress, cashier, and model for art classes. While visiting a girlfriend who was recovering from drug addiction, Dorothy was arrested in a police raid on "a disorderly house," which was actually a union headquarters.[1023] About this experience [in jail] she writes, "I think that for a long time one is stunned by such experiences. They seem to be quickly forgotten, but they leave a scar that is never removed."[1024]

Catholic friends had impressed and inspired Dorothy everywhere she went. In Brooklyn, she and a Catholic nurse regularly attended Sunday Mass together. In Chicago, her three roommates attended Sunday Mass weekly without miss. Also in Chicago, when Dorothy was about ten, she was running through a railroad flat apartment, looking for her playmate, when she saw the girl's mother praying on her knees at her bedside. The mother, without interrupting her prayers, and without embarrassment, simply directed Dorothy to where she could find her friend. About these experiences Dorothy writes humbly, "Worship, adoration, thanksgiving, supplication — these were the noblest acts of which men were capable in this life."[1025] In New Orleans, Dorothy attended Sunday night Benediction at the cathedral at Jackson Square, and learned to pray the rosary. Dorothy was attracted to the Church because of its liturgy and devotions, and because it was "the Church of the immigrants, the Church of the poor."[1026]

After she published her first book, *The Eleventh Virgin*, a company bought the movie rights for five thousand dollars. With that sum in hand, Dorothy moved to Staten Island, where she bought a beach home. She invited Forster Battleham to move in with her; the two lived a common-law marriage for the next four years.

At twenty-eight, Dorothy gave birth to her daughter Tamar [Therese]. Dorothy writes, "When the little one was born, my joy was so great that I sat up in bed in the hospital and wrote an article for the *New Masses* about my child, wanting to share my joy with the world."[1027] Later, the mother wrote, "I wanted my child to believe, and if belonging to a Church would give her so inestimable a grace as faith in God, and the companionable love of the Saints, then the thing to do was to have her baptized a Catholic."[1028] Dorothy comments, "I was not going to have her [daughter Tamar] floundering through many years as I had done, doubting and hesitating, undisciplined and amoral. I felt it was the greatest thing I could do for my child."[1029] The father, an atheist and anarchist, "would not talk about the faith and would relapse into complete silence if I [Dorothy] tried to bring up the subject."[1030] He was averse to any ceremony before officials of either Church or state."[1031] At thirty, Dorothy cries onto the page, "I loved him. It was killing me to think of leaving him."[1032] Tamar was baptized in July 1927, and Dorothy was received into the Church on December 28, 1927, the day after she left Forster.

Five years after converting to Catholicism, Dorothy was anguished while she was reporting on a labor protest in Washington, D.C, containing both Communists and non-politically involved workers.

> Where was the Catholic leadership in the gathering of bands of men and women together, for the actual works of mercy that the comrades had always made part of their technique in reaching the workers? . . . . I kept thinking to myself. They were His [Jesus'] friends, His comrades, and who knows how close to His heart in their attempt to work for justice.[1033]

Reflecting on her situation, Dorothy went directly from the White House to the National Shrine of the Immaculate Conception. There she begged God on that December 8th afternoon, "that some way would open up for me" to work more effectively for the poor.[1034] After the bus ride back to New York City, she entered her apartment, and sitting there was a stranger who introduced himself as Peter Maurin.

Peter explained that after having read Dorothy's articles he believed that they together could effect major changes in Catholic social thinking and acting. He suggested that he and she conduct round-table discussions, publish a paper, promote Houses of Hospitality, and open agronomic universities, "where workers would become scholars and scholars workers."[1035] Dorothy listened. At their next meeting, Dorothy commented about Peter's suggestion of publishing a newspaper, "I would like nothing better."[1036] Peter suggested the title *The Catholic Radical*. Dorothy, with her exposure to Communism, countered with *The Catholic Worker*. Peter replied humorously, "Man proposes, but woman disposes." [1037] The first issue of *The Catholic Worker* appeared on May Day 1933, and its twenty-five hundred copies were sold at Union Square for a penny apiece. By the year's end, a hundred thousand copies were published for each issue. Three years later, the number of copies mushroomed to one hundred eighty thousand. The newspaper's masthead read, "Published and edited by Dorothy Day," and its mission was:

> It's time there was a Catholic paper printed for the unemployed. The fundamental aim of most radical sheets is the con-

version of its readers to radicalism and atheism. Is it not possible to be radical and not atheist? Is it not possible to protest, to expose, to complain, to point out abuses and demand reforms without desiring the overthrow of religion? In an attempt to popularize and make known the encyclicals of the Popes in regard to social justice and the program put forth by the Church for the "reconstruction of the social order," this news sheet, *The Catholic Worker*, is started.[1038]

Within six months of its origin, the Catholic Worker movement began providing hospitality to the needy. Dorothy writes, "We must recognize the hard fact, that no matter how good a social order, there will always be the lame, the halt and the blind who must be helped, those poor of Christ, the least of his children, whom he loved, and through whom there is a swift and easy road to find him."[1039] By 1936, thirty-three Hospitality Houses had been founded from coast to coast. When a reporter asked Dorothy how long the "clients" would receive free hospitality, she replied, "We let them stay forever. They live with us, they die with us, and we give them a Christian burial. We pray for them after they are dead. Once they are taken in, they become members of the family. Or rather always were members of the family. They are our brothers and sisters in Christ.[1040]

Hospitality homes evolved into Catholic Worker farms. Beginning in 1935, Catholic Worker Farms were started at Easton, Pennsylvania; near Newburg, New York; on Staten Island, and in the Hudson Valley villages of Tivoli and Marlboro.

Dorothy promoted faith-based opposition to war. When the United States' Catholic hierarchy, clergy, and laity overwhelmingly supported General Franco in the Spanish Civil War, many supporters abandoned her. Parishes and schools canceled block subscriptions to *The Catholic Worker*. Readership plummeted from almost two hundred thousand copies per issue to fifty thousand. Fifteen Hospitality Houses closed.

Dorothy refused to abandon her pacifist stand. She perceived war as a "tearing asunder of the body of Christ."[1041] Experience, study, and prayer had taught her that Peter Maurin was right that the true revolution lay in "the gentle personalism of traditional Christianity."[1042]

Because wars continued, Dorothy Day joined a group of fifty Mothers for Peace, who in 1963 traveled to Rome to thank Pope John XXIII for his encyclical *Pacem in Terris*. Two years later, Dorothy returned to Rome, where she fasted publicly as a plea that the pope and the bishops at Vatican Council II might condemn all wars. Soon, the Council in its *Constitution on the Church in the Modern World* condemned nuclear war as a crime against humanity, and declared as criminal any military action against innocent and defenseless non-combatants.

Dorothy authored over a thousand articles for *The Catholic Worker*, and another three hundred fifty articles for other magazines, plus seven books including her autobiographical novel, *The Eleventh Virgin* (1923); the account of her spiritual journey, *From Union Square to Rome* (1938); and her autobiography, *The Long Loneliness* (1952).

Ever since her college days, Dorothy had involved herself in support of the powerless and voiceless: garment industry employees, streetcar operators, iron workers, farm workers, seamen, prisoners, and conscientious objectors to military conscription. She advocated not just improved living conditions, working conditions, and material benefits, but also the inherent dignity of the poor and workers. The last time she was jailed was in 1973 when she was picketing in support of farm workers.

At seventy-six, Dorothy suffered a heart attack at Tivoli after returning from the Eucharistic Congress in Philadelphia where she, along with Mother Teresa and Cardinal Karol Wojtyla (later Pope John Paul II), had spoken. After that point, she wrote and spoke little in public.

At her death, she left a loosely structured but highly spirited movement. It is unlikely that any religious community was ever less structured than the Catholic Worker. Each community is autonomous. There is no board of directors, no sponsor, no system of governance, no endowment, no pay checks, no pension plans. Since Dorothy Day's death, there has been no central leader.[1043]

*For further information, contact*
The Dorothy Day Guild
New York Catholic Center
1011 First Avenue
New York, N.Y. 10022 U.S.A.

# DECEMBER

✢

## 8. ✢ Gloria María Elizondo García

*Place: Monterrey, Nuevo León; Ciudad Victoria*
*and Tampico, Tamaulipas*
*Fame: "The good God, the good God." Imaginative and effective*
*lay apostle who served the poor for decades, then entered*
*the convent and was elected Superior General.*

Gloria María Elizondo García (1908-65) was blessed with great compassion.[1044] She achieved extraordinary good whatever she did, wherever she went, for whomever she served.

As a child, she herself needed help. As a one-year-old, she lay at death's door. Her family at Durango gathered around her bed. Her relatives traveled almost four hundred miles from Monterrey to pray for her. By the grace of God, she survived. At five, the family's living quarters on the second floor above the government's Office of Housing was burned down by a political-minded arsonist. The family escaped, but the father felt he had to move his family. They went to the major city of Monterrey. The family prayed often before the statue of the Infant of Prague, which helped to sustain them. At thirteen, María graduated from the business course at the local school, and found employment in the accounting department of a local company. She was given ever-increasing responsibility as the company expanded.

Her compassion found expression in action. At twenty, she regularly visited the mental hospital and women's penitentiary, and distributed to the patients and inmates gifts of candies, clothing, and other desired items. At Christmas, she prepared special meals for those confined in these institutions.

Southeast of Monterrey, in the state of Nuevo León, lies the industrial town of Ciudad Victoria in the state of Tamaulipas. Because the poor people there needed jobs, Gloria planned and founded a fish-packing plant. She named the product, *Cruz de Oro* (Cross of Gold). She treated her employees like family members. Noticing in the neighborhood an indifference to religion, she organized programs of religious instruction. Heeding the pope's exhortation to the faithful to form Catholic Action groups, she organized professionals, teachers and parents into round-table discussion groups to inspire and instruct them in the faith. For the children, she established five catechetical centers. On Saturdays, she rented a truck and drove around the Colonia Tamatán to pick up idle children and transport them to the distant parish of Nuestra Señora del Refugio to attend Mass and afterwards play games outside. On Sundays, she made similar trips with the truck to pick up adults so that they could attend Mass. In 1948, she prevailed upon some businessmen to donate land in Tamatán, where she planned and oversaw the construction of a chapel, which the bishop came and blessed. To assist her in the people-projects, she successfully invited into Cuidad Victoria, the women's religious communities of the Madres de la Caridad del Refugio, and the Misioneras Catequistas de los Pobres. The sisters soon began to work with fishermen and their families. Through María's efforts, hundreds of children received baptism and First Communion; and one Sunday, eighty couples in the same ceremony received the sacrament of matrimony.[1045] Because girls who had been without work often became prostitutes in Ciudad Victoria, María initiated for them a program of instruction with the sisters, at first in Monterrey, and eventually, right in Ciudad Victoria.

In 1950, María moved back to Monterrey. She missed her family. She also wanted to discuss with them a possible career change. Back home, she shared that she wanted to enter the convent. Her aging mother resisted and insisted that María might take care of her mother. María delayed her entrance.

María entered the Congregación de las Madres Misioneras Catequistas de los Pobres on July 16, 1954. In 1956, she published the book *Jesuscristo*, in order to communicate the message of Jesus to the simple people. The book sold ninety thousand copies. Almost three years later, in April, she took her temporary vows and the religious name Sister Gloria María de Jesús. Two years later, she was appointed Mistress of Postulants. In May 1961, a virtually unprecedented situation arose when the community elected her superior general and she was not yet in final vows. The archbishop was contacted for approval of the election. He was shocked, but he listened and acceded. Sister Gloria María de

Jesús was appointed superior general, and two days later she took final vows.

The community of sisters loved and admired Mother Gloria. She modeled for them a life of prayer and service that was innovative and effective. In 1962, she introduced at Monterrey the Christian Cursillo Movement for Women. When some of the community's convents opened their doors to host meetings, some consternation erupted among the sisters. One sister describes Mother's role in resolving the dispute. "Mother Gloria called together the community. With firmness in her decision, she said to us that our mission was to work in each diocese for whatever the Good God would love and bless for all people, and that the Movement was a grace from God in our community. She asked that we continue assisting this Movement for the good of the Church."[1046]

In mid-1965, Mother Gloria was diagnosed with cancer. She suffered significantly. In mid-November 1966, she received the sacrament of the Anointing of the Sick. Mother requested that as many sisters as possible might be present for the anointing. She spoke to them:

> Do not think that I am going to forget you. If here on earth everyday I look out for each one of you and for your families, there above [in heaven] where I will have no other occupation, how much more will I desire what is good for you. I promise you that I will intercede for you. There I will be able to do for the congregation much more than I can do here.[1047]

On December 8, 1966, Mother Gloria died. At the funeral Mass, the archbishop quoted her oft-repeated favorite phrase, "The good God, the good God." Mother Gloria had lived and died in praise of and service to "the good God."

*For further information, contact*
La Causa de Sor Gloria María
Las Misioneras Catequistas de los Pobres
5 de Mayo 419 Ote.
Monterrey, Nuevo León, México

# 9. ✠ Saint Juan Diego

*Place: México City, D.F.*
*Fame: Convert to Christianity. Received apparitions*
*of Our Lady of Guadalupe.*

Within four days, the Blessed Mother appeared four times to the Aztec Indian, Juan Diego (c. 1474-1548).[1048]

JUAN DIEGO

Juan had been "born... in the Tlayacac highlands in the Méxican Cuauhtitlan region, where in 1168 the Nahua people had settled and which in 1476 was conquered by the Aztec chief Axayacati.... Juan Diego was a member of the lowest and most numerous class of the Aztec people and he worked the land. He married but had no children. Around 1524-25 he and his wife became Christians and they were baptized Juan Diego and Maria Lucia. Maria Lucia died in 1529. Even before becoming a Christian, Juan Diego was a very religious person. He was reserved and loved silence.[1049]

Mary addressed Juan as "Juanito, Juan Dieguito," indicating her affection for him and his humble way of life.[1050] She appeared with Indian features, dark complexion, typical dress, and spoke the native Nahuatl language. She identified herself as "the perfect always Virgin Holy Mary, Mother of the most true God through whom one lives."[1051] These apparitions and the rapid spread of the news resulted within six years of the conversion of nine million Indians. Our Lady of Guadalupe and her agent Juan Diego have been credited as being the most effective evangelizers in the history of the Catholic Church. The following summary is provided from a study of the original documents.

Very early on Saturday, December 9, 1531, as Juan Diego was taking his daily fifteen-mile walk through the Tepeyac hills on the northwest outskirts of México City to attend Mass in México City, Mary first appeared to him. Juan relates that he had heard soft and gentle singing, as if coming from many unseen birds on the hilltop. He stopped and asked himself why he was so lucky to hear this sound. He wondered if he were dreaming. From the eastern side of the hill, the wonderful singing stopped, and he heard his name being called. His advance was blocked, but he felt no fear, only peace and contentment throughout his whole body. Arriving at the top of the hill, he saw the Doncella standing there. She possessed a perfect grandeur. Her clothing shook and shone like the sun. Rocks beneath her feet released rays of light. The ground and grass shined like jewels in the snow. She spoke in his native Nahuati language, "Listen, my son, my lowly one, where are you going?" He replied, "My Queen, my Muchachita," I am going to your house to do the things that our priests give us to do." She explained, "My littlest son, I am the perfect always Virgin Mary, Mother of the truest God, . . . Queen of heaven and earth. I desire that a sacred house be built here. And I will give to people all my love through my compassionate seeing, assistance, and salvation, because I am their compassionate Mother. I will listen to your crying and sadness, in order to cure all your pains, miseries, sufferings."[1052]

Bishop Juan de Zumárraga received Juan and listened respectfully to his report of the appearance of the Virgin. The elderly bishop suggested that Juan come back another day. That evening, when Juan was on his way home, the Blessed Mother met him and inquired about the progress of her request. Juan reported that he had difficulty first, in getting in to see the bishop, and next, getting the attentive bishop listening to take action. The next day, Sunday evening, the Virgin again met Juan and inquired about the progress of her expressed desire. Juan explained that the bishop had requested a sign from the Lady. The Lady asked Juan to come back on Monday morning, when she would provide a sign. On that morning, however, Juan was preoccupied with caring for his dying uncle, and he failed to return to the place where Our Lady had met him previously.

On December 12, Tuesday morning, Juan was hurrying to ask a priest to come for his uncle. Juan thought it best to avoid the path on which he had encountered the Lady. He walked on the opposite side of the hill, but the Lady still intercepted his path. She assured him that his uncle would be cured. She invited Juan to gather roses from the rocky top of the hill, and to take these as a sign for the bishop that the Virgin Mary wished a house to be built in her honor on that hill. The humble Indian did as he had been asked. Juan was surprised that any flowers, let alone roses, were growing among the rocks in this cold weather. The obedient devotee, however, did as Mary asked. He gathered roses amidst the rocks and carried them in his *tilma* (cloak).

At the residence, after the bishop received Juan, the lowly Indian opened his *tilma* to display the bunch of roses. As the flowers fell out of the cloak and on to the ground, the bishop and his staff fell to the ground in prayer and amazement. Portrayed on the mantle was the image known popularly as Our Lady of Guadalupe.

After the Virgin's apparition in 1531, the first sanctuary was constructed two years later on the site designated by Mary, on top of the foundation of the earlier parish church. In 1556, Bishop Zumárraga's successor began the second church. The present Basilica of Our Lady of Guadalupe was begun in 1695 and was consecrated in 1709. Further significant additions were made in 1883 and 1930, which resulted in the present edifice.

This event has been documented many times. Juan González, the interpreter for the Spanish-speaking Bishop Zumárraga and the non-Spanish speaking Juan Diego, took notes on the conversations held between the two protagonists. These notes remain extant. About 1560, the Jesuit priest Antonio Valeriano compiled in his native Nahuatl an account of the facts of the apparitions and the miracles attributed to the Virgin. At least fifteen other accounts of the Jesuits' relations with the Indian population testify to the popular belief in the apparitions of the Virgin. Bishop Montufar, Zumárraga's successor, indirectly but significantly contributed to the promotion of devotion to Our Lady of Guadalupe. "In the Provincial Council [of bishops] of 1555, he, along with other bishops, formulated canons that indirectly approved the apparitions, for the order to abolish and prevent the worship of images and the propagation of traditions not well founded did not mention the Guadalupean image and devotion to it."[1053]

Within a generation of the apparition, Jesuit missionaries carried the news of the apparition to the Philippines, Puerto Rico, and Spain. In

1754, Pope Benedict XIV proclaimed a Mass and Office for Our Lady of Guadalupe. In 1910, Pope Pius X declared Our Lady of Guadalupe the patroness of Latin America, and in 1945, Pope Pius XII declared Our Lady of Guadalupe the Queen of México and Empress of the Americas.

*For further information, contact*
Basilica de Santa María de Guadalupe
Plaza de las Américas
Villa de Guadalupe, D.F., México

✳

## 9. ✠ Fulton J. Sheen

*Place: Peoria, Illinois; New York City and Rochester, New York*
*Fame: "Single most important Catholic in twentieth-century America."*
*Host of the TV series "Life is Worth Living."*

Critics have acclaimed Bishop Fulton J. Sheen (1895-1979) as "the twentieth century's most famous Catholic preacher," "one of the greatest preachers of this century," and "perhaps the most popular and influential American Catholic of the twentieth century."[1054] These critics were, respectively, noted Catholic historian John Tracy Ellis, internationally famous Baptist preacher Billy Graham, and the publishing board of Our Sunday Visitor's *2000 Catholic Almanac*.[1055]

FULTON J. SHEEN

This first of four sons was born to Newton Morris Sheen and Delia Fulton Sheen in a second-floor bedroom above the family's hardware store in El Paso, Illinois. The couple baptized their boy Peter, he took John as his confirmation name, and, upon admission to the Catholic high school of the all-male Spalding Institute, he identified himself as Fulton, which was his mother's maiden name. At St. Viator College in Bourbonnais, Illinois, Fulton Sheen received an A.B. degree in 1916. His bishop assigned him to study at St. Paul Seminary in St. Paul,

Minnesota. Upon completing his seminary studies, Sheen took summer courses at St. Viator and earned an M.A. in 1919. On September 20, 1919, the bishop of Peoria ordained Fulton J. Sheen a priest. The next year, the young priest received the licentiate in Sacred Theology (STL) and bachelor's of Canon Law (JCB) at the Catholic University of America. Desirous of plumbing the depths of the philosophical underpinnings of Western European culture, he studied at Louvain, where he earned his doctorate in philosophy (Ph.D.) in 1923.

Bishop Sheen achieved excellence in half a dozen fields.

As an academician, he received in 1925 the rarely bestowed and highly coveted *Agrege en philosophie* award from the prestigious Catholic University of Louvain. The next year, he became the first American to be awarded the Cardinal Mercier International Prize in Philosophy. When his doctoral dissertation was published in 1926, the work was acclaimed "a philosophic masterpiece."[1056] After ordination in 1926, Sheen spent a few months in an inner-city parish in Peoria before teaching for almost a quarter of a century as a professor of theology and then philosophy at the Catholic University of America in Washington, D.C. "Three of Sheen's books, published between 1925 and 1934, were major contributions to scholastic philosophy, earning widespread applause from scholars and exhibiting a breadth of knowledge that was truly exceptional."[1057]

As an author, he published sixty-six books, sixty-two booklets, and thousands of articles. Granted, most of his books "were invariably repetitive reworkings of his public platform addresses."[1058] More than twelve of his books remain in print over two decades after the bishop's death.

As director of the Society for the Propagation of the Faith from 1950 to 1966, "Sheen raised more money for the poor than any other American Catholic, an effort that was augmented by the donation of more than ten million dollars of his personal earnings."[1059]

As an ecumenist and convert-maker, he presented the Catholic Church positively during an initially anti-Catholic era, which led to the acceptance of the Church by many persons formerly opposed to her. He presented his subject matter in a way "in which the Catholic Church comes forward as the one and only real champion of reason."[1060] *America* magazine, in 1979, called Sheen "the greatest evangelizer in the history of the Catholic Church in the United States."[1061]

Sheen's most famous converts include author, diplomat, and United States Congresswoman Clare Booth Luce, business magnate Henry Ford II, actress Loretta Young, leftist newspaper columnist Heywood Broun, and world renowned violinist Fritz Kreisler. Two fallen-away Catholics whom Sheen brought back to the fold were Communist newspaper editor Louis Budenz and former Communist spy Elizabeth T. Bentley.

Perhaps Sheen is remembered most popularly as a radio and television apologist, whose radio show, "The Catholic Hour," was broadcast weekly from 1928 to 1950; and whose television show, "Life Is Worth Living," was broadcast weekly from 1952 to 1957. Over the decades, more than seven million listeners heard his radio program; and each week, over five million viewers watched his TV program. For his "No. 1 TV show in America," Sheen won two Emmy Awards.[1062] His TV time slot ran opposite and drew larger audiences than "Mr. Television," the comedian Milton Berle. When Sheen beat out Berle in the ratings, a reporter asked him how this could happen. Berle joked, "Bishop Sheen had better writers."[1063] Sheen made the cover of magazines such as *Time*, *Look*, *Colliers*, and *TV Guide*.

As a churchman, Sheen was ordained in 1919 and named Auxiliary Bishop of New York in 1951 and Bishop of Rochester in 1966. As Bishop of Rochester, he was the first bishop in the U.S.A. to begin to implement the changes recommended by Vatican Council II. "He immediately created territorial vicars, a diocesan priests' council, a board of counselors that included several laypersons, and a new Vicar for Urban Ministry."[1064] During the Vietnam War, he was the first bishop to call for the end of the war. In October 1969, seven months ahead of the compulsory retirement age of seventy-five, the Vatican accepted Sheen's resignation from the see of Rochester. At the same time, Pope John Paul II named Sheen titular archbishop of Newport, Wales, and appointed the ecumenist to the Papal Commission for Nonbelievers. For the next ten years, until his death in 1979, Sheen traveled worldwide preaching retreats. When Pope John Paul II visited St. Patrick's Cathedral in October 1979, he personally asked to see Bishop Sheen. When the bishop appeared, the pope said, "You have written and spoken well of the Lord Jesus, and you are a loyal son of the Church."[1065] Sheen regarded these words as the highest praise he had ever received. Immediately after his death in 1979, he was buried at St. Patrick's Cathedral in the crypt.[1066]

Underlying these accomplishments is the spirituality that permeated these good works. Bishop Sheen attributes his practice of praying a Holy Hour before the Blessed Sacrament as providing the "fuel" for all that he did. Every day for sixty years, from priesthood ordination until his death, Sheen practiced a Holy Hour, whose three-fold purpose was: "sharing in Our Lord's work of redemption, fulfilling Our Lord's desire for our companionship, and growing into the likeness of Our Lord."[1067]

Sheen did not escape suffering in his relationships with people, despite his extraordinary intellect, wit, charm, and grace. At the Catholic University of America, theology faculty members challenged whether Sheen was suitably qualified to teach theology. Within months of his arrival, therefore, he was transferred to the department of philosophy, where his credentials were impeccable. Scholars then challenged the quality of his scholarship. Sheen soon realized he could not pursue both courses simultaneously: serious scholarship, and popular communication of the faith. Sheen resigned from the university in order to dedicate himself entirely to communicating the message of Jesus to the largest number of people. Another hurt occurred many years later when, as auxiliary bishop of New York, Bishop Sheen had a run-in with Cardinal Spellman. Spellman insisted that Sheen, as director of the Society for the Propagation of the Faith, "reimburse the archdiocese for large quantities of powdered milk acquired by Spellman as head of the Military Ordinate during the Korean conflict."[1068] Sheen refused. He knew that Spellman had received the milk as a donation. Sheen reasoned that since the archdiocese had paid nothing, the archdiocese needed to receive nothing. Spellman, furious, appealed to the pope. Pope Pius XII sided with Sheen. Months later, the cardinal refused to approve the bishop's continuing his TV program. The bishop, forced by the cardinal to resign, announced that he was leaving the "No. 1 TV show in America" for "personal reasons."[1069] Spellman took occasion to exile Sheen from New York City by intervening to have Sheen appointed Bishop of Rochester.

Bishop Sheen seemed to be misfit for the Rochester assignment. He was a man of ideas, not details; a visionary, not an administrator. Under the banner of supporting subsidiarity, the bishop created numerous diocesan committees, but in reality he rarely used them. And the bishop, singularly gifted as a communicator, failed to communicate that he was closing an inner-city parish and giving its property to HUD (The Federal Department of Housing and Urban Development). The bishop broke the news through *The New York Times* in New York City rather than through the Gannett newspapers in upstate New York. Diocesan officials knew nothing about the decision and were taken completely by surprise. The parishioners learned from the national news agencies that their parish was being closed and its property being given to the federal government. After three years as bishop at Rochester, Sheen resigned.

*For further information, contact*
Archbishop Fulton J. Sheen Communication Room
"The Depot"
17 E. Main Street
El Paso, IL 61738 U.S.A.

## 14. ✠ Catherine de Hueck Doherty

*Place: Toronto and Combermere, Ontario; New York City, New York*
*Fame: "Love. Love. Love. Never count the cost."*
*Foundress of Madonna House lay apostolate and mystic.*

"Fifty years ahead of her time," was how the archbishop of Toronto described Catherine de Hueck Doherty (1896-1985).[1070] Long before Vatican II promulgated its decree on the laity, Catherine had founded the lay apostolic movements of Friendship House at Toronto, and Madonna House at Combermere, Ontario.[1071] The latter movement invited lay people to join a community committed to living the gospel without compromise. Catherine's "Little Mandate" reveals her faith-vision.

CATHERINE DE HUECK
DOHERTY

Arise — go! Sell all you possess . . . give it directly, personally to the poor. Take up their cross (My cross) and follow Me — going to the poor — being poor — being one with them — one with Me. Little — be always little — simple — poor — childlike. Preach the gospel with your life — without compromise. Listen to the Spirit — He will lead you. Do little things exceedingly well for love of Me. Love — love — love, never counting the cost. Go into the marketplace and stay with Me. . . pray . . . fast. . . . pray always. . . . fast. Be hidden. Be a light to your neighbor's feet. Go without fear into the depths of men's hearts. I shall be with you. Pray always. I will be your rest.[1072]

In living with and for the poor, Catherine begged for food, and literally shared her bed with the homeless. She spoke and acted on behalf of the poor. She wrote hundreds of articles and over thirty books. By the time of her death, Catherine's community of laity had grown to more than two hundred members living in twenty-two houses on three continents. This community consisted of lay men and women and priests, all of whom take promises of chastity, poverty and obedience; plus priest-associates who, while continuing to work in their home dioceses, dedicate themselves to the spirit of Madonna House. Catherine describes in the *Constitution* the community of service.

He who touches God, who is in love with God, must touch and be in love with humanity. Not with humanity as a whole, but with each individual in it. But being in love with humanity means serving humanity in every dimension in which man exists. Of course it embraces the spiritual works of mercy, but it should embrace all of life — politics, economics, technology, science, sports, name it — every activity of man, for in each there are directions to be given, goals to be led to, and services to offer. Moreover, if my right hand, symbolically speaking, touches God, and my left hand touches man, then I am cruciform and when I am cruciform I am more united to Christ, which is the reason I was baptized.[1073]

Catherine lived an extraordinarily full life. Catherine Kolyschkine was born in Russia to parents who faithfully attended the Russian

Orthodox liturgies; her father was Russian Orthodox, and her mother, Lutheran. The parents regularly took Catherine with them on visits to the homes of the poor. As a child, Catherine learned what oftentimes she repeated later on, "A love that is not incarnate is not real love."[1074] Catherine grew up respecting and recognizing in all people their God-given dignity. Her father's occupation required extensive travel, resulting in Catherine's spending long periods of her youth in a suburb of Alexandria, Egypt; and at Constantinople, Turkey. At Alexandria, she studied in a school operated by Roman Catholic nuns, and became exposed to the Church's western tradition. As a child, she spoke six languages and understood three more. Her parents raised her with a passionate love for God and God's people, especially the poor, and the Church, which Jesus had founded.

At fifteen, she married her aristocratic cousin Boris de Hueck. The eruption of World War I in 1914, and the Bolshevik Revolution three years later, soon subjected the couple to abject poverty, refugee status, persecution, and near starvation. The couple emigrated to Canada in 1921, when their son was born. Nine years later, Boris and Catherine separated. Eventually, the couple divorced, and had their marriage annulled. She supported herself by successive jobs as laundress, waitress, sales clerk, and public lecturer. "Catherine found herself being pulled in two conflicting directions. She realized she was a single parent with a small child to support. Yet she felt hounded by Christ's words to the rich young man in the Gospel verse: 'Sell what you possess and give to the poor . . . and come, follow me' (Mt 19:21)."[1075]

With the encouragement of Neil McNeil, Bishop of Toronto, Ontario, Catherine pursued her emerging vocation of living the gospel without compromise. She moved into the slums of Toronto in order to know, love and serve the poor. Here, she founded the first Friendship House. Later, other Friendship Houses were established in other Canadian and United States cities throughout the 1930s and 1940s. Though Catherine had been helping the bishop fight against the inroads of Communism, rumors spread inside and outside the Church that Catherine herself was a Communist. With her credibility shattered, Catherine felt forced to leave the city.

In 1938, Catherine moved to 138th Street in Harlem, where she continued her personal call to love. In the U.S.A., she became a forerunner of the civil rights movement, advocating locally and lecturing nationally, for natural civil rights regardless of race. During the Spanish Civil War and World War II, she served in Europe as a journalist for Catholic periodicals. Her writings and social justice activities occasioned much criticism, causing her to feel like "a stranger in a strange land."[1076] Countless clergy and laity criticized her while the bishops generally protected and encouraged her.

In the midst of these tumultuous years, in 1943, Catherine met and married Eddie Doherty, who at that time was America's highest paid journalist. Suffering rejection again, this time from the Friendship House staff in the United States, she and Eddie moved in 1947 to Combermere, Ontario. Broken by all that had happened to her, she suffered heart problems and describes herself as "sick in both heart and mind."[1077] To Combermere, however, traveled a continuous stream of people who desired to live and work with her. From these devotees emerged the Madonna House apostolate.

Catherine's vision of service was rooted in silence. Encountering the Lord in silence compelled her to encounter him in activity also. She sought out the Lord and his image in every person, especially the poor. She describes the experience of silence.

> If we are to witness to Christ in today's marketplaces, where there are constant demands on our whole person, we need silence. If we are always available, not only physically, but by empathy, sympathy, friendship, understanding, and boundless *caritas*, we need silence. To be able to give joyous, unflagging hospitality, not only of house and food, but of mind, heart, body, and soul, we need silence. True silence is the search of man for God. True silence is a suspension bridge that a soul in love with God builds to cross the dark, frightening gullies of its own mind, the strange chasm of temptation, the depthless precipices of its own fears that impede its way to God.[1078]

Ever the idealist and realist, Catherine instructs at the conclusion of her thirty-six page *Constitution* how inevitable differences in community life are to be resolved. "If there is a disagreement about the interpretation of the *Constitution* of these guide lines, let us fast and pray, trusting in the power of the Spirit to teach us God's will if we listen to Him and to one another. Let us search the Scriptures and remember that our spirit is a spirit of freedom, not of rigidity, one of love, not of contention."[1079]

The author of an award-winning popular biography about Catherine makes this observation:

> Catherine believed in God on a personal and profound level. She claims to have heard God's voice leading her into the hearts of people all over the world. Some call her a modern-day saint, and have started a movement for her canonization by the Catholic Church. Others insist she was a charlatan. By some standards, her life was a shining success, and by other standards, a folly, a failure. Yet no one can deny that the story of her life and her constant struggle with joy and sorrow, passion and pain, doubts, loneliness, and rejection are anything less than extraordinary.[1080]

*For further information, contact*
Madonna House Apostolate
2888 Dafoe Road
Combermere ON K0J 1L0 Canada

✢

## 16. ✢ Venerable María Dolores Medina Zepeda

*Place: México City, D.F.; and Toluca, México*
*Fame: Self-taught at home, she earned at thirteen an elementary teacher's license. Foundress of the Hijas de la Pasión de Jesuscristo y de María Dolorosa.*

Founders and foundresses are almost always highly gifted people. Led by faith, they possess both a vision and a practical way of embodying that vision. Natural leaders, they attract people who wish to follow the leader's direction. Flexible and creative administrators, they keep adjusting to ever-arising internal and external challenges to the nascent institution. Mother María Dolores Medina Zepeda (1860-1925) possessed all these gifts.

Born in México City, and baptized Lolita, she was the oldest of three girls and two boys of her father's second marriage. She received her education at home.

When Lolita was twelve, the Lerdo Laws called for the expulsion of foreign clergy, which resulted in the closing of many schools. The adolescent, with the permission of her mother, converted part of her family's home into a school and invited the local schoolchildren to continue their education in religion and the three R's in the Medina home. Beginning at twelve, Lolita studied for a teacher's license. At thirteen, she took the examination and was awarded the license to teach elementary school. As incredible as this achievement at this young age seems, postulators for her cause have investigated and have affirmed this fact. The *Archivo Histórico del Ayuntamiento* authorized her license on November 18, 1873.[1081]

When Lolita's sister took ill in 1884, the family moved from México City to Tacubaya. Three years later, Lolita suffered an immobilization of her spine. "Her family made a novena to the Sacred Heart of Jesus, seeking the good health of their daughter. Immediately the illness dissipated, but later she relapsed, and Lolita always had to work under conditions of poor health."[1082] While sick in bed, Lolita read the biography of St. Paul of the Cross, who had founded the Passionist Fathers in 1725 and whose Passionist Fathers were serving in her local parish, San Diego. She felt attracted to the saint's spirituality. When she recovered from her illness, she founded a local society of the *Hijas de Maria*. Other women soon joined Lolita in this ministry among the *Hijas de Maria*. The women called their group, which Lolita formed on December 12, 1889, the *Hijas de la Pasión de Jesuscristo y de María Dolorosa* (Daughters of the Passion and Death of Jesus, and of the Pain of the Most Holy Mary), who are known popularly as the *Hermanas Pasionistas de México* (the Passionists Sisters of México). The women involved the young *Hijas de Maria* in catechizing young children.

In July 1892, Dolores and two other women began a *Circulo Católico* (Catholic Circle) to teach the Catholic faith to children. Although the three taught together, they lived separately. Each woman was testing the waters for living the religious life of prayer, poverty, and chastity. Also, they did not want by living together to attract the unwanted attention of the political authorities who had outlawed religious orders. The government had closed the religious communities' institutions and had confiscated their properties.

In 1894, Dolores and three companions left their individual homes, and began to live a communal life in the building which housed the Circulo. To all external appearances they were teachers living together at the school where they taught. Inside the house, they followed a life of communal prayer, meditation, and sharing of resources. Soon, five more women joined them. The archbishop saw what was emerging, and asked that this burgeoning community submit to him a *Constitution*, which he soon approved. A Paulist Father, Diego Alberici, assisted the women in composing the *Constitution*; he is regarded as a co-founder of the community. In February 1896, the women adopted a religious habit, and took religious names. Lolita chose Sister Maria Dolores of the Wound from the Side of Christ. She was elected superior general, and was named the directress of novices. The next year, the women professed religious vows for the first time.

In 1897, two difficult situations arose. Paulist Father Diego Alberici was recalled to Rome, Italy, by the Paulist superior general. Subsequently, the sisters missed dearly his wise consul, and kind assistance. And, Mother Dolores' illness flared up again.

For the next ten years, Mother served as superior general. In 1908, the archbishop, who had gotten wind of grumbling within the religious community, suggested that the community conduct another election, but one in which Mother would not be permitted to be a candidate for the superior general. Mother and the sisters complied. Although not elected superior general, she was elected the first consultor. The next year, she was transferred from México City to Toluca, where she opened a *colegio* for young girls. In 1916, like members of many Mexican religious orders, she went to Cuba, where the faith and religion could be practiced freely, unlike in México. At Cuba, she opened three more *colegios* between 1916 and 1919. In 1919, when she was reelected superior general, she left Cuba and returned to México.

Soon into this new term, beginning in 1919, Mother felt called to the difficult task of removing two sisters from the community. One sister had been among the first group of sisters. Unfortunately, this sister "had upset the communal living."[1083] Mother also removed her predecessor, Madre Paz Muñoz-Ledo "whose continual departures from the convent to the city's streets, her lax life, and lack of communal living in the last few years had created a counter-witness."[1084] At the same time, the archbishop required the sisters to work in the diocesan seminary, which further upset many of the sisters. These were difficult years for Madre Dolores.

At the conclusion of the six-year term as superior general, she was reelected at the beginning of 1925. Within months, however, she suffered a relapse of her sickness and became bed-ridden. Madre described her sufferings as "a hell."[1085] By the end of the year, on December 16, she died.

*For further information, contact*
Casa Generalizia
José Gómez de la Corina, 6
Col. San Miguel
Chapultepec 11850 México, D.F. México

⚬

## 24. ✠ Josefa Parra and Coleta Meléndez

*Place: Degollado, Jalisco*
*Fame: Martyrs. Preferred to die rather than suffer rape.*

After six years of armed revolution, México held elections, and in March 1917, elected Venustiano Carranza as president.[1086] Although peace and prosperity began to take shape in México City, general lawlessness continued in the states of Jalisco and Michoacán. And the new federal government seemed helpless to protect the people and to prevent trouble.

In Jalisco, about a hundred miles southeast of Guadalajara, the bandit Inés Chávez García was terrorizing the citizens. On Christmas Eve 1917, he and his group of more than one thousand desperados appeared at daybreak at the gates of Degollado. A terrifying gun battle ensued. Throughout the day, the townsmen held off the thieves. The locals had positioned themselves in the bell tower of the church and at the main entrances to the town. For hours, the fighting went on. It is reported that García lost approximately two hundred men, which losses enraged the barbarous bandit. By noon, the tide of the fighting began shifting;

the townsmen could not hold out much longer. They had hoped for support from federal troops, but these troops had marched towards Degollado, yet set up camp about five miles away, where they were preparing a dinner for themselves. About six o'clock in the evening, Inés Chávez García's men overran the last bastion of the defenders of the city. The final few protectors were shot in the town's central plaza.

What followed on that memorable night is indescribable: Chávez García, like the Barbarians of whom history recounts great horrors, allowed his men license to satisfy their worst instincts of blood and sensuality at the cost of the local people and their families. García's troops assassinated without pity the men of the village, burned homes and businesses, and made sport of countless young people. In the middle of this orgy, some of García's gunmen chased Josefa [Parra] and Coleta [Meléndez]. The girls knew what was awaiting them at the hands of these savage men. Remembering the great love with which they had promised to protect their purity, they resolved in a heroic act that they would suffer death rather than suffer rape. Passing a butcher shop which was ablaze, in a dash, they escaped from the men, and ran into the fire-engulfed building. The flames soon consumed the bodies of these two innocent young women.[1087]

Josefa Parra (1892-1917) had been born on the ranch El Sabinito in the area of La Piedad, in the state of Michoacán. She was baptized three days later, and was confirmed two months before her first birthday. When her parents purchased land near Degollado, in Jalisco, the family moved there. At eight, Josefa started school. Because her mother died when Josefa was in sixth grade, the young girl had to leave school in order to take care of the home, her father, and her siblings. Her teacher reports that Josefa was a conscientious student, and, among other virtues, practiced an exemplary degree of modesty. Because Josefa's father enjoyed a certain financial success, the family members dressed "elegantly," in current fashions, and in good style.[1088] Josefa, at the same time, always dressed modestly.

Josefa practiced devotions to the Passion of Our Lord and to the Eucharist. One of her classmates reports that Josefa used to read the Passion daily, and, on at least one occasion, while reading the Passion quietly by a brook, broke into tears during her reflection on the Lord's suffering, dying, and rising for sinners. Josefa often attended daily Mass, and received Communion. Her periods of prayerful thanksgiving after Mass were very edifying. On one occasion, she appeared to be in deep ecstasy after receiving Communion. At fourteen, she became a member of the *Hijas de María* and faithfully followed the religious obligations of the society.

Coleta Meléndez (1897-1917) had been born at Tierras Blancas, in the state of Guanajuato. The very poor family moved to the ranch El Refugio, about ten miles outside of Degollado, Jalisco. Coleta's father found work on the ranch owned by Josefa's father. The two girls developed a great friendship, and often passed their days in each other's homes. Josefa, five years older than Coleta, instructed the younger friend in the Catholic faith and religion. In her home, Josefa prepared Coleta for her First Communion. The two frequently traveled to Degollado for daily Mass and would pray the rosary along the way. When Coleta came of the proper age, she too joined the *Hijas de Maria*.

Observers have reported that Josefa led the way of escaping from the girls' attackers and similarly led the way into the burning building. Josefa and Coleta are referred to respectfully as *"Las Quemaditas"* (the burned ones).

*For further information, contact*
Causa de Canonización de Las Quemaditas
Padre J. Jesus Vasquez Ruiz
Apartado Postal #20
Defensores 20
Degollado, Jalisco, México

## 30. ✛ Maria de la Luz Camacho González

*Place: Coyoacán, México City, D.F.*
*Fame: Lay catechist. Shot dead while defending the church
and the children inside when the Communist Red Shirts
came to burn down the church.*

"*Viva* the first martyr of Catholic Action," exclaimed the archbishop of México at the funeral Mass for Maria de la Luz Camacho González (1907-34).[1089] Immediately, the congregation began chanting: "*Viva* the first martyr of Catholic Action."[1090] Thirty thousand people, in defiance of the anti-Catholic government, gathered to honor Maria. The crowd lined the streets from her home in the Coyoacán section of México City, filled the church and its plaza to overflowing, and accompanied her corpse to the local cemetery. She had been killed at the front doors of her parish church by gunshots fired by a mob of forty or more fourteen to eighteen-year-old members of the Camisas Rojas.

On the day before the funeral, around nine o'clock in the morning on December 30, at the same time that a Children's Mass was being celebrated inside the Church of San Juan Bautista, word spread that the Camisas Rojas were amassing in the park across from the church, and that they intended to burn down the church. This was no idle threat. The Camisas Rojas had been founded by Tómas Garrido Canabal, the former governor of Tabasco, who had burned down all but two of the churches in the state of Tabasco. This group had assassinated priests, inflamed the youth, and prohibited the singing of hymns. In one of the churches he burned, two nuns died in the fire. Notoriously known as "the Scourge of Tabasco," Canabal was a ruthless lackey, whom President Cardenas just thirty days before had appointed Secretary of Agriculture.

Someone rushed to Maria's home with the news about the gathering of the Camisas Rojas. Maria, taking along her younger sister, ran to the church. The twenty-seven-year-old catechist positioned herself on the steps of the church, invited other faithful Catholics nearby to join her, and indicated to the opposing Camisas Rojas that she intended to prohibit, over her dead body, the enemies of Christ from destroying Christ's church. The mob taunted her: threatening to kill the priests and to raze the church. [1091] To the Camisas Rojas's curses and threats, she replied, "We have no fear. We are ready to die for Christ, and we would be happy to do that."[1092] One of the Camisas Rojas approached Maria. As one of her former students, he begged her, "Miss Camacho, please go to safety."[1093] She refused to budge, and instead urged him to leave. She was going to do her best to protect the church building and the children inside it from these malefactors.

The mob started shouting, "Damned be Christ the King. Damned be the Virgin of Guadalupe."[1094] Maria shouted back, "*¡Viva Cristo Rey! ¡Viva Santa Maria de Guadalupe!*"[1095] A pregnant pause emerged. A verbal signal was given: "*¡Viva la revolución!*"[1096] With that, shots rang out. The Camisas opened fire against the unarmed defenders of the Church. Maria was shot in the chest. As she died, she was heard to have whispered, "*¡Viva Cristo ...*"[1097]

> "*¡Viva Cristo...*" A final triumphant declaration of faith in the One King, and the young woman fell. The red blood spilled over her green dress with its white collar; red, white, green ... the colors of México. The colors reminded observers of the reason that the stalwart defenders stood in front of the parish church. God was not dead, and the sturdy Mexican Catholics would defend their beliefs, even at the risk of death.[1098]

At least six persons were killed: Maria and four defenders of the church, and one of the Camisas Rojas, whom a crowd of Catholics captured and lynched.

Maria had grown up with her family in México City. As her parents' first child, at seven months Maria suffered the death of her mother. Her father remarried within two years, and her step mother died nine years later. After four years without a mother for his children, the father married, in 1922, the children's aunt, i.e., their birth-mother's sister. Between the marriages, Maria and her two brothers and two sisters were raised by both their maternal grandmother and this aunt-stepmother. For her education, Maria attended a boarding school in Puebla and two local schools in the Federal District. She finished her formal education at fourteen.

At fifteen, while continuing to perform her domestic chores, Maria dedicated herself to an apostolic life. She began catechizing children, and eventually she conducted the classes in her own home; each Saturday she would bring into her home eighty children for religious instruction. She started a library of doctrinal and apologetic books, so that Catholics might be more able to explain and defend their faith. Blessed with a gift for acting, she wrote and directed short plays as a means to instruct children and adults about their faith. She possessed a number of talents: a beautiful singing voice and skills in embroidery, painting, and playing the violin. Because she avoided participating in her peers' preoccupation of talking about boys, she suffered at times calumny and isolation; she knew, however, that God was calling her to a vocation other than the married state. Maria's peers elected her to the diocesan Central Catechetical Committee, which bore and fulfilled the responsibility of providing religious instruction to the city's thirty thousand children.[1099] The catechetical ministry of Maria and hundreds of people like her was essential to the promotion of the faith because the government had shut down religious schools. After the closure, the city's children received their religious instruction in private homes.

In January 1930, immediately after Pope Pius XI called for the creation of Catholic Action groups to be founded to confront the rising tide of atheistic secularism, the Archbishop of México City initiated Catholic Action and its youth arm, the *Associación Católica Juventud Mexicana*. Right away, Maria joined Catholic Action. Around this same time, she pondered entering religious life. She wrote to her father, explaining that she wanted to give her entire life to God, but she did not want to burden him with the cost of the traditional dowry when a young woman entered the convent. She suggested that she would work, and earn money to provide her own dowry. Two years later, in 1932, she joined the Third Order Franciscans. She dedicated her days to prayer and service, especially to the catechizing of young children. In 1934, her life ended abruptly on the steps of her parish church.

*For further information, contact*
Arquidiócesis Primada de México
Curia: Durango #90
Col. Roma - Apartado Postal #24-433
06700 México, D.F. México

# ENDNOTES

❧

[1] The author thanks Sister Betty Ann McNeil, D.C., archivist, for providing information and reviewing the draft of this biography.

[2] Betty Ann McNeil, D.C., *Fifteen Days Of Prayer With Saint Elizabeth Ann Seton* (Liguori, MO: Liguori Press, 2002), p. 24.

[3] McNeil, p. 38.

[4] McNeil, p. 27.

[5] Annabelle M. Melville, *Elizabeth Bayley Seton*, 1774-1821. (New York, N.Y.: Charles Scribner's Sons, 1951), p. 31.

[6] Private correspondence with Sister Betty Ann McNeil, D.C.

[7] McNeil, p. 17.

[8] McNeil, p. 22.

[9] McNeil, p. 38.

[10] Melville, p. 87.

[11] McNeil, pp. 37-38.

[12] McNeil, p. 38.

[13] Melville, p. 95.

[14] In 1808, Carroll was raised to archbishop, when the diocese of Baltimore was elevated to the status of archdiocese.

[15] McNeil, p. 3.

[16] McNeil, p. 9.

[17] McNeil, p. 26.

[18] The author thanks Father Michael Hopkins, C.Ss.R, assistant pastor St. Peter the Apostle Church, and Mary Argenbright, office manager of the National Shrine of St. John Neumann, for providing information and reviewing the draft of this biography.

[19] Journal, p. 124

[20] Private correspondence with Father Michael Hopkins, C.Ss.R.

[21] Michael J. Curley, *Bishop John Neumann, C.Ss.R. A Biography*. (Philadelphia, PA: Bishop Neumann Center, 1952), p. 399.

[22] *John Neumann, C.SS.R., The Immigrant Shepherd*, p. 20.

[23] Private correspondence with Father Michael Hopkins, C.Ss.R.

[24] The author thanks Father Robert Choquette, C.S.C., vice postulator, for providing information and reviewing the draft of this biography.

[25] www.ewtn.com/library/Mary/Bessette.htm; p. 1.

[26] Jean-Guy Dubuc, *Brother André*. Tr. by Robert Prud'homme. (L'Eclaireru, Beauceville: Editions Fides, 1999), p. 96.

[27] www.ewtn, ibid)

[28] Bernard LaFreniere, *Brother André According to Witnesses.* (Montréal, QC: St. Joseph's Oratory, 1990), p. 60.

[29] Dubuc, p. 95.

[30] N.B. Oil was used as an instrument in curing the sick, in Mt 6:15 and Js 5:14.

[31] Dubuc, p. 114.

[32] Dubuc, p. 127.

[33] Dubuc, p. 53.

[34] Dubuc, p. 57.

[35] Dubuc, p. 30.

[36] Dubuc, p. 33.

[37] Dubuc, p. 41.

[38] LaFreniere, p. 44.

[39] Dubuc, p. 52.

[40] Dubuc, p. 54.

[41] Henri-Paul Bergeron, C.S.C., *Brother Andre: The Wonder Man Of Mount Royal.* Tr. by Real Boudreau, C.S.C. Tenth Printing. (Montréal, QC: St. Joseph's Oratory, 1988), p. 164.

[42] Bergeron, p. 165.

[43] Bergeron, p. 165.

[44] The author thanks Father Roberto Saldivar, M.Sp.S., and Father Juan José González, M.Sp.S, for providing information and reviewing the draft of this biography.

[45] Pamphlet: "Quien Es Félix de Jesús Rougier?," p. 1.

[46] Levy, p. 23.

[47] www.zenit.org/english/archive/0007/ZE00072.html; p. 3.

[48] Levy, p. 120.

[49] Levy p. 124.

[50] The author thanks Sister Patricia Simpson, C.N.D., author, for providing information and reviewing the draft of this biography.

[51] Simone Poissant, C.N.D., *Marguerite Bouregouys, 1620-1700.* Tr. by Frances Kirwan. (Canada: Bellarmin, 1993), p. 19.

[52] Poissant, p. 27.

[53] Poissant, p. 29.

[54] Private correspondence with Sister Patricia Simpson, C.N.D.

[55] Simpson, p. 6.

[56] Poissant, p. 69.

[57] The author thanks Judy Ballant, archivist, for providing information and reviewing the draft of this biography, and Elizabeth Delene, of the Bishop Baraga Association, for her assistance with information on Frederic Baraga.

[58] *The Snowshoe Priest.* (Duluth, MN: Lake Superior Port Cities Magazine, 1984), p. 1.

[59] John W. McGee, *The Catholic Church In The Grand River Valley, 1833-1950.* (Lansing, MI: Franklin Dekleine Company, 1950), pp. 66-67.

[60] No author, brochure: "Welcome to Lansing, Bishop Baraga Days, 53rd Annual Celebration, The Snowshoe Priest, Frederic Baraga 1797-1868," p 4.

[61] The author thanks Mother Mary Suzanne, O. Carm., superior general, and Sister Maria Agnes, O. Carm., prioress, for providing information and reviewing the draft of this biography.

[62] Jude Mead, C.P., *The Servant of God Mother M. Angeline Teresa, O. Carm. (1893-11984), Daughter of Carmel, Mother to the Aged. A Critical/Historical Biography.* (Petersham, MA: St. Bede's Publication, 1990), p. 5.

[63] Loretta Pastva, S.N.D., ed., *The Carmelite Sisters for the Aged and Infirm. Mother Mary Angeline Teresa McCrory, O. Carm., Servant of God, Foundress.* (Torino, Italy: Éditions du Signe, 2000), p. 5.

[64] Mother M. Bernadette de Lourdes, *Woman of Faith, Foundress, Mother M. Angeline Teresa, O. Carm.*, (U.S.A.: Carmelite Sisters for the Aged and Infirm, 1984), p. 24.

[65] Mead, p. 22.

[66] Ann Ball, *Faces Of Holiness. Modern Saints In Photos And Words.* (Huntington, IN: Our Sunday Visitor, Inc., 1998), p. 25.

[67] Ball, p. 26.

[68] Lourdes, p. 467.

[69] Miguel Angel Villa Roiz and Carlos Villa Roiz, *De América Al Cielo.* (1999), p. 211.

[70] Roiz, p. 213.

[71] The author thanks Sister Virginie Fish, O.S.P., vice postulator, and Sister Madeline Swaboski, IHM, for providing information and reviewing the draft of this biography.

[72] Maria M. Lannon, *Response to Love. The Story of Mother Mary Elizabeth Lange, O.S.P.* (Washington, D.C.: Josephite Pastoral Center, 1992), pp. 20-21.

[73] Lannon, p. 12.

[74] Lannon, p. 12.

[75] Lannon, p. 7.

[76] Lannon, p. 3.

[77] Lannon, p. 11.

[78] The author thanks Sister Pauline Longtin, M.I.C., vice postulator, for providing information and reviewing the draft of this biography.

[79] *Forerunner in the Church. Délia Tétreault. Foundress of the Institute of the Missionary Sisters of the Immaculate Conception (1865-1941).* (Laval, QC.: Bureau de la Cause Délia Tétreault, n.d.), p. 4.

[80] *Forerunner*, p. 27.

[81] Fernand Ouelette, ed., *L'Experiénce De Dieu Avec Délia Tétreault.* (Québec City, QC: Fides, 2000), p. 23.

[82] Ouellette, p. 21.

[83] Ouellette, p. 25.

[84] Ouelette, p. 28.

[85] Ouellette, p. 29.

[86] Ouelette, pp. 30-31.

[87] Ouellette, p. 33.

[88] *A l'avant-garde dans l'Église. Délia Tétreault, fondatrice d'Institut des Soeurs Missionaires d'Immaculée Conception, 1865-1941.* (Laval, QC: Bureau de la Cause Délia Tétreault, n.d.), pp. 30-31.

[89] Ouellette, pp. 85-86.

[90] M. A. Habig, *Saints of the Americas.* (Chicago, IL: Franciscan Herald Press, 1982), p. 126.

[91] Roiz, p. 86.

[92] Roiz, p. 86.

[93] Habig, p. 128.

[94] Habig, p. 128.

[95] Herbert Thurston and Donald Attwater, *Butler's Lives of the Saints*. Vol. I, p.259.

[96] *Butler's*, I, p. 259.

[97] *Butler's*, I, p. 260.

[98] The author thanks Father Russell Smith, postulator, for providing information and reviewing the draft of this biography.

[99] (www.richmonddiocese.org/parater/seminarian.htm; "The Servant of God, p. 1.

[100] Ibid.

[101] www.richmonddiocese.org/parater/seminarian.htm; "The Servant of God, p. 2.

[102] www.richmonddiocese.org/parater/civilwar.htm; p. 2.

[103] www.richmonddiocese.org/parater/civilwar.htm; p. 3.

[104] The author thanks Father Russell Smith, postulator, for providing information and reviewing the draft of this biography.

[105] "The Spanish Jesuit Mission to Virginia," p. 5.

[106] "The Spanish Jesuit Mission," p. 5.

[107] Albert J. Nevins, M.M., "The Colony That Failed," in *Our American Catholic Heritage*. (Huntington, IN: Our Sunday Visitor, 1972). p. 55.

[108] Albert J. Nevins, M.M., *American Martyrs From 1542*. (Huntington, IN: Our Sunday Visitor, 1987), p. 31.

[109] Nevins, *American Martyrs*, p. 31.

[110] The Spanish Jesuit Mission, p. 5.

[111] The Spanish Jesuit Mission, p. 5.

[112] The Spanish Jesuit Mission, p. 2.

[113] The Spanish Jesuit Mission, p. 4.

[114] The author thanks Ann Ball, author, for providing information and reviewing the draft of this biography.

[115] Guillermo Ma. Havers, *Testigos de Cristo en México*. (Guadalajara, Jal: 1986), Ediciones Promesa, p. 193).

[116] Havers, *Testigos de Cristoen México*, p. 193.

[117] Havers, *Testigos de Cristoen México*, pp. 193-94.

[118] Havers, *Testigos de Cristoen México*, p. 194.

[119] The author thanks Sister Mary Jeanne, O.C.D. for providing information and reviewing the draft of this biography.

[120] Helenita Colbert, *To Love Me In Truth. Mother Maria Luisa Josefa of the Blessed Sacrament, Servnt of God, 1866-1937*. (Los Angeles, CA: Carmelite Sisters of the Most Sacred Heart of Los Angeles, 1987), p. 14.

[121] Colbert, p. 14.

[122] Colbert, p. 16.

[123] Private correspondence with Sr. Jeanne, O.C.D.

[124] Colbert, p. 19.

[125] Colbert, pp. 20-21.

[126] Colbert, p. 140.

[127] *Mother Maria Luisa Josefa of the Blessed Sacrament (Mother Luisita), In Love's Safekeeping*. Tr. by Basil Frison, C.M.F., and Sister Maria de la Paz Ayon. (Los Angeles, CA: Carmelite Sisters of the Most Sacred Heart of Los Angeles, 1999), pp. 948-49.

[128] The author thanks Father James Wolf, O.F.M. Cap., archivist, for providing information and reviewing the draft of this biography.

[129] The Messenger of the Province of St. Joseph, Vol. 1, No. 5, March 1923, p. 31.

[130] Nerius of Hallgarten, O.F.M. Cap., *Articles of Testimonial Proof.* (Milwaukee, WI: Sentinel Bindery and Printing Co., 1951), p. 4, para. # 22.

[131] Nerius of Hallgarten, p. 5, para. # 35.

[132] Joseph N. Tylenda, "Eckert, John (Stephen) (1869-1923)." In *The Encyclopedia of American Catholic History.* (Collegeville, MN: A Michael Glazier Book, 1997), p. 475.

[133] Glazier, p. 475.

[134] Nerius of Hallgarten, p. 12, para. # 93-94)

[135] Nerius of Hallgarten, p. 32, para. #235.

[136] Nerius of Hallgarten, p. 32, para. #238.

[137] Messenger, p. 21.

[138] Tylenda, p. 476.

[139] Havers, *en México*, p. 227.

[140] Havers, *Testigos de Cristo en Jalisco.* (Guadalajara, Jal.: Ediciones Promesas, S. A.; 1988), p. 3.

[141] Havers, *Testigos de Cristo en Jalisco,* pp. 3-4.

[142] Havers, *Testigos de Cristo en Jalisco,* p. 6.

[143] Roiz, pp. 264-65.

[144] Pierre Dufresne, web site, Perre-Joseph-Marie-Chaumonot, Diocese of Edmunston, p. 2.

[145] The author thanks Gilles Drolet, promoter, for providing information and reviewing the draft of this biography.

[146] Gilles Drolet, *Un Missionaire Au Coeur Marial. Le Père Pierre-Joseph-Marie Chaumonot, Jésuite, 1611-1693.* (Sillery, QC: Collection: Aux sources mariales de;' Eglise canadienne; 1993), p. 15.

[147] Joseph N. Tylenda, *Jesuit Saints And Martyrs.* (Chicago, IL: Loyola Press, 1998), pp. 55-56.

[148] Tylenda, *Jesuit Saints and Martyrs*, p. 53.

[149] Dufresne, p. 2.

[150] The author thanks Frere Real Provost, O.F.M., for providing information and reviewing the draft of this biography.

[151] www.stjohnsarchdiocese.nf.ca/monitor/didace.html; p. 2.

[152] Ibid, p. 1.

[153] www.diocese-edmundston.ca/les-saints-chez-nous/frere.didace.pelletier.htm; p. 2.

[154] www.diocese-edmundston.ca/les-saints-chez-nous/frere.didace.pelletier.htm; p. 2.

[155] Mary Nona McGreal, O.P., "Wherever God Calls, Father Samuel Mazzuchelli, O.P. (1800-1864)," in Tylenda, *Portraits*, p. 157.

[156] The author thanks Sister Mary Nona McGreal, O.P., author of the candidate's *positio*, for providing information and reviewing the draft of this biography.

[157] www.sinsinawa.org/About US/History/Mazzuchelli/Mazzuchelli.html; p. 1.

[158] McGreal, p. 158.

[159] Samuel Mazzuchelli, The *Memoirie of Father Samuel Mazzuchelli, O.P.* (Chicago, IL: The Priory Press, 1967), p. 8-9.

[160] James Bernard Walker, O.P., "Mazzuchelli, Samuel," in *New Catholic Encyclopedia*, vol. 9, p. 525.

[161] McGreal, p. 160.

[162] Habig, *Saints Of The Americas*, p. 148.

[163] Habig, p. 149.

[164] The author thanks Bishop Felipe Estevez, S.T.D., for providing information and reviewing the draft of this biography.

[165] John Egan, *Catholic New York*. June 2003. Vol. XXII, No. 9; p. 5.

[166] Egan, p. 5.

[167] Egan, pp. 5, 38.

[168] www.fiu.edu/ñfef/varela93097.html; p. 1.

[169] www.pfvarela.org/Espanol/Sintesis.htm; p. 2.

[170] The author thanks Sister Marie De L'Euchariste, M.S. Gen., for providing information and reviewing the draft of this biography.

[171] Madeleine Guertin, S.J.M., "Alexis-Louis Mangin, Cofondateur des Servantes de Jésus-Marie. (Diocese of Edmundston web site), p. 2.

[172] Raymond Maric, *Alexis-Louis Mangin, Marie-Zita De Jesus. Fondateur et Fondatrice de la Congrégation des Servantes de Jésus-Marie*. (Turin, Italy: Sadifa Media, 1986), p. 29.

[173] *Constitutions.*, p. XV.

[174] Maric, p. X.

[175] Maric, p. IX.

[176] The author thanks Brother Robert Taylor, O.S.A, for providing information and reviewing the draft of this biography.

[177] Marion A. Habig, *Saints of the Americas*. (Huntington, IN: Our Sunday Visitor, 1974), p. 176.

[178] Habig, *Saints of the Americas*, p. 178.

[179] Habig, *Saints of the Americas*, p.178.

[180] Habig, *Saints of the Americas*, p.178.

[181] Arnulf Charles Hartmann, O.S.A, "Gutiérrez Rodríguez, Bartolomé, Bl." in *New Catholic Encyclopedia*, vol. 6. p. 868.

[182] The author thanks Stephanie Morris, director of archives, and Sister Maria E. McCall, S.B.S., assistant director of archives, for providing information and reviewing the draft of this biography.

[183] Boniface Hanley, O.F.M., *A Philadelphia Story*. [Mother Katharine Drexel] (Paterson, N.J.: The Anthonian, 1984), p. 15.

[184] Katharine Drexel, S.B.S., *Reflections on Religious Life, found in the writings of Mother M. Katherine Drexel*. (Philadelphia, PA: Mother Mary Katharine Drexel Guild, 1983), p. 3.

[185] Lou Baldwin, *A Call to Sanctity. The Formation and Life of Mother Katharine Drexel*. (Philadelphia, PA: The Catholic Standard and Times, 1988), p. 24.

[186] Baldwin, p. 33.

[187] Baldwin, p. 33.

[188] Baldwin, p. 34.

[189] Baldwin, Call, pp. 37-38.

[190] Katharine Drexel, S.B.S., *Reflections on Life in the Vine, found in the writings of Mother M. Katherine Drexel*. (Philadelphia, PA: Mother Mary Katharine Drexel Guild, 1983), p. 20.

[191] Drexel, *Life in the Vine*, p. 16.

[192] The author thanks Father Roberto Saldivar, M.Sp.S., and Sister M. Elizabeth Sadowska, R.C.S.C.J., superior, for providing information and reviewing the draft of this biography.

[193] Marie-Michel Philipon, *Conchita: A Modern Mystic*. Tr. by Susan Hall. Revised by María Luisa Icaza de Medina Mora. (Coyoacán, MX: Editorial Cimiento, A.C., n.d.), p. 25.

[194] Philipon, p. 20.

[195] Philipon, p. 20.

[196] Philipon, p. 21.

[197] Philipon, p. 23.

[198] Philipon. p. 19.

[199] Philipon, p. 13.

[200] Phil,ipon, p. 17.

[201] Philipon, p. 18.

[202] Concepción Cabrera de Armida, *I Am. Eucharistic Meditations on the Gospel*. (Staten Island, N.Y.: Alba House, 2001), pp. 96-98.

[203] The author thanks Roger Quesnel, promoter, for providing information and reviewing the draft of this biography.

[204] Private correspondence with Roger Quesnel.

[205] Private correspondence with Roger Quesnel: Georges-Philias Vanier's Inaugural Address, p. 3.

[206] Fintan Benedict Warren, O.F.M., "Quiroga, Vasco De," in *New Catholic Encyclopedia*, vol.12, p. 32.

[207] Jim Tuck, www.mexconnect.com/mex_/history/jtuck/jtvascoquiroga.html; p. 3.

[208] Warren, p. 32.

[209] Father Eusebio Francisco Kino at www.desertusa.com/mag98/april/papr/du_kino.html; p. 1.

The author thanks Father Charles Polzner, S.J., for providing information and for reviewing the draft of this biography.

[210] "Father Eusebio Francisco Kino: Missionary and Explorer," at www.padrekino.org/documentienglish/uksonoraadesert.htm; p. 2.

[211] Eusebino Kino. *Kino's Historical Memoir of Pimería Alta, a Contemporary Account of the Beginning Of California, Sonora, and Arizona*. Tr. and ed. by Herbert Eugene Bolton. (Berkeley, CA: University of California Press, 1948), vol. 1, pp. 288-89.

[212] The author thanks Roger Quesnel, promoter, for providing information and reviewing the draft of this biography.

[213] Women of Faith, Pauline Vanier; www.k12connect.ca/-splamondon1/PaulineVanier.html, p. 1.

[214] Émile-Marie Brière, *Under Mary's Mantle. Our Lady's Love For Canada*. (Combermere, ON: Madonna House Publications, 2000), p. 181.

[215] www.k12connect.ca-splamondon1/PaulineVanier.html, p. 2.

[216] Private correspondence with Roger Quesnel.

[217] www.k12connect.ca/splamondon1/PaulineVanier.html, p. 3.

[218] www.k12connect.ca/-splamondon1/PaulineVanier.html, p. 2.

[219] www.silk.net.RetEd/ezineromero, p. 1.

[220] Placido Erdozain, *Archbishop Romero, Martyr of Salvador*, tr. by John McFadden and Ruth Warner. (Maryknoll, N.Y.: Orbis Books, 1981), p. 76.

[221] www.salt.claretianspubs.org/romero/romero.html; p. 2.

[222] www.salt.claretianpubs.org/romero/intro.html; p. 2.

[223] www.salt.claretianpubs.org/romero/romero.html; p. 2.

[224] www.salt.claretianpubs.org/romero/romero.html; p. 1.

[225] Erdozain, pp. 77-78.

[226] Erdozain, pp. 75-76.

[227] www.icomm.ca/carecen/page41.html; p. 2.

[228] www.salt.claretianpubs.org/romero/romero.html; p. 1.

[229] James R. Brockman, complier and translator, *The Church Is All of You. Thoughts of Archbishop Oscar Romero.* (Minneapolis, MN: Winston Press, 1984), p. 94.

[230] Miguel Angel Villa Roiz and Carlos Villa Roiz, *De América Al Cielo. Santos, Beatos, Mártires, y Siervos de Dios Hacia el tercer milenio.* (México City, MX: 2000), p. 247.

[231] Arquidiócesis de Guadalajara, *Anacleto Gonzalez Flores Y Compañeros,* (Guadalajara, Jal: Comisión Diocesana de Causas de Canonización, 2001), p. 18.

[232] Villa Roiz and Villa Roiz, p. 245.

[233] Villa Roiz and Villa Roiz, 246.

[234] Villa Roiz and Villa Roiz, 246.

[235] Guillermo María Havers, *Testigos de Cristo en Jalisco.* (Guadalajara, Jal: Ediciones Promesas, S.A., 1988), pp. 120-21.

[236] The author thanks Sister Guadalupe Mondregan, H.J., religious superior, for providing information and reviewing the draft of this biography.

[237] No author, *Santoral De La Familia Vicentina.* (México D.F., MX: Ediciones Familia Vicentina, ca. 2000), pp. 230-31.

[238] *Santoral,* pp. 221-22.

[239] Gerardo Sánchez Sánchez, coordinator, and George Herbert Foulkes, editor, *Fase Romana En Los Procesos De Canonización,* (Ciudad de México, MX: Comision para las causas de los Santos Arquidiócesis de México, 2000), p. 75.

[240] Sister Paul-Émilie Guay, S.C.O. , *A Pioneer in Bilingual Education,* (Ottawa, ON: Centre for the Cause of beatification of Mother Elisabeth Bruyère, 1998), p. 2.

[241] The author thanks Sister Gabrielle Laramée, S.C.O., member of the Centre Cause d'Elisabeth Bruyère, for providing information and reviewing the draft of this biography.

[242] Jean-Charles Taché, "Foyer Domestique," in *Domestique,* 1876, p. 133.

[243] Émilien Lamirande, *Élisabeth Bruyère (1818-1876), Foundress of the Sisters of Charity of Ottawa* (Grey Nuns of the Cross). Tr. by Sister Gabrielle L. Jean. (Ottawa, ON: Sisters of Charity of Ottawa, 1995), p. 48.

[244] Angelo Mitri, *Brief Statement on the Life and Cause of Beatification of the Servant of God, Mother Elisabeth Bruyère, Foundress of the Sisters of Charity of Ottawa, (1818-1876).* (Private publication, 2001), p. 5.

[245] Mitri, p. 5.

[246] Bibiane Lavictoire, S.C.O., *Mother Elisabeth Bruyère, Recommendations to the Sisters, August 22, 1872* (Private publication, 2000); pp. 7-8.

[247] Lavictoire, S.C.O.,p. 14.

[248] Gabrielle Laramée, *Mother Bruyère, Daughter of the Church,* tr. by Yvonne Laperle, (Canada: Notre-Dame, Inc.; n.d.), p. 10.

[249] Mitri, p. 12.

[250] Mitri, p. 12.

[251] Mitri, p. 13.

[252] The author thanks Sister Gisèle Boucher, S.M., postulator of the Cause of Rosalie-Cadron-Jetté, for providing information and reviewing the draft of this biography.

[253] Yvon Langlois, *A Lantern In The Night: Rosalie, Midwife.* Tr. by Irene Morisette, C.N.D. (Montréal, QC: Arrimage Gestion Impression, Inc.;1996), p. 23.

[254] Langlois, p. 20.

[255] Langlois, p. 25.

[256] Langlois, p. 26.

[257] Langlois, p. 43.

[258] Langlois, p. 29.

[259] Gisèle Boucher, "Rosalie Cadron-Jetté, Une page de l'Evangile de la vie," p. 2. (Internet, Edmundston Diocese, Saints, Rosalie Cadron-Jetté), p. 2.

[260] Boucher, p. 2.

[261] Langlois, p. 50.

[262] Boucher, p. 2.

[263] Langlois, p. 48.

[264] Langlois p. 72.

[265] Langlois, p. 53.

[266] During the 1840's, Sister Marcelle had witnessed other Sisters of Charity of Montréal, who volunteered to leave the motherhouse to begin new foundations at Saint-Hyacinthe, Rivière-Rouge (now Saint-Boniface, Manitoba), and Bytown (now Ottawa).

The author thanks Sister Viola Greene, S.C.Q., Directress of Mother Mallet Centre at www.centremarcellemallet.com, for providing information and for reviewing the draft of this biography.

[267] André-Marie Cimichella, *Good Mother Marcelle Mallet, Foundress of The Sisters of Charity of Québec,* tr. by Marguerite B. Lyons. (Québec, QC: L'Imprimerie Vitray Inc., 1986), p. 28.

[268] Ibid., pp. 29-30.

[269] Ibid., p. 45.

[270] Ibid., p. 30.

[271] Ibid., p. 60.

[272] Ibid., p. 20.

[273] www.centremarcellemallet.com/biography.html; p. 2.

[274] www.centremarcellemallet.com/biography.html; p. 2.

[275] Brière, p. 104.

[276] The author thanks Father Kevin Kenny, O.F.M. Conv., director National Shrine of Blessed Kateri Tekakwitha, for providing information and reviewing the draft of this biography.

[277] Thomas J. Coffey, *Kateri Tekakwitha, America's Marvelous Maiden.* Rev. ed. (Gloversville, N.Y.: The Leader-Herald, 1994), p. 14.

[278] No author, *Positio of the Servant of God, Katharine Tekakwitha, The Lily of the Mohawks.* (New York, N.Y.: Fordham University Press, 1940), p. 78)

[279] No author, *Positio of the Servant of God, Katharine Tekakwitha, The Lily of the Mohawks,* p. 69.

[280] Coffey, p. 25.

[281] *Butler's Lives Of The Saints*, ed. by Herbert J. Thurston, S.J. and Donald Attwater, four volumes. (Westminster, MD: Christian Classics, 1990), vol. IV, p. 157.

[282] Coffey, p. 27.

[283] Coffey, pp. 28-29.

[284] Coffey, p. 29.

[285] The author thanks Sister Margaret Petcavage, S.S.C., for providing information and reviewing the draft of this biography.

[286] Margaret Petcavage, S.S.C., monograph: "Was She a Smuggler?" p. 1.

[287] Petcavage, brochure: "Mother Maria Kaupas," p. 2

[288] Maria Kaupas, ed by Mary Cabrini Durkin, O.S.U., *Loving You, Mother Maria. Walking in the Spirit of Mother Maria Kaupas*. (Strasbourg, France: Éditions du Signe, 1999), p. 35.

[289] Kaupas, p. 33

[290] Kaupas, p. 25.

[291] The author thanks Sister Jeannine Serres, S.S.A., director of Centre Mère Marie-Anne-Blondin, for providing information and reviewing the draft of this biography.

[292] Vincent J. O'Malley, C.M., *Ordinary Sufferings of Extraordinary Saints*. (Huntington, IN: Our Sunday Visitor, 2000), pp. 130-39.

[293] Endnote: In 1884, when the Vatican gave formal recognition to the community of the Sisters of St. Anne, Roman officials repeated the same error as to the place of origin. The error was corrected in 1903, long after Mother had died.

[294] Ephesians 4:25.

[295] Christine Mailloux, S.S.A., *Esther Blondin, Prophet for Today*. Tr. by Eileen Gallagher, S.S.A. (Montréal, QC: Éditions Paulines, 1989), p. 61.

[296] Mailloux, pp. 25-26.

[297] André-M. Cimichella, O.S.M., *Mother Marie Anne Blondin, Woman of Hope*. Second edition. (Lachine, QC: The Sisters of Saint Anne, 2000), p. 34.

[298] Mailloux, p. 32.

[299] Cimichella, p. 67.

[300] Cimichella, p. 38.

[301] Cimichella, p. 40.

[302] The author thanks Sister Helena Mayer, S.H.C.J., archivist, for providing information and reviewing the draft of this biography.

[303] Mary Andrew Armour, in collaboration with Ursula Blake and Annette Dawson, *Cornelia. The Story of Cornelia Connelly, 1809-1879, Foundress of the Society of the Holy Child Jesus*. (Pompano Beach, FL: Exposition Press of Florida, Inc.; 1984), p. 5.

[304] Armour, p. 13

[305] Armour, p. 13.

[306] Armour, p. 20.

[307] Armour, p. 22.

[308] Armour, p. 23.

[309] Boniface Hanley, O.F.M., *Cornelia Connelly, Foundress of the Sisters of the Holy Child Jesus: The Grace to Know Your Will*. (Paterson, NJ: St. Anthony's Guild, n.d.), p. 18.

[310] Armour, p. 34.

[311] Armour, p. 34.

[312] Armour, p. 36.

[313] Armour, p. 47.

[314] Hanley, p. 22.

[315] Armour, p. 45.

[316] Private correspondence with Sister Helena Mayer, S.H.C.J.

[317] The author thanks George H. Foulkes, lay postulator, and Sister Dolores, H.M.S.S., promoter, for providing information and reviewing the draft of this biography.

[318] George Herbert Foulkes, *Maria Del Refugio Aguilar, Apostle of the Eucharist For The New Millenium,* tr. by John Wainwright, (Rome, Italy: Mercedarian sisters of the Blessed Sacrament, 2000), p. 4.

[319] Foulkes, *Apostle.* pp. 5-6.

[320] George Herbert Foulkes, *María Del Refugio Aguilar. Apóstol de la Eucaristía Para El Nuevo Milenio.* (México, D.F., MX: Causa De María Del Refugio, 2000), p. 14.

[321] Foulkes, *Apostle,* p. 22.

[322] Foulkes, *Apóstol* pp. 26-27.

[323] No author, monograph: "Mercedarian Sisters of the Blessed Sacrament," (Cleveland, OH: n.d.), pp. 5-6.

[324] Foulkes, p. 29.

[325] Brière, p. 156.

[326] Diocese of Edmundston, Canada; web site for Théophanius-Léo Chatillon; p. 1.

[327] Brière, p. 155.

[328] The author thanks Sister Jeannine Couture, S.J.S.H., author, for providing information and reviewing the draft of this biography.

[329] No author, pamphlet: "Mother Elisabeth Bergeron, Foundress of the Congregation of the Sisters of Saint Joseph of Saint-Hyacinthe." (Canada: 1991), p. 2.

[330] Private correspondence with Sister Jeannine Couture, S.J.S.H., Words of Elisabeth Bergeron, p. 1.

[331] Catherine Farmer and others, *Elisabeth Bergeron, Witness of God's Affection, Foundress of the Sisters of Saint Joseph of Saint-Hyacinthe.* Tr. by Helen Shaver. Series: Great Moments In Canadian Church History. (Tunisia: Sadifa Media, n.d.), p. 1.

[332] Private correspondence with Sister Jeannine Couture, S.J.S.H,; "Words of Elisabeth Bergeron," p. 1.

[333] Farmer, p. 31.

[334] Pamphlet, p. 3.

[335] Robert Michel, O.M.I., *Bienheureuse Marie de l'Incarnation, Saints of Canada.* Web site: Diocese of Edmundston, "Marie de l'Incarnation," p 2.

[336] The author thanks Sister Gabrielle Noel, O.S.U., for providing information and reviewing the draft of this biography.

[337] Website: patron saints Index, Marie of the Incarnation Guyart, p. 1.

[338] Website: Patron Saints Index: Blessed Marie of the Incarnation Guyart, p. 1.

[339] Lorraine Letourneau, *Marie de l'Incarnation.* Series: Célébrités Canadiennes. (Montréal, QC: Lidec, Inc.; 1990), p. 31.

[340] Létourneau, p. 45.

[341] Letourneau, p. 53.

[342] The author thanks Sister Thérèse Gendron, Little Sisters of the Holy Family, secretary for Le Centre Marie-Léonie Paradis, for providing information and reviewing the draft of the biography.

[343] André-M. Cimichella, O.S.M., *Blessed Marie Paradis, Her Multiple and Mysterious Ways (1840-1912)*. Tr. by Marguerite Lyons. (Sherbrooke, QC: Éditions Mont Sainte-Famille, 1984), p. 11.

[344] Cimichella., p. 11.

[345] Cimichella, pp. 22-23.

[346] Cimichella, pp. 26-27.

[347] Private correspondence with Sister Thérèse Gendron, "Maxims of the Servant of God, Mother Mary Leonie," #10.

[348] Cimichella, p. 89.

[349] Private correspondence with Sister Thérèse Gendron, anonymous monograph: "A Brief History of the Little Sisters of the Holy Family." (n.d.), p. 3.

[350] Cimichella, p. 65.

[351] www.centre.francois.laval@patrimonie-religieuse.com; p. 1.

[352] The author thanks Marie-France Cossette, assistant for the François de Laval Animation Center, for providing information and reviewing the draft of the biography.

[353] George E. Demers, *The Ven. Msgr. de Laval*. Tr. by Georges Abel. (Québec, QC: Cause De Msgr. de Laval, Seminaire de Québec, 1967), p. 11.

[354] Raymond J. Lahey, *The First Thousand Years: A Brief History Of The Catholic Church In Canada*. (Ottawa, ON: St. Paul University, 2002), p. 33.

[355] Demers, p. 37.

[356] The author thanks Betty Seymour, promoter, for providing information and reviewing the draft of this biography.

[357] Maziliauskas, *Pioneer Prince*, p. 30.

[358] Bunson and Bunson, p. 23.

[359] Matthew Bunson, *"How Beautiful Upon the Mountains," An Illustrated History of the Diocese of Altoona-Johnstown, 1901-2001*. (Hollidaysburg, PA: Diocese of Altoona-Johnstown, 2001). p. 18. The first priest to be ordained in the U.S.A. was Stephen Theodore Badin, who arrived in the country already a deacon, and was ordained by Bishop Carroll on May 25, 1793.

[360] Cicognani, p. 210.

[361] Bunson and Bunson, pp. 62-63.

[362] Ferdinand Kittell, "Demetrius Augustine Gallitzin," in *The Catholic Encyclopedia*. www.newadvent.org/cathen/06367b.htm; p. 3.

[363] Amleto Giovanni Cicognani, *Sanctity In America*. (Paterson, N.J.: St. Anthony Guild Press, 1940), p. 211.

[364] Matthew Bunson, p. 20.

[365] Matthew Bunson, p. 19.

[366] www.newadvent.org/cathen/06367b.htm; p. 3.

[367] The author thanks Sister Thérèse Caron, A.M.J., director of the Centre Catherine de Saint-Augustin, for providing information and reviewing the draft of the biography.

[368] Lorraine Létourneau, *Catherine de Saint-Augustin*. Series: Célébritiés Canadiennes. (Montréal, QC: Lidec, Inc.; 1990), p. 58.

[369] www.osa-west.org/blessedmariecatherine.html;

[370] website: Vies des Saints, for April 12, p. 3.

[371] Vies des Saints, p. 3.

[372] Vies des Saints, p.3.

[373] The author thanks Sister Francis Maria Cassidy, S.C., for providing information and reviewing the draft of the biography.

[374] Theodore Maynard, *Great Catholics In American History*. (Garden City, N.Y.: Hanover House, 1957), p. 238.

[375] Margaret Conklin, *An American Teresa*. (Long Island City, N.Y.: Color Graphic Press, Inc.; 1981), p. 26.

[376] Conklin, p. 29

[377] Private correspondence with Sister Francis Maria Cassidy, S.C.

[378] Miriam Teresa Demjanovich, S.C., *Greater Perfection Conferences*, ed. by Charles C. Demjanovich. (Paterson, N.J.: Charles C. Demjanovich, 1983), pp. 304-05.

[379] Conklin, p. 36.

[380] Maynard, p. 251.

[381] Maynard, p. 251.

[382] Maynard, p. 251.

[383] The author thanks Father David P. Reid, SS.CC., provincial, for providing information and reviewing the draft of this biography.

[384] Herman Gomes, *Damien, Servant of God, Servant of Humanity*. (Honolulu, HA: Hawaiian Province of the Congregation of the Sacred Hearts of Jesus and Mary, 2002). Revised, 2002., p. 2.

[385] No author, pamphlet: "Blessed Damien of Molokai." (Honolulu, HA: Knights of Columbus, Kamiano Council #11743; 1997), p. 2.

[386] Pamphlet: p. 2.

[387] Joseph N. Tylenda, S.J., "A Greater Love, Damien de Veuster, SS.CC. (1840-1889)," in *Portraits in American Sanctity*. (Chicago, IL: Franciscan Herald Press, 1982), p. 68)

[388] Tylenda, p. 71.

[389] Tylenda, p. 71.

[390] Vital Jourdain, *The Heart of Father Damien*. Tr. by Francis Larkin and Charles Davenport. (Milwaukee, WI: The Bruce Publishing Company, 1955), p. 253.

[391] Tylenda, p. 72.

[392] Miguel Angel Villa Roiz, and Carlos Villa Roiz, *De America Al Cielo. Santos, Beatos, Mártires, y Siervos de Dios Hacia al tercer milenio*. (México City, MX:, 1999), p. 282.

[393] Gerardo Sánchez Sánchez, ed. *Proceso Diocesano Para Las Causas De Canonización*. (México City, MX: 1998), p. 23

[394] Sánchez Sánchez, p. 23.

[395] Sánchez Sánchez, p. 22.

[396] Sánchez Sánchez, p. 22.

[397] Luciano Rivas Piccorelli, S.J., *27 Nuevos Santos Mexicanos. Canonizados por el Papa Juan Pablo II*. (Ciudad de México, MX: Obra Nacional De La Buena Prensa, A.C.; 2000), p. 11.

[398] Piccorelli, p. 11.

[399] www.catholic.net/rec/Peridoical/Ingress; "Blessed Miguel Pro and the New Mexican Martyrs;" July 2000, p. 2.

[400] The author thanks Father Denis Lépine, chancellor of the Diocese of Saint-Hyacinthe, for providing information and reviewing the draft of this biography.

[401] Jean Houpert and Jules Beaulac, *The Good Bishop Moreau*. (Saint-Hyacinthe, QC: Soeurs de Saint-Joseph De Saint-Hyacinthe, 1987), p. 8.

[402] Houpert and Beaulac, p. 3.

[403] Houpert and Beaulac, p. 8.

[404] Houpert, and Beaulac, p. 8.

[405] Houpert and Beaulac, p. 10.

[406] Houpert and Beaulac, p. 10.

[407] Houpert and Beaulac, p. 10.

[408] Houpert and Beaulac, p. 11.

[409] Houpert and Beaulac, p. 11.

[410] Ghislaine Salvail, S.J.S.H., "Le Bienheureux Louis-Zéphirin Moreau," website of Diocèse of Edmundston, p. 2.

[411] The author thanks Sister Marie-de-L'Eucharistie, S.J.M., M.S. Gen., for providing information and reviewing the draft of this biography.

[412] Raymond Maric, *Alexis-Louis Mangin, Marie-Zita De Jésus. Fondateur et Fondatrice de la Congrégacion des Servantes de Jésus-Marie.* (Turin, Italy: Sadafa Media, 1986), p. VI.

[413] Maric, p. VI.

[414] Madeleine Guertin, s.j.m., www.dioceseofedmunston.org, "éléonore potvin," p.2.

[415] Private correspondence with Sister Marie-de-L'Eucharistie, S.J.M., p. 1.

[416] Maric, p. VII.

[417] Maric, p. VII.

[418] Private correspondence with Sister Marie-de-L'Eucharistie, S.J.M., *Constitutions de la Congrégacion des Servantes de Jésus-Marie*, p. III.

[419] The author thanks Father Ebner, director of the Centre Vital Grandin, for providing information and reviewing the draft of this biography

[420] No author, booklet: "Venerable Bishop Vital Grandin, Oblate of Mary Immaculate." (1958), p. 10.

[421] *Venerable Vital Grandin*, p. 13.

[422] *Venerable Vital Grandin*, p. 14.

[423] Emile-Marie Briere, *Under Mary's Mantle. Our Lady's Love For Canada.* (Combermere, ON: Madonna House Publications, 2000), pp. 126-27.

[424] *Venerable Vital Grandin*, p. 27.

[425] Fidel de Jesús Chauvet, O.F.M., "Zumárraga, Juan De," *New Catholic Encyclopedia*, vol. 14, p. 1137.

[426] Website, "Juan De Zumárraga," in *The Catholic Encyclopedia*, Vol. XV, 1912, p. 3.

[427] Website, p. 1.

[428] Marion A. Habig, *The Franciscan Book of Saints*. Revised edition. (Chicago, IL: Franciscan Herald Press, 1979), p. 449.

[429] Website, p. 2

[430] Matthew Bunson, Margaret Bunson, and Stephen Bunson, *John Paul II's Book Of Saints*. (Huntington, IN: Our Sunday Visitor, 1999), p. 339.

[431] The author thanks Sister Raquel Rodríguez Aguayo, S.S.M.M.P., for providing information and reviewing the draft of this biography.

[432] María del Rosario Plácito Aguirre, *Una Mujer Que Se Forja Y Consume al Calor Del Corazon De Cristo. Breve biografia de la Sierva de Dios, R. M. Ma. Guadalupe García Zavala.* (Guadalajara, Jal.: Arquidiócesis de Guadalajara, 1988), pp. 43-44.

[433] Plácito Aguirre, p. 26.

[434] Plácito Aguirre, p. 32.

[435] The author thanks Father William D. McCarthy, M.M., Center for Mission Research and Study at Maryknoll, for providing information and reviewing the draft of this biography.

[436] Private correspondence with William D. McCarthy, M.M., *Father James Anthony Walsh Discourses*, p. 3; as found in *Selections from the writings of James Anthony Walsh and Thomas Frederick Price, Cofounders of the Maryknoll Society*, p. 1; privately compiled by William D. McCarthy, M.M.

[437] Private correspondence with William D. McCarthy, M.M., *James Anthony Walsh Discourses*, p. 361, as found in *Selections* by McCarthy, p.1.

[438] Robert E. Sheridan, M.M., *The Founders Of Maryknoll. Historical Reflections.* (Maryknoll, N.Y.: Catholic Foreign Mission Society of America, Inc.; 1980), pp. 33-34.

[439] *James Anthony Walsh Discourses,* p. 360.

[440] *James Anthony Walsh Discourses*, p. 347.

[441] William D. McCarthy, M.M., "Walsh, James Anthony (1867-1936)," in *The Encyclopedia Of American Catholic History*, p. 1455.

[442] James Anthony Walsh, in *The Field Afar*, April 1922, p. 100; as found in *Selections from the writings of James Anthony Walsh and Thomas Frederick Price, Cofounders of the Maryknoll Society*; privately compiled by William D. McCarthy, M.M.; p. 3.

[443] The author thanks Father William D. McCarthy, M.M., Center for Mission Research and Study at Maryknoll, for providing information and reviewing the draft of this biography.

[444] Sheridan, pp. 19-25.

[445] Sheridan, p. 19.

[446] James E. Walsh, M.M., sermon preached on the occasion of the internment of Father Price in the Maryknoll cemetery at Maryknoll, New York, December 8, 1936; found in *Very Reverend Thomas Frederick Price, M.M.*, ed. by Robert Sheridan, (Brookline, MA: privately printed, and reissued with supplement, at Maryknoll, N.Y., 1981), p. 273.

[447] The author thanks Sister Luisa María Valdez, C.F.M.M., regional superior, for providing information and reviewing the draft of this biography.

[448] Private correspondence with Sister Luisa María Valdez, found in Ojeda, p. 10.

[449] Private correspondence with Sister Luisa Maria Valdez, p. 2.

[450] Private correspondence with Sister Luisa María Valdez, found in Ojeda, p. 402-03.

[451] The author thanks Monsignor Robert M. O'Connell, vice postulator, for providing information and reviewing the draft of this biography.

[452] M. N. L. Couve de Murville, *Slave from Haiti: A Saint for New York? The Life of Pierre Toussaint.* (London, England: Catholic Truth Society Publications, 1995), p. 4.

[453] Couve de Murville, p. 6.

[454] No author, pamphlet: "Venerable Pierre Toussaint," (Bronx, NY: Pierre Toussaint Guild, ca. 1997), p. 4. Quoting Sister Marie Emmanuel, in Immaculata Magazine (Libertyville, IL: Franciscan Friars, n.d.).

[455] Couve de Murville, p. 10.

[456] Emmanuel, p. 6.

[457] Couve de Murville, p. 111.

[458] Emmanuel, p. 6.

[459] Emmanuel, p. 7.

[460] Tarry, pp. 343-44.

[461] Emmanuel, p. 8.

[462] The author thanks Brother Timothy Arthur, O.F.M., archivist, for providing information and reviewing the draft of this biography.

[463] Antoine Tibesar,O.F.M., "Always Forward! Father Junípero Serra, O.F.M. (1713-1784)" in Joseph N. Tylenda, S.J., *Portraits in American Sanctity.* (Chicago, IL: Franciscan Herald Press, 1982), p. 111.

[464] Tibesar, p. 112.

[465] Tibesar, p. 115.

[466] Tibesar, p. 118.

[467] The author thanks Father Jean-Guy Sauvageau, Representative of the Seminary of Quebec for the Cause de Gérard Raymond, for providing information and reviewing the draft of this biography.

[468] Les Amis de Gérard Raymond, *Gérard Raymond.* (Québec, QC: Les Amis de Gérard Raymond, 1983), p. 7.

[469] Les Amis, p. 4.

[470] Les Amis, p.5.

[471] Les Amis, p. 13.

[472] Les Amis, p. 9.

[473] Les Amis, p. 10.

[474] Les Amis, p. 14.

[475] Les Amis, p. 21.

[476] Les Amis, pp. 22-23.

[477] Les Amis, p. 25.

[478] Les Amis, p. 27.

[479] Gérard Mercier, O.S.B., *Her Spiritual Journey. A Woman with an Overwhelming Charisma: Catherine-Aurélie Caouette.* Tr. from the French. Abridged edition. (Sisters of the Precious Blood of the American Federation, n.d.), p. 7.

[480] The author thanks Sister Rose Mary, A.P.B.; and Sister Jeanette Héon, A.P.S., for providing information and reviewing the draft of this biography.

[481] Mercier, p. 6.

[482] Mercier, p. 8.

[483] Mercier, p. 8.

[484] Mercier, p. 10.

[485] Mercier, p. 11.

[486] Mercier, p. 12.

[487] Mercier, p. 12.

[488] Website: Diocese of Edmundston, p. 1.

[489] Mercier, p. 207

[490] Mercier, p. 203.

[491] Mercier, p. 204.

[492] Mercier, p. 234.

[493] Mercier, p. 195.

[494] Mercier, p. 196.

[495] Catherine-Aurélie Caouette, A.P.S., *"Sitio ... I thirst."* (Saint-Hyacinthe, QC: Centre Aurélie Caouette, 1984), p. 6.

[496] Caouette, p. 14.

[497] No author, *With Dyed Garments, Mother Catherine Aurélie of the Precious Blood.* Tr. by A Religious of the Precious Blood. (Brooklyn, N.Y.: Sisters Adorers of the Most Precious Blood, 1947), pp. 174-80.

[498] Ibid., p. 66.

[499] Ibid.

[500] Mercier, p. 239.

[501] Nidia A. Varela, F.M.A., *Itinerario Historico-Espiritual De La Venerable Sor María Romero Meneses, Hija De María Auxiliadora.* (San José, Costa Rica: Oficina del Proceso de la Venerable Sor María Romero, 2001), p. 10

[502] Nora María Herrara, F.MA., *Vida Breve De Sor María Romero. Hija de María Auxiliadora para jóvenes y adultos.* (San José, Costa Rica: Editorial e Imprenta Ludovico, 2001), p. 6.

[503] Varela, p. 13.

[504] Varela, p. 12.

[505] Varela, p. 17.

[506] Varela, p. 19.

[507] Varela, p. 19.

[508] Varela, p. 20.

[509] Varela, p. 21.

[510] María Romero Meneses, F.M.A., "Pensamientos," (www.ctv.es/USERS/jalolo/pensamientosmr.html; p.1.

[511] No author, pamphlet: "At the Service of the Least: María Romero." (Roma: F.M.A., 2002), p. 6.

[512] Varela, p. 37.

[513] Pamphlet, p. 7-8.

[514] Varela, p. 28.

[515] Varela, p. 35.

[516] www.ctv.es/USERS/jalolo/pensamientosmr.html, p. 1.

[517] "At the Service of the Least: María Romero.", p. 10.

[518] The author thanks Sister Mary de Paul, O.P., archivist for The Dominican Sisters of Hawthorne, for providing information and reviewing the draft of this biography.

[519] Mary Joseph Blessington, O.P., *Out of Many Hearts. Mother M. Alphonsa Lathrop, and Her Work.* (Hawthorne, N.Y.: The Servants of Relief for Incurable Cancer, 1965), p. 19.

[520] Blessington, p. 13.

[521] Dominican Sisters of Hawthorne, *Fidelity, 1900-2000.* (Strasbourg, France: Editons du Signe, n.d.), p. 15.

[522] Dominican Sisters, *Fidelity,* p. 13.

[523] Boniface Hanley, O.F.M., *"The More Things Change, the More They Are the Same."* [Life of Rose Hawthorne Lathrop] (Paterson, N.J.: St. Anthony's Guild, 1985), p. 19.

[524] Dominican Sisters, *Fidelity,* p.18.

[525] Dominican Sisters, *Fidelity,* p. 19.

[526] The author thanks Father Zygmunt Musielski, O.M.I., vice postulator; and Robin Charlesworth, assistant director of planning and communications for the Cause of Anthony Kowalczyk, for providing information and reviewing the draft of this biography.

[527] P. J. Klita, O.M.I., *Servant of God, Brother Anthony Kowalczyk, Oblate of Mary Immaculate.* (Edmonton, AL: Accent Printing LTD, n.d.), p. 7.

[528] Klita, p. 9.

[529] Klita, p. 11.

[530] Klita, p. 22.

[531] Klita, p. 22.

[532] Website: Geoff McMaster, "Holy janitor's humble abode crumbles to dust," June 18, 1999; p. 2.

[533] Klita, p. 28.

[534] Klita, p. 28.

[535] www.puertorico-herald.org/issues/2001/vol15no8/CarManRodr-en.shtml; p.

[536] Francisco Aguiló, ed. *Carlos M. Rodríguez (1918-1963), un santo Puertorriqueño.* (San Juan, P.R.: Circulo Carlos M. Rodríguez, 2001), pp. 121-23.

[537] Aguiló, p. 129.

[538] The author thanks Sister Mary Martha Blandford, O.S.C., for providing information and reviewing the draft of this biography.

[539] Pius J. Barth, O.F.M., "With Light Step and Unstumbling Feet, Mother Maria Maddalena Bentivoglio, O.S.C. (1834-1905)," in Joseph N. Tylenda's *Portraits in American* Sanctity. (Chicago, IL: Franciscan Herald Press, 1982), p. 226)

[540] Barth, p. 227.

[541] Barth, p. 227.

[542] Barth, p. 229.

[543] Barth, pp. 230-31.

[544] Barth, p. 231.

[545] Zarrella, p. 50.

[546] Zarrella p. 50.

[547] Zarrella p. 54.

[548] Barth, p. 233.

[549] www.angelfire.com/in/jesusmaryjoseph/martyr.html; p. 2.

[550] ibid.

[551] ibid., p.2.

[552] www.ibid; p. 2.

[553] www.ibid; p. 2.

[554] ibid.

[555] www.angelfire.com/in/jesusmaryjoseph/prologue.html; p. 1.

[556] www.angelfire.com/in/jesusmaryjoseph/martyr.html; pp.3-4.

[557] The author thanks Monsignor Robert C. Wurtz, director of the National Shrine of Our Lady of Victory, for providing information and reviewing the draft of this biography.

[558] *Buffalo Times,* July 1936.

[559] Boniface Hanley, O.F.M., *Servant of God, Monsignor Nelson H. Baker (1841-1936), One Lifetime.* (Paterson, N.J.: St. Anthony's Guild, n.d.), p. 12.

[560] Hanley, p. 29.

[561] Hanley, p. 19.

[562] Hanley, p. 22.

[563] Hanley, p. 29.

[564] Hanley, pp. 10, 12.

[565] Buffalo News, Dec. 24, 2000; p. A-6.

566 Hanley, p. 12.

567 The author thanks Father Gregory Gay, C.M., provincial of the Central American Province, and Sister Adelaide Bocanegra, Beth., superior, for providing information and reviewing the draft of this biography.

568 No author, *De Tenerife a Guatemala: la historia de santidad de un prergrino canario. Hermano Pedro De San José Betancur, Fundador de la Orden Bethlemita.* (Bogota, Colombia: Congregación De Hermanas Bethlemitas, 2002), p. 16.

569 No author, "Saint Peter Of Saint Joseph Betancur, Founder of the Bethlemite Order." (Bogota, Colombia: Congregation of Bethlemite Sisters, ca. 2002), p. 2.

570 www.Zenit.org; July 30, 2002, p. 1.

571 *De Tenerife*, p. 24.

572 No author, Congregación De Hermanas Bethlemitas, "Beato Hermano Pedro de San José de Bethancur." (Guatemala: Santa Lucia M.A. Sac., n.d.), p. 4.

573 www.newadvent.org/cathen/02534b.htm; p. 2.

574 Ibid,, below, p. 3.

575 No author, "Como vivio El Hermano Pedro Las Virtudes Teologicas Y Cardinales?", p. 3.

576 *De Tenerife*, p. 55.

577 ibid. p. 7.

578 Miguel Angel Villa Roiz and Carlos Villa Roiz, *De América Al Cielo.* (1999), p. 220.

579 The author thanks Sister Dolores Salazaar, Siervas de la Santíssima Trinidad y de los Pobres, for providing information and reviewing the draft of this biography.

580 John Guimond, *Thanks Be To God. The Spirit And Life Of Venerable Solanus Casey, Capuchin.* (Detroit, MI: The Father Solanus Guild, 1978), p. 25.

581 The author thanks Brother Leo Wollenweber, O.F.M. Cap., vice postulator, for providing information and reviewing the draft of this biography.

582 Albert H. LeDoux, "Casey, Solanus (1870-1957)," *The Encyclopedia of American Catholic History,* (Collegeville, MN: A Michael Glazier Book, 1997) p. 232.

583 Boniface Hanley, O.F.M., *The Doorkeeper, The Story of Father Solanus Casey, Capuchin.* (Paterson, N.J.: St. Anthony's Guild, 1987), p. 12.

584 Michael Crosby, ed., *Solanus Casey. The Official Account of a Virtuous American Life.* (New York, N.Y.: The Crossroad Publishing Company, 2000), p. 50.

585 Crosby, p. 73.

586 Crosby, p. 84.

587 Crosby, p. 84.

588 Hanley, p. 28.

589 Hanley, p. 30.

590 Hanley, p. 30.

591 The author thanks Father Gentil Turcotte, O.F.M., director of the Musée du Père Frédéric, for providing information and reviewing the draft of this biography.

592 Kevin Kidd, O.F.M., *Good Father Frederick. A Franciscan Apostle, 1838-1916.* From the French text prepared by Léandre Poirier, O.F.M. (Trois-Rivières, QC: Éditions du Bien Publique, 1995), p. 16.

593 Kidd, p. 24.

594 Kidd p. 27.

595 Kidd, p. 28.

596 Good, p. 24.

[597] Kidd, p. 38.

[598] Marion A. Habig, O.F.M., *The Franciscan Book of Saints*. (Chicago, IL: Franciscan Herald Press, 1979), p. 591.

[599] Brière, p. 148.

[600] Good, p. 21.

[601] Brière, p. 148.

[602] The author thanks Father Barnabas Diekemper, O.F.M., historian; Mary Nell Davis, director of the Margil House of Studies; and sister Mary Paul Valdez, C.D.P.; for providing information and reviewing the draft of this biography.

[603] Gary James, ed. "The Magnificent Saga of Father Antonio Margil de Jesus, 'The Apostle of New Spain'." Video. Houston, TX: The Margil House of Studies, 1999.

[604] Hughes, Vat. Archives, 1993.

[605] Patrick Linbeck, "Venerable Antonio Margil, O.F.M. (1657-1726): The Apostle of New Spain." *The Dunwoodie Review*, 1995, p. 139.

[606] Linbeck, p. 147.

[607] The author thanks Sister Mary Laurence Hanley, O.S.F., director of Mother Marianne's Cause, for providing information and reviewing the draft of this biography.

[608] Durkin with Hanley, p. 14.

[609] Mary Laurence Hanley, O.S.F., "Missionary and Nurse to the Lepers of Hawaii. Mother Marianne Cope, O.S.F. (1838-1918)", in Joseph N. Tylenda's *Portraits In American Sanctity*. (Chicago, IL: Franciscan Herald Press, 1982), p. 242.

[610] Durkin with Hanley, p. 15.

[611] Hanley, p. 243.

[612] The Catholic Sun, diocese of Syracuse, NY; July 12-25, 2001; vol. 120, No. 26; pp. 1,4.

[613] Private correspondence with Mary Laurence Hanley, O.S.F., "Representative Writings of the Servant of God Mother Marianne of Molokai." (Syracuse, N.Y.: Sisters of the Third Franciscan Order, n.d.), p. 11: letter to the Bishop of Olba, Honolulu, 9/15/1888.

[614] Representative Writings, p. 12, May 16, 1889.

[615] Representative Writings, p. 17.

[616] Hanley, p. 246.

[617] The author thanks Susan H. Brosnan, archivist for the Knights Of Columbus Museum, for providing information and reviewing the draft of this biography.

[618] Christopher J. Kauffman, *Faith & Fraternalism: The History of the Knights of Columbus, 1882-1982*. (New York, N.Y.: Harper & Row, Publishers, 1982), p. 26.

[619] Robert Leeney and others. "Father Michael J. McGivney, 1852-1890." Columbia Magazine, January 1990, p. 6.

[620] At this moment in American history, numerous ethnic and cultural organizations had formed to preserve Old World language and traditions, while providing financial insurance in case of injury or death to the family's bread-winner. Some of these societies, e.g., the Freemasons, were unabashedly anti-Catholic, yet attracted Catholics, who put their faith and religion at risk, because of the financial benefits they needed for their families. The Church needed a society to counter the anti-Catholic bigotry common at that time.

[621] Kauffman, p. 21.

[622] Kauffman, p. 40.

[623] Kauffman, p. 45.

[624] Kauffman, p. 72.

[625] The author thanks Sister Rita Bérubé, R.S.R., vice postulator for the Cause of Élisabeth-Turgeon, for providing information and reviewing the draft of this biography.

[626] Marthe Saint-Pierre, R.S.R., *Une Grande Amie Des Jeunes: Élisabeth Turgeon.* (Rimouski, QC: Les Publications R.S.R., 2002), pp. 16-17.

[627] Giselle Huot, tr. by Edwina Bouchard, R.S.R., *An Unbelievable Dream... Thousands of Youngsters.* (Rimouski, QC: Les Publications R.S.R, 1996), p. 15.

[628] Vivian Bond, R.S.R., *She Was For Real.* (Rimouski, QC: Valley Publishing Company, 1999), p. 19.

[629] June 2002, p. 136.

[630] Bond, p. 22.

[631] No author, pamphlet: "Élisabeth Turgeon (Mother Mary Elisabeth)." Letter: July 31, 1880; p. 2.

[632] Bond, p. 24.

[633] Bond, p. 24.

[634] The author thanks Brother Robert Taylor, O.S.A., for providing information and reviewing the draft of this biography.

[635] Marion A. Habig, O.F.M., *Saints of the Americas*, (Huntington, IN: Our Sunday Visitor, 1974), p. 161.

[636] Habig, p. 164.

[637] Habig, p. 168.

[638] Habig, p. 170.

[639] Habig, p. 170.

[640] Marguerite Jean, S.C.I.M., *A Woman of Yesterday, Today, and Tomorrow. Marie Josephte Fitzbach, Mother Mary of the Sacred Heart 1806-1885.* (Québec, QC: Imprimerie Le Renouveau, 1989), p. 13.

[641] The author thanks Sister Denise Rodrigue, S.C.I.M. vice postulator for the Cause of Marie Fitzbach, for providing information and reviewing the draft of this biography.

[642] Jean, p. 8.

[643] Jean, p. 7.

[644] Georgianna Juneau, S.C.I.M., *Mother Mary of the Sacred Heart and Her Collaborators (1806-1885). Foundress of the Good Shepherd Congregation of Québec.* (Québec, QC: Les Soeurs du Bon-Pasteur de Québec, 1989), p. 38.

[645] Juneau, p. 63.

[646] Juneau, p. 84.

[647] Juneau, p. 92.

[648] Juneau, p. 85.

[649] Juneau, p. 115.

[650] Jean, p. 21.

[651] Private correspondence with Marguerite Jean, S.C.I.M.

[652] The author thanks Maurice da Silva, promoter, for providing information and reviewing the draft of this biography.

[653] Marion A. Habig, O.F.M., *Saints of the Americas.* (Huntington, IN: Our Sunday Visitor, 1974), pp. 110-11.

[654] Habig, p. 112.

655 Dina Bélanger, R.J.M., *The Autobiography of Dina Bélanger (Marie Sainte-Cecile de Rome, Religious of Jesus and Mary)*. Tr. by Mary St. Stephen, R.J.M. Rev. by Felicity Moody, R.J.M. (Sillery, QC: Les Religieuses de Jésus-Marie, 1997), p. 54.

The author thanks Sister Marcelle Lachance, R.J.M., and Sister Agathe Lagueux, R.J.M., for providing information and for reviewing the draft of this biography.

656 Bélanger, p. 115.

657 Bélanger, p. 133.

658 Ghislaine Boucher, R.J.M., *In Dina's Footsteps, 1897-1929*. Tr. by Florestine Audette, R.J.M. (Québec, QC: The Religious of Jesus and Mary, 1994), p. 8.

659 *Positio Super Virtutibus*. [Dina Bélanger] (Rome, Italy: Congregatio Pro Causis Sanctorum, 1987), vol. IV, part 1, p. 27.

660 Bélanger, p. 16

661 Boucher, p. 33

662 Boucher, p. 19.

663 Bélanger. p. 57.

664 Bélanger, p. 57.

665 Bélanger, p. 59.

666 Bélanger, p. 61.

667 Bélanger, p. 102

668 Bélanger, pp. 55-56

669 Bélanger, p. 67

670 Boucher, p. 25.

671 Bélanger p. 79.

672 Bélanger, p. 92.

673 Bélanger, p. 93.

674 Bélanger, p. 110.

675 Bélanger, p. 104.

676 Bélanger, p. 111.

677 Bélanger, p. 112.

678 Bélanger, p. 12.

679 Bélanger, p. 118.

680 Boucher, p. 53.

681 Bélanger, p. 143.

682 Bélanger, p. 215.

683 *Positio*, p. 124: "Q.: Against which virtue were directed the temptations of the demon that you mentioned? Were they against faith, against hope, against charity? Were they against humility, against chastity or other virtue? A.: These temptations were directed against chastity. She told me sometimes that she would have missed communion had she not held on obedience to her confessor. That made me understand that these temptations were sometimes violent."

684 Bélanger, p. 154.

685 Bélanger, p. 363.

686 Habig, p. 166.

687 Habig, p. 153.

688 Habig, p. 154.

689 Habig, p. 154.

690 *Butler's Lives Of The Saints*, vol. III, pp. 533-34.

[691] The author thanks Father Conrad L. Harkins, O.F.M., vice postulator for the Cause of the Georgia Martyrs, for providing information and reviewing the draft of this biography.

[692] Succession was matrilineal, i.e., succession was awarded to a sister's son, or a daughter's husband, and not to the chief's son

[693] Gillian Brown, *The Franciscan Missions of Coastal Georgia*. (Boston, MA: The Cause of the Georgia Martyrs, 1985), p. 10.

[694] Alexander Wyse, O.F.M., "The Martyrs of Georgia. Father Pedro de Corpa, O.F.M. and His Four Companions (+ 1597)," in Joseph N. Tylenda's *Portraits of American Sanctity*. (Chicago, IL: Franciscan Herald Press, 1982), p. 82.

[695] Albert J. Nevins, M.M., *American Martyrs From 1542*. (Huntington, IN: Our Sunday Visitor, 1987), p. 36.

[696] Brown, p. 11.

[697] Wyse, pp. 11,13.

[698] Wyse, p. 87.

[699] Nevins, pp. 37-38.

[700] Brown, p. 20.

[701] Private correspondence with Gerardo Sánchez Sánchez.

[702] Private correspondence with Gerardo Sánchez Sánchez.

[703] Private correspondence with Gerardo Sánchez Sánchez.

[704] The author thanks Hermana Romelia Chacon Murguia, S.S.C.I.P., for providing information and reviewing the draft of this biography.

[705] The author thanks Sister Mary Francis Clare Radke, O.S.F., general minister; and Valerie Ensalaco, corporate vice president for institutional advancement, for providing information and reviewing the draft of this biography.

[706] Anne Marie Knawa, O.S.F., *As God Shall Ordain: A History of the Franciscan Sisters of Chicago, 1894-1987*. (Lemont, IL: Worzalla Publishing Company, 1989), pp. 9-10.

[707] Knawa, p. 26.

[708] Josephine Dudzik, O.S.F., "Chronicle." (Chicago, IL: Franciscan Sisters of Chicago, 1910), p. 1.

[709] Knawa, p.65.

[710] Chronicle of Mother Mary Theresa Dudzik, p.6.

[711] Dudzik p.18.

[712] Dudzik p. 45.

[713] Knawa, p. 366.

[714] The author thanks Sister Thérèse Frigon, S.P., of the Bureau de la Cause de Émilie Gamelin, for providing information and reviewing the draft of this biography.

[715] Therese Carignan, S.P., ed. and tr. *Mother Gamelin, A Woman of Compassion*, (Monrtréal, QC: Imprimerie Hermès Inc., 1984), p. 71.

[716] website, Patron Saints index, Bl. Émilie Tavernier-Gamelin, p. 1.

[717] Carignan, p. 27.

[718] Denise Robillard. *Émilie Tavernier-Gamelin*. Tr. by Lina Gaudette, S.P. (Montréal, QC: Éditions du Méridien, 1992), p. 97.

[719] Web site: Bl. Émilie Tavernier Gamelin, p. 1.

[720] Robillard, p. 101.

[721] André-M. Cimichella, O.S.M., *Emilie Tavernier Gamelin. The Great Lady of Montreal, Foundress of the Sisters of Providence.* (Outremont, QC: Editions Carte Blanche, 2002), p. 46.

[722] Robillard, p. 144.

[723] Cimichella, p. 48.

[724] Cimichella, p. 58.

[725] Chimicella, p. 71.

[726] Cimichella, p. 71.

[727] Carignan, p. 62.

[728] Carignan, p. 51.

[729] The author thanks Father Robert Wong, S.J., director of Martyrs' Shrine, for providing information and reviewing the draft of this biography.

[730] Jean de Brébeuf, *The Huron Relation of 1635*, tr. by A. J. Macdougall, S.J., and J. S. McGivern, S.J., (Midland, ON: A Martyrs' Shrine Publication, 1993), p. 12.

[731] de Brébeuf, p. 12.

[732] Elmer O'Brien, *The Inner Flame of St. John de Brébeuf.* (Midland, ON: Martyrs' Shrine, 1984), p. 7.

[733] Office of Readings: "From the spiritual diaries of Saint John de Brébeuf, priest and martyr." *The Liturgy of the Hours*, (New York, N.Y.: Catholic Book Publishing Co., 1975), vol. IV, pp. 2020-21.

[734] O'Brien, pp. 5-6.

[735] The author thanks Father Robert Wong, S.J., director of Martyrs' Shrine, for providing information and reviewing the draft of this biography.

[736] *Butler's Lives of the Saints*, vol. III, p. 650.

[737] Joseph N. Tylenda, S.J. *Jesuit Saints & Martyrs* (Chicago, IL: Loyola Press, 1998), p. 201.

[738] Tylenda, *Jesuit Saints & Martyrs* p. 201.

[739] Tylenda, *Jesuit Saints & Martyrs* p. 432.

[740] The author thanks Father Robert Wong, S.J., director of Martyrs' Shrine, for providing information and reviewing the draft of this biography.

[741] Tylenda, *Jesuit Saints & Martyrs* p. 432.

[742] *Butler's Lives of the Saints*, vol. III, p. 651.

[743] The author thanks Father Robert Wong, S.J., director of Martyrs' Shrine, for providing information and reviewing the draft of this biography.

[744] *Butler's Lives of the Saints*, vol. III, p. 650.

[745] The author thanks Father Robert Wong, S.J., director of Martyrs' Shrine, for providing information and reviewing the draft of this biography.

[746] Tylenda, *Jesuit Saints & Martyrs* p. 434.

[747] Tylenda, *Jesuit Saints & Martyrs* p. 435.

[748] Tylenda, *Jesuit Saints & Martyrs* p. 435.

[749] The author thanks Père Jacques Rinfret, O.M.I., vice postulator, and Père Réal Mathieu, O.M.I., for providing information and reviewing the draft of this biography.

[750] Vincent J. O'Malley, C.M., *Saintly Companions.* (Staten Island, N.Y.: Alba House, 1995), pp. 247-74.

[751] Alphonse Nadeau, O.M.I., *Le Père Lelièvre, Oblat de Marie-Immaculée. "L'Apôtre de Sacré-Coeur."* (Neuville, QC: Imprimerie A. Garneau, Inc., n.d.), p. 12.

[752] Nadeau, p. 12.

[753] Nadeau, pp. 12-13.

[754] Nadeau, p. 13.

[755] Villa Roiz and Villa Roiz, p. 282.

[756] This author's translation cannot do justice to Marina's melliflous rhyme and rhythm.

[757] Roberto Octavio Balmori, ed., *Siervos de Dios Esposos, Eugenio Balmori Martinez Y Marina Marina Francisca Cinta Sarrelangue, Datos Biograficos, Fragmentos de Cartas, Poemas.* (Coatzalcoalcos, Veracruz: 2002; p. 58.

[758] Gerardo Sánchez Sánchez, *Proceso, Diocesano Para Las Causas De Canonización.* (México, MX: 1998), p. 23

[759] The author thanks Père Gerard Desrochers, C.Ss.R., for providing information and reviewing the draft of this biography.

[760] Gerard Desrochers, C.Ss.R. *Alfred Pampalon, Redemptorist. He loved Mary. He loved Saint Anne.* Tr. by Gabriel Bergeron. Rev. by Margaret Burton. (St. Anne de Beaupré, QC: Secretariat of the Shrine of St. Anne de Beaupré, 2001), pp. 29-30.

[761] Desrochers, p. 39.

[762] Desrochers, pp. 40-41.

[763] Desrochers, p. 45.

[764] Desrochers, p. 52.

[765] Desrochers, p. 53.

[766] Desrochers, p. 54.

[767] Desrochers, p. 59.

[768] Desrochers, p. 60-61.

[769] Desrochers, p. 63.

[770] Desrochers, p. 69.

[771] Desrochers, p. 88.

[772] Desrochers, p. 68.

[773] Desrochers, p. 133.

[774] Desrochers, p. 133.

[775] Desrochers, pp. 151-52.

[776] Desrochers, p. 105.

[777] Desrochers, p. 179.

[778] Desrochers, p. 180.

[779] Helena Pereña de Malagón, "Palafox Y Mendoza, Juan De, Ven." In *New Catholic Encyclopedia*, vol. 10, p. 872.

[780] www.upaep.mx/puebla/palafox.html; p. 2.

[781] The author thanks Sister Kate Misbauer, S.L., archivist for the Loretto Archives, for providing information and reviewing the draft of this biography.

[782] Camillus Paul Maes, *The Life Of Rev. Charles Nerinckx: With A Chapter On The Early Catholic Missions of Kentucky.* (Cincinnati, OH: Robert Clarke & Co., 1880), p. 27.

[783] Maes, p. 31.

[784] Maes, p. 63.

[785] Maes, p. 265.

[786] Maes, pp. 75-76.

[787] Maes, p. 187.

[788] Helene Magaret, *Giant in the Wilderness. A Biography of Father Charles Nerinckx.* (Milwaukee, WI: The Bruce Publishing Company, 1952), p. 199.

[789] Private correspondence with Kate Misbauer, S.L. *I Am the Way: Constitutions of the Sisters of Loretto at the Foot of the Cross.* (Nerinx, KY: Sisters of Loretto, 1997), pp. 2 and 4.

[790] *I Am The Way,* p. 2.

[791] Maes, pp. 412-13.

[792] The author thanks Sister Marie Kevin Tighe, S.P., vice postulator; Sister Mary Roger Madden, S.P., author and historian, and Sister Eileen Ann Kelly, S.P., archivist; for providing information and reviewing the draft of this biography.

[793] Private correspondence with Eileen Ann Kelly, S.P.

[794] Joseph Eleanor Ryan, S.P., "With Courage and Faith, Mother Theodore Guerin, S.P. (1798-1856)," in Joseph N. Tylenda's *Portraits In American Sanctity,* (Chicago, IL: Franciscan Herald Press, 1982), p. 140.

[795] Private correspondence with Eileen Ann Kelly, S.P.

[796] Herman Joseph Alerding, *History of the Catholic Church in the Diocese of Vincennes.* (Indianapolis, IN: 1883), p. 3.

[797] Mitchell, p. 51.

[798] Mitchell, pp. 90-91.

[799] Mitchell, p. 83.

[800] Mitchell, p. 92.

[801] Mitchell, p. 92.

[802] Mitchell, p. 94.

[803] Private correspondence with Eileen Ann Kelly, S.P.

[804] Mitchell, p. 100.

[805] Mitchell, p. 107.

[806] Mitchell, p. 82.

[807] Durkin, p. 20.

[808] The author thanks Sister Hélène Tremblay, C.N.D., Director of the Centre Jeanne-LeBer, for providing information and reviewing the draft of this biography.

[809] Céline Langelier, C.N.D., and Helene Tremblay, C.N.D., *The Recluse of Montréal: Jeanne LeBer, 1662-1714.* Tr. by Elizabeth Jane Fraser, C.N.D. and Patricia Simpson, C.N.D. (Montréal, QC: Congrégation de Notre-Dame, 1996), pp. 8-9.

[810] Langelier, p. 17.

[811] Langelier, p. 17.

[812] Langelier, p. 18.

[813] Langelier, p. 19.

[814] Langelier, p. 20.

[815] The author thanks Father Carl Hoegerl, C.Ss.R., archivist for the Redemptorist Provincial Archives for the Baltimore Province, for providing information and reviewing the draft of this biography.

[816] Carl W. Hoegerl, C.Ss.R. and Alicia Von Stamwitz, *A Life of Blessed Francis Xavier Seelos, Redemptorist, (1819-1867).* (Ligouri, MO: Liguori, 2000), p. 22.

[817] Hoegerl, p. 27.

[818] Hoegerl, p. 67.

[819] The author thanks Sister Simone Perras, S.N.J.M., for providing information and reviewing the draft of this biography.

[820] Yolande Laberge, S.N.J.M., *Mère Marie-Rose: Eulalie Durocher 1811-1849.* Series: Célébrités Canadiennes. (Montréal, QC: Lidec Inc., 2000), p. 28.

[821] Laberge, p. 43.

[822] Monique Thériault, S.N.J.M., *Eulalie-MélanieDurocher, Mère Marie-Rose. Synthèse d'une rencontre a la Maison générale en 1991 en vue de 'émission de télévision Videotron.* (Longueuil, QC: Private publication, rev. in 1995), p. 3.

[823] Laberge, p. 50.

[824] The author thanks Sister Rose Patrice Sasso, O.P., executive director of The Cardinal Cooke Guild, and Patricia Handal, coordinator of The Cardinal Cooke Guild, for providing information and reviewing the draft of this biography.

[825] Benedict J. Groeschel, C.F.R., and Terrence L. Weber, *Thy Will Be Done. A Spiritual Portrait of Terence Cardinal Cooke.* (Staten Island, N.Y.: Alba House, 1990), pp. 96-97.

[826] Groeschel and Weber, p. 105.

[827] Groeschel and Weber, p. 105.

[828] www.priestsforlife.org/magisterium/cardcookeltr.htm, p. 1; Letter of Terence Cardinal Cooke, to the people of the Archdiocese, to be read at all Masses on October 8-9, after his death on October 6.

[829] Groeschel and Weber, p. 40.

[830] Groeschel and Weber, p. 40.

[831] Groeschel and Weber, p. 99.

[832] The author thanks Hermana Raquel Rodríguez Aguayo, S.S.M.M.P. for providing information and reviewing the draft of this biography.

[833] Margaret Mary Alacoque would be canonized on May 13, 1920

[834] Maria del Rosario Plácito Aguirre, S.S.M.M.P., *Semblanza del Padre Cipriano Iñiguez Martín del Campo.* (Guadalajara, Jal.: Editorial Jus, S.A. de C.V., 1993), p. 42.

[835] Plácito, p. 73, 75.

[836] Plácito, p. 80.

[837] Plácito, p. 93.

[838] Plácito, p. 91.

[839] www.osa-west.org/blessedeliasdelsocorro.html; p. 1.

[840] ibid.

[841] ibid.

[842] The author thanks Sister Albertine, O.S.F., archivist, and secretary for the Board of the Father Walter Ciszek Prayer League, for providing information and reviewing the draft of this biography.

[843] Walter Ciszek, S.J., with Daniel L. Flaherty, S.J. *With God in Russia.* (New York, N.Y.: The America Press, 1964), p. 1.

[844] Ciszek, *With God*, p. 3.

[845] Ciszek *With God*, pp. 6-7.

[846] Ciszek *With God*, p. 7.

[847] Edmund Murphy, S.J., *The Father Ciszek Story.* (Scranton, PA: Association of Jesuit University Presses, n.d.), pp. 14-15.

[848] Ciszek *With God*, p. 14.

[849] Murphy, p. 15.

[850] Murphy, p. 21.

[851] Murphy, pp. 24-25.

[852] Murphy, pp. 25-26.

[853] Murphy, p. 27.

[854] Ciszek *With God*, p. 201.

[855] Murphy, p. 29.

[856] Charles Edward Ronan, S.J., "Aguilar Y Seiyas, Francisco," in the *New Catholic Encyclopedia*, vol. 1, p. 221.

[857] The author thanks Father John E. Rybolt, C.M., author, and Morgan MacIntosh, archivist for the De Andreis-Rosati Memorial Archives in the John T. Richardson Library at DePaul University; and for providing information and reviewing the draft of this biography.

[858] Frederick J. Easterly, C.M., "Many Things in a Short Time, Venerable Felix De Andreis, C.M., (1778-1820)" in Tylenda's *Portraits In American Sanctity*, (Chicago, IL: Franciscan Herald Press, 1982), p. 46.

[859] Easterly, p. 47.

[860] Rybolt., p. 13.

[861] Rybolt., p. 20.

[862] Easterly, p. 52.

[863] Easterly, p. 53.

[864] Easterly, p. 53.

[865] Rybolt., p. 24.

[866] Rybolt, p. 54.

[867] The author thanks Sister Jacqueline Saint-Yves, S.G.M., secretary general of the Sisters of Charity of Montreal "Grey Nuns," for providing information and reviewing the draft of this biography.

[868] Marie Cecilia Lefèvre, S.G.M., and Rose Alma Lemire, S.G.M., *A Journey of Love. The Life Story of Marguerite d'Youville.* (Private publication, ca. 1991), p. 9.

[869] Lefèvre and Lemire, p. 11.

[870] Mary Pauline Fitts, G.N.S.H., *Hands to the Needy. Blessed Marguerite d'Youville: Apostle to the Poor.* (Garden City, N.Y.: Doubleday & Company, Inc., 1971), p. 166.

[871] Fitts, p. 239.

[872] Fitts, p. 239.

[873] The author thanks Father John Marzolf, S.J., director of the Shrine of Our Lady of Martyrs, for providing information and reviewing the draft of this biography.

[874] *Butler's Lives of the Saints*, vol. III, p. 649.

[875] Reuben Gold Thwaites, ed. *Jesuit Relations.* (Cleveland, OH: Burrows Bros., Co; 1896), vol. 30, ch. IV, para. 3.

[876] Joseph N. Tylenda, *Jesuit Saints & Martyrs*, (Chicago, IL: Loyola Press, 1998), pp. 322-23; 351.

[877] www.wyandot.org/jogues.htm

[878] Bert Ghezzi, *Voices Of The Saints. A Year of Readings.* (New York, N.Y.: Doubleday, 2000), p. 322.

[879] Joseph N. Tylenda, S.J., *Jesuit Saints & Martyrs.* (Chicago, IL: Loyola Press, 1998), p. 323.

[880] Tylenda, p. 323.

[881] Tylenda, p. 323.

[882] Thwaites, vol. 28, p. 131.

[883] Thwaites, vol. 25, p. 49.

[884] Angus Macdougall, S.J., "Isaac Jogues, 1607-1646." (www.wyandot.org/jogues.htm), p. 5.

[885] Tylenda, p. 352.

[886] Macdougall, p. 5.

[887] The author thanks Father John Marzolf, S.J., director of the Shrine of Our Lady of Martyrs, for providing information and reviewing the draft of this biography.

[888] Tylenda, p. 353.

[889] Tylenda, p. 353.

[890] Nevins, p. 49.

[891] The author thanks Father John Marzolf, S.J., director of the Shrine of Our Lady of Martyrs, for providing information and reviewing the draft of this biography.

[892] Tylenda, p. 322.

[893] Tylenda, p. 323.

[894] Thwaites vol. 28, pp. 127-29.

[895] The author thanks Father Len Brown, C.M.F., provincial of the Eastern Province of the Claretian Missionaries, and Margaret Todd, archivist for the Claretian Missionaries Archives, for providing information and reviewing the draft of this biography.

[896] Anthony Mary Claret, *Autobiography*. Ed. by José María Viñas, C.M.F. (Chicago, IL: Claretian Publications, 1976), para. 8,9, and 15.

[897] Claret, para. 38.

[898] Claret, para. 68.

[899] Habig, p. 117.

[900] Habig, p. 117.

[901] Claret, para. 494.

[902] Claret, para. 496.

[903] Claret., para. 495.

[904] Claret. para. 620-21.

[905] Habig, p. 121.

[906] Claret, para. 199.

[907] No author. *"May Everything be Lost but Charity." Blessed Mother María Encarnación Rosal, Synthesis of Her Life.* (Santafé de Bogota, Colombia: Editorial Kimpres Ltda, 1998), p. 11.

[908] *Synthesis*, p. 12.

[909] Carlos E. Mesa, C.M.F., *Encarnación Rosal: una vida, un compromiso.* (Guatemala: Editorial del Ejército, 1985), p. 220.

[910] *Synthesis*, p. 19.

[911] The author thanks Père Jacques Rinfret, O.M.I., vice postulator, and Père Réal Mathieu, O.M.I., for providing information and reviewing the draft of this biography.

[912] Alphonse Nadeau, O.M.I. *Le Père Lelièvre, Oblate de Marie-Immaculée, "L'Apotre du Sacré-Coeur."* (Neuville, QC: Imprimerie A Garneau, n.d.), p. 1.

[913] Nadeau, p. 3.

[914] Laurent Tremblay, O.M.I. *L'inoubliable Llelièvre, O.M.I.* (Québec City, QC: Maison Jésus-Ouvrier, 1995), p. 2.

[915] Tremblay, p. 2.

[916] Tremblay, p. 2.

[917] Tremblay, p. 2.

[918] The author thanks Sister Georgette Desjardins, R.H.S.J., of the Bureau Des Fondateurs des R.H.S.J., for providing information and reviewing the draft of this biography.

[919] Georgette Desjardins, R.H.S.J., and Juline Roberge, R.H.S.J., "Jerome Le Royer, Sieur de la Dauversière," in *Jésus Marie et notre temps.* Juillet 2002, #347, p. 5.

[920] Georgette Desjardins, R.H.S.J., pamphlet: *"Jerome Le Royer, Sir De La Dauversière, At the service of God and poor, (1597-1659)."* p. 4.

[921] website: patron saints, Jerome Le Royer, p. 1

[922] Desjardins, p. 2.

[923] Web site: p. 1.

[924] Desjardins and Roberge, p. 5.

[925] Desjardins, p. 2.

[926] Raymond J. Lahey, *The First Thousand Years. A Brief History of the Catholic Church in Canada.* (Ottawa, ON: Saint Paul University, 2002), p. 26.

[927] The author thanks Hermana Ana María González Aguilar, MSCC, coordinator of the Commission for the Cause of José de Jesús López y González.

[928] Xorge Chargooy, *José a Jesús López , La sonrise de Dios.* No. 184 in series: Vidas Ejemplares, (Obra Nacional de la Buenad Prensa, A.C.; n.d.), p. 4.

[929] Chargooy, p. 22.

[930] Chargooy, p. 23.

[931] Private correspondence with Hermana Ana María González Aguilar, MSCC.

[932] Chargooy, p. 23.

[933] The author thanks Sister Thérèse Payer, R.H.S.J., and Sister Georgette Desjardins, R.H.S.J., both of the Bureau Des Fondateurs des R.H.S.J., for providing information and reviewing the draft of this biography.

[934] No author, "Jeanne Mance, A Misé Sur Le Roc De Sa Foi En Dieu," in Bulletin du Centre Jeanne-Mance, vol. XVIX (sic), December 2000, pp. 1-4.

[935] H. E. MacDermot, *Jeanne Mance.* (Canada: 1947), Reprinted from The Canadian Medical Association Journal, p. 5.

[936] Émile-Marie Brière, *Under Mary's Mantle. Our Lady's Love For Canada.* (Combermere, ON: Madonna House Publications, 2000), p. 84.

[937] MacDermot, p. 6.

[938] Jeanne-Mance, Bulletin, p. 4.

[939] Mary Louise Sullivan, M.S.C., *Mother Cabrini: "Italian Immigrant of the Century."* (New York, N.Y.: Center for Migration Studies, 1992), p. 247.

[940] The author thanks Sister Mary Louise Sullivan, M.S.C., author, for providing information and reviewing the draft of this biography.

[941] Mary Ann Clark, Jerri Pogue, and Diane Rickard. *Great American Catholics.* (Notre Dame, IN: Ave Maria Press, 1976), p. 125.

[942] Sullivan, p. 28.

[943] Sullivan, p. 30.

[944] Sullivan, p. 31.

[945] Sullivan, p. 36.

[946] Sullivan, p. 45.

[947] Sullivan, p. 54.

[948] Frances Xavier Cabrini, *Letters Of Saint Frances Xavier Cabrini.* Tr. by Ursula Infante, M.S.C. (1970), pp. 458-59.

[949] The author thanks Sister Doris Goudeaux, S.S.F., director of Friends of Henriette Delille Commission Office, for providing information and reviewing the draft of this biography.

[950] Virginia Meacham Gould and Charles E. Nolan, *Henriette Delille: "Servant of Slaves."* (New Orleans, LA: Sisters of the Holy Family, 1999), p. 9.

[951] Gould and Nolan, pp. 9-10.

[952] Gould and Nolan, p. 10.

[953] Gould and Nolan, p. 10.

[954] Gould and Nolan, p. 10.

[955] Gould and Nolan, p. 13.

[956] Gould and Nolan, p. 18.

[957] Gould and Nolan, p. 17.

[958] Gould and Nolan, pp. 18-19.

[959] The author thanks Sister Margaret Phelon, R.S.C.J., archivist, for providing information and reviewing the draft of this biography

[960] Louise Callan, R.S.C.J., *Philippine Duchesne, Frontier Missionary of the Sacred Heart*. Abridged Edition. (Westminster, MD: The Newman Press, 1965), p. 5.

[961] Callan, p. 427.

[962] Callan, p. 430.

[963] Callan, pp. 40-31.

[964] Callan, p. 4.

[965] Callan, p. 442.

[966] Callan, p. 477.

[967] Herbert J. Thurston, S.J. and Donald Attwater, ed. *Butler's Lives of the Saints*, vol. IV, p. 381.

[968] Callan, p. 486.

[969] Callan, p. 23.

[970] No author, *Bishop Ovide Charlebois, O.M.I., Apostle And Friend Of The Indians*. (Richelieu, QC: Keewatin Indian Missions, 1959), p. 5.

[971] *Bishop Ovide Charlebois*, p. 21.

[972] *Bishop Ovide Charlebois*, p. 15.

[973] *Bishop Ovide Charlebois*, p. 11.

[974] *Bishop Ovide Charlebois*, p. 11.

[975] *Bishop Ovide Charlebois*, p. 4.

[976] *Bishop Ovide Charlebois*, p. 8.

[977] *Bishop Ovide Charlebois*, p. 8.

[978] *Bishop Ovide Charlebois*, p. 5.

[979] *Bishop Ovide Charlebois*, p. 7.

[980] *Bishop Ovide Charlebois*, p. 11.

[981] *Bishop Ovide Charlebois*, p. 16.

[982] *Bishop Ovide Charlebois*, p. 16.

[983] *Bishop Ovide Charlebois*, p. 17.

[984] *Bishop Ovide Charlebois*, p. 16.

[985] *Bishop Ovide Charlebois*, p. 18.

[986] The author thanks Sister Jovita Mendez, M.D.P.V.M., for providing information and reviewing the draft of this biography.

[987] Julia Navarette y Guerrero, *Mi Camino. Recuerdos de mi vida. Autobiografía de Julia Navarette, una mística mexicana de nuestros tiempos*. (México: Centro de Estudios de los Valores Humanos; 1993), p. 81.

[988] Navarette y Guerrero, p. 82.

[989] Navarette y Guerrero, p. 84.

[990] Navarette y Guerrero, p. 111.

[991] Corbala, p. 170.

[992] Joseph N. Tylenda, S.J., "Beloved of God and Men, Father Magin Catalá, O.F.M. (1761-1830)," in *Portraits In American Sanctity*. (Chicago, IL: Franciscan Herald Press, 1982), p. 126.

[993] Tylenda, p. 127.

[994] Tylenda, p. 129.

[995] Prayer card: The Servant of God, Father Magin Catala, University of Santa Clara; 1962.

[996] Tylenda, p. 129.

[997] www.newadvnt.org/cathen/09530a.htm

[998] Prayer card, ibid.

[999] Tylenda, *Portraits*, p. 124.

[1000] The author thanks Ann Ball, author, for providing information and reviewing the draft of this biography.

[1001] Ann Ball, *Blessed Miguel Pro, 20th Century Mexican Martyr*. (Rockford, IL: Tan Books And Publishers, Inc., 1996), p.3.

[1002] Ball, p. 21.

[1003] Ball, p. 36.

[1004] Ball, p. 49.

[1005] www.catholic-forum.com/saints/saintm16.htm; p. 1.

[1006] Ball, p. 78.

[1007] Ball, p. 80.

[1008] Ball, p. 109.

[1009] Wilfrid DuFault, A.A. *Marie-Clement Staub, A.A. 1876-1936. Apostle and Founder*. ( Sillery, QC: Sisters of Saint Joan of Arc, 1990), p. 6.

[1010] DuFault, p. 8.

[1011] The author thanks Sister Gilberte Paquet, S.J.A., vice postulator, for providing information and reviewing the draft of this biography.

[1012] Serge Saint-Michel, *Landmarks In The Canadian Church: Marie-Clement Staub, A.A, and Mother Jeanne Of The Sacred Heart*. Ed. by The Congregation Of The Sisters Of Saint Joan Of Arc. (France: Girold, 1989), p. 23.

[1013] Saint-Michel, p. 43.

[1014] DuFault, p. 13.

[1015] Yvon Le Floc'h, A.A., *The Founding of the Congregation of the Sisters of Saint Joan of Arc, 1913-1921*. Tr. by Mrs. Edward Murphy. (Sillery, QC: Mother House Publication, 1965), p. 10.

[1016] DuFault, p. 22.

[1017] Saint-Michel, p. 29.

[1018] The author thanks Deacon Tom Cornell, of the Peter Maurin Catholic Worker Farm, for providing information and reviewing the draft of this biography.

[1019] Phyllis Zagano, ed., *Dorothy Day, In My Own Words*. (Liguori, MO: Liguori, 2003), p. 108.

[1020] Day, p. 62.

[1021] Private correspondence with Deacon Tom Cornell.

[1022] Day, p. 94.

[1023] Day, p. 100.

[1024] Day, p. 105.

[1025] Day, p. 107.

[1026] Jim Forest, "Day, Dorothy (1879-1980)," in *The Encyclopedia of American Catholic History.* (Collegeville, MN: A Michael Glazier Book, 1997), p. 414.

[1027] Day, p. 137.

[1028] Forest, p. 414.

[1029] Dorothy Day, *The Long Loneliness. An Autobiography.* (San Francisco, CA: Harper San Francisco, 1952), p. 136.

[1030] Day, p.147.

[1031] Day, pp. 147-48.

[1032] Day, pp. 148.

[1033] Day, pp. 165-66.

[1034] Day, p. 166.

[1035] James Allaire and Rosemary Broughton, *Praying with Dorothy Day.* Series: Companions for the Journey. (Winona, MN: St. Mary's Press, 1995). p. 21.

[1036] Private correspondence with Deacon Tom Cornell.

[1037] Day, p. 175.

[1038] Zagano, p. xvi.

[1039] Zagano, p. 29.

[1040] Margaret Gabriel, "Dorothy Day Onstage," in *St. Anthony Messenger*, April 2003, vol. 110, No. 11, p. 24.

[1041] Private correspondence with Deacon Tom Cornell.

[1042] Private correspondence with Deacon Tom Cornell.

[1043] Jim Forest, www.catholicworker.org/hisotrytext.cfm; p. 2.

[1044] The author thanks Sister María Teresa Zamora V. M.C.P., vice postulator, for providing information and reviewing the draft of this biography.

[1045] No author, *Sierva de Dios, Sor Gloria María Elizondo García, Misionera Catequista de los Pobres.* (Las Misioneras de los Pobres, 1997), p. 9.

[1046] *Sierva de Dios*, p. 19.

[1047] *Sierva de Dios*, p. 20.

[1048] Numerous historians, including clergy and laity, Mexicans and non-Mexicans, have suggested that Juan Diego may never have lived. These scholars admit that Juan Diego has served a symbolic role, but that insufficient evidence exists to support that he was an historical figure. These critics base their position on the following grounds: between 1531 and 1648, "there was not one verified reference to or mention of Juan Diego," by the Church's missionaries in México; that the popularly-revered and allegedly miraculously-preserved *tilma* is actually deteriorating; and that the anti-apparitionists' views received little or no hearing during the process in preparation for the canonization of Juan Diego. Cf. Stafford Poole, C.M., "Did Juan Diego Exist, Questions on the eve of Canonization.", *Commonweal*, June 14, 2002, pp. 9, 11.

[1049] Norberto Rivera Carrera, Cardinal Archbishop of México City, (www.fides.org/home-ing.html;, 3/07/2002), p. 2.

[1050] Guadalupe Pimentel, D.C., *Juan Diego.* (San Pedrito Tlaquepaque, Jal.: Editorial Alba, 2001), p. 81.

[1051] Pimentel, p. 85.

[1052] Pimentel, pp. 78-86, #'s 6-29.

[1053] Angel María Garibay Kintane, "Guadalupe, Our Lady of," *New Catholic Encyclopedia*, vol. 6, p. 821.

[1054] www.chnonline.org/2002-01-03/newstory3.html; pp. 1-2.

[1055] The author thanks Karen L. Fulte, foundress of the Archbishop Fulton J. Sheen Communication Room, for providing information for this biography.

[1056] Thomas J. McSweeney, "Sheen, Fulton John (1895-1979)," in *The Encyclopedia of American Catholic History*, p. 1286.

[1057] Thomas C. Reeves, *America's Bishop. The Life And Times Of Fulton J. Sheen*, (San Francisco, CA: Encounter Books, 2001), p. 3.

[1058] McSweeney, p. 1286.

[1059] Reeves, p. 4.

[1060] McSweeney, p. 1286.

[1061] Reeves, p. 4.

[1062] www.elpaso.net/~bank/elpasohistory/sheen/shnpjs01.htm; p. 2.

[1063] www.elpaso.net/~bank/elpasohistory/sheen/shnpjs01.htm; p. 3.

[1064] McSweeney, p. 1288.

[1065] McSweeney, p 1288.

[1066] Buried along with the cardinals, and Bishop Sheen, are the Servant of God Pierre Toussaint, Auxiliary Bishop John McGuire, plus Monsignor Michil Lavelle, who served as rector of the cathedral for half a century, from 1889-1939.

[1067] Michael DuBruiel, *Praying In The Presence Of Our Lord, With Fulton J. Sheen*. Series Editor: Benedict J. Groeschel, C.F.R. (Huntington, IN: Our Sunday Visitor, 2001), p. 23.

[1068] McSweeney, p.1287.

[1069] McSweeney p. 1287.

[1070] Catherine de Hueck Doherty, *Fragments of My Life*. (Combermere, ON: Madonna House Publications, 1996), p. 96.

[1071] The author thanks Kathleen Janet Thompson, vice postulator; Lori Duquin, author; and Peggy Cartwell and Rochelle Greenwood of the Muskegon, Michigan Madonna House; for providing information and reviewing the draft of this biography.

[1072] De Hueck Doherty, *Fragments*, p. 95.

[1073] Private correspondence with Rochelle Greenwood: Catherine's *Constitutions*, private edition, p. 11.

[1074] "Who is Catherine Doherty? A Woman In Love With God." www.madonnahouse.org; p. 3.

[1075] www.madonnahouse.org/doherty/index.html, pp. 3, 4.

[1076] De Hueck Doherty, *Fragments*, pp. 152-56.

[1077] De Hueck Doherty, *Fragments*, p. 172.

[1078] De Hueck Doherty, *Poustinia: Encountering God in Silence, Solitude and Prayer*. (Combermere, ON: Madonna House Publications, 2000), p. 20.

[1079] Private correspondence with Rochelle Greenwood: Catherine's *Constitutions*, p. 36.

[1080] Lorene Hanley Duquin, *They Called Her the Baroness. The Life of Catherine de Hueck Doherty*. (Staten Island, N.Y: Alba House, 1995), p.3.

[1081] Gerardo Sánchez Sánchez, coordinator. George Herbert Foulkes, general editor. *Fase Romana En Los Procesos De Canonización*. (México D.F., MX: 2000), p. 64.

[1082] Villa Ruiz, and Villa Ruiz, p. 214.

[1083] Sánchez Sánchez, p. 62.

[1084] Sánchez Sánchez, p. 62.

[1085] Sánchez, p. 62.

[1086] The author thanks Father Severino P. Lopez, relative of Josefa Parra, for providing information and reviewing the draft of this biography.

[1087] No author, pamphlet: *Sacrificio De Las Siervas.* [Josefa Parra y Coleta Meléndez] (n.d.), p. 2.

[1088] No author, pamphlet: *Datos de la Vida y Muerte de la Sierva de Dios, Josefa Parra.* (n.d.), p. 2.

[1089] Guillermo Havers Ma., *Testigos de Cristo en México.* V. Centenario de Evangelización en América Latina; 1492-1992. (Guadalajara, Jal.: Ediciones Promesas, S.A.; 1986), p. 213

[1090] The author thanks Ann Ball, author, for providing information and reviewing the draft of this biography.

[1091] Havers, p. 212.

[1092] Havers, p. 212.

[1093] Ann Ball, *Faces Of Holiness: Modern Saints In Photos And Words.* (Huntington, IN: Our Sunday Visitor, 1998), p. 155.

[1094] Havers, p. 212.

[1095] Havers, p. 212.

[1096] Havers, p. 212.

[1097] Havers, 213.

[1098] Ball, p. 155.

[1099] Sánchez Sánchez, p. 41.

# COUNTRIES, PROVINCES, AND STATES IN WHICH SAINTS LIVED AND MINISTERED

## Canada

Alberta — Anthony Kowalczyk, Vital Grandin

Manitoba — Ovide Charlebois, Vital Grandin

New Brunswick — Marie-Leonie Paradis, Vital Grandin

Northwest Territories — Vital Grandin

Ontario — Catherine de Hueck Doherty, Elizabeth Bruyère, Frederic Baraga, Georges Vanier, Jean de Brébeuf, Pauline Vanier, Stephen Eckert

Québec — Adolphe Chatillon, Alexis-Louis Mangin, Alfred Pampalon, André Bessette, André Grasset de Saint-Sauveur, Catherine-Aurélie Caouette, Catherine-de-Saint-Augustine, Délia Tétreault, Didace Pelletier, Dina Bélanger, Eléonore Potvin, Elizabeth Bergeron, Elizabeth Turgeon, Emilie Tavernier-Gamelin, François de Montmorency Laval, Frédéric Jansoone, Georges-Philias Vanier, Gérard Raymond, Isaac Jogues, Jeanne Le Ber, Jeanne Mance, Jérôme Le Royer de la Dauversière, Kateri Tekakwitha, Louis Emond, Louis-Zéphirin Moreau, Magin Catalá, Marcelle Mallet, Marguerite Bourgeoys,

| | Marguerite d'Youville, Marie-Anne Blondin, Marie-Clément Staub, Marie-Guyart de l'Incarnation, Marie-Léonie Paradis, Marie-Rose Durocher, Marie Fitzbach, Michael McGivney, Ovide Charlebois, Pauline Vanier, Pierre-Joseph-Marie Chaumonot, Rosalie Cadron-Jetté, Victor Lelièvre |
|---|---|
| Saskatchewan | Ovide Charlebois |
| Vancouver | Magin Catala |

## Caribbean Islands

| | |
|---|---|
| Cuba | Anthony Mary Claret, Félix Varela, Maria del Refugio Aguilar |
| Haiti | Mary Elizabeth Lange, Pierre Toussaint |
| Puerto Rico | Carlos Manuel Rodriguez, Félix Varela |

## Central America

| | |
|---|---|
| Costa Rica | Antonio Margil, Maria Romero Menenses |
| El Salvador | Oscar Arnulfo Romero |
| Guatemala | Antonio Margil, Pedro de San José Betancur, Maria Encarnación Rosal |
| Nicaragua | Maria Romero Menenses |

## México

| | |
|---|---|
| Aguascalientes | José a Jesús López y González, Julia Navarette y Guerrero |
| Baja California | Eusebio Kino |
| Chiapas | Francisco Orozco y Jimenez |
| Chihuahua | Pedro de Jesús Maldonado |

| | |
|---|---|
| Coahuila | Antonio Margil |
| Colima | Miguel de la Mora |
| Durango | Mateo Correa |
| Guanajuato | Elias del Socorro Nieves, José Maria de Yermo y Parres, Pablo Anda y Padilla |
| Guerrero | Bartolomé Laurel Dias, José Ramon Ibarra y González, Margarito Flores |
| Jalisco | Anacleto González Flores and Companions, Atílano Cruz Alvarado, Augustin S. Caloca, Cipriano Iñiguez, Coleta Meléndez Josefa Parra, Cristóbal Magallanes, David Glavan Bermúdez, Francisco Orozco y Jimenez, Jenaro Sánchez, José Maria Robles, José Isabel Flores, Julio Alvarez Mendoza, Justino Orona Madrigal, Maria de Jesus Sacramentado Venegas, Maria Guadalupe Garcia Zavala, Maria Luisa Josefa de la Peña Navarro, Maria Vicenta Chavez Orozco, Miguel Pro, Pedro Esqueda Ramirez, Rámon Adame Rosales, Rodrigo Aguilar Alemán, Sabás Reyes Salazar, Toribio Romo González, Tranquilino Ubiarco |
| México | Maria Dolores Medina Zepeda |
| México D.F. | Bartolomé Gutiérrez Rodriguez, Concepción Cabrera de Armida, Eugenio Balmori Martinez, Felipe de Jesús de las Casas, Félix de Jesús Rougier, Francisco Agular y Seijas, José Maria Vilaseca Agilera, José Plancarte y Labastida, José Ramon Ibarra y González, Juan de Zumarraga, Loiis Fores, Louis Sasada, Maria de la Luz Camacho González, Maria del Refugio Aguilar y Torres, Maria Dolores Medina Zepeda, Marina Francisca Cinta Sarrelangue, Pedro Baptist Blasquez and |

| | |
|---|---|
| | Companions, Pedro Manrique de Zuñiga, Rafael Guizar y Valencia, Richard Trouvé of Saint Ann, Sabastian de Aparicio, Vicente Ramirez de San José |
| Michoacán | Francisco Aguilar y Seijas, Jesús Méndez Montoya, José Plancarte y Labastida, José Sánchez del Rio, Maria Vicenta Chavez Orozco, Vasco de Quiroga |
| Morelos | David Uribe Velasco, Rafael Guizar y Valencia |
| Nuevo León | Antonio Margil |
| Nyarit | Antonio Margil |
| Oaxaca | Martyrs of Oaxaca: Jacinto de los Ángeles and Juan Bautista |
| Puebla | José Maria de Yermo y Parres, José Ramon Ibarra y González, Juan de Palafox y Mendoza, Juan Diego, Rafael Guizar Y Valencia, Sebastian de Aparicio |
| Querétaro | Antonio Margil, Bartolomé Laurel Dias |
| San Luis Potosi | Concepción Cabrera de Armida, Pablo Anda y Padilla |
| Sonora | Eusebio Kino, Maria Guadalupe Garcia Zavala |
| Tabasco | Antonio Margil |
| Tlaxcala | Teen Martyrs of Tlaxcala |
| Veracruz | Dario Acosta Zurita, Eugenio Balmori Martinez, Marina Francisca Cinta Sarrelangue Rafael Guizar y Valencia, Sebastian de Aparicio |
| Yucatan | Antonio Margil |
| Zacatecas | Antonio Margil, David Roldan Lara, Luis Batis Sáinz, Manuel Morales, Salvador Lara Puenta, Sebastian de Aparicio |

# United States of America

| | |
|---|---|
| Arizona | Eusebio Kino |
| California | Dorothy Day, Eusebio Kino, Frances Xavier Cabrini, Junipero Serra, Magin Catalá, Maria Luisa Josefa de la Peña Navarro |
| Colorado | Frances Xavier Cabrini |
| Connecticut | Michael J. McGivney |
| Florida | Martyrs of Virginia |
| Georgia | Martyrs of Georgia |
| Hawaii | Damien de Veuster, Marianne Cope |
| Illinois | Dorothy Day, Fulton J. Sheen, Frances Xavier Cabrini, Maria Kaupas, Mary Therese Dudzik, Samuel Mazzuchelli |
| Indiana | Anna Bentivoglio, Solanus Casey, Theodore Guerin |
| Iowa | Samuel Mazzuchelli |
| Kansas | Rose Philippine Duchesne |
| Kentucky | Charles Nerinckx, Felix de Andreis |
| Louisiana | Anna Bentivoglio, Antonio Margil, Cornelia Connelly, Frances Xavier Cabrini, Henriette Delille, Rose Philippine Duchesne |
| Maryland | Francis Xavier Seelos, John Neumann, Mary Elizabeth Lange, Michael McGivney, Elizabeth Ann Seton |
| Massachusetts | James A. Walsh, Marie Clement Staub |
| Michigan | Frederic Baraga, Samuel Mazzuchelli, Solanus Casey, Stephen Eckert |
| Minnesota | Frederic Baraga |
| Missouri | Felix de Andreis, Rose Philippine Duchesne |

| | |
|---|---|
| Mississippi | Cornelia Connelly |
| Nebraska | Anna Bentivoglio, Katharine Drexel |
| New Jersey | Frances Xavier Cabrini, Miriam Teresa Demjanovich |
| New Mexico | Eusebio Kino, Maria Kaupas |
| New York | Angeline Teresa McCrory, Catherine de Hueck Doherty, Dina Belanger, Dorothy Day, Elizabeth Ann Seton, Felix Varela, Fulton J. Sheen, Frances Xavier Cabrini, Isaac Jogues and Companions, James A. Walsh, John Neumann, Kateri Tekakwitha, Marianne Cope, Michael McGivney, Nelson Baker, Pierre Toussaint, Rose Hawthorne Lathrop, Solanus Casey, Stephen Eckert, Terence J. Cooke, Thomas F. Price, Walter Ciszek |
| North Carolina | Thomas F. Price |
| Pennsylvania | Cornelia Connelly, Demetrius Augustine Gallitzin, Frances Xavier Cabrini, Francis Xavier Seelos, John Neumann, Katharine Drexel, Maria Kaupas, Walter Ciszek |
| Texas | Antonio Margil, Eusebio Kino |
| Virginia | Frank Parater, Martyrs of Virginia |
| Washington | Frances Xavier Cabrini |
| Wisconsin | Frederick Baraga, Samuel Mazzuchelli, Solanus Casey, Stephen Eckert |

# INDEX OF SAINTS
# AND FEAST DAYS

❦

Didace Pelletier, Bl., Feb. 21

Dina Bélanger, Bl., Sept. 4

Dorothy Day, Nov. 29

Éléonore Potvin, May 30

Elias del Socorro Nieves, Bl., Oct. 11

Élisabeth Bergeron, Ven., Apr. 29

Élisabeth Bruyère, Apr. 5

Élisabeth Turgeon, Aug. 17

Elizabeth Ann Seton, Mother, St., Jan. 4

Émilie Tavernier-Gamelin, Bl., Sept. 24

Eugenio Balmori Martínez, May 14

Eusebio Francisco Kino, Mar. 15

Felipe de Jesús de las Casas, St., Feb. 5

Felix De Andreis, Ven., Oct. 15

Félix de Jesús Rougier, Ven.,Jan. 10

Félix Varela, Feb. 25

Frances Xavier Cabrini, Mother, St., Nov. 13

Francis Xavier Seelos, Bl., Oct. 5

Francisco Aguilar y Seijas, Oct. 14

Francisco Orozco y Jimenez, Feb. 18

François de Montmorency Laval, Bl., May 6

Frank Parater, Feb. 7

Frederic Baraga, Jan. 19

Frédéric Jansoone, Aug. 5

Fulton J. Sheen, Dec. 9

Gabriel Lalement, St., Sept., 26

George-Philias Vanier, Mar. 7

Gérard Raymond, Jul. 5

Gloria María Elizondo García, Dec. 8

Henriette Delille, Nov. 16

Isaac Jogues, St., Oct. 19

Jacinto de los Angeles, Sept. 16

James A. Walsh, Jun. 29

Jean de Brébeuf, St., Sept. 26

Jean de Lalande, St., Oct. 19

Jeanne LeBer, Oct. 3

Jeanne Mance, Nov. 12

Jérôme Le Royer de la Dauversière, Nov. 6

John Neumann, St., Jan. 5

José Antonio Plancarte y Labastida, Apr. 26

José de Jesús López y González, Nov. 11
José María de Yermo y Parres, St., Sept. 20
José María Vilaseca Aguilera, Apr. 3
José Ramon Ibarra y González, Ven., Feb. 1
José Sánchez del Río, Feb. 10
Josefa Parra and Coleta Meléndez, Dec. 24
Juan Bautista, Sept. 16
Juan de Zumárraga, Jun. 3
Juan Diego, St., Dec. 9
Juan Palafox y Mendoza, Ven., Oct. 1
Julia Navarette Guerrero, Ven., Nov. 21
Junípero Serra, Bl., Jul. 1
Kateri Tekakwitha, Bl., Apr. 17
Katharine Drexel, St., Mar. 3
Louis Émond, Sept. 26
Louis Flores, Bl., Aug. 19
Louis Sasada, Bl., Aug. 25
Louis-Zéphirin Moreau, Bl., May 24
Magin Catalá, Nov. 22
Marcelle Mallet, Apr. 9
Marguerite Bourgeoys, St., Jan. 12
Marguerite d'Youville, St., Oct. 16
María de Jesus Sacramentado Venegas, St., Jul. 30
Maria de la Luz Camacho González, Dec. 30
María del Refugio Aguilar y Torres, Apr. 24
María Dolores Medina Zepeda, Ven., Dec. 16
María Encarnación Rosal, Bl., Oct. 27
María Guadalupe García Zavala, Ven., Jun. 24
Maria Kaupas, Mother, Apr. 17
Maria Luisa Josefa of the Blessed Sacrament, Ven., Feb. 11
María Romero Meneses, Bl., Jul. 7
María Vicenta Chavez Orózco, Bl., Jul. 30
Marianne Cope, Ven., Aug. 9
Marie Anne Blondin, Bl., Apr. 18
Marie Fitzbach, Sept. 1
Marie Guyart de l'Incarnation, Bl., Apr. 30
Marie-Clément Staub, Nov. 23
Marie-Léonie Paradis, Bl., May 4
Marie-Rose Durocher, Bl., Oct. 6
Marina Francisca Cinta Sarrelangue, Sept. 29

Martyrs of Georgia, Sept. 14
Martyrs of Oaxaca, Sept. 16
Martyrs of Virginia, Feb. 9
Mary Lange, Mother, Feb. 3
Mary Theresa Dudzik, Mother, Ven., Sept. 20
Michael J. McGivney, Aug. 14
Miguel Pro, Bl., Nov. 23
Miriam Teresa Demjanovich, May 8
Nelson Baker, Jul. 29
Noel Chabanel, St., Sept. 26
Oscar Arnulfo Romero, Mar. 24
Ovide Charlebois, Nov. 20
Pablo Anda y Padilla, Ven., Jun. 29
Pauline Vanier, Mar. 23
Pedro Baptist Blasquez and Companions, St., Feb. 26
Pedro de San José Betancur, St., Jul. 30
Pedro Manrique de Zuñiga, Bl., Aug. 19
Pierre Toussaint, Ven., Jun. 30
Pierre-Joseph-Marie Chaumonot, Feb. 20
Rafael Guizar y Valencia, Bl., Jun. 6
René Goupil, St., Oct. 19
Richard Trouvé of St. Ann, Bl., Sept. 10
Rosalie Cadron-Jetté, Apr. 5
Rose Hawthorne Lathrop, Jul. 9
Rose Philippine Duchesne, St., Nov. 17
Samuel Mazzuchelli, Ven., Feb. 23
Sebastian de Aparicio, Bl., Feb. 25
Solanus Casey, Ven., Jul. 31
Stephen Eckert, O.F.M. Cap., Feb. 16
Teen Martyrs of Tlaxcala, Bl., Sept. 23
Terence J. Cooke, Oct. 6
Theodore Guerin, Mother, Bl., Oct. 3
Thomas F. Price, Jun. 29
Vasco de Quiroga, Mar. 14
Vicente Ramírez de San José, Bl., Sept. 10
Victor Lelièvre, Nov. 3
Vital Grandin, Bl., Jun. 3
Walter Ciszek, Oct. 12